Essential Expositions of the Psalms by Saint Augustine

Augustinian Heritage Institute

Board of Directors

+John E. Rotelle, O.S.A. (1939–2002), founding director
Joseph L. Farrell, O.S.A.　　　David Hunter
Joseph T. Kelley　　　　　　　Patricia H. Lo
Jane E. Merdinger　　　　　　Boniface Ramsey
Jonathan Yates

Translation Advisory Board

Allan D. Fitzgerald, O.S.A.　　Edmund Hill, O.P.
Joseph McGowan　　　　　　Boniface Ramsey

THE WORKS OF SAINT AUGUSTINE
A Translation for the 21st Century

Essential Expositions of the Psalms by Saint Augustine

Selected and Introduced by
Michael Cameron

Expositions and Psalms, translation and notes by
Maria Boulding, OSB

Edited by
Boniface Ramsey

New City Press
of the Focolare
Hyde Park, NY

Published in the United States by
New City Press of the Focolare
202 Comforter Blvd., Hyde Park, New York 12538
©2015 Augustinian Heritage Institute

Cover artwork by Leandro DeLeon
Book design by Steven Cordiviola

Library of Congress Cataloging-in-Publication Data:

Augustine, Saint, Bishop of Hippo.
  [Enarrationes in Psalmos. Selections. English]
  Essential Expositions of the Psalms / by Saint Augustine; selected and introduced by Michael Cameron; Expositions and Psalms translated by Maria Boulding; edited by Boniface Ramsey.
      pages cm
  Includes bibliographical references and index.
  ISBN 978-1-56548-510-5 (alk. paper)
1. Bible. Psalms--Criticism, interpretation, etc.--Early works to 1800. I. Ramsey, Boniface, editor. II. Title.
  BR1430.52.A9413 2015
  223'.206--dc23
                    2015013217

Printed in the United States of America

This book is dedicated to the memory of three extraordinary priests:

    Rev. Thomas R. Seitz, St. Thomas the Apostle Church, Chicago (+2007)
    Rev. Thomas F. Martin, O.S.A., Villanova University (+2009)
    Rev. J. William Harmless, S.J., Creighton University (+2014)

Wise mentors, passionate preachers, treasured friends

Contents

Preface 11
General Introduction 13

   I. On watching Augustine work 13
      A. Psalms and sermons and word cascades 13
      B. How to read with Augustine 15

   II. Restless heart reading: Texts that lie on Augustine's lap 17
      A. Scripture's importance (as a whole) to Augustine 17
      B. The Psalms' importance (in particular) to Augustine 21

   III. What Augustine thought about on Sunday morning 24
      A. Public exegesis: Reading with new eyes 24
      B. Strategies for preaching conversion 29
      C. Readers on risers: Audiences that escalate 38

   IV. Segue: Working with this book 44
      A. Structure of the anthology 44
      B. Numbering the Psalms and the Expositions 48

Notes 51

PART I
ENTERING THE PSALTER'S GREAT HOUSE OF PRAYER

Exposition of Psalm 119 59
   Synopsis 59
   Augustine's Text of Psalm 119 60
   Exposition 60

Exposition of Psalm 120 73
   Synopsis 73
   Augustine's Text of Psalm 120 74
   Exposition 74

Exposition of Psalm 121 93
   Synopsis 93
   Augustine's Text of Psalm 121 94
   Exposition 94

PART II
EXPLORING CHRIST'S BEAUTIFUL MYSTERY

Exposition 1 of Psalm 33 113
Synopsis 113
Augustine's Text of Psalm 33:1 114
Augustine's Text of 1 Samuel 21:12–13 114
Exposition 114

Exposition of Psalm 44 125
Synopsis 125
Augustine's Text of Psalm 44 126
Exposition 127

Exposition of Psalm 56 157
Synopsis 157
Augustine's Text of Psalm 56 158
Exposition 159

Exposition of Psalm 138 177
Synopsis 177
Augustine's Text of Psalm 138 178
Exposition 180

PART III
RECOVERING OUR BEARINGS

Exposition 2 of Psalm 30: 1–11 209
Synopsis 209
Augustine's Text of Psalm 30:1–11 210
Exposition 210

Exposition 2 of Psalm 32 225
Synopsis 225
Augustine's Text of Psalm 32:1–5 226
Exposition 226

Exposition of Psalm 72 241
Synopsis 241
Augustine's Text of Psalm 72 242
Exposition 243

Exposition of Psalm 140 ... 267
   Synopsis ... 267
   Augustine's Text of Psalm 140 ... 268
   Exposition ... 269

PART IV

EXERCISING THE SPIRITUAL MIND

Exposition 3 of Psalm 30 ... 297
   Synopsis ... 297
   Augustine's Text of Psalm 30:8–16 ... 298
   Exposition ... 298

Exposition 2 of Psalm 31 ... 311
   Synopsis ... 311
   Augustine's Text of Psalm 31 ... 312
   Exposition ... 313

Exposition of Psalm 54 ... 339
   Synopsis ... 339
   Augustine's Text of Psalm 54 ... 340
   Exposition ... 342

Exposition of Psalm 142 ... 369
   Synopsis ... 369
   Augustine's Text of Psalm 142 ... 370
   Exposition ... 371

PART V

GAZING UPWARD IN LOVE

Exposition of Psalm 38 ... 389
   Synopsis ... 389
   Augustine's Text of Psalm 38 ... 390
   Exposition ... 391

Exposition of Psalm 41 ... 417
   Synopsis ... 417
   Augustine's Text of Psalm 41 ... 418
   Exposition ... 419

Exposition of Psalm 42 437
    Synopsis 437
    Augustine's Text of Psalm 42 438
    Exposition 438

EPILOGUE

VIEW FROM THE ROOF

Exposition of Psalm 122 449
    Synopsis 449
    Augustine's Text of Psalm 122 450
    Exposition 450

Select Bibliography 465

Abbreviations of Biblical Books 471

Names and Places Index 473

Index of Scripture References 477

Subject Index 487

Preface

My hope is that this anthology may serve several purposes. Certainly it offers the curious a manageable sampling of Augustine's preached exegesis in general and of his massive *Expositions of the Psalms* in particular. But for a book like this the stakes are higher because the needs are deeper. Many anxiously search Scripture today, not to locate disembodied and timeless "meanings," but to relearn from the ground up *how* to read in a way that is both theologically coherent and faithful to the texts' own concerns. In a movement that crosses confessional borders many seekers today have apprenticed themselves to the early Christian readers of Scripture in order to learn not only *what* they learned but also *how they learned it*. Of course, we can't simply replicate the results of an earlier era; but that isn't the point. The best apprentices want to incarnate their masters' attitudes and impersonate their practices; that is, they seek not merely to *imitate* but somehow to *become* their teachers—in their own way. An anthology like this offers an opportunity to get inside a great spiritual-theological mind like Augustine's so that we may learn how to see our issues through his eyes. Though great chasms of time and cultural change separate us from him, Augustine's main concerns remain recognizable and relevant. We too ask of the texts, "What's going on here?" We too wish to learn freshly how to read, how to understand, how to appropriate these texts as living words from God. After making the appropriate adjustments, each of us may learn to become what Augustine became as he searched out Scripture's mysteries with his people: reader and questioner, searcher and believer, finder and preacher. Beyond conducting a tour of Augustine's fascinating ideas, I hope this book channels the restless spirit of holy inquiry that runs through his *Expositions* and conveys the deep enthrallment with Scripture that pervades its pages for our own reading, exegesis, and preaching.

I wish to thank two dear friends and acute readers, William Harmless, S. J., and Allan Fitzgerald, O.S.A., for their work of reviewing the volume's arrangement and offering critiques of the General Introduction. Their sage counsel and many solid suggestions have substantially improved the work presented here. This book was already in the publisher's hands when the news hit like a bullet that Fr. Bill Harmless had died unexpectedly on 14 October 2014. The loss for the world of scholarship, and for many other worlds, is incalculable. For me Bill was a close companion, smiling critic, and wise mentor. His fingerprints are all over this volume, and those who know Bill's ways will sense him. In God all things work together for good, as St. Paul said; but in the short term some of those things wreak havoc. Reluctantly we release Bill entirely to the God he loved, as he himself did every day. *Requiescat in pace.*

Thanks go to the people at New City Press for their patient willingness to await a volume that was long in preparation. This book also has been fortunate to have Boniface Ramsey as its editor; his practical wisdom and drive for clarity infused a quality that it would not otherwise have had. I am deeply grateful to my wife, Lorie Simmons, for dinner conversations and breaks for movies and warm encouragement all along the way.

Portland, Oregon
3 March 2015
Second Week of Lent

General Introduction

I. On watching Augustine work

> When a letter from the Apostle was read just now, brothers and sisters, you heard in it an admonition and a request.... *Keep watch prayerfully. Pray also for us, that God may open to us a door for the word, whereby we may speak of his mystery and make it known, as it is my duty to speak* (Col 4:2–4). I ask you, please, to regard these words as my own. In the Holy Scriptures there are profound mysteries which are hidden so that no one may approach them disrespectfully. But we must search for them and allow them to exercise our minds, knowing that when they are opened they will nourish us. The Psalm we have just sung is an example, for its meaning is somewhat obscure in many places. But, as with the Lord's help its message begins to be teased out and explained, you will see that what you are hearing is something you knew already (*Exposition of Psalm* 140,1).[1]

Here we get a first glimpse of Augustine working. He speaks directly to his North African congregation. They are in the middle of the liturgy. They have already listened to a reading from an epistle of Paul and have just sung Ps 140. Augustine has just begun to preach. Here we get to overhear him beginning to guide his people on a journey into mystery.

A. Psalms and sermons and word cascades

This is the Augustine we are going to explore in this anthology. It's not the Augustine most people are familiar with. Many know the Augustine of the *Confessions* or of *The City of God*. Augustine the preacher, the Augustine we watch here speaking directly to his hearers about a Psalm they have just sung, is much less known to us. Few today know the vast trove of sermons (some newly rediscovered) and works of preached exegesis on John's Gospel, the First Epistle of John, and the Psalms. Transcribed by stenographers scribbling busily as they listened, stored in the Hippo cathedral library, and preserved from invaders and the ravages of time, the sermons of Augustine show him speaking across 1600 years to our day. Taken together, nearly a thousand of them have survived. It's only a fraction of his preaching—but a spectacular treasure nonetheless. Among them the exegetical sermons form a special class of public discourses that interpret portions of sacred Scripture line by line for a worshiping congregation in a liturgical setting.

Augustine devoted the prime years of his career as priest and bishop (from about the mid 390s to the late 410s) to preaching his way verse by verse through all 150 Psalms. He treated several Psalms more than once and broke up some into several sermons. After adding in a few dictated sermon-like works, Augustine considered the complete collection of more than two hundred "expositions" on the Psalms to be a single work. It has been known since the 16th century as the *Enarrationes in psalmos,* or "running explanations of the Psalms."[2] It is Augustine's longest work, more than twice the length of *The City of God* and longer than all other early church writers' works on the Psalms combined. Eagerly copied by medieval monks looking for help in their contemplative rumination on Scripture, the *Expositions* remained the most influential work on the Psalms in the West for the next thousand years.

In this introduction, I'd like to equip you with some reading tools and to suggest a frame of mind for approaching this sprawling and beautiful but somewhat baffling work. These biblical commentaries are, first and foremost, sermons. So we won't find complete coverage of all aspects of the biblical texts, whether historical, philological, or even theological. We won't find detailed descriptions of historical settings or explanations of a psalmist's original intention or pronouncements of definitive meaning. (For Augustine the author of many of the Psalms was the historical King David, "to whom the whole Psalter is attributed" [9,35]. He thought David consciously spoke prophetically using the voice of Christ, the future Son of David who was also the Son of God.) However, we will find impassioned and exacting investigations of the words of Scripture delivered orally for live audiences, undertaken in faith as explorations of the canonical Christian Scriptures, venerated by the Church as God's living word intended for the spiritual conversion of real people.[3] For Augustine—as for all Jewish and Christian interpreters before the eighteenth century (and for many since)—Scripture mediates God's presence, first by revealing a divinely ordered structure of saving history in Israel, Christ, and the Church, then by portraying an array of saintly models for human living in faith, justice, and love, and finally by opening a cache of saving grace for those who know how to read rightly. In order to watch and work with Augustine as he reads Scripture, we need to take up his angle of vision on the texts.

The best way to learn from Augustine, whether Augustine the exacting exegete, the provocative theologian, the stirring preacher, the probing philosopher, the authoritative bishop, or what-have-you, is to ponder his practice before attending to his theory. That is, don't start, much less stop, with abstractions about him, put forward either by himself or by scholars who write on him. Rather, take time first to watch Augustine *doing* what he does: apprentice yourself to him while witnessing him practice his craft, noting the patterns of thought and action that recur as he works. After doing that, theory, whether his or that of his commentators, will become helpful for naming and analyzing his practice. But prioritizing theory tends to substitute explanations for the things to be explained and to lose what Augustine's best-known biographer, Peter Brown, has called "the tang of life."[4] This is particularly true when we watch Augustine read and preach Scripture. Too often, a bloodless analysis of his treatise *Teaching Christianity* (*De doctrina Christiana*) substitutes for observing Augustine the practicing exegete and preacher. *Teaching Christianity* is a treasured and important work, a genuine classic of western culture; yet it only begins to convey Augustine's full perspective on reading and preaching the Bible and doesn't at all suggest the sheer *zest* that he poured into doing that work over the course of more than four decades. For that we must go first to the sermons and expositions themselves. Only then can we profitably probe the richness that lies beneath the understated simplicity of *Teaching Christianity*.

This anthology offers an opportunity to watch Augustine the interpreter and preacher at work in his native habitat: before a living congregation, with codex splayed open before him, among sweating, murmuring people who hungered for his words, who thrilled to his verbal displays, and who sighed at his descriptions of God's design for salvation.[5] For Augustine, all the people, from the simple to the sophisticated, were creatures made in God's image; yet they were also needy, contending daily with the dangers and unknown destinies that held sway amidst life's uncertainties (just as we do). But he tirelessly reminded them that they were safe in the body of Christ, loved by God, and poised to learn God's will (just as we are). From the moment of his ordination he fretted about how to turn what he knew to benefit people's salvation (see Letter 21,4). While we can't access Augustine's hearers' full experience, we can access what they heard: his words. These words don't say everything, but they say a lot. More than many historical figures, Augustine *lived* what he read and thought and spoke, he *communicated* his convictions with an unmatched power and artistry, and he had the good fortune that his words have *survived* the cascades of history. Millions of his words have flowed down to us. Like a water main break in the middle of Late Antiquity, Augustine's geyser across the ages floods our libraries with books and our minds with questions. We're asking a few of these questions in this introduction.

B. How to read with Augustine

How can we get inside these *Expositions*? You might enter through one of several doors. You might read them doctrinally for Augustine's teaching on some theme like christology or grace; you might test the ways that faith informed Augustine's philosophical views about being or time or the human will; you might go further afield to study the *Expositions* historically and culturally for what they reveal about daily life and customs in late Roman North Africa, its social structures, family customs, educational practices, and the like; and the list could go on indefinitely. Such studies have all been undertaken and are constantly being multiplied. They offer legitimate angles and fruitful approaches for creating context and portraying depth, but in a sense they read against the grain and beside the point of Augustine's *purpose* in the *Expositions*. How do we read *with* Augustine?

The *Expositions* contains many rich and poetic statements, evocative in their density, captivating in their beauty. But they are, at first sight, both beguiling and bewildering to the modern reader. Perusing them is one thing, but understanding what's going on in them isn't as simple as we might hope. Certainly the *Expositions* arise from a peculiar context that must be reconstructed, and their method of exegesis is hardly what we're used to from modern biblical scholarship. But even reading the *Expositions* on their own terms presents challenges as we soon run into their apparently shapeless form. On reflection, even the concept of exegetical sermons seems strange. They appear wordy, diffuse, rambling, more propelled by Augustine's interpretive ingenuity and the biblical text's craggy phrasing than by any central purpose. It helps to remember that Augustine preached extemporaneously, improvising on sets of stock themes like a jazz musician.[6] But we may still come away with an impression of planless verbiage containing interesting episodes with a barely intelligible goal, a pastiche of garrulous Augustine's thoughts for the day. This restless meandering, while sometimes intriguing, can seem random and pointless, just as hitting balls and running bases is mere chaos to one who doesn't understand the rules of baseball. The "running explanations" label thus seems apt. Do they run somewhere in particular?

Perhaps we need to re-imagine. Is there a method in the meandering, a plan lying hidden somewhere in the open field of play? What if the rambling isn't incidental but actually central to Augustine's purpose, and a larger coherence underlies the wild variety, as he himself discovered that Scripture itself had? I suggest that if we patiently watch Augustine work at his craft of exegesis and preaching, a subtle pattern begins to suggest itself, *a pattern formed by the process of conversion.* It begins to appear that he constructed the episodes of exegesis to stir in hearers and readers a continual movement of spiritual change, and that the format of running exegesis had something to do with that. He pursued a process that led people to undertake a journey even more than merely to learn a map. He worked to stir up the restless heart of his congregation to seek rest in God by bringing them out of the grandstands and into the arena of wrestling with Scripture. This exegetical process kept hearers' hearts seeking and their spiritual feet moving in transit to God, not outwardly but inwardly, as Augustine never tired of repeating (e.g., 119,1). Thus each episode of exegesis was training. It was a set of exercises that coached hearts up the steps of ascent toward spiritual love and commitment.

Before we begin, it's important to gain a sense of the overall project of this introduction. Readers should take a multi-pronged approach to a massive work like the *Expositions* and should travel as many avenues toward understanding as possible. Usable *conceptual* introductions and synoptic overviews exist for Augustine's concept of Scripture,[7] for his preaching and the Sermons,[8] and for the *Expositions*,[9] so I won't repeat here what's readily available elsewhere. This introduction takes a *practical* approach by supplying readers with an orienting framework for reading the texts. We're going to use texts that you now have in your hands to let Augustine himself teach us how to read them. Can we get Augustine to help us read and understand these sermons? This introduction is an orientation session to help you let him do that.

Readers should approach the *Expositions* with at least three themes in mind: first, Augustine's understanding of his purpose in performing the *public exegesis of Scripture,* and the shift of perception required for reading properly; second, his steady aim at *spiritual conversion* that runs through all his preaching, and the rhetorical strategies he used to induce it; and finally, his idea about *the needs of multiple audiences* who stand on different steps of the spiritual conversion stairway, and the use of "spiritual exercises" in communal reading that he tailored to each audience. We'll shortly examine each of these three themes more closely. But before starting with the first I need to offer a quick orientation to how Scripture (as a whole) and the Psalms (in particular) function for Augustine.

II. Restless heart reading: Texts that lie on Augustine's lap

A. Scripture's importance (as a whole) to Augustine

Augustine aimed to transform believing hearts and minds by training them in the skill of how to read (hear) and think with Scripture. Then as now, this process requires above all that Christians soak themselves in Scripture's language, stories, images, values, and thought forms. That allows Scripture to gradually shape the soul, even though the process isn't automatic, or simple, or brief. Augustine himself once confessed to a friend that, despite studying Scripture for decades, he still felt like a novice.

> For the depth of the Christian writings is so great that I would daily make progress in them if I tried with the greatest leisure, the highest desire, and greater talent to master them alone from the beginning of boyhood up to decrepit old age. It is not that one comes to those matters that are necessary for salvation with such great difficulty, but, though each person grasps them in the faith without which one does not live a pious and upright life, there remain to be understood by those making progress so many things, and things

cloaked in such shadows of mysteries, and there lies hidden so great a depth of wisdom, not only in the words by which they are stated that way but also in the realities that are to be understood, that those who are the oldest, the most intelligent, and the most ardent with the desire to learn, experience what the same Scripture says in another passage, *When a human being has come to the end, then he is at the beginning* (Sir 18:6). (Letter 137,3)[10]

Augustine clearly continues to read not just to gain more Scripture knowledge but also to learn how to better judge what he reads. In other words, he's concerned to develop a *skill in reading Scripture* that is closely tied to his sense of its purpose in bringing about conversion. "Conversion" here refers not to a moment but to a process of change; it means not only initially entering upon the life of faith but also continually "making progress" in attaining spiritual wisdom. It follows that Augustine's conversion-oriented exegesis would constantly return to the same themes of salvation and community, even as he continually turns the knobs on Scripture's kaleidoscope of images that relate to Christ and the Church, orienting everything toward the embrace of divine love that is conversion.

Scripture words themselves, Augustine believed, were the best means of producing that conversion. So his work of preaching does not so much *take from* Scripture as it *takes form from* and *builds upon* Scripture; that is, he does not abstract from the texts some higher idea above them that they are *really* about and where all the real action is; rather, he thinks and speaks and dwells within the world of Scripture as he imagines it. This is why his sermons are knee-deep in biblical allusions and quotations.

Augustine's zigzag personal history with the Bible suggests how he attained his idea of the dimensions and possibilities of reading, his grasp of the exegetical task, and his understanding of preaching's importance. This story says less about the way he formed his concept of Scripture and more about how he attained a working perspective on the Bible after years of struggling with it. He had been aware of the Bible through his church-going mother Monica. Going away to school in Carthage and becoming a late-teen lover of rhetoric ignited a Cicero-inspired ardor for wisdom; but he recoiled from the Bible under the impression that it was ungainly and crude, presuming that its lack of lofty style meant that it lacked wisdom. Then a long Manichean interlude further bollixed up his search for wisdom by deleting the Old Testament and a truly human Christ from his spiritual awareness. But Ambrose helped him to recover a Catholic sense of Scripture by reckoning God as a speechmaker who composed the Bible as coherent divine discourse assembled from diverse human elements. Augustine soon came to see Christ, divine and human, as the organizing center of the Old and New Testaments. God the Word coming down to human flesh exactly paralleled the Word of God accommodating human speech. As he later told fellow readers in his congregation:

> There is but one single utterance of God amplified throughout all the Scriptures, dearly beloved. Through the mouths of many holy persons a single Word makes itself heard, that Word who, being God-with-God in the beginning, has no syllables, because he is not confined by time. Yet we should not find it surprising that to meet our weakness he descended to the discrete sounds that we use, for he also descended to take to himself the weakness of our human body. (103, 4th exp. 1)

This perspective pervades Augustine's sense of Scripture throughout the *Expositions* and affects his preaching in a number of interlocking ways. Let me briefly summarize several dominating perspectives.

1. Christ in history and prophecy. Christ is Scripture's center and culmination. All parts of the salvation story either anticipate or recall him. He fits together every character, age, custom, event, and institution, sometimes obviously, sometimes obscurely. He fulfills the covenant of Moses, both its moral and prophetic dimensions, by giving grace and truth (Jn 1:17). His grace fulfills the commandments in the law of Moses that never change, and Christians empowered by grace obey these moral commands as written. Meanwhile his truth fulfills the Old Testament prophecies, whose ritual aspect as commands to be literally fulfilled (for example, the sabbath rest) once pointed forward but which now, as illustrated in *Answer to Faustus, a Manichean* (e.g., VI,4), point backward as testimonies to be figuratively read. Christians intentionally do not carry out the prophetic commands, and their not doing so shows that they no longer function prophetically. Now they witness to Christ's fulfillment and confirm that they should be read and understood in terms of *hodie*, "today," the present time of fulfillment.

2. One flesh, one voice, one book. Christ's voice sounds throughout Scripture, especially in the Psalms. The Lord's own words from the cross witness to this: *My God, my God, why have you forsaken me?* (Ps 21:2; Mt 27:46) These words come at the high point of the passion drama and capture the instant of the exchange of redemption. But they also represent authoritative Scriptural exegesis from the lips of the dying Lord himself, demonstrating that his own voice sounds in the words of all the Psalms. Since one discourse and one voice echoes through the two Testaments, we know that they form one Book. This means first that the gospel was preached even before Christ came, though in hidden form. As Augustine famously put it, "New in Old concealed, Old in New revealed."[11] But it also means exegetically that the different forms of the gospel found in the Old and New Testaments are mutually interpreting.

3. Redemption fulfills the law. When Jesus took up the voice of sinful humanity as his own, he displayed the transaction of redemption, the moment of exchanging sin for justice, death for life, condemnation for grace. This humble act disclosed and bestowed divine love for humanity. But it also disclosed Christ's distinctly human love that fulfilled Scripture's central double-pronged command of love for God and neighbor. This command, proclaimed to Israel in the Old Testament (Dt 6:5; Lv 19:18), was ratified in the New by Jesus (*On these two commands hang all the law and prophets* [Mt 22:37–40]) and Paul (*Love fulfills the law* [Rom 13:10]). Christ's self-sacrifice fulfilled this command of love utterly, thus turning the letter of the law to spirit, a power within the heart rather than a prescription from without.

4. Transformed Christian hearts adore God. This divine-human love was not a static thing but a power that overcame sin and united heaven and earth. God's love poured out on the cross decisively affected our attitude toward God and our ability to know and show that same love to others. By its nature God's love effects change; to receive it is to live out of the same humility and grace that gave it. Love begins when faith sees Christ sacrifice himself for our sake, humble divinity lying "prostrate at our feet," wearing our mortal robe, dying our death, and so lancing pride and lifting us up (*Confessions* VII,18,24). Faith breeds hope, and hope enlarges the heart for love. All good preachers and teachers, Augustine explains, tell the salvation story in such a way that listeners "by hearing it may believe, by believing may hope, and by hoping may love" (*Instructing Beginners in Faith* 4,8).

Christ's strategy of assuming human weakness and suffering was an act of redemption that included us; thus, when the Lord spoke on the cross or in the Garden of Gethsemane (*Let this cup pass from me* [Mt 26:39]), he actually displayed the voice of our mortal fear as a prayer of intercession to God. He prayed as our priest not only *for* us or even *in* us; rather he prayed *as* us, assuming our words, our identity, and our history as condemned sinners. Conjoining us to himself, he created or rather unveiled the unity of "the whole Christ" (*totus Christus*), a central theme of the *Expositions*. Christ suffered and died not for himself alone but *for* his people.[12] Thus Christ and Church join in a single body whose mystery grounds the entirety of Scripture (*Exp. Ps.* 79,1). This is especially clear in the Psalms, where the voices of the head and the body converge not merely to alternate with one another but even to impersonate one another. He speaks our words and we speak his; in reading we learn of him and of ourselves. Augustine became enthralled with this vision of the whole Christ as he read the Psalms and constantly sought to enthrall his hearers with it as well, teaching them to see themselves in the texts because they are included in Christ himself. Indeed, Augustine stunned his hearers by announcing to them, "We are Christ too" (26, 2nd exp. 2).[13]

5. Christian reading practices transformed. This process impacts the way Christians read Scripture; being lifted to love's vantage point, they can spot *caritas* throughout Scripture. Though it's obvious enough in certain passages (consider 1 Cor 13), most often love lies hidden in the obscurity of events and words that seem to have nothing explicitly to do with Christ or salvation or love. And yet, says Augustine, the reader transformed by love knows how to find it because like Christ, or rather through Christ, Scripture everywhere acclaims or implies it. *Teaching Christianity* makes this point famously by calling love Scripture's "end," that is, its goal and fullest expression (I,35,39; see 1 Tm 1:5). The *Exposition of Psalm* 140 makes the same point but more clearly grounds it in the crucified Christ:

> Whatever salutary idea anyone may conceive or formulate in words, whatever truth may be dug out from any page of the Divine Scriptures, it tends toward one end only, and that is charity.... You need look for nothing else in Scripture, and let no one lay upon you any other command. Wherever there is an obscure passage of Scripture, charity is concealed in it, and wherever the sense is plain, charity is proclaimed. If it were nowhere plain to see, it would not nourish you; if it were nowhere concealed, it would not exercise you. The same charity cries out from a pure heart in the words of the Psalm and from hearts like his who prays here. And who this is, I can tell you in a word: it is Christ. (140,2)

6. The logic of Scripture's obscurity. The passage just quoted mentions that what Scripture conceals "exercises" the reader. The point is crucial. For Augustine the Bible's accounts are, like Rembrandt's paintings, portraits in chiaroscuro.[14] God left some places bright-lit, open and obvious, while others lie darkened by shadow and mystery. Both parts are necessary. Augustine compares them to the opening and closing of "God's eyelids" (10,8). Scripture's dark "secrets" are part of a strategy that keeps seekers hungry, puts freeloaders off track, and prompts new Christians to look for more. The text's literal sense or "letter" has inherent integrity and value, but Augustine is looking for the big picture in a small compass. He is typically more concerned, like Blake seeing the world in a grain of sand, "to pass through the letter and to search for the mysteries it conceals" (131,2). This does not mean, though, that the letter is left behind like an empty husk; rather, the spiritual sense empowers the letter to lift the soul toward wisdom from God. Paul importantly said, *The letter kills* (2 Cor 3:6), as Augustine learned from Ambrose (*Confessions* VI,4,6); but that's true only when the letter is left to itself. Augustine unfolds Paul's bigger picture in his important treatise *Answer to Faustus, a Manichean*. When the letter cradles this deeper spiritual sense, he writes, it mediates life, just as knowledge, when it is alone, puffs up, but edifies when combined with love (1 Cor 8:1; *Answer to Faustus, a Manichean* XV,8).

B. The Psalms' importance (in particular) to Augustine

The Book of Psalms surfaced at crucial moments in Augustine's life. At his post-conversion retreat in Cassiciacum outside Milan in 386, the first Old Testament text on which Augustine set his newly-opened eyes was a Psalm (*Confessions* IX,4,8).[15] Forty-four years later, as the Vandals were preparing their siege of Hippo in 430, we find the aged and infirm Augustine on his deathbed asking for Psalms to be hung around him in large letters to console his final hours.[16] The years in between witnessed him not only praying the Psalms daily with his little community of monastic brothers but also preparing and preaching the *Expositions*.

Augustine conceived a series of Psalms studies soon after ordination, perhaps originally for his small community living on the cathedral grounds at Hippo. Just before he became bishop, probably about 394–395, Augustine completed studies of the first 32 Psalms (33 in modern Bibles; see pp. 49–50 below for an explanation about numbering the Psalms and the *Expositions*). His work was not without at least one personal model, since, when he listened to Ambrose's sermons in Milan, it is quite likely that Ambrose included the Psalms among the Old Testament writings that he preached on. But when Augustine himself started preaching, he went beyond these early experiences to immerse himself in the tradition of Christian Psalm interpretation, already centuries old by his time. The roots of the Christian reading of the Psalms lay in the New Testament, which used them to find the person and work of Christ in the Old Testament's "vast forest of prophecy."[17] The gospels picture Jesus using the Psalms to explain his identity, his message, and above all his passion. Matthew and Mark cast the story of the crucifixion in terms of Psalms of lamentation, especially Ps 21 (Mt 27:46; Mk 15:34), Ps 30 (Lk 23:46) and Ps 68 (Mt 27:34). Luke's post-resurrection Jesus taught the apostles everything about himself in the Law, the Prophets, *and the Psalms* (Lk 24:44). Apostolic preaching and teaching presented the Psalms as prophecies of the messianic age in general and of the messiah in particular (Acts 2:25–28; 4:25–26; 13:33–37; Rom 15:8–11; Heb 1:5–13). But Christians also read the Psalter as the Book of Christ in another way, not only as an "objective" account of fulfilled prophecy but also as a revelation of his human soul, in fact as a virtual transcript of his inner life as he accomplished the work of redemption. Paul particularly taught Christians to read the Psalms as echoes of the voice of Christ.[18] Second-century writers like Ignatius of Antioch, Justin Martyr and Irenaeus continued the christological reading of the Psalms; so did Tertullian, Cyprian, Clement of Alexandria and Origen in the third century. In the fourth century, the Christ of the Psalms was important to Athanasius, Basil of Caesarea, Gregory of Nazianzus, Gregory of Nyssa and John Chrysostom in the East, and to Hilary of Poitiers, Jerome and Ambrose of Milan in the West. But Augustine took the traditional christological reading of the Psalms to unprecedented heights.

The Psalms were ripe for Augustine's close study and teaching because traditional Christian exegesis of the Psalter—perhaps Valerius, the bishop of Hippo for whom Augustine had been ordained to the presbyterate in 391, had awakened him to this—focused on Christ's humanity, which was of intense interest in the earliest days of his ministry. Augustine's search for Christ's humanity in the Psalms wasn't the product of mere theological curiosity. All early Christians saw Christ's human life, death, and resurrection as the starting point for salvation. But as a new presbyter Augustine faced the pastoral challenge of ministering to simple believing folk who would never become the kind of spiritual expert that he was. Augustine became supremely concerned to understand the inner workings of faith and to find effective ways to assist simple people to make progress in conversion. Orienting them to the humility and humanity of Christ was essential to this. So, while still serving as an "apprentice" under bishop Valerius, Augustine took up the Psalms in order to think deeply and exactly about the human Christ and his function in salvation. The Psalms became a kind of school for learning and teaching how "in Christ your Son our Lord and by your Scriptures" God showed "the way of salvation" (*Confessions* VII,7,11).

Augustine's attraction to studying the often vehement prayers of the Psalms is hardly a surprise. His restless spirit entered easily into the Psalter and its words, which channeled the most primitive human desires, cravings, fears, sorrows, and joys into the search for God. An intensely analytical mind combined with a natural sensitivity to create "a sort of preset harmony between the text of the Psalms and the soul of Augustine."[19] These texts made an ideal laboratory for analyzing the movements of the religious soul. Their emotional intensity fit Augustine's perception of how to seek truth from a sense of personal longing, and he read the Psalms for both their "diagnostic" and their "therapeutic" properties.[20] As Augustine examined the human soul's darker depths under the Psalms' intense spiritual light, each verse became a mini-exercise in spiritual living and a catalyst for "the conversion of the affections."[21] Their dialogical literary form shifted Augustine's early lofty but solitary intention to "know God and the soul, nothing more" (*Soliloquies* I,2,7). The study of the Psalms provided a mode of communal spiritual searching. But Augustine also gradually discovered in the Psalms a vast field of biblical prophecies whose fulfillment in Christ brilliantly illumined the contours of Christianity and invited every Christian reader to savor its riches. The Psalms—as ongoing conversation with God—thus became a mirror in which Augustine examined his soul, a lens through which he viewed Old Testament prophecies of Christ, and a prism through which he read the entire Bible.

The *Expositions* became a vehicle for Augustine to explore many different aspects of Christian life, thought, and practice. He constantly thinks about Christ, human and divine. Although he speaks with prescience and preciseness about the Savior's two natures and their unity (thus influencing the Church's later dogma about Christ), he's less interested in philosophical-theological precision than in pastoral effectiveness. Because Christ is so intimately bound to the Church, the *Expositions* are rich in ecclesial teachings, particularly in the theme of "the whole Christ," about which more will be said later in this introduction. But, even apart from the whole Christ, the reality of the Church is also especially important in the *Expositions*. Augustine considers the Church from many angles: as one (54,16–25), holy (even though mixed with bad Christians) (80,20–22), universal (147,16–19). Many biblical images of the Church appear in the *Expositions*: winepress and threshing floor (8,1), divine chariot (67,24), moon (10,3), vineyard (79,1), sparrow's nest (83,7), school of Christ (143,1), mother (57,5), daughter (43,23), wife (56,11) and maidservant (85,22). Among other theological themes, along the way Augustine muses on the nature of faith (109,12), the sacraments (26, 2nd exp. 2), the image of God in humanity (42,6), original sin (50,10), prayer (119,9), peace (121,12), and many other topics. Ethical concerns appear often, but usually serve to reinforce the perspective of wisdom in which those concerns take shape. Augustine's preaching against social injustices could be quite pointed, but it usually aids his pastoral effort to form the right spiritual attitudes rather than to prescribe certain actions (e.g., 38,11–12). See, for instance, how Augustine commends the wisdom of the ant that hoards resources against the day of hardship (66,3), or disparages the fool who puts off repentance under the illusion of being able to control time (76,8).

Augustine mocks pagan attitudes about the Church (148,16) and anticipates his polemic against them in the "two cities" imagery at the basis of *The City of God* (see 64,2). A common theme is the already traditional polemic against Jews (117,6; 138,8; 58, 1st exp. 1; 108,1). Several examples of Augustine's anti-Judaism appear in the anthology, which features perspectives that the Church has repudiated since the Second Vatican Council (1962–1965). On the other hand, as Paula Fredriksen has shown, Augustine's attitude toward Jews was relatively forward-looking for its time, and elements of his teaching bucked the hostility evident in other quarters of early Christianity.[22] Impressively, he found an ongoing role for Jews *as Jews* in the Christian economy—even if it was a subservient role next to triumphal Christianity. A few passages in the *Expositions* argue against the Manicheans and some others combat Pelagian views. But by far the most prominent opponent was the Donatists, whom we meet in several of the *Expositions* included here. Donatists carried over a sense of the Church's purity from the age of persecution before the peace of Constantine. In the spirit of Cyprian of Carthage (d. 258) they complained about Catholic accommodations that sullied the purity of the enclosed garden and the one dove (see Sg 4:12, 6:9); which were for them favored, because exclusivistic, images of the Church. The rival Christianities, Donatist and Catholic, fueled hot passions on every street corner in late fourth- and early fifth-century North Africa, though the fight was less a duel of theology than a conflict of imaginations over the picture of the true Church (e.g., 54,15–22).

III. What Augustine thought about on Sunday morning

A. Public exegesis: Reading with new eyes

We have seen in broad terms how Augustine approached the Bible in general and the Psalms in particular. Now let's turn to the three major thematic lenses for viewing the *Expositions* as mentioned above, *public exegesis, the goal of preaching for conversion,* and *the needs of different audiences.* To help keep focus as we watch Augustine work, for each of these I'll begin by suggesting a short passage from the *Expositions* to read that will frame the discussion of the theme to follow. The discussion will not so much unfold the passage as enlarge upon the theme that it suggests as a reading lens.

1. First focus exercise: *Exp. Ps.* 44,1–3

Let's look now at the first key point: Augustine's public exegesis. In order to focus on just one example, I ask you to read 44,1–3 (below, pp. 127–131). The core of these sections is the theme of *achieving spiritual understanding*, that is, using what Augustine calls the believer's "different kind of eyes" in order to discern the truth about Christ and look into Scripture's hidden depths. Here is a synopsis to get started.

1. Ps 44 is a wedding song for the Word and the bridal Church. It requires a spiritual perspective to read it rightly. According to the title, attendees must dress "properly" by clothing themselves with spiritual "understanding" that belongs to "the children of Korah." The Hebrew name "Korah" means "bald" (*calvus*) in Latin. Since the very word *calvus* suggests the one who died on Calvary, the "children of Korah" must point, Augustine says, to those who "understand" the cross of Christ. For people who read it in that light, the Psalm can't help but "germinate, burst into flower, grow, reach perfection, and yield fruit for harvesting."

2. The title also prophesies about "those things which will be changed"— not just society's cultural change from pagan to Christian, but even the more individual change "from an old self into a new self," from thieving to giving, from cheating to chastity, from crankiness to kindliness. But who has made the changes happen?

3. Christ, the bridegroom, is the change agent. People see differently because of him. He said, *Whoever sees me sees the Father* (Jn 14:9), while looking for those who can see him with "a different kind of eyes." Here is the center of Augustine's exegesis: the *way of seeing* that makes all the difference. In fact, that "different kind of eyes" allows us, who entered as guests at the wedding, to discover with astonishment that *we ourselves are the bride*! So we ask, what does the bridegroom look like? Consider, says Augustine, Jn 1:1 and *the Word in the beginning with God, the Word who is God*, which is Christ in majesty. But he came down to remove our ugliness in sin by his love, which reveals the beauty of Jn 1:14, *the Word made flesh*. The "different kind of eyes" now sees beauty in every scene of his life, from birth to death. "Let the bridegroom come forth and show himself to us," Augustine cries, "and let us love him.... Let him come to us, so that we may gaze on him with the eyes of our spirit."

2. First wide-angle view: Seeing the way Augustine sees

The *Expositions* commend seeing with "a different kind of eyes." The Scripture scholar Luke Timothy Johnson has written that the recovery of Scripture's immediate vitality by modern people will require a shift of viewpoint. He says that we must "imagine the world that Scripture imagines," that is, we must read while approximating a pre-modern immediacy to God and an unsecularized outlook.[23] It's not unlike trying to watch a 3D movie. You wear a special set of glasses that translates the raw off-kilter images into pictures of striking depth and texture. Imaginatively we enter into a different visual process. Augustine saw Scripture from within "the world that Scripture imagines." By extension, entering into Augustine's way of seeing biblical texts will help us make sense of his sermons. We watch and join Augustine imaginatively entering the world of Scripture as he read the Psalms with his congregation. In order to read his *Expositions*, we must work with him and, so to say, imagine the world *that Augustine imagines* that Scripture imagines. How do we do that?

a. Love as a way of seeing

For a moment let's ponder how truly radical the Christian way of seeing is. Christianity's first word is not about dogma, institution, ritual, tradition, mystical visions or spiritual enlightenment, though it ultimately entails these things. It doesn't build up from soaring emotion, deep intellectuality, or heroic obedience, though its fullness may include these. Rather, as the Canadian theologian Bernard Lonergan concluded after a long career in theology, Christianity's first word is about *falling in love with God*. Lonergan wrote:

> It is as though a room were filled with music, though one can have no sure knowledge of its source. There is in the world, as it were, *a charged field of love and meaning;* here and there it reaches a notable intensity; but it is ever unobtrusive, hidden, inviting each of us to join. And join we must if we are to perceive it, for our perceiving is through our own loving.[24]

Lonergan, the modern Canadian, wasn't thinking of Augustine, the ancient North African, when he wrote this. But Augustine used remarkably similar terms to describe the Christian ascent to God while reading Scripture. A memorable passage of the *Expositions* (included below, pp. 419–423) treats Ps 41's famous image of the deer that longs for the springs of water. Augustine saw in this an image of the spiritual seeker. Like Ps 44, this Psalm was dedicated to *the children of Korah*, so Augustine thought it expressed the deer's pining for "the font of understanding" (41,2) that led the deer to say, *I poured out my soul above myself* (Ps 41:5, Latin). This is right, says Augustine: only by pouring out my soul *above myself* (i.e., in love) can I find the lofty *home of God* (*domus Dei*). But how do I get there? God has provided a way, Augustine explains. Besides his abode on high, God also has a tent on earth, his *tabernaculum*, the Church. The road (*via*) to the *domus Dei* stretches up through that Church-tent to heaven. But, someone asks, isn't the Church only a way station? Yes, he answers; but look for the saints living in the tent who model the pilgrimage to heaven by how they obey God, endure suffering, and practice justice and love. One such saint wrote Ps 72, Augustine declares, and there recalled his costly and dangerous struggle to answer questions about why evildoers prospered while good people suffered. His foot nearly slipped, the Psalmist says, but after considering his saintly forebears he ascended to the *domus Dei,* where he learned that bad people's good fortune only readied them for punishment, while good people's bad fortune trained them for their inheritance. (The word "trained" here is *exercere,* "to exercise.") So the Psalmist's question got a provisional answer; but it was available only from that higher perspective. What drew him there? It was a kind of music, Augustine exclaims, anticipating Lonergan—music not unlike that of a wedding reception, a celebration of love like the one in Ps 44.

> He was drawn toward a kind of sweetness, an inward, secret pleasure that cannot be described, as though some musical instrument were sounding delightfully from God's house. As he still walked about in the tent he could hear this inner music; he was drawn to its sweet tones, following its melodies and distancing himself from the din of flesh and blood, until he found his way even into the house of God. He tells us about the road he took and the manner in which he was led, as though we had asked him, "You admire the tent on earth, but how did you reach the secret precincts of God's house?" *By the voice of exultation and praise,* he says, *the sounds of one celebrating a festival....* From that eternal, unfading festival melodious and delightful sound reaches the ears of the heart, but only if the world's din does not drown it. The sweet strains of that celebration are wafted into the ears of one who walks in the tent and ponders the wonderful works of God in the redemption of believers, and they drag[25] the deer toward the springs of water. (41,9)

This is love talking. *The voice of exultation and praise,* which draws him like a mysterious melody into God's house, moves the Psalmist *to ponder the wonderful works of God.* This is precisely what Augustine's public exegesis of the Psalms was designed to do.

Lonergan addresses the root Christian experience, but he also captures well Augustine's vision for preaching Scripture in the Church. Lonergan's "charged field of love and meaning" equates to Augustine's community of Christ's body, the whole Christ of head and members, wherein each speaks in his or her own voice but also in the voice of the other, the head for the body, and the body for the head. The whole Christ is the context for all Augustine's exegesis of the Psalms; he repeatedly reminds his hearers about being part of the body at the beginning of many of the *Expositions* (e.g., 30, 2nd exp. 3; 54,3; 140,3; etc.). The members of the whole Christ see with "another kind of eyes" because they look through the eyes of Christ their head; they seek, as it were, to read as Christ reads. Jesus in a sense rewrote the ancient Psalms with the ink of his grace and the stylus of his cross, and bequeathed these rewritten Psalms to his members. In a real sense this is the text that Augustine expounds, the Scripture that Christ rewrote and reads in his members. Augustine's episodes of exegesis function as training exercises for members of the whole Christ to read the Psalms through the eyes of their head.

b. Audible sacrament: the word in the liturgy

Imagining the liturgical setting is crucial. Augustine was nothing if not an orator fired up by a living encounter, ever moved by the plights and pleasures that showed in the faces of a live audience grappling with God's word. In these *Expositions* we can still sense Augustine's juices flow when he warms to his text and feels the living circulation of spirit in the liturgy. We may be separated by time but in our own way we are still participants. Augustine's "different kind of eyes" opened upon the texts as he presided over the Church's liturgy. To read the *Expositions* rightly we can't forget that liturgy framed everything that Augustine said and made sense of everything that people heard. The worship service didn't merely showcase his preaching; importantly, it also anticipated—implicitly for inquirers and catechumens who were dismissed after the sermon, and explicitly for the baptized—communion in the sacrament of the Lord's body and blood, the Eucharist.

The physical space within the church where the community gathered around Scripture and sacrament gave a heightened sense of participating in an otherworldly enterprise; it both symbolized and catalyzed an alternative way of being human.[26] Looking with "a different kind of eyes," the people read Scripture through a lens honed in baptism and held in place by the sacrament of the altar. This "higher" way of seeing became particularly apparent in the ancient opening words of the Eucharistic prayer, still used today, "Lift up your hearts." To this the people responded, then as now, "We have lifted them up to the Lord."[27] Augustine urged believers to closely consider their response so that they would speak these words truthfully. If they did, then their "different kind of eyes" would help them to *envision* themselves in the Eucharist, and thus *to be* Christ's body, while also helping them to assume their responsibility *to become* Christ's body. As he famously urged catechumens approaching the altar for the first time, "Be what you see, and receive what you are" (Sermon 272).[28] But something parallel occurred in preaching Scripture, for just as he urged the people to *see* themselves in Christ's body on the altar, he wanted them also to *hear* themselves in Christ's voice in the Psalms. He implicitly urged them to listen with "a different kind of ears." Augustine's preaching in effect said to hearers, "Be what you hear, and receive what you are."

In this sense Augustine's preaching was sacramental. A sacrament, he thought, resulted when God's word conjoined with a sensory element. His provocatively paradoxical phrase to describe this is well known: a sacrament was "a visible word" (*Homilies on the Gospel of John* 80,3). So the Eucharist, marking the presence of Christ on the altar, was a "visible word" that taught not only the head's redeeming story but also revealed the redeemed body's dignified identity and exalted responsibility. It turns out that Augustine first used this phrase early in his career to describe events of Scripture's Exodus story, when God used "visible words" like "sounds and letters, smoke, and a column of fire and cloud" to teach our childish minds and cure our inner eyes (*True Religion* 50,98, from about 390). So, if the sacrament of the altar was a "visible word," then we might call Augustine's publicly preached exegesis of Scripture an "audible sacrament." Thus the "different kind of eyes" lifts Christian readers up to an alternative consciousness as they read Scripture. We should stay keyed in to that consciousness as we read the *Expositions*.

B. Strategies for preaching conversion

Although Scripture's basic message about love is simple, it is difficult to interiorize and put into practice. Augustine refers to it as the Bible's "peak," or *summa* (*Teaching Christianity* I,35,39). Climbing that peak and understanding that message requires a long-term commitment and effort to investigate many different images and models of love that Scripture provides and preached exegesis unfolds. Meanwhile, living out that reality requires constant practice that results in conversion.

1. Second focus exercise: *Exp. Ps.* 140,1–3

Now let's turn to the second of our three themes, Augustine's practice of preaching for *conversion*. For this let's read 140, 1–3 (below, pp. 269–272). This passage shows Augustine commending the sweaty push-and-pull process of reading Scripture slowly, questioningly, and meditatively, as a tool for changing the heart. As we play God's game of hide-and-seek among the words of the text, we learn how to "win" by finding its central truths, while each victory moves us closer to living out God's will. Here is a synopsis of the passage.

a. Scripture consistently hides its cache of mysteries. Why? Because truth refuses to serve itself up on a platter in order to ensure that we won't "hold it cheap."[29] Truth isn't an artifact you can buy and mount on your mantel; because it's alive it makes ongoing demands on one who claims it. In other words, we have to put ourselves out to discover and unpack its mysteries. We need "exercises of the soul."

b. What do readers keep looking for in Scripture? Love, of course. Any Scripture text you find has "love" written in it, either in large plain letters or in code. What kind of love? Paul defines it as "charity from a pure heart" (1 Tm 1:5)—in other words, love that accords with God's will. This love cries out in the Psalm and also gives a clue to the speaker's identity. Who is this? "I can tell you in a word," says Augustine. "It is Christ."

c. But why then does the Psalmist pray for protection from sin? Would Christ do that? Augustine answers that we must understand who Christ is. It is not just Christ the Lord who cries out here; *it is also we ourselves.* "Charity cries out *to* Christ from our hearts, and charity cries out *from* Christ on our behalf." But Augustine doesn't stop with assigning voices; he also unearths the astonishing exchange wherein the head speaks *for* the members and the body claims the head's voice as its own. Think, he says, of a stubbed toe that makes the tongue cry out, "That hurt *me!*" Christ speaks not for himself alone but for the whole Church and for every Christian. This unity of two in one body and two in one voice is basic to Augustine's understanding of the Christ who speaks in the Psalms. Here we have Augustine's majestic theme of *totus Christus,* the whole Christ (140,4).

2. Second wide-angle view: You become what you hear

Augustine points to the Psalm's obscurity as strategic, for purposes of exercise. What's going on here? It's not immediately obvious why Augustine should adopt a strategy of preaching his exegesis. Its form is odd, if for no other reason than that by adhering closely to the text's wording he surrenders control of the discourse's "arrangement" (*dispositio*), a classic component of rhetorical construction.[30] With the biblical text itself as the organizing principle, Augustine and his co-readers must ride the rapids of the uneven, unpredictable, and at times unintelligible word flow of the Old Latin Bible. Yet for Augustine it seems that something essential for spiritual understanding and progress is at stake, something that reflects the character of the Christian life itself. What might that be?

Augustine follows the biblical text closely and thoroughly (if our manuscripts are accurate, he rarely leaves out a phrase), and urges hearers to join his "sweaty" work of exegetical performance.[31] Clearly he thinks something here is critical for the *hearer's* understanding—not just for his sermon preparation. In short, for Augustine the preacher, process is purpose and purpose is process. That is to say, his approach ensures that hearers will not take away from the texts some disembodied "meaning" but rather will inwardly situate their hearts within a vital understanding to be adopted, loved, and lived. For Augustine, commentary is plaited Bible, so to speak, a weaving of the preacher's words in and through the Bible's words. He hews closely to each text because every word is packed with power on the verge of detonation in the exchange between careful preached exegesis and openhearted hearing.

Extended reading of the sermons shows that Augustine allied the exegetical sermon form with his message. He charged the very sound and rhythm of his words with something of their meaning. The feature is obvious in a figure of speech beloved of poets, onomatopoeia. Many schoolchildren learn about it from Edgar Allan Poe's "jingling, tinkling, rhyming, chiming, bells, bells, bells, bells," as the words intonate the clanging spoken of in "The Bells." Music lovers become aware of this in feeling the rolling seas in Debussy's *La Mer,* or the calm after the storm in Beethoven's Sixth, or "Pastoral," Symphony. The form of something does not point to something else more real and actual, but form overlaps and channels content. Ancient rhetorical theory was aware that certain figures of speech acted this way, as in the device called hyperbaton, wherein an irregular rhythm of speech conveyed turbulent emotion.[32] The conscious use and theoretical acknowledgement of such devices by writers both ancient and modern suggest that they don't so much name a technique as identify a sensibility.

In visual terms that are not unrelated to faith practices, we might say that joining form and content this way is like painting an icon. Recent rhetorical studies have taken up this analogy to make sense of patterns of speech.[33] They note that an icon is a visual sign with a non-arbitrary relationship to the thing it represents. Speech may be called "iconic" if it conveys to the mind something of the reality it represents, like a painting of the sun that works because the yellow configuration looks something like what it portrays. The representation in a sense participates in the reality it seeks to convey; and the medium at least partly makes the message. The icon does not simply point to the thing being portrayed but also opens a way to vitally know it by providing a primitive experience of its mystery. I suggest that Augustine's preached exegesis is often similarly iconic. That is, he crafts the exegesis not only to indicate and map and describe spiritual transformation, but he also seeks *to rhetorically advance the movement involved in conversion.* We need to savor this. Augustine doesn't just talk about a reality he finds in the Bible's words; he makes his Scripture-soaked words induce the experience of it.

How does this happen? Augustine works on this by creating an undulating rhythm of sense, a flow of verbal movement that builds and releases a feeling of tension within the hearer. A variety of rhetorical devices binds and looses the hearer's attention, stirring anticipation one moment and then relaxing it the next. Augustine asks questions, intensifies ideas, shifts perspectives, enlarges reference frames, abbreviates phrasing, stages dialogues, impersonates speakers, imports texts, reverses angles, stockpiles images, launches rhymed sequences, and so forth.[34] Undoubtedly in person he intensified these dynamics using voice modulation, varied pacing, facial expressions, and bodily gestures.

a. How tension devices work

Let's return to the *Exposition of Psalm* 140 to watch Augustine work with this "tensive" approach. His exegesis is comparatively unremarkable among the *Expositions,* but just for that reason it gives a feel for the kind of rhetorical shaping that was second nature and practically unconscious for him. I translate literally to pick up cadences of the lines, which are numbered for keying to the analysis that follows. Augustine is dealing with the first line of the Psalm, "I have cried to you, O Lord; hear me."

1. I don't say it, the whole Christ says it—
2. But more in the person of his body is it said.
3. For even when he was here, he prayed while he bore flesh,
4. And from the person of his body, he prayed to the Father.
5. When he prayed, dripping blood oozed from his whole body.
6. That's written in the gospel: Jesus prayed with intense prayer and sweat blood.[35]
7. What's the effusion of blood from the whole body,
8. Except the suffering of martyrs from the whole Church?
9. But nevertheless we were there too in figural form.
10. What of him hung from the wood, except what he received of us?
11. And how would God the Father ever dismiss and desert the only Son,
12. Especially him, who was one God with him?
13. So that's the evening sacrifice—
14. The Lord's passion, the Lord's cross, a saving victim offered, a holocaust God accepted.
15. That evening sacrifice, in resurrection, made up the morning offering.
16. What I read in the Psalm, this I hear from the Lord.
17. In him too, I learn in the Psalm what I read in the gospel....
18. All this as foretold has happened just so
19. As we've heard, so we've also seen.

Here's a simple list of observations, not exhaustive, of places where Augustine builds and releases rhetorical tension as he

— contrasts perspectives (1: "I"/whole Christ; 2: head/member; 15: evening/morning; 16: read/hear);

— reframes Psalm within gospel narrative (1–8: prayer in Psalm, prayer during passion);

— stirs pathos by vivid imagery (5–6: blood oozing from beloved Lord as he suffers);

— transitions sharply from Christ to martyrs (5–8: blood of Jesus becomes blood of martyrs);

— recasts scene to include hearers suddenly (9: "we were there too");

— questions with expected yes, logic implying coherence (10: Where but from us did he get flesh?);

— questions with expected no, logic implying incoherence (11–12: God abandons Son? One God with him?);

— sprays short phrasing in rapid bursts (15: passion, cross, victim, holocaust);

- conjoins Old and New Testaments (16–17: Psalm and the Lord's voice, Psalm and gospel);
- syncopates and rhymes (7–8, 15–17, 19[36]).

Note that part of what makes the tension-and-release scheme work is the shortness of each line, which lends itself to epigrammatic rhythms of rising and falling, not unlike wisdom sayings found in the Book of Proverbs, whose parallelism rhymes not sound but sense.

Following closely the contours of the text while weaving in these devices creates a series of verbal mini-dramas that keeps the discourse perpetually moving like a pendulum, swinging from puzzle to solution and back, from mystery to revelation and back, from image to truth and back, from unknown to known and back. At the same time his hearers' hearts continually swing from tension to release, from restlessness to rest, from the anxiety of questioning to the peace of understanding. This is Augustine's catch and release, the rhythm of his inhaling-and-exhaling discourse. Each act of posing and resolving the text's obscurities reenacts in miniature the movement of conversion that characterizes Christian life. It is the systole and diastole of the sermonic heart.

b. Scripture-induced conversion

This way of commenting on Scripture is a world away from our all-too-self-removed and scholastically detached way of thinking about the Bible. We often look for "meanings" that have been severed from the words like cut flowers and favor abstractions that press a text's historical, theological, or devotional essence between the pages of a closed book. But Augustine didn't cut and dry texts that way, and neither did other ancient Christian interpreters. Augustine looked for ways to find and savor the living divine mystery that lay nestled within the Bible's words. Wreathing commentary in and around its words created the sensation of traveling the twisting lanes of the Christian pilgrimage itself, a mimesis of conversion's route from death to life. Such a process didn't merely add knowledge or infuse warmth; it immersed hearers in the text's own *movement*, and trained them to negotiate the ever-new demands on faith's journey toward understanding.[37] Preached exegesis exercised over and over the skills for plumbing texts in a way that released spiritual reason's power to ripen faith into understanding.

Augustine was inventive, but he hardly invented this approach. He was putting his own stamp on an ancient tradition of wisdom built up by sages over many centuries and from many cultures, including, of course, ancient Jewish culture. These wisdom teachers not only opened learners to imagine some new conceptual path of understanding but also pushed them to walk it themselves. The key here is to see Augustine preaching not simply to inform but also *to show*, not merely to organize insight but also *to practice wisdom*.[38]

Something Augustine did in the fourth book of *Teaching Christianity* helps to vivify this. Despite the way it is sometimes read, this text isn't an abstract treatise on rhetorical principles but rather a rough guide to rhetorical practice that grew out of fifty years of public speaking experience, thirty-five of them preaching Christianity. Examining Scripture and the early Church for examples of writing that met the criteria for good rhetoric (note the easy transition between writing and speaking), Augustine drew freely on his boyhood rhetorical hero, Cicero. Augustine memorably baptizes for Christian use Cicero's three great tasks of discourse, "to instruct, to delight, to sway" (*docere, delectare, flectare*). But as Hildegund Müller has noted, Augustine was bending his old master's language to his new Christian purpose. He tweaked the word used for the last of Cicero's tasks, *flectare*, "to sway," by turning it into a word adaptable to conversion, *movere*, "to move." (*Teaching Christianity* IV,17,34) [39] This subtle change highlights Augustine's conviction that a preacher's highest purpose is to carry hearers forward in a flow of dynamic *spiritual change*, that is, not only to stir minds and hearts but also to impel them toward new action and new life—namely, to conversion born of love. After all, Augustine could sling lots of Christian theology at his audiences if he wanted to, but for him loving things, not knowing things, was what mattered.

Augustine enlarges on this in a different treatise on Christian communication, *Instructing Beginners in Faith*. Written more than twenty years before the fourth book of *Teaching Christianity*, it is in some ways more instructive about his process.[40] There he writes that it is not enough to talk about attaining the goal of "love from a pure heart"; we must also "move and direct" our hearers' attention toward that love (*Instructing Beginners in Faith* 3,6). That is, it's fine to tell hearers *that* we are to love, but we must also show and train them *how* we are to love.

To keep our heads above water, then, in the stream of Augustine's *Expositions of the Psalms*, we need to learn to float with his constant effort to *turn* his hearers to God. This perspective allows one reading the pages of the *Expositions* to see in them, and to breathe with them, the spirit of Augustine's famous "restless heart" (*Confessions* I,1,1). How did Augustine immerse himself in these texts? I suggest that he pursued at least two practices, which I'll call *inhabitation* and *accommodation*.

c. Inhabitation: "We dwell in each other" (*Instructing Beginners in Faith* 12,17)

Augustine recast a quite traditional audience-centered rhetorical approach within a Christian theological framework by approaching communication as a form of indwelling others in "the bond of love" (*Instructing Beginners in Faith* 12,17). He confesses in effect, "I think a lot of great thoughts but am almost always disappointed by my poor way of expressing them" (ibid. 2,3) (even Augustine?!). Yet Christian teachers, he continues, aren't allowed to mope about their inability to grace the world with all they know. Any discrepancy between knowing and speaking, after all, pales in comparison with the Son of God's astonishing descent from high heaven to lowly earth. Augustine practically shouts his point: *Christ's humble love, not superior understanding, motivates the Christian teacher and preacher.* And when you speak in love, Augustine says, you soon discover two joyous facts. First, as charity descends to serve the least in the community, it activates unexpected strength and peace as it seeks to impress people with nothing except the desire for their salvation (ibid. 10,15). And second, the bond of love mysteriously incarnates your personal presence within your hearers, who now welcome what you say as if your words were their words. In a memorable passage Augustine declares, "So great is the power of feeling in soul-sympathy, that when listeners are affected by us as we speak, and we are affected by them as they learn, *we dwell within each other.* In that way listeners sort of 'speak' in us what they hear, and in a sense we 'learn' in them what we teach" (ibid. 12,17). Outwardly we speak and they listen, but inwardly—through love—they teach and we learn. Only love can reciprocate that way, only love can make the radical translation whereby hearers learn by taking up the voice of the teacher, and teachers relearn by hearing what they already know for the first time, again. This "ego-emptying" not only features constantly in Augustine's preaching; it's elementary to his understanding of human learning. The "love-feast" of understanding doesn't merely lay out raw verbal vegetables from its stockroom but rather dices them, tosses them, seasons them, cooks them, presents them. In short, true knowledge breathes the accommodating spirit of loving service, and love infuses *a way into* understanding as part of understanding itself.[41]

The main model for this is the Incarnation. A christological pattern lies beneath all the *Expositions* like a grid conducting electric current. The Psalms apply everywhere to us because they apply everywhere to Christ, and Christ is always together with us. That's because, by taking our flesh and especially by enduring our death, Christ hardwired us into himself. The way Augustine often put this was to say that Christ "transfigured us in himself," that is, he incorporated us into him and his redemptive suffering by "the wonderful exchange, the divine business deal" (30, 2nd exp. 3). He took our death, we took his life; he took our sin, we took his righteousness. As marvelous as this exchange was, however, not even that was an end in itself. Its ultimate purpose was to drive the body of Christ's ongoing conversion of ascent from embracing the Lord's humanity to contemplating his divinity. Augustine called this the *transitus,* "passage," which pictures the flowing "movement" between the head and members of Christ's body (142,9). As we've seen, this kind of movement stirs the heart to love. The Psalms captured the gospel love story's pathos and energy and bottled it, so to speak, for the whole Christ, to fuel its conversion ascent from flesh to spirit. This indwelling comes to splendid expression in the words of the Psalms, whose exegesis irradiates love's energy.

Augustine the preacher not only identified with the Lord's story but also modeled himself on Christ's model follower, Paul the Apostle (1 Cor 11:1), the Christian pastor and preacher *par excellence.* Playing on the Latin *paulus*, meaning "little," Augustine says that Paul deigned to become "small Paul" (44,22) and to nourish new converts "like a wet nurse pampering her children" (1 Thes 2:7). Paul didn't mind acting like a mother happily offering her baby juicy tidbits, or like a hen covering her little clutch with warm wings (*Instructing Beginners in Faith* 10,15). That's the self-image a Christian teacher and preacher should have, says Augustine. This mutual indwelling was elemental to Augustine's theological thinking about Christ, the Church, and salvation—and to his practice of publicly preaching his exegesis as a way to move people toward conversion.

d. Accommodation: "We speak in a fashion you can understand" (*Exp. Ps.* 119,2)

Augustine's practice of preaching exegesis for conversion drew on common ancient rhetorical understandings of how to create a discourse. In fact "transfiguration" was conceptually based on the rhetorical practice of impersonation, a device of imitating the voice of an opponent or a partner or even inventing a voice for an inanimate object. Augustine saw this as a template for understanding theologically how redemption works. But rhetorically it articulated a potent way to accommodate speech to the needs and capacity of an audience.[42] Rhetoric, "the art of speaking" (*ars loquendi*), was above all the "art of accommodation."[43] According to this understanding, orators looked for ways to adapt their speech to the capacity of their hearers. Accommodation shows that a particular act of speech does not intend to create an absolute and timeless universal statement, relevant to all at large because aimed at none in particular; rather it addresses some local audience in a specific situation. This concreteness of speech carries a number of implications for understanding the sermonic form and the *Expositions* you're going to read.

Ancient students of oratory named the preeminent way that speakers accommodated particular rhetorical situations *decorum*.[44] This referred not to mere polite talk and good behavior in delicate situations. For them *decorum* refers to a discourse's appropriateness or "fittingness," by which an orator adapts speech to the capacity of the audience, to the tenor of the situation, to the scope of the subject, and to the resources of language. *Decorum*, the ancients taught, implies a power of discernment that can't be taught in rulebooks. It presumes an intangible skill of judgment—a shrewdness for determining who the audience is, what their specific needs are, what the appropriate mindset might be, and what proper feelings to have, and then to custom-tailor words that will move hearts, sway minds, and shape actions.[45] *Decorum* has often been limited to matters of speaking style alone as a kind of decorative act that makes finished ideas palatable. But recent study has shown that, at least in the Ciceronian tradition that

Augustine was trained in, decorum straddled the concerns for *both* speech's format ("elocution") *and* the creation of its substance ("invention"). In other words, decorum affected both form and content.

The take-away is that *decorum* highlights speech as intended *for* an audience. It's not merely a stylistic accommodation, as though an idea is fully formed first, and all I need to do in order to get it across is to dumb it down or sweeten it up, depending on whom I'm talking to. Rather, presuming that form is a part of content, *decorum* builds upon the transaction that takes place between the speaker and the hearer. That is to say, *decorum* embeds *the way to understand in what is to be understood*. Study of the practice of *decorum* reveals that, because discourse is inherently audience-oriented, audience reception is a structural feature of discourse.[46] Not that the audience usurps the speaker's privileged role of determining what to say; rather, by shaping the speaker's concern to communicate, the audience leaves an imprint upon the discourse. Hearers therefore affect the discourse's structure and sense, and they come back to play a role later when the now past discourse needs to be interpreted and understood by people who weren't there to hear it fresh. I argue that this is the case with Augustine's *Expositions*, and that recognizing the dynamics of *decorum* will help us understand what's going on in them.[47]

How did Augustine embed his strategy for bringing understanding to his hearers in the *Expositions*? The aim of conversion shaped Augustine's preached exegesis. Of course he wanted to proclaim truth in order to convey right information; but even more he wanted to stir his hearer's desire to ascend to spiritual change and understanding, that is, to tap into the power of conversion. Augustine's evident practice of rhetorical accommodation, adapted to preaching the Christian Scriptures, considered not just his hearers' intellectual and spiritual capacities but even more their spiritual progress. For the Church, the Bible mysteriously conveys the word of the transcendent God, and Scripture's own constant aim is conversion to this God. So Augustine and all the other early Christian readers of Scripture weren't importing something alien into the interpretive process by emphasizing this. To their minds conversion–oriented exegesis, from a Greek word meaning "leading out," led out Scripture's own deepest intent. In the *Expositions* we watch Augustine the headmaster teaching people *how to read* within the *schola Christi*, "the school of Christ" (79,1). But he comes across less like a professor of exegesis giving instruction in a school than a spiritual director giving counsel in confidence. Part of that counsel was giving practical models and training exercises in reading to the members of the whole Christ. He wanted to see them keep wading into Scripture's waters, whatever their level of spiritual attainment. To do this, Augustine not only baby-stepped beginners in the shallows of Scripture's wording; he also dove with advanced learners down to its more obscure spiritual recesses, toward the spiritual aquifer below where whole lakes of refreshment awaited discovery.

How amazing is the profundity of your words! We are confronted with a superficial meaning that offers easy access to the unlettered; yet how amazing their profundity, O my God, how amazingly deep they are! To look into that depth makes me shudder, but it is the shudder of awe, the trembling of love. (*Confessions* XII,14,17)

Augustine was similarly awed by Scripture's ability to attract the simplest believers and challenge the most advanced thinkers simultaneously.[48] He tried to mimic that approach in his sermons. His congregations included people at every level of spiritual progress, from all walks and states of life. He dealt with all kinds.[49] Who were the most advanced? If it's true for believers as for preachers that entering Christ's humble love, not attaining superior understanding, marks the stages of spiritual progress, then social and cultural studies may help only marginally. We can't equate class, station, status or training with progress in spiritual wisdom. The very advanced in society may find the simplicity of the Christian Scriptures unbearably crass.[50] On the other hand, even someone untutored like Augustine's mother Monica might become a "citadel of [spiritual] philosophy" and ascend with him to the highest reaches of spiritual vision available to Christians in this life.[51]

C. Readers on risers: Audiences that escalate

For Augustine, Scripture not only *reveals* the will of God so that it can be stated and known; it also *empowers* people actively seeking to obey the will of God. The humble form that so dismayed the young Ciceronian actually imparts the humility it portrays, the very condition necessary not only to understand Scripture but also to access the salvation it offers. Likewise, exegesis actively grows understanding, and preaching actively stirs conversion. Exegesis leads out the sense of the text *to* someone in order to re-embody it in life. By definition, therefore, real audiences shape preached exegesis, which carries the imprint of those audiences. Since we encounter this imprint in the *Expositions*, might we organize an approach to reading them that reflects Augustine's effort to accommodate his audience?[52] For our third and final theme, we'll look at Augustine's vision of the different audiences that he had before him while delivering his sermons on the Psalms, and we'll try to make sense of how the hearers shaped what the preacher had to say.

1. Third focus exercise: *Exp. Ps.* 119,1–2

For this exercise dealing with Augustine's audiences, let's read 119,1–2 (below, pp. 60–64). This exegesis worked on the first Step-Song, which began the sequence of Pss 119–133, often referred to as the Gradual Psalms (from *gradus*, the Latin word for "step") and which, since the days when the Jews sang them on pilgrimage to the Second Temple, have been viewed as a single collection. Augustine uses his opening sections to frame their imagery within the Christian spiritual ascent of conversion. Here is a synopsis.

a. Christians ascend, says Augustine, not by bodily feet but by desire for God. Augustine prepares to view the Step-Songs by looking at them through the prism of Ps 83:6–7: *God arranges his ascents in his heart, in the valley of weeping, to the place he has appointed*. That is, God has arranged the path of spiritual ascent from humility to glory. The spiritual journey from mortal life on earth to eternal joy in heaven is like climbing a mountain. Beginning down low, "in the valley of weeping," it aspires to an undreamt height which, Paul said, *eye has not seen, nor ear heard, nor has it risen* (ascendit) *in the human heart* (1 Cor 2:9). Well, if it hasn't "ascended" within the human heart, said Augustine, "then let the human heart ascend to it." That's what these Psalms help people do.

b. Christ helps us to climb by the example of his humility as our starting point and his glorification as our goal. Mention of the "valley" implies the nearby "mountain," the one suggesting humility, the other, sublimity. No one but our Lord embraces both, so we begin climbing by believing in his humble flesh while ascending toward his transcendent divinity. "He is the starting point of your ascent and the goal of your ascent." Christ is present at both ends of conversion's rise from darkness to light, and from flesh to spirit.

c. But discernment and maturity levels in the Christian community are extremely varied; people stand everywhere on the conversion stairway. Many mount only the first step, others sweat up the steps just above, and a few get to the top stairs. Augustine's language for these groups, partly borrowed from Paul (1 Cor 3:1–2) speaks of "little ones" (*parvuli*), "climbers" (*ascendentes*), and "spirituals" (*spiritales*).[53] The "little ones" suckle on Christ's crucified humanity; the "spirituals" find a perch of wisdom and understanding where they behold rays of Christ's divinity; the "climbers" move in the liminal space in between. John's Gospel marks the bottom and top steps: *the Word was made flesh* (1:14) and *the Word was God* (1:1) signal the beginning and end, respectively, of the conversion staircase. Meanwhile, the prophecy in Is 11:2–3 about the qualities of Jesse's royal "stump" names the steps in descending order: wisdom at the top is just above understanding, then counsel, strength, knowledge, and piety cascade down to fear of the Lord, which Scripture calls *the beginning of wisdom* (Ps 110:10). Like Isaiah, the Apostle Paul christologically constructed his message to accommodate believers at the top and the bottom of the stairs. Though Paul's unspeakable visions were at the top, he accommodated his language to all audiences in order to "speak in a fashion you can understand" (as Augustine paraphrased 2 Cor 5:13). Augustine, besides remarkably but subtly ranking his insight and authority alongside the Apostle's, clearly modeled his ministry to mixed groups on Paul's astute and inclusive strategies of accommodation.

2. Third wide-angle view: Mapping Augustine's congregation

The experience of hearing Augustine preach was undoubtedly extraordinary, yet those who gathered to hear him were probably an ordinary mix of people from all stations of life and levels of spiritual attainment.[54] If indeed his sermons carry the imprint of his congregation, what can we discern about its spiritual composition? Augustine evidently saw his listeners as differing groups of spiritual climbers who were being impelled by the power of word and sacrament up the steps of conversion. Everything he said tried to incline them toward greater loving contemplation of God and justice-giving love for the neighbor. Preached exegesis mediated the power of Scripture for that spiritual ascent. For him spiritual conversion was the achievement of wisdom: spiritual understanding produced by knowledge that had been transfigured by love for the eternal. Here's his thumbnail description of what he was aiming for: "Not unfittingly we understand wisdom to be the knowledge and love of that which abidingly is, and unchangingly remains, which God is" (135,8).

Getting a sense of how the *Expositions* reflect Augustine's view of his people's progress toward wisdom is the key to understanding them. The process of exegesis serves as an instrument in attaining that goal. Augustine doesn't interpret texts with a view to unearthing and announcing some definitive "meaning"; rather sermonic exegesis aids hearers in their specific need to constantly move toward conversion. His close readings of Scripture were intended *for* different spiritual types of people according the stages of conversion; that is, we might say that Augustine aimed at different *implied audiences* that were mixed together in his congregation. The shape of each sermon embodied Augustine's designs for persuasion to conversion, and so each tells us something about these audiences *as Augustine conceived of them*. We might imagine him distributing them on a sort of mental graph, plotting the coordinates of various people's spiritual progress, strategizing for what people needed to continue their climb to the next step. In a word, *each exposition accommodated different actual audiences in order to shape them into the audiences they needed to become.*[55]

Augustine's "implied audiences" combined actual people standing before him at the liturgy with his idealized sense of the groups named by Paul. He "spoke to their condition" as he moved through the texts. All were on the same path of progress but stood on different "steps" on the conversion stairway. The lessons were interactive between groups. Those lower aspired to go higher, while those higher were to exercise the humility of their estate by descending lower to help others.

a. On the steps of conversion

From the very beginning of his Christian life after baptism, Augustine thought of spiritual progress as a series of steps. He used early philosophically oriented works as learning exercises for a cadre of like-minded seekers.

Soon he began a project that transposed elements of the traditional liberal arts curriculum keyed to deepening spiritual conversion. Though never completed, the project showed him already composing "spiritual exercises" for inquisitive minds. After being unexpectedly drafted into the presbyterate at Hippo, Augustine began to seriously explore Scripture as the basis for ascent. Language for the steps to spiritual maturity became biblical, drawn principally from two sources: the Beatitudes, from the Sermon on the Mount in Mt 5:3–8, and the messianic spiritual gifts named in Is 11:2–3. Undoubtedly the schemes were originally designed for serious spiritual truth-seekers like himself. But as his ministerial duties and preaching opportunities multiplied, he broadened his concern to embrace all levels of maturity. *The steps describe stages of the soul's spiritual ascent from immaturity to maturity.*

b. The mix of groups

The "steps" or modes built upon one another and interacted with one another. The first led to the second, third, and fourth; but the second didn't leave behind the first, nor did the third or fourth leave behind the second. Conversion is a cumulative process, so those on higher steps of the ascent to spiritual *understanding* continued to stand on what they learned on the lower steps of *faith*. These "spirituals" continually renewed themselves at faith's "home base," the humanity of Christ crucified, by God's word received along with the Eucharist. Indeed, their high standing depended on continuing to receive the same grace that nourished the "little ones." Beginners and advanced shared different forms of the same food, as Augustine explained:

> Solid food is not incompatible with milk, even so much so that solid food itself turns into milk whereby it can be suitable for infants to whom it comes through the flesh of a mother or nurse (see 1 Cor 3:1–2).... Accordingly, little ones neither must be suckled in such a way that they always fail to understand [that] Christ [is] God, nor must they be weaned in such a way that they forsake Christ the man. (*Homilies on the Gospel of John* 98,6)[56]

But in order to clarify the continuity of the conversion and growth process, Augustine was willing to adjust his beloved imagery of infants nursing on the Incarnation. The image should not be mistaken for insisting that all believers remain babies. But just in case, he said, let's talk about buildings instead:

> The crucified Christ is both milk for the suckling and food for those advancing. In fact, therefore, the similitude of the foundation is more suitable (1 Cor 3:10); for, in order that what is being built might be completed, the building is added on, the foundation is not removed (ibid.).

Exegesis not aimed directly at one group was not wasted on the others. "Little ones" heard particular episodes of preached exegesis for "spirituals" in the way that was appropriate to them, and "climbers" heard in their own way, and so on. For example, "spirituals" were clearly the target of

Augustine's advanced teaching about the "being" of God, who in Latin is called *idipsum*, "Being-Itself," or "the Selfsame" (121,5). Though it was beyond them, "little ones" and "climbers" heard the same teaching (as did catechumens and perhaps outsiders). Every teacher recognizes the pedagogical problem of balancing efforts to challenge quicker-witted students on the one hand and to encourage the slower ones on the other. For Augustine this was a matter of stirring *the desire to understand*. He once wrote to some obstructive Manicheans, "We should not at present work with you in order that you may now understand these ideas, for that is not possible, but *in order that you may desire to understand them* at some point" (*The Catholic Way of Life and the Manichean Way of Life* I,17,31). Presumably the less mature believers listening to Augustine's preaching did desire to understand. He addresses them briefly in some asides of *Exp. Ps.* 38, where he puzzles over the problem of truth that "leaps beyond" the capacity of some hearers. He warns people not to make hasty judgments or to jump to premature conclusions, but rather to work on their *desire* to understand (38,7: "we speak to all of you, to those who have such a longing and to those who do not have it yet"). The Lord's own disciples, Augustine recalled (38,3), were avid and eager to learn, but were "not able to bear" many things he had to say (see Jn 16:12). Paul lamented that he could not speak to the Corinthians as to spiritual persons but only as to "little children" (see 1 Cor 3:1–2). However, Augustine continued, Paul knew that the less mature "were not to be despaired of, for all that, but nourished" (38,3). So Augustine counseled his "little ones" this way: "Do not be in a hurry (*festinare*, "hasten," "rush"), then, to hear what you cannot yet take in, but grow up so that you may become capable of it" (ibid.). Augustine's use of "hear" (*audire*) refers to "listening with understanding", so that the soul grasps, agrees, and follows through in action. He says in so many words, "Listen in, this is fine; but be patient and learn to walk before you run." This ties in with Augustine's staple conviction, learned early and repeated often throughout his works, taken from Is 7:9 in the Old Latin translation of the Greek Old Testament (the Septuagint), "Unless you believe, you will not understand" (see *The Teacher* 11,37; *Faith and the Creed* 1,1; *Exp. Ps.* 8,6). Faith in authority precedes spiritual understanding (see *True Religion* 24,45; *Exp. Pss.* 35,1; 54,23). For now the less mature must learn to "hear" with faith rather than understanding. Like children at the side table who overhear the adult discussion at Thanksgiving dinner, the less mature must grow in order to understand what the mature are talking about. In terms of the ascending steps of conversion, little ones should hear the higher truths openly stated in a way that spurs their desire to climb toward understanding.

Meanwhile, simpler lessons renewed those higher up with basics (after all, lower steps are not removed). Furthermore, the advanced needed to return below to fulfill their obligation to help lower believers rise higher as a duty of humble service. Full-orbed Christian community life included all the modes, and each one either anticipated or recalled the others.

The members of the whole Christ worked together on the model of Christ their head and learned different lessons: that they must nurture a sense of unity and responsibility for each other; that exercising love binds members together; that care for one another continually resorts to and builds upon the humility of Christ; that an imperative for service is inherent in the higher levels of spiritual attainment. Thus the congregation assembled before Augustine was not unlike a one-room schoolhouse wherein a single instructor teaches at several levels simultaneously, while students imitate and instruct one another.[57]

c. Charting the audiences

While maintaining a perception of these different groups that Augustine himself would recognize, I propose that we read the *Expositions* according to the group structure mentioned in 119,2: *little ones, climbers,* and *spirituals*. Augustine surveyed the progress of conversion in a statement that reflects these groups: "Truth first came to us clad in flesh [*little ones*], and through his flesh healed the inner eye of our hearts [*climbers*], so that we might one day have the strength to see him face to face [*spirituals*]" (56,17).

I'd like to tweak this slightly, however. Augustine seems to differentiate between weaker and stronger *climbers*, according to a focus on either overcoming weakness of the will or attaining the strength of a spiritual perspective: "The first stage of understanding is to recognize that you are a sinner. The second stage of understanding is that when, having received the gift of faith, you begin to do good by choosing to love, you attribute this not to your own power but to the grace of God" (31, 2nd exp. 9). These seem keyed to two dominating metaphors in the *Expositions*: medicine and education. The images represent Augustine's modes of encouragement to hearers at the two middle stages: one to take up the difficult work of self-correction and mastering wayward desire, and the other to reorient the will toward increasing delight in God. So I will split the *climbers* into two groups: the relatively less mature but aspiring *convalescents*, and the relatively more mature and vigorous *strivers*.

Thus four groups commingled in the congregation that listened to Augustine's sermons: *little ones, convalescents, strivers,* and *spirituals*. Augustine tries to deal with each and all while neither over-challenging those who stand lower nor under-challenging those who stand higher. To some extent this accounts for the meandering of the *Expositions*: multiple groups needed different kinds of care and feeding, and he moved from group to group as prompted by the texts and guided by his personal judgment.[58] By definition this scenario presupposes the permeability of each group, since the concern for conversion sought to stir constant movement of both ascent for progress and descent for service.

These categories are lenses through which to see, and against which to measure, the restless movement of conversion Augustine hoped to catalyze. As he treats each text, many vectors meet: his view of Scripture, his understanding of the salvation story, perspectives on the Trinity and the Incarnation, unity and reciprocity of Christ and Church, grace and sin within individuals, threats from outsiders and schismatics. Augustine structured the steps of spiritual conversion to include all those concerns implicitly, while explicitly addressing the needs of particular hearers. Thus the *Expositions* maintained awareness of the larger constellation of Christian convictions and values while negotiating the rhetorical situation with specific groups by accommodation and decorum.

IV. Segue: Working with this book

A. Structure of the anthology

The anthology is divided into six sections that contain the complete text for nineteen of Augustine's *Expositions of the Psalms*. Short prefaces oriented to the analysis above precede each of the six sections, while brief synopses preceding the selected expositions provide a frame and a stimulus for reading. Augustine follows the verses and the wording of each Psalm closely and in order. For ease of referring back to the Psalm, the translation of Augustine's Latin text of a given Psalm taken from the Boulding translation appears before each exposition.

The *Expositions* that follow, arranged according to the groups sketched above, offer an interpretive device for locating essential threads that run through the sermons and help us to read them coherently. In a sense Augustine followed a similar approach while reading the Psalms. The *Expositions* show that he sought first to gain perspective on a Psalm by locating a unifying motif. He worked, he says, to find the Psalm's "soul (*anima*) as though hiding in the Psalm's body, that is, the inner understanding within the outer words" (104,35; see 65,2). For example, he thought Ps 70's teaching on grace was "the gist of the Psalm, the message that resounds from nearly every syllable in it" (70,1.2). He saw good understanding "flow down" from another Psalm's first verse (132,1). But most often the Psalm's title, its superscript, uncovered the key to its coherence. He compared it to the doorway of a house, or its lintel, or façade, that sign that announces to guests and passersby "what's going on inside" (58,1.1). It ensured that visitors didn't enter either too boldly or else too hesitantly, and that once inside they didn't get lost (53,1; 55,1).

For Augustine, I think, the Step-Song collection (Pss 119–133) was a sort of doorway into the great house of the Psalter. Its stairway imagery fit well with the trajectory of spiritual ascent at the center of Augustine's conversion-oriented thought and spirituality. These ascending "steps" suggested the soul's urge toward self-transcendence by a gradual mounting up into God's presence. Though its upward journey will end only in the future life, the soul makes a genuine beginning here below, fueled by liturgy, sacraments, humility, grace, prayer, the practice of love—and reading Scripture in community. This ascent of the soul occurs within a great house—the house of the Psalter. Accordingly I have blended the step imagery into a figure of a large house or building whose entryway invites a view of the building's great height and whose stairs climb gradually from the entry level and lower floors to the upper floors and roof. The imagery represents the movement of ascent toward full spiritual conversion.

Let me briefly characterize each of the groups in terms of the ascending steps in a great house in order to portray the progress of conversion. I will key the different parts of the anthology to this image.

PART I. Entering the Psalter's Great House of Prayer:
The View from the Threshold

> Let us picture to ourselves a man or woman called to make the ascent. Where will it take place? In the heart. What is the starting point? Humility, the valley of weeping. Whither is he to ascend? To a reality that cannot be put into words, of which another Psalm says, *To the place God has appointed.* (119,2)

The first part of the anthology envisions looking from a vantage point within an open-spaced building that allows one to look up to survey its height. The "threshold view" of the anthology's opening section uses the first three *Expositions* of the Step-Song series—on Pss 119, 120, and 121—to survey Augustine's vision of the spiritual climb from flesh to spirit, and the steps of learning that lie in between. These three sermons offer a global look, a sort of *Expositions*-in-miniature, which captures in brief the approach, method, scope and purpose of the entire group of more than two hundred expositions—and so also of the whole anthology. After this opening survey, the collection of *Expositions* coheres around the four categories as focusing lenses through which to read.

PART II. Exploring Christ's Beautiful Mystery:
Steps to the First Floor

> He is humility, the humility that slew pride. So when I say "Christ," my brothers and sisters, I am drawing attention most especially to his humility. It was by humility that he opened a way for us. (33, 1st exp. 4)

The second part uses Augustine's expositions of Pss 33 (1st exp.), 44, 56, and 138 to highlight the Psalter's "steps to the first floor," that is, the lowest levels of ascent on the upward way of conversion. These relate to Scripture's words and stories about the humanity of Christ. Divine Wisdom, by lowering itself into human flesh even to the ignominy of the cross, became the food that we could take. Thus God met our alienation and blindness at the precise spot where we might open ourselves to grace: our *flesh*. With faith and baptism one embraces Christ's mystery, and the gift of salvation by grace is sealed in baptism. Scripture's words unfold Christ's mystery for the newly baptized as well as for the spiritually advanced. The divine

Word spoke to us of redeeming love in a way that even the simplest might understand. "To little ones the humility of Christ is preached, and the flesh of Christ and the crucifixion of Christ, because this is the milk suited to little ones" (120,6). Like infants during a midnight feeding, little ones see the shining moon of the Church that reflects the light of Christ inasmuch as "the flesh of Christ is the head of the Church" (ibid.). Augustine's emphasis is heavily christological, with a focus on Christ's human life; but it is equally ecclesial, with a stress on the Church's life in Scripture and the sacraments. Scripture exercises for *little ones* crossing into Christ's mystery—or for more advanced believers renewing themselves at faith's foundations—consist in rehearsing again and again the story of Christ's incarnate humility and of the divine love poured out in his death and resurrection for the sake of his bride, the Church.

PART III. Recovering Our Bearings: *Steps to the Mezzanine*

> This is a hard question [the Psalmist] has set himself. His soul is perplexed; but it is a soul destined to make the passage to a state where it will despise earthly things and long for those of eternity, and here we see something of that passover. The searching inquiry is itself the passage; the soul is tossed by storms but sure of reaching the harbor. (72,20)

The third part uses Augustine's expositions of Pss 30 (2nd exp.), 32 (2nd exp.), 72, and 140 to highlight the "steps to the mezzanine," that is, the steps up to the beginnings of a serious ascent to conversion as a life practice. Their words warn of the dangers and difficulties that await those starting out on a serious commitment to the Christian life. The first great metaphor for ascending the steps of conversion imagines the state of the soul in relation to sickness, medicine and healing. Common elements of soul-sickness are self-absorption, delusions of self-importance, vulnerability to flattery, obsession with useless knowledge, bursts of anger, lusts of the flesh, skewed judgment, and hardhearted pride (Sir 10:15). If the primary human problem is not lack of knowledge but presumption about having knowledge, then our prime need for getting beyond ourselves is self-scrutiny. Believers bathed in the dawning light of Christ slowly awaken to their mental and moral weaknesses, despite the desire to do good (Rom 7:13–25). Imperfection, of course, had long been evident in the crooked timber of humanity. Ancient philosophy had also worked on these weaknesses and sought various cures for the soul, practices of healing wisdom that drew on a long tradition of soul-therapy. Pushing souls toward healing was a practice known as "psychagogy," literally, "soul-leading."[59] But this healing process for Christians began in candidly confessing sin and weakness (42,7). Scripture exercises for *convalescents* focused on practicing confession, examining one's outlook and motives, and shunning the world's blandishments of fame, pleasure, and power.

PART IV. Exercising the Spiritual Mind: *Steps to the Upper Floors*

> We are in some measure educated through visible things toward apprehension of the invisible. (44,6)

The fourth part uses Augustine's expositions of Pss 30 (3rd exp.), 31 (2nd exp.), 54, and 142 to highlight the "steps to the upper floors," that is, to the upper middle heights of the conversion ascent. They relate to Scripture's words and encouragements about the attractions and pleasures that await those aspiring to the more advanced stages of healing, wherein lost rational-spiritual perception is restored and active. The other great metaphor of progress in conversion relates to education, that is, enlightening the rational-spiritual mind in order to rid the soul of ignorance of God's will and to reorient oneself to spiritual reality. Sin and rebellion not only defaced God's image in the soul or mind but also stunted its ability to perceive the realm of spirit properly. The higher, earth-transcending spiritual mind became enervated when it yielded to the lower, earth-pandering carnal mind (Rom 8:6). But as the believing soul recovered, God's image began to reappear, along with fresh strength to perceive, gauge and act upon spiritual reality. After this rebirth, says Augustine, we discover that "with our mind we apprehend what is just and unjust, and with it we distinguish the true from the false" (42,6). To lead a soul along toward enlightenment was a form of spiritual pedagogy. Those empowered by spiritual reason now were moved less by the dictates of external spiritual authority and more by inner-directed reason. Doctrine, dogma, and ethical axioms worked not as detached theorems but as spiritual reason's organizing principles for loving perception and action. Scripture exercises for *strivers* reworked spiritual reason's powers through, among other things, logical argumentation, question-and-answer drills, the tracking of semantic inferences, the ferreting out of falsehoods, and the admiration of truth's beauty.

PART V. Gazing Upward in Love: *Steps to the Top Floor*

> Although I have leapt beyond earthly pleasures, although fleeting pleasures do not hold me fast, although I now despise those lower things and climb to what is better, I find it enough to enjoy in God's presence the understanding I have from these better things. (38,3)

The fifth part uses Augustine's expositions of Pss 38, 41, and 42 to highlight the "steps to the top floor," that is, the uppermost steps of the ascent to conversion. They relate Scripture's words and images to the bliss and responsibility of spiritual contemplation in love. For Augustine the peak of human experience in the present life is the contemplation of God in love, which leads inexorably to loving one's neighbor in justice and compassion for God's sake. What begins in faith, and grows in hope, matures into a love that understands and rests in God's wisdom. In the way appropriate for this present age, the soul knows and loves God for himself and for no other reward than knowing the eternal "I AM." The full scope of human spiritual development is reserved for the future life, when we shall perceive God immediately. But in the interim, spiritual understanding stands as proxy for the future vision of God.[60] Scripture exercises for *spirituals* stoke desire for the spiritual mind to mount up from earthly realities so that it may, in the words of Augustine's much-loved Pauline text, *understand the invisible things of God through those that have been made* (Rom 1:20).

Epilogue: *View from the Roof*

A retrospective epilogue uses Augustine's exposition of Ps 122 to review the distance traveled in the ascent to conversion. This Psalm's "downward look" over where the soul has come from is the basis for the fourth in the sequence of Step-Song expositions, and recalls the first three that provided the "upward look" on where the soul was aspiring in Part I. This exposition reflects upon, restates, and explores Scripture's vision for the soul's maturity. It recalls how the ascending reader's spiritual conversion takes place in the practice of love.

As I have been suggesting, the *Expositions* groupings in each category frame a way of reading that locates a central focus in each of the respective sermons. This way into the *Expositions* unveils images of Augustine the impassioned believer and the astute preacher that contrast with other more common and perhaps superficial images of him as the stained-glass saint or the austere predestinarian or the pleasure-scorning killjoy. But I must throw in a disclaimer. These categories cannot and do not explain everything going on in any particular sermon. Augustine's mental map of people and places along the way of conversion isn't a sociological description of an actual audience; the breakdown and group sketches offered here don't offer catchall descriptions or airtight explanations of either the *Expositions* or their first hearers. The framework of the anthology offers a set of lenses through which to view these remarkable examples of early Christian preaching, and an opportunity to peer deep into the mind and heart of an extraordinarily gifted teacher and deeply devoted lover of people and of the Bible. But it stands to reason that, given their richness and variety, the *Expositions* should be read from multiple angles. Readers are therefore invited to correct this book's perspective, or to construct another, and perhaps to view these many-sided texts from some more promising angle.

B. Numbering the Psalms and the *Expositions*

Augustine's numbering of the Psalms differs from that of modern Bibles. Also, the numbering of the *Expositions* can be confusing on several counts, so let me append an explanation here for both.

1. Numbering the Psalms. Augustine's Latin text followed the numbering of the Greek Old Testament (the Septuagint), which combined the Hebrew

Pss 9 and 10 into one Psalm; thus the Septuagint Pss 9(b)-147 were one behind the Hebrew enumeration that has been adopted for use in modern Bibles. Augustine's translation, known as the Old Latin version (*Vetus Latina* in Latin), followed the Septuagint. Other small irregularities occur, but the versions catch up at Ps 147. *Note that this anthology uses the Septuagint and Old Latin enumeration both for the* Expositions *and for internal references to the Psalms.* By contrast, the nineteenth-century English translation of the Oxford *Library of the Fathers* series renumbered Augustine's *Expositions* according to the Hebrew numbering of the Psalms. That translation was abridged for the series *Nicene and Post-Nicene Fathers*, which has often been reprinted. Moreover, online users of the public-domain translation of the *Expositions* should be aware that sites like newadvent.org use that nineteenth-century Oxford translation with the Hebrew Psalm numbering.

2. Numbering Augustine's first series of Expositions. Augustine treated Pss 1–32 (Hebrew 1–33) during his presbyterate (391–396). References to these reflect the Psalm and section number assigned by the seventeenth-century French Benedictine editors of Augustine's works. J. P. Migne reproduced these in his nineteenth-century *Patrologia Latina*, which was then followed by the modern critical editions and translations. Thus "21.1" refers to the *Exposition of Psalm* 21, first series, first section.

3. Numbering Augustine's second series. However, Augustine treated Pss 18, 25, 26, and 29–32 a second time during his years as a bishop (396–430). These have traditionally been called "*Exposition* 2 *of Psalm* 30," and so forth. The Boulding system used in this volume differs slightly by referring to "*Exp.* 2 *of Ps.* 30," and so forth. This anthology includes a few of these, namely from Pss 30, 31 and 32. This anthology follows the Boulding numbering for ease of cross-referencing to the complete translation, with the small tweak that places the exposition number after the Psalm number; thus, "*Exp. Ps.* 30, 2nd exp.," and so on.

4. Numbering multiple sermons on one Psalm. Augustine not infrequently preached several sermons on a single Psalm, so it is necessary to differentiate them. These multiple sermons are part of Augustine's "second" series as bishop (see #3 above), traditional numbering made references like "*Exp.* 2 of *Ps.* 30.2.1," (that is, exposition of Ps 30 [Hebrew Ps 31], second series, second sermon, first section. But the complete Boulding translation of the *Expositions* ignores the double series arrangement and numbers the expositions for a single Psalm in a sequence. Thus what the traditional system calls "*Exp.* 2 of *Ps.* 30.2.1" Boulding refers to as "*Exp.* 3 *of Ps.* 30.1. The same reference in this anthology will be "*Exp. Ps.* 30, 3rd exp."

5. Numbering sections The last number in the sequence refers to the section number of the exposition itself rather than to a verse in the Psalm being preached on (although sometimes the number of the section and that of the verse coincide). Typically a section is at most a few paragraphs long. Thus for both the traditional "*Exp. Ps.* 30.2.1" and for this volume's "*Exp. Ps.* 30, 3rd exp. 1," the number 1 at the end refers to the section number.

Notes

1. From this point untitled attributions refer to Augustine's *Expositions of the Psalms*. All translations of this work in the introduction and anthology are taken from the six-volume translation of Maria Boulding, *Expositions of the Psalms*, ed. John E. Rotelle and Boniface Ramsey, Works of Saint Augustine III/15–20 (Hyde Park, N.Y.: New City Press, 2000–2004). (This series is hereafter referred to as WSA.) Boulding's own footnotes, except for a few minor corrections, are unchanged from the original.

2. The great early modern humanist Erasmus of Rotterdam (d. 1536) first referred to the collection as *enarrationes*, and the term stuck.

3. It's important to recognize that in the *Expositions* Augustine reads and interprets the Psalms of the so-called *Vetus Latina* (VL), the "Old Latin" translation of the Bible. The VL was not a translation from the Hebrew, as virtually all modern Bibles are. Rather it was a rough and not infrequently inaccurate translation of the Septuagint, the Greek translation of the Jewish Scriptures made two centuries before Christianity by a legendary Jewish team known as "the Seventy" (thus abbreviated LXX). The LXX was authoritative for early Christians, from the writers of the New Testament up to and including Augustine. This fact remains to be fully explored by Christian scholars, especially theologians. (See Timothy Michael Law, *When God Spoke Greek: The Septuagint and the Making of the Christian Bible* [New York: Oxford University Press, 2013].) Augustine considered the LXX a divinely inspired translation. The VL was assembled perhaps two centuries before Augustine; it had been venerated by North Africans for generations by his time, not unlike the way some Christians still revere the King James Bible. Augustine told Jerome that when some townspeople heard his new Vulgate version of the book of Jonah as replacing the VL, they nearly started a riot (Letter 71,3,5). But the VL's wooden closeness to the phrasing of the LXX made for a number of awkward readings, several of which you'll encounter in the *Expositions*. Augustine often referred to the Greek of the LXX as part of his exegesis (e.g., *Exp. Ps.* 30.2), and sometimes corrected the Old Latin in light of it, especially late in his career.

4. In the foreword to Henry Chadwick's fine short biography, *Augustine of Hippo: A Life* (New York: Oxford University Press, 2009) ix.

5. See the lively description in William Harmless, *Augustine and the Catechumenate*, rev. ed. (Collegeville: Liturgical Press, 2014) 186–197.

6. See William Harmless, "A Love Supreme: Augustine's 'Jazz' of Theology," in *Augustinian Studies* 43 (2012) 149–177. Their improvisational character has been recognized by Augustinian scholars for a century, ever since the studies of Roy J. Deferrari, "Reports of Augustine's Unwritten Sermons," in *Transactions and Proceedings of the American Philological Association* 46 (1915) 35–45; "St. Augustine's Method of Composing and Delivering Sermons," in *The American Journal of Philology* 43 (1922) 97–123, 193–219.

7. For Augustine's concept of Scripture see Pamela Bright, "St. Augustine," in *Christian Theologies of Scripture: A Comparative Introduction*, ed. Justin S. Holcomb (New York: New York University Press, 2006) 39–59; Tarmo Toom, "Augustine on Scripture," in *The T & T Clark Companion to Augustine and Modern Theology* (London: Bloomsbury T & T Clark, 2013) 75–90. See also my essay "Augustine and Scripture" in *The Blackwell Companion to Augustine* (Oxford: Wiley-Blackwell, 2012) 200–214. I address issues around Augustine's early development in hermeneutics and reading, particularly the figurative dimension, in *Christ Meets Me Everywhere: Augustine's Early Figurative Exegesis* (New York: Oxford University Press, 2012).

8. For Augustine's preaching, its context, themes, style, and method, see Michele Pellegrino, "General Introduction" to *Sermons,* ed. John E. Rotelle, WSA III/1 (Hyde Park, N.Y.: New City Press, 1990) 13–163. See also George Lawless, "Augustine of Hippo as Preacher," in *Saint Augustine as Bishop: A Book of Essays,* ed. Fannie Le Moine and Christopher Kleinhenz (New York: Garland, 1994) 13–37; Éric Rebillard, "*Sermones,*" in *Augustine through the Ages: An Encyclopedia,* ed. Allan Fitzgerald, (Grand Rapids: Eerdmans, 1999) 773–792; William Harmless, ed., *Augustine: In His Own Words* (Washington: The Catholic University of America Press, 2010), chap. 4, "Augustine the Preacher"; Peter Sanlon, *Augustine's Theology of Preaching* (Minneapolis: Fortress Press, 2014). Older but still useful chapters on Augustine the preacher appear in F. Van der Meer, *Augustine the Bishop,* trans. Brian Battershaw and G. R. Lamb (New York: Harper Torchbooks, 1960) 405–452. With the discovery of new, or rather lost, sermons of Augustine in the last several decades, scholarly study of Augustine's sermons is intensifying. For a thorough review of scholarly progress and prospects, with detailed bibliography, see Anthony Dupont, *Gratia in Augustine's* Sermones ad populum *during the Pelagian Controversy* (Leiden: Brill, 2013) 3–35. For general orientation to the phenomenon of preaching in early Christianity, see Carol Harrison, *The Art of Listening in the Early Church* (Oxford: Oxford University Press, 2013).

9. For serious consideration of the *Expositions,* English readers should consult Michael Fiedrowicz's "General Introduction" in *Expositions of the Psalms* (1–32), WSA 3/15 (2000) 13–66. That essay abridges his book-length study, the most complete available: *Psalmus Vox Totius Christi: Studien zu Augustins 'Enarrationes in Psalmos'* (Freiburg: Herder, 1997). See also Fiedrowicz and Hildegund Müller, "*Enarrationes in psalmos,*" in *Augustinus-Lexikon* 2, ed. C. P. Mayer (Basel: Schwabe, 1996–2002) 804–857. Rowan Williams gives a reader-friendly introduction, "Augustine and the Psalms," in *Interpretation* 58 (2004) 17–27; as does Andrew Louth, "'Heart in Pilgrimage': St Augustine as Interpreter of the Psalms," in *Orthodox Readings of Augustine,* ed. G. E. Demacopoulos and A. Papanikolaou (Crestwood, N.Y.: St Vladimir's Seminary Press, 2008) 291–304. I give an overview of the *Expositions* in *"Enarrationes in psalmos,"* in *Augustine through the Ages* 290–296. Several essay collections have appeared recently: *Meditations of the Heart: The Psalms in Early Christian Thought and Practice; Essays in Honor of Andrew Louth* (Turnhout: Brepols, 2011); *The Harp of Prophecy: Early Christian Interpretation of the Psalms,* ed. Brian E. Daley and Paul R. Kolbet (Notre Dame: University of Notre Dame Press, 2015). See also the essays by Michael C. McCarthy: "An Ecclesiology of Groaning: Augustine, the Psalms, and the Making of Church," in *Theological Studies* 66 (2005) 23–48; "Creation through the Psalms in Augustine's *Enarrationes in Psalmos,*" in *Augustinian Studies* 37 (2006) 191–218. For the "Psalms of Ascent" or "Step-Songs" (Psalms 119–133), which are central to the organization of the present anthology, see McCarthy's essay, "The Psalms of Ascent as Word of God in Augustine's *Enarrationes in psalmos,*" in *Augustinian Studies* 41 (2010) 109–120. Now also see Gerard McLarney, *St. Augustine's Interpretation of the Psalms of Ascent* (Washington: The Catholic University of America Press, 2014). I thank Professor McLarney for kindly allowing me to see his book in the proof stage.

10. This and all other translations, unless noted, come from WSA.

11. *Questions on the Heptateuch* II,73. This principle was so crucial that Augustine developed several rhyming jingles to teach people to remember it. The passage just referred to uses the rhyme *lateat/pateat* ("concealed/revealed"). *Instructing Beginners in Faith* 4,8 says that the New Testament has a "secret hideaway" in the Old, and the Old is put on "open display" in the New (*occultatio/manifestatio*). The word play appears also in *Exp. Ps.* 105,36, which rhymes the pair "revealed/veiled" (*revelatum/velatum*).

12. For this reason, Augustine's understanding of Christ leads organically and inexorably to his understanding of the Church and of salvation.
13. Gerard McLarney calls this Augustine's "hermeneutic of alignment." *St. Augustine's Interpretation of the Psalms of Ascent* 7–8, 33–43, 199–214.
14. I thank Bill Harmless for this striking image.
15. Annemaré Kotzé, "Reading Psalm 4 to the Manicheans" in *Vigiliae Christianae* 55 (2001) 119–136.
16. Recounted by Augustine's friend and biographer Possidius, *Life of Augustine* 31,2.
17. The phrase comes from the Donatist exegete Tyconius, whose celebrated *Book of Rules* appeared perhaps in the 380's. Augustine speaks of reading this book about the time he began preaching the *Expositions* (Letter 41,2).
18. Richard Hays, "Christ Prays the Psalms: Israel's Psalter as the Matrix of Early Christology," in *The Conversion of the Imagination: Paul as Interpreter of Israel's Scripture* (Grand Rapids: Eerdmans, 2005) 101–118: "The interpretation of the lament psalms as *prayers of the Messiah* is already a presupposition of the earliest stratum of New Testament tradition" (117, emphasis in text).
19. The statement comes from Gustave Bardy, who added, "Those who want to know the foundation of the interior life of the bishop of Hippo should read the *Enarrationes*" (quoted in Fiedrowicz, *Psalmus Vox Totius Christi* 47). Fiedrowicz refers to Augustine's "special affinity and connatural relationship" with the Psalms ("General Introduction," WSA 3/15 [2000] 3).
20. Fiedrowicz, "General Introduction" 37–40.
21. Ibid. 40–43.
22. Paula Fredriksen, *Augustine and the Jews: A Christian Defense of Jews and Judaism* (New Haven: Yale University Press, 2010).
23. Luke Timothy Johnson and William S. Kurz, *The Future of Catholic Biblical Scholarship* (Grand Rapids: Eerdmans, 2002) 120. The book's brief chapter on Augustine (91–118) is helpful, despite needing some adjustment.
24. *Method in Theology* (New York: Herder, 1972) 290, quoted in Michael Paul Gallagher, *Faith Maps* (New York: Paulist Press, 2010) 72, with emphasis added. Lonergan was drawing on a text of the French thinker Olivier Rabut.
25. The Latin is *rapio*, "carry off," "seize by force." Augustine's own experience lies just below the surface. He used this word in *Confessions* VII,17,23 to tell God about the first time he felt the divine presence as spirit. "I was caught up to you by your beauty," he wrote, in the Henry Chadwick translation. Boulding translates rather blandly, "I was drawn toward you." The contemporary of Shakespeare, William Watts (1631), vividly translates, "I was ravished to thee by thine own beauty." Anyone who has been "carried away" after truly "falling" in love knows the aptness of these otherwise violent images.
26. Hildegund Müller notes that the people gathered within the walls of the church physically symbolized their separation from the world and their sense of unity. See her "Preacher: Augustine and His Congregation," in *The Blackwell Companion to Augustine* 302.
27. Augustine discusses this liturgical exchange in Sermon 227, among other places. Harmless, *Augustine in His Own Words* 154–155.
28. Harmless, *Augustine and the Catechumenate,* rev. ed., 372–381.

29. Augustine's word is *vilesco*, "make worthless"; Boulding translates "approach disrespectfully."
30. Harmless, "A Love Supreme" 155–157.
31. Augustine demanded that hearers sweat together with him in the work of exegesis. The imagery fits the afflictions of African heat; but it also draws on the Adam and Eve story, the sinning couple of Eden who were sentenced to sweat for their bread in Gn 3:19. "Proclaiming the word of truth is hard work, and so is listening to it.... Accordingly, if God's word is our bread, let us sweat away at listening to it" (*Exp. 3 Ps.* 32,1).
32. Harrison, *The Art of Listening in the Early Church* 43
33. Michael C. Leff and Andrew Sachs, "Words the Most Like Things: Iconicity and the Rhetorical Text," in *Western Journal of Speech Communication* 54 (1990) 252–273.
34. Harrison, *The Art of Listening in the Early Church* 42–43. McLarney refers to various devices as "*phrases fictives*" in *St. Augustine's Interpretation of the Psalms of Ascent* 133–135.
35. Augustine follows a popular misreading (which remains widespread) of Jesus sweating blood during his Agony in the Garden (Lk 22:44). Luke (presuming the text is original) wrote that Jesus' drops of sweat were "like" great drops of blood. But in view of the impending crucifixion, Luke clearly intended the blood-sweat connection. Raymond E. Brown, *The Death of the Messiah* I (New York: Doubleday, 1994) xx.
36. Reading the lines aloud one can feel their rhythm and hear the rhyming. Here I underline words to stress the syncopation: Lines 7–8: *Quid est de toto corpore sanguinis effluxio / nisi de tota ecclesia martyrum passio?* Line 15: *Illud sacrificium vespertinum fecit in resurrectione munus matutinum.* Line 16: *Quod lego in psalmo, hoc audio a Domino.* Line 17: *In ipso etiam, psalmum agnosco quod in evangelio lego.* Line 19: *sicut audivimus, ita et vidimus* (actually a quote from Ps 47:9). Harmless entertainingly demonstrates what he calls Augustine's "Rap Latin" in *Augustine in His Own Words* 131–132.
37. Augustine professed not to understand why he loved figuration so much, when the plain or bottom-line versions of an idea added up to knowing the same thing. Why is it so much sweeter, he asked, to think of a group of newly baptized people like a flock of shorn ewes coming up from washing, rather than just saying plainly what they are? (*Teaching Christianity* II,6,7) He didn't answer the question. But he wondered the same thing later in a letter and guessed that it had something to do with creating love together with knowledge. Realities wrapped in figures, he wrote, "arouse and kindle love more than if they were set forth bare without any likenesses of the sacraments" (Letter 55,21). The critical feature is the *movement* from the figure to the reality: for the soul is "confronted with bodily likenesses and brought from there to spiritual realities that are symbolized by those likenesses, *it is strengthened by this passage (transitus)*, and is set aflame like the fire in a coal when stirred up, and is carried with a more ardent love toward rest" (ibid.).
38. Etienne Gilson astutely observed long ago, after reading Augustine for his philosophy in order to compare him to Thomas Aquinas: "If we are dealing not so much with knowledge as with love, then the philosopher's task is not so much to cause knowledge as to cause love.... Now in order to arouse love we do not prove, we show. Augustine never tires of doing this." *The Christian Philosophy of Saint Augustine,* trans. L.E.M. Lynch (New York: Vintage Books, 1960) 236. Augustine loved philosophy, but for the sake of his congregation didn't philosophize in his sermons. But the reverse was not true. Apparently one could take the philosopher out of the preacher, but not the preacher out of the philosopher.
39. Müller, "Preacher: Augustine and His Congregation" 306–307.

40. For details on this work, see Raymond Canning's introduction to his translation, *Instructing Beginners in Faith* (Hyde Park, N.Y.: New City Press, 2006) 9–38.
41. In a remarkable throwaway half-line of *Answer to Faustus, a Manichean,* Augustine writes, "No one enters into truth except through love" (XXXII,18).
42. *Miscellany of Questions in Response to Simplician* I,1,1. On impersonation (*prosopopoeia*), see my *Christ Meets Me Everywhere* 179–185, 196–200, 290–292.
43. Kathy Eden, *Hermeneutics and the Rhetorical Tradition* (New Haven: Yale University Press, 1997) 14.
44. Robert Dodaro has recalled the importance of decorum in studying Augustine's theological formulations in a series of articles. The latest is "Language Matters: Augustine's Use of Literary Decorum in Theological Argument," in *Augustinian Studies* 45 (2014) 1–28. See the bibliography for previous articles. Modern rhetorical studies have aimed to recover the importance of decorum by analyzing its importance in classical Latin oratory; see Michael C. Leff, "Decorum and Rhetorical Interpretation: The Latin Humanistic Tradition and Contemporary Critical Theory," in *Vichiana*, 3rd series (1990) 107–126.
45. "The sermons are defined not so much by their content as by their effect on the listener." Müller, "Preacher: Augustine and His Congregation" 306.
46. This is a relatively new way to think about the sermons. Anthony Dupont has recently pointed out in *Gratia in Augustine's* Sermones ad populum 10, n. 21, "As far as Augustine's preaching activity is concerned, 'preacher-audience analysis' is still in its infancy."
47. Harrison, *The Art of Listening in the Early Church* 49, calls this analysis "auditory criticism," a term that emphasizes "the role of the hearer in rhetorical practice." This approach addresses "how a text is arranged and presented in order to communicate with a hearer, to facilitate their understanding and effect their response in particular circumstances."
48. Ambrose helped Augustine's early steps toward conversion by showing him that the Bible was "all the more deserving of reverence and divine faith in that Scripture was easily accessible to every reader, while yet guarding a mysterious dignity in its deeper sense" (*Confessions* VI,5,8). Eventually Augustine spoke of the experience of Scripture's becoming deeper as one's understanding grew: "Scripture is a reality that grows along with little children (*parvuli*)" (ibid. III,5,9). These "little ones" will be discussed below. Almost two centuries after Augustine, his devotee Gregory the Great wrote, "Scripture is like a kind of river that is both shallow and deep, in which the lamb may wade and the elephant can swim" (*Letter to Leander* 4).
49. We get a sense of the variety of people, as well as Augustine's concern to accommodate the way he spoke to them, in *Instructing Beginners in Faith* 15,23.
50. A point Augustine emphasizes ibid. 8,12–9,13.
51. On "citadel of philosophy" see *The Happy Life* 10; on their spiritual ascent, see the famous vision at Ostia in *Confessions* IX,10,23–26.
52. Harrison, *The Art of Listening in the Early Church* 37–38: "We can learn a great deal about the silent hearer...simply by bearing in mind that what is said, and how it is said, in so many different contexts, is shaped by their presence, and by a desire to inform, move and persuade them by what they heard."
53. This echoed language that Jesus had used in speaking about those to whom God's revelations were given (Mt 11:25–27). Moreover, in North Africa the newly baptized were called *infantes* ("newborns"). To our ear, talking about adults as "little ones"

can sound arrogant or elitist. In fact, the meaning intended the exact opposite; this language reflects the reverse perspectives embedded in Scripture's logic of conversion, wherein the first are last, the last first, and only those with child-like humility enter the kingdom of God (cf. Matt 18:1–5; 19:30). Moreover, the mature Augustine realized that in many ways he himself remained a "little one" (*Answer to Faustus, a Manichean* XII,48). See G. G. Stroumsa, "Milk and Meat: Augustine and the End of Esotericism," in *Hidden Wisdom: Esoteric Traditions and the Roots of Christian Mysticism,* ed. Aleida and Jan Assmann (Leiden: Brill, 1996) 132–146.

54. Hildegund Müller writes, "The sermon was preached in front of a mixed audience of pagans, catechumens and baptized Christians, providing the preacher with a handy image of the *civitates permixtae* (the 'intermingled' communities of the respective followers of God and the World)." "Preacher: Augustine and His Congregation" 302. See Harmless's richly imagined experience of being inside Augustine's basilica in *Augustine in His Own Words* 122–124.

55. "The author makes his readers.... If he makes them well—that is, makes them see what they have never seen before, moves them into a new order of perception and experience altogether—he finds his reward in the peers he has created." Wayne Booth, *The Rhetoric of Fiction* (Chicago: University of Chicago Press, 1961) 397–398.

56. *Tractates on the Gospel of John 55–111*, trans. John W. Rettig, *Fathers of the Church* 90, (Washington: The Catholic University of America Press, 1994) 214.

57. I thank Lorie Simmons for this vivid image. This helps to make some sense out of Augustine's otherwise puzzling statement in *Teaching Christianity* I,39,43 that those who have attained the highest level of spiritual maturity—those with a firm habit of living by faith, hope and charity—"have no need of the Scriptures except for instructing others."

58. Exercising wise discernment and shrewd judgment was routinely expected of a bishop in other, often mundane, matters. Perhaps it's not unreasonable to imagine it playing a role while working with a congregation in matters of liturgy, preaching, and exegesis. See Kevin Uhalde, *Expectations of Justice in the Age of Augustine* (Philadelphia: University of Pennsylvania Press, 2007) 44–65.

59. Elizabeth Asmis, "'Psychagogia' in Plato's Phaedrus," in *Illinois Classical Studies* 11 (1986) 153–172; Michael Cameron, "*Totus Christus* and the Psychagogy of Augustine's Sermons," in *Augustinian Studies* 36 (2005) 59–70; and now Paul R. Kolbet, *Augustine and the Cure of Souls* (Notre Dame: University of Notre Dame Press, 2010) (on *psychagogia* in pre-Christian philosophical use, 8, 31–61; on psychagogic practice in Ambrose, 77; in Augustine, 117–128).

60. Augustine wrote to a correspondent who had asked about the relation between faith and spiritually regenerated reason: "If, then, we are already believers, we have come to the way of faith, and, if we do not give it up, we shall undoubtedly come not only to as great an understanding of incorporeal and immutable things as can be grasped in this life, though not by all, but also to the peak of contemplation, which the Apostle calls *face to face* (1 Cor 13:12)" (Letter 120,1,4).

PART I

ENTERING THE PSALTER'S GREAT HOUSE OF PRAYER

View from the Threshold

Exposition of Psalm 119

Synopsis

    This short Psalm, the first of the Step-Songs, profitably repays the labor to understand it, for it surveys the spiritual ascent to God's domain. No one has imagined this divine place; we're too weighed down by the flesh. But Christ came down to help us ascend from the valley to the mountain. He is both the starting point and the goal: the valley is his humble flesh, and the mountain his glorious divinity. He didn't "fall," like Adam, but rather "descended." Likewise, teachers like Paul have descended to help "little ones" who feed on milk so that they may ascend to become "spirituals" who eat solid food. Isaiah's prophecy shows you the stages of ascent, starting with fear of the Lord, the beginning of wisdom (1–2).

    Anyone who is serious about climbing quickly runs into challenges within and without; earthly loves are hard to shake. But the "sharp arrows" of God's word and the "hot coals" of saintly examples give a much-needed boost (3–5). The higher one climbs, however, the clearer and more disappointing becomes the issue of the "mixed body" of good and bad in the Church. The climber then echoes the Church bemoaning "my long-drawn-out exile." The allegory of Abraham's two sons illustrates the dilemma by displaying two peoples, two Jerusalems, and two covenants, old and new. But charity remains the only key to progress (6–7).

    The journey of ascent goes on spiritually, not physically. "If you are in love with God, you are climbing toward him" (8). But love for neighbor must follow. Peace is easy to talk about; but its truth does not penetrate the heart until one begins to practice it. The climber's great challenge is to learn how to deal peaceably with people who hate peace. We face that daily with the schismatics (9).

Augustine's Text of Psalm 119

(1) A Song of Steps.

    I cried to you, Lord, when I was troubled, and you heard me.

(2) Lord, rescue my soul from wicked lips and the guileful tongue.

(3) What is to be given to you, what shall be provided for you,

    That you may withstand the guileful tongue?

(4) Sharp arrows of the mighty one, with destructive, all-devouring coals.

(5) Alas, alas, how long-drawn-out is my exile!

    I have been dwelling among the tents of Kedar.

(6) My soul has been on pilgrimage for a long time.

(7) I dealt peaceably with those who hated peace.

    When I spoke to them, they waged war on me without justification.

Exposition

A Sermon to the People

General introduction to the "Songs of Ascents"

1. The psalm we have just heard, and to which we have sung our response, is a short one, and very profitable for our instruction. Listening to it will not be too long a job for you, and when you put it into practice your labor will not be unfruitful.

As the title that prefaces the psalm informs us, this is a *Song of Ascents*.[1] In Greek the title is *αναβαθμῶν*. Now ascents, or steps, can be used for either going up or going down, but the steps that appear in these psalms represent people going up. We too are to ascend, but we must not try to climb with our bodily feet; rather should we remember what was written in another psalm: *God arranges ascents in his heart, in the valley of weeping, to the place he has appointed* (Ps 83:6–7(84:5–6)).[2] *Ascents*, it said. Where? In the heart. What is the starting point? The valley of weeping. But whither are we mounting? That is hard to say, for human speech falters and the destination

---

1. Psalms 119–133(120–134) were regarded by Jewish tradition as a distinct group. In his *Expositions* Augustine also viewed them so, as mutually connected and different from the rest of the Psalter. His explanation of the overall title, given here at the beginning of his *Exposition of Psalm* 119, is an introduction to all of them; the essential themes of his treatment are found here. It appears that his sermons on these *Songs of Ascents* were preached at Hippo between December 406 and April 407, or, less probably, a year later.
2. A key text for Augustine's interpretation of these psalms.

cannot be described, perhaps cannot even be conceived in thought. When the lesson from the apostle was read just now, you heard about something that *eye has not seen, nor ear heard, nor has it risen into the human heart* (1 Cor 2:9). So it has not risen into the human heart? Then let the human heart ascend to it instead. But if *eye has not seen, nor ear heard nor has it risen into the human heart*, how can we say anything about that place to which we are called to ascend? Since it is indescribable, the earlier psalm simply says, *To the place he has appointed*. The psalmist, through whom the Holy Spirit was speaking, seems to say, "What else can I tell you about it? That we are going to a place like this... or like that...? Whatever I say to you, you will think in earthly terms, you who crawl along the ground with your burden of flesh, for *the corruptible body weighs down the soul, and this earthly dwelling oppresses a mind that considers many things* (Wis 9:15). To whom can I speak? Who will hear? Can anyone comprehend where we shall be after the present life, if we have ascended in our hearts? No, no one; and you will do better to hope for a place of happiness beyond all telling, which he who arranged ascents in your heart has appointed for you."

But where did God arrange them? *In the valley of weeping*. This closed-in valley[3] symbolizes humility, as a mountain stands for height. The mountain we have to climb is a height of the spirit. Who is the mountain? Who else but our Lord Jesus? He made himself into a valley of weeping for you in his passion; and he is the mountain of your ascent because he remains where he has always been. What is the valley of weeping? *The Word was made flesh, and dwelt among us* (Jn 1:14). What is the valley of weeping? *He offered his cheek to one who struck him; he was drenched with insults* (Lam 3:30). He was punched, smeared with spittle, crowned with thorns, and crucified. This is the valley of weeping from which your upward climb must begin.

But whither are you to ascend? *In the beginning was the Word, and the Word was with God; he was God* (Jn 1:1). It was this same Word who *was made flesh, and dwelt among us*. He came down to you, but in such wise that he remained in himself; he came down to you so that for you he might become a valley of weeping, but he remained in himself so that he might be for you the mountain of your ascent. *In the last days the mountain of the Lord's house shall be revealed on the summit of all mountains* (Is 2:2), says Isaiah. To that height you are to climb, but do not imagine some earthly expedition. When you hear of the mountain, do not think of elevated ground; when you hear of a rock or a stone,[4] do not let your mind conjure up something flinty; when you hear Christ called a lion,[5] do not suppose that he is fierce; and when you hear of a lamb,[6] do not picture an animal to yourself. In himself he is none of these things, but he became

---

3. *Convallis*, a valley enclosed on all sides.
4. See 1 Cor 10:4.
5. See Rv 5:5.
6. See Jn 1:29; Rv 5:6.

all of them for you. He is the starting point of your ascent and the goal of your ascent; you climb from his example to his divinity. He gave you an example by humbling himself.

When certain of his friends disdained to begin from the valley of weeping, he rebuked them. They were ambitious for an over-hasty ascent; they aspired to high honors but gave no thought to the route of humility. Mark what I am saying, beloved.[7] Two disciples wanted to sit beside the Lord, one at his right, the other at his left. The Lord saw that they were getting things back to front and thinking about honors prematurely, for they should have been learning first of all how to be humbled in order to be exalted.[8] So he said to them, *Are you able to drink the cup I am to drink?* (Mt 20:22). He was destined to drink the cup of suffering in the valley of weeping; but they, paying no heed to Christ's humility, wanted to seize the high dignity of Christ. He recalled them to the way like lost travelers, not because he meant to refuse them what they wanted but in order to show them how to reach it.

2. Therefore, my brothers and sisters, since we are to ascend in our hearts, let us sing this psalm about ascending. A certain descent occurred first, a descent right down to our level, without which no ascent would have been possible for us. Jacob saw a vision of ladders, and on those ladders some were shown to him mounting and others coming down; he saw the movement in both directions.[9] We may perhaps think that the climbers he saw were those making progress,[10] and those coming down were backsliders, because this is in fact what we find in the people of God: that some make progress and others fall away. The ladders may possibly suggest these, but perhaps it is better to think that all those on the ladders, whether ascending or descending, are good people; for it was no accident that the text spoke of some as descending, not as falling down. There is a vast difference between descending and falling, for it was because Adam fell that Christ descended. The one fell, the other descended; the one fell through pride, the other descended in mercy. Yet he did not descend alone. Well, yes, he did descend alone from heaven, of course, but there are many holy people who imitate him by descending to us, and have done so in the past. On what a height must the apostle have been accustomed to dwell when he said, *If we are beside ourselves, it is for God!* (2 Cor 5:13) By going forth in his mind he had gone forth to God. Mentally leaving behind all human frailty, all the temporal concerns of this world, all these transient things that dwindle to nothing as they are born and sink into death, his heart dwelt in a contemplation that defied description, insofar as such a state was possible for him. Of that state he said that the one who experienced

---

7. *Caritas vestra.*
8. See Mt 23:12; Lk 14:11; 18:14.
9. See Gn 28:12.
10. *Visos proficientes.* Variant: *viros proficientes*, "men making progress."

it *heard things beyond utterance, of which no human tongue may speak* (2 Cor 12:4). Of those realities he could not speak to you, but he himself was able to see them in some degree, though he could not pass them on. If therefore he had chosen to tarry for ever in what he saw but could not express, he would not have lifted you to a height where you too could see them. But what did he do? He came down. In the same letter he says, *If we are beside ourselves, it is for God; if we restrain ourselves, it is for you* (2 Cor 5:13). What does he mean by *restrain ourselves*? "We speak in a fashion you can understand." And this was because Christ also, by being born and suffering, made himself such that people could talk about him; for humans easily talk about another human. Can any mortal talk about God, as God truly is? But men and women readily speak about someone human like themselves. If great people were to come down to little ones and yet speak to them only of HIM WHO IS great, it was necessary for him who was great to become little himself, so that great human teachers could speak of him to little people. And this he did.

What I am telling you now is what you heard about when the lesson from the apostle was read. If your ears were attentive you heard him say, *Not as spiritual persons could I speak to you, but only as carnal* (1 Cor 3:1). On the heights he conversed with spiritual beings, but in order to speak to those who are carnal he comes down. And when he comes down, he speaks of the one who himself descended. If you are not sure of this, listen to what John said of Christ when he was abiding in himself: *In the beginning was the Word, and the Word was with God; he was God. He was with God in the beginning. Everything was made through him; no part of created being was made without him* (Jn 1:1–3). Take that in, if you can. Seize it, for it is solid nourishment. But you will say to me, "Yes, he is solid food, to be sure, but I am an infant. What I need is milk, so that I can grow up and become capable of eating solids." Christ knew this. He is solid food, but you can only take milk; and so he who was solid food was processed through flesh to reach your palate. A mother does this: she eats solid food and processes it through her flesh to pass it on to her baby in the form of milk; similarly the Word, the Lord, the food of angels, was made flesh, and so the apostle could say, *I gave you milk to drink, rather than solid food. You were not capable of it then, nor are you even now* (1 Cor 3:2). He descended to little ones to give them milk, and because he descended, he gave them the one who descended; for he asked them, *Did I ever claim to know anything among you, save Jesus Christ and him crucified?* (1 Cor 2:2) If he had said simply, *save Jesus Christ*, we might have thought he meant Jesus Christ in his divinity, in his reality as the Word with God, Jesus Christ the Son of God. But him the little ones cannot grasp—not when he is spoken of like that. How can they take him in, these little ones who can take only milk? *Jesus Christ, crucified*, says the apostle. Suck what he became for you, and you will grow toward what he is.

There are climbers, and there are some who descend. On those ladders, some mount, some descend. Who are the climbers? Those who are making progress toward an understanding of spiritual things. Who are the ones who descend? People who, though they enjoy as much understanding of spiritual things as human beings can, nonetheless come down to the level of the little ones to tell them all they can take in. Thus these little ones, nourished on milk, may grow fit and strong until they are able to absorb solid spiritual food. Consider, brothers and sisters, how Isaiah too was one of the teachers who came down to us. The very stages of his descent can be discerned. When he spoke of the Holy Spirit he put the Spirit's gifts in a definite order: *The spirit of wisdom and understanding shall rest upon him, the spirit of counsel and strength, the spirit of knowledge and piety, and the spirit of fear of the Lord* (Is 11:2–3). He began with wisdom and brought the list down to the fear of the Lord. As he, your teacher, descended from wisdom to fear, so you, the learner, must ascend from fear to wisdom if you are to make progress; for Scripture says, *The fear of the Lord is the beginning of wisdom* (Ps 110(111):10; Prv 1:7; 9:10; Sir 1:16).

Listen now to the psalm. Let us picture to ourselves a man or woman called to make the ascent. Where will it take place? In the heart. What is the starting point? Humility, the valley of weeping. Whither is he to ascend? To a reality that cannot be put into words, of which another psalm says, *To the place* God *has appointed* (Ps 83:6–7(84:5–6)).

Verses 1–2. The would-be climber encounters cunning dissuaders

3. When someone thus addresses himself to the ascent—or, rather, to put it more plainly, when a Christian begins to think about making headway—he or she soon suffers from the tongues of people with opposing ideas. Anyone who has not yet had any trouble of this kind has not yet made any progress; and if anyone is not prepared to endure it, that person had better not make any attempt to advance. Does such a one[11] want to understand what we are saying? It is more a matter of our listening together, and reflecting on our own experience. Let anyone begin to move forward, begin to want to make the ascent, begin to scorn earthly, perishable, temporal things and to set little store by the prosperity this world offers; let such a one begin to think of God alone, disdain to gloat over his gains or lament his losses; let him even resolve to sell all he owns, give the proceeds to the poor, and follow Christ. What happens? Let us see how he has to put up with the talk of people who try to pull him back,[12] who raise all kinds of objections, and—what is worse—attempt to turn him away from salvation as though they had his best interests at heart. Anyone who genuinely wants to promote another's interests wants that person's salvation, wants whatever will profit the other; but the false counselor holds the other back

---

11. Variant: "Do you...?" (plural).
12. Variant: "disparage him."

from salvation. Cloaked as an adviser, he dispenses a murderer's venom, and so he is reckoned a guileful tongue. The person essaying the climb should therefore pray to God first of all for protection against such tongues. This is what the psalmist did: *I cried to you, Lord, when I was troubled, and you heard me.* How did the Lord hear him? In such a way as to set him on the steps, ready to ascend.

4. As he prepared to ascend, his plea was heard. What does he pray now? *O Lord, rescue my soul from wicked lips and the guileful tongue.* What is a guileful tongue? A sly tongue, one that feigns friendliness but does real mischief. People of guileful speech ask, "Do you mean to attempt what no one else has done? Do you aim to be the only real Christian?" If the aspiring climber points to others who are doing the same, and reads out the gospel passages where the Lord commanded it, or reads the Acts of the Apostles, what is the reply of people with cunning tongues and iniquitous lips? "But you may not have the strength for that. What you propose is too arduous an undertaking." Some try to deter him by discouragement, others make it even harder for him by their positive commendation; for this is the way of life that has conquered the world, and so great is Christ's authority that not even a pagan dare criticize Christ. So he who is above criticism is read out, and we hear him counseling, *Go and sell all you possess and give the money to the poor. Then come, follow me* (Mt 19:21). Christ cannot be faulted, then? The gospel cannot be gainsaid? Very well, the guileful tongue resorts to deterrence through praise. If you want to praise him, guileful tongue, you should be encouraging me; why make things difficult for me with your praise? You would do better to insult the Christian enterprise than to praise it deviously. If you were to insult it openly, what would you say? "Have nothing to do with it! That is a foul way of life, a wicked course!" But you know that if you take that line you can be refuted by the authority of the gospel, so you turn to a different tactic to dissuade me: by your insincere praise you try to hold me back from true praise; indeed, by praising Christ you attempt to hold me back from Christ. You say, "But what does it mean? Others have achieved it, have they? Wonderful! But you will probably not be strong enough. Are you setting out to climb? You will fall." The speaker may sound like an adviser, but he is a snake, with a guileful tongue, and venomous. Pray against a tongue like that, if you want to ascend. Say to your God, *O Lord, rescue my soul from wicked lips and the guileful tongue.*

Verses 3–4. The climber is armed with sharp arrows and burning coals: God's words and the examples of the saints

5. The Lord your God says to you, *What is to be given to you, what shall be provided for you, that you may withstand the guileful tongue?* What defense will you have, he asks, against the guileful tongue, with what weapon will you meet the guileful tongue, how are you to arm yourself against the guileful tongue, *what is to be given to you, what shall be*

provided for you? He asks to test you, for he is going to answer his own questions. He responds to his own interrogation: *Sharp arrows of the mighty one, with destructive, all-devouring coals.* Whether you say *destructive* or *all-devouring*—for there are variations among the codices—it comes to the same. Look at it like this: coals are called all-devouring because by laying waste and depopulating a region they quickly reduce it to desolation. Now what are these coals? It would be better if you were first to understand what the arrows are, beloved. *Sharp arrows of the mighty one* are the words of God. Watch them as they are launched, and see how they pierce hearts! But when human hearts are transfixed by the arrows of God's word, the effect is not death but the arousal of love. The Lord is a skilled marksman with his eye on love, and no one shoots more accurately at love than he who shoots with the word. He shoots at his lover's heart for the good of the lover; he shoots to turn you into his lover. We shoot with his arrows when we deal in words.

What about the all-devouring coals? It is not enough to counter the sly tongue and the wicked lips with words. Words alone are insufficient; we need examples too. The destructive coals are examples. You shall have a brief explanation, beloved, as to why they are called destructive; but first consider how we should use examples. A sly tongue can devise nothing more insidious than to say, "Take care, you may not be able to carry your enterprise through. It is too much for you to tackle." Now you have made the gospel precept your own, and so you have an arrow, but as yet you have no coals. There is some danger that an arrow alone may not prevail against the guileful tongue; but there are still coals. Suppose, for instance, you hear God beginning to say to you, "If you are not strong enough to do this, how can that other person do it? Or how was So-and-So able to manage it? You are hardly more delicate than that senator, are you? Are you weaker in health than X or Y?[13] Are you weaker even than women? If women have been strong enough to follow this way of life, is it too much for men? Rich people, delicately nurtured, have been robust enough: is it too rough for the poor?" The person so challenged replies, "But I have committed so many sins; I am a wretched sinner." Then he is reminded of how many people have sinned greatly, and loved all the more because they were forgiven more. As the gospel tells us, *one who is forgiven little loves little* (Lk 7:47).

All these arguments have been rehearsed, and the names have been listed of people who found the necessary strength. The hearer who had already been pierced to the heart by God's word now has destructive coals heaped upon him, and his earthly way of thinking is purged. What does it mean, to be despoiled and depopulated? It means the place is left bare and empty. Plenty of rank plants used to flourish in him: many carnal thoughts, many worldly loves. All these are burnt up by the destructive coals to

---

13. Variant: "weaker than this or that invalid?"

leave a clean, empty place. In this pure place God can erect his building, for the devil's abode has been dismantled and Christ is now being built up there. As long as the devil makes it his home, Christ cannot be built. But the destructive coals arrive and demolish the evil building. Then on the desolate site the edifice of perpetual happiness is raised.

Consider now why they are called coals. When people are converted to the Lord they pass from death to life. But live coals were once extinct, dead, before they were kindled. Coals that are not on fire can be called dead; burning ones are called live coals. Thus the examples of the many sinful people who have been converted to God are called coals. You may hear others marveling at what has happened, saying, "I knew him once. I knew what a drunkard he was, what a scoundrel, what a fan of the circus and the amphitheater, and how dishonest. But now, look how he serves God, and what a blameless life he leads!" Do not be surprised. He is a piece of coal. You rejoice to see him a live coal, because you deplored his dead state. But while you praise this live coal—if you praise him wisely—you will apply him to another who is dead, and set fire to him or her as well. What I mean is this: if anyone is still reluctant to follow God, put the coal that used to be dead near him. Equip yourself with the arrow of God's word and the destructive coal, and so go out to confront the iniquitous lips and the sly tongue.

Verse 5–6. *The miseries of exile, living among the dark tents of Kedar*

6. What comes next? The speaker has taken up his burning arrows; let him now take the destructive coals as well. He is already fending off the sly tongue and the wicked lips, already mounting the first step and beginning to make headway; but he is still living among bad people, among the wicked. The winnowing has not taken place yet. Think of it this way: does the mature condition of the grain mean that it is already in the barn? Clearly not. Inevitably it is still pressed down under a load of straw; and so it is with Christians. The more progress they make, the more evident and serious in their eyes are scandals among the people; for if they are not advancing themselves they will not notice prevalent sins, and if they are not true Christians themselves they will not detect impostors. The Lord teaches us this in the parable about the wheat and the tares, brothers and sisters. *When the shoots had grown up and borne fruit, then the weeds became apparent* (Mt 13:26). This suggests that no one notices bad people except an observer who has become good, for only *when the shoots had grown up and borne fruit* did the weeds really show up. The psalmist is one who is beginning to make progress. He therefore notices bad people and many evils of which he was previously unaware; and so he cries out to God, *"Alas, alas, how long-drawn-out is my exile!* I have gone so far away from you. My pilgrimage is so wearisome! I have not yet arrived in

that homeland where I shall live untroubled by any evil.[14] Not yet have I attained to the fellowship of the angels, where I shall have no scandals to dread. Why am I not yet there? Because *my exile is so long-drawn-out.*" An exile[15] implies a pilgrimage or journey abroad. A person who lives in a foreign land, away from his own country, is called an exile. Thus the psalmist laments, *How long-drawn-out is my exile!* And where is he, in this prolonged exile?

It sometimes happens that someone on a journey lives among more congenial people than perhaps he did back at home; but this is not the case with us when we remember that we are travelers, far away from the heavenly Jerusalem. A person may leave his own country and find himself better off during his travels: he comes across trustworthy friends on the journey, unlike any he found at home. Indeed, in his own land he had enemies; that was why he was driven out and forced to journey abroad; and on his way he finds what he never found in his homeland. But Jerusalem, our homeland, is not like that, for there all the citizens are good. Anyone on a journey away from Jerusalem is thrust among bad people and cannot escape from them, except by returning to the society of the angels, to be at home in that place from which he is distanced by his travels. There dwell all the righteous and holy ones who enjoy God's word without reading, without letters, for what is written on the page for us they behold in the face of God. What kind of homeland is it? A very great country, and wretched are they who are so far from home.

7. But what of the psalmist; what has he to say? *How long-drawn-out is my exile!* This is definitely the voice of pilgrims and exiles, the voice of the Church as it struggles along on earth. It is the voice of one who cries out from far-off countries in another psalm: *From the ends of the earth I have called to you* (Ps 60:3(61:2)). Is there any one of us who cries from the ends of the earth? No: not I, nor you, nor he, nor she; but the whole Church[16] cries from the ends of the earth. The whole inheritance of Christ cries out, and of the Church a psalm said in prophecy, *Ask of me, and I will give you the nations as your inheritance, and the ends of the earth for your possession* (Ps 2:8). Christ's domain extends to the furthest bounds of the earth; all the saints are his possession; and all the saints form a single person in Christ because the Church is a holy unity. Therefore it is this single person who laments, *From the ends of the earth I have called to you, as my heart was wrung with pain* (Ps 60:3(61:2)).

Perhaps this one person might be asked, "With whom are you living, then, that you groan like this?" He reiterates, *My pilgrimage is so long-drawn-out.* Yes, but might he not have good neighbors? No, for if he had, he would hardly say *Alas*, would he? *Alas* is a word that indicates misery; it

---

14. Or "by any bad person."
15. *Incolatus.*
16. Variant: "only the Church."

is a sound of calamity and unhappiness, yet it also expresses hope, because the one who uses it has at last learned to grieve. There are many others, just as wretched, who do not grieve; they are exiles too, but have no desire to go home.

The psalmist certainly does want to go home, for he experiences the misery of his exile. Because he recognizes it he is on the way already. He is beginning his ascent, for he is beginning to sing the Song of Ascents. Where is he groaning, then? Among whom is he living? *I have been dwelling among the tents of Kedar.* That is a Hebrew word, and I am sure you did not understand it. What does the phrase mean: *I have been dwelling among the tents of Kedar*? As far as I remember the interpretation of Hebrew names,[17] Kedar signifies "darkness." We can take Kedar as equivalent to "darkness" in our language.

Now you know that Abraham had two sons.[18] The apostle refers to them and makes them stand for the two covenants, one being born from the slave-girl, the other from the free wife.[19] Ishmael was born from the maid-servant; but Isaac, conceived through faith in what seemed a hopeless situation, was born from the free Sarah.[20] Both were Abraham's offspring, but they were not both Abraham's heirs. One of them, though born from Abraham, was not born to an inheritance. The other was his heir: not only his son, but his heir too. Ishmael personifies all who worship God from carnal motives. Their province is the Old Covenant, for the apostle says to them, *You who want to be subject to the law, have you not heard the law? It is written that Abraham had two sons, one by the slave-girl, and the other by the free woman; and this story is symbolic. The two allegorically prefigure the two covenants* (Gal 4:21–22.24). What covenants does he mean? The old and the new. The Old Covenant was from God, and the New Covenant is from God, just as both Ishmael and Isaac were sons of Abraham. But Ishmael was destined for earthly rule, Isaac for a heavenly kingdom. The Old Covenant embodied earthly promises: an earthly Jerusalem, an earthly Palestine,[21] an earthly kingdom, earthly salvation,[22] the subjugation of enemies, plenty of children, abundant harvests. All these are earthly promises. But they can be understood in a spiritual sense, as symbols, for the earthly Jerusalem was a shadow of the heavenly city and the earthly kingdom a shadow of the kingdom of heaven. Ishmael was in shadow, Isaac in the light. And if Ishmael was in shadow, we might as well say he was in darkness, for darkness is nothing but deeper shadow.

---

17. See Jerome, *Hebrew Names* 4,6.
18. See Gn 16:15; 21:2.
19. See Gal 4:22–31.
20. Or perhaps "…was born from the free Sarah through faith, once she had given up her despairing attitude"; see Gn 18:10–15.
21. Augustine seldom uses this name for the Holy Land in his *Expositions*.
22. Or possibly "good health."

If, then, Ishmael's place was in darkness, but Isaac's in light, we can say that all those who, even in the Church, seek earthly prosperity from God still belong to Ishmael. These are the same ones who oppose spiritually-minded persons who are making progress and disparage them. They have iniquitous lips and sly tongues.

Our psalmist on his upward journey prayed against them, and he was supplied with destructive coals and the sharp arrows of a mighty warrior, for he still has to live among such people until the whole threshing-floor is cleared at winnowing-time. This is why he complained, *I have been dwelling among the tents of Kedar.* Ishmael's tents bear this name, Kedar. Genesis indicates this, for it tells us that Kedar belonged to Ishmael.[23] Isaac and Ishmael are represented as close companions, which signifies that people who belong to Isaac live among those who belong to Ishmael. The former want to ascend, but the latter try to pin them down below. The former long to fly to God, but the latter try to pluck out their wings. The apostle gives hints of this, for he says, *As at that time the son begotten according to the flesh persecuted the one begotten according to the Spirit, so it is today* (Gal 4:29). Spiritual persons suffer persecution from the carnally-minded. But what does Scripture say? *Cast out the slave-girl and her son. The son of a slave-girl shall not be heir with my son Isaac* (Gn 21:10). But when will that command be implemented: *Cast them out*? When winnowing begins on the threshing-floor. But for the present, before they are expelled, *alas, how long-drawn-out is my exile! I have been dwelling among the tents of Kedar.* Thus the psalm indicates to us whom it means by the tents of Kedar.

8. *My soul has been on pilgrimage for a long time.* He says it is his soul that has been on pilgrimage, to make sure you do not think only of bodily journeys. The body travels from place to place; the soul travels by its affections. If you are in love with the earth, your journey is taking you far from God. If you are in love with God, you are climbing toward him. Let us exert ourselves in charity toward God and our neighbor, that we may make our way back to charity. If we fall to earth we wither and become moldy. The psalmist had fallen, but a descent had occurred for his sake, down to his level, so that he might ascend. Reflecting on the time his pilgrimage had lasted, he says he is an exile in the tents of Kedar. Why? Because *my soul has been on pilgrimage for a long time.* His pilgrimage is going on in the place where he is to ascend. Just as his pilgrimage is not a bodily one, so his ascent will not be in the body either. Where does he ascend? *The ascents are in his heart,* we were told in another psalm.[24] If he is to ascend in his heart, there can be no ascent for him unless his soul is on pilgrimage. But until he arrives, he complains, *My soul has been on pilgrimage for a long time.* Where? In the tents of Kedar.

---

23. See Gn 25:13.
24. See Ps 83:6(84:5).

Verse 7. A plea for peace and unity addressed to the Donatists

9. *I dealt peaceably with those who hated peace.* I want you to hear how true these words are, brothers and sisters. You can test the truth of what you are singing only if you are beginning to act in harmony with your song. However much I say about this, in whatever way I explain it, whatever words I use, the truth will not penetrate anyone's heart unless he or she has already begun to practice it. Begin to act on it, and then see for yourselves what we are telling you. Then your tears will flow at every word; then as the psalm is sung your heart will be engaged in what it sings. How many people there are who make plenty of noise with their voices but are dumb in their hearts! And how many others have no sound on their lips but shout with their love! God's ears are alert to the human heart. Just as a person's ears are open to the speech of another, so are God's ears open to a person's heart. Many are heard without opening their mouths, and many others are not heard even though they shout loudly.

We must pray with our affections, and say, *My soul has been on pilgrimage for a long time; I dealt peaceably with those who hated peace.*[25] "Learn to know peace; love peace," we say to them. "You call yourselves righteous. If you were righteous you would be genuine wheat, yes; but you would be still among the straw, groaning there." There are wheat-grains in the Catholic Church—real grains. They put up with the straw until the time comes for winnowing on the threshing-floor and they keep crying out, *Alas, how long-drawn-out is my exile! I have been dwelling among the tents of Kedar.* "I have lived among the straw," they imply. But as burning straw gives off thick smoke, so does thick darkness emanate from Kedar. *I have been dwelling among the tents of Kedar, and my soul has been on pilgrimage for a long time.* This is the authentic voice of the wheat-grains, groaning amid the chaff.

We point out these things to those who hate peace. We say to them, *I have dealt peaceably with those who hate peace.* Who are the ones who hate peace? Those who tear our unity apart. If they had not hated peace, they would have stayed within that unity. But their motive for seceding was the desire to be righteous, and not be mixed up with the unrighteous.[26] Whose voice is it in this psalm—ours or theirs? You must decide! The Catholic Church says, "Unity must not be sacrificed; God's Church must not be rent

---

25. The following lines make it clear that the Donatists are in Augustine's mind. In 406–407, the probable date of his *Expositions* of the "Songs of Steps," the conflict with the Donatists was still a burning issue.
26. At the heart of the Donatist crisis were two different conceptions of the Church. For the schismatics, the Church was meant to be the society of the pure; for Augustine it was a mixed crop of good and bad, growing together until judgment day, with the hope that some of the weeds would be revealed as wheat in the end. Meanwhile, the bad serve God's purposes by exercising the good in tolerance and charity.

apart. God will judge later between the bad and the good. If the bad people cannot be sorted out from the good now, they must be borne with for the time being. Bad people can be with us on the threshing-floor, but cannot be in the barn. In any case, those who appear to be bad today may be good tomorrow, just as those who today are proud of their own goodness may tomorrow turn out to be bad. Anyone who humbly tolerates bad people for a time will attain everlasting rest." This is the Catholic voice.

What tone do they adopt, those who understand *neither what they are saying nor the matters on which they pronounce?* (1 Tm 1:7) *Touch nothing unclean* (Is 52:11; 2 Cor 6:17), they say. *"Anyone who touches what is unclean shall be defiled* (Lv 22:4). Let us take ourselves off; we don't want to get mixed up with bad people."

We plead with them, "Love peace, set your hearts on unity. Don't you realize how many good people you are leaving behind when you stigmatize them all as evil?" But they are ferociously angry when we say this; they even try to kill us. Their open attacks have often been notorious, and so too the traps they have set. Since we have to live among the ambushes they lay for us, and since the very people whom we exhort to love peace range themselves against us, can we not recognize our own voice in the psalm? *I have dealt peaceably with those who hate peace; when I spoke to them, they waged war on me without justification.*

What is the force of those last words, brothers and sisters? *They waged war on me?* That would not amount to much, if the psalm had not added, *without justification.* When we say to them, "Love peace, love Christ," do we say, "And pay honor to us"? Certainly not! We say, "Pay honor to Christ." We want him to be venerated, not ourselves. How unimportant we are by comparison with the apostle Paul! Yet he kept saying to those little ones of his, whom wicked people and evil counselors tried to drag away from unity into schism—what did he keep saying to them? *Was Paul crucified for you, or were you baptized in Paul's name?* (1 Cor 1:13) We are saying the same: "Love peace, love Christ." If they love peace, they will love Christ, for in saying, "Love peace," we are implicitly urging them to love Christ. You ask why? Because the apostle says of Christ, *He is himself our peace, since he united the two* (Eph 2:14).

If Christ is peace because he made two into one, how can you make one into two? In what sense are you promoters of peace, if when Christ makes two into one, you make one into two? When we say these things to them, we deal peaceably with those who hate peace. And whenever we have spoken to these haters of peace, they have waged war on us without justification.

Exposition of Psalm 120

Synopsis

Ascents in the heart occur "by a good intention, in faith, hope and charity, in a desire for eternity and everlasting life." We must never forget that the starting place for ascent is "the valley of weeping." The martyrs did not forget, but they went to death scattering seeds of faith. We don't know what will happen, but ignorance about the future keeps us on alert (1–3).

For encouragement we lift our eyes to *the mountains* by learning the deeds of Scripture's great figures. However, our help comes not from these mountains themselves but from the one who created the mountains (4). We concentrate on him so as not to lose our footing on the steps of ascent. God is the guardian of Israel, whose name means "seeing God." How do we "become Israel"? Go back to the story of Moses on the mountain asking to see God's glory. God refused, but he did allow him to see his "back." We become Israel by looking with Moses at God's "back," that is, Christ's human passing from death to life, his "passover." Believe what Christ became for you and you will "see" God and thus become Israel (5–6).

The Lord defends Israel better than "the hand of your right hand." This mysterious phrase suggests that the left hand relates to temporal things and the right hand to what is eternal. Many confuse these, but Job did not. The Song of Songs and Proverbs portray the right attitude of love for what is eternal. If "hand" symbolizes power, then *the hand of your right hand* refers to our power to stand at Christ's right hand at the final judgment. That power is faith (7–11).

Yet God must still protect us from scandals that relate to failures either to love God or to love one's neighbor. One is to be "burned by the sun" (which refers to errors about Christ's divinity), and the other is to be "burned by the moon" (which refers to errors about Christ's humanity or about the Church) (12). The Lord guards us as he guarded the martyr Crispina, who was sorely tested. Faith yields nothing to temptation because it relies on God for protection (13).

Augustine's Text of Psalm 120

(1) A Song of Steps.

   I lift up my eyes to the mountains, whence comes my help.

(2) My help is from the Lord, who made heaven and earth.

(3) Do not let my foot be dislodged.

   "Neither let him grow drowsy, your guardian."

(4) Lo, he will not be drowsy or sleep, the guardian of Israel.

(5) The Lord will guard you. The Lord will be your defense,

   Better than the hand of your right hand.

(6) The sun will not burn you by day, nor the moon at night.

(7) The Lord will guard you from every evil.

   May the Lord guard your soul.

(8) May the Lord guard your going in, and your coming out henceforth and forever.

Exposition

A Sermon to the People[1]

A "Song of Ascents" is appropriate to the festival of a martyr; the need for perpetual vigilance

1. We now approach the second psalm in the collection entitled *Songs of Ascents*. This is a group of psalms which deal with our[2] upward climb, as you have heard already in our exposition of the first one. The ascent is made in our hearts as we mount toward God through the valley of weeping, which symbolizes the humility of our very distressed condition. The ascent can succeed for us only if we are first of all humbled and remember that it is from this valley[3] that our climb must begin. A valley[4] is a sunken region of the earth: just as high areas are called mountains, so is a lowly place called a valley. Were we to forget that this must be our starting-point we would be getting things upside down and seeking exaltation before the proper time; and then we would not ascend but fall headlong. The Lord himself taught

---

1. Preached on the festival of the martyr Saint Crispina (see section 13), probably on 5 December 406 or 407, a few days after the *Exposition of Psalm* 119.
2. Variant: "your."
3. Variant: "... only if we are first of all mindful that it is from this valley of humility."
4. The word in these lines is *convallis*, literally a valley closed in on all sides.

us that there can be no ascent except from the valley of weeping. For our sake he graciously willed to be humbled even to death on a cross and to suffer. Let us not neglect his example. The martyrs understood about the valley of weeping. How did they gain understanding? You ask how? By mounting in their turn from the valley of weeping, to receive their crowns.

2. This *Song of Ascents* is apposite today,[5] for of the martyrs Scripture says, *They went on their way weeping, as they scattered their seed* (Ps 125(126):6). This is the activity proper to the valley of weeping, where seeds are scattered by people in tears. What are these seeds? Good works performed amid earthly woes. One who is diligent in good works in the valley of weeping is like a farmer who sows in the winter. Is he deterred from his job by the cold? Definitely not. Nor should we be deterred by the hardships of this world from doing good; for notice what comes next in that passage of Scripture: *When they come back they will come leaping for joy, carrying their sheaves.*[6]

3. These songs have only one thing to teach us, brothers and sisters, and that is how to ascend. But our ascent must be made in the heart, by a good intention, in faith and hope and charity, in a desire for eternity and everlasting life. That is what the ascent is. Now we need to explain[7] how to accomplish it.

You heard plenty of rather terrifying things when the gospel was read, beloved![8] You are well aware that *the Lord's hour will come like a thief in the night* (1 Thes 5:2). *If the householder had known at what hour the thief would come, I tell you truly, he would not have allowed his wall to be breached* (Mt 24:43). Now you are saying, "But if the hour will come like a thief, who can know the time of the Lord's coming?" You don't know the time of it? Be vigilant all the time, then, so that even if you don't know when he is coming he will find you prepared when he does. Perhaps the very purpose of your being kept ignorant of the time is to ensure that you are always ready. It is the householder in the story who will be overtaken suddenly by the unexpected timing, and the householder represents proud persons. Take care not to aim at being a householder, and then it will not overtake you unawares. "What am I to be, then?" you ask. Another psalm showed you the kind of person you must be: *I am poor and sorrowful* (Ps 68:30(69:29)); for if you are poor and sorrowful you will not be a householder, to be overtaken suddenly by that hour and suddenly overwhelmed. Householders are the kind who promote their greedy impulses, dissipate their energies on the pleasures of this world, become swollen with pride and overbearing toward humble folk, and insult holy people who recognize

---

5. The feast of Saint Crispina.
6. The best reading seems to be *gremia*, perhaps "bunches"; compare Sermon 313D, 3. Variant: "sheaves."
7. Variant: "learn."
8. *Caritas vestra.*

the narrow way that leads to life.[9] The hour will come suddenly upon such persons. That was how some were behaving in the days of Noah; you heard their story in the gospel. *The coming of the Son of Man will be as it was in the days of Noah. People were eating and drinking, marrying and taking wives, setting out new plants and building, until Noah entered the ark. Then the flood came, and destroyed them all* (Mt 24:37-39; Lk 17:26-27).

How are we to understand this passage? Does it mean that all who engage in these activities will perish—all who are given in marriage or take wives, all who set out new plants, all who build? No; but those who put their whole reliance on doing such things, who prefer these things to God, or are ready to offend God for the sake of them: these will perish. Others, who either disengage themselves from such insubstantial occupations or else engage in them without being totally engaged,[10] people who rely more on the giver than the gifts, who even amid the gifts are sensitive to his consolation and his mercy and not so completely taken over by the gifts that they fall away from the giver—these will not be found unprepared when the hour strikes like a thief.

To persons so disposed the apostle said, *You are not in darkness, that the day should catch you out like a thief, for you are all children of light and children of the day* (1 Thes 5:4-5). When the Lord warned us to be as wary of that hour as of a thief, he likened it to night, as did also the apostle: *The day of the Lord will come like a thief in the night* (1 Thes 5:2). Are you hoping that it will not catch you unprepared? Take care not to live in the night. What does that mean? *You are children of light and children of the day; we do not belong to the night or to the darkness* (1 Thes 5:5). Who are the children of night and darkness? The wicked, the godless, and unbelievers.

Verses 1-2. The Lord's light reaches us from the mountains

4. But even the careless must hearken before the hour strikes. Let the apostle remind them: *You were darkness once, but now you are light in the Lord* (Eph 5:8). Let them be vigilant, as our psalm urges them.[11] The mountains are already bathed in light; why are these people still asleep? Let them lift their eyes to the mountains, whence comes their help. What does it mean to say that the mountains are illumined already? The sun of righteousness has risen,[12] the gospel has been preached by the apostles, the Scriptures have been promulgated, all the sacraments[13] are thrown

---

9. See Mt 7:14.
10. See 1 Cor 7:31.
11. Some witnesses here insert the first two verses: *I have lifted my eyes to the mountains, from where comes help for me. My help is from the Lord, who made heaven and earth.*
12. See Ml 4:2. This was a favorite image for Christ's resurrection.
13. Or perhaps more generally, "the mysteries of the faith."

open, the veil is rent apart,[14] and the secret recess of the temple lies open. Now at last let them lift their eyes to the mountains, whence comes help for them. Thus does the psalm command, this psalm which is the second in the collection called *Songs of Ascents*.

But they must not on that account put their trust in the mountains, because the mountains do not give off light of their own. They transmit light from him of whom Scripture says, *He was the true light, which illumines every human person who comes into this world* (Jn 1:9). We can take the mountains to be symbols of great and illustrious people. And is anything greater than John the Baptist? What a mountain he was! Of him the Lord himself testified, *There has never arisen a mother's son greater than he* (Mt 11:11). You can certainly see in him a lofty mountain bathed in light; but listen to his confession: *From his fullness we have all received* (Jn 1:16). Help comes to you not from the mountains themselves but from him whose plenitude endows the mountains. All the same, unless you lift your eyes to the mountains through the Scriptures, you will not be brought near[15] to be illuminated by him.

Verses 3–4. How to keep your footing. Israel's unsleeping guardian

5. Well then, sing the next verses of the psalm. If you want to hear how to set your feet very firmly on the steps, so that you will be in no danger of either growing tired in the climb or slipping and falling, say the next verse: *Do not let my foot be dislodged*. How do feet get dislodged? In the same way as someone's foot was dislodged in paradise. But before thinking about him, reflect how one whose place used to be among the angels was dislodged, and fell, and was transformed from an angel into a devil; for he fell when his foot slipped. Inquire why he fell: he fell through pride. Pride is the only thing that dislodges a foot. Pride alone causes someone to lose his foothold and come crashing down. Charity moves us to walk and make progress; pride pushes us into a fall.

In view of this, what does the speaker say in another psalm? *The children of men will hope in the protection of your wings* (Ps 35:8(36:7)). If they are under his protection they are always humble, ever hopeful of God, and never reliant on themselves. They *will hope in the protection of your wings*, Lord, because they are not sated with happiness deriving from themselves. What comes next? *They will be inebriated by the rich abundance of your house, and you will give them the torrent of your delights to drink* (Ps 35:9(36:8)). They are athirst, and they have been inebriated; they are thirsty, and they drink; but they do not drink from themselves; they are not their own fountain. Whence do they drink? *They will hope in the protection of your wings*. They cannot help being humble if they are under God's wings. Why? *With you is the fountain of life* (Ps 35:10(36:9)), says the psalm. The

---

14. See Mt 27:57.
15. Variants: "will not draw near"; "will not be instructed."

mountains are not irrigated from their own source, any more than they are illumined with their own light; for see what follows: *In your light we will see light* (Ps 35:10(36:9)).

If then we shall see light in his light, who can fall away from the light? Only the one who tries to be a light to himself and will not have the Lord for his light: this is the one who falls out of the light that enlightens him. The psalmist well knew that no one falls except one who wants to be a light unto himself, whereas of himself he is darkness; and so he immediately added the prayer, *Let not the foot of pride come near me, nor the hand of sinners dislodge me* (Ps 35:12(36:11)). Let not any imitation of the ways of sinners impel me, he means, and cause me to fall away from you. But why were you afraid, psalmist? Why did you pray, *Let not the foot of pride come near me*? He answers, Because *that was how they fell, all who work iniquity* (Ps 35:13(36:12)). The ones you see working iniquity now are already condemned, but they earned their condemnation by falling, there where the foot of pride first approached them.

The would-be climber who does not wish to fall in his ascent has heard this lesson aright. He wants to make progress from his starting-point in the valley of weeping, and not faint or fail through swollen pride. He prays to God, *Do not let my foot be dislodged*. And God replies, *Neither let him grow drowsy, your guardian*. Consider this carefully, beloved. Two voices speak, but they are saying almost the same thing. The human speaker is climbing up and singing his Song of Ascents: *Do not let my foot be dislodged*; and God seems to be answering him, "You are making your plea to me, *Do not let my foot be dislodged*. But add a further plea: *Neither let him grow drowsy, your guardian*, and then your foot will not be dislodged."

6. Now suppose the climber responds, "But is it in my power to determine whether he who guards me falls asleep? I certainly hope he will not sleep or grow drowsy." If that is what you want, choose a guardian for yourself who will not sleep or grow drowsy, and then your foothold will be assured. God is never sleepy. You want an unsleeping guardian? You are right, perfectly right, to pray, *Do not let my foot be dislodged*, but he says something further to you: *Neither let him grow drowsy, your guardian*. Perhaps you were on the point of turning to human protectors, and asking, "Whom can I find who will not fall asleep? What person can ward off drowsiness? Whom shall I find? Where shall I go? Where am I to turn?" God shows you: *Lo, he will not be drowsy or sleep, the guardian of Israel*. Do you want a guardian who never dozes off or feels drowsy? *Lo, he will not be drowsy or sleep, the guardian of Israel*, for Christ is Israel's guardian.

That means you must be Israel. What is Israel? The name is interpreted as "One who sees God."[16] But who sees God? We see him first by faith,

---

16. A popular etymology. The aspiration of the true Israel is to see God; compare Jn 1:46–51.

later by vision.[17] If you cannot yet behold him by sight, see him by faith. If you cannot behold his face, because sight would be needed for that, see his back. That was what the Lord told Moses: *You cannot see my face. But you shall see my back when I pass by* (Ex 33:20.22–23). Are you waiting for him to pass? He has passed already, so you can see his back. When and where did he pass? Listen to John: *When the hour had come, at which Jesus was to pass from this world to the Father...* (Jn 13:1). Our Lord Jesus Christ has already accomplished his passover. The word "pasch" means a crossing over. It is a Hebrew word; some people think it is Greek, and associated with "passion," "suffering"; but this is not true. Careful and learned scholars have proved that the word "pasch" is Hebrew, and means not passion but passover. By his passion the Lord passed over from death to life and opened a way for us who believe in his resurrection, that we too may pass over from death to life. It is no great thing to believe that Christ died: pagans and Jews and all bad people believe that. All of them are sure that he died. The faith of Christians is in Christ's resurrection. This is what matters to us, that we believe he rose from the dead.

This is why he wanted to be seen precisely when he "passed by," that is to say, when he had risen. He wanted us to believe in him when he passed by, because *He was delivered to death for our transgressions, and rose for our justification* (Rom 4:25). It was faith in Christ's resurrection that the apostle emphasized more than anything else, for *if you believe in your heart that God raised him from the dead, you will be saved* (Rom 10:9). He did not say, "If you believe that Christ died," for pagans and Jews and all his enemies believed that. He said, *If you believe in your heart that God raised him from the dead, you will be saved.* To believe that is to be Israel, one who sees God. Perhaps all you see is his back, but if you have believed in his back, you will attain to the vision of his face.

What does that mean? What is his face, in the beginning? *In the beginning was the Word, and the Word was with God; he was God* (Jn 1:1). And his back, his state afterward, what was that? *The Word was made flesh, and dwelt among us* (Jn 1:14). If you have believed in what Christ afterward[18] became for you, if you have believed in what Christ afterward assumed for you, if you believe in what the Word became for you, if you believe that he rose in the flesh to save you from despairing about your own flesh, you will become Israel.

When you have become Israel, he who guards you will not grow drowsy or fall asleep, because you are Israel now, and you have heard the psalm's assurance, *Lo, he will not be drowsy or sleep, the guardian of Israel.* Christ did sleep indeed, but he arose. What does he say in another psalm? *I slept,*

---

17. See 2 Cor 5:7.
18. *Posterius,* "later," "afterward." There is a pun, difficult to convey in translation, on the *posteriora,* the "after parts" or "back" of God in Moses' encounter with him (Ex 33), and what Christ became "later" (*posterius*) in the Incarnation.

and took my rest. Did he remain asleep? No, for he continues, *I arose, because the Lord upheld me* (Ps 3:6(5)). If he has arisen, then, he has already passed over, and if he has passed over, contemplate his back. What does it mean, to contemplate his back? Believe in his resurrection. Remember how the apostle said, *Though he was crucified in weakness, he is alive by the power of God* (2 Cor 13:4), and again, *Rising from the dead, Christ will never die again, nor will death ever again have the mastery over him* (Rom 6:9). The psalm has good reason therefore to sing to you, *Lo, he will not be drowsy or sleep, the guardian of Israel.*

But you, with your carnal mind, are you perhaps still wondering, "Is there anyone who will not sooner or later be drowsy and sleep?" If you look for one among ordinary human beings you will never find such a one. Do not rely on any of them, for everyone dozes off or grows sleepy. When do ordinary men or women get drowsy? When they are carrying weak flesh. When do they sleep? When they die so you cannot rely on them. A mortal may grow drowsy; and when he dies, he falls asleep. It is no good looking for an unsleeping guardian among your fellow men and women.

Verse 5. The hand of your right hand; the significance of right and left

7. And who, you ask, will guard me? Who will neither grow drowsy nor sleep? Listen to the next words: *The Lord will guard you.* Not some drowsy, sleepy fellow-human, but the Lord guards you.

How does he guard you? *The Lord will be your defense, better than the hand of your right hand.*[19] Well, brothers and sisters, let us try to understand with the Lord's assistance what is meant by the words: *The Lord will be your defense, Better than the hand of your right hand.* I think there must be some hidden reason why the psalm did not say simply, *The Lord will be your defense,* and leave it at that, but added, *better than the hand of your right hand.* What can it mean? Does the Lord guard our right side but not our left? Did he not make the whole of us? Did not he who made a right hand for us make a left hand too? But in any case, if the psalm wanted to affirm something concerning the right hand only, why did it say, *better than the hand of your right hand,*[20] rather than just "better than your right hand"?[21] Why did it speak so? Surely because some secret meaning is hidden here, which we are to discover by knocking at its door.[22] It could have said either,

---

19. *Super manum dexterae tuae,* an almost meaningless phrase, translated literally from a variant in the Greek of the Septuagint. It is necessary to retain it in this awkward form in English because Augustine, believing that any obscure expression could invite him and his hearers to search for hidden spiritual mystery, meditates on it in the following paragraphs, and further in section 11.
20. *Super manum dexterae tuae.*
21. *Super dexteram tua.*
22. See Mt 7:7.

The Lord will be your defense, and added nothing else; or, if it wanted to mention the right side, it could have said, "The Lord will be your defense at your right"; or again, if the hand had to be mentioned, it could have said, "The Lord will be your defense, better than your right hand."[23] There was no need for the awkward phrase, *super manum dexterae tuae,* was there?

I will set before you the ideas that the Lord may himself suggest to me. He dwells in you too and will undoubtedly cause you to recognize the truth of what I say. At the moment you do not know what we are about to tell you, but once we have said it there will be no need for us to prove to you that what we say is true; you will yourselves acknowledge the truth of it. And how will you do that? The Lord who dwells in you will himself demonstrate it, insofar as you belong to the number of those who pray, *Do not let my foot be dislodged,* those to whom it is said, *Let him not grow drowsy, your guardian.* It is important that Christ should not sleep within you; and if he does not, you will understand that what we say is true. Are you going to ask me what I mean by that? If your faith goes to sleep, Christ is asleep in you; for your faith in Christ is the means by which he dwells in your heart. The apostle prays that *Christ may dwell in your hearts through faith* (Eph 3:17). In a person whose faith does not go to sleep, Christ is wakeful. And if perhaps your faith was asleep, and you were therefore tossed about by this difficult passage, you were like the boat which was battered in a storm while Christ was aboard and sleeping.[24] Wake him up, and the storms will subside.

8. I want to put a few questions to your faith, then, dearest friends.[25] Because you are children of the Church, and have made progress in the Church, and are making progress in the Church, and will make progress in the Church if you are not doing so already, and, if you have already made progress, need to be helped in the Church to make even more,[26] I am asking you what you customarily understand by the saying in the gospel, *Do not let your left hand know what your right hand is doing* (Mt 6:3). If you have understood that, you will discover what the right hand is, and what the left. You will realize that though God made both, the left has nonetheless no business to know what the right hand is up to.

---

23. *Super manum dexteram tuam.*
24. See Mt 8:24–26; Mk 4:37–39; Lk 8:23–24.
25. *Carissimi.*
26. Conjectural translation: *Et in ecclesia profecistis... proficietis qui nondum profecistis, et in ecclesia proficiendi estis.* The last verb is difficult since a gerundive is normally passive, and there seem to be few, if any, examples of the use of the verb *proficere* in the passive with a personal subject. It may be that Augustine's rhetoric was sweeping him along, and the enthusiasm of the people for the build-up in the sentence led him to stretch grammar a little. Some copyists smoothed the difficulty by substituting *perficiendi,* "you need to be made perfect."

Our left hand symbolizes all we have in the temporal sphere; the right hand stands for all the eternal, unchangeable goods the Lord promises us. He who will one day give us eternal life also comforts us in our present life with temporal things, and thus it is evident that he made both right hand and left. A psalm of David says of certain people, *Their mouths have spoken empty words, and their right hand is a hand that deals unjustly* (Ps 143(144):11). It appears that he found people he needed to rebuke, because they regarded their right hand as their left, and treated their real left hand as though it were the right. He explains shortly afterward who these people are. If anyone thinks that the only happiness available to human beings cannot exist except amid temporal possessions and a profusion of the wealth this world offers, such a person is foolish and misguided, and has made what should be his left hand into his right. The kind of people rebuked by the psalm were like that. It was not as though even their temporal possessions were anything but God-given; but because they thought that a happy life consisted solely in such goods and sought nothing further, they deserved the rebuke. Listen to how they are characterized in the following lines: *Their mouths have spoken empty words, and their right hand is a hand that deals unjustly*, the psalm has said; then it continues, *Their sons are like well-set saplings, their daughters are adorned and gathered round them like the pillars of the temple, their storerooms are full to overflowing, their ewes fruitful, increasing at every lambing-time, and their oxen are sturdy. Never is their hedge broken down or their property invaded, nor is there rioting in their streets* (Ps 143(144):11–14). This is a description of the great good fortune enjoyed by some. A just person could have had the same good fortune as Job did, but Job regarded it all as his left hand; he did not mistake it for his right. The only kind of happiness he looked upon as his right hand was perpetual, unending happiness with God. His left hand was made vulnerable, but his right hand was enough for him. How was his left hand injured? By the devil's temptations. The devil suddenly took all his possessions away, though only by God's permission, in order that a just man might be proved, and the wicked one punished. Job knew his left hand for a left hand, and knew his right hand for what it was: his right hand. How did he support himself with his right hand, how did he exult in the Lord? He was comforted over his losses, for he suffered no loss of interior riches: he had a heart full of God. *The Lord gave, and the Lord has taken away*, he said. *This has happened as the Lord willed: may the Lord's name be blessed* (Jb 1:21). That was his right hand: the Lord himself, eternal life, the light that was in him, the fountain of light, the vision of light in God's light. *They will be inebriated by the rich abundance of your house* (Ps 35:9(36:8)). All this was his right hand. His left hand had been there as a help and comfort, but not as the foundation of his happiness; for his true, genuine happiness was God.

What of the others, the ones of whom David said that *their mouths have spoken empty words, and their right hand is a hand that deals unjustly*? He did not rebuke them because they had a profusion of goods, but because *their mouths spoke empty words*. How do we know this? Because after listing all their wealth he continued, *They have called blessed people who have these things*. The empty words they mouthed consisted in this, that they reckoned as blessed all who have such riches. But what is your judgment, you who know what your left hand is, and what your right? You will say what the psalm goes on to say: *Blessed rather is the people whose God is the Lord* (Ps 143(144):15).

9. Now give me your attention, beloved.[27] We have seen the left hand, and we have also observed the right. Listen to how our interpretation is confirmed in the Song of Songs. *His left hand is beneath my head*, we read. The bride is speaking of the bridegroom; the Church is speaking of embracing Christ in fidelity and love. What does the bride say? *His left hand is beneath my head, and his right hand will embrace me* (Sg 2:6). What should we gather from the fact that when he embraces her the bridegroom places his right hand on top, and his left beneath? He places his left hand below to comfort her, and his right hand above for her protection. *His left hand is beneath my head*, she says. The left hand is God's gift; it is called *his* left hand, for he gives all temporal things. How empty-headed they are, and how impious, who beg for such things from idols, from demons! And what a lot of people beg them from demons, and do not get them! There are others who do not beg them from demons, and yet have them; but these goods are not given by demons. On the other hand, many beg them from God, and do not get them, for he who calls us to the happiness of the right hand well knows how best to dispense the goods of the left.

If you possess this left-hand fortune, let it be your left hand; let it be under your head, and let your head rest upon it. By that I mean let your faith be above it, for in your faith Christ dwells. Do not give temporal things precedence over your faith, and then the left hand will not be on top of your head. Subordinate all temporal things to your faith, and let your faith be supreme over all of them. Then his left hand will be under your head, and his right hand will embrace you.

10. The Book of Proverbs also clarifies what is meant by the right hand and the left. Listen to what it says about Wisdom: *Length of days and years of life are in her right hand, but in her left are riches and fame* (Prv 3:16, LXX). This *length of days* is eternity. Scripture is in the habit of calling what is eternal "long," for anything that comes to an end is short. In another passage God promises, *I will fill him completely with length of days* (Ps 90(91):16). If length of days did not signify eternal life, would God be pledging anything special when he commands, *Honor your father and your mother, that you may have a long life in the land?* (Ex 20:12) To what land does this refer if not the land of which the psalmist says to God, *You are my hope, my portion in the land of the living?* (Ps 141:6(142:5)) And

---

27. *Caritas vestra.*

what does it mean to enjoy a long life there? What else but to live for ever? After all, what does a long life in this world entail? Arriving at old age! Our span of life here may seem long, but when it is complete[28] we see how short it was, because it has ended. Moreover, there are many who speak ill of their parents and yet grow old on this earth, whereas many others who are dutiful toward their parents go quickly to the Lord. The promise of long life is hardly fulfilled, is it, if it refers to the present life? Scripture must be using long life as a symbol of eternity. This kind of long life is in Wisdom's right hand; but riches and fame, which represent all we need in the present and all that popular opinion reckons good, are the gifts of Wisdom's left hand.

Now suppose someone comes along and wants to wound you in your right hand. He wants to take your faith away from you. You have been slapped on your right hand: offer him your left. Let him take away anything that is temporal, but not your eternal possessions. Listen to how the apostle Paul did this. People were hounding him because he was a Christian: that is, they were hitting his right hand. He retaliated with his left, warning them, "I am a Roman citizen."[29] They despised his right hand, but he scared them with his left. They could not feel threatened by his right hand, because they had not believed in Christ.

Well now, if Christ's right hand embraces you, and his left hand is beneath your head, what is the meaning of the gospel command, *Do not let your left hand know what your right hand is doing?* (Mt 6:3) It means, "When you perform a good work, do it in view of eternal life." If you do some good deed on earth with the object of acquiring a wealth of earthly commodities, your left hand knows what your right is doing, and you have mixed up your right hand with your left. Act only with a view to eternal life. If you do that, you will act with a tranquil mind, for it was for this purpose that God tempted him.[30] If you act in whatever you are doing solely for the sake of gaining some human advantage, with no motive apart from the present life, your left hand is working alone. If you act for the sake of eternal life your right hand is working alone. If, however, your will is directed toward eternal life, but some covetousness associated with temporal life creeps into your motive, so that you keep this also in view as you perform your good work and hope for some reward here, your left hand is interfering with the activities of your right, and this God forbids.

---

28. Variant: "when death comes."
29. See Acts 22:25.
30. *Ad hoc enim tentavit Deus eum,* so the codices. If this is correct, the reference may be to Job, who was mentioned in section 8. Variant: *hoc enim mandavit Deus* ("for this is what God commanded").

The power of your right hand is God-given, but the Lord himself must defend it

11. Now let us go back to the words of the psalm, *The Lord will be your defense, better than the hand of your right hand.* The psalm calls power a hand. How can we prove this? From the fact that God's own power is referred to as a hand. When the devil tempted Job he said to God, *Just stretch out your hand and touch all his belongings* (Jb 1:11).[31] What else can the challenge, *Stretch out your hand,* mean except, "Put forth your power"? But listen to a still clearer proof, my brother, my sister, for you may still be thinking in carnal terms and supposing that God is distributed among many bodily organs. Listen to a still clearer piece of evidence, then. Scripture says somewhere, *Death and life are in the hands of the tongue* (Prv 18:21). We know what tongues are: small pieces of flesh that by moving in our mouths and striking against the palate and the teeth produce the distinct sounds with which we speak. So now let someone show me the hands of the tongue. Surely the tongue does not have hands? Yet it does, in a way. What are its hands? The power of the tongue; for what is meant by the warning, *Death and life are in the hands of the tongue*? The gospel tells us: *Out of your mouth you will be justified, and out of your mouth you will be condemned* (Mt 12:37).

If the hand represents power, what is the hand of the right hand? I can think of no better way of understanding it than to assume that the power of the right hand is the power God has given you to be at Christ's right hand, if you choose. All the impious will be at his left, and all God's good sons and daughters at his right. To these he will say, *Come, you who are blessed by my Father, take possession of the kingdom prepared for you since the creation of the world* (Mt 25:34). But you have received power to be at his right, power to become a child of God. What power is that? The power of which John speaks: *He gave them power to become children of God.* And how did that power come to you? Through faith, for John specifies, *To those, that is, who believe in his name* (Jn 1:12). If you are a believer, this power has been given to you, the power to be among the children of God. But to be among the children of God is to be entitled to a place at Christ's right hand. This means that your faith is *the hand of your right hand.* The power conferred on you to find a place among God's children is therefore *the hand of your right hand.*

But what is the use of even this power given to us, if the Lord does not protect it? A Christian is someone who has come to believe and is already walking in faith. But he or she is weak, and is harassed by temptations, by all sorts of distress, by the allurements of sensuality, by stirrings of avarice, by the crafty tricks and traps of the enemy. Can the power a believer

---

31. Some witnesses continue the quotation: *and see if he does not curse you to your face.*

has received hold out against all these? Is it enough that he has believed in Christ, so as to be numbered among God's children? Woe betide him if the Lord does not also protect the faith he has. Your chances are poor unless the Lord ensures that you are not tried beyond your strength, as the apostle guarantees that he will: *God is faithful, and he will not allow you to be tempted more fiercely than you can bear* (1 Cor 10:13). God it is who does not allow us to be tried beyond our strength, even though we are already believers, even though the hand of our right hand is already within us; and God it is who covers us with a defense better than the hand of our right hand. It is not enough for us to have the hand of our right hand, unless he protects this very gift, the hand of our right hand.

Verse 6. The danger of being burnt by scandals related to either the sun or the moon

12. I said all that with reference to trials and temptations; now observe what follows. The Lord protects you *better than the hand of your right hand*, I told you, and I think you recognized the truth of that. If you had not recognized it—and, moreover, recognized it as taught by the Scriptures—you would not be raising your voices to demonstrate to me that you have understood. Well then, brothers and sisters, since you have understood, consider the next verse. Think why the Lord needs to protect you, even better than the hand of your right hand. He is a better guardian for us even than faith itself, through which we have received power to become children of God and claim a place at Christ's right hand.

Why is it necessary for the Lord to protect us? Because of scandals. But where do scandals come from? We must beware of scandals from two sources, which correspond to the two commandments on which the law and the prophets depend: namely, love for God and love for our neighbor.[32] The Church is loved for our neighbor's sake, but God for his own sake. The psalm speaks figuratively of God as the sun and figuratively of the Church as the moon. A person may go wrong by holding mistaken beliefs about God: for instance, by not believing that the Father and the Son and the Holy Spirit are of one and the same substance. If such a person, deceived by the cunning of the heretics, especially the Arians,[33] believes that either the Son or the Holy Spirit is in any sense less than the Father, he or she has stumbled over a scandal concerning God. But again, anyone may be scandalized concerning the Church, thinking that it exists in one region only[34] and failing to see that it is spread throughout the whole wide world; or he may put his faith in those who say, *Look, here is Christ!* or, *There he is!* (Mk 13:21) as you heard just now when the gospel was read. Persons

---

32. See Mt 22:40.
33. Augustine's language is reminiscent of the Council of Nicea (325). On the Arians, see the note at *Exposition of Psalm* 54, 22.
34. The Donatists' contention.

so deceived do not realize that Christ, by paying such an enormous price, purchased the whole world; and thus they could be said to have stumbled over a scandal concerning their neighbors. They are burnt by the moon.

We conclude, then, that anyone who wanders into error touching the very substance of the truth is burnt by the sun, and burnt in daylight, for he or she has strayed from the wisdom of which Scripture says, *Day speaks the word to succeeding day* (Ps 18:3(19:2)). This is why the apostle speaks of *interpreting spiritual truths to people possessed of the Spirit* (1 Cor 2:13). *Day speaks the word to succeeding day: interpreting spiritual truths to people possessed of the Spirit. Day speaks the word to succeeding day: we speak wisdom among the perfect* (1 Cor 2:6). But what does the rest of that psalm-verse suggest: *And night imparts knowledge to night?* (Ps 18:3(19:2)) To little ones the humility of Christ is preached, and the flesh of Christ and the crucifixion of Christ, because this is the milk suited to little ones. These little ones are not abandoned in the night, because the moon shines then; this symbolizes the Church which is preached through the reality of Christ's flesh; for the very flesh of Christ is the head of the Church. Those who are not scandalized over this, not made to stumble over the Church or over the flesh of Christ, are not burnt by the moon. Those who are not made to stumble over the truth that exists unchangeably and beyond the reach of defilement are not burnt by the sun. In this context the sun does not mean the sun in the sky, which flies and cattle see along with us, but that sun of which the impious will say at the end, *What good has our pride done us, or what benefit has come to us from our vaunted wealth? All these things have passed away like a shadow.* And they will continue, *No doubt of it, we strayed from the path of truth. On us the light of righteousness did not shine, nor did the sun rise for us* (Wis 5:8–9.6). We cannot think, can we, that the sun we see in the sky does not rise for wicked people? God has arranged that it shall; of him it is said, *He causes his sun to rise over the good and the wicked* (Mt 5:45). There is a sun which God has made, which he causes to rise over good and bad people alike, the sun which both good and bad can see; but there is another sun which is not made but begotten, he through whom all things were made, and in whom is the understanding of unchangeable truth. Of this sun the wicked lament, *The sun did not rise for us* (Wis 5:6). Those who do not go astray from wisdom itself are not burnt by the sun. Those who do not go astray concerning the Church, or the flesh of the Lord,[35] or all those things done for our sake in his temporal dispensation, are not burnt by the moon. But all of us, even though already believers in Christ, will fall into error concerning the one or the other, unless the promise made in the psalm is fulfilled in us: *The Lord will be your defense, better than the hand of your right hand.* This is why, after the psalm has made that promise, the believer seems to be inquiring further, "But look: I have the hand of my

---

35. Variant: "the resurrection of the Lord."

right hand, for I have already chosen to believe in Christ. I have received the power to be numbered among the children of God. Why do I still need God to defend me even more effectively, better than does the hand of my right hand?" The psalm explains: *The sun will not burn you by day, nor the moon at night.* The Lord gives you extra protection, even better than that afforded by the hand of your right hand, so that neither the sun in the daytime nor the moon at night may scorch you.

This assurance is enough to make you understand, brothers and sisters, that the language is figurative. If we think literally of the visible sun, we know that it certainly can burn us during the day; but does the moon burn us at night? No, of course it doesn't. But what does burning suggest? Scandal. Listen to what the apostle says on that subject: *Is anyone weak, and I am not weak too? Is anyone tripped up, without my being afire with indignation?* (2 Cor 11:29)

Verses 6–8. The example of Saint Crispina

13. *The sun will not burn you by day, nor the moon at night.* Why not? Because *the Lord will guard*[36] *you from every evil.* May he guard you[37] from scandals relating to the sun, scandals relating to the moon, and every kind of disaster, for he is *your defense, better than the hand of your right hand,* and *he does not sleep or grow drowsy.* Why do we need such protection? Because we are beset by temptations. *The Lord will guard*[38] *you from every evil.*

May the Lord guard your soul. Yes, your very soul. *May the Lord guard*[39] *your going in, and your coming out henceforth and for ever.* It does not say he will guard your body, for the martyrs were slain as to their bodies; rather *may the Lord guard*[40] *your soul,* because as far as their souls were concerned the martyrs did not yield. The persecutors turned their rage against Crispina,[41] whose birthday[42] we celebrate today. They unleashed their savagery against a rich woman, delicately nurtured; but she was strong, because the Lord was for her a better defense than the hand of her right hand, and he was guarding her. Is there anyone in Africa

---

36. Variant: "guards."
37. Variant: "he will guard you."
38. Variant: "guards."
39. Variant: "the Lord will guard."
40. Variant: "the Lord will guard."
41. Born at Thagara in the Province of Africa, Crispina was a noble Roman matron and the mother of children. During the persecution of Diocletian she was brought before the tribunal and ordered to worship the gods. She steadfastly refused, despite the tearful pleas of her children. She was executed on 5 December 304, and her festival was celebrated on that day in Augustine's time.
42. I.e., her birthday into eternal life, the day of her martyrdom.

who does not know about these events, brothers and sisters? Scarcely, for she was extremely famous, of noble stock and very wealthy. But all these advantages belonged to the left hand and were under her head. The enemy attacked, intent on striking her head, but all that was presented to him was the left hand, which was beneath her head. The head was on top, and Christ's right hand was embracing her from above. Had the persecutor power to do anything, even against so delicate a woman? She was of the weaker sex, perhaps enfeebled by riches and quite frail in body in consequence of the life to which she had been accustomed. But what did all this signify, compared with the bridegroom whose left hand was beneath her head, whose right hand was embracing her? Was the enemy ever likely to overthrow one so fortified? He struck her, certainly, but only in the body. What does the psalm say? *May the Lord guard your soul.* The soul did not yield, though the body was struck down. And even the body was slain only for a time, for it is destined to rise again at the end. He who graciously willed to be the Church's head surrendered his own body to be killed, but only for a time. He raised his flesh to life again on the third day, and he will raise ours at the end. The head was raised that the body might wait expectantly and not faint.

May the Lord guard your soul. May it not yield; may your soul not be shattered against stumbling-blocks when persecutions arise and tribulations surround you. May it not faint or give way,[43] for the Lord bids us, *Do not be afraid of those who kill the body, but cannot kill the soul. Fear him rather who has the power to kill both soul and body in hell* (Mt 10:28). May the Lord guard this soul of yours, so that you never yield to an evil persuader, never yield to one who makes false promises, and never yield to anyone who threatens you with temporal disaster. *May the Lord guard*[44] *your soul.*

We "go in" when tempted and "come out" from temptation; the Lord guards us in both cases

14. Finally, *may the Lord guard your going in, and your coming out henceforth and for ever.* Notice how it says, *Your coming out henceforth and for ever,* whereas your *going in* is only for a time. Focus your attention on this: *may the Lord guard your going in, and your coming out henceforth and for ever.* May he *guard your coming out.* What is our *going in*? What is our *coming out*? When we are tempted, we go in; when we conquer the temptation, we come out. Listen to what Scripture has to say about going in and coming out: *Pots are proved in the kiln, and righteous persons in temptation and trouble* (Sir 27:6). If good people are like a potter's vessels, it is necessary for them to be put into the fire like pots. Not when they go in is the potter free from anxiety, but only when they have come out. The Lord, by contrast, is free from anxiety all the time, because he *knows his*

---

43. Variant: "fall."
44. Variant: "the Lord guards."

own (2 Tm 2:19) and knows which ones will not crack. The ones who do not crack are those in whom are trapped no bubbles of pride.

Thus humility is your guardian in all temptation, for we are climbing up from the valley of weeping, singing our Song of Ascents; and the Lord is guarding our entrance that we may go into it and be safe. When temptation comes upon us let us keep our faith whole and strong. Then he will guard our *coming out henceforth and for ever*, for when we have finally come through all temptation there will be no further temptation to daunt us for all eternity, no concupiscence ever again to make its insolent demands. Listen to the apostle reminding you, as I reminded you myself not long since, that *God is faithful, and he does not*[45] *allow you to be tempted more fiercely than you can bear.* So you see, your going in is guarded. When God does not allow any temptation to befall you that you cannot bear, he is guarding your going in; now see whether he also guards your coming out. The apostle continues, *But along with the temptation he ordains*[46] *the outcome, so that you may withstand it* (1 Cor 10:13). Can we offer any other interpretation of the psalm than the one taught us by the apostle's words, brothers and sisters? Guard yourselves, but not by any strength of your own, for the Lord is your defense and your guardian, the Lord who neither grows drowsy nor sleeps. Once only did he sleep for us; but he rose again, and now he will never sleep any more.

None of us must rely on ourselves. We are ascending from the valley of weeping; let us not linger on the way. There are steps ahead of us, and we must neither linger nor fall through pride. Let us pray to God, "Do not let our feet slip." Let him not sleep, your guardian. It is up to us[47] to make him our guardian, the Lord who neither sleeps nor gets drowsy, the Lord who guards Israel. What "Israel" is this? The one who sees God. Thus will your help come from the Lord; thus will he be *your defense, better than the hand of your right hand*; thus will your going in be guarded, and your coming out *henceforth and for ever*. If you rely on yourself, your foot has slipped already; and if your foot has slipped, you will be deceived into thinking you have already mounted to some particular step. You will fall off it, if you are proud. The humble person in the valley of weeping prays, *Do not let my foot be dislodged*.

Conclusion: this has been a rich feast of the word

15. Although this is a short psalm, our examination of it has taken a long time, and this sermon has been a long one. Put it to yourselves this way, brothers and sisters: I invited you to blessed Crispina's birthday party, and I have prolonged the banquet somewhat beyond what was expected.

---

45. Variant: "will not."
46. Variant: "will ordain."
47. Some witnesses insert "by God's grace."

But could this not happen to you if some officer[48] invited you to his table, and compelled you to drink more than you meant to? Well then, we ought to be allowed to do the same with God's word, leaving you inebriated and filled with it. Just so has the Lord in his gracious mercy drenched the earth with his seasonal rain.[49] This has prevented us from going with greater joy to the shrine of the martyrs,[50] as we promised yesterday. Beyond all suffering and toil, the martyrs are here with us.

---

48. *Militaris.*
49. Or perhaps "his temporal, material rain," in contrast to the spiritual potations of which Augustine has spoken.
50. *Dominus pluvia sua temporali terram dignatus est irrigare, ut cum maiore gaudio nos non sineret ire ad locum martyrum.* The translation offered above follows the CSEL text. But weighty witnesses, followed by the CCL edition, omit the *non*; if this is correct, the sentence could be differently understood, as follows: "Just so has the Lord drenched the earth with his seasonal rain, sending us with all the more joy to the shrine of the martyrs... ."

Exposition of Psalm 121

Synopsis

Love is the soul's rudder. All human beings live in love but must be attentive to the type and aim of their love. This Step-Song helps lovers climb heavenward with fellow travelers who shout their encouragement along the way (1–2). Pilgrims fire each other up by imagining themselves standing in the forecourt of the heavenly Jerusalem. But at present that spiritual city is still under construction, being built out of the living stones of saints (3–4).

The saints contemplate God, whose name is "I AM WHO AM" or "the Selfsame," which might be called "Being-Itself." If this is all too much for you to take in, then just hold on to the flesh of Christ, that is, believe what Christ became for you as human, so that you may participate in him as divine, the Word who is Being-Itself. Our years fail because we do not have being in ourselves, but his years never fail (5–6). The "tribes of the Lord" ascend to the city that shares in Being-Itself, though they are mixed with bad tribes that do not ascend. Those that ascend make up the true Israel, whose name means "seeing God." That is, "true Israelites" see "the one who is" in order to confess his name (7–8).

How should we understand the puzzling phrase, *the seats sat in judgment*? How can seats sit? Scripture elsewhere says that heaven is God's "throne" and that *the heavens proclaim God's glory*. Connect God's "seats" to the apostles, because the Lord says that they will sit on twelve thrones judging Israel. Now, it's the job of judges to ask questions. What questions do the apostles ask? They inquire, *What makes for the peace of Jerusalem?* Answer: only love is strong enough to bring peace (9–11).

Love is Jerusalem's strength; it brings peace to the heavenly city. Love is very powerful! If you can't perform some divine duty, then love someone who does that duty, and it is the same as doing it yourself. Or give just a cup of cold water to a thirsty person in love, and it is equal to giving away riches. Christ's preachers constantly proclaim love; it brings the peace of the heavenly city into this earthly exile (12–14).

Augustine's Text of Psalm 121

(1) A Song of Steps.

    I rejoiced over those who told me, "We are going to the Lord's house."

(2) Our feet were standing in the forecourts of Jerusalem,

(3) The Jerusalem that is being built like a city.

    It shares in the Selfsame [Being-Itself].

(4) Thither have the tribes ascended, the tribes of the Lord,

    A testimony to Israel, to confess your name, O Lord.

(5) There the seats sat in judgment over the house of David.

(6) "Ask what makes for the peace of Jerusalem."

    There are abundant riches for those who love you.

(7) May peace reign in your strength and abundance in your towers.

(8) For the sake of my brethren and kin,

    I always spoke of your peace.

(9) For the sake of the house of the Lord my God,

    I have sought your good.

Exposition

A Sermon to the People[1]

Introduction: the power of love to lift us to Jerusalem

1. Impure love inflames the soul, lures it toward the pursuit of earthly things which are desirable but doomed to perish, and plunges it headlong into the deepest turpitude.[2] Holy love raises the soul to heavenly thoughts and kindles in it a longing for eternal realities, arousing its desire for what neither passes nor dies, and lifting it from the depth of hell to heaven. Every kind of love has its own energy, and in the soul of a lover love cannot be idle; it must lead somewhere. Do you want to discern the character of a person's love? Notice where it leads. We do not admonish you to love nothing, but we do admonish you to withhold your love from the world, so that you may be free to love him who made the world. A soul enmeshed in

---

1. According to Possidius (*Indiculus* 10,4) Augustine preached two *Expositions* of this psalm, of which the earlier is apparently lost. The one given here is the second.
2. An abrupt opening, but it introduces immediately the theme of the two loves, which will run through the sermon.

earthly love has sticky wings and is unable to fly. But once it is cleansed from filthy, mundane attachments its wings can spread freely. The two commandments of love—love of God and love of neighbor[3]—are like a pair of wings, and as soon as they are disentangled from every impediment the soul flies. And whither does it fly? Where else but to God? It mounts to God in flight because it mounts by love. Before it gains the power to do this, it groans on the ground, if the longing to fly is already in it. *Who will give me wings, as though to a dove? Then I will fly away and find rest* (Ps 54:7(55:6)), it moans. Whither shall it fly? Away from the hindrances that surround it, the hindrances that evoke the sighs of the psalmist. He longs to fly away from them, from this place where he is mixed up with bad people, from the place where the grains of wheat are mingled with the straw. He longs to fly to a place where he need no longer suffer close contact and association with any impious person but may live in holy fellowship with the angelic citizens of the eternal Jerusalem.

Verse 1. Mutual encouragement along the road

2. The psalm which we have undertaken to study with you today, holy brethren,[4] is a psalm of longing for that Jerusalem. The one who voices the longing is one who in this psalm is ascending, for this is a Song of Steps.[5] As we have often explained to you, beloved, the steps in question are not for going down but for going up. The psalmist is someone who wants to ascend. And whither would he want to ascend if not to heaven? What is there in heaven to attract him? Does he want to climb up there in order to be with the sun and the moon and the stars? No, of course not. In heaven is the eternal Jerusalem, where dwell the angels, our fellow-citizens. For a little while we are absent from those compatriots of ours, while we are journeying on earth. On our pilgrimage we sigh, but in our own city we shall rejoice.

Yet even while we are still on the journey we find companions who have already seen that city and they invite us to run toward it. The speaker in the psalm is happy about the encouragement they offer, and he says, *I rejoiced over those who told me, We are going to the Lord's house.* Dearly beloved brothers and sisters, call to mind a scene familiar to you. When some festival of the martyrs falls due, perhaps, and some holy place is named at which all are to assemble to celebrate the solemn rites, remember how the throngs incite one another, how people encourage each other, saying, "Come on, let's go, let's go!" Others ask, "Where are we going?" And they are told, "To that place, to the holy site." People talk to each other and catch

---

3. See Mt 22:40.
4. *Sanctitati vestrae.*
5. On this group of psalms and the probable dating of Augustine's expositions of them, see his general introduction in *Exposition of Psalm* 119,1 and the note there.

fire with enthusiasm, and all the separate flames unite into a single flame. This one flame that springs up from the conversation of many people who enkindle one another seizes them all and sweeps them along to the holy place. Their devout resolve sanctifies them. If, then, holy love energizes people and tugs them to a material place, what kind of love must it be that tugs persons united in heart toward heaven, as they say to each other, *We are going to the Lord's house*? Let's run, let's run fast, they say, for *we are going to the Lord's house!* Let's run and not weary, because we shall reach a place where fatigue will never touch us. Let's run to the Lord's house, and let our soul be gladdened by those who tell us these things; for those who cheer us on have seen our homeland before we have, and they shout from afar to us latecomers, "We are going to the Lord's house! Walk! Run!" The apostles have seen it, and they exhort us, "Run, walk, follow: we are going to the Lord's house!" And what do we reply, every one of us? *"I rejoiced over those who told me, We are going to the Lord's house.* I rejoiced over the prophets and I rejoiced over the apostles, for all of them have told us, *We are going to the Lord's house."*

Verse 2. Think of yourself as though you were there already

3. *Our feet were standing in the forecourts of Jerusalem.*[6] If you were wondering what the Lord's house is, you know now. In that house of the Lord the founder of the house is praised. He is the delight of all who dwell in the house; he alone is our hope here, as he will be our fulfillment there.

What should the eager runners keep in mind, then? How should they think of it? As though they were there already and standing within it, for it is a wonderful thing to stand there among the angels and never lose one's place. One there was who did lose his place and fall away, because *he did not stand in the truth* (Jn 8:44). All the others, those who have not fallen away, do stand in the truth. The one who stands fast is the one who finds joy in God.[7] They fall, who try to find their joy in themselves. But who tries to find enjoyment in himself? A proud person. Very different was the hope of one whose ambition was to stand for ever in the courts of Jerusalem; he said to God, "*In your light we will see light,* not in my light. *With you is the fountain of life,* not with me." And did he have anything further to say about this? Yes: *Let not the foot of pride come near me, nor the hands of sinners dislodge me. There they have fallen, all those who work iniquity; they have been driven out, unable to stand* (Ps 35:10.12–13(36:9.11–12)).

Well then, if some were unable to stand because they were proud, make sure that you ascend humbly, so that you may say, *Our feet were standing in the forecourts of Jerusalem.* Think of yourself as you will be when you get there. You are still on the way, but keep your future destiny before

---

6. Variant: *in your forecourts, O Jerusalem.*
7. *Qui Deo fruitur,* a key idea for Augustine. God is to be enjoyed for his own sake; everything else is to be used as a means.

your eyes as though you were standing there and already rejoicing with the angels in a joy that can never be taken away from you. Bear yourself as though the prophecy in another psalm were already a reality for you: *Blessed are they who dwell in your house; they will praise you for ever and ever* (Ps 83:5(84:4)).

Our feet were standing in the forecourts of Jerusalem. What Jerusalem does this mean? There is another Jerusalem, an earthly city of which people speak often, but it is no more than a shadow of the real one. Would it be any great matter to stand in the earthly Jerusalem when that city itself could not even stand but was reduced to ruins? If the earthly Jerusalem were envisaged, would the Holy Spirit be suggesting any great thing when he evoked from the burning heart of a lover the cry, *Our feet were standing in the forecourts of Jerusalem*? Is not the terrestrial Jerusalem the city to which the Lord addressed his reproach, *Jerusalem, Jerusalem, you kill the prophets and stone those who are sent to you?* (Mt 23:37) Would our psalmist have been aspiring to any special privilege if he had wanted to stand among those who used to kill the prophets and stone those sent to them? Let any notion of the earthly Jerusalem be banished from the mind of one who is in love, who is afire, who longs to reach that Jerusalem which is our mother,[8] which the apostle calls our *everlasting home in heaven* (2 Cor 5:1).

Verse 3. The holy city is still being built

4. But don't just take my word for it; listen to the next verse, for that indicates to which Jerusalem the psalm means us to direct our minds. It states, *Our feet were standing in the forecourts of Jerusalem*, but then it seems to anticipate a question from someone, "What Jerusalem do you mean? About which Jerusalem are you speaking?" The psalm immediately adds a clarification: *The Jerusalem that is being built like a city.* When David said that, brothers and sisters, the city was already complete; it was not still under construction. The psalm must therefore be speaking of some other city which is being built even now. Living stones are hastening toward it, those of which Peter says, *You too must allow yourselves to be built, like living stones, into a spiritual house* (1 Pt 2:5), into a holy temple for God. What is implied by *allow yourselves to be built, like living stones*? You are alive if you believe; and if you believe you are being made into God's temple, for the apostle Paul teaches, *God's temple is holy, and that temple is yourselves* (1 Cor 3:17). This is the city which is now a-building. Stones are hewn out of the mountains by the hands of those who preach the truth, and squared to fit into an everlasting structure. There are still many stones in the builder's hands; he does not drop them,[9] for he means to shape them to perfection, ready to be built in with the rest into the fabric of the temple. This is *the Jerusalem that is being built like a city.* Christ is its foundation,

---

8. See Gal 4:26.
9. Variant: "may they not fall from his hands."

for Paul the apostle says, *No one can lay any other foundation than that which is laid, which is Christ Jesus* (1 Cor 3:11).

Now, when a foundation is laid in the earth, the walls are built up on top of it. The weight of the walls bears downward, down to the bottom where the foundation has been laid. But if our foundation is in heaven, the weight of our building bears upward, toward heaven.[10] Look at the lofty, spacious basilica all round you. It was raised by physical work and, because it was a matter of bodily labor, the builders laid the foundations underneath. We, on the contrary, are being built spiritually, and so our foundation is established in heaven. Let us run to the place where we are to be built in, for of that Jerusalem the psalm says, *Our feet were standing in the forecourts of Jerusalem.* But what Jerusalem is it? *The Jerusalem that is being built like a city.*

Perhaps, though, the indication is not yet clear enough. The psalm has pointed to the Jerusalem *that is being built like a city,* but that might still be taken in a material sense. Suppose there is someone who argues, "Yes, when these things were said in David's time and these verses were sung, the city was complete: I grant you that. But David foresaw in spirit that it would be destroyed and built up anew. In fact his city was overthrown and the people were taken captive and deported to Babylon. Scripture calls this 'the transmigration to Babylon.'[11] Then Jeremiah prophesied that when seventy years had elapsed the city could be rebuilt,[12] that city which had been destroyed by the attackers." Someone might argue in this way. "David saw in spirit that the city of Jerusalem would be razed by its enemies," he might say, "and he also saw that it could be rebuilt after seventy years; that was why he said, *Jerusalem, that is being built like a city.* You need not refer the text to the Jerusalem which consists of holy persons, built up like living stones."

Let us clear up this ambiguity by looking at the next lines. The psalmist says, "*Our feet were standing in the forecourts of Jerusalem.* Which Jerusalem do I mean? Not the one that you see to be built of material walls but *the Jerusalem that is being built like a city.*" Why *like a city*? Why not just say "a city"? Surely because the edifice with material walls, the earthly Jerusalem, was a visible city; it was a city properly so called, it was what is called a city in common parlance. But the heavenly Jerusalem is being built up *like a city,* just as the living components that are being built into it are *like living stones,* for they are not literally stones. And just as they are not stones, but like stones, so the heavenly Jerusalem is not a literal city but *like a city.*

---

10. Compare his meditation in *Confessions* XIII,9,10 on love as the "weight" that bears things toward their place of rest.
11. See Mt 1:11.
12. See Jer 25:11–12; 29:10.

We should note that by using the word *built* the psalm clearly meant us to think of a growing structure and the interlocking of component parts and walls. Strictly speaking, of course, a city means the people who live there; but the psalmist indicates that he means us to think of an actual place by using the verb *is being built*. The spiritual edifice bears a certain resemblance to a material building, and so he says it *is being built like a city*.

5. But let the psalmist continue and exclude all doubt, because we must not think in a materialistic way about this Jerusalem, the *Jerusalem that is being built like a city*.

It participates in the being of God

It shares in the Selfsame.[13] Now, brothers and sisters, if anyone can apply the keen edge of the mind, if anyone can lay aside the murk of the flesh, if anyone can cleanse the eye of the heart, let him or her look up and see. What is *idipsum*? It is simply *idipsum*, Being-Itself. How can I say anything about it, except that it is Being-Itself? Grasp it if you can, brothers and sisters, for whatever else I may say, I shall not have defined Being-Itself. All the same, let us attempt to direct the gaze of our minds,[14] to steer our feeble intelligence, to thinking about Being-Itself, making use of certain words and meanings that have some affinity with it.

What is Being-Itself? That which always exists unchangingly, which is not now one thing, now another. What is Being-Itself, Absolute Being, the Selfsame? That Which Is. What is That Which Is? The eternal, for anything that is constantly changing does not truly exist, because it does not abide—not that it is entirely nonexistent, but it does not exist in the highest sense. And what is That Which Is if not he who, when he wished to give Moses his mission, said to him, *I AM WHO AM?* (Ex 3:14) What is That Which Is if not he who, when his servant objected, *So you are sending me. But what shall I say to the sons of Israel if they challenge me, Who sent you to us?* (Ex 3:13), refused to give himself any other name than *I AM WHO AM?* He reiterated, *Thus shall you say to the children of Israel, HE WHO IS has sent me to you* (Ex 3:14). This is Being-Itself, the Selfsame: *I AM WHO AM. HE WHO IS has sent me to you.*

You cannot take it in, for this is too much to understand, too much to grasp. Hold on instead to what he whom you cannot understand became for you. Hold onto the flesh of Christ, onto which you, sick and helpless, left wounded and half dead by robbers, are hoisted, that you may be taken

---

13. *Cuius participatio eius in idipsum*. The redundant *eius* is a Hebraism. Here, as in *Confessions* IX,4,11, where he is meditating on Psalm 4:9, Augustine understands the word *idipsum* ("the Selfsame") as an echo of the mysterious, ineffable name of God, who is infinite, immutable Being. Compare also *Confessions* VII,17,23; IX,10,24; XII,7,7.
14. Some witnesses omit "direct the gaze of our minds."

to the inn and healed there.[15] Let us run to the house of the Lord, run all the way to that city, so that our feet may stand there, in that place which *is being built like a city, which shares in the Selfsame*. To what am I telling you to hold fast? Hold onto what Christ became for you, because Christ himself, even Christ, is rightly understood by this name, *I AM WHO AM*, inasmuch as he is in the form of God. In that nature wherein *he deemed it no robbery to be God's equal* (Phil 2:6), there he is Being-Itself. But that you might participate in Being-Itself, he first of all became a participant in what you are; *the Word was made flesh* (Jn 1:14) so that flesh might participate in the Word.

But God speaks to weak people, telling them that this Word which was made flesh and lived among us came from the stock of Abraham (for the promise was made to Abraham and Isaac and Jacob that through their seed all nations would be blessed,[16] and that is why we see the Church spread throughout the whole world). God looked for strong hearts when he said, *I AM WHO AM*; he looked for strong hearts and the keen, focused gaze of contemplation when he told Moses to say, *HE WHO IS has sent me to you*. But perhaps you do not yet practice contemplation.[17] Do not be put off, do not despair. HE WHO IS willed to become a human being like you, so he had more to say when Moses was terrified of his name. What name? The name, HE WHO IS. But he said more: "*I am the God of Abraham, the God of Isaac and the God of Jacob; this is my name for ever* (Ex 3:15). Do not despair of your own prospects because I have told you, *I AM WHO AM, and HE WHO IS has sent me to you*. Do not despair, reflecting how you are tossed to and fro, and precluded from sharing in the Selfsame by the mutability of all human things and the inconstant state of mortals. I am coming down to you, because you cannot come up to me. *I am the God of Abraham, the God of Isaac and the God of Jacob*. Put your hope in Abraham's seed, that you may be strengthened to see the one who is coming to you from Abraham's seed."

6. This is the Selfsame to whom another psalm says, *You will discard them like a garment, and so they will be changed, but you are the Selfsame, and your years will not fail* (Ps 101:27–28(102:26–27)). He whose *years will not fail*, he alone is Being-Itself. Do not our years fail every day, brothers and sisters? Do they ever stand still? The years that have come exist no longer; those which are still to come have no existence yet. The years that have passed have already failed us, and the years of our future will fail us in their turn. The same is true, brothers and sisters, even of a single day. Take today: we are talking now, at this moment, but the earlier hours have slipped away and the later hours have not yet arrived. When they have arrived, they too will slip away and fail. Are there any years that fail not?

---

15. See Lk 10:30–34.
16. See Gn 12:3; 22:18; 26:4.
17. See Ex 3:14–15.

Only the years that stand. There beyond are the years that stand, and there the stable years are but one year, and that one year that abides is one single day, because that one abiding day knows neither sunrise nor sunset; it does not succeed yesterday nor is it chased away by tomorrow, but it abides for ever as this one day—if you want to call it a day. If you prefer to think of it as years, call it so; if you want to call it a day, it is a day; but, however you think of it, it stands.

The city that *shares in the Selfsame* shares in that stability, and because it does so the speaker in the psalm, who is running toward the city, cries out, *Our feet were standing in the forecourts of Jerusalem*; for there all things stand, and nothing passes away. Do you too hope to stand there immovably? Run thither. No one has absolute being as of himself. Think hard about this, brothers and sisters. A person has a body, but the body is not absolute being, because it has no stability in itself. It changes with the passing stages of life, it changes as we move from place to place and changes with the seasons, it is changed by disease and the infirmities of the flesh. In itself it cannot stand. Nor do the heavenly bodies stand in themselves, for they too undergo certain mutations, even though some of these are concealed from us. They obviously move from place to place, rising from the east and traveling to the west and then finding their way back to the east once more. They too are powerless to stand, for they are not Being-Itself. Not even the human soul can stand. What a variety of thoughts flit across it! What intense feelings of pleasure[18] sway it! How fiercely it is pulled this way and that and stretched[19] by its desires! The human mind itself, the so-called rational mind, is mutable, for it is not Being-Itself. One moment it wants something, and then it wants it no longer; now it knows something, and then it does not know; now it remembers, now it forgets. No one of himself has absolute being.

One there was who arrogated absolute existence to himself, as of right, one who desired to be his own absolute; and he fell. An angel fell and became a devil. He then offered the fatal drink of pride to humans and in his envy dragged down with him the man and woman who had been standing. They too began to want to be their own selfsame; they tried to be their own rulers, to exercise lordship over their own lives. They refused their real Lord, who truly is the Selfsame, to whom a psalmist said, *You will discard them like a garment, and so they will be changed, but you are the Selfsame* (Ps 101:27–28(102:26–27)). But now at last, after such protracted sickness, after such grievous disease, struggles and toil, let the humbled soul turn back to HIM WHO IS Absolute Being and find its place in the city that *shares in the Selfsame*.

---

18. Variant: "acts of will."
19. Variant: "cut and torn."

Verse 4. The tribes of the Lord, the true Israel

7. *Thither have the tribes ascended.* We told you earlier that in this psalm we hear the voice of people ascending, the voice of the Church as it makes the ascent, and so we were prompted to inquire where fallen humans are going in their climb. Are we still wondering about their goal? The height they are bound for, the end of their climb, the goal of their ascent, is that place *whither the tribes have ascended*, as our psalm now tells us. But where is that? Where *have the tribes ascended*? Into that city which *shares in Being-Itself.* That is the goal of our ascent—Jerusalem. There was once a man who, instead of mounting to Jerusalem, went down from Jerusalem to Jericho[20] and fell among robbers. If he had not gone down, he would not have fallen foul of them. Anyone who has fallen among robbers on his downward path must change course and climb up instead and encounter angels. Let such a one mount to that place, for *thither have the tribes ascended.*

But what are these tribes? Many know the answer, but many do not. Let those of us who know what the tribes are go down to those who do not know, so that they may ascend with us to the place whither the tribes have gone. "Tribes" can also be called *curiae*, if this word is used loosely. There is no exact synonym for the term "tribe," though *curia* comes somewhere near it.[21] In the strict sense we use *curia* for the council which sits in an individual city, whence are derived the names *curiales* and *decuriones*,[22] so called because they are members of a *curia* or a *decuria*. You know how every city has one *curia* of this kind. But there are also (or formerly were) groups of people in these same cities, each of which could be called a *curia*. When the word is used in this sense we can say that each city has many of them; Rome has thirty-five. These may be styled "tribes." The people of Israel had twelve, corresponding to the number of Jacob's sons.

8. The people of Israel comprised twelve tribes, but among them were both bad people and good. What a bad tribe they were, what a wicked party, that crucified the Lord! And what a good fraternity acknowledged the Lord! The clans that crucified the Lord are the tribes of the devil. The psalm says not merely, *Thither have the tribes ascended*; it specifies *the tribes of the Lord* to make it clear that not all the tribes are meant. What, then, are these *tribes of the Lord*? Those who knew the Lord. Among the twelve bad tribes were some good people, members of good clans that acknowledged the architect of the city. They were grains of wheat among

---

20. See Lk 10:30.
21. A *curia* was originally one of the thirty divisions of the Roman people established by Romulus for voting purposes. Thereafter the name came to be used for the meeting place of the Roman Senate or for that of the local senate in other cities. As Augustine points out, the word was often used more widely.
22. The *decuriones* were municipal councillors. A municipal senate was supposed to consist of ten divisions of ten men each.

the tribes, but they were mixed up with the chaff. They went up, but not in the company of the chaff; they went up as sifted, purified, elect tribes, as *tribes of the Lord. Thither have the tribes ascended, the tribes of the Lord.*

Now what else is said about *the tribes of the Lord*? That they are *the testimony to Israel.*[23] Listen, brothers and sisters, and understand what this *testimony to Israel* is, who these people are in whom the proof of the true Israel may be discerned. What does "Israel" mean? The interpretation of the name has been mentioned before, but it is as well to repeat it frequently, for it may have slipped the minds of some, even though we spoke of it not long ago. By repeating it we make sure that it is not forgotten even by those unable or unwilling to read; let us serve as a book for them. "Israel" is taken to mean "seeing God." Or rather, if we analyze the name more exactly, we can say that "Israel" means "the seeing one is."[24] So when we put these two interpretations together we get "the one who sees God, is." No human being *is* in his or her own right, for we are inconstant and subject to change, unless we participate in HIM WHO IS the Selfsame. A human being truly *is* when he sees God. He *is* when he sees HIM WHO IS, for, in seeing HIM WHO IS, the creature too comes to be in his measure. Thus he becomes Israel, for Israel is the seeing one.

A proud person is not Israel, for, instead of sharing in Being-Itself, the proud person wants to be his own absolute being. Anyone who tries to be the source of his own being is no Israel. No impostor can be Israel, and every proud person is an impostor. What I mean is this, brothers and sisters: any proud person pretends to be something he is not; he cannot do otherwise. It would not be so bad if a proud person tried to appear what he is not in the sense, say, of wanting to be thought a flautist,[25] when he is no such thing. He could soon be proved bogus if people said to him, "Go on, then, sing. Let's hear what you can do." If he could not, he would be shown up as having made false claims when he tried to appear as something he was not. Or again, if someone said he was a fluent orator, we could say to him, "Very well; give us a speech, and prove it." As soon as he began to speak, he would be shown up; he would not be what he claimed to be.[26]

But what is much worse is the claim of a proud person to be righteous when he is not. Righteousness is difficult to discern, and hence it is not easy to detect proud persons. Yet the proud want to seem what they are not, and therefore they do not share in Being-Itself, and they do not belong to Israel, "the one who sees God."

---

23. *Testimonium Israel*: "a testimony to Israel," or "a guarantee of Israel," or "a proof that Israel.
24. *Est videns*.
25. *Choraula*, see *Exposition of Psalm* 96,10; but it is evident from the present passage that the flautist was also expected to sing.
26. The two examples touch on areas where Augustine himself was expert and sensitive.

Who, then, does belong to Israel? One who *shares in the Selfsame*. And who is that? One who confesses that he is not what God is and that he holds from God whatever good he can claim to have, that of himself he is nothing but sin and that he possesses righteousness only as a gift from God. Such a person is one in whom there is no guile. What did the Lord say on catching sight of Nathanael? *Look, there is a true Israelite, in whom there is no guile* (Jn 1:47). If the true Israelite is one in whom no guile is to be found, we infer that the tribes that have ascended to Jerusalem are those found free of guile. They are the authentic Israel, the ones who give proof of being the real thing, because through them it can be seen that there were grains of wheat among the straw all the time, even though to an onlooker the threshing-floor seemed to contain nothing but chaff. The grains were there among it, but when they have ascended in heavenly splendor and the winnowing is finished, then will the *testimony to Israel* be rendered, for then will all the evildoers say to each other, "When the whole lot looked bad to us, there really were righteous people among the bad. We thought everyone was as bad as we were ourselves." Thus the good are a *testimony to Israel*.

Why do they ascend? *To confess to your name, O Lord*. No more glorious motive could be envisaged. As pride makes one presumptuous, so does humility prompt confession. As a presumptuous person tries to pose as something he is not, so a confessing person has no wish to appear other than he is but loves what God is. The Israelites in whom there is no guile mount to this confession because they are truly Israelites. In them is the testimony to Israel, and they ascend for this purpose: *to confess to your name, O Lord*.

Verse 5. The apostles sit on seats to judge, but they are themselves the Lord's seat

9. *There the seats sat in judgment*. This is a puzzling expression and likely to raise problems unless it is rightly understood. Our translation renders as *seats* what the Greeks call θρόνοι. The Greeks use the word θρόνοι for benches of honor, or sedilia. There is nothing remarkable, brothers and sisters, about people sitting on seats or judicial benches. But how are we to understand a statement that the seats themselves sit down? It is as strange as though someone were to say, "Let the bishop's chair sit here, and the benches sit there." People sit on benches, on seats, and on chairs. Seats are for sitting on; the seats themselves do not sit.

What can the psalm mean, then, by saying, *There the seats sat to exercise judgment*? Well, you are certainly familiar with a saying of the Lord, *Heaven is my throne, but the earth is my footstool* (Is 66:1; Acts 7:49). This amounts to God telling us that his seat is heaven. But now who are the heavens? Who else but just persons? These heavens are a single heaven, just as the individual churches are the one Church: they are many, but in such a way as to form one; and the same is true in the inverse sense of the just, for they are heaven, but in their separate individuality they are heavens. God has his seat in them, and from them God exercises judgment. A psalm had good reason to say, *The heavens proclaim God's glory* (Ps 18:2(19:1)), for the apostles were made into heaven. How did that come about? By their being justified. As a sinner was made into earth when he was told, *Earth you are, and back to earth you shall go* (Gn 3:19), so were the justified made into heaven. They carried God, and from them God constantly flashed the lightning of his miracles, thundered his terrors, and rained down his consolations. They were heaven; they truly were. And they incessantly proclaimed the glory of God. The psalm left you no room for doubt about the apostles being heaven, for it went on to say, *Their sound went forth throughout the world, their words to the ends of the earth* (Ps 18:5(19:4)). Whose sound, whose words? Those of the heavens.

Well now, if heaven is God's seat, and the apostles are heaven, it follows that they are God's seat, God's throne. Scripture says elsewhere, *The soul of a just person is the throne of wisdom* (Prv 12:23, LXX). That is a tremendous statement: *The soul of a just person is the throne of wisdom*; it implies that in the soul of a righteous person wisdom sits as on a judicial bench, or a throne, and from there judges all things. The apostles were thrones for wisdom and yet the Lord said to them, *You will sit upon twelve thrones, judging the twelve tribes of Israel* (Mt 19:28). It seems, then, that they will themselves sit upon the twelve seats, but at the same time they are seats for God. This is what our present psalm teaches when it speaks of the seats sitting: *There the seats sat.* Who sat? *The seats.* And who are *the seats*? The heavens. Who are the heavens? Heaven. And what is heaven? That of which the Lord said, *Heaven is my seat* (Is 66:1; Acts 7:49).

We are taught three things, therefore. The just are seats, and they have seats, and it is in Jerusalem that the seats will sit. To what purpose? For judgment. The Lord promised, *You will sit upon twelve seats*, you who yourselves are my seats, *judging the twelve tribes of Israel*. Whom will they judge? Those below, on earth. Who will judge? Those who have become heaven.

Those amenable to their judgment will be divided into two groups, one to the right, the other to the left. The saints will join Christ in judging; as Isaiah says, *the Lord will come in judgment, with the elders of his people* (Is 3:14). Those who will collaborate with him are distinct from those subject to his judgment and to theirs. The people facing judgment will be segregated into two groups.[27] One will be placed at his right, and the acts of mercy they have performed will be enumerated to them. The others will be relegated to his left, and they will be reminded of their cruelty and their barrenness where mercy was called for. To those stationed at his right the invitation will be extended, *Come, you who are blessed by my Father, take possession of the kingdom prepared for you since the creation of the world.*

---

27. The repetition in these sentences may be due to Augustine's having suddenly remembered another text he could adduce, that of Is 3:14.

And why? *I was hungry, and you fed me*, he will tell them. But they will protest, *When did we see you hungry?* He will reply, *When you did that for even the least of those who are mine, you did it for me* (Mt 25:34–35.37.40).

What is the implication, brothers and sisters? The apostles will judge concerning those people who have been advised to make friends for themselves by using iniquitous mammon, *so that they may welcome you into the tents of eternity* (Lk 16:9). The saints will sit in judgment with the Lord, marking carefully who among those before them have performed acts of mercy; they will take into their company those placed at the Lord's right and welcome them into the kingdom of heaven. And this, even this, is the peace of Jerusalem. In what does the peace of Jerusalem consist? In the conjunction of corporal works of mercy with spiritual works of preaching, so that in both giving and receiving there may be peace. The apostle saw almsdeeds as a matter of due payment and receipts,[28] for he said, *If we have sown spiritual seeds for your benefit, is it too much to ask that we reap a carnal harvest from you?* (1 Cor 9:11) On the same subject he said in another passage, *The one who gathered much had no surplus, and the one who gathered little, no lack* (2 Cor 8:15). Why did the one who had gathered a great deal have nothing left over? Because anyone who had more than enough gave to someone in need. And why did the one who gathered little not go short? Because he received from someone else who had plenty. This was done *that there might be equality* (2 Cor 8:14). And this is the peace for which our psalm prays, *May peace reign in your strength*.

Verse 6. The peace of Jerusalem is founded on love

10. What we have just said is certain, for the psalm makes it clear. It has told us that *there the seats sat in judgment over the house of David*, which means "over Christ's household," to which they conscientiously gave food in due season.[29] But immediately after this the psalm turns to the seats and admonishes them, "*Ask*[30] *what makes for the peace of Jerusalem*. You are the seats that are sitting to judge. You have become the Lord's seats and so you function as judges. But it is the duty of judges to ask questions, and of those before them to answer when questions are put to them. So then, *ask what makes for the peace of Jerusalem*." What will their interrogation reveal? That some people have been active in works of mercy and others have not. They will call into Jerusalem those who have performed works of mercy, for these are the things that *make for the peace of Jerusalem*.

Love[31] is a powerful thing, brothers and sisters; love is a powerful thing. Would you like a proof of how strong it is? Consider, then: if someone is prevented by circumstances from carrying out a duty enjoined by God, let

---

28. See Phil 4:15.
29. See Mt 24:45.
30. *Interrogate*.
31. *Dilectio*, the love of free choice.

him love someone else who performs that duty, and he fulfils it through that other. Note this carefully, beloved. Suppose, for instance, a man has a wife whom he cannot leave. He must obey the apostle's orders, *Let the husband render his debt to his wife* (1 Cor 7:3), and again, *Are you bound to a wife? Then do not seek to be unbound* (1 Cor 7:27). It will occur to him that there is a better way of life, concerning which the same apostle says, *I wish everyone were as I am* (1 Cor 7:7). He marks those who have taken this course, he loves them for it, and in them he carries out what he is unable to do himself. Love is a powerful thing. It is our strength, and anything else we may have is useless without it. *If I speak with human tongue or angel's tongue, but have no charity, I have become like a booming gong or a clashing cymbal*, warns the apostle; and then he adds something even weightier: *If I distribute all my resources to feed the poor, and deliver my body to be burnt, yet have no charity, it profits me nothing* (1 Cor 13:1.3). If charity exists alone and has no goods to distribute to the poor, let it simply love and give only a cup of cold water,[32] and the act will be judged as meritorious as that of Zacchaeus, who gave half his patrimony to the poor.[33] How can that be? The one gave so little, the other so much. How can the one be as highly deserving as the other? Yet he is indeed just as deserving. The material possibilities were not comparable, but charity was equal in the two cases.

11. The judges are questioning you, then, and you must assess what you are. We have been told, *We are going to the Lord's house*. We were certainly gladdened by those who gave us those tidings: *We are going to the Lord's house*. Find out, then, if we are truly going there. We travel not on foot but by our affections. Test whether we are on the way. Each one of you must question himself about his attitude to the holy poor person, the needy brother or sister, the penurious beggar. Let each one check that his compassion is not too narrow, because the seats which will sit in judgment will have to interrogate you, and their duty is to seek out what makes for the peace of Jerusalem. How will they conduct their interrogation? As seats for God. Is God interrogating you, then? Does anything lie hidden from God, and can anything elude those interrogators who are bidden, *Ask what makes for the peace of Jerusalem*?

But what makes for the peace of Jerusalem? *There are abundant riches for those who love you*. The psalmist has now turned to address Jerusalem herself. There are great riches for those who love her—riches after poverty, for here below her lovers are in need, but affluent there; here they are weak, there strong; here in penury, there in wealth. How did they become rich? Here below they gave away what they had received from God for a limited time, and there they receive the reward that God will give them for eternity. Here on earth, brothers and sisters, even the rich are paupers. A rich man

---

32. See Mt 10:42.
33. See Lk 19:8.

is lucky if he recognizes his poverty, for if he thinks himself full, that is no more than puffed-up pride, not plenitude. Let him acknowledge that he is empty so that he may be deserve to be filled. What does he possess? Gold. What does he not yet possess? Eternal life. Let him take stock of what he has and recognize what he has not. Let him give to others from what he has, brothers and sisters, that he may receive what he has not; let him use what he has to buy himself what he does not have, and there will be abundant riches for those who love Jerusalem.

Verse 7. Love is the city's strength

12. *May peace reign in your strength.* O Jerusalem, city being built like a city, city whose share is in Being-Itself, *may peace reign in your strength.* Let there be peace in your love, for your strength lies in your love. Listen to the Song of Songs: *Love is as mighty as death* (Sg 8:6). That is a solemn utterance, brothers and sisters: *Love is as mighty as death.* There could be no more glorious assertion of the strength of charity than *Love is as mighty as death,* for who can stand firm against death? Fire, water, the sword—against all these we can make a stand; we can resist potentates, we can resist kings. But death, death alone, no one can resist. This is why death is used as a comparison to suggest the power of love: *Love is as mighty as death.*[34] Moreover, love itself effects a kind of death in us, for charity slays what we once were so that we may become what we were not. The man who said, *The world has been crucified to me, and I to the world* (Gal 6:14), had died that death, and so too had those to whom he said, *You are dead, and your life is hidden with Christ in God* (Col 3:3). *Love is as mighty as death.* If it is mighty, it has great power and force; it is strength itself. Through love weak people are ruled by the strong, earth by heaven, the nations by the seats; and therefore the psalm prays, *May peace reign in your strength,* may peace reign in your love.

What is more, through that strength, through that love, through that peace, may there be *abundance in your towers,* which means in your elevated places. Only a few will sit in judgment, but the great crowds at Christ's right hand make up the population of the city. There are many under the protection of each one of the exalted judges, many who are welcomed by the judges into the tents of eternity;[35] and thus there will be abundance in its towers. God himself is the fullness of delights and our all-sufficient riches. He is Being-Itself, in which the city participates; in this will our abundance consist.[36] But how can this be? Through charity, which is to say, through the city's strength. But who has charity, brothers and sisters? The person who in this life is not self-seeking.[37] The apostle Paul was a

---

34. Compare a similar passage in *Exposition of Psalm* 47,13.
35. See Lk 16:9.
36. Variant: "He himself will be our abundance."
37. See Phil 2:4.21.

man of charity. Listen to what he tells us: *Try to appease everyone in all circumstances, as I too make myself agreeable to all in every respect* (1 Cor 10:33). What has become of the claim you made elsewhere, Paul? You said, *If I were still out to please men, I would not be Christ's servant* (Gal 1:10), yet now you say that you try to mollify others, and you exhort your disciples to do the same! But in denying that he tried to please men he omitted to mention the object some have in making such efforts; they curry favor with others for their own advantage, not for the promotion of charity. The person who is intent on his own reputation is not seeking the salvation of other people. But Paul elaborates: *Try to appease everyone... as I too make myself agreeable to all in every respect, seeking not my own advantage but the profit of the many, that they may be saved* (1 Cor 10:33).

Verses 8–9. Fraternal charity is the reason for preaching of Jerusalem's peace

13. The psalmist[38] has been speaking about charity, and in the same vein he continues, *For the sake of my brethren and kin I spoke always of your peace.* O Jerusalem, you are the city that shares in Being-Itself, but I am still in the midst of this life on earth, a pilgrim poor and groaning. I do not yet enjoy your peace, but I preach of your peace to others. I preach it not for my own gain, as do the heretics who seek their own advancement as they say, "Peace be with you," when in truth they do not have the peace they preach to the peoples. If they had, they would not tear apart the unity of the Church.

But I, says the psalmist, *I spoke always of your peace*. From what motive? *For the sake of my brethren and kin*, not to win a reputation for myself, not for money, not even to save my life, for *life to me is Christ, and death is gain* (Phil 1:21). But *I spoke always of your peace for the sake of my brethren and kin*. He was longing[39] *to die and to be with Christ* (Phil 1:23), but this man who preached peace to his brethren and kin knew that it was necessary for them that he remain in the flesh.[40] *For the sake of my brethren and kin I spoke always of your peace.*

14. *For the sake of the house of the Lord my God I have sought your good.* I have sought good things indeed, but not for myself, for then I would have been seeking good not for you but for me, and I would not even have gained any good myself, because I was not seeking it for you. No, it is *for the sake of the house of the Lord my God* that I have preached: for the Church, for the saints, for the pilgrims, for the needy, so that they may make the ascent. To them we say, *We are going to the Lord's house*. It is *for the sake of the house of the Lord my God* that *I have sought your good*.

---

38. *Hic* ("he") apparently refers to the psalmist, but the reference throughout section 13 could be to Paul.
39. Variant: "I was longing."
40. See Phil 1:23–24.

This exposition has been rather long, brothers and sisters, but it was necessary. Pluck fruit from it, eat, drink, grow strong, and seize the prize.

PART II

EXPLORING CHRIST'S BEAUTIFUL MYSTERY

Steps to the First Floor

Exposition 1 of Psalm 33

Synopsis

The Psalm itself is straightforward, but not its title. So let hearers knock with me at the door of its "deep and vast mystery." The story line about David is strange: he *altered his behavior in the presence of Abimelech, and forsook him, and went away.* This reflects a story in the First Book of Samuel in which David affects madness, drums on the city doors, gets "carried in his own hands," falls down outside on a threshold, and dribbles spittle on his beard. Moreover, a name change occurs; in Samuel the priest's name was Achis, but here it's Abimelech. Such oddities nudge us to study the Psalm title carefully in light of the Samuel story (1–2). As Paul said, *All these things happened with symbolic import* (1–3).

How do we relate it to Christ? Hebrew name interpretation helps. "Abimelech" signifies "my father's kingdom," "Achis" means "How can this be?" and "David" means "strong of hand." Here's my understanding: The tribe of Levi performed temple sacrifices, but we know that Melchizedek's sacrifices surpassed them, because Levi's ancestor Abraham gave him tribute (see the Epistle to the Hebrews). Our Lord was a priest of the order of Melchizedek, as David himself prophesied in another Psalm. David symbolized this change by "altering his behavior" before the Levite priest. Christ altered his behavior in the "new sacrifice" that gave the bread of angels to human beings, fed through human flesh like milk for little ones (4–6). He spoke about this in the presence of the Jews (Jn 6), that is to Abimelech, "my father's kingdom." Like the other Levite priest, Achis, they asked "How can this be?" They lacked understanding about the Eucharist. So Christ "forsook" the Jews and went to the gentiles (7–8). Further actions of David described in the narrative point to aspects of Christ's passion story and to the Eucharist (9–11).

Augustine's Text of Psalm 33:1

(1) A psalm of David, when he altered his behavior in the presence of Abimelech,
> And forsook him, and went away.

Augustine's Text of 1 Samuel 21:12–13

(Augustine combines his exegesis of the psalm title with the story told here.)

(12) David was afraid of him [Saul] as well,
> And altered his behavior in front of them all, affecting madness.

(13) He drummed on the doors into the city, and was carried in his own hands,
> And fell down outside on the threshold, as saliva dribbled down his beard.

Exposition

First Sermon

Introduction: knock, and it shall be opened to you

1. There seems to be nothing in the text of this psalm that is obscure or needs explanation, but its title calls for careful attention and invites us to knock on its door. And since in this psalm we find it written that anyone who hopes in the Lord is blessed, let us all hope that when we knock he will open to us.[1] He would not have exhorted us to knock unless he were willing to open the door to us when we do. It sometimes happens that someone who had decided to keep his door shut is nevertheless so wearied by repeated knocking that he changes his mind, gets up, and opens, so that he may not have to put up with the persistent caller any longer;[2] have we then not much better reason to hope that God will quickly open to us, when he himself has commanded, *Knock, and the door will be opened to you?* (Mt 7:7) With all the earnestness of my heart that is what I am doing now, knocking at the door of the Lord God, asking him graciously to reveal this mystery to us; and I beg you too, beloved,[3] to join me in knocking, with the intention of listening and in a spirit of humble readiness to pray for me; for we must admit that it is a deep and vast mystery we have here.

---

1. See Mt 7:7–8.
2. See Lk 11:8.
3. *Caritas vestra.*

He begins to expound the title: David before Abimelech/Achis

2. This is how the title reads: *A psalm of David, when he altered his behavior in the presence of Abimelech, and forsook him, and went away.* We need to look through what Scripture relates about David's exploits to find out when this happened, as we did when examining the title of another psalm, *when David was in flight from the face of Abessalon, his son* (Ps 3:1). In that connection we read in the Books of Kings[4] how David was on the run from his son Abessalon. This is something that really happened, and what happened has been written down; so that although the title of that psalm was assigned very mysteriously, it was, all the same, derived from an event that really occurred.[5]

I think the position is the same with our present psalm, and that we shall find this episode, that *David altered his behavior in the presence of Abimelech, and forsook him, and went away,* also recorded in the Books of Kings,[6] where everything about David's exploits is told. We do not find this story precisely, but we do find an event from which the story seems to be derived. Scripture records that when David was fleeing from his persecutor, Saul, he took refuge with Achis, King of Gath;[7] this man was king of a territory bordering on that of the Judeans. There David lay low to escape Saul's hostility. But the memory of David's triumph was still fresh, the triumph that had earned him hatred for the good he had done in killing Goliath, and winning both honor and safety for kingdom and king in a single fight.[8] While Goliath was uttering his taunts Saul had seethed with rage, but as soon as Goliath had been overthrown Saul's attitude changed into enmity for the man whose hand had slain his foe, and he became jealous of David's reputation. This was more especially the case because the people were ecstatic with joy, and the women danced and sang of David's prowess, crying that Saul had slain thousands, but David tens of thousands.[9] As a result Saul was very upset, because this boy was beginning to acquire higher renown than himself through one fight, and was being exalted above the king in the praises sung by all. As Saul fell prey to sickly malice and worldly pride, he began to be jealous of David and to hound him. This was when David took refuge with the King of Gath, as I have said. This king's name was Achis.

But the attendants of Achis pointed out to him that the fugitive he was sheltering could be none other than the man who had won great glory among the Judeans. They said to him, *Isn't this David, the man to whom the*

---

4. Second Book of Samuel in our usage. "Abessalon" is the reading of the best manuscripts.
5. See 2 S 15:14.
6. Samuel.
7. See 1 S 21:10–15.
8. See 1 S 17:41–54.
9. See 1 S 18:7.

chorus of Israelite women sang, "Saul has slain thousands, and David tens of thousands"? (1 S 21:11). Now if that reputation had begun to arouse Saul to jealous hatred, did not David have reason to fear that this other king, with whom he had sought refuge, might be minded to treat him badly? David could be an enemy on his very doorstep if he let him live, or so the king might think. So Scripture tells us, *David was afraid of him as well, and altered his behavior in front of them all, affecting madness. He drummed on the doors into the city and was carried in his own hands, and fell down outside on the threshold, as saliva dribbled down his beard.* The king in whose country he was hiding saw him and demanded of his attendants, *What have you brought this madman to me for? Do you think I want him in my house?* (1 S 21:12–15). The king threw him out and banished him, and so David departed unharmed, thanks to this feigned insanity.

It is because of the pretended insanity that the title of our psalm seems to relate to this story: *A psalm of David, when he altered his behavior in the presence of Abimelech, and forsook him, and went away.* In the story it was Achis, not Abimelech, but the only disagreement is in the name, for the event has been described in the psalm's title in almost the same words as in the Book of Kings. This fact should prompt us to seek more carefully the mysterious reason[10] for the change of name. Clearly it has been changed; but not without reason. It signifies something. The episode was recalled, yet the name was altered, and there must be some reason for this.

Why has the name been changed?

3. The profundity of these mysteries must be obvious to you, brothers and sisters. If it was no mystery that Goliath was killed by a mere boy, then neither was it a mystery that David altered his bearing, and feigned madness, and drummed on the door, and fell down at the city gates and on the threshold, and that saliva trickled down his beard. How is it possible that all this had no significance? The apostle tells us plainly, *All these things happened to them, but with symbolic import, for they are written down as a rebuke to us, upon whom the climax of the ages has come* (1 Cor 10:11). Did the manna signify nothing, the manna of which the apostle said, *They ate spiritual food?* (1 Cor 10:3) What of the parting of the sea, and the leading of the people safely through it so that they might escape from Pharaoh's persecution—did that mean nothing, when the apostle declares, *I would not have you ignorant, brothers and sisters, that all our ancestors walked under the cloud, and all crossed the sea, and all were through Moses baptized in cloud and sea?* (1 Cor 10:1–2) What about the rock that was struck, so that water gushed out—is that void of significance, in view of the apostle's statement that *the rock was Christ?* (1 Cor 10:4) Do all these things, historical events as they were, have no further meaning? Finally, think of Abraham's two sons, born in the natural way, yet called by the

---

10. *Sacramentum.*

apostle figures of the two covenants, old and new. *These are two covenants, allegorically prefigured,* he says (Gal 4:24). If all these signify nothing, in spite of the statement backed by apostolic authority that they happened as mysterious types of what was to come, then we are right to think that what I read to you just now about David from the Book of Kings had no further meaning either. Nor, consequently, is there any significance in the change of name when the psalm says, *In the presence of Abimelech.*

Christ cut down the devil by humility

4. Let me have your attention now, please. Everything that I have been saying has been said as from a knocking hand; the door has not been opened yet. I was knocking while I said it, you were knocking as you listened; now let us all persevere in knocking and praying that the Lord may open to us. We have an interpretation of the Hebrew names, for there has been no lack of learned men[11] to translate these names from Hebrew into Greek, and thence into Latin. If we look up these names we find that Abimelech means "My father's kingdom" and Achis "How can this be?" Let us consider the names carefully, for perhaps the door is beginning to open for us. If you ask, "What does Achis mean?" you are told it means, "How can this be?" But "How can this be" is what a person says who is bewildered, and cannot understand. Abimelech means "my father's kingdom," and David means "strong of hand." David represented Christ, as Goliath represented the devil, and when David laid Goliath low he prefigured Christ, who crushed the devil. But what is Christ, who cut down the devil? He is humility, the humility that slew pride. So when I say, "Christ," my brothers and sisters, I am drawing attention most especially to his humility. It was by humility that he opened a way for us. We had wandered far from God by pride, and could not find our way back except through humility; yet we had no model of humility to hold before us and imitate. The whole mortal race of humans had swollen with pride. Even if someone of humble spirit did emerge, such as the prophets and patriarchs, humankind disdained to imitate humble humans. To overcome their unwillingness to do so, God himself became humble, so that at any rate human pride would not disdain to follow in the footsteps of God.

Melchizedek's sacrifice

5. As you know, the Jews of old offered sacrifices proper to the order of Aaron, using animals as victims. This was a mysterious prophetic sign. The sacrifice of the Lord's body and blood had not yet been offered; the faithful know about this, as do all who have read the gospel, and this sacrifice is now widespread throughout the world. Keep both kinds of sacrifice before your mind's eye, the one after the order of Aaron, the other after the order of Melchizedek; for Scripture says, *The Lord has sworn, and will*

---

11. Such as Jerome.

not revoke it: you are a priest for ever, after the order of Melchizedek (Ps 109(110):4). Now of whom is this said, *You are a priest for ever, after the order of Melchizedek?* Of our Lord Jesus Christ. Who was Melchizedek? He was King of Salem. Salem was the ancient city, but the city in the same place in later days was called Jerusalem, according to the experts. So before ever the Jews established their kingdom the priest Melchizedek was there, and Genesis describes him as a priest of God Most High.[12] On the occasion when Abraham delivered Lot from the power of his enemies, Melchizedek met him. Abraham had struck down Lot's captors and set his kinsman free, and it was after this rescue that Melchizedek came out to meet him. So great was Melchizedek that he could confer a blessing on Abraham. He set forth bread and wine, and blessed Abraham; and Abraham gave him tithes. Consider what he set forth, and who the man was to whom he gave his blessing. Then, later on, Scripture says to someone, *You are a priest for ever, after the order of Melchizedek.* David said this in spirit[13] long after Abraham's day, yet Melchizedek was Abraham's contemporary. To whom, then, does the prophecy refer, *you are a priest for ever, after the order of Melchizedek?* To whom else, but the one whose sacrifice is known to you?

The Word makes himself assimilable to mortals

6. The sacrifice of Aaron was therefore superseded, and the sacrifice according to the order of Melchizedek came into being. To this end, someone *altered his behavior.* Who is this someone? Let him not be just "someone," for our Lord Jesus Christ is known to us.[14] He willed us to find salvation in his body and blood. But how could he make his body and blood available to us? Through his humility; for if he had not been humble, he could not have been eaten and drunk. Contemplate his lofty divinity: *in the beginning was the Word, and the Word was with God; he was God* (Jn 1:1). That is eternal food. The angels eat it, the celestial powers eat it, the blessed spirits eat it, and in eating they are totally satisfied, yet this food that fills them and gives them joy remains undiminished. What human being could aspire to that food? Where could a human heart be found fit to eat food like that?

It was necessary for that banquet to be converted into milk if it was to become available to little ones. But how does food become milk? How can food be turned into milk, except by being passed through flesh? This is what a mother does. What the mother eats the baby eats too, but since the baby is unable to digest bread, the mother turns the bread into her own flesh, and through the humility of the breast and its supply of milk she feeds her baby with the same bread. How then does the Wisdom of God feed us

---

12. See Gn 14:18.
13. Or "in the Spirit."
14. A variant in punctuation, supported by some witnesses, translates as "Who is this someone? A Someone well known, for our Lord Jesus Christ is known to us."

with that supernal bread? *The Word was made flesh, and dwelt among us* (Jn 1:14). Think of the humility of it: humans have eaten the bread of angels, as Scripture says: *He gave them bread from heaven; mortals ate the bread of angels* (Ps 77(78):24–25). The eternal Word on whom the angels feed, the Word who is equal to the Father, this Word human beings have eaten. He who, *being in the form of God, deemed it no robbery to be God's equal*, he on whom the angels feed to their total satisfaction, *emptied himself and took on the form of a slave. Bearing the human likeness, sharing the human lot, he humbled himself and was made obedient to the point of death, even death on a cross* (Phil 2:6–8), so that from the cross the Lord's flesh and blood might be delivered to us today as the new sacrifice. This was because *he altered his behavior in the presence of Abimelech*, that is, in the presence of "his father's kingdom," for "my father's kingdom" was the kingdom of the Jews. In what sense could that be called his father's kingdom? In that it was David's kingdom, Abraham's kingdom. The kingdom of God the Father is the Church, rather than the Jewish people; but with regard to Christ's human descent the people of Israel was "his father's kingdom." It was said of him, *The Lord God will give him the throne of his father, David* (Lk 1:32). This proves that according to carnal descent David was the father of our Lord, though in his divinity Christ was not David's son but David's Lord. The Jews were familiar with Christ in the flesh, but had no knowledge of his divinity. Accordingly he put to them the question, *What do you think of Christ? Whose son is he? They replied, "David's." Jesus said to them, Then how is it that David in Spirit calls him "Lord," saying, The Lord said to my Lord, "Sit at my right hand, until I make your enemies into your footstool"? If David in the spirit calls him "Lord," how can he be David's son? And they had no answer to give him* (Mt 22:42–46), because all they knew of Christ was what they could see in him with their eyes, not what was to be understood with the heart. If only they had had eyes within as they had eyes without, they would have recognized David's son from what they saw outwardly, but from what they understood inwardly they would have recognized him as David's Lord.

He turned from the Jews to the Gentiles

7. So *he altered his behavior in the presence of Abimelech*. What does *in the presence of Abimelech* mean? In the presence of his father's kingdom. And what does that mean? In the presence of the Jews. *And he forsook him and went away.* Whom did he forsake? He forsook the Jewish people, and went away. Look for Christ today among the Jews, and you do not find him. Why did he forsake them and go away? Because although he *altered his behavior* they clung to the old sacrifice after the order of Aaron, and did not grasp the sacrifice according to the order of Melchizedek; so they lost Christ, and the gentiles came to possess him, even though he had not previously sent any preachers to them. He had sent plenty of preachers to the Israelites: David himself, and Abraham, Isaac and Jacob, Isaiah,

Jeremiah and the other prophets. All these he had sent, but in spite of it few had come to know him, or at any rate few in comparison with those who were lost, for they were many. We read of thousands. Scripture says, *A remnant shall be saved* (Rom 9:27);[15] but if you look for Christians today among the circumcised, you find none. Earlier in the Christian era, not so long ago, there were many thousands of Christians from the circumcised, but if you look for them now you will not find them; and it is with good reason that you find none, for Christ *altered his behavior in the presence of Abimelech, and forsook them and went away.*

But it was in the presence of Achis that David altered his behavior, and forsook him and went away. The names were changed deliberately, to alert us to the mystery this change signified. Otherwise we might have thought that what the psalm recalled and related was nothing more than the event recounted in the Books of Kings; then we would not have sought out any prefiguration of future happenings, but read it simply as the story of past events. But the names are changed, and what does this tell you? That there is something still closed here. Knock then. Do not remain stuck in the letter, for the letter is death-dealing,[16] but desire the spiritual meaning, for the Spirit gives life, and spiritual understanding saves the believer.

The scandal of the eucharist

8. Listen now, brothers and sisters, to how he forsook King Achis. I have told you that the name Achis means "How can this be?" Now recall the occasion in the gospel when our Lord Jesus Christ was speaking about his body, and said, *Unless you eat my flesh and drink my blood, you will not have life in you, for my flesh really is food, and my blood really is drink* (Jn 6:54.56). The disciples who were following him were appalled, and shuddered at what he said. They did not understand it, and thought the Lord was making some dreadful proposal: that they were to eat that flesh of his that they could see, and drink the blood. They could not bear it, and it was as though they were asking, "How can this be?" Their mistake, their ignorance, their stupidity, were prefigured in King Achis, for when someone asks, "How can this be?" it indicates a lack of understanding, and where there is no understanding, there is the darkness of ignorance. So ignorance, like King Achis, held sway over them; over them the kingdom of error held sway. But Christ went on, saying, *Unless you eat my flesh and drink my blood....* He had "altered his behavior," and so the notion of giving his flesh to people to eat, and his blood to drink, seemed to them dementia, insanity. David likewise seemed insane to Achis, who protested, "You have brought a madman into my house." Indeed, does it not sound like insanity to say, "Eat my flesh, drink my blood"? Yet here is Christ saying, *Unless you eat my flesh and drink my blood, you will not have life*

---

15. See Is 10:22.
16. See 2 Cor 3:6.

in you. He seems to be mad. But it is to King Achis that he seems to be mad, that is, to the stupid and ignorant. Accordingly he forsakes them and goes away; understanding has fled from their hearts, so that they cannot comprehend him. What had they to say? *"How can this be?"* which is what the name Achis means. They objected, *"How can this man give us his flesh to eat?"* (Jn 6:53). They thought the Lord was a madman, that he did not know what he was saying, that he was raving. But he knew very well what he was saying by this alteration in his behavior; by making use of apparent madness and insanity he was proclaiming his sacraments, so he affected madness, and drummed on the doors into the city.

The tender affection of Christ

9. We must inquire next the meaning of the phrases, "he affected," and "he drummed on the doors into the city." Moreover it was not without some good reason that Scripture said, *He fell down outside on the threshold, and saliva trickled down his beard.* No, it was by no means without good reason. A somewhat long-winded explanation will not seem burdensome to us if it rewards us with insight. Now you are aware, brothers and sisters, that the Jews, in whose presence he altered his behavior, whom he forsook when he went away, are having a holiday today.[17] They have lost Christ; he has left them and gone away, so their holiday is an empty one. But we enjoy a fruitful holiday, with the opportunity to understand Christ who left them and came to us. Nothing in all this is without purpose, even in David's crazy behavior, where he is said to have *affected madness, and drummed on the doors into the city; he was carried in his own hands, and fell down outside on the threshold, and saliva dribbled down his beard.* We are told that he *affected madness*; what does *affected* suggest? He had affection. But what is it to have affection, or be affectionate? He had compassion on our infirmities; that was why he willed to assume that very flesh in which he could slay death. He had compassion on us; it is saying that he had tender affection for us. The apostle rebukes people who are hard-hearted and without affection. Censuring some people of this type, he says they are *without affection, devoid of mercy* (Rom 1:31). Where there is affection, there will mercy be. Where did we find mercy? In him who was merciful to us from above. If he had been unwilling to empty himself, and had chosen rather to remain where he is—eternal, and equal to the Father—we would have remained in eternal death; but in order to free us from that eternal death into which the sin of pride had plunged us, he humbled himself, and became obedient unto death, even the death of the cross. This is where his affection for us took him, as far as dying on the cross.

---

17. The sermon was preached on a Saturday, as is clear from its closing words.

The drum

Now when someone is crucified, he is stretched out on a wooden instrument. But when you want to make a drum, you stretch out flesh—skin, that is—over a wooden frame. This is why Scripture has it that *he drummed*; it means that he was crucified, he was stretched out on a wooden frame. *He affected*: that is, he felt affectionate tenderness for us, even to the point of laying down his life for his sheep.[18] And *he drummed*. How? *At the doors into the city*. This door is the one that is opened to us so that we may believe in God. We had closed our doors against Christ, and opened them to the devil; our hearts were closed against eternal life. But because we humans had our hearts shut against eternal life and could not see that Word on whom the angels gaze, our Lord God himself opened the hearts of mortals; he drummed on the doors of the city.

Eucharist and humility

10. *And he was carried in his own hands.* How on earth are we to understand this, my brothers and sisters, how is it humanly possible? How can someone be carried in his own hands? A person can be carried in the hands of others, but not in his own. Well, we have no way of knowing what it literally means in David's case; but we can make sense of it with regard to Christ. Christ was being carried in his own hands when he handed over his body, saying, *This is my body* (Mt 26:26); for he was holding that very body in his hands as he spoke. Such is the humility of our Lord Jesus Christ, and this humility is what he recommends to us most strongly. He exhorts us to practice it too, brothers and sisters, so that by imitating his humility we may have life. By holding fast to Christ's humility we can strike down Goliath and conquer our pride. *He fell down outside on the threshold.* What does that signify, *he fell down*? He threw himself down into humility. But why *on the threshold*? At the place where we make our entrance into faith, that entrance that admits us to salvation. There is no way in except through this preliminary faith, as the Song of Songs declares, *You will come and pass through, beginning from faith* (Sg 4:8, LXX). We too shall come, and see him face to face, as Scripture promises: *Dearly beloved, we are children of God already, but what we shall be has not yet appeared. We know that when he appears, we shall be like him, because we shall see him as he is* (1 Jn 3:2). When shall we see him? When all these other things have passed away. Listen to a similar testimony from the apostle Paul: *Now we see a tantalizing reflection in a mirror, but then face to face* (1 Cor 13:12). Until we come to see the Word face to face, as the angels see him, we still need the threshold where the Lord fell down, humbling himself even to death.

---

18. See Jn 10:15.

Childlike words concealing strength

11. What significance is there in *the saliva dribbled down his beard*? This is part of the way in which he *altered his behavior in the presence of Abimelech* (or Achis); and then *he forsook him and went away*. He forsook those who did not understand. And to whom did he go? To the gentiles. Let us then try to understand what they found incomprehensible. Saliva dribbled down David's beard; what is saliva? It represents the babbling of infants, for babies do plenty of dribbling. And were these words not like baby-talk: "Eat my flesh, drink my blood"? Yet these infantile words masked virile strength, for virile strength[19] is symbolized by the beard. So then, what else does saliva dribbling down his beard represent, but the weak words that concealed his strength?

Conclusion

I think you have understood the title of this psalm now, holy brethren.[20] If we were to attempt to explain the psalm itself now, there would be a risk that what you have heard might slip your memories. But tomorrow is Sunday, when we owe you a sermon, so let us put the rest off till then, so that you may be ready to listen to the text of the psalm with fresh enjoyment. We shall have dealt with the title, in the name of our Lord Jesus Christ.

---

19. *Virtus.*
20. *Sanctitas vestra.*

Exposition of Psalm 44

Synopsis

The Psalm demands the proper "attire" of spiritual understanding from *the children of Korah* (*calvus* in Latin), that is, the children of Calvary, those who *understand* Christ crucified and his marriage to the Church. They represent "things to be changed" in the conversion from old to new — not just from pagan to Christian, but from bad persons to good ones. The reality dawns on the wedding guests that they are themselves the bride, who sees Christ with "a different set of eyes" and perceives the beauty of his flesh and humble death. The Church also sees its own beauty since Christ erased sin's ugliness (1–3).

The Father *overflows with a good Word*, that is, the Word of God spoken from all eternity. All God's works are found in this Word (4–6). As human, Christ is *fair beyond all humankind* because saving grace pours forth from his lips (7–8). Alternatively the text can be heard as spoken by the prophet (9–10). The prophet now speaks to Christ. *Gird your sword on your thigh* must refer to the severance that the gospel can cause within families. But this sword also severs us from the devil, and it severs Christians from the synagogue. In a sense, taking flesh severed Christ from the Father, and his teaching severed him from his mother, the synagogue. The thigh refers to a prophecy about Abraham's seed (11–13). Christ, who is that seed, rides forth to seize his kingdom, wearing a robe of beauty, dignity, faithfulness, gentleness, and justice. His piercing words arouse love, as in the Song of Songs (14–16). His divine throne stands forever, unlike that of Israel's kings, who ruled only for a time. His *scepter of righteous rule* untwists people's crooked hearts and bends their will to God's will. Because he *loved justice and hated iniquity*, he strikes fear in the hearts of resisters (17–18).

God "anointed" God, reflecting the root of the term "Christ." Jacob elaborately signified this when he anointed the stone upon which he dreamed of angels ascending and descending from heaven. The stone was set at Jacob's head: so the rejected stone would become the cornerstone, and Christ would become "head" of "the Man," that is, the Church. Preachers like Paul ascend to the divinity and descend to the humanity of the Son of Man.

The "anointed God" became human to share his immortality (19–21). Sweet scents exude from the "garments" of his body, the saints. *The king's daughters from ivory palaces* are the apostles and the churches, which together form the Queen (22–24). The prophet urges her to *hearken and see,* so that all believers may see the King and thus forget the sinful kingdom they came from. Christ desires the beauty that he himself created in his bride (25–26).

The Tyrian maidens, converts from all the gentile races, pay homage with their alms. The Queen's beauty isn't outward but inward, in her purity of conscience. *The virgins conducted to the king* foretell the streams of women who have come from throughout the world to dedicate themselves to Christ. However, some schismatics remain outside the Church (27–31). Meanwhile, the sons born to take the place of the fathers are the bishops appointed in the churches. Generation after generation will confess to God in this great city until the consummation of the age, when she is set free to reign with God. Then all hearts will be transparent, and all charity will be perfect. The bride will fully "know herself," for now she remains mostly hidden from herself (32–33).

Augustine's Text of Psalm 44

(1) For those things which will be changed, for the children of Korah,
   for understanding. A song for the beloved one.

(2) My heart overflows with a good word;
   I tell my works to the king.
   My tongue is the pen of a scribe writing swiftly,

(3) Fair are you beyond all humankind;
   Grace bedews your lips; therefore God has blessed you forever.

(4) Gird your sword upon your thigh, mighty warrior.

(5) In your beauty and dignity, ride forth victoriously and seize your kingdom,
   By your faithfulness, gentleness, and justice.

(6) Your arrows are sharp and very powerful; peoples will fall under your assault.
   In the hearts of the king's enemies your arrows will find their mark.

(7) Your throne, O God, stands forever and ever.
   Your royal scepter is a scepter of righteous rule.

(8) You have loved justice and hated iniquity.
   For God, your God, has anointed you with the oil of joy,

(9) For your garments drift the perfumes of myrrh, spices and cassia.
Kings' daughters from ivory palaces have found favor with you.
(10) Kings' daughters come to do you honor.
The queen has taken her place at your right hand,
In a golden gown, decked with variety.
(11) Hearken, my daughter, and see, and bend you ear.
Forget your own people, and your father's house.
(12) For the king has desired your beauty.
He is your God [and they adore him].
(13) And Tyrian maidens will pay homage to him with their gifts.
All the rich among the people will seek favor with you.
(14) All the glory of the king's daughter is within, with her gold fringes.
(15) She is girdled with varied embroidery.
Virgins will be conducted after her to the king;
Her nearest and dearest will bend to you.
(16) They shall be conducted with joy and gladness;
They shall be ushered into the temple of the king.
(17) To take the place of your fathers, sons have been born to you,
And you will appoint them princes all over the world.
(18) They will be mindful of your name in generation after generation.
Therefore peoples will confess to you for ever, and for unending ages.

Exposition

A Sermon preached in the Restored Basilica on Wednesday, 2 September[1]

Verse 1. Childish mockery of a bald man

1. We have joyfully sung this psalm with you, and now I beg you to study it carefully with us. It is a song about a sacred marriage, about a bridegroom and his bride, a king and his people, the Savior and those who are to be saved. Anyone who has arrived at this wedding properly dressed in wedding clothes (not to attract attention to himself or herself, but in honor

---

1. Possibly in A.D. 403.

of the bridegroom) will not be content just to listen eagerly. That is what people ordinarily do when all they are looking for is entertainment, and they have no intention of letting what they see or hear affect their behavior. But a properly disposed guest also takes to heart a word that will not lie there idle, but will germinate, burst into flower, grow, reach perfection, and yield fruit for harvesting. As the title of the psalm indicates, we must be the children of Korah. No doubt the original children of Korah were historical persons; but every title found in the divine Scriptures offers a hint to alert minds, demanding not merely a hearer, but a perceptive one. We can investigate the meaning of the Hebrew word, and find out what "Korah" means and, as is the case with all the words in Scripture, an interpretation is at hand. "The children of Korah" means "the children of the bald man." You must not think that funny. We do not want to be like those tittering boys with their childish minds, whom we read about in the Book of the Kingdoms.[2] They mocked the prophet Elisha by shouting after him, *Off you go, baldy, off you go, baldy!* Those silly, prattling children jeered at him to their own destruction, for wild beasts came out of the woods and devoured them. This is what Scripture says, and we have reminded you where it was written.[3] Let those who remember it recognize the reference, and those who do not remember look it up, and those who have not read it at all take our word for it. Since that episode was a symbol of future realities, it should not upset us. Those boys represented stupid people, people with ignorant minds, and the apostle does not want us to be like that. *Do not be childish in your outlook*, he says. But then he qualifies it, because he remembers that the Lord invited us to imitate children when he placed a little child before him and warned us, *Only someone who becomes like this child will enter the kingdom of heaven* (Mt 18:3). So after bidding us grow out of childish attitudes, the apostle is careful to remind us in what sense we must be childlike: *Do not be childish in your outlook*, he says. *Be babes in your innocence of evil, but mature in mind* (1 Cor 14:20). Anyone who delights to be childlike is not delighted by the immaturity of children, but by their innocence; for it was immaturity that incited the boys to jeer at God's holy man for his baldness, and shout after him, *Baldy! Baldy!* So it came about that they were devoured by wild animals, and represented people who with the same childish attitude mocked at a certain man who could be called "bald" because he was crucified at a place named Calvary. Such people behaved as though they had been seized by wild beasts, because they were in fact possessed by demons, by the devil and his angels, for he is at work in God's rebellious subjects[4] Childish onlookers they were who stood before the sacred tree wagging their heads and saying, *Let him come down from the cross, if he is the Son of God* (Mt 27:42).

---

2. That is, 2 K 2:23–24, in our system.
3. See note at *Exposition of Psalm* 41, 2.
4. See Eph 2:2.

We are Christ's children, because we are the children of the bridegroom,[5] and this psalm is written for us, as its title proclaims: *For the children of Korah, for those things which will be changed.*[6]

The world has changed, and so have we

2. There is no need, is there, for me to explain what is meant by *for those things which will be changed*? What should I say about it? Anyone who has been changed will recognize from personal experience what it means. Let all who hear this phrase, *for those things which will be changed*, reflect on what they once were, and what they are now. And let them consider first of all how the world has altered. Not long ago it worshiped idols, now it worships God; until recently it paid cult to the things he made, but now to him who made it. Notice when this was said, "for those things which will be changed." The pagans who are still left are terrified by the changed state of affairs; unwilling to be changed themselves, they see our churches brought into commission again and their temples abandoned, celebration in the one and desolation in the other. They are astonished at the change, but let them read the prophecies that announced it; let them bend an ear to him who promised it, and believe him now that he has made his promise good.

But that is not all, brothers and sisters. Each one of us is being changed from an old self into a new self, from an unbeliever into a believer, from a thief into a generous giver, from an adulterer into a chaste person, from a spiteful troublemaker into a kindly neighbor. So let the psalm be sung for us, *for those things which will be changed*; and now let him be delineated through whom the changes are brought about.[7]

The Word weds the Church; the bridegroom's beauty

3. The full title is, *For those things which will be changed, for the children of Korah, for understanding. A song for the beloved one.* This beloved one was seen by his persecutors, but not for their understanding, for if they had known him, they would never have crucified the Lord of glory.[8] It was for the purpose of understanding that he himself was seeking a different kind of eyes when he said, *Whoever sees me sees the Father* (Jn 14:9). Let the psalm now sing of him, and let us rejoice at his marriage, and so be among those of whom the marriage is made, who are invited to the wedding: these invited guests are themselves the bride, for the Church is the bride, and Christ the Bridegroom. It is customary for appropriate

---

5. See Mt 9:15; Lk 5:34.
6. One codex has "Unto the end, for the children...." The CCL editors amend the second clause to "for those [people] who will be changed."
7. *Per quem commutata sunt*, "through whom these [things] have been changed"; but the CCL editors amend to *per quem commutati sunt*, "through whom they [Christians] have been changed."
8. See 1 Cor 2:8.

songs to be sung by students[9] to both spouses. These songs are called epithalamia, and are devoted to honoring bridegroom and bride. Perhaps you are wondering whether there is any bridal chamber[10] at this wedding to which we have been invited? Yes, there is; why else would another psalm say, *He has pitched his tent in the sun, and he is like a bridegroom coming forth from his tent?* (Ps 18:6(19:5)) The nuptial union is effected between the Word and human flesh, and the place where the union is consummated is the Virgin's womb. It is flesh, very flesh, that is united to the Word; as Scripture says, *They are two no longer, but one flesh* (Mt 19:6; see Eph 5:31). The Church was drawn from the human race, so that flesh united to the Word might be the Head of the Church, and all the rest of us believers might be the limbs that belong to that Head.

Do you want to see who he is, who has come to his wedding? *In the beginning was the Word, and the Word was with God; he was God* (Jn 1:1). Let the bride be happy, then, for she has been loved by God. And when was she loved? While she was still ugly, for, as the apostle says, *All have sinned, and are in need of the glory of God*, and again, *Christ died for the impious* (Rom 3:23; 5:6). She was loved in her ugliness, that she might not remain ugly. It was not because she was ugly that she was loved; her ugliness was not itself the object of his love. If he had loved that, he would have preserved it, but in fact he rid her of her ugliness and formed beauty in her.

To what kind of bride did he come, and what did he make of her? Let him come himself in the words of the prophets, let him come now. Let the bridegroom come forth and show himself to us, and let us love him. But if we find any trace of ugliness in him, let us love him not. What a strange thing! He found plenty of ugly features in us, yet he loved us; but if we find anything ugly in him, we must not love him. It is true that he put on our flesh in such a way that it could be said of him, *We saw him, and there was no fair form or comeliness in him* (Is 53:2), but if you take account of the mercy that caused him to be reduced to such a state, he is beautiful even in his deformity. The prophet was speaking from the standpoint of the Jews when he said, *We saw him, and there was no fair form or comeliness in him.* Why is that so? Because his lowly state was no use to them *for understanding.* For all who do understand, the truth that *the Word was made flesh* (Jn 1:14) is supremely beautiful. A friend of the bridegroom prayed, *Far be it from me to boast, save in the cross of our Lord Jesus Christ* (Gal 6:14). It would be a mean-spirited thing merely not to be ashamed of it; you must boast of it. Why did Christ have neither fair form nor comeliness? Because Christ crucified was a scandal to the Jews, and foolishness to gentiles. But in what sense was he fair of form on the cross? Because God's foolishness is

---

9. *Ab scholasticis.* The CCL editors supply a doubtful suggestion from one codex that the word should be *scoliasticis*, derived from a Greek word for a festive song sung between servings of drinks at a banquet.
10. *Thalamus.*

wiser than human wisdom, and God's weakness more powerful than human strength.[11] Let us therefore, who believe, run to meet a bridegroom who is beautiful wherever he is. Beautiful as God, as the Word who is with God, he is beautiful in the Virgin's womb, where he did not lose his Godhead but assumed our humanity. Beautiful he is as a baby, as the Word unable to speak,[12] because while he was still without speech, still a baby in arms and nourished at his mother's breast, the heavens spoke for him, a star guided the magi, and he was adored in the manger as food for the humble. He was beautiful in heaven, then, and beautiful on earth: beautiful in the womb, and beautiful in his parents' arms. He was beautiful in his miracles but just as beautiful under the scourges, beautiful as he invited us to life, but beautiful too in not shrinking from death, beautiful in laying down his life and beautiful in taking it up again, beautiful on the cross, beautiful in the tomb, and beautiful in heaven.

Listen to this song to further your understanding, and do not allow the weakness of his flesh to blind you to the splendor of his beauty. The supreme and most real beauty is justice: if you can catch him out in any injustice, you will not find him beautiful in that regard; but if he is found to be just at every point, then he is lovely in all respects. Let him come to us, so that we may gaze on him with the eyes of our spirit, as he has been delineated for us by the prophet who sang his praises, and began, *My heart overflows with a good word.*

Verse 2. The Father speaks

4. *My heart overflows with a good word.* Who is speaking here—the Father, or the prophet? Some have understood these words to be spoken by the Father, who by saying, *My heart overflows with a good word*, gives us an inkling of a birth beyond the power of human telling. But notice that he says, *Cor meum*; this is to save you from any mistaken idea that God needed to undertake something in order to beget a Son. A human being does have to undertake something, namely sexual union, in order to procreate children; without this human parents cannot bring children to birth. But you must not suppose that God needed any such union in order to beget his Son; and to exclude that mistake he says, *My heart overflows with a good word.* Think, every one of you: this very day your heart generates a plan, but your heart does not need to seek a wife in order to do so. Through this plan that has been born from your heart you perhaps build something. Before your construction stands there built, it stands already in your plan; what you are going to construct is already present in your intelligence, through which you are going to make it. So you can take satisfaction in an edifice that does not yet exist, not because you can see it as a building but because

---

11. See 1 Cor 1:23.25.
12. *Infans Verbum.*

you have brought it to birth as a plan, though no one else can approve your plan unless you have told others about it, or they see the finished job.

If, then, all things were made through the Word, and the Word is from God, contemplate the fabric that was made through the Word, and proceed from the completed building to admire the master-plan. What must the Word be like, if through him were made the sky and the earth, and all the sky's array, all the earth's fecundity, the vast expanse of the sea, the wide air, the shining stars and the radiance of sun and moon? All these things are visible; but pass beyond even these, and consider the angels, the authorities, thrones, sovereignties and powers;[13] all these were made through him. And how comes it that all these things were created good? Because the *good Word* was uttered, through whom they came to be. So the Word is good, and this Word was addressed by someone as *Good Teacher*, yet the Word himself deprecated this address: *Why do you ask me about what is good? No one is good, except the one God* (Mt 19:17; Mk 10:18). How are we to interpret this? Someone addressed him as *Good Teacher*, and he asked, *Why do you ask me about what is good?* He even added, *No one is good, except the one God.* How then can he himself be good? Because he himself is God, and moreover is one God together with the Father; for when he said, *No one is good, except the one God*, he did not separate himself from the Father, but asserted their unity. *My heart overflows with a good Word*: this can be understood, then, as God the Father's statement about his good Word, our God, our benefactor, that good Word through whom alone whatever we have of goodness is possible.

5. The next line is, *I tell my works to the king*. Is this still the Father speaking? If it is, let us see how we can also interpret this consistently with the true Catholic faith. *I tell my works to the king*. If it means that the Father tells his Son, our King, about his works, what can it mean? What works can the Father tell his Son about, when all the Father's works are performed through the Son?

Perhaps the verb, *I tell*, refers to the eternal generation of the Son? Can that be it? I am afraid that this explanation may at some points be difficult for those of slower intelligence to grasp; but I will offer it all the same, and let anyone follow who can. It is better so, because if I don't explain at all, even those capable of following will not have the chance. Here we are, then: in another psalm we read, *Only once has God spoken* (Ps 61:12(62:11)). He spoke many times through the prophets, and many times through the apostles; today he speaks through his saints; yet the psalm says, *Only once has God spoken*. How can he be said to have spoken once only, unless we take it to mean his utterance of his Word? In the preceding line we understood *my heart overflows with a good Word* to mean the begetting of the Son, and this next line seems to me to be a repetition of the same truth: *my heart overflows with a good Word* is reiterated in the verb, *I tell*. After

---

13. See Col 1:16.

all, what does *I tell* mean? "I bring forth a word." And from where does God bring forth a Word, if not from his heart, from his innermost being? Any word you speak yourself you bring forth from your heart; there is no other source for the word that sounds audibly and then fades away. Are you surprised that the same should be true for God? But there is this difference: God's speaking is eternal. You say something now, because you were silent a moment ago. Or perhaps you do not yet speak your word, you hold it back. When you do begin to bring it out you are breaking your silence and giving birth to a word that did not previously exist. Not in this manner did God generate his Word, for God's speaking has no beginning and no end; yet he speaks one Word only. He could speak another only if what he had spoken could pass away; but as he by whom the Word is spoken abides eternally, so too does the Word he speaks abide. This Word is spoken once, and never ceases to be spoken; nor had the speaking of it any beginning; nor is it spoken twice, for what is spoken once never passes away. Accordingly *my heart overflows with a good Word* signifies the same as *I tell my works to the King*.

But still, why does it say, *I tell my works*? Because in this uttered Word are all the works of God. Whatever God was to create was already present in the Word. Nothing could have existed in the created order that was not present in the Word, just as nothing can be in your own handiwork that was not present in your plan. The gospel makes this plain by saying, *What was made was alive in his life* (Jn 1:3–4). Created beings existed, but only in the Word; they were there in the Word, though they had as yet no existence in themselves. But the Word was, and this Word was God; this Word was with God and was the Son of God, and was one God with the Father. *I tell my works to the King*. Let anyone who understands about this Word listen to the Speaker, and contemplate both the Father and his everlasting Word, in whom are present all things that will come to be in the future, as are present still all those that have passed away. These are the works of God: works in his Word, in his only-begotten Son, in the Word of God.

6. Now, how does the psalm continue? *My tongue is the pen of a scribe writing swiftly.* What possible resemblance can there be, brothers and sisters, between God's tongue and a scribe's pen? Well, what resemblance is there between a rock and Christ? Or a lamb and our Savior? Or a lion and the strength of the only-begotten Son?[14] Yet these comparisons were made, and it is only because they were that we are in some measure educated through visible things toward apprehension of the invisible. So too with this humble metaphor of the pen: we should neither equate it with the excellent reality it points to, nor reject it as unworthy. But I wonder why God willed to call his tongue the pen of a swiftly-writing scribe? After all, however rapidly a scribe might be able to write, it would not bear comparison with the speed of which another psalm speaks: *Very swiftly runs his word* (Ps 147:15).

---

14. See 1 Cor 10:4; Jn 1:29; Rv 5:5.

However, insofar as the human mind may presume to understand, I think that this comparison, *my tongue is the pen of a scribe,* may also be taken as spoken by the Father. Ordinarily what is spoken with the tongue makes a sound and then fades away, whereas what is written endures; but when God speaks his Word, it does not make a transient sound and then fade, but is spoken and abides, and therefore God has chosen to compare it with the abiding written word rather than with sounds. By adding, *A scribe writing swiftly,* he has prodded our minds toward further understanding; and they must not be lazy, content to think of those who copy ancient texts, or very nimble secretaries. If we concentrate on these, our minds will proceed no further. Think swiftly of the word, *swiftly;* turn that word, *swiftly,* over in your mind. What does it suggest—*swiftly?* God's speed is so great that nothing could be swifter. When people write they form letter after letter, syllable after syllable, word after word; and there is no passing on to the next until the one before has been properly written. But with God there are not many words, nor is anything left out, but all things are comprised in one Word; so nothing could be swifter.

Verse 3. The bridegroom brings grace

7. But look—this eternal Word so uttered, the coeternal Word of the eternal Father, will come as bridegroom. *Fair are you beyond all humankind.* Why does it not say, "Beyond the angels"? What did it imply by *beyond humankind?* Surely, that he too is human. But to ensure that you do not put the man Christ on a par with any other human, it says that he is *fair beyond all humankind.* He is human indeed, but beyond all humans; he is among humans, but beyond them; he takes his human birth from humankind, but he is beyond all humankind. *Grace bedews your lips.* Elsewhere we read, *The law was given through Moses, grace and truth came through Jesus Christ* (Jn 1:17). *Grace bedews your lips.* Truly such help was necessary for me, because *I take great delight in God's law as far as my inner self is concerned, but I am aware of a different law in my members that opposes the law of my mind, and imprisons me under the law of sin inherent in my members. Who will deliver me from this death-ridden body, wretch that I am? Only the grace of God, through Jesus Christ our Lord* (Rom 7:22–25). This is why our psalm says, *Grace bedews your lips.* He came to us with the word of grace on his lips, with the kiss of grace. What could be sweeter than grace like this? And with what is it concerned? *Blessed are those whose iniquities are forgiven, and whose sins are covered* (Ps 31(32):1). If he had come as a strict judge, without this grace bedewing his lips, who would have had any hope of salvation? Would anyone have been unafraid of what was owing to a sinner? But he came bringing grace, and so far from demanding what was owed to God, he paid a debt he did not owe. Did one who was sinless owe a debt to death? But you, what was owing to you? Punishment. He canceled your debts, and paid off debts that were none of his. This is mighty grace. Grace—why "grace"? Because it

is given gratis. It is up to you to give thanks, then, but not to repay him, for that you cannot do. Looking for some means of making recompense to God, a psalmist asked, *What return shall I make to the Lord for all his bounty to me?* Then he seemed to find something: *I will take in my hands the cup of salvation, and call on the name of the Lord* (Ps 115(116):12–13). So you think to make sufficient repayment to him, because you take in your hands the cup of salvation, and call on the name of the Lord? But who gave you this cup of salvation?

The psalmist confined himself to thanksgiving, since he fell far short of making due recompense. Find something that you can give to God that you did not receive from him, and then you will be in a position to make proper repayment. But be careful, because when you look for something to render to him that you did not first receive from him, you may find it, certainly, but all you will find is your sin. That certainly you did not receive from him, but neither is it fit for you to offer. That is what the Jews gave him—evil for good. They received rain from him, but yielded him no fruit, only painful thorns. Whatever good there is in you that you want to give to God, you will discover that you received it from no one else but God. This is the grace of God, bedewing Christ's lips. He made you, and made you gratis, for he could not give anything to you before you were there to receive it. Then when you had gone to ruin, he sought you; he found you and called you back again. He did not hold your past sins against you, and he promised you good things for the future. Truly, O Christ, *grace bedews your lips*.

8. *Therefore God has blessed you for ever*, says the psalm. It would be straining the text to understand this phrase also—*therefore God has blessed you for ever*—as spoken by God the Father. It seems better to assume that the prophet is speaking here in his own person. Sudden changes of speaker, even entirely unexpected changes, are commonly found in the sacred Scriptures; anyone who looks carefully will find that the pages of holy writ are full of them. For instance, another psalm prays, *O Lord, rescue my soul from wicked lips and the guileful tongue*; but immediately it continues, *What is to be given to you, what shall be added to you, that you may withstand the deceitful tongue?* Obviously there are two different speakers here, one making a petition, the other responding with help. One speaker says, *Sharp arrows of the mighty one, with all-devouring coals*, the same one who asked, *What is to be given to you, what shall be added to you?* But in the next line the petitioner resumes, *Alas, how long-drawn-out is my wayfaring!* (Ps 119(120):2–5). Such frequent switches within a few lines alert us to use our intelligence. The place where the speaker changes is not noted; there is no indication, "Man says this; God says that"; but the words themselves make clear to us which belong to the human speaker, and which to God.

It was a man who said, *My heart overflows with a good word; I tell my works to the king*. A man said this, the man who wrote the psalm, but he said it in God's name. But now he begins to speak in his own person: *Therefore God has blessed you for ever.* God had said, *Grace bedews your lips*, to the one whom he had made fair beyond all humankind, for this Son whom he had begotten before all ages, this eternal Son whom he, the eternal Father, had brought forth, God had also made to be a man. On this account the prophet was filled with a joy that he could scarcely express. He had spoken earlier as from God, but now, contemplating what God the Father would reveal about his Son to humankind, the prophet says as from himself, *Therefore God has blessed you for ever.* Why blessed? Because of grace. With what is grace concerned? With the kingdom of heaven. The Old Testament had promised a land; but the reward promised to those subject to the old law was different from that promised to us under grace. The land slipped away from them, and that land was all the kingdom that they were destined for, those people subject to the law; but the kingdom of heaven that belongs to the children of grace does not slip away. That is why our psalm says here, *God has blessed you*, not for a time only, but *for ever.*

An alternative interpretation: the psalmist has spoken throughout

9. However, some people have preferred to consider all the words we have so far considered as spoken by the prophet himself. Thus the line, *My heart overflows with a good word*, would be the prophet's way of announcing his hymn (for when anyone sings a hymn to God, his or her heart is blurting out a good word, just as when anyone blasphemes God, that person's heart is belching out a bad word). On this showing the next line, *I tell my works to the king*, would signify that the highest duty of every human being is to praise God. It is proper to God to delight you by his beauty, and your business to praise him with thanksgiving. If your works are not praise offered to God, you are beginning to be in love with yourself, and to join the company of those people of whom the apostle predicts, *They will be lovers of themselves* (2 Tm 3:2). Find no pleasure in yourself, and let him be your delight who made you; because what you find displeasing in yourself is what you have yourself brought about in you. Let your work be praise offered to God; let your heart overflow with this good word. Tell your works to the King, because the King has created you for this purpose, and himself given you what you are to offer him. Give back to him his own gifts; do not try to snatch a share of your inheritance and go off abroad, there to squander it on harlots and feed pigs. Remember that story in the gospel. But of us too the glad cry has gone up, *He was dead, but has come back to life; he had perished, but is found* (Lk 15:24.32).

10. *My tongue is the pen of a scribe writing swiftly.* There have been interpreters who similarly understood this in the sense that the prophet indicated what he was going to write, and therefore compared his tongue with a scribe's pen. He would have mentioned in particular a scribe writing at speed to suggest that he would write about things which would come to pass swiftly. So we should understand "writing swiftly" to mean "writing

about swift matters," or events which were not to be long delayed. In fact God did not delay long before sending Christ. How quickly time seems to have rolled by, once it is past! Recall the generations that preceded you, and you will find that Adam seems to have been made only yesterday. In the same way we read about all the things that have happened since that beginning, and they seem to have been accomplished very swiftly. The day of judgment will arrive swiftly too, so you must forestall it by even greater promptitude. It will come quickly, so you must be even quicker about changing your life. The face of the judge will be upon us, but look to the prophet's advice: *Let us hasten before his face confessing* (Ps 94(95):2). *Grace bedews your lips, therefore God has blessed you for ever.*

Verse 4. The sword of division

11. *Gird your sword upon your thigh, mighty warrior.*[15] What sword is this? Surely your word. With that sword he laid low his enemies, and with that sword he severed son from father, daughter from mother, daughter-in-law from mother-in-law; for in the gospel we read, *I have come to bring not peace, but a sword*, and again, *There will be five in one household ranged in opposition, two against three, and three pitted against two: a son against his father, a daughter against her mother, and a daughter-in-law against her mother-in-law* (Mt 10:34; Lk 12:52–53). What sword sliced them apart, if not the sword Christ brought? Truly, brothers and sisters, even now we see the same thing happening daily. Some young man decides to serve God, and thereby offends his father; they are at loggerheads, one promising an earthly estate, the other in love with a heavenly inheritance, one promising one thing and the other setting his heart on something quite different. The father should not think himself slighted, for no one except God is being preferred to him, yet he goes to law against this son who wants to serve God. Nonetheless the spiritual sword that divides them is more powerful than the bonds of flesh that unite them. The same division is effected between a daughter and her mother, and far more so between a daughter-in-law and her mother-in-law,[16] for sometimes in one household where there is a daughter-in-law and her mother-in-law, one may be heretical and the other Catholic. But where this sword is powerfully at work, we need not fear

---

15. This and the following paragraph are quoted by Eugippius (A.D. c.455–535), in his compilation of extracts from Augustine, much used in the middle ages; he thus provides an independent witness to the text. The discrepancies are minor.
16. Possibly he is thinking of Monica's tact in handling difficulties between herself and her mother-in-law, as described in his *Confessions* IX,9,20. The division was all the more likely to be felt in this relationship, where only one party might be Christian, though he goes on to consider the situation where both are Christian, but one Catholic and the other heretic (or schismatic).

any repetition of baptism.[17] If a daughter can be set in opposition against her mother, how much more a daughter-in-law against her mother-in-law?

12. This division has taken place also on a larger scale, affecting the whole human race: a son has been severed from his father, because we were once children of the devil. To people who were still unbelievers it was said, *You are children of your father, the devil* (Jn 8:44); and where did all our unbelief come from, if it was not handed down to us from him? He was not our father by creating us, but we made ourselves his children by imitating him. But now we see the child set against the father, divided from him. The sword has come into play, the sons and daughters have found another father and another mother. The devil, who presented himself as our model, made us into children doomed to death, but the two parents we have found bring us forth to eternal life.[18] So a son has been divided against his father.

There is also an instance of the division between a daughter and her mother, because those of the Jewish race who became believers were divided from the synagogue. Again, a daughter-in-law was set against her mother-in-law, because the Christian people of gentile origin could be called a daughter-in-law, since its bridegroom, Christ, was a son of the synagogue. Yes, he was; for where did his human birth in the flesh come from? From the synagogue. He left his father and mother to cleave to his wife, that they might be two in one flesh. This is not some fancy of mine, but a truth attested by the apostle, who says, *This is a great mystery, but I am referring it to Christ and the Church* (Eph 5:32). In a certain sense he did leave his Father: not that he was ever separated from him, but in that he took human flesh. How was that a leaving of his Father? Inasmuch as *being in the form of God he deemed it no robbery to be God's equal, yet he emptied himself and took on the form of a slave* (Phil 2:6–7). And how did he leave his mother? By leaving the Jewish race, as represented by the synagogue, which clung to the old rites. This was symbolically suggested by the episode where he asked, *Who is my mother, who are my brothers?* (Mt 12:48; Mk 3:33). He was teaching inside[19] but they were standing outside. Think about it: aren't the Jews standing outside like that even now, while Christ is teaching in the Church? Now, who is the mother-in-law? The bridegroom's mother. And the mother of our bridegroom, our Lord Jesus Christ, is the synagogue. Obviously her daughter-in-law is the Church, which has come from the gentiles and will have no truck with circumcision

---

17. Presumably because the elder relative, if Donatist, might try to insist on it, but a Catholic daughter-in-law would accept the inevitability of division, and refuse.
18. Evidently God and holy mother Church. But Eugippius has *terrenam* (earthly) instead of *aeternam* (eternal), presumably understanding it of biological parents who are Christians.
19. Variant: "was leading them within."

of the flesh, so she is set against her mother-in-law. *Gird on your sword.* We have indicated its power.

The sacredness of the thigh

13. *Gird on your sword*—your word, that is; and gird it *upon your thigh, mighty warrior.* Buckle your sword to your thigh. What significance is there in the thigh? It represents the flesh. That is why a prophecy said, *The scepter shall not be taken from Judah, nor a leader from his thighs* (Gn 49:10). And remember Abraham: he had been promised that in his seed all nations would be blessed,[20] and the time came for him to send his servant to find and bring home a wife for his son. It was from this son that would descend the holy seed in whom all nations would be blessed. Abraham, holding fast in faith to the great name that would come through the apparent lowliness of his own seed, that is, the Son of God who would be born from the human race as Abraham's descendant, ordered the servant he was dispatching to swear to him by using a special gesture. *Place your hand under my thigh,* he said, *and so swear* (Gn 24:2–3). It was like saying, "Place your hand on the altar," or "on the gospel," or "on the prophet," or on anything sacred. "Put your hand under my thigh," he said, because he had faith, and so far from fearing any suggestion of indecency, he understood the truth. This is why the psalm says, *Gird your sword upon your thigh, mighty warrior.*

You are a mighty warrior even in respect of your thigh, for God's weakness is stronger than any human power.[21] *Mighty warrior.*

Verse 5. Gentleness and power

14. *In your beauty and dignity.* Receive your endowment of justice, because in your justice you are always beautiful and dignified. *Ride forth victoriously and seize your kingdom.* Do we not see this fulfilled already? It has undeniably taken place. Look round at the whole world: he has ridden forth victoriously and seized his kingdom, for all nations are his subjects. What was it like, to see all this in spirit? Just what it is for us to experience it now. When these things were spoken, Christ was not yet reigning, he had not yet ridden forth victoriously. These things were preached, but now they have been manifested in reality, and they are within our grasp. We know God to be a faithful keeper of his promises in very many matters; in only a few does he still owe us a fulfillment. *Ride forth victoriously and seize your kingdom.*

15. *By your faithfulness, gentleness and justice.* He kept his promise about truth and faithfulness when faithfulness sprang up from the earth, and justice looked down from heaven.[22] Christ was revealed to an expectant human race, so that in Abraham's offspring all nations might be blessed.

---

20. See Gn 1:3.
21. See 1 Cor 1:25.
22. See Ps 84:12(85:11).

The gospel was preached, and truth was faithfully imparted. What about gentleness? The martyrs suffered, and thereby God's victorious cause was greatly advanced, and his reign extended throughout all nations. The martyrs neither flinched nor resisted; they spoke up frankly, concealing nothing; they were ready for any fate and refused none. This was mighty gentleness! It was the body of Christ that achieved this, because it had learned the lesson from its Head. He had been the foremost to be led like a sheep to the slaughter, like a lamb that does not open its mouth in the presence of the shearer.[23] So gentle was he that hanging on the cross he prayed, *Father, forgive them, for they do not know what they are doing* (Lk 23:34). But what of his justice? He will come to judge, and to requite each of us in accordance with our deeds.[24] He spoke the truth, he endured injustice,[25] but he will settle matters equitably. *Your right hand will conduct you wonderfully.* We are conducted by his right hand, but he himself by his own. He is God, we are human. By his right hand he was conducted: by his power, that is; for whatever power the Father has, Christ has also, as he also possesses the same immortality as the Father, the same divinity as the Father, the same eternity as the Father, and the strength of the Father. His right hand will conduct him wonderfully as he does good, shares human suffering, and foils the malice of his human enemies by his goodness. He is still being conducted to places where he does not yet reign, and it is his right hand that conducts him, for what takes him there is the gift he has given to his saints. *Your right hand will conduct you wonderfully.*

Verse 6. Christ's piercing shafts

16. *Your arrows are sharp and very powerful.*[26] These are his piercing words that arouse love. In the Song of Songs the bride moans, *I am wounded by love*,[27] by which she means that she is in love, she is afire with love, and she is yearning for her bridegroom, who has pierced her with the arrows of his word. *Your arrows are sharp and very powerful,* penetrating and effective. *Peoples will fall under your assault.* Who are these who have fallen? Those who were struck, and so brought low. But though we see peoples subject to Christ, we do not see them falling, so the psalm goes on to explain where this falling occurs: *in the heart*. There they exalted themselves against Christ, and there they fall before Christ. Saul was accustomed to blaspheme Christ, and stood proudly erect; but now he prays to Christ, for he was struck down and fell prostrate. Christ's enemy

---

23. See Is 53:7.
24. See Rom 2:6.
25. Variant: "he displayed meekness."
26. *Potentissimae*, agreeing with "arrows;" but a variant supported by the CCL editors has *potentissime*, agreeing with "Christ" (understood). The following lines support the former alternative.
27. See Sg 2:5; 5:8.

was slain so that Christ's disciple might be raised to life. From heaven the arrow was aimed, and Saul was struck in his heart. It was in Saul that it found its mark, for he was not Paul yet, but still Saul, still upright, not yet fallen flat. But the arrow struck him and he fell low in his heart. This falling down in his heart was not a consequence of his falling on his face; it happened when he asked, *What do you want me to do, Lord?* (Acts 9:6). So recently you were putting Christians in chains, Saul, and dragging them off to punishment; and now you are saying to Christ, *What do you want me to do?* What a sharp arrow that must have been, what a potent arrow, which felled the wounded Saul to turn him into Paul! As he fell, so too did the peoples; look at the gentiles and see how they have been brought into subjection to Christ. This is why the psalm says, *Peoples will fall under your assault, in the hearts of the king's enemies your arrows will find their mark.* Your enemies, it means, for the psalmist calls you a king, and knows that is what you truly are. *Peoples will fall under your assault, in the hearts of the king's enemies your arrows will find their mark.* They were your enemies, they were wounded by your arrows, and they fell before you. So from enemies they were transformed into friends; your enemies died, and your friends live. This is the same transformation that the title of our psalm proclaimed: *for those things that will be changed.* We study to understand individual words and particular verses of the psalm, but we study in such a way that none of us may doubt that the whole refers to Christ. *Peoples will fall under your assault, in the hearts of the king's enemies your arrows will find their mark.*

Verse 7. The straight ruler

17. *Your throne, O God, stands for ever and ever,* because God has blessed you for ever by the grace that bedews your lips. The throne that stood in the Jewish kingdom stood for a time only, as befitted those who were under the law, but not those under grace. Then he came to deliver those who were under the law, and establish them under the regime of grace. *Your throne, O God, stands for ever and ever.* Why? If the throne that belonged to that former kingdom was a temporary one only, how is it that this throne will stand for ever and ever? Because it is God's. *Your throne, O God, stands for ever and ever.* O eternal Godhead![28] God could not possibly have a temporary throne. *Your throne, O God, stands for ever and ever, your royal scepter is a scepter of righteous rule.* It is a scepter of righteous rule because it guides us aright. People were bent, distorted, they wanted regal power for themselves, they were in love with themselves, they cherished their own evil ways. They did not submit their wills to God, but sought to bend the will of God to their own lusts. A sinner or an unjust person often gets angry with God for dropping no rain on him, but he does

---

28. *O aeternitatis divinitas!* But a variant has *divitias*: "Oh the riches of eternity!"

not want God to get angry with him for dropping so low himself.[29] Nearly every day people sit down to find fault with God: "He ought to have done this...that other arrangement was not a good idea." You see what you ought to do, evidently, but you think he doesn't? You are twisted out of shape, but he is perfectly straight. How can you make a twisted thing sit well with a straight one? They cannot be aligned. You may attempt to lay a warped beam along a level floor, but it does not meet or fit properly, it will not lie flush with the pavement. The floor is perfectly level all over, but the beam is warped and will not fit a flat surface. In the same way, God's will is level and yours is bent. You think his will is not straight because you cannot fit in with it; but you must straighten yourself to fit his will, not attempt to bend his to suit you. You can't, anyway. Your effort is futile, because his will is always perfectly straight. Do you want to be united with him? Then allow yourself to be corrected. Then it will be his rod or scepter that rules you, his scepter of righteous rule. That is why we speak of a sovereign as a "ruler"; and anyone who does not correct his subjects is a defective ruler. Our ruler is sovereign over those who have been made straight. As he is a priest because he sanctifies us,[30] so too he is our king or ruler because he rules us.[31] But what does Scripture say in another text? *With a holy person you will be holy, and with the innocent man you will be innocent. With the chosen you will be chosen, and with the perverse you will deal perversely* (Ps 17:26–27(18:25–26)). This does not mean that God is perverse, but that those who are perverse themselves think him so. If you take delight in what is good, you find God good; if the good does not please you, you think God depraved. If God seems tortuous to you, it is your own tortuousness that is the trouble, for his rectitude abides unchangeably. Listen to the testimony of another psalm: *How good God is to Israel, to those of straightforward hearts!* (Ps 72(73):1).

Verse 8. Attend to your sins before God does

18. *Your royal scepter is the scepter of righteous rule. You have loved justice and hated iniquity.* Here you see what the scepter of righteous rule is: *you have loved justice and hated iniquity.* Draw near to this scepter and let Christ be your king, allow this scepter to rule you, because otherwise it may break you; it is an iron rod, and inflexible. What did another psalm have to say about it? *You will rule them with an iron rod, and you will dash them to pieces like a potter's vessel* (Ps 2:9). Some it rules, others it breaks; it rules the spiritual, but breaks the carnal. Come near to this scepter, then. What are you afraid of about it? The whole of the scepter is summed up

---

29. A slightly forced pun this time, not as good as some of Augustine's others: *"Deo quia non pluit; et non vult sibi Deum irasci, quia fluit."*
30. *Sacerdos a sanctificando nos.*
31. Variant: "... a priest for the purpose of sanctifying us ... a king/ruler to rule us."

in this: *you have loved justice and hated iniquity.* What are you afraid of? Perhaps you were an iniquitous person, and you hear that your king hates iniquity, so you are afraid. But he is what you make him to be. What does he hate? Iniquity. He doesn't hate you, does he? But there is iniquity in you? All right. God hates it, so you must hate it as well, so that both of you are in accord, hating the same thing. You will become God's friend if you hate what he hates. So too will you be his friend if you love what he loves. Let the iniquity that is in you become loathsome to you, and let what he has created delight you. You are a human being, and you are sinful. There, look, I have called you by two names: "human being," and "sinful." One of these names indicates your nature, the other your guilt; one was made for you by God, the other you made yourself. Love what God made, and hate what you made, because he hates it too. Now look how you are beginning to find yourself united to him, since you hate what he hates! He will punish sin, because his royal scepter is a scepter of righteous rule. Would you wish him not to punish sin? That is impossible. Sin demands to be punished; if it did not, it would not be sin. Forestall him, then; if you don't want him to punish your sin, punish it yourself. It is to this very end that he continues to spare you, putting it off, holding his hand, bending his bow, threatening you. Would he make such a display of shouting that he is going to strike you, if striking you was what he really wanted? No, and that is why he delays in dealing with your sins; but you must not delay. Turn your attention to punishing your sins, because it is not possible for them to go unpunished in the long run. They must needs be punished, either by yourself or by him. Admit them, so that he may remit them.[32] A penitential psalm exemplifies this attitude: *Turn your face away from my sins* (Ps 50:11(51:9)). Did it say, "from me"? No, it didn't, and in another place a psalm expressly begs God, *Do not turn your face away from me* (Ps 26(27):9). Accordingly we must understand the first one to mean, "I don't want you to see my sins," because for God to see something means to take it into account. When a judge is said to take something into account, it means that he turns his attention to it, and therefore must punish it, because he is a judge. And God is a judge too. *Turn your face away from my sins.* But you, for your part, should not turn your face away, if you want God to turn his face away from them. In that same psalm this very offer is made to God: *I know my wrongdoing, and my sin confronts me all the time* (Ps 50:5(51:3)). He wants it to be before his own eyes, but not before God's. *Your royal scepter is a scepter of righteous rule.* No one should be complacent about God's mercy, for his scepter is a scepter of righteous rule. Are we saying that God is not merciful? Far from it; what could be more merciful than God, who so generously spares sinners, God who takes no notice of any past sins in any of those who turn back to him? Love him for his mercy, but in such fashion that you want him to be true to himself; for his mercy cannot diminish his justice, nor

---

32. *Tu agnosce, ut ille ignoscat.*

his justice his mercy. In the meantime, as long as he delays, be sure that you do not delay, because his royal scepter is a scepter of righteous rule.

God's anointing of God

19. *You have loved justice and hated iniquity, for, O God, your God has anointed you.* That is why he anointed you, so that you might love justice and hate iniquity. Notice how this is phrased: *for, O God, your God has anointed you.*[33] It means, "Oh you who are God, your God has anointed you." God is anointed by God. In Latin it looks as though the word "God" is just repeated in the nominative case, but in Greek the distinction is perfectly clear: one name belongs to the person addressed, and the second to the person who addresses him, saying, *O God, he has anointed you.* So the phrase, "O you who are God, your God has anointed you," is like saying, "This is why your God has anointed you, O God." You have to accept this and understand the verse in this way, because it is quite clear in the Greek.[34]

Who, then, is the God who was anointed by God? Let the Jews tell us that. After all, these Scriptures are theirs as well as ours. God was anointed by God, and when you hear the word, "anointed," understand that it means Christ, for "Christ" is derived from "chrism," and the name "Christ" means "Anointed one." Nowhere else were kings and priests anointed; it was done only in that kingdom where Christ's coming was prophesied, where he was anointed, and from where the name Christ was to come. Nowhere else at all do we find this, in any other nation or kingdom. So God was anointed by God, and with what kind of oil? Spiritual, obviously. Visible oil is a sign; invisible oil is a sacramental mystery,[35] for the spiritual oil is within. God was anointed for us, and sent to us. He was God, but he became man so that he could be anointed; yet he was man in such wise that he was God, and he was God in such a way that he did not disdain to be man. He is true man and true God, and there is no falsehood in him, for he is in every respect true, in every respect the very Truth. God became man, and it can be said that "God was anointed," because God became man, became Christ the Anointed One.

Jacob's anointed stone and Jacob's ladder

20. We have a prefiguration of this in the episode where Jacob had put a stone under his head and gone to sleep.[36] The patriarch Jacob used the

---

33. *Propterea unxit te, Deus, Deus tuus.*
34. In the Septuagint, as in the quotation of the verse by Heb 1:9, it runs as follows: Διά τοῦτο ἔχρισέν σε ὁ Θεός ὁ Θεός σου. Since in Greek, as equally in Latin, the first noun could be either nominative or vocative, only the punctuation as inserted here makes Augustine's point.
35. A variant supported by two codices makes the thought slightly clearer: "Visible oil functions as a sign of invisible oil, for it is a sacrament...."
36. See Gn 28:11–22.

stone as a pillow for his head, and while he was asleep he saw the heavens opened, and a ladder extending from heaven to earth, with angels passing up and down on it. When he awoke he poured oil on the stone and went away. In that stone he recognized Christ; that was why he anointed it. Notice what a long time ago preaching about Christ began. Now what is the significance of that act of anointing a stone, particularly among the patriarchs, who worshiped the one God? It was a symbol only, and Jacob left it at that. It was not as though he anointed the stone and came back to it regularly, and offered sacrifice there; the mystery was given symbolic expression and that was all; there was no initiation of sacrilegious cult.

Now consider the stone, and remember another text: *the stone rejected by the builders has become the headstone of the corner* (Ps 117(118):22). The stone was placed at Jacob's head because Christ is the head of a man.[37] Think about this carefully, for there is a great mystery here. The stone is Christ; he is *the living stone, rejected by men, but chosen by God* (1 Pt 2:4), and the place for a stone is at a man's head, because Christ is the head of a man. The stone was anointed because Christ's name is derived from chrism. By Christ's revelation ladders were shown to Jacob, stretching from earth to heaven, or from heaven to earth, with angels ascending and descending on them. We shall understand the significance of this more clearly if we recall the statement made by the Lord himself in the gospel. Now you are aware that Jacob is the same person as Israel. His name was changed to Israel when he was wrestling with the angel, and winning; he received a blessing from the opponent he was beginning to overcome.[38] Similarly Israel—the people of Israel, I mean—overcame Christ in the sense that they crucified him, yet in the persons of those Israelites who came to believe in Christ, Israel was blessed by the one it had defeated. However, many of them did not believe, and the crippling of Jacob symbolizes this. A blessing, and a lameness. A blessing, certainly, in those who believed, and we know that very many from their race did come to believe later. But a crippling in those who did not believe. And because those who did not were many, and those who did were comparatively few, the adversary touched the broad part of Jacob's thigh to strike him lame. What is "the broad part of the thigh"? The majority of his race.

Now for the ladders. In the gospel, when the Lord saw Nathanael, he said, *Look, there is a true Israelite, in whom there is no guile* (Jn 1:47). Something like that had been said about Jacob: *Jacob was a man without guile, who lived at home* (Gn 25:27); and the Lord remembered that description when he caught sight of Nathanael, a man free from guile who came from that same people. So he said, *Look, there is a true Israelite, in whom there is no guile*. He called Nathanael a guileless Israelite because he had Jacob in mind. But Nathanael replied, *How did you come to know me?* to

---

37. See 1 Cor 11:3.
38. See Gn 32:24–31.

which the Lord answered, *When you were under the fig tree, I saw you.* That means, "Even when you were among a people subject to the law, which spread its material shade over them as a protection, I saw you." And what is implied by "I saw you?" It means, "Even there, I took pity on you." Nathanael remembered that he really had been under a fig tree, and he was amazed, because he thought no one had seen him there, so he confessed, *You are the Son of God, you are the King of Israel.* Who said that? None other than the man who had just been told that he was a true Israelite, and that there was no deceit in him. The Lord continued, *Have you believed because I said, "I saw you under the fig tree?" You will see greater things than that.* He is talking to Jacob, to Israel, to the man who had put a stone under his head. *You will see greater things that that.* What greater things can he have in mind? The stone is already at Jacob's head. *To all of you I say, you will see heaven opened, and God's angels ascending and descending over the Son of Man* (Jn 1:47–51). May this be true now, in the Church; may it be true that God's angels ascend and descend on those ladders. The angels of God are charged with announcing the truth. Let them mount high and see that *in the beginning was the Word, and the Word was with God; he was God.* Then let them come down and see that *the Word was made flesh, and dwelt among us* (Jn 1:1.14). Let them ascend, and lift up the great, but let them descend to nourish the little ones. Look how Paul ascended: *If I seem to be out of my mind, it is because I am talking to God*; but then watch him coming down again: *but if I am talking sense, it is for you* (2 Cor 5:13). Then, see, up he goes again: *We speak wisdom among the perfect*, and down: *I gave you milk to drink, rather than solid food* (1 Cor 2:6; 3:2). And this is what happens all the time in the Church: God's angels ascend and descend upon the Son of Man, because the Son of Man is enthroned on high, and to him we ascend in our hearts; in this respect he is our Head. But the Son of Man is here below, inasmuch as his body is on earth. His members are here, the Head is in heaven; we ascend to the Head, and descend to his members. Christ is there, and Christ is here. If he were present above only, and not here, how could the voice from heaven have demanded, *Saul, Saul, why are you persecuting me?* (Acts 9:4). Who was giving him any trouble in heaven? No one, neither the Jews, nor Saul, nor the diabolical tempter; no one was causing him trouble in heaven, but he complained, just as when our foot is trodden on, our tongue yells, because of the organic unity of the human body.

21. *You have loved justice and hated iniquity, for, O God, your God has anointed you.* We have already spoken about this anointed God, that is, about Christ. There was no clearer way in which Christ's name could have been expressed, than by calling him "Anointed God." As he is *fair beyond all humankind*, so too he is anointed *with the oil of joy, more abundantly than all who share with him.* Who share with him? The children of men, because he is the Son of Man, who became a sharer in their mortality in order to make them sharers in his immortality.

Verse 9. The scent of Christ

22. *From your garments drift the perfumes of myrrh, spices and cassia.* Your clothing diffuses sweet scents. His garments are his saints, his elect, the whole Church which he makes fit for himself, free from spot or wrinkle;[39] for he washed away its every spot in his blood, and smoothed out every wrinkle as he stretched it on the cross. From him proceeds the sweet scent evoked by the various plants named in the psalm. Listen to Paul, the smallest of men,[40] who was like that fringe of the Lord's garment which a woman with a hemorrhage touched, and was healed;[41] listen to him: *We are the fragrance of Christ offered to God in every place, both for those who are on the way to salvation, and for those who are perishing* (2 Cor 2:15). You will notice that he did not say, "We are a sweet scent for those on the way to salvation, but a foul stench for those who are perishing." What he said was, *We are a sweet fragrance, both for those who are on the way to salvation, and for those who are perishing.* We may well believe that a person can be saved by a good scent; there is nothing improbable about that. But how could anyone be destroyed by a good scent? This is something profound, a great truth is here; even if we find it impossible to grasp, it is true nonetheless. Paul himself indicates that it is difficult, for he immediately adds, *Who is equal to this?* How can anyone understand why people should die from a sweet perfume? But I will make a suggestion, brothers and sisters. Paul was preaching the gospel. Many loved him for doing so, but many others were jealous of him. Those who loved him were in process of being saved by the delicate perfume, but this same perfume was provoking the jealous to their own destruction. So for those who were on their way to perdition it was not a bad smell; it was a good scent, and that made them all the more jealous of Paul, because it was obvious that God's good grace had its way with him. No one is jealous of a miserable person. Paul was glorious in his preaching of God's word, and was living under the guidance of the scepter of righteous rule. All those who loved Christ in him, and were running after Christ's beautiful perfume, loved Paul. The bride, who says in the Song of Songs, *Let us run toward the fragrance of your ointments* (Sg 1:3), loved her bridegroom's friend; but the others were all the more tormented by jealousy as they saw Paul glorious in his preaching of the gospel and blameless in his life, so they were slain by the sweet scent.

---

39. See Eph 5:27.
40. His name resembles the Latin *paulus*, "small," and he called himself *the least of the apostles*, 1 Cor 15:9.
41. See Mk 5:28; Mt 9:20; Lk 8:44.

Verse 10. The apostles' daughters

23. *From your garments drift the perfumes of myrrh, spices and cassia; kings' daughters from ivory palaces have found favor with you.* Whichever ivory palaces, whichever great houses or regal mansions you care to name, there have been kings' daughters from there who have been pleasing to Christ. Would you like me to suggest to you a spiritual interpretation of these ivory palaces? The great houses, the mighty tabernacles of God are the hearts of the saints, and the kings who live there are royal because they rule their flesh, subordinate their crowding human affections to their will, chastise their bodies and bring them into submission. This is how you should understand the palaces, and from there come the kings' daughters in whom Christ finds his joy, because when these kings preach and spread the gospel, many souls are born to them, and all these souls are "the daughters of kings." The churches are the apostles' daughters, kings' daughters. Christ is the *King of kings* (Rv 19:16), and under him the apostles too are kings, for to them it was said, *You will sit upon twelve thrones, judging the twelve tribes of Israel* (Mt 19:28). They preached the word of truth, and through it they begot churches, not for themselves but for him. In the law it was laid down that *if a man dies, his brother shall marry the dead man's wife, and raise up offspring for his brother* (Dt 25:5). The brother is to *marry the dead man's wife, and raise up offspring,* not for himself, but *for his brother.* Now Christ himself used the expression, *Tell my brothers* (Mt 28:10);[42] and in a psalm he said, *I will tell of your name to my brothers* (Ps 21:23(22:22)). Christ died, he rose again, he ascended, and he withdrew his bodily presence, so his brothers took his wife for the purpose of begetting children through the preaching of the gospel—not by their own power, but through the gospel—so that their Brother's name might be perpetuated. That is why Paul said, *In Christ Jesus through the gospel I have begotten you* (1 Cor 4:15). Accordingly, as they were raising up offspring for their Brother, they did not call the children they begot "Paulines" or "Petrines," but "Christians." The same wide-awake caution is to be found in these verses too. Examine them, and see if this is not the case, for after speaking of *ivory palaces,* and evoking royal, spacious, beautiful, comfortable dwellings, such as are the hearts of the saints, the psalmist added, *kings' daughters from ivory palaces have found favor with you, and come to do you honor.* They are the daughters of kings, certainly, for they are the daughters of your apostles, but they come *to do you honor,* because the apostles have raised up offspring for their Brother. Paul had raised some up for his Brother, and when he saw some of them running after his own name he exclaimed, *Was Paul crucified for you?* (1 Cor 1:13). What does the law enjoin? That the newborn should be named after the dead man.[43]

---

42. Compare Jn 20:17.
43. See Dt 25:6.

Let the child be born to the dead man, and bear the dead man's name. Paul observes this prescription and recalls his converts to their senses when they try to adopt his name: *Was Paul crucified for you?* And what about the time when you begot them, Paul; did you put your own name on them? No, for he continues, *Or were you baptized in Paul's name?* (1 Cor 1:13). *Kings' daughters have found favor with you, and come to do you honor.* Hold onto that phrase, *to do you honor,* keep it in mind always, for this is what it means to wear the wedding garment: that you seek his honor, his glory.

The daughters of kings can also be taken to represent the cities which have believed in Christ, and were founded by kings; and the phrase, *from ivory palaces* can be understood to mean that they were founded by the rich, the proud, the arrogant. *Kings' daughters have found favor with you, and come to do you honor,* because they are no longer seeking to promote the reputation of their city fathers, but are concerned to honor you. Let anyone point out to me in Rome any temple of Romulus that is held in anything like the same veneration as the memorial of Peter, which I can point out! And who is being honored in Peter, if not the one who died for us? For we are Christians, not Petrines. Even though fathered by the dead man's brother, we are named after the dead man. We came to birth through Peter, but we are born to Christ. As Rome, so too Carthage, and many another noble city: all of them are daughters of kings, but they have found favor with their true King and come to do him honor. And from all of them is formed one single queen.

The queen's apparel

24. What a nuptial hymn this is! As songs full of joy are resounding, the bride herself enters. Until now it was the bridegroom's coming that preoccupied us, and he was being described throughout; all eyes were on him. But now it is time for the bride's entry. *The queen has taken her place at your right hand.* If she were on your left, she would not be a queen. There are indeed some persons at your left, but to them will be said, *Depart from me into the eternal fire* (Mt 25:41). Your queen will stand to your right, and to her will the invitation be spoken, *Come, you who are blessed by my Father, take possession of the kingdom prepared for you since the creation of the world* (Mt 25:34). *The queen has taken her place at your right hand in a golden gown, decked with variety.* What is this queenly apparel? It is precious, and of varied colors; this represents the mysteries of our teaching, and the variety of languages in which they are expressed. The African tongue is one, the Syriac another, the Greek another, the Hebrew another...and many others there are. These languages make up the variety with which the queen's gown is adorned. Just as all the different colors in a dress harmonize to form a unity, so do all these tongues express the one faith. Let there be plenty of variety in the garment, but no tear made.

So we have interpreted the variety as the diversity of languages, and the gown itself as unity; but now what does the gold represent amid this variety? It symbolizes wisdom. However great the variety of languages, it is one and the same gold that is preached. The gold itself does not vary, but there is variety in the way the gold is spoken about. All tongues preach the same wisdom, the same doctrine and discipline. There is variety in the languages, but gold in their meaning.

Verse 11. The admonition to the bride

25. The prophet now addresses the queen, and delighted he is to sing to her. He addresses each one of us too, provided we know where we belong, and try to be members of that body, and persevere in faith and hope, united with one another as limbs of Christ. He addresses us, *Hearken, my daughter, and see.* He speaks as one of the fathers to a daughter, even though the speaker is a prophet or an apostle (for after all, we speak of "our fathers the prophets," and "our fathers the apostles," and if we call them our fathers, they have the right to call us their children). The daughters of these kings are being addressed, therefore, but the admonition is delivered by a single fatherly voice, and to one single daughter: *Hearken, my daughter, and see.* Listen first, and afterwards see. The gospel was brought to us, and realities we do not yet see have been preached to us; we have believed on the strength of what we have heard, and by believing we shall come to see. The bridegroom mentions this in another psalm: *A people I never knew has come to serve me, and as soon as they heard me they obeyed me* (Ps 17:45(18:43–44)). Why does he say, *As soon as they heard me?* Because that people has not yet seen. The Jews saw him, and crucified him; the gentiles did not see him, but believed. Let the queen make her entry from amid the gentiles, let her come in a golden gown, bedecked with variety; let her come from the gentiles adorned with all the foreign tongues but with a single undivided wisdom, and let the admonition be spoken to her, *Hearken, my daughter, and see.* Unless you hear first, you will not see. Hear, so that you may cleanse your heart by faith, as the apostle said in the Acts of the Apostles: God was *cleansing their hearts by faith.*[44] This is why we must hear what we are to believe before we see it: our hearts need to be cleansed first by believing, so that we may be able to see with them. Listen, so that you may believe; cleanse your heart by faith. "And when I have cleansed my heart, what am I going to see?" *Blessed are the pure of heart, for they shall see God* (Mt 5:8).

Hearken, my daughter, and see, and bend your ear. Merely to hear would not be enough; we must hear with humility, so *bend your ear. And forget your own people and your father's house.* In another nation, in another father's house, you were born. The nation was Babylon,[45] and its

---

44. Acts 15:9. It was Peter who said this, though usually by the title, "the apostle," Augustine means Paul.
45. Babylon is for Augustine the type of the earthly city; he will develop the theme later in *The City of God.* See also *Confessions* II,3,8.

king the devil. From whatever quarter the gentiles have come flocking in, they have come from their father, the devil; but they have repudiated him.[46] *Forget your own people and your father's house.* The devil begot you as an ugly child when he made you a sinner; but God who justifies the ungodly gives you new birth as a beautiful creature. *Forget your own people and your father's house.*

Verse 12. Her beauty is the king's gift

26. *For the king has desired your beauty.* What beauty is this, if not what he himself created in her? He has desired beauty, but whose? The beauty of a sinner, a wicked, ungodly woman, as she was in the house of her father the devil, and among her own people? No, no; but the beauty of the bride described in the Song of Songs: *Who is this who comes up washed white?* (Sg 6:10.6). She was not white before, but now she has been washed pure white: as the Lord promises through a prophet, "Even if your sins are brilliant red, I will wash you white as snow."[47] *He has desired your beauty.* But who is this king? *He is your God.* See now how right it is for you to abandon that other father, and that other nation that was yours, and come to this King who is your God. He is your God and your King, your King and your bridegroom. The King you are marrying is God; he provides you with your portion, by him you are adorned, by him redeemed, by him healed. Whatever you have in you that can please him, you have as his gift.

Verse 13. The homage of the Gentiles and of the rich

27. *And Tyrian maidens will pay homage to him with their gifts.* It is to your King, your God, that these *Tyrian maidens will pay homage with their gifts*. The maidens from Tyre represent maidens from all gentile races: the part stands for the whole. Tyre was a neighbor to the land where prophecy flourished, so Tyre symbolized the gentiles who were to believe in Christ. From there came the Canaanite woman who was at first called a dog; you remember where she came from, because the gospel says, *He withdrew to the region of Tyre and Sidon, and a Canaanite woman who lived in those parts came out and kept shouting* (Mt 15:22). And the rest of the story you know. She had been a "dog" earlier, in her father's house and among her own people, but by crying out and coming to the King she became beautiful through her faith in him. So she deserved to hear, *Woman, your faith is great* (Mt 15:28). *The king has desired your beauty. And Tyrian maidens will pay homage to him with their gifts.* Even so does the King will to be approached and to see his treasury filled; and he himself has provided the gifts with which they are to be filled, filled by you.[48] Let them come, says the psalm, let them come to pay him homage with their gifts. What kind

---

46. Possibly an allusion to the renunciations preceding baptism.
47. See Is 1:18.
48. Variant: "and they are filled for you/us."

of gifts are acceptable? *Do not lay up treasures for yourselves on earth, where moth and rust will destroy, and thieves may break in and steal them; lay up for yourselves treasures in heaven, where neither thief nor moth can touch them. For where your treasure is, your heart will be too* (Mt 6:19–21). *Come with your gifts, give alms, and everything will be clean for you* (Lk 11:41). Come with your gifts to him who says, *I want mercy rather than sacrifice* (Hos 6:6; Mt 9:13; 12:7). In days of old there was a temple that foreshadowed what was to come, and people used to bring bulls, rams, goats, and various other animals for sacrifice. By their blood-shedding one thing was done, but something else signified. But now blood has been shed for us, the blood prefigured by all those sacrifices; the King himself has come, and he demands gifts. What gifts? Alms. For he will sit in judgment, and will himself award gifts to certain people. *Come, you who are blessed by my Father*, he will say, *take possession of the kingdom prepared for you since the creation of the world*. And why? Because *I was hungry, and you fed me; I was thirsty, and you gave me a drink; naked, and you clothed me; a stranger, and you made me welcome; sick and in prison, and you visited me*. These are the gifts that the Tyrian maidens bring as homage to the King, for when they ask him, *When did we see you so?* he who is both enthroned on high and present here below can say, thinking of those who go up the ladder and those who come down, *When you did that for even the least of those who are mine, you did it for me* (Mt 25:34–38).

28. *Tyrian maidens will pay homage to him with their gifts*. The psalmist now intends to state more clearly who the daughters of Tyre are, and how they are to do homage to the king. *All the rich among the people will seek favor with you*. So these daughters of Tyre who come with their gifts are the rich citizens for whom the bridegroom's friend has this advice: *Instruct the rich of this world not to be high-minded, nor to put their trust in unreliable wealth, but in the living God, who gives us everything to enjoy in abundance. Let them be rich in good works, give readily, and share what they have*. Let them do honor to the King with their gifts, but not think that they are losing what they give. They should have no anxiety about putting it where they will find it again for ever. *Let them use their wealth to lay a good foundation for the future, and so attain true life* (1 Tm 6:17–19). As they do honor to the King with their gifts they *will seek favor with you*, for they all come to the Church and give alms there. They should not do it elsewhere, outside; the Church is the right place to do it, because a favorable reception from this bride and queen will be to their advantage when they give alms. This is why we read that people who sold their goods used to come with the proceeds to seek the queen's acceptance, and what they brought they would lay at the feet of the apostles.[49] Love grew very strong in the Church. The queen with her gracious countenance is the Church, but the daughters of Tyre who pay homage—the wealthy who bring gifts, that

---

49. See Acts 4:34–35.

is—they are the Church too. *All the rich among the people will seek favor with you.* Both those who seek acceptance, and the queen whose acceptance is entreated, are all the one bride, all one queen, for mother and children together all belong to Christ, belong to the Head.⁵⁰

Verses 14–15. Inner beauty

29. Good works and almsgiving can trap us in human pride, however, so the Lord warns, *Be careful not to do your good works in the sight of other people, to attract their attention* (Mt 6:1). Yet he also tells us in what sense these things must be done publicly, in order to win the bride's favor: *Let your deeds shine before men and women in such a way that they see the good you do, and bless your Father who is in heaven* (Mt 5:16). Do not seek recognition for yourselves by the good works you carry out in public, but seek the honor of God. Someone objects, perhaps, "But who knows whether it is God's glory I am seeking, or my own? If I give something to a poor person, I can be seen doing it, but who sees what my intention is?" The one who sees can take care of that; he who will reward you sees your intention. He who sees you within loves you within; he loves you within, and you must love him within, for he fashions your inner beauty. Do not seek your reward in being seen by onlookers, and praised for what you do; consider the next words of the psalm: *All the glory of the king's daughter is within.* Not only does she wear an outer garment of gold, decked with variety; he who has fallen in love with her knows her to be inwardly lovely as well. What is the inner face of beauty? Beauty of conscience. There Christ regards us, there Christ loves us, there Christ punishes, there Christ bestows the crown. Let your almsgiving be done in secret, then, for *all the glory of the king's daughter is within. With her golden fringes she is girdled with varied embroidery.* Her beauty is within, but in her fringes is a variety of tongues, setting forth the splendor of her teaching. But what would be the use of them, if there were no beauty within?

30. *Virgins will be conducted after her to the king.* Yes, this surely has happened. The Church has believed, and the Church has spread throughout all nations. Look how virgins now long to be pleasing to the King! What motivates them? That the Church has led the way. *Virgins will be conducted after her to the king, her nearest and dearest will be led to you.* Those who are conducted are no strangers, but her nearest and dearest, those who belong to her. Notice that the psalm first said, "To the king," then turned toward him and said, "To you." *Her nearest and dearest will be led to you.*

Verse 16. The joyful entry of the virgins

31. *They shall be conducted with joy and gladness, they shall be ushered into the temple of the king.* The temple of the king is the Church itself, and

---

50. The paradox Augustine plays with in this paragraph, that the Church is the people, yet more than the people, is taken up again in sections 31 and 33 below.

yet the Church enters his temple. Of what is the temple built? Of the people who enter the temple. Who are its living stones?[51] God's faithful. These are the ones who *will be ushered into the temple of the king.* There are virgins outside the King's temple, heretical nuns; virgins they are indeed, but what advantage is that to them if they are not brought into the King's temple? The King's temple stands firm in unity; it is not a tumbledown place, or torn apart, or divided against itself. The mortar binding its stones together is the charity of those who live there. *They shall be ushered into the temple of the king.*

Verse 17. Sons to take the place of fathers for the Church

32. *To take the place of your fathers, sons have been born to you.* Nothing could be more obvious. Look carefully at this temple of the king, because the psalmist speaks on its behalf, with its worldwide unity in mind. Those who have chosen to remain virgins cannot be pleasing to the bridegroom unless they are brought into his temple. *To take the place of your fathers, sons have been born to you.* The apostles begot you; they were sent out, they preached, they are the Church's fathers. But was it possible for them to remain with us in bodily form for ever? It is true that one of them said, *I long to die and to be with Christ, for that is much the best; but it is necessary for you that I remain in the flesh* (Phil 1:23–24). Yes, he said that, but how long was he able to stay? Even until our day?

Even into the future? No; but was the Church abandoned when the apostles departed? Far from it. *To take the place of your fathers, sons have been born to you.* What does that mean? The apostles were sent to be your fathers, but in their place sons have been born to you, because bishops have been appointed. Where did they spring from, the bishops who are found throughout the world today? The Church calls them "fathers," although the Church itself brought them forth, and appointed them to the sees of the fathers. Do not imagine yourself forsaken then, O Church, because you do not see Peter, do not see Paul, do not see any of those from whom you were born. A new fatherhood has grown up for you from your own offspring. *To take the place of your fathers, sons have been born to you; and you will appoint them princes all over the world.* Look how widely the King's temple has been extended, and let any virgins who are not being ushered into it learn from this that they have no place at the wedding. *To take the place of your fathers, sons have been born to you; and you will appoint them princes all over the world.* This is the Catholic Church: her sons have been set up as princes worldwide, her sons have been appointed in her fathers' stead. Let those who are cut off from us recognize the truth, let them come back into unity, let them be led into the temple of the King. God has built his Church in every place, laying the firm foundations of the

---

51. See 1 Pt 2:5.

prophets and apostles.[52] The Church has given birth to sons, and appointed them in place of our fathers as princes over the whole earth.

Verse 18. The city of God

33. *They will be mindful of your name in generation after generation. Therefore the peoples will confess to you.* What is the use of confessing, if it is done outside the temple? What is the point of praying, if prayer is not offered on the mountain? *With my voice I have cried to the Lord,* says another psalm, *and he heard me from his holy mountain* (Ps 3:5(4)). And what mountain is that? The mountain of which Scripture says, *A city founded upon a mountain cannot be hidden* (Mt 5:14). What mountain? The mountain Daniel saw growing from a small stone, and smashing all earthly kingdoms, and filling all the surface of the earth.[53]

Let anyone who hopes to receive, worship there; let anyone who wants to be heard, ask there; let anyone who wants to be forgiven, confess there. *Therefore the peoples will confess to you for ever, and for unending ages,* for though in eternal life there will no longer be any groaning sinners, the everlasting confession of sheer happiness will never cease in the praises sung to God in that heavenly, imperishable city. To this same city will the peoples confess in praise for ever, this city to which another psalm sings, *Glorious things are spoken of you, city of God* (Ps 86(87):3). To her who is Christ's bride, who is a queen, a king's daughter and a King's wife, will they sing, for her princes are mindful of her name in generation after generation, which means as long as this age shall last, this age which rolls on through succeeding generations. So long shall they continue to care lovingly for her, until she is set free from this passing world to reign with God for ever. Therefore will the peoples confess to her through all eternity, for there will the hearts of all be transparent and manifest as they shine with charity made perfect. Thus she will know herself entirely in utter fullness, she who is in many of her parts hidden now even from herself. This is why we are warned by the apostle to pass no judgment prematurely, before the Lord comes to light up all that is hidden in darkness, and lay bare the thoughts of all hearts; then each one will receive due commendation from God.[54] That holy city will in some sort confess to herself, for the peoples who form her will confess for ever to the city. No part of her may remain hidden from herself, for nothing in any one of her citizens will be hidden from sight.

---

52. See Eph 2:20.
53. See Dn 2:35.
54. See 1 Cor 4:5.

Exposition of Psalm 56

Synopsis

We just heard about the Lord's example of love and about his commandment of love: the two go together. He enacted what he taught, and he also helps us to fulfill what he commands. The Psalm too speaks of this in terms of the whole Christ, *totus Christus,* the head and the body that speak in and for each other (1).

The Psalm title's words about David are familiar enough, but what do they have to do with Christ? The phrase *title for David himself that is not to be tampered with* gives a clue. Since David's story never mentions a title, we know it refers to the sign with the title *King of the Jews* over Jesus on the cross. The Jews complained about the placard, but Pilate refused to change it (2–3). Then it says that David fled into a cave. That's Christ taking on human flesh to hide his divinity, even to the point of death and burial in the earth. But he arose untouched by decay (4).

In the Psalm Christ prays as a single human being with soul and flesh united to the divine Word. But the whole Christ speaks here, so it's our voice that prays for protection from evil (5–6). We pray to God *Most High*; majesty stoops to listen and deals kindly with us. God raised Christ from the dead, but elsewhere it says that Christ raised himself (7–8). His crucifiers did not understand that he was God; now they've been scattered and disgraced. But in God's providence the Jews continue to survive in order to carry our Scriptures for us; that is, their writings are impartial witnesses that anticipated the coming of Christ. God sent Christ as mercy that suffers with us and as truth that requites us. He slept in death of his own accord, though his sleep was "disturbed" by the Jews who accused him, using "teeth and tongues" as weapons (9–12).

Now the prophet speaks of Christ's glory that pervades the whole earth. The rebellious Donatists do not recognize this (13). Then Christ again speaks, affirming that his persecutors *dug a pit in front of me but fell into it themselves.* Readers with "Christian eyes" know that it's typical for evildoers to get tangled up in their own crimes (14).

People who are ready to embrace God's will with patience sing these Psalms in their sufferings. Christ exclaims, *Arise, O my glory! Arise, psaltery and lyre!* These two instruments portray Christ as divine and as human. The expression, *mercy to the heavens, truth to the clouds*, is initially confusing, but it makes figurative sense in terms of God's grace. Truth came in flesh to heal our inner eye so that we might see him face to face (17).

Augustine's Text of Psalm 56

(1) For the end, as a title for David himself that is not to be tampered with,
   When he fled into a cave from Saul's pursuit.

(2) Have mercy on me, O God, have mercy, for my soul trusts in you,
   And beneath the shadow of your wings I will hope, until iniquity shall pass.

(3) I will cry to God Most High, to God who has dealt kindly with me.

(4) He sent from heaven and saved me;
   Those who trampled on me he has consigned to disgrace.
   He sent his mercy and truth,

(5) And he rescued my soul from amid the lion-cubs.
   Though disturbed, I lay down to sleep.
   Their teeth are weapons and arrows, their tongue a sharp sword.

(6) Be lifted up above the heavens, O God,
   And may your glory pervade the whole earth.

(7) They set a snare for my feet, and bent my soul down.
   They dug a pit in front of me, but fell into it themselves.

(8) My heart is ready, O God, my heart is ready.
   I will sing and play the psaltery.

(9) Arise, O my glory! Arise, psaltery and lyre!
   I will arise at dawn.

(10) I will praise you among the peoples, Lord,
   And sing psalms to you among the Gentiles.

(11) For your mercy is magnified even to the heavens,
   And your truth reaches to the clouds.

(12) Be lifted up above the heavens, O God,
   And may your glory pervade the whole earth.

Exposition

A Sermon to the People

Introduction: Christ's command and example of love; head and body

1. My brothers and sisters, we have just heard in the gospel how dearly our Lord and Savior loves us. As God he is intimate with the Father, as man he is intimate with us. He is from our race, yet now enthroned at the right hand of the Father, and you have heard how much he loves us. He spoke of the measure of his charity, and required the same measure of us, telling us of his commandment: that we love one another. Perhaps we might have been doubtful and perplexed as to how much we should love one another, and what the perfect charity might be that pleases God, for perfect charity is that charity which cannot be surpassed. So to dispel our doubts he put the standard into words himself, and taught us. *No one can have greater charity than this*, he said, *to lay down one's life for one's friends* (Jn 15:12). He acted himself in accordance with what he taught, the apostles acted as they had learned from him, and then they preached to us that we must do the same. Let us do likewise; for though if we think of him as our Creator we are not what he is, we are what he is with regard to what he became for our sake. If he alone had achieved it, perhaps no one among us would aspire to imitate him, for though human, he was human in such a way that he was also God. But human he was, and so servants have imitated their Master, and disciples have imitated their Teacher, and our predecessors in his family have done it, people who though they were our ancestors are yet our fellow-servants. Moreover, God would not have commanded us to do likewise if he had judged it impossible for human beings to love like that. When you take your weakness into account, do you feel yourself collapsing under the weight of this commandment? Draw strength from his example, then. Or do you find even his example overwhelming? Be confident: he who gave you the example is at hand, to give you help as well.

Let us listen to him in this psalm. Most opportunely, and by the Lord's disposition, it happens that the gospel chimes in with the psalm, for while the gospel reminds us of the love of Christ, who laid down his life for us so that we might lay down ours for our brothers and sisters, the psalm shows us how he laid down his life, for it sings about his passion. So the conformity and harmony between gospel and psalm are evident.

Now the whole Christ consists of head and body. You are certainly aware of this. The head is our Savior himself, who suffered under Pontius Pilate and now, after rising from the dead, is seated at the Father's right hand. His body is the Church: not this or that local church, but the Church that extends throughout the world. It is made up not only of people alive today, for those who have gone before us belong to the Church too, and so do those who will come after us, even to the end of time. All the faithful are Christ's members, and the Church is thus made up of all who believe.

The head of the Church is enthroned in heaven, from where he rules and guides his body; and though the body is still debarred from the vision of him, it is linked to him by charity.

Since, then, the whole Christ consists of the head and his body, we must be alert to the accents of the head in all the psalms in such a way that we catch the voices of the body too. He would not have us speaking apart from him, any more than he wants to be apart from us, for he said, *Lo, I am with you even to the end of the ages* (Mt 28:20). If he is with us, he speaks in us, speaks about our concerns, and speaks through us, because we also speak in him; and only because we speak in him do we speak the truth.[1] If we attempt to speak in our own persons and of ourselves, we shall linger in lies.

Verse 1. The Jews, imitating Saul, persecuted the true David

2. The psalm sings of our Lord's passion, so let us look at the title it bears: *To the end*. The "end" is Christ.[2] Why is he called "the end"? Not because he consumes anything, but because he consummates it. To consume a thing means to destroy it; to consummate means to bring it to perfection. When we say a thing is "finished," we derive the phrase from the notion of "the end."[3] But we say it in two different senses: "the bread is finished," and "the tunic is finished." The bread is finished up, all eaten; the tunic is finished when the weaver has completed the job. The bread comes to an end in the sense of being used up, but the weaving of the tunic is ended when it has been brought to perfection.

Now Christ is the end of all our striving, because however hard we try, we are made perfect only in him and by him. Our perfection is to reach him. But when you reach him you will look for nothing further, for he is your end. When you are on a journey, your end is the place you are making for, and when you reach it, there you will stay. Similarly the end of your endeavor, of your enterprise, of your striving and your intention, is he to whom you are making your way; and when you reach him, you will desire nothing further, because you could never have anything better. Christ has set us an example of how to live our lives here, and he will give us our reward in the life to come.

3. *For the end, as a title for David himself that is not to be tampered with, when he fled into a cave from Saul's pursuit*. On referring to sacred Scripture we find that David, King of Israel (from whom the Davidic Psalter takes its name), was indeed pursued by King Saul. Many of you are familiar with the story, because you have had the Scriptures in your hands, or have listened to them. David was persecuted by Saul. But David was very moderate, and Saul very fierce, David gentle and Saul jealous, the one long-suffering and the other cruel, the one kind and the other ungrateful.

---

1. This sentence epitomizes Augustine's teaching on the psalms.
2. See Rom 10:4.
3. More obvious in Latin: *finitum* ("finished") from *finis* ("end").

David treated Saul with such leniency that when he had him in his power he laid no hand upon him, nor harmed him at all.[4]

David was given by the Lord God an opportunity to kill Saul if he chose, but he preferred to spare him. Yet not even by such kindness was Saul persuaded to give up his persecution. So we have found that in those days, when Saul was persecuting David, there was a king already repudiated pursuing one who was destined to be king in the future, and that David fled from Saul into a cave.

What has this to do with Christ? If the events of that time prefigured what was to come, we can find Christ in this story, and very clearly indeed; for I do not see how the words, *a title that is not to be tampered with*, can apply to David. There was no title written for David which Saul attempted to falsify. But we do see that in our Lord's passion a title was inscribed: *King of the Jews*, a title calculated to rebuke the effrontery of those who did not keep their hands off their king. In them Saul was present, and in Christ, David. As the gospel that derives from the apostles testifies, and as we know, as we confess, Christ was *from David's line, according to the flesh* (Rom 1:3), but only according to the flesh, for in his divinity he is far above David, above heaven and earth, above all things visible and invisible; for everything was made through him, and apart from him nothing was made.[5] Yet when he came to us he deigned to become man from the lineage of David, for the Virgin Mary, who bore Christ, was of David's line, and so Christ was born into David's tribe.

Well then, a title was inscribed: *King of the Jews*. As we have said, Saul represented the Jewish people, as David stood for Christ. And there it was, the title, *King of the Jews*. The Jews were incensed at it, for they were ashamed to acknowledge as their king someone they had the power to crucify. They did not foresee that the cross to which they nailed him would one day adorn the brows of kings. In their indignation at the title they went to the judge, Pilate, to whom they had delivered Christ for crucifixion; and they said to him, *Do not put "The King of the Jews"; put "He said, I am the King of the Jews"* (Jn 19:21). And because under the guidance of the Holy Spirit Scripture had long ago sung, *For the end, as a title that is not to be tampered with*, Pilate answered, "*What I have written, I have written.* How dare you prompt me to lie? I do not distort the truth."

How Christ, like David, hid in a cave

4. Now that we have heard what that phrase means, *a title that is not to be tampered with*, let us pass on to the next: *when David fled into a cave from Saul's pursuit*. What does that signify? The David of the Old Testament certainly did this, but we did not find in him any connection with the writing of a title; now, conversely, let us see whether flight into a cave has

---

4. See 1 S 24.
5. See Jn 1:3.

any relevance to the new David. That cave which the old David used to cover himself prefigured something. Why did he cover himself? In order to remain hidden; he did not want to be found. But what does being covered by a cave suggest? Being covered by earth. If a person takes refuge in a cave, he is covered over completely by the earth, and so cannot be seen. Jesus went about carrying earth, since the flesh he wore had been taken from the earth, and he was concealed by it so that his Godhead might not be discovered by the Jews; for if they had known it, they would never have crucified the Lord of glory.[6] How was it that they did not discover the Lord of glory? Because he had covered himself with a cave. What I mean is this: he displayed before their eyes the weakness of his flesh, but kept the majesty of his Godhead covered over by his body, as though hidden in the earth. Consequently they failed to realize that he was God, and crucified him as a man. He was not capable of dying, except in his humanity, or of being crucified, except in his humanity, or of being held prisoner, except in his humanity. He exposed the earth in him to those who sought him with evil intent, and kept his life for those who seek him in the right way. His flesh, then, was his means of fleeing from Saul into a cave. You can take the idea further, if you like, and say that the Lord fled from Saul into a cave in the sense that he underwent his passion and hid himself from the Jews even to the point of dying. The Jews unleashed their utmost savagery against him, yet they still went on thinking, until the moment of his death, that he might be set free, and prove by some miracle that he was indeed the Son of God. These events had been foretold in the Book of Wisdom: *Let us condemn him to the most shameful of deaths, for his claims will be taken care of, according to his own account. If he truly is the Son of God, he will deliver him from the hands of his adversaries* (Wis 2:20.18). Since, therefore, he was hanging on the cross and not being rescued, they concluded that he was not God's Son. They insulted him as he hung there, shaking their heads and saying, *If you are the Son of God, come down from the cross! He saved others, but he can't save himself!*[7] And as they said it, the prophecy in the Book of Wisdom came true: *So they thought, but they were mistaken, for their malice completely blinded them* (Wis 2:21). Would it have been a great feat to come down from the cross, for someone who so easily rose from the grave?

Why was it his will to suffer even to the point of death? This was another way in which he fled from Saul into a cave. A cave, you see, can be thought of as a place underground. Now it is well known to us all that his body was laid in a tomb that had been hewn out of rock; and this tomb was therefore a kind of cave, and there he took refuge from Saul. The Jews persecuted him to the very moment when he was laid in that cave. How do I prove that their persecution went on as long as that, even to his burial? Well, consider:

---

6. See 1 Cor 2:8.
7. See Mt 27:40.42.

even after he was dead, but still hanging on the cross, they wounded his body;[8] but when he had been wrapped with due care in burial cloths and placed in the cave, the Jews could inflict no further outrage on his flesh. Then the Lord arose from that cave where he had taken refuge from Saul; he arose unhurt, untouched by decay, and, while concealing himself from those impious people whom Saul had foreshadowed, he showed himself to his own members. The limbs of the Risen One were handled by those who were themselves limbs of his body, and they believed.[9] And so Saul achieved nothing.

We have spent enough time discussing the title, as the Lord graciously enabled us. Now let us listen to the psalm.

Verse 2. The whole Christ prays, and teaches us to pray

5. *Have mercy on me, O God, have mercy, for my soul trusts in you.* Christ is praying in his passion, *Have mercy on me, O God.* God is saying to God, *Have mercy on me.* He who, together with the Father, has mercy on you is crying out in you, *Have mercy on me.* Something in him that belongs to you is crying out, *Have mercy on me,* something that he took from you; for he clothed himself in flesh to set you free. Now this same flesh is pleading, *Have mercy on me, O God, have mercy*; the whole man is pleading, the man who is soul and flesh, for the Word assumed our entire humanity, the Word became a complete man. True, the evangelist expresses it by saying, *The Word was made flesh, and dwelt among us* (Jn 1:14), but you must not take this to mean that he had no human soul. This is far from the truth. In the language of Scripture, "flesh" means "human being." So Scripture says elsewhere, *All flesh will see the salvation of God* (Is 40:5; Lk 3:6). This does not mean that flesh alone will see it, and the soul will have no place, does it? Again, the Lord himself, referring to the human race, says, *As you have given him power over all flesh* (Jn 17:2). Surely he did not mean that his power extended over flesh only, and not, much more importantly, over souls? Was it not his primary reason for coming, to set souls free? So in the case of our Lord himself, the soul was there and the flesh was there; a whole man was there. This whole man was one with the Word, and the Word was one with this human being; the man and the Word together were one single human being, and the Word and the man together were one God. Let him say, then, *Have mercy on me, O God, have mercy*, and let us not take fright when we hear the voice of one who both pleads for mercy and grants it. He pleads for it precisely because he also grants it, for he became man because he is merciful. He was born not by any necessity of his condition, but to set us free from our condition of necessity. *Have mercy on me, O God, have mercy on me, for my soul trusts in you.* You hear your Teacher praying, so learn to pray. He prayed for this very reason, to

---

8. See Jn 19:34.
9. See Lk 24:39; Jn 20:27–28.

teach us to pray, just as he suffered to teach us to suffer, and rose from the dead to teach us to hope for resurrection.

6. *And beneath the shadow of your wings I will hope, until iniquity shall pass away.* This is certainly the whole Christ speaking; here is our voice too. Iniquity has not passed away yet; no indeed, iniquity is still at the boiling-point. The Lord himself indicated that in the last days iniquity will be very widespread: *with iniquity increasing mightily, the love of many will grow cold, but whoever perseveres to the end will be saved* (Mt 24:12–13). But who will persevere to the end, until iniquity has passed away? Only the one who is within Christ's body, who is among the members of Christ, and has learned from the body's head the long-suffering that perseveres. You as an individual pass away, and at once your personal temptations have passed away with you. If you have led a holy life, you go away into another life, into which other holy people have entered already. Into that life the martyrs entered, and if you become a martyr you pass into that other life too. But does this mean that because you have passed beyond this life, iniquity has gone away as well? Clearly not. Other bad people are born all the time, just as other bad people die. And just as other bad people are being born and other bad people are always dying, so too other righteous people are taking leave of us and others being born. Until the end of time there will always be iniquity causing affliction and righteousness enduring it. *And beneath the shadow of your wings I will hope, until iniquity shall pass away.* This means: "You, Lord, will protect me, so that I do not get scorched under the sun of iniquity. You will provide shade for me."

Verse 3. God is most high, yet near

7. *I will cry to God Most High.* If he is most high, how can he hear your crying? "My confidence is born from experience," the psalmist replies, "because I am praying to *God, who has dealt kindly with me.* If he dealt kindly with me before I sought him, will he not hear me now that I am crying out to him?" The Lord God dealt kindly with us by sending us our Savior Jesus Christ, to die for our misdeeds and rise for our justification.[10] And for what kind of people did God will his Son to die? For the godless. The godless were not seeking God, but God sought them. He is "most high" indeed, but in such a way that our wretchedness and our groans are not far from him, for the Lord is close to those who have bruised their hearts.[11] *I will cry to God Most High, to God who has dealt kindly with me.*

Verse 4. Prophecy fulfilled:
Christ is raised, and the Jews carry the Scriptures for us

8. *He sent from heaven and saved me.* It is quite obvious that the man Jesus, this very flesh, this very Son of God, has been saved already insofar

---

10. See Rom 4:25.
11. See Ps 33:19(34:18).

as he partakes of our nature. The Father did send from heaven and save him; the Father sent from heaven and saved him from the dead. But you need to keep in mind that the Lord also raised himself. Both truths are stated in Scripture—that the Father raised him and that he raised himself. Affirming that the Father raised Christ, the apostle says, *He was made obedient to the point of death, even death on a cross, which is why God raised him high and gave him a name above every other name* (Phil 2:8–9). You have there a statement that the Father raised and exalted his Son. Now listen to another, showing that the Son also raised up his own flesh. Using the imagery of the temple he said to the Jews, *Dismantle this temple, and in three days I will raise it up again*; and the evangelist explained to us what he meant: *He was speaking of the temple of his body* (Jn 2:19.21). But now he speaks in the person of one praying, of a human being, of a being of flesh, and he says, God *sent from heaven, and saved me*.

9. *Those who trampled on me he has consigned to disgrace.* He has reduced to disgrace those who trampled on Christ, insulted him after his death, and crucified him as a mere man because they did not understand that he was God. This has happened already, hasn't it? We are not being asked to believe in something future; we only need to observe what is already accomplished. The Jews raged against Christ, and persecuted him in their pride—but where? In the city of Jerusalem. In the stronghold of that kingdom about which they were so conceited, there they raised their arrogant heads against him. But after the Lord's passion they were uprooted, and they lost the kingdom where they had refused to acknowledge Christ as king. Consider how completely they have been consigned to disgrace: they have been scattered throughout all nations, with no stability anywhere, and nowhere any secure home.

But the Jews survive still, and for a special purpose: so that they may carry our books, to their own confusion. When we want to prove to the pagans that Christ's coming was prophesied, we produce these Scriptures. But possibly pagans obstinately opposed to the faith might have alleged that we Christians had composed them, fabricating prophecies to buttress the gospel we preach. They might have thought that we were trying to pass off our message by pretending that it had been foreshadowed in prophecy. But we can convince them of their error by pointing out that all those Scriptures which long ago spoke of Christ are the property of the Jews. Yes, the Jews recognize these very writings. We take books from our enemies to confute other enemies!

In what sort of disgrace do the Jews find themselves? A Jew carries the book which is the foundation of faith for a Christian. Jews act as book-bearers for us, like the slaves who are accustomed to walk behind their masters carrying their books, so that while the slaves sink under the weight, the masters make great strides through reading.¹² Such is the shameful position to which the Jews have been reduced, and the prophecy uttered so long ago has been fulfilled: *those who trampled on me he has consigned to disgrace.* What a disgrace it is indeed for them, brothers and sisters, that they can read this verse like blind people looking into their own mirror! In that Holy Scripture which they are carrying the Jews are reflected in the same way as a blind person's face is reflected: it is seen by others, but the blind man cannot see himself. *Those who trampled on me he has consigned to disgrace.*

Christ is mercy and truth

10. Perhaps when the psalm said, *He sent from heaven and saved me*, you wondered, "What did he send from heaven? Whom did he send from heaven? Did he send an angel to save Christ, a servant to save the Lord?" No. All the angels form part of the creation that is at Christ's service. Angels could be sent to obey, they could be sent to render services, but not to help Christ. Admittedly it is written that angels ministered to him,¹³ but not like merciful beings ministering to one in need: rather as subjects to the Omnipotent. What, then, did he *send from heaven* to save me? In the next line we hear what he sent from heaven: *He sent his mercy and his truth.* To what purpose? *And he rescued my soul from amid the lion-cubs.* The psalm says, *He sent* from heaven *his mercy and his truth*; and Christ himself declared, *I am the truth* (Jn 14:6). Truth was sent here to rescue my soul from amid the lion-cubs, and mercy too was sent. So we find that Christ is both mercy and truth: mercy that suffers with us, and truth that requites us. This is connected with what I said a moment ago about Christ raising himself from the dead. If Truth raised Christ, and if Truth delivered Christ's soul from amid the lion-cubs, then as he was merciful in dying for us, so was he true in rising to justify us. He had said that he would rise again, and Truth cannot lie. Because he was Truth and spoke truly, he displayed real scars, as he had received real wounds. The disciples touched these scars, handled them and assured themselves of their reality. The one who put his fingers into the pierced side exclaimed, *My Lord and my God!* (Jn 20:28), confessing that Christ had in mercy died for him, and in truth had risen and shown himself to him.

He sent from heaven *his mercy and his truth, and rescued my soul from amid the lion-cubs.* Who are these lion-cubs? They are the little people who were cruelly deceived and wickedly seduced by the Jewish leaders;¹⁴ the

---

12. *Illi portando deficiant, illi legendo proficiant.* Possibly the image of the *paedagogus* referred to in Gal 3:24 is also in Augustine's mind. Compare his *Exposition of Psalm* 40, 14. A *librarius* (his word here) was more often either a copyist, scribe, secretary, or bookseller.
13. See Mt 4:11; Mk 1:13; Lk 22:43.
14. Variant: "by the chief priests."

leaders were lions, and the common people lion-cubs. But they all roared, and all killed. In the succeeding verses of the psalm we shall hear about the slaughter they wrought.

Verse 5. Christ's willing sleep; Jewish responsibility

11. *He rescued my soul from amid the lion-cubs*, says the psalm. Why do you say, *He rescued my soul*? What had you endured, that you needed to be rescued? *Though disturbed, I lay down to sleep*. This is Christ's way of indicating his death. We read that the Old Testament David fled into a cave, but not that he slept in it; so one David was in the cave, but it is the other David who says here, *Though disturbed, I lay down to sleep*. It must be a special kind of disturbance that is meant, for it seems he was not subject to disturbance, even though they were disturbing him. He described himself as "disturbed" with reference only to the belief of his furious enemies, not from any consciousness of having yielded to them. They thought they had disturbed him, they thought they had won; but he, *though disturbed, lay down to sleep*. This "disturbed" man was so placid that he slept when he wanted to. No one who is genuinely disturbed can sleep. All who suffer disturbance are either awakened from sleep, or prevented from sinking into it. Yet this man was "disturbed," and fell asleep. Great was the humility of this "disturbed" man, and great the power of the sleeper. What power enabled him to sleep? That power of which he testified, *I have the power to lay down my life, and I have the power to take it up again. No one takes it away from me; but I lay it down of my own accord, that I may take it up again* (Jn 10:18.17). They disturbed him, but he lay down to sleep.

In this respect Adam was a type of Christ. God sent a deep sleep upon Adam, in order to fashion a wife for him from his side.[15] Was God unable to make a wife for the first man by taking her from his side while he was awake? Surely not. Or was it that God wanted Adam to be asleep so that he would not feel it when one of his ribs was pulled out? But who sleeps so soundly as not to be aroused if a bone is torn out? If God had power to remove a rib from a sleeping man without causing pain, he could have done so equally well when the man was awake. So why did he want to do it while Adam slept? Because in Christ's case, a bride was made for him as he slept on the cross, and made from his side. With a lance his side was struck as he hung there, and out flowed the sacraments of the Church.[16]

Though disturbed, I lay down to sleep, he says. He made the same point in another psalm, where he said, *I rested and fell asleep*; he there indicated his power. He could perfectly well have said, *I slept*, without the personal pronoun, as he does in our present psalm; so why did he say, *I*

---

15. See Gn 2:21.
16. See Jn 19:34. This imagery became commonplace in the Fathers, and was further developed in the middle ages with reference to the devotion to the Sacred Heart; see especially Bonaventure, *Lignum Vitae* 29–30.

slept, with the emphatic pronoun included?[17] Clearly he meant to imply, "I slept because I chose to do so. They did not put me to sleep by force, against my will. I slept voluntarily in accordance with my claim *I have the power to lay down my life, and I have the power to take it up again.*" That is why he goes on to say, in the earlier psalm, *I rested and fell asleep, and I arose because the Lord will uphold me* (Ps 3:6(5)).

12. *Though disturbed, I lay down to sleep.* What was disturbing him? Who were causing the disturbance? Let us see how he brands the Jews with the stigma of a bad conscience, though they meant to hold themselves not guilty of killing the Lord. Their motive in delivering him to the judge was to make it look as though they had not killed him themselves, as the gospel makes plain. Pilate, who sat as judge at the time, had said to them, *Take him, and try him according to your own law*; but they replied, *It is not lawful for us to put anyone to death* (Jn 18:31). So it was unlawful for you to kill anyone, but lawful to hand him over to be killed? Who is really killing him, anyway? The man who yielded on hearing the uproar, or the one who by raising the uproar extorted the death sentence? Let the Lord give his own evidence as to who killed him. Was it Pilate, who killed him reluctantly? Because he was so unwilling he even had Jesus scourged, clothed him in a ridiculous garment, and after the scourging brought him out into full view before them, in the hope that they would be sated by the punishment of flogging and not insist on his being put to death. For the same reason, when he saw that they were not relenting, he went so far as to wash his hands, as we read in the gospel, and protested, *I am innocent of the blood of this just man* (Mt 27:24). Make up your mind whether he was truly innocent, even though he only gave way in response to their clamor. But even if he was not, much more guilty were they who tried to force him by their shouting to kill Christ.

Let us question the Lord himself and listen to what he has to say, and to whom he attributed his death. He has told us, *Though disturbed, I lay down to sleep.* So let us press him further. If you were disturbed, yet lay down to sleep, who persecuted you? Who put you to death? Was it Pilate, who handed you over to his soldiers to hang you up on the tree and fasten you with nails? No? Listen, he says, and I will tell you who it was: simply *human beings*.[18] Those, he tells us, those are the persecutors I had to endure. But how did they put him to death, if they carried no weapon? They unsheathed no sword, launched no frontal attack on him; so how did

---

17. Some paraphrase has been used in the translation to convey the contrast Augustine is pointing out between *dormivi* in the Psalm he is commenting on, and *ego dormivi* in Psalm 3.
18. *Filii hominum*, literally "sons of men." In other contexts, such as *Exposition of Psalm* 8, 10–11 and *Exposition of Psalm* 35, 12–14, Augustine makes a special point of this expression, associating it with Christ's own title, "Son of Man." But in the present context he does not insist on this.

they kill him? *Their teeth are weapons and arrows, their tongue a sharp sword.* Ignore the weaponless hands and watch the armed mouth, for that is where the sword is wielded that slew Christ; so too from Christ's own mouth proceeded the sword with which the Jews would in their turn be slain. He has a sharp, two-edged sword[19] and when he rose from the dead he smote them, and severed from their company those he meant to make his faithful followers. They had an evil sword, he a good sword; they had wicked arrows, he good arrows; for truly he does have his store of good arrows, which are his good words. He shoots them into every believing heart, that he may win its love. Quite different are their arrows, and their sword. *The teeth of human beings are weapons and arrows, their tongue a sharp sword.* The tongue of these people is a sharp sword,[20] and their teeth are offensive weapons and arrows. When did they strike at him? When they shouted, *Crucify, crucify!* (Jn 19:6).

Verse 6. Christ's glory pervades the earth

13. And what did they achieve against you, Lord? Let the prophet dance for joy now. All the preceding verses were spoken by the Lord—and by the prophet, of course, but only because the Lord was speaking in him. And equally, now that the prophet begins to speak as from himself, the Lord still speaks through him, inasmuch as the Lord dictates to him the truth he speaks. You have good reason, then, brothers and sisters, to listen to the prophet when he speaks in his own name. Moved by the Spirit,[21] this prophet beheld the Lord humiliated, buffeted, scourged, punched, slapped, spat on, crowned with thorns and hung on the tree. He beheld the executioners behaving savagely and Christ enduring it; he saw in the Spirit[22] them triumphing and him apparently defeated. He saw too that after all his humiliation and their savagery Christ rose again, and that all the furious Jews had done had come to nothing. The prophet was transported with joy, as though he saw it all happening, and he cried, "*Be lifted up above the heavens, O God.* A man you were on the cross, but God above the heavens. Let them remain on earth to rant, but you be in heaven to judge." Where are they who rampaged? Where are those teeth of theirs, teeth that were *weapons and arrows*? Is it not true of them that *the wounds they inflict are like those from the arrows of mere children?* (Ps 63:8(64:7)) This is what a psalm says of them elsewhere, intending to suggest how futile was their fury, and how uselessly they had worked themselves into their rage. *The wounds they inflicted were like those from the arrows of mere children*, for they were powerless against Christ, who was crucified for an hour or two, but then rose again and is seated in heaven. How do young children

---

19. See Rv 1:16.
20. *Machaera*, a single-edged sword. In the lines above he has been using *gladius*.
21. Or "in spirit."
22. Or "in spirit."

fashion arrows for themselves? Out of reeds. And what sort of arrows are they, what force do they have? What kind of bow launches them? Is that a real shot? Does it wound anyone?

Be lifted up above the heavens, O God, and may your glory pervade the whole earth. Why, O God, are you exalted above the heavens? Think about this, brothers and sisters: we do not see him as God exalted above the heavens, but we believe him to be so, whereas we not only believe that his glory spreads over the earth, for we see that it does. I put it to you, then: consider what madness afflicts the heretics who have severed themselves from the bonded unity of Christ's Church. Clinging to a part and thereby losing the whole, they refuse to be in communion with the entire world, where Christ's glory is diffused. We Catholics, on the contrary, are present all over the earth, because we are in communion with the whole of it, wherever Christ's glory is deployed. We see now that what was sung in the psalm has been perfectly realized. Our God has been exalted above the heavens, and his glory shines over all the earth. How mad you are, you heretic! What you cannot see, you believe, in company with me; but what you can see, you deny. Along with me you believe Christ to be exalted above the heavens, though we cannot see this; yet you deny that his glory irradiates the whole earth, which we do see! *Be lifted up above the heavens, O God, and may your glory pervade the whole earth.*

Verse 7. Sinners always entrap themselves

14. Now the psalm takes up the Lord's own words again. The Lord himself begins to teach us, as though he were speaking directly to us, even while the psalmist goes on joyfully shouting, *Be lifted up above the heavens, O God, and may your glory pervade the whole earth!* Yes, the Lord in person encourages us, as though demanding of us, "What were they able to effect against me, those persecutors of mine?" But why is he talking to us? Because the persecutors attack us in the same way. But though they have made similar attempts on us, they achieve nothing. Consider, then, beloved,[23] how the Lord addresses us and spurs us on by his own example. *They set a snare*[24] *for my feet, and bent my soul down.* They almost thought to dethrone him from heaven, and thrust him into the depths: *they dug a pit in front of me, but fell into it themselves.* Am I the one they harmed, or did they harm themselves? See him exalted above the heavens as God, and see his glory shining over all the earth. Christ's kingdom is plain to see, but where is the kingdom of the Jews? What they ought not to have done, they did; now the justice they ought to suffer is done to them. They *dug a pit, and fell into it themselves.* Their persecution of Christ did him no ultimate harm, but ultimately harmed them.

---

23. *Caritas vestra.*
24. Literally "mousetrap."

Do not suppose that this happened to them alone, brothers and sisters. Anyone at all who digs a pit for a brother or sister must of necessity fall into it. Give me your close attention now, and look at the matter with Christian eyes. Do not be taken in by appearances. Perhaps when I say this, someone comes into your mind, someone who tried to trick a brother or sister, and meant to contrive a hidden snare. He laid it, it worked, and his brother fell into the trap. The victim was despoiled and wronged, perhaps unjustly imprisoned through perjured testimony or some malicious accusation. It looks as though this unhappy person is the oppressed and the other the oppressor, as though he is conquered and the other his conqueror. So you will think we are talking nonsense when we say that whoever has dug a pit for his brother or sister will fall into it himself. But I have a question to put to you as Christians, because as Christians you can read the answer from our own experience. The pagans persecuted the martyrs. The martyrs were arrested, bound, thrown into prison, exposed to the beasts. Others were executed with the sword, others again burnt to death. Now, does this mean that the persecutors were victorious, and the martyrs vanquished? Far from it! Look hard, and you will see the glory of the martyrs before God; look for the pit that the pagans dug, and you will find it in their torn consciences, for that is where the hole gapes, where the godless come to grief—in their bad consciences. Can you suppose that someone who has lost the light of Christ and been struck blind has not fallen into a pit? If such a one had not fallen into it he would see where he is putting his feet. But in fact he does not know where he is going. If someone is on his way, and then falls into a hole, he has lost his way. So you see, all evildoers lose their way, and become entangled in their crimes.

All the same, perhaps your enemy has thrown you into a robber's clutches, or into the hands of some villain, of some judge he has bribed; you are in a tight spot. But he is delighted; he is crowing over you. Do not look at the case with pagan eyes. I have said this already, and say it again: do not look at it as a pagan would, but with Christian eyes. You see him jumping for joy, yes, and his very jumping is the trap that will get him. Better the grief of someone suffering wrong than the joy of someone doing wrong. The joy of someone who does wrong is itself a snare, and anyone who falls into it loses the power of sight. Are you sorry for yourself because you have lost your coat, and not sorry for the person who has lost integrity?[25] Which of you has sustained the graver loss? He kills, and you are killed; does that mean that he is alive, and you are dead? Heaven forbid! Where is your faith, your Christian faith?[26] Where are those who die—for a while? Let them hearken to their Lord: *Any who believe in me, though they die, shall yet live* (Jn 11:25). It follows that one who does not believe, though

---

25. *Fidem*; but he means "good faith," "honesty."
26. Or perhaps, "What becomes of Christians who keep faith?"

he lives, is dead. *They dug a pit in front of me, and fell into it themselves.* This is what happens to all bad people, unavoidably.

Verse 8. The prepared heart

15. With hearts prepared, good people embrace the will of God with patience, and in patience they even glory in their sufferings, crying, *My heart is ready, O God, my heart is ready. I will sing and play the psaltery.* What has my enemy achieved against me? He prepared a trap, but my heart was prepared too. He has prepared a snare to cheat me, and shall I not prepare my heart to endure it steadfastly? He has prepared a trap to afflict me; shall I not prepare my heart to bear it? He will fall into it himself, but I will sing and play the psaltery. Listen to how fully prepared the apostle's heart was as he imitated his Lord: *We even glory in our sufferings,* he says, *knowing that suffering fosters endurance, and endurance constancy, and constancy hope; but hope does not disappoint us, because the love of God has been poured out into our hearts through the Holy Spirit who has been given us* (Rom 5:3–5). Paul was beset by harsh conditions, in chains, in prison, beaten, enduring hunger and thirst, cold and in need of clothing, desolate amid all his labors and afflictions, yet he kept saying, *We glory in our sufferings.* How could he say it? Only because his heart was prepared. Accordingly he sang and played psalms: *My heart is ready, O God, my heart is ready. I will sing and play the psaltery.*

Verse 9. One risen flesh, two melodies

16. *Arise, O my glory!* The man who fled from Saul into a cave is speaking. *Arise, O my glory!* May Jesus be glorified after his passion. *Arise, psaltery and lyre!* What is he calling out to, what does he command to arise? I find two instruments mentioned here, yet I perceive Christ's body to be one. It was one single flesh that rose; yet in a sense two instruments did rise. The psaltery is one kind of musical instrument, the lyre another.[27] Whatever is made to accompany singing, and is a bodily object a singer can use, is called a musical instrument.[28] But these instruments differ from each other; and insofar as the Lord enables me, I want to suggest to you how psaltery and lyre differ, why they are distinct, and why the summons, *Arise!* is addressed to both.[29] We have already pointed out that the Lord's

---

27. Some liberty has been taken in the translation here. Augustine refers to both psaltery and lyre as types of "organ," and goes on to say that it is not only the large instrument inflated with bellows that can be called an "organ," but any other musical instrument too. Since this is alien to our usage, a phrase has been omitted.
28. *Organum.* The reference to "a bodily object" prepares the following development on the flesh of Christ.
29. The verb, "arise," is singular throughout, even when psaltery and lyre are jointly addressed; the point is important for Augustine's interpretation.

flesh arose single and undivided, yet two instruments are addressed: *Arise, psaltery and lyre!* The psaltery, as you know, is an instrument which is held in the hands of the player. It has strings stretched across it. But the wooden, concave sounding-chamber which lends resonance to the strings, the vaulted piece which resounds to the touch because it is filled with air, is in a psaltery located in the upper part. A lyre, on the contrary, has its concave, wooden sounding-chamber at the bottom.[30] This means that in a psaltery the strings derive their resonance from above, whereas in the lyre they derive it from the lower part. This is the difference between a psaltery and a lyre.

What, then, do these instruments symbolize for us? The Lord Christ, our God, arouses both his psaltery and his lyre, and prophesies, *I will arise at dawn.* You do not need to be told that this is a reference to our Lord's resurrection. We have read about it in the gospel; notice this allusion to the time at which he rose. How long was Christ being sought[31] through the shadows? He shone forth; let him be acknowledged; he arose at dawn. But still, what is the psaltery? What is the lyre? The Lord used his flesh for two kinds of operations: miracles and sufferings. The miracles came from above, the sufferings from below. The miracles he performed were divine, but he worked them through his body, he wrought them through his flesh. So when the flesh performs divine works, it is a psaltery; but when the flesh suffers human pain it is a lyre. Let the psaltery give forth its melody: let the blind see the light of day, the deaf hear, the paralytics feel their muscles toned up, the lame walk, the sick spring from their beds, the dead arise. All this is the sound of the psaltery. But the lyre must give its voice too: let Christ hunger, thirst, sleep, and be arrested, scourged, mocked, crucified, and buried. In his flesh you hear some music sounding from above, and some from below; yet it was one flesh only that arose, and in that one flesh we catch the notes of both psaltery and lyre. These two types of action fill the gospel. And so is he preached among the nations, for both the miracles and the sufferings of the Lord are proclaimed.

Verses 10–12. Mercy as high as heaven, truth down to the clouds

17. Both psaltery and lyre arose[32] at dawn, and now give praise to the Lord. What does the psalm say next? *I will praise you among the peoples, Lord, and sing psalms to you among the Gentiles; for your mercy is magnified even to the heavens, and your truth reaches to the clouds.* The heavens are above the clouds, and the clouds below the heavens, yet the clouds

---

30. This difference was a favorite theme for Augustine. Compare his *Exposition 2 of Psalm* 32, 5; *Exposition of Psalm* 42, 5; *Exposition 2 of Psalm* 70, 11; *Exposition of Psalm* 80, 5.
31. So the codices. The editors of the CCL text change the indicative to a subjunctive: "How long should Christ be sought...?"
32. Singlar verb.

belong to that region of the sky which is quite near to us. They thicken at that height which is so close to us that sometimes the clouds envelop our mountains. The higher region of heaven is above this; there is the home of Angels, Thrones, Sovereignties, Authorities, and Powers.[33] In view of this it would seem that the psalm ought to have said, "Your truth is magnified even to the heavens, and your mercy reaches down to the clouds." Yes, surely it should have put it that way round? In heaven the angels praise God, contemplating the very form of truth in totally unclouded vision, with no trace of falsehood to distort it. They see him, love him, praise him, and never tire. There is the place of truth. But our miserable state here is the appropriate place for mercy, for it is to the miserable that mercy must be shown. There is no need for it above, where no one is miserable. I make this point to explain why I suggested that it would have been more fitting to say, "Your truth is magnified even to the heavens, and your mercy reaches down to the clouds."

But we understand "clouds" to be the preachers of truth, mere mortals carrying this murky flesh, we might say, but clouds nonetheless from which the Lord flashes the lightning of his miracles and thunders his commandments. Moreover these are the clouds Isaiah mentions when, speaking in the Lord's name, he rebukes a wicked, barren, thorn-choked vineyard, threatening, *I will forbid my clouds to send rain upon it* (Is 5:6); which is to say, "I will give orders to my apostles to abandon the Jews and offer them the gospel no more, but to evangelize in the good soil of the gentiles, which will produce not thorns, but grapes." We know that those who preach the truth—the prophets, the apostles, and all who duly offer the word of truth—are God's clouds. There is light concealed within them, just as the clouds have an inner luminosity whence they produce lightning. Mortal preachers are clouds.

What, then, is the meaning of this verse, Lord: *your mercy is magnified even to the heavens, and your truth to the clouds*? Truth resides predominantly in the angels, but you have granted it to humans too, and brought it down as far as the clouds. Angels, on the contrary,[34] do not seem to need mercy. But you deal mercifully with miserable mortals; you grant them mercy by giving them a share in the resurrection, and so you make them equal to the angels. This is how your mercy reaches even up to the heavens.

Glory be to our Lord, and to his mercy, and to his truth, because in his mercy he has not ceased to bless us through his grace, nor yet deprived us of his truth. Truth first came to us clad in flesh, and through his flesh healed the inner eye of our hearts, so that we might one day have the strength to see him face to face.[35]

---

33. See Col 1:16.
34. *Rursus*, with all the codices; but the editors of the CCL text read *sursum*, "above."
35. See 1 Cor 13:12.

Let us give thanks to him, and in harmony with the psalm say these last lines, which occurred earlier as well: *Be lifted up above the heavens, O God, and may your glory pervade the whole earth.* The prophet said that to God many, many years ago; we see now that it has come true, so let us say it with him.

Exposition of Psalm 138

Synopsis

The reader recited the wrong Psalm, but we'll take that as a sign of God's will. Since we must sweat for our bread, let's be sure it's Christ's bread we're sweating for. Christ often speaks through the prophets in his own person as ruler, bridegroom, redeemer, and head. But the head has a body; that's who we are, the Church, the whole Christ, two in one flesh, one "Man" (including women), who speaks with a single voice that includes us (1–2).

Christ the human being was tested and known by God (3). He sat down and rose up in death and resurrection. His body also speaks here, for it sits in the confession of sin and rises in justification by grace (4). *You have understood my thought from afar* recalls the story of the prodigal son, whose return home was seen by his father from far away. God sees us from afar. The Church confesses to God without dissimulation but nevertheless still feels his punishing hand (5–7).

The confession, *Your knowledge is too wonderful for me*, recalls the mysterious story of Moses asking to see God. Using words understandable to human beings, God invited Moses to see God's "back" as the Lord "passed by." This is the "passover" of Christ's human suffering. The hand conspicuously placed over Moses' face prophesied Jewish blindness to Christ. But not all were blind, for some became believers (8). They took up "wings" that carried them from God's displeasure to God's welcome: the "wings" of God's double commandment to love God and neighbor. Christ helped us to re-grow "wings" of love so that we might fly where God's hand might lead us (9–13).

With Christ's descent to earth, even human life's darkness became instructive. God was like the woman of the parable who searched for a lost coin: we are that coin, for his image is etched upon us (14). All worldly woe is medicinal and educational; bitterness mingled with pleasures gives perspective regarding the "day" of good fortune and the "night" of adversity. God wants us to achieve detached indifference (15–16). Job is a prime model of this because God changed his inner desires that once belonged to the old city of sin, Babylon (17–19).

The "bone" of Christ's body is its inner strength before God under persecution (20). But Christ speaks also for weaker members of his body. Peter was "imperfect" when he denied the Lord; thus, when the Lord spoke in the Psalm of *my imperfection*, he included "my Peter." Scripture says, *All are written in your book*—not only the perfect but also the imperfect. Peter went wrong by rebuking the Lord for talk of his passion, and all the disciples went wrong by fleeing his suffering. Yet later they all became "firm bone" in Christ's body after the resurrection (21–23), and through them a great many people believe, *more numerous than grains of sand*. But because the Church is a mixed body of good and bad people, whole groups have defected from Christ's unity because the mixture offends their sense of purity (24–26). The Church indignantly protests that it too hates sin as it reserves judgment on God's enemies until the end of time; for now it obeys the Lord's command, *Love your enemies*. Thus the Psalmist's *perfect hatred* hates the sin but loves the sinner (27–28). Meanwhile the Church sighs in patience on its pilgrimage to the heavenly Jerusalem. It prays, *Lead me in the eternal way*, that is, lead me in Christ, *the way, the truth, and the life* (29–30). This Psalm's great mysteries have been more sweetly opened for being so obscure! God mixed a marvelous love-potion for us! You learned what you didn't know, and renewed the knowledge that you already had (31).

Augustine's Text of Psalm 138

(1) To the end, a Psalm of David.

(2) O Lord, you have tested me and you know me.
   You know my sitting down and my rising up.

(3) You have understood my thoughts from afar;
   You have traced my path and my boundary.

(4) You have foreseen all my ways, for there is no guile on my tongue.

(5) Now, Lord, you know everything about me, most recent things and things of long ago;
   You fashioned me, and you have laid your hand upon me.

(6) Your knowledge is too wonderful for me;
   Mighty it is, beyond my reach.

(7) Whither shall I go from your spirit,
   And whither flee from your face?

(8) If I mount to heaven, you are there;
   If I sink down to hell, even there you are present.

(9) If I take once more the wings that will carry me straightforward,
And dwell at the uttermost parts of the sea,
(10) Even there your hand will lead me, your right hand bring me through.
(11) I said, perhaps the darkness will overwhelm me;
Yet the very night was my illumination in my delight,
(12) For the darkness will not be further darkened by you, Lord.
And night will be as bright as the day;
Its darkness is all one with its light.
(13) For you have taken possession of my inmost parts;
O Lord, you took me to yourself even from the womb of my mother.
(14) I will confess to you, O Lord, for you have revealed yourself as wonderful and terrible.
Wonderful are your works, and my soul knows it.
(15) My bone is not hidden from you, for it was you who created it in that secret place,
As you also formed my nature in the lower regions of the earth.
(16) Your eyes beheld my imperfection,
And in your book all shall be written.
They will go wrong concerning the day, and not one of them will be there.
(17) But your friends have become for me exceedingly honorable, O God;
Their preeminence has been most firmly established.
(18) I will count them, and they will be more numerous than grains of sand.
I have risen, and I am still with you.
(19) If you slay sinners, O God, then, men of blood, depart from me.
(20) Because you will say in your thoughts,
They will capture their cities in vain.
(21) Do I not hate those who hate you, O Lord?
Have I not been consumed with indignation over your enemies?
(22) With a perfect hatred I have hated them;
They have become foes to me.
(23) Test me, O God, and know my heart;
Examine me, and take cognizance of my ways,
(24) And see if there is any way of sin in me,
And lead me in the eternal way.

Exposition

A Sermon to the People

A mistake has been made by the reader, but we can profit from it

1. We had prepared a short psalm for our consideration today[1] and indicated to the reader that this was the psalm to be recited. But at the last minute he apparently became flustered and read this one instead. We have deemed it preferable to see in the reader's mistake a sign of the will of God and to follow that rather than to do our own will by sticking to our original plan. If, therefore, it turns out that we have detained you for a long time on account of the length of this psalm, you must not blame us but believe that God has willed us to work in such a way as to be fruitful. There was good reason for the punishment imposed on us at the time of the first sin: that we must eat our bread in the sweat of our brow.[2] Only be sure that what you eat is really bread. It is true bread if it is Christ; as he said of himself, *I am the living bread which has come down from heaven* (Jn 6:51). We find him manifested in the gospel; let us look for him also in the prophets. The people over whose hearts a veil still lies[3] cannot see him there, but you heard something about that veil yesterday, beloved. For us the situation has changed, because the evening sacrifice of the Lord's cross tore the veil apart, laying bare the secret recesses of the temple.[4] Whenever Christ is preached to us there is bread for us to eat, even though it be at the cost of labor and sweat.

Christ and the Church, head and members, two in one flesh and one voice

2. Now our Lord Jesus Christ sometimes speaks through the prophets in his identity as our head, for he is Christ, our savior. He is seated at the right hand of the Father,[5] but for our sake he was also born of the Virgin and suffered under Pontius Pilate. You know how he suffered: his innocent blood was poured out as our ransom. He redeemed us, guilty prisoners that we were in the devil's clutches, and forgave us our transgressions, using his own blood, our ransom price, to blot out the record of our debt.[6] He is the ruler, the bridegroom, and the redeemer of the Church, and he is our head.

Now, if he is the head, obviously he must have a body. His body is holy Church, and she, to whom the apostle says, *You are Christ's body, and his members* (1 Cor 12:27), is also his bride. The whole Christ, head and body

---

1. Possibly Psalm 137(138); see the note at section 18 below.
2. See Gn 3:19.
3. See 2 Cor 3:15.
4. See Mt 27:51.
5. See Mk 16:19.
6. See Col 2:13–14.

together, constitute a perfect man.[7] Women are included in this, for woman was formed from man and belongs with him. Of the first marriage it was written, *They will be two in one flesh* (Gn 2:24), and the apostle interprets this saying in the light of the mystery, for the statement was made about those two original humans only because in them the marriage of Christ and the Church was prefigured. This is how the apostle explains it: *They will be two in one flesh. This is a great mystery, but I am referring it to Christ and the Church* (Eph 5:31–32). He tells us elsewhere that Adam foreshadowed Christ: *Adam was a type of the one who was to come* (Rom 5:14). And, as Adam was a type of Christ, so too was the creation of Eve from the sleeping Adam a prefiguration of the creation of the Church from the side of the Lord as he slept, for as he suffered and died on the cross and was struck by a lance, the sacraments which formed the Church flowed forth from him.[8] By Christ's sleeping we are to understand his passion. This image is used in another psalm, which says in his name, *I rested, and fell asleep, and I arose because the Lord will uphold me* (Ps 3:6(5)). As Eve came from the side of the sleeping Adam, so the Church was born from the side of the suffering Christ.

As you know, our Lord Jesus Christ speaks through the prophets sometimes with his own voice and at other times with ours, because he makes himself one with us; as Scripture says, *They will be two in one flesh* (Gn 2:24). Indeed, the Lord referred to this himself when, speaking about marriage in the gospel, he emphasized, *So they are two no longer, but one flesh* (Mt 19:6). One flesh, because Christ took flesh from our mortal stock, but not one Godhead, because he is the creator and we are creatures. Yet because of our union with him, whatever the Lord says in virtue of the fleshly nature he assumed can be taken as said both by the head who has now ascended into heaven and by the members who still struggle along on their earthly pilgrimage. When Saul was persecuting Christ's earthly members, Christ cried out from heaven in the person of those suffering members, *Saul, Saul, why are you persecuting me?* (Acts 9:4)

Let us now listen to the Lord Jesus Christ speaking in our psalm's prophetic words and remember that, though the psalms were sung long before the Lord was born from Mary, they were not sung before he was the Lord. From the beginning of time he is the creator of all that is, but at a certain point in time he was born from a creature. Let us believe in his Godhead and understand, to the best of our ability, that he is equal to the Father. But that divine person, equal to the Father, became a sharer in our mortality, a mortality that belonged not to him but to us, so that we might share the divine nature that belongs not to us but to him.

---

7. *Vir.*
8. See Jn 19:34.

Verses 1–2. The form of God and the form of a servant; death and resurrection

3. *O Lord, you have tested me and you know me.* It is quite possible for the Lord Jesus Christ himself to say this: even he can rightly say *Lord* to the Father. His Father would not be his Lord had he not graciously willed to be born according to the flesh. In his divine nature God is his Father; in his humanity God is his Lord. Shall I tell you to whom God stands as Father? To the Son who is his equal. So the apostle says, *Being in the form of God he deemed it no robbery to be God's equal* (Phil 2:6). God is Father to Christ in this coequal *form*, Father to his only-begotten Son who is born from his own substance. But the only-begotten Son became a participant in our mortality, as I have reminded you, in order that we might be created anew and be made participants in his divinity, being restored to eternal life. After saying of him, *Being in the form of God he deemed it no robbery to be God's equal*, what else does the apostle say? *Yet he emptied himself and took on the form of a slave; and, bearing the human likeness, he was revealed as man* (Phil 2:7). In the form of God he is equal to the Father, but he took the form of a servant whereby he is less than the Father. He states both these truths in the gospel. *I and the Father are one* (Jn 10:30), he says, and also, *the Father is greater than I* (Jn 14:28). He can say, *I and the Father are one*, when he speaks in the form of God, and *the Father is greater than I*, when he speaks from his servile nature. God is therefore both his Father and his Lord: Father to him in his divine nature and Lord to him as servant. Let him say, then, *O Lord, you have tested me and you know me*, and let us not be surprised or shocked to hear the only-begotten Son of God saying this.

You have tested me and you know me. This does not mean that God did not know him already; it means that he made him known to others through the testing. *You have tested me*, he acknowledges, *and you know me*.

4. *You know my sitting down and my rising up.* What is this sitting? And this rising up? To sit is to humble oneself. Thus the Lord sat down in his passion and rose up in his resurrection. *You know this*, he says to God: you willed it, you approved it, it was done according to your purpose.

Alternatively, you may prefer to hear the voice of the body speaking in these words of its head. In this case we ourselves can say, *You know my sitting down and my rising up.* We sit down when we humble ourselves in repentance, and we rise up when our sins have been forgiven, for then we rise up toward the hope of eternal life. This is why another psalm advises, *Rise up after sitting down, you who eat the bread of sorrow* (Ps 126(127):2). In yet another psalm penitents are eating the bread of sorrow when they sing, *My tears have been bread to me day and night* (Ps 41:4(42:3)). What does the admonition mean, then, *Rise up after sitting down*? Take care that you are not exalted unless you have first been humbled. Plenty of people aspire to rise up before they have sat down: they want to be thought holy before they have confessed that they are sinners.

You can take the verse either way, then. If you hear in it the head speaking in his own name, the words, *You know my sitting down and my rising up,* will mean "my passion and my resurrection." If you prefer to hear the body speaking, the same words will mean, "In your sight I have both confessed my sins and been justified by your grace."

Verses 3–4. The prodigal son seems to be speaking here

5. *You have understood my thoughts from afar; you have traced my path and my boundary, and foreseen all my ways.* What do the words *from afar* suggest? While I am still on pilgrimage, before I reach my homeland, my mind is already an open book to you. Refer this to the younger son in the parable, for he too became part of Christ's body. He represents the Church gathered from the gentiles, this younger son who had departed for a distant country. *A certain man, the head of a family, had two sons.*[9] The elder did not go far away; he used to work on the estate, and he represents the holy people of the Old Testament who carried out the duties imposed by the law and kept its commandments. But the rest of the human race had strayed away into the worship of idols, which was like wandering off into a far country. For what is more distant from him who made you than an artifact that you made for yourself? So this younger son set off for a far-off region, taking his money with him, and, as we know from the gospel, he squandered it by reckless living in the company of prostitutes. Then he began to feel hungry, and he applied to a leading citizen in the district, who gave him a job feeding pigs. He longed to satisfy his hunger with the pods thrown to the pigs, but he could not. Laboring, miserable, ground down by want, he remembered his father and wanted to go home. *I will rise up and return to my father* (Lk 15:18), he resolved. *I will rise up,* he said, for he had been sitting. Catch the sound of his voice in the words of the psalm, *You know my sitting down and my rising up.* I sat down in my poverty, I rose up by longing for your bread. *You have understood my thoughts from afar* for, although I had wandered far off, is there any place where you are not present, you whom I had abandoned? *You have understood my thoughts from afar*: this is why the Lord says in the gospel, *While he was still on his way his father ran to meet him* (Lk 15:20), for he had understood the boy's thoughts even when he was far away. *You have traced my path and my boundary.* He mentions his *path,* and what path can he mean except the bad path he had taken in abandoning his father—as though he could ever be hidden from the eyes of the one who would see justice done?

But we could understand it in another way. Would he ever have been crushed by poverty, or set to feed pigs, if his father had not willed to chastise him while he was far off in order to welcome him when he came

---

9. See Lk 15:11–32.

back? He was caught like a fugitive, pursued by the righteous punishment of God. Wherever we flee, however far we may have gone, God punishes our willfulness. Like a recaptured fugitive the errant son declares, *You have traced my path and my boundary.* What does *my path* mean? The way on which I first set out. And what is *my boundary*? The very limit of my wandering. *You have traced my path and my boundary.* The most distant place I reached was not too far away for you to see; I had traveled many miles, but you were there. *You have traced my path and my boundary.*

6. *You have foreseen all my ways.* Notice that he says not "seen" but *foreseen.*

Before I went along those ways, before ever I began to walk in them, you foresaw them, and you allowed me to weary myself in my own ways so that, when I could endure the weariness no longer, I would return to your ways.

For there is no guile on my tongue. Why did he say that? "See, Lord, I am making this confession to you: I went away from you, in whose company all was well with me; and when I was away from you everything went badly. But this was for my good, for, if I had been happy without you, perhaps I would never have wanted to return." This is Christ's body speaking, confessing its sins, and justified not of itself but by his grace. Therefore it can say, *There is no guile on my tongue.*

Verses 5–6. God's mysterious wisdom in blinding part of Israel, with a view to ultimate mercy

7. *Now, Lord, you know everything about me, most recent things and things of long ago.* You know all about my most recent plight, when I was reduced to feeding pigs, and you know my ancient sin, when I demanded from you my share of your wealth. My ancient deeds were the root of my most recent woes. With our ancient sin we fell, and we suffered our later punishment when we were born into this wearisome, perilous, mortal life. Please God this may be our final punishment! It will be, provided we are now willing to return to him,, but there is a still later punishment, a final one, reserved for certain godless people who will hear the sentence, *Depart from me into the eternal fire which was prepared for the devil and his angels* (Mt 25:41).

What about ourselves, brothers and sisters? Even if we have hitherto turned our backs on God, let our toil be limited to this mortal life. Let us remember the bread offered to us by our Father, let us recall the happiness of our Father's house, and let us not hanker for the pigs' husks, the doctrines of demons. *Now, Lord, you know everything about me, most recent things and things of long ago*: the latest state to which I am reduced and the most ancient sin whereby I offended you.

You fashioned me, and you have laid your hand upon me. Where did you fashion me? In this mortal condition, destined for hard labor, to which all of us were born. Everyone who is born has been fashioned by God in the womb of his mother, for there is no creature that is not shaped by him. But *you fashioned me* in this toilsome existence, *and you have laid your hand upon me*, a punishing hand that lies heavy on the proud. It has thrown down all the self-important for their own good, so that it may raise them up humbled. *You fashioned me, and you have laid your hand upon me.*

8. *Your knowledge is too wonderful for me; mighty it is, beyond my reach.* Now, brothers and sisters, it is time for you to listen to something that is admittedly somewhat obscure but most rewarding in its sweetness once it is understood.

Moses was a holy servant of God. With him God spoke through a cloud, because, when God chose to communicate with any of his servants in time, he customarily did so through some created medium; that is to say, he did not speak through his own substance but by employing some material, created thing, through which his words might be transmitted and made audible to human, mortal ears. That was God's ordinary way of speaking to people; he did not speak to them as he speaks through his own substance. How does he speak in his own substance? The speaking of God is the Word of God, and Christ is the Word of God. That divine Word does not sound forth and then fade away. The Word through whom all things came into being[10] abides immutably for ever. This Word is also the wisdom of God, and to the Word a psalm says concerning created things, *You will discard them, and so they will be changed, but you are the Selfsame* (Ps 101:27–28(102:26–27)). Similarly in another passage Scripture says of divine wisdom, *Abiding in herself, she renews all things* (Wis 7:27). Wisdom stands firm—if we can properly say that she stands; the expression connotes immutability, not immobility—and stands in total self-consistency, varying in no place nor at any time. Nowhere is she other than she is here or there, never is she different from what she is now or was formerly. This is what God's utterance is.

But the communication of God with Moses was a form of speech addressed to a human being, making use of transitory sounds. It could not have taken this form if God had not pressed into service some created, corporeal medium, through which his words could be made intelligible. Moses desired and earnestly longed to see God's very form, and as God spoke to him he pleaded, *If I have found favor in your sight, show me yourself* (Ex 33:13). He longed intensely for this, and tried to cajole God by alleging the friendly intimacy of which he, Moses, had been found worthy. So he entreated God to allow him to see his majestic glory and his face—insofar as we can speak about the face of God. But God's answer was, *You cannot see my face, for no one has seen my face and lived. But I will place you in this crevice in the rock, and I will cover you with my hand. When I pass by, you shall see my back* (Ex 33:20.22–23). These words in their turn give rise to a further riddle, or rather they are an obscure figure

---

10. See Jn 1:3.

of the way things are. *When I pass by, you shall see my back*, says God, as though his face were in front, and his back behind him. Yet far be it from us to think of his majestic reality in this way. If anyone does think of God in those terms, how has he profited from the closing of the temples? He is fashioning an idol in his own heart.

Evidently these words conceal great mysteries. The Lord was speaking to his servant through some created medium, as I have indicated—speaking in a way of his own choosing, and some intimation is given here of the person of our Lord and savior Jesus Christ. Inasmuch as he is in the form of God, and thus equal to the Father,[11] he is invisible to human eyes, just as the Father too is invisible. For if not even human wisdom can be perceived with our eyes, can the power and wisdom of God[12] be seen with the eyes of the body? But in the fullness of time our Lord was to assume human flesh and make himself visible even to fleshly eyes, so that our inward minds, so sorely in need of healing, might be cured. Therefore God enigmatically foretold that future manifestation to Moses, promising him, *You cannot see my face. You shall see my back*, but only *when I pass by*. To ensure that you do not see my face, my hand will shade you. What does it mean by suggesting that the Lord would *pass by*? Surely nothing else but what the evangelist meant by saying, *When the hour had come, Jesus was to pass from this world to the Father* (Jn 13:1). This is what the Pasch signifies, for the word "Pasch" means "Passover." "Pasch" is a Hebrew word, and the Latin equivalent is *transitus*. What, then, is meant when God promises, *You cannot see my face* but *you shall see my back*? Whom did Moses represent when he was told, *You cannot see my face* but *you shall see my back*, and that only *when I pass by*, and also warned that, in order that he not see God's face, *I will cover you with my hand*?

The Lord called his early deeds his *face*, but his passing from this world in the passion was in a sense his *back*. He appeared to the Jews and they did not recognize him. Moses represented them at this time when he was told, *You cannot see my face*. Why was it that they could not see God when he was present to them in the flesh? Because the hand of the Lord lay heavy upon them. Isaiah had said concerning them, *Blind this people's heart, O Lord, and make their eyes heavy* (Is 6:10), and the voice of this same Jewish people is heard in another psalm acknowledging that *your hand lay heavy upon me* (Ps 31(32):4). But this heaviness was God's doing, designed to make sure they would not recognize Christ's divinity for, if they had known it, they would never have crucified the Lord of glory,[13] and, if the Lord had not been crucified, his blood would not have redeemed the whole world. What, then, did God's action mean? Surely it was a manifestation of the rich depths of his wisdom and knowledge, of which the apostle exclaims,

---

11. See Phil 2:6.
12. See 1 Cor 1:24.
13. See 1 Cor 2:8.

O how deep are God's wisdom and knowledge, how unfathomable his decisions and inscrutable his ways! Who has understood the mind of the Lord, or been his counsellor? Who ever forestalled him in giving, and so deserved a recompense? From him are all things, through him are all things, in him are all things. To him be the glory for ever and ever (Rom 11:33–36). The apostle utters this cry after pointing out that *blindness has fallen upon part of Israel so that the full tally of the Gentiles may come in, and so all Israel may be saved* (Rom 11:25–26). As a punishment for their pride, some of the Jewish people were blinded, for they had declared themselves righteous, and in their blindness they crucified the Lord. He laid his hand upon them to prevent them from seeing him until he had passed from this world to the Father.

But did they not see his back after his passing? The Lord arose and appeared to his disciples and to all who had believed in him. He did not appear to others, to those who had crucified him, because he had covered them with his hand until his passover. After spending forty days with his disciples, however, he ascended into heaven and, when in the fullness of time the day of Pentecost arrived, he sent the Holy Spirit to them. Filled with the Holy Spirit, these men, who had all been born into one mother tongue and had learned no other, began to speak in the languages of all nations.[14] The thousands of hearers who had crucified the Lord were terrified and pierced to the heart at such a wondrous sign. After listening to the apostles preaching Christ to them and marveling that such unlearned people could speak in all tongues, they sought advice from the apostles as to what they should do. Peter proclaimed Christ to them, Christ whom they had despised as he hung on the cross, whom they had mocked as no more than a mortal man, whom they had jeered at because he did not come down from the cross, though in fact he did something much greater than coming down from the cross: he rose from the grave. Hearing Christ so proclaimed, the crowds asked, *What shall we do?* (Acts 2:37) These people who raged against the Lord when they could see him were now asking advice about their salvation! They were told, *Repent, and let every one of you be baptized in the name of the Lord Jesus Christ, that your sins may be forgiven* (Acts 2:38). So they did see his back, though they had not managed to see his face. His hand had been covering their eyes, not permanently, but until his passover. After he had passed from this world he took his hand away from their eyes and, once it had been removed, they asked the disciples, *What shall we do?* At first they were enraged but later devout, at first angry but later fearful, at first blind but afterwards illuminated.

9. I think that in our psalm too we should hear the voices of such people recalling their unbelief, for *God imprisoned all in unbelief, that he might have mercy upon all* (Rom 11:32). The psalm recalls his act: *You fashioned me, and you laid your hand upon me. Your knowledge is too wonderful for*

---

14. See Acts 2:4 ff.

me; mighty it is, beyond my reach. It seems to imply, "It was when you laid your hand upon me that you became wonderful to me." I do not understand you. Yet I used to live with you. How easily accessible to me was my father's face when I said, *Give me the portion of the property that is due to me* (Lk 15:12). But, now that I have departed to a distant country and find myself worn down by hunger, it is beyond my perception; *it is too hard for me* (Ps 72(73):16), and I can no longer see what I left behind. *Your knowledge is too wonderful for me*, the psalmist confesses. As a consequence of my sin it became too wonderful, and to me incomprehensible. It was easy for me to contemplate you before I abandoned you in my pride. But now *your knowledge is too wonderful for me; mighty it is, beyond my reach.* I cannot reach it by my own efforts, he means. When I do reach it, I shall reach it by your grace.

Verses 7–10. You cannot get away from God, but let the wings of charity lift you

10. By now you realize that this runaway, however far his flight has carried him, cannot be hidden from the eyes of God, from whom he is trying to escape. Where is he to turn now, when even his boundary has been traced? Listen to his question: *Whither shall I go from your spirit?* If the Spirit of the Lord fills the whole earth,[15] where can anyone go to escape this all-pervading Spirit? *Whither shall I go from your spirit, and whither flee from your face?* He is looking for a place to which he can run to escape God's anger. But what place is going to give sanctuary to one who is a fugitive from God? People do sometimes take in fugitives, but only after enquiring from whom they have escaped. If they ascertain that a runaway slave belongs to a master who is not very powerful, they are not so anxious, reassuring themselves that the poor wretch is not likely to be discovered by a master like that. But, if they find out that he belongs to a powerful owner, they either refuse to take him in or do so only in great fear, comforting themselves that a man, even a powerful one, can after all be deceived. But is there any place from which God is absent? Can anyone deceive God? Is anyone invisible to him? If someone runs away from him, will he not demand his fleeing servant back from anyone who harbors him? Where, then, can a fugitive go from God's face? He scurries hither and thither, looking for a refuge.

11. *If I mount to heaven, you are there; if I sink down to hell, even there you are present,* he says. So you have understood at last, have you, poor runaway, that you cannot possibly put any distance between yourself and him from whom you tried to flee so far? Now you see that he is everywhere. Where do you plan to go?

The fugitive has stumbled upon sound advice, inspired by God, who in his mercy has deigned to call him back. *If I mount to heaven, you are*

---

15. See Wis 1:7.

there; if I sink down to hell, even there you are present. If I exalt myself, I find you there in my high station ready to push me down. If I hide, I know you are searching for me, and not only searching me out but subjecting me to your scrutiny; for, if I am proud on the score of my own pretended righteousness, you are there, you who alone are truly righteous. If my sins plunge me into the depths of evil, and I refuse to confess,[16] saying, *Who will see me? Who will confess to you in hell?* (Sir 23:25; Ps 6:6(5)) still you are there to punish me. Where am I to go in order to escape from your face? Is there any place where I shall not feel you present and angry?

12. But he has hit upon a good plan. "I know how to flee from your face," he says. "I know how I can get away from your Spirit. I will flee from your avenging Spirit, from your stern, menacing countenance." And how will you do that? *If I take once more the wings that will carry me straightforward, and dwell at the uttermost parts of the sea*, then I shall be able to escape from your face.

Is he right? He thinks he can hide from God's face in the uttermost regions of the sea. But will God not be there too, since of him the fugitive has already admitted, *If I sink down to hell, even there you are present*? It would be strange if he who is not absent even from the world below were not present also at the furthest bounds of the sea.

But the runaway insists, "I know how to escape from your anger. I need to get back my wings, wings that will take me straight ahead, not off course: wings that will neither allow me to mount in proud presumption nor sink me into despair and ruin." What are these wings he means to take? Surely the paired wings of the twin commands of charity, the paired commandments on which both the law and the prophets depend.[17] "If I take these wings," he says, "if I equip myself with these two pinions, and make my dwelling at the uttermost edge of the sea, I can flee from your face to your face, from the frown of your anger to the smiling countenance of your appeasement." For what does the uttermost edge of the sea signify if not the end of the world? Let us fly thither even now in hope and desire, borne upon the paired wings of twofold charity; and let us seek no rest except that which awaits us at the furthest bounds of the sea. If we seek rest anywhere else, into the sea we shall plunge. Let us fly toward that boundary where the sea ends. Let us keep ourselves aloft on the two wings of love. Let us fly to God in hope, even now, in this in-between time, and through faithful hope fix our thoughts in advance on that final shore.

13. Observe now who is to be our guide. He it is, and no other, from whose angry presence we are trying to escape; for how does the psalm continue? *If I sink down to hell, even there you are present. If I take once more the wings that will carry me straightforward* (notice that he speaks of taking them once more, so we know he has lost them) *and dwell at the uttermost*

---

16. See Prv 18:3.
17. See Mt 22:40.

parts of the sea, even there your hand will lead me, your right hand bring me through. Let us ponder this truth, beloved brothers and sisters; let it be our hope and our comfort. Let us recover through charity the wings we lost by indulging inordinate desires. These self-indulgent desires have become like sticky birdlime hampering our wings and dashing us down from our free flight in our native air, in the free breezes of God's Spirit. Struck down from this air we lost our wings and fell into the clutches of the fowler. But Christ bought us back by his blood, though it was our attempt to escape from him that led to our captivity. With his commandments he nourishes the new growth of our wings so that now we can soar again, free from our sticky impediment. Let us not be enamored of the sea, then, but fly beyond it, even to its furthest end. Let no one be afraid, but neither let anyone trust in the power of his wings because, even though we are winged creatures once more, we shall plunge into the depths of the ocean, exhausted and weary, if we rely on our own strength rather than allowing him to lead us. Both things are needful: that we have wings and that he lead us on, for he is our helper. We have free will, but how much can our free will achieve if he who commands us does not also help us? *Even there your hand will lead me, your right hand bring me through.*

Verse 11. Christ illumines our night

14. He has come a long way. He looks back, and how does he reflect on the journey? *I said, Perhaps the darkness will overwhelm me.* I have already put my faith in Christ, certainly, and already I am borne aloft on the wings of twofold charity. But iniquity is rampant in this world and, as it increases, the charity of many people cools down. The Lord warned that it would be so: *With iniquity increasing mightily, the love of many will grow cold* (Mt 24:12). And here I am, in this life, beset by such great scandals, so many sins, such hordes of temptations and evil suggestions with every passing day. What am I to do? How will I ever reach those distant limits of the sea? I hear the Lord's dreadful warning, *With iniquity increasing mightily, the love of many will grow cold*, and then the promise that he attached to it: *Whoever perseveres to the end will be saved* (Mt 24:13). But I quail at the length of the journey, and I say to myself, *Perhaps the darkness will overwhelm me.*

Yet the very night was my illumination in my delight. The night itself proved to be light for me, because in the night of my despair—despair of ever having the strength to cross the vast sea, or to sustain so long a flight, or to reach the furthest shore by persevering to the end—he sought me out and found me as I fled. Thanks be to him who struck at my fleeing back with his whip, and called me, and pulled me away from disaster, and so made my night radiant.

As long as we are in this life, it is night for us. How was our night illumined? By Christ's descent into the night. Christ took flesh from this world and lit up the night for us. A woman in the gospel had lost a drachma,[18] and she lighted a lamp. The wisdom of God had also lost a drachma. What is a drachma? A coin, but on it is stamped the image of our emperor himself, for men and women were made in the image of God,[19] and they were lost. What did that wise woman do? She lighted a lamp. A lamp is made from clay, but it carries a light by which the drachma can be found. Wisdom's lamp was the flesh of Christ; it was made from earth's clay, but it shone with the light of the Word and found those who were lost. *The very night was my illumination in my delight*; night itself held delight for us, because Christ is our delight. Think how we should rejoice in him. These shouts of yours, this evidence of your joy[20]—what prompts them? Your delight, obviously. But where does your delight spring from? Surely from a night that has become radiant with light because Christ the Lord is preached to us? He sought you before you began to seek him, and he found you so that you might find him. *The very night was my illumination in my delight.*

Verse 12. Through recognition of God's remedial punishments, and holy indifference to varying fortunes, believers meet light and darkness with equanimity

15. *For the darkness will not be further darkened by you, Lord.* But make sure that you yourself do not make your darkness darker. God will not do so: he enlightens our darkness. This is why another psalm says, *You, Lord, will light my lamp; my God, you will enlighten my darkness* (Ps 17:29(18:28)). Are there any people who do deepen their own darkness, which God never does? Yes, there are. Bad people, perverted people, are obviously darkness when they sin, but if they refuse to confess the sins they have committed, and even go so far as to defend them, they are making their darkness darker still. If you have sinned, you are in darkness, but if you confess your darkness, you will deserve to have your darkness turned into light. If, however, you defend your darkness, you are making your darkness darker than ever. And when will you ever get out of this doubly dark darkness, when even in simple darkness you were blundering about?

How can we say that the Lord does not further darken our darkness? He does not allow us to go unpunished when we sin; he chastises us through the very confusion and unhappiness we create for ourselves, and he teaches us through the experience. You must understand, brothers and sisters, that all the misery of the human race, all the woe in which the world groans, is a medicinal pain, not a penal sentence. You observe pain on all sides, everywhere fear, everywhere deprivation, everywhere hardship. Avarice increases, certainly, but only in bad people. If God is educating us by means

---

18. See Lk 15:8–9.
19. See Gn 1:26–27.
20. Evidently Augustine's congregation was signifying its assent noisily.

of such chastisements[21] to prevent our darkness from growing deeper still, we should acknowledge that we are under his disciplinary scourge. Let us bless God, who mingles bitterness into the sweetness we find in our temporal life lest we become so desensitized by immersion in temporal pleasures that we lose our desire for eternal joys, no longer wanting the sea to end for us so that we may dwell beyond its utmost bounds. Let the ocean's waves roar as they will. The more they rage and foam, the more surely does the dove[22] soar above them on its outspread wings. God does not darken our darkness. He ensures that our sins entail their own suffering, and he sprinkles bitterness over our depraved pleasures. Let us, then, not darken our own darkness by defending our sins, and then night itself will be our illumination in our delight, *for the darkness will not be further darkened by you.*

16. *And the night will be as bright as the day.* The psalm speaks of a night that is like day. By *day* it means here worldly good fortune, and by *night* the adversity we encounter in this life. If we acknowledge that the adversity we endure is the just punishment for our sins, the chastisement laid upon us by our Father will even seem sweet to us, since we thereby avoid the bitter sentence of a judge. Thus we shall regard the darkness of our night as all one with the light of this night.

But if it is a night, how can there be any light in it? It is night because the human race has gone astray in this world; it is night because we have not yet reached that day which is not hemmed in by either yesterday or tomorrow, that everlasting day which knows no sunrise because its sun never sets. It is therefore still night for us in this world, but a night that has a kind of light of its own, as well as its own darkness. We have already explained why it is called night in a general, overall sense. But what is there within it that can be called light? Worldly prosperity and happiness, temporal enjoyment, temporal honor and renown—these are a kind of luminosity in the night. But adversity, bitter troubles, and disgrace are like this night's darkness. During this night, during this mortal life, human beings experience both light and darkness: the light of prosperity and the darkness of misfortune. But when Christ has come and made the soul his own dwelling through its faith, when he has promised a different light, when he has inspired and granted patience, when he has counseled men and women not to be too happy over prosperity lest they be crushed by adversity—then believers begin to treat the present world with detached indifference. No longer are they elated when things chance to go well with them, nor are they shattered when things turn out badly. They bless the Lord in all circumstances, not only in abundance but also in loss, not only in health but also in sickness.

---

21. Variant: "delivers us from such chastisements."
22. This dove is not mentioned in the present psalm in either the Hebrew or the Septuagint. It seems to have flown in from Augustine's *Exposition of Psalm* 54,8–9, of which there are several echoes here.

The promise sung of in another psalm is kept in their lives: *I will bless the Lord at all times; his praise shall be in my mouth always* (Ps 33:2(34:1)). If it is to be *always*, his praise must be on your lips when this present night is enlightened and when it is dark, when prosperity smiles upon you and when misfortune brings sadness. Then will the promise of our present psalm come true for you: *Its darkness will be all one with its light.* Its darkness does not crush me underfoot, because its light does not elate me.

17. Job was an example of one who lived in this world's light, for initially he possessed ample wealth. At first we are given a description of the light that shone on him during the night, the light of his riches. So abundant were his goods and resources that they seemed like light for him, even while he dwelt in the night. The enemy therefore concluded that such a man must be a worshiper of God simply because so much had been given to him, and he begged that it be taken away. Thus Job's night, formerly so well lighted, became deep darkness. But whether it was luminous or dark, Job knew that it was night in either case, a night in which he was still a wayfarer, not yet at home with his God. This God of his was his inner light, and in its radiance he treated the light and the darkness of this night with calm indifference. When the night was enlightened for him by his abundant wealth, he worshiped God. When all these things were taken away and the darkness was total, what did he say? *The Lord gave, and the Lord has taken away. This has happened as the Lord willed: may the Lord's name be blessed* (Jb 1:21). Throughout this life I am in the night, he seems to say. But my Lord dwells within my heart. When he lavished temporal wealth on me he enlightened the night with comforts of a sort, and when he withdrew that temporal light it seemed that the night grew darker. But I know that *its darkness is all one with its light*, and so I can say, *The Lord gave, and the Lord has taken away. This has happened as the Lord willed: may the Lord's name be blessed.* I am not sad in this night, because *its darkness is all one with its light*. Both of them are passing, and therefore let the joyful be as though they did not rejoice and mourners as though they were not weeping,[23] for *its darkness is all one with its light.*

Verses 13–14. The secret of this inner freedom and detachment

18. *For you have taken possession of my inmost parts,*[24] *O Lord.* I am well able to say, "The night's *darkness is all one with its light*," because I am the property of him who dwells within me. He is the owner not of my heart alone but of my inmost parts too, not only of my thoughts but also of my passions. He therefore possesses that part of me which could be tempted to take pleasure in some glimmer of light in the night. He controls the source

---

23. See 1 Cor 7:30.
24. Literally *kidneys*, regarded by the ancients as the seat of the passions and affections, as the heart represented the locus of thoughts.

of my feelings and affections, and I cannot take delight in anything but the inner light of his wisdom.

What are you saying, psalmist? Can you not feel pleasure in the success of your business, in seasons of happiness, honors, riches, or a contented household? No, he replies. Why not? Because *its darkness is all one with its light.* But what is the source of this indifference of yours, this detached attitude that makes you regard this night's darkness and this night's light as all one? Where does it spring from? He answers, *You have taken possession of my inmost parts, O Lord; you took me to yourself*[25] *even from the womb of my mother.* While I was in my mother's womb, I could not regard the darkness of this night as all one with its light, for my mother's womb symbolizes the standards of the city to which I then belonged. What city is that? The city that brought us to birth in captivity. We know all about that city, Babylon, of which we spoke yesterday.[26] Believers leave that city and set their course for the heavenly light of Jerusalem.[27] This is why I said that from my mother's womb I was taken up by the Lord; this is why there is now for me no difference between the darkness of the present night and its light. Those who are still in the womb of Babylon, their mother, rejoice over this world's successes and are shattered by its calamities. They know no rejoicing except that which comes to them when some temporal affair turns out well, and they are strangers to sadness except when their temporal enterprises go wrong.

But you, for your part, leave Babylon. Strike up a hymn to the Lord. Come forth and be born! The Lord will take you up even as you leave your mother's womb. Who is God? None other than the God of the apostle Paul, who testified, *It pleased God, who set me apart from my mother's womb, to reveal his Son in me* (Gal 1:15–16). Who was Paul's mother? The synagogue. And what had he learned there except what the Jews, all the Jewish people, had held and learned[28] there? They professed to praise God, but no corresponding deeds were to be found in them. The words of God, though cherished among them, were only like leaves; there was no fruit anywhere. As you know, when the Lord came across a tree like that, he cursed it and made it wither.[29] He found leaves on it, but no fruit. Now this episode was recounted to turn our minds toward a different tree, for in

---

25. *Suscepisti me.* In the present context the idea of a father picking up his newborn child seems to be present.
26. If he is referring to his *Exposition of Psalm* 136, which treats extensively of Babylon, it may be that the "short psalm" he had intended to preach on today was Psalm 137(138), inadvertently skipped by the reader. See section 1 of the present exposition.
27. Variant: "the light of the heavenly Jerusalem."
28. Many codices omit "and learned."
29. See Mt 21:19.

the natural order it was not yet the season for fruit,[30] and, if everyone knew that, is it possible that the designer of heaven and earth did not?

Well then, he who set Paul apart from his mother's womb has likewise set us apart from our mother's womb. Who was our mother? The city of Babylon. Taken up and acknowledged by him, we are already beginning[31] to cherish a different hope. Brothers and sisters, his promise has given you cause for joy; take root in that different hope and produce fruit. From now on we know no disaster except to offend God and to refuse to let him lead us to the reward he has promised, and we know no happiness except to deserve God and to be led to the fulfillment of his promise. What do this world's goods, or this world's woes, mean to us? Let them be all one to us, for now that we have been taken up by God from the womb of that mother who bore us, we can view both with detachment, saying, *Its darkness will be all one with its light*. Successes in this world do not make us happy, nor do its troubles make us miserable. All we need is to hold fast to righteous conduct, love the faith, hope in God, love God, and also love our neighbor. After all our efforts we shall have unquenchable light, we shall enjoy a day that knows no sunset. Whatever has been a glimmer of light in our night, along with its darkness, will have passed away, for *you have taken possession of my inmost parts, O Lord; you took me to yourself even from the womb of my mother*.

19. *I will confess to you, O Lord, for you have revealed yourself as wonderful and terrible*. The psalm says that in his wonderful being God shows himself as terrible. Even as we marvel at you, Lord, you are terrible in our eyes, and we rejoice with fear. We are afraid that, if we bear ourselves proudly on account of the gifts you have given, we may lose through pride what we gained by humility. *I will confess to you, O Lord, for you have revealed yourself as wonderful and terrible; wonderful are your works, and my soul knows it*. My soul has reached this keen perception now, because you took me to yourself from the womb of my mother, but even before that your knowledge of me was wonderful. It had become so powerful that I could not reach it. I mean that it had become so powerful, as far as I and my understanding were concerned: so powerful as to be beyond my grasp.

Why has my soul attained to this keen awareness? Because the night has itself become my enlightenment in my delight, and your grace came to me to enlighten my darkness. It could have happened only because you took possession of my inmost parts and embraced me even from the womb of my mother.

Verse 15. Strong inner support

20. *My bone is not hidden from you, for it was you who created it in that secret place*. He speaks of his bone, *os*, another form of which in popular

---

30. See Mk 11:13.
31. Variant: "let us now begin."

Latin is *ossum*. This meaning is clear in the Greek. If we had no access to the Greek we might have thought he meant *os* ("mouth"), of which the plural is *ora*, rather that *os* ("bone").[32] *My bone is not hidden from you*, he says, *for it was you who created it in that secret place*. I have a certain *ossum* hidden within me (we prefer to use the word *ossum*; better that linguistic experts should find fault with us than that people should not understand). This *ossum* of mine is hidden inside me; you made it for me secretly within, and therefore it is not hidden from you. Though you made it secretly, it is no secret from you, is it? Other people do not see this interior *ossum*; they know nothing about it. But you know it because you made it.

Now what is this bone that he is talking about, brothers and sisters? Since it is not immediately visible, we must look for it. But because we are Christians speaking in the name of the Lord to other Christians, we have already had experience of this special kind of bone. It is an inner firmness or strength, suitably called a bone because firmness and strength are what we expect in bones. Similarly there is an inner firmness in the soul, which saves it from breaking down.[33]

Whatever sufferings come our way, whatever distress, whatever the misfortunes of this world that seethe around us, the inner structure that God has made firm in us cannot break or even bend under pressure. The steady strength of our endurance is the Lord's creation. As another psalm says, *To God will my soul be subject, for my patience comes from him* (Ps 61:6(62:5)). Think of the apostle Paul and how he manifested the firmness that was within him. *As if sorrowful, we always have cause for joy* (2 Cor 6:10), he says. Why did he say, *As if sorrowful*?[34] Because the apostles had to withstand abuse, reproaches, persecutions, beatings, blows, stoning, prison, and chains. Would anyone have thought them anything other than wretched then? The persecutors themselves would not have bothered to treat them so badly if they had not been confident of reducing the apostles to misery by their onslaughts. But the persecutors based that judgment on their own weakness, for they did not have the hidden bone within them. The victims, who did possess it, appeared outwardly wretched to onlookers, but they were rejoicing inwardly to God, from whom their inner bony structure was not concealed, because he had built it in secret.

---

32. The two words are *os, ossis* (" bone") and *os, oris* ("mouth" or "face"). They coincide only in the nominative and accusative singular, and only there if the length of the vowel is disregarded. Augustine goes on to say that he will use the collateral form *ossum* ("bone") to avoid ambiguity. He says this is a popular form, though it is found in ancient classical examples.
33. Variant: "an inner strength in the soul, a firmness that does not break down."
34. See the powerful meditation on the "as if" quality of Christian sadness in *Exposition 2 of Psalm* 48,5. Christian life may be "as if" sad, but it is joy without qualification.

But the same apostle, Paul, gives us a glimpse of that bone which God had secretly made, when he says, *What is more, we even glory in our sufferings* (Rom 5:3). If you are simply saying that you are not sad, Paul, that does not amount to much. But do you even glory in your sufferings? Surely it would be enough if you warded off sadness? No, he replies, that would not be enough for Christians. God has made such a strong bone, and hidden it inside me, that I would not be satisfied with not breaking. I must also glory! And what are you glorying about? *Our sufferings, knowing that suffering fosters endurance.* Then he describes the process whereby this inner firmness is established in the heart: we know that *suffering fosters endurance, and endurance constancy, and constancy hope; but hope does not disappoint us, because the charity of God has been poured out into our hearts through the Holy Spirit who has been given us* (Rom 5:3–5). So well formed, so firmly set, is the hidden bone that it causes us to glory in our sufferings. Yet we appear wretched to other people, because what we have within us is hidden from them.

But *my bone is not hidden from you, for it was you who created it in that secret place, as you also formed my nature in the lower regions of the earth.* My nature is endued with flesh and is therefore at home in the lower regions of the earth. Yet I have within me the bone you formed, thanks to which I do not collapse under any persecutions I meet in this lower region where my natural self lives.

Would it be surprising if an angel proved strong? No, but it is a great achievement if flesh is strong. And whence would flesh derive its strength, where would the strength of a fragile vessel come from, if that bone had not been fashioned in secret? *You formed my nature in the lower regions of the earth.*

Verses 16–17. Christ's imperfect members

21. What about those who are less firm? As I have already reminded you, Christ speaks in this psalm. Many things have been said in the name of his body, but the head is speaking too, though not in the sense that they are distinct from each other like two persons: now the head and now the body. To distinguish them like that would be to divide them, and then they would not be two in one flesh.[35] But if they are two in one flesh, do not be surprised if the two speak with one voice.

Now when our Lord Jesus Christ suffered, his disciples did not yet have that bone within them. The strength to suffer had not yet been firmly established in them, and so they hid. They had no realistic idea of their own strength or weakness. Thus Peter made bold to promise the Lord that he would stay with him in his passion, even to death. He did not realize that he was a sick man, but his physician knew it. What happened? *I will go with you even to death* (Lk 22:33), promised Peter. And the Lord replied,

---

35. See Eph 5:31–32.

Truly I tell you, before cockcrow you will deny me three times (Mt 26:34). The doctor's assessment proved truer than the sick man's presumptuous assertion.

When, therefore, the psalm says, *My bone is not hidden from you, for it was you who created it in that secret place*, it is speaking of those in whom strong, firm bone has developed within. But this is true above all of the steady courage of our Lord and Savior Jesus Christ himself in confronting his passion. When he willed, he sat down; and when he willed, he rose up.[36] When he willed, he slept, and when he willed, he awoke; as he said, *I have the power to lay down my life, and I have the power to take it up again* (Jn 10:18). But what of those in whom such fortitude had not been formed or firmly established? What has the psalm to say about them? Observe what Christ says to God, his Father: *Your eyes beheld my imperfection*. "My imperfection includes my Peter, making promises and then denying me, presumptuous and then failing through fear. Yet your eyes have seen him." It was when the Lord himself had looked at Peter after his third denial that Peter was reminded of the Lord's prediction to him, and then, as the gospel relates, *he went outside, and wept bitterly* (Lk 22:62). Those tears were evoked by God's gaze upon him, for *your eyes beheld my imperfection*, as the psalm says.

That imperfect man who tottered during the Lord's passion would undoubtedly have perished, but your eyes saw him and, along with him, all those who had been imperfect until they were made firm by Christ's resurrection. Then it was made plain before their eyes that the Lord's mortal body—that body in which he had died—had not perished. Strong bone was then secretly formed within them, so that they too might have no fear of dying.

Your eyes beheld my imperfection, and in your book all shall be written: not only the perfect, but *all*, and therefore the imperfect as well. Let the imperfect not be afraid but make progress. They must not take my injunction not to be afraid as an excuse for being complacent about their imperfection and remaining stuck where they were when grace found them. Let them simply make as much progress as they can. They must grow daily, and daily draw closer to Christ. What matters above all is that they do not leave the body of the Lord. Provided that they are part of this one body, conjoined with all its other members, they will deserve to hear this voice and know that it applies to them: *Your eyes beheld my imperfection, and in your book all shall be written*.

22. *They will go wrong concerning the day, and not one of them will be there*. Before the passion, our Lord Jesus Christ was the "day" still with them, as he indicated himself by telling them, *Walk, while you have daylight* (Jn 12:35). But his imperfect members *will go wrong concerning the day*. They, even they, thought that our Lord Jesus Christ was nothing

---

36. See section 4 above.

more than a man, that there was no hidden Godhead in him, that he was not in his invisible nature God, and that there was no more to him than what could be seen. Even they held this opinion—even Peter. We shall speak of Peter in particular, because in him we are given an example to encourage us not to despair of our own weakness.[37]

Earlier the Lord had questioned his disciples as to what people thought about him, and Peter answered, *You are the Christ, the Son of the living God.* The Lord said to him in reply, *Blessed are you, Simon, son of Jonah. It is not flesh and blood that revealed this to you, but my Father, who is in heaven* (Mt 16:16–17). Why did the Lord say that? Because Peter had called him the Son of God. But immediately after this, in the same context, we hear the Lord beginning to speak of his approaching passion. Then this same Peter, the one who had confessed Jesus to be the Son of God, was afraid that he might die like any son of man. He was certainly the Son of God, but he was also a son of man: the Son of God because he was in the form of God and equal to the Father, and a son of man because he had taken the form of a servant, in which he is less than the Father.[38]

He was confronting his passion in the form of a servant, but what grounds had Peter for fearing that the form of God would perish along with the form of a servant, rather than taking it for granted that from the form of God the servant-form would come to life again? Yet Peter was afraid and said to him, *Far be it from you, Lord, have some pity for yourself* (Mt 16:22). And the Lord, who a moment before had declared Peter blessed, now said, *Get behind me, Satan. You have no taste for the things of God, but only for human things* (Mt 16:23). Directly after Peter had confessed, *You are the Christ, the Son of the living God,* he heard the words, *It is not flesh and blood that revealed this to you, but my Father, who is in heaven*: he was the rock, he was blessed, on account of his confession. But now he was called *Satan* because he had spoken not at the prompting of any revelation from the Father but out of the weakness of his flesh. *You have no taste for the things of God, but only for human things,* Christ told him.

Think of it, brothers and sisters: Christ was there with them. This was the Christ who had gone about among them, who had commanded the waves and walked on the waters before their eyes,[39] who had raised up a man dead for four days as they looked on,[40] who had performed other mighty miracles before their eyes;[41] and yet they were terrified during his passion, as though they had lost someone in whom they had hoped in vain. *They will go wrong concerning the day, and not one of them will be there.* Not a single one of them, not even he who had said, *I will go with you even*

---

37. Variant: "our own strength," in a potential sense, presumably.
38. See Phil 2:6–7; Jn 14:28.
39. See Mk 4:39; Mt 14:25.
40. See Jn 11:39–44.
41. See Jn 11:47.

to death (Lk 22:33). Jesus had foretold it, saying, *The hour is coming when each of you will go his own way, leaving me alone. Yet I am not alone, for the Father is with me* (Jn 16:32). The Father was with him, and he was with the Father; the Father was in him, and he was in the Father.[42] He and the Father are one,[43] yet the disciples were frightened when he died. Why? Because they went wrong concerning the day, and so not one of them was there. The psalm foresaw it: *They will go wrong concerning the day, and not one of them will be there.*

23. What else is implied in that prophecy, *They will go wrong concerning the day*? Does it mean they will be lost? Surely not, for then what would become of the promise, *Your eyes beheld my imperfection, and in your book all shall be written*? When did they go wrong about the day? When they failed to understand the Lord dwelling among them on earth. Yet how does the psalm continue? *But your friends have become for me exceedingly honorable, O God.* These same disciples who went wrong concerning the day, these same men of whom not a single one was to be found when Christ suffered, became your friends and were made exceedingly honorable in my eyes. After the Lord's resurrection that firm bone was secretly built within them, and they themselves suffered for the name of Christ, at whose passion they had been terrified. *Your friends have become for me exceedingly honorable, O God; their pre-eminence has been most firmly established.* They were made apostles, they became leaders of the Church, they took their places as rams leading the flock;[44] *their pre-eminence has been most firmly established.*

Verses 18–20. The Church is a mixed collection of people

24. *I will count them, and they will be more numerous than grains of sand.* Through those disciples who went wrong concerning the day, through those of whom not one was there, so great a multitude has come to birth that, like grains of sand, they are beyond counting, except by God. He said, *They will be more numerous than grains of sand*, yet he also said, *I will count them.* Counted they have been, even though more in number than grains of sand, for grains of sand have themselves been counted by him who knows the number of the hairs on our heads.[45] *I will count them, and they will be more numerous than grains of sand.*

25. *I have risen, and I am still with you.* What does he mean by this: *I have risen, and I am still with you*? I have undergone my passion, he is saying; I was buried, and now I have arisen, and they do not yet understand that I am with them. *I am still with you*,[46] but not yet with them, for they do

---

42. See Jn 14:10.
43. See Jn 10:30.
44. See *Exposition of Psalm* 64,18.
45. See Mt 10:30.
46. The Father.

not yet recognize me. This is attested by the gospel, where we read that after the resurrection of our Lord Jesus Christ the disciples did not immediately recognize him when he appeared to them.

Another interpretation is possible. *I have risen, and I am still with you* could refer to the present era, when he is still hidden at the right hand of the Father, before being revealed in his glory when he comes to judge the living and the dead.

26. Now he tells us what he is suffering in his body, the Church, throughout this whole long period when he is risen and still with the Father. These sufferings are caused by the presence of sinners in the midst of the Church and by the heretics who separate themselves from it. Thus the psalm continues, *If you slay sinners, O God, then, men of blood, depart from me; because you will say in your thoughts, They will capture their cities in vain*. I think the sequence of ideas here is as follows: *If you slay sinners, O God, they will capture their cities in vain*. The psalmist wishes us to understand that these sinners are slain because, when they become puffed up with pride, they lose the grace which was their true life. *The holy spirit of discipline rejects falsehood, and withdraws from stupid thinking* (Wis 1:5). This is how sinners are slain: darkened in their understanding, they are alienated from the life of God.[47] Through self-exaltation they lose hold of their confession, and so they are killed, and the warning of Scripture is exemplified in them: *No confession can be made by a dead person: he is as though nonexistent* (Sir 17:26).

Thus it happens that they *capture their cities in vain*, for *cities* represent the empty-headed people whom these sinners persuade to follow their own empty-headed errors. Inflated by their reputation for holiness, the leaders persuade blind and ill-educated folk to follow them as though they were more trustworthy, tearing apart the Church's bond of unity. They often find an excuse for separating themselves from our unity in Christ by accusing some among us of evil lives and pretending to shun communion with such persons. It may be that in so doing they not only defame the innocent, whom they pretend to avoid as evildoers, but also make true allegations about others as bad as themselves. There are such bad persons among us, and the true wheat of Christ[48] groans in their company but still keeps the bond of unity intact.[49] In the voice of those who suffer in this mixed company, the psalm cries, *Men of blood, depart from me; because you will say in your thoughts, They will capture their cities in vain*. It means this: the reason why the heretics will lure their disciples away into their own sects, there to be

---

47. See Eph 4:18.
48. See Mt 3:12; 13:30.
49. As he often does, Augustine defends the idea of the Church found in the gospels: a mixture of wheat and weeds, good fish and bad, during this time before the judgment. His target in this section is obviously the different notion of the Donatists, that the Church is the society of the pure.

corrupted by their stupid notions, is that *you will say in your thoughts, Men of blood, depart from me.* Heretical leaders, spiritually slain as a punishment for their pride, capture their cities in vain, which is a figurative way of saying that they seduce their followers in vain, luring them into vain errors, tearing apart the Church's unity and deserting the good wheat on the pretext of taking offence at the straw mixed with it. But the psalm has a warning also for the wheat itself, the good, faithful people: they must not openly separate themselves from the wicked before the final winnowing, which will sort them out at the end. If they did so prematurely, they might also distance themselves from the good who are still mingled with the bad. Rather should good people, through their praiseworthy conduct and plainly different way of life, tacitly say every day, *Men of blood, depart from me.* This is said to the wicked by God's voice, but his voice speaks in the thoughts of holy people, as the psalm indicates.

Who are the *men of blood*? Who else but those who hate their brothers and sisters? John says, *Everyone who hates his brother is a murderer* (1 Jn 3:15). But sinners, spiritually slain, do not understand how God says to the wicked, using the thoughts of his good followers as his medium, *Men of blood, depart from me.* They therefore rebuke the faithful for maintaining communion with bad people, and, using this reproach as an excuse for separating themselves from the Church, they *capture their cities in vain.* This dismissal is spoken to the wicked only in the thoughts of good people at the present time, but one day it will be spoken to them aloud and openly, when they hear from our head himself, *I never knew you; depart from me, all you who act unjustly* (Mt 7:23).

Verses 21–22. Love your enemies, and hate their sins

27. But now Christ's body, the Church, protests, "How can the proud slander me, alleging that the sins of others defile me? How can they make that a pretext for separating from me and so capturing *their cities in vain*? *Do I not hate those who hate you, O Lord*? How can they demand that I separate physically from bad people, when they who make the demand are worse themselves? Were I to do as they ask, the wheat would be uprooted with the weeds before harvest-time,[50] and I would lose the patience that enables me to bear with my straw until the final winnowing.[51] I would tear apart the nets of unity before the mixed catch of fish is hauled ashore for sorting at the end of the world.[52] Do the sacraments I receive belong to

---

50. See Mt 13:29.
51. See Mt 3:12.
52. See Mt 13:47–48; Lk 5:6. Elsewhere Augustine thinks of the fishing episode in Lk 5 as a symbol of the Church's mixed catch in the present age, where the nets are in danger of tearing. In the other fishing episode, in Jn 21:1–8, the catch represents for him the netful of the elect, who do not tear the nets. See *Exposition 3 of Psalm 30,2* and *Exposition of Psalm 49,9.*

those evildoers? Do I, by consent, communicate with their way of life or their deeds? *Do I not hate those who hate you, O Lord? Have I not been consumed with indignation over your enemies?* Was I not furious, did not zeal for your house devour me,[53] when I saw how senseless they were? Did not disgust always possess me at the sinners who abandon your law?[54] And who are your enemies, if not those who prove by their lies that they hate your law? If, then, I have hated them, how can people who *capture their cities in vain* impute to me the sins of those I have hated, the sins of those over whom I have been filled with disgust out of zeal for your house?"

But what has become of the Lord's injunction, *Love your enemies*? Do you think that, because he mentioned only yours, God's enemies fall outside its scope? It is true that he said, *Do good to those who hate you* (Mt 5:44), not "to those who hate God." The psalm too asks, *Do I not hate those who hate you, O Lord?* It does not say, "Those who hate me." And it continues, *Have I not been consumed with indignation over your enemies?* Not "over mine." But if people hate us and are enemies to us because we serve God, are they not hating him and making themselves his enemies? It cannot be right, then, can it, for us to withhold our love from enemies such as these? When the Lord went on to say, *Pray for those who persecute you* (Mt 5:44), surely he implied that those to whom he spoke would suffer persecution on God's account. We need to seek clarification from the psalm's next verse.

28. *With a perfect hatred I have hated them.* What is *perfect hatred*? It means, I hated the sins in them but I always loved your creation. To hate with perfect hatred implies that you neither hate the persons because of their vices nor love the vices because of the persons. This interpretation is confirmed by the next words, *They have become foes to me*; the psalmist shows that they are not only God's enemies but his own as well. How, then, is he to do justice both to his own declaration, *Do I not hate those who hate you?* and to the Lord's command, *Love your enemies*? How is he to do justice to both, except through a *perfect hatred*, whereby he hates everything in them that makes them sinful and at the same time loves them because they are human beings? Even in the period covered by the Old Covenant, when a carnal people was customarily kept in line by visible punishments, there was a man whose insight gave him kinship with the New Covenant. This was God's servant, Moses. How could he have hated sinners when he prayed for them?[55] But, equally, how could he not have hated them when he killed them?[56] The answer must be that he hated them with a perfect hatred. In the perfection of this hatred he hated the iniquity he was punishing, but in such a way that he loved the human beings for whom he habitually prayed.

---

53. See Ps 68:10(69:9).
54. See Ps 118(119):53.
55. See Ex 32:11–13.
56. See Ex 32:26–28.

*Verses 23–24. God reads the Church's heart and
leads it in the eternal way, Christ*

29. This, then, is our situation. Although at the end Christ's body will be separated from godless and wicked folk even physically, for this time in between it must still sigh among them. The sinners who have been spiritually slain denounce good people in the Church for maintaining communion with bad members and make the presence of these bad members a pretext for separating themselves from the good and innocent ones. Thus the schismatic leaders *capture their cities*, but *in vain*. Meanwhile plenty of bad people refuse to follow the breakaway movements and remain in the Church, mixed inextricably with its good members, so that the good will have to tolerate them to the end.

What does the body of Christ do amid these trials? What must it do, in order to bring forth fruit in patience,[57] a harvest of a hundred-, sixty-, or thirty-fold?[58]

Christ's beloved is among maidens like a lily amid thorns.[59] What is she to do? What does she ask? How does she understand herself? What is the beauty of the king's daughter like, that beauty which she hides within?[60]

Listen to the Church's prayer. *Test me, O God, and know my heart.* It is for you to test me, O God; I pray that you will know me—not any heretic who cannot test or know my heart, for there in my heart you test me and know that I do not consent to the deeds of the wicked, though they believe that I am contaminated by sins that are not mine. As I persevere in my long pilgrimage I am mindful of the groan I uttered in another psalm, that I must deal peaceably with those who hate peace,[61] until I reach that vision of peace which is the name of Jerusalem, the mother of us all, our eternal city in heaven. By their quarrelsome calumnies and by their separation from me my enemies may capture cities for themselves, but not cities that will last for eternity. *They will capture their cities in vain.*

Test me, then, *O God, and know my heart; examine me, and take cognizance of my ways.* To what end? Listen to the remaining verse.

30. *See whether there is any way of sin in me, and lead me in the eternal way.* The psalmist prays, *Take cognizance of my ways*—that is, of my plans and thoughts—*and see whether there is any way of sin in me*, through action or through consent. Then *lead me in the eternal way*. What else does this mean but "Lead me in Christ"? Who is the *eternal way* if not he who is eternal life? He is eternal, he who said, *I am the way, the truth, and the life* (Jn 14:6). Perhaps you may find something in the way I am walking that is displeasing in your eyes, for my way is mortal. *Lead me*, then, *in*

---

57. See Lk 8:15.
58. See Mt 13:23.
59. See Sg 2:2.
60. See Ps 44:14(45:13).
61. See Ps 119:7(120:6–7).

the eternal way, where there is no sin, for *if anyone has sinned, we have an advocate with the Father, Jesus Christ the righteous one, and he himself is the expiation for our sins* (1 Jn 2:1–2). He is our *eternal way* beyond sin, and he is eternal life beyond all punishment.

Conclusion

31. These are profound and holy signs, brothers and sisters. How wonderfully does the Spirit of God speak to us! And what delights he prepares for us in this our night! But how does it happen, brothers and sisters? How is it that these truths are all the sweeter to us for being more obscure?[62] With marvelous skill he mixes a love-potion for us. He has made his own words so wonderful that when we tell you things you already know, the fact that we draw them forth from what seemed to be obscure passages makes them like a fresh discovery for you. You see what I mean? You already knew, didn't you, that bad people must be borne with in the Church of God and that schisms are to be avoided? And you surely knew before now that we have to hold out and persevere in these nets which hold both good and bad fish until we reach the final shore. You knew that in the meantime the nets are not to be torn, because when they are brought ashore the good will be put into containers and the bad thrown away.[63] You knew all this, didn't you? But you did not understand the corresponding verses in this psalm. So now what you did not understand has been explained, and what you already understood has been made new.

---

62. Variant: "These truths are sweeter to us for their very obscurity."
63. See Mt 13:47–48.

PART III

RECOVERING OUR BEARINGS

Steps to the Mezzanine

Exposition 2 of Psalm 30: 1–11

Synopsis

Let's chisel out a sermon for you from this Psalm's secrets. In the title, the "end" refers to Christ. But what is "ecstasy"? Its root sense, "out of one's mind," refers to an altered state induced by either fear or exaltation. Paul was exalted in heavenly visions (1–2). But if it refers to fear, it relates to Christ's being fearful as he prayed in the garden before his death. Yet in reality Christ was portraying *our* fear, having taken up our flesh and voice in redemption's "wonderful exchange." As a part of Christ, one person with him, "we too are Christ." He helps us do all things (3–4).

We pray that we may not be ashamed forever. This can only happen in God's justice, not our own. God's grace alone justifies; given gratis, it cannot be earned either by efforts or merits (5–6). We ask God to "make haste" to save us, but this refers to how *we* count time, which is not as God counts it. God is our only refuge, especially from ourselves. We were left half-dead by the side of the road, but Christ our Good Samaritan pitied us (7–8). He nourishes us with mother's milk of mercy until we are strong enough to eat the bread of angels. Enemies lay their traps of error and terror, but our Commander left an example of how to fight. The body of Christ suffers temptation in many places, but not all suffer at the same time, and temptation takes different forms (9–10).

Christ prayed on the cross, *Into your hands I commit my spirit*, in order to teach you that he speaks in this Psalm (11). Fear of physical death ironically leads people to spiritual death when they lie or cling to empty earthly things to avoid it. But the human soul's constraints are unavoidable, whether they be ignorance of other people's hearts, ignorance of one's own heart, the inescapability of death, or the chains of bad habits. Who can deliver us except Christ? (12–13) A good death frees us from the devil's clutches. Though the path is narrow, God guides us into free and open spaces (14–16).

Augustine's Text of Psalm 30:1–11

(1) A psalm for David, an ecstasy.
(2) In you, O Lord, I have put my trust; let me not be shamed forever.
   In your justice set me free, and rescue me.
(3) Bend your ear toward me: make haste to rescue me.
   Be to me a protecting God, and a home of refuge to save me.
(4) You are my fortified place and my refuge.
   For the honor of your name you will be my leader,
   And you will nourish me.
(5) You will lead me out of this trap they have hidden for me,
   For you are my protector.
(6) Into your hands I commit my spirit.
   You have redeemed me, Lord God of truth.
(7) You hate all those who pay futile regard to vain things.
   But I have put my trust in the Lord.
(8) I will exult and be glad in your mercy,
   Because you have looked kindly on my humble state,
   You have saved my soul from its constraints.
(9) You have not shut me up into the power of the enemy;
   You have guided my feet into open spaces.
(10) Have mercy on me, Lord, for I am in distress.
   Under your anger my eye is confused, my soul too and my belly.
(11) For my soul faltered in the pain, and my years faded amid sighs....

Exposition

The First Sermon to the People[1]

Verse 1

1. Let us try to probe the secrets of this psalm we have just sung, and chisel out from it a sermon to offer to your ears and minds. The title of the psalm is *To the end, a psalm for David himself, an ecstasy.* If we have

---

1. Probably preached at a country church near Carthage, possibly in the summer of 411.

come to know Christ, we know what *to the end* means, because the apostle tells us that *Christ is the end of the law, so that everyone who believes may be justified* (Rom 10:4). He is an "end" not in the sense of finishing it off, but of bringing it to its perfection. You know how we speak of the "end" of something in two different ways: either what puts out of existence something that did exist, or what brings to full perfection something that had only begun to exist. So you can see that *to the end* means "to Christ."

What does "ecstasy" imply?

2. *A psalm for David, an ecstasy.* The word *ecstasy* is Greek. Its meaning is best conveyed for us by the phrase "standing outside," but ecstasy strictly means being out of one's mind, or "being beside oneself." Now, we can think of two possible reasons for this condition: one is fear; the other is the contemplation of heavenly things so intense that the realities of life here below seem to slip out of the mind. The saints experienced this kind of ecstasy, all those saints at least to whom were revealed the hidden mysteries of God that transcend this world. Paul spoke about being beside oneself, being in ecstasy, and hinted that he was referring to himself, when he said, *Whether we are beside ourselves, for God, or in our right mind, for you, the charity of Christ constrains us* (2 Cor 5:13–14). What he means is: "If we choose to do nothing else, and simply contemplate what we see when we are beside ourselves, we would not be available to you, but would be so rapt in heavenly things as to seem uncaring about you. And when you with your uncertain steps tried to follow us to those higher, heavenly realms, would we not still seem uncaring, but for the fact that the charity of Christ constrains us, so that we consider ourselves your servants? And so out of gratitude to him who had granted us higher graces we would not disdain lower needs for the sake of the weak, and would accommodate ourselves to people who could not join us in the vision of heavenly realities, like Christ, who *being in the form of God, deemed it no robbery to be God's equal, yet emptied himself and took on the form of a slave"* (Phil 2:6–7).[2] You notice that Paul says, *Whether we are beside ourselves, for God,* because God alone sees his own mystery and only he can reveal his secrets; we only see them in ecstasy. And the man who is speaking here is the one who testifies that he was seized and carried off to the third heaven,

---

2. The preceding passage could be understood in a slightly different way: "... when you with your uncertain steps tried to follow us to those higher, heavenly realms, would we consider ourselves your servants? Would we not deem it right, and not ungrateful to him who had granted us higher graces, to refuse to neglect lower needs and our ministry to the weak? Would we accommodate ourselves to people who could not join us in the vision of heavenly realities—would we, if the charity of Christ did not constrain us? This is the Christ who....", etc.

where he heard inexpressible words, which no human being may utter.³ So completely was he beside himself that he could say, *Whether in the body or out of the body I do not know; God knows* (2 Cor 12:2).

If the title of our psalm refers to ecstasy like this, if it envisages this mode of being beside oneself, we must certainly expect its author to have weighty and profound things to say. The author is the prophet, but more truly the Holy Spirit who spoke through the prophet.

Could Christ be genuinely afraid?

3. But suppose "ecstasy" means fear? The text of our psalm will have plenty of relevance to this other meaning of the word, for it looks as though it is going to talk about the passion, in which fear played a part. Whose fear? Christ's certainly, since the psalm was entitled, *to the end*, and we understand "the end" to be Christ. Or our fear, perhaps? Surely we cannot attribute fear to Christ as his passion loomed, when we know that was what he had come for? When he had reached that suffering for which he had come, was he afraid of imminent death? Surely even if he had been human only, not God, he could have been more joyful at the prospect of future resurrection than fearful because he was about to die, couldn't he?

Head and body speak as one

But in fact he who deigned to assume the form of a slave, and within that form to clothe us with himself, he who did not disdain to take us up into himself, did not disdain either to transfigure us into himself, and to speak in our words, so that we in our turn might speak in his.⁴ This is the wonderful exchange, the divine business deal, the transaction effected in this world by the heavenly dealer. He came to receive insults and give honors, he came to drain the cup of suffering and give salvation, he came to undergo death and give life. Facing death, then, because of what he had from us, he was afraid, not in himself but in us. When he said that his soul was sorrowful to the point of death,⁵ we all unquestionably said it with him. Without him, we are nothing, but in him we too are Christ. Why? Because the whole Christ consists of Head and body. The Head is he who is the savior of his body,⁶ he who has already ascended into heaven; but

---

3. See 2 Cor 12:2.4.
4. Here and in the following paragraphs Augustine articulates his most profound conviction on the psalms: the "I" who speaks is always Christ, either Christ in his own person, or Christ in the person of his members, or the *totus Christus*, Head and members, bridegroom and bride. The texts he quotes (Acts 9:4; Eph 5:31–32; Is 61:10) are among his favorites for making the point, and recur frequently, as do the key phrases, *transfigurare nos in se, una quaedam persona, una vox*.
5. See Mt 26:38.
6. See Eph 5:23.

the body is the Church, toiling on earth. Were it not for the body's linkage with its Head through the bond of charity, so close a link that Head and body speak as one, he could not have rebuked a certain persecutor from heaven with the question, *Saul, Saul, why are you persecuting me?* (Acts 9:4). Already enthroned in heaven, Christ was not being touched by any human assailant, so how could Saul, by raging against the Christians on earth, inflict injury on him in any way? He does not say, "Why are you persecuting my saints?" or "my servants," but *Why are you persecuting me?* This is tantamount to asking, "Why attack my limbs?" The Head was crying out on behalf of the members, and the Head was transfiguring the members into himself. It is like the tongue speaking in the foot's name. It may happen that someone's foot is trodden on in a crowd, and it hurts: the tongue cries out, "You"re treading on me!" It does not say, "You are treading on my foot"; it says it is being trodden on. Nobody has touched it, but the crushed foot is not severed from the tongue.

This will help us to understand about the ecstasy of fear. What am I to say, brothers and sisters? If people who were destined to suffer were completely fearless, why would that prophecy have been made to Peter, the one we heard on the feast day of the apostles? The Lord foretold Peter's future passion by saying to him, *When you were younger you fastened your belt and went where you liked; but when you have grown old, someone else will fasten it for you, and take you where you do not want to go.* He said this, Scripture asserts, *indicating how Peter would die* (Jn 21:18–19). If the apostle Peter was so perfect that he willingly went where he did not want to[7] (I mean he did not want to die, but he did want to win his crown), why wonder if there is some fear when the righteous suffer, even the saints? Fear springs from human weakness, hope from the divine promise. Your fear is your own, your hope is God's gift in you. In your fear you know yourself better, so that once you are set free you may glorify him who made you. Let human weakness be afraid, then, for divine mercy does not desert us in our fear.

So it is a frightened person who begins the psalm: *In you, O Lord, have I put my trust; let me not be shamed for ever.* He or she is both afraid and trustful, you see; and you see too that the fear is not devoid of hope. Even if there is some turmoil in this human heart, divine comfort has not left it alone.

4. Christ is speaking here in the prophet; no, I would dare to go further and say simply, Christ is speaking. He is going to say certain things in this psalm that we might think inappropriate to Christ, to the excellent dignity of our Head, and especially to the Word who was God with God in the beginning. Some of the things said here may not even seem suitable for

---

7. Variants: "unwillingly went where he did not want to"; "went as though willingly where he did not want to"; "was led where he did not want to go, though also willing it."

him in the form of a servant, that form which he took from the Virgin; and yet it is Christ who is speaking, because in the members of Christ there is Christ. I want you to understand that Head and body together are called one Christ. To make this quite clear he says, when speaking of marriage, *They will be two in one flesh; so they are two no longer, but one flesh* (Mt 19:5-6). But perhaps it might be thought that he only means this to apply to any ordinary marriage? No, because listen to what Paul tells us: *They will be two in one flesh*, he says. *This is a great mystery, but I am referring it to Christ and the Church* (Eph 5:31-32). So out of two people one single person comes to be, the single person that is Head and body, bridegroom and bride. The wonderful, surpassing unity of this person is celebrated also by the prophet Isaiah, for Christ speaks prophetically in him too: *The Lord has arrayed me like a bridegroom adorned with his wreath, or a bride decked with her jewels* (Is 61:10). He calls himself bridegroom and he calls himself bride: how can he say he is both bridegroom and bride, except because they will be two in one flesh? And if two in one flesh, why not two in one voice? Let Christ speak, then, because in Christ the Church speaks, and in the Church Christ speaks, and the body speaks in the Head, and the Head in the body. Listen again to the apostle as he expresses this even more plainly: *As the body is a unit and has many members, and yet all the members of the body, many though they be, are one body, so too is Christ* (1 Cor 12:12). He was speaking about Christ's members—the faithful, that is—but he did not say, "So too are Christ's members." He called the whole entity he had spoken about, "Christ." A body is one single unit, with many members, but all the members of the body, numerous as they are, constitute one body; and it is the same with Christ. Many members, one body: Christ. All of us together with our Head are Christ, and without our Head we are helpless. Why? Because united with our Head we are the vine, but if cut off from our Head (God forbid!) we are only loppings, of no use to the vine-tenders and fit only for the bonfire. This is why Christ himself says in the gospel, *I am the vine, you are the branches, and my Father is the vine-dresser*; and he warns us, *Without me you can do nothing* (Jn 15:5.1). If we can achieve nothing without you, Lord, we can do everything in you. Yes, because whatever work he does through us seems to be our work. He can do plenty, or rather everything, without us, but we can do nothing without him.

Verse 2. Profitable shame

5. Whether the speaker's ecstasy is the product of fear or of being beside himself, let him speak on, then, because either way what is to be said befits him. Let us who are within Christ's body say—and let us all say it as one, because we are a unity—*In you, O Lord, I have put my trust; let me not be shamed for ever*. The shame I truly dread, he says, is the shame that lasts for eternity. There is a temporary shame that is profitable to us, the shame of the mind that reviews its sins, and is horrified by the review, and

ashamed at the horror, and is shamed into correcting itself. This is why the apostle too asks, *What glory did you have in those doings of which you are now ashamed?* (Rom 6:21); he is saying that the believers are ashamed not of their present gifts, but of their past sins. A Christian does not fear that kind of shame; indeed, if we have not undergone it, we shall be ashamed for ever. What is eternal shame? That of which Scripture says, *Their lawless actions will convict them to their faces* (Wis 4:20). The wicked flock will gather at the Lord's left hand as their iniquities convict them to their faces and the goats are separated from the sheep, and they will hear their sentence: *Depart from me, you accursed, into the eternal fire which was prepared for the devil and his angels.* And if they ask why? *I was hungry and you did not feed me* (Mt 25:41.42). They were contemptuous, then, when they refused food to Christ in his hunger, refused him a drink when he was thirsty, gave him no clothing when he was naked, did not take him in when he was a traveler, failed to visit him when he was sick; they were contemptuous then. But when this list begins to be read out to them they will be ashamed, and this shame will last for all eternity. This is the shame that the speaker in the psalm fears when he is either terrified out of his mind, or beside himself for God, and prays, *In you, O Lord, have I put my trust; let me not be shamed for ever.*

Justification is God's work

6. *In your justice set me free, and rescue me,* for if you take my "justice" into account, you cannot but damn me. *In your justice set me free.* There is a justice that belongs to God, but becomes ours as well when it is given to us. It is called God's justice to ensure that humans do not imagine that they have any justice as from themselves. Paul affirms this by saying, *When someone believes in him who justifies the impious, that faith is reckoned as justice to the believer* (Rom 4:5). What does that mean, God who "justifies the impious"? It means he changes one who was impious into a just person.

The Jews, on the contrary, assumed that they were able to achieve perfect justice by their own efforts, and in consequence they tripped over the stumbling-stone, the rock of scandal,[8] and failed to recognize the grace of Christ. All they received was a law that could show them up as guilty, not one by which they could be freed from their guilt. What does the apostle have to say about that? *I bear this witness against them: they have zeal for God, indeed, but it is not informed by knowledge* (Rom 10:2). What does he mean by saying that the Jews *have zeal for God,* but then adding that *it is not informed by knowledge*? Listen: he goes on to point out the consequence of this lack of knowledge: *They failed to recognize the righteousness that comes from God, and by seeking to set up a righteousness of their own, they did not submit to God's righteousness* (Rom 10:3). If their uninformed zeal for God consists in ignorance of God's justice and the wish to set up

---

8. See Rom 9:32.

their own, as though they could become just by their own efforts, it follows that the reason why they did not recognize God's grace was that they did not want to be saved gratis. For who is saved gratis? Everyone in whom the Savior has found nothing to crown, but only what he must condemn, one in whom he has found nothing that deserves rewards but only what merits torments. If he is to act as the law's provisions truly demand, the sin must be condemned. If he were to act on that principle, whom could he acquit? He found all of us to be sinners; he alone, who found us sinners, himself came without sin. The apostle confirms this: *All have sinned, and are in need of the glory of God* (Rom 3:23). And what does that mean, *are in need of the glory of God*? That you need him to set you free, for you cannot do it by yourself. Because you have no power to liberate yourself you need a liberator. What have you to boast about? How can you give yourself airs about the law and righteousness? Do you not see what the law collides with inside you, what it testifies about you, and against you? Do you not hear someone fighting, confessing, and imploring help in the struggle? Do you not hear the Lord's athlete begging the superintendent of the games to help him in his contest? God does not look on as you compete, in the same way as the one who puts on the games watches you if you are fighting in the amphitheater. This man can award you the prize if you win, but cannot help you if you are in danger. God does not look on like that. No, indeed not; notice what Paul says: *I take great delight in God's law as far as my inner self is concerned, but I am aware of a different law in my members that opposes the law of my mind, and imprisons me under the law of sin inherent in my members. Who will deliver me from this death-ridden body, wretch that I am? Only the grace of God, through Jesus Christ our Lord* (Rom 7:22–25). Why call it "grace"? Because it is given gratis. And why is it given gratis? Because there were no preceding merits on your part; God's benefits forestalled you. To him, then, be the glory, to him who sets us free, *for all have sinned, and are in need of the glory of God*.

With this in mind, *in you, O Lord, have I put my trust*, not in myself. *Let me not be shamed for ever*, because I trust in him who does not shame me.[9] *In your justice set me free, and rescue me*. Because you have found in me no justice of my own, set me free in yours; let me be freed by what renders me just, what makes a godless person godly, what enables a blind person to see, what raises up one who is falling, what makes a mourner rejoice. That is what sets me free; I do not liberate myself. *In your justice set me free, and rescue me*.

Verse 3. Time is very short

7. *Bend your ear toward me*. God did this when he sent Christ himself to us, for he sent one who bent his head low and wrote in the earth when

---

9. Variant: "because whoever trusts in him is not shamed."

an adulterous woman was presented to him as deserving of punishment.[10] Already he had bent down to the earth; for God had bent down to the humans who had been told, *Earth you are, and back to earth you shall go* (Gn 3:19). God does not bend his ear to us by some kind of shift in bodily position, nor is he confined by a determined bodily shape, as we are. We must exclude any human fantasies of this kind when thinking about God. God is Truth. Now truth is neither square, nor round, nor long. Truth is everywhere, if the eye of the heart is open to it. But God bends his ear to us when he pours down his mercy upon us. What greater mercy could there be, than that he should send his only Son, not to live with us, but to die for us? *Bend your ear toward me.*

8. *Make haste to rescue me.* His prayer, *make haste*, is heard. This verb was used to help you understand that the whole stretch of time during which the world rolls on its way, this time that seems to us so long, is really no more than a moment. Anything that has an end is not long. The time from Adam to the present day is over and done with, and certainly far more time has passed than remains ahead, yet if Adam were still alive, and were to die today, what difference would it have made to him to have been here so long, to have had such a long life? So why this prayer for haste? Because the years are flying past, and what seems to you long-drawn is very brief in God's eyes. In his ecstasy the psalmist had understood how quickly time passes.

You cannot escape from God

Make haste to rescue me. Be to me a protecting God, and a home of refuge to save me. Be a home of refuge for me, O God my protector, a home of refuge; for sometimes I am in peril, and I want to flee—but where? What place can I flee to, and be safe? A mountain? A cave somewhere? Some fortified building? What fortress can I hold? What defensive walls put up around me? Wherever I go, there is someone following me: myself. You can flee from anything and everything, poor mortal, except your conscience. Go into your house, lie down on your bed, seek the ultimate privacy: you will find no secret place to run to from your conscience, if your sins are gnawing you. But in saying, "Make haste to rescue me, and set me free by your justice, forgive my sins and build up your own justice in me," he is saying, "You will be the home where I can take refuge, and to you I flee for safety; for where else can I run to, away from you?" If God is angry with you, where will you run? Listen to what is said in another psalm by someone who fears God: *Whither shall I go from your spirit, and whither flee from your face? If I mount to heaven, you are there; if I sink down to hell, even there you are present* (Ps 138(139):7–8). Wherever I go, I find you there. If you are angry, I find you as an avenger, if you are appeased, as a helper. Nothing is left to me but to flee, not from you but to you. My

---

10. See Jn 8:6.

brothers and sisters, if any one of you is a servant, and you want to evade your master, you run to some place where your master is absent; but if you want to evade God, it is to the Lord that you must run, for there is no place where you can go to escape God. All things are immediately present and naked to the eyes of the Almighty.[11]

The Lord is the good Samaritan

"Do you yourself be my home, then," prays the psalm, "a home where I can take refuge. If I have not been saved, how can I escape? Heal me, and I will take refuge in you. I cannot walk unless you heal me, so how will I be able to run?" Where could a person go, or run to, if he was unable to walk and lying half-dead in the road, after being wounded by robbers? A priest passed him by, a Levite passed him by, but a Samaritan who chanced that way took pity on him (see Lk 10:30–35); and this is our Lord, who took pity on the human race. The word "Samaritan" means "guardian." And who will guard us, if he abandons us? The Jews said to him, *Are we not right to say that you are a Samaritan, and that you have a demon?* and they spoke truly, even though they meant it as vilification. The Lord rejected one charge but embraced the other: *I have no demon*, he said (Jn 8:48–49); but he did not say, "I am no Samaritan," because he wanted it to be understood that he is our guardian. In his loving pity he drew near to the wounded traveler, healed him, took him to the tavern, and lavished his mercy on him in every way. The patient can now walk, and therefore can also run, and where should he run to, if not to God, where there is a home of refuge waiting for him?

Verse 4. God our mother

9. *You are my fortified place and my refuge. For the honor of your name you will be my leader, and you will nourish me.* Not for my deserts, but *for the honor of your name*, so that you may be glorified; and not because I am worthy of it, *you will be my leader*, so that I do not stray away from you; and *you will nourish me*, so that I may be strong enough to eat the food you give the angels. He who has promised us the food of heaven has nourished us here below with milk, in his motherly mercy. A nursing mother causes the food which her child is not yet capable of eating to pass through her own flesh, and pours it out again as milk; the baby gets the same food he would have received at table, but because it has passed through her flesh it is suitable for a young child. So too the Lord put on flesh and came to us, to make his wisdom palatable for us as milk. The body of Christ speaks here: *You will nourish me.*

---

11. See Heb 4:13.

Verse 5. Temptation

10. *You will lead me out of this trap[12] they have hidden for me.* Already there is a hint of the passion here: *you will lead me out of this trap they have hidden for me.* But it does not refer only to the passion of our Lord Jesus Christ, for the devil has set his trap for all time. Woe betide anyone who falls into that trap; and fall into it anyone will, who does not trust in the Lord, and does not say, *In you, O Lord, have I put my trust; let me not be shamed for ever. In your justice set me free, and rescue me.* The enemy's trap is stretched out ready; there are twin loops in it, error and terror: error to entice, terror to break and grip us. You must shut the door of greed against error, and the door of fear against terror; and then you will be led clear of the trap.

Your Commander gave you an example of how to fight in this way. He deigned even to be tempted for your sake, and displayed the example in himself. At first he was tempted by alluring possibilities, as the devil tried the door of greed in him, suggesting, *Say to these stones, "Become loaves of bread." Worship me, and I will confer these kingdoms on you. "Throw yourself down, for scripture says, 'He has charged his angels to take care of you, and they will carry you in their hands, so that you will not even stub your foot on a stone'"* (Mt 4:3.9.6). All this was enticement, meant to tempt him to greed. But when the devil discovered that in Christ, who was being tempted for us, the door of greed was closed, he changed his tactics and tried the door of fear instead, preparing the passion for him. That is why the evangelist ends the story with the words, *when all the temptation was finished, the devil left him, biding his time* (Lk 4:13). What does that suggest, *biding his time*? That he meant to return and try the door of fear, having found the door of greed shut.

Now the whole body of Christ undergoes temptation to the very end. Think, my brothers and sisters, how it was when some harmful measure was enacted against Christians. The whole body was hit at once, the whole body took the thrust; that is why a psalm contained the words, *I was pushed at like a heap of sand to make me topple, but the Lord held me up* (Ps 117(118):13). Then when all those attempts to strike down the whole body were over, temptation began to assail separate parts. The body of Christ is still tempted: although one church may not be suffering persecution, another will be feeling the blows. It no longer has to suffer the fury of an emperor, but it endures the rage of a wicked populace. How much devastation has been caused by mobs?[13] How much harm has been done to the Church by bad Christians? They are like the fish that were caught in the net and became so numerous that they weighed down the fishermen's boats, on that

---

12. *Muscipula*, literally a mousetrap.
13. Perhaps an allusion to the Circumcellions. See *Exposition of Psalm 54*, 26 and the note there.

occasion when the Lord aided their catch before his passion.[14] A similar load of temptation is never lacking. Let none of us tell ourselves, "This is not a time of temptation." Any who think so are promising themselves peace, but those who promise themselves peace are invaded unawares. Let the whole body of Christ pray, *You will lead me out of this trap they have hidden for me,* for our Head has been led out of the trap they concealed for him, those people we heard about just now in the gospel. They were all ready to say, *This is the heir. Come on, let's kill him and the inheritance will be for us.* But when the Lord questioned them they pronounced sentence against themselves. *"What will the landlord do to those rascally tenants?" "He will bring those wretches to a wretched end, and let the vineyard to other gardeners." "What? Have you never read the text, The stone rejected by the builders has become the headstone of the corner?"* The phrase, *rejected by the builders,* has the same implication as *they threw him out of the vineyard and killed him* (Mt 21:38.40–42.39). Christ was delivered; our Head is there on high, and free. Let us cling to him now by love, so that later on we may be even more strongly cemented to him by immortality; and let us all say, *You will lead me out of this trap they have hidden for me, for you are my protector.*

Verse 6. Christ is speaking in the psalms

11. Let us listen now to something our Lord said on the cross: *Into your hands I commit my spirit* (Lk 23:46). When we hear those words of his in the gospel, and recognize them as part of this psalm, we should not doubt that here in this psalm it is Christ himself who is speaking. The gospel makes it clear. He said, *Into your hands I commit my spirit; and bowing his head he breathed forth his spirit* (Lk 23:46; Jn 19:30). He had good reason for making the words of the psalm his own, for he wanted to teach you that in the psalm he is speaking. Look for him in it. Bear in mind how he wanted you to look for him in another psalm, the one "for his taking up in the morning,"[15] where he said, *They dug holes in my hands and my feet, they numbered all my bones. These same people looked on and watched me. They shared out my garments among them, and cast lots for my tunic* (Ps 21:17–19(22:16–18)). He wanted to make sure you would understand that this whole prophecy was fulfilled in himself, so he made the opening verse of that same psalm his own cry: *O God, my God, why have you forsaken me?* Yet all the same he transfigured the body's cry as he made it his own, for the Father never did forsake his only Son. *You have redeemed me, Lord God of truth,* carrying through what you promised, unfailing in your pledge, O God of truth.

---

14. See Lk 5:7.
15. See the title of Psalm 21(22).

Verse 7. Futile preoccupations

12. *You hate all those who pay futile regard to vain things.* Who does so? Anyone who dies by fearing death. Such a person tells lies out of fear of dying, and so dies before the time comes for death, even though the object of the lies was to carry on living. You are afraid to die, and so you want to tell lies, so you tell lies and you die! While attempting to evade one death, which you may postpone but cannot banish altogether, you fall into two deaths, dying first in your soul and later in your body. How does this come about, if not through paying futile regard to vain things? And all because this passing day is pleasant to you, and those years that fly by are pleasant; yet you can catch hold of no part of them and, what is more, you are caught yourself. *You hate all those who pay futile regard to vain things. But I,* who do not, *have put my trust in the Lord.* If you put your trust in money, you are paying futile regard to vain things; if you put your trust in high office or some exalted rank in human government, you are paying futile regard to vain things; if you put your trust in some powerful friend, you are paying futile regard to vain things. When you put your trust in all these, either you expire, and leave them all behind, or they will crumble while you are still alive, and what you trusted will have let you down. Isaiah points to futility like this: *All flesh is but grass, and all its splendor like the flower of the field; the grass is dried up and its flower wilted, but the word of the Lord abides for ever* (Is 40:6–8). For my part, I do not put my trust in empty things as they do, nor pay futile regard to them; I have put my trust in the Lord, who is not empty.

Verse 8. The soul's constraints

13. *I will exult and be glad in your mercy,* not in any righteousness of my own. *Because you have looked kindly on my humble state, you have saved my soul from its constraints, and have not shut me up into the power of the enemy.* What are these constraints, from which we want our souls plucked free? Could anyone list them? Or heap them up, so that we can size them aright? Or suggest suitable means to avoid or escape them? The first constraint that hems in the human race, and a harsh one it is, is our ignorance of anyone else's heart, our tendency often to think badly of a faithful friend and to value an unfaithful one. This is a hard constraint indeed! What are you going to do about it, to gain insight into the hearts of others? What kind of eye can you bring to the job, you weak, pathetic mortals? What do you propose to do today, to read the heart of your brother or sister? You have not the wherewithal.

Another major constraint is that you do not even see what your own heart will be like tomorrow. And what am I to say about the constraints of mortality itself? We are constrained to die, and no one wants to. Nobody wants something that constrains us all. No one wants something that will happen whether we like it or not. That is a mighty constraint, to dislike something unavoidable. If it were possible, we would certainly choose not to die; we would wish to become like the angels, but by some transformation that did not involve dying, as the apostle suggests: *We have a building from God, a home not made by hands, an everlasting home in heaven. We groan over our present condition, longing to have our heavenly dwelling put on over this one, so that being clothed in it we may not be found naked. Yes, we who are still in this earthly dwelling groan under our burden; not that we want to be stripped of it, but wishing to be invested with the other one on top, so that what is mortal may be swallowed up by life* (2 Cor 5:1–4). We want to reach God's kingdom, but not to travel there through death; yet constraint stands there saying, "This way." Do you hesitate to go that way, poor mortal, when by that same route God has come to you?

Then what about the constraints of overcoming bad habits? Conquering a habit entails a hard fight, as you well know. You see that your behavior is wrong, that it is detestable and makes you unhappy, yet you go on behaving in the same way. You did so yesterday, and you will today. If you are so uncomfortable when I put it to you like this, how much more uncomfortable does it make you to think about it yourself? Yet you will go on doing it. What is dragging you along? Who is leading you off captive? Could it be the law in your members that is in conflict with the law in your mind? If so, cry out, *Who will deliver me from this death-ridden body, wretch that I am? Only the grace of God, through Jesus Christ our Lord* (Rom 7:24–25). Then the psalm-verse we have just read will be true for you: *I have put my trust in the Lord. I will exult and be glad in your mercy. Because you have looked kindly on my humble state, you have saved my soul from its constraints.* How was it saved from its constraints? Only because he looked kindly on your humble state. He who had the power to free you from constraints would not have heard your plea unless you had first humbled yourself, as that man humbled himself who cried, *Who will deliver me from this death-ridden body, wretch that I am?* But the Jews were not humbled, the Jews who *failed to recognize the righteousness that comes from God, and by seeking to set up a righteousness of their own, did not submit to God's righteousness* (Rom 10:3).

Verse 9. Freedom from the real enemy

14. *You have not shut me up into the clutches of the enemy.* This does not mean the clutches of your neighbor, or your business-partner, or someone you fought with and wounded, or someone you may have chanced to injure in your town. For people like that we are bound to pray.[16] We have a different enemy, the devil, the ancient serpent. All of us are set free from his clutches when we die, provided we meet death well; but any who die a bad death, who die in their iniquities, are shut up into his power, to be damned with him at the end. The Lord our God delivers us from the clutches of our

---

16. See Mt 5:44.

enemy, but the enemy tries to entrap us through our lusts. When these lusts are powerful, and we submit to them, they are justly called constraints. So if God sets us free from our constraints, what will there be in us for the enemy to grab? How can we then be imprisoned in his clutches?

15. *You have guided my feet into open spaces.* Well, yes, the path is narrow.[17] To the laborious plodder it is narrow, but to the lover it is wide. The same path which seemed narrow now seems to have widened. *You have guided my feet into open spaces,* says the psalm, for if my feet were squeezed too close together they might tread on each other and trip me up. So what does he mean by saying, *You have guided my feet into open spaces*? It must mean, "You have made right living easy for me, though it was once so difficult." That is what the line means: *you have guided my feet into open spaces.*

Verses 10–11. A hurried conclusion

16. *Have mercy on me, Lord, for I am in distress. Under your anger my eye is confused, my soul too and my belly. For my soul faltered in the pain, and my years faded amid sighs.* This will have to do for now, dearest friends.[18] With the Lord's help I may be able to make up what is still due, and go home with the psalm finished.[19]

---

17. See Mt 7:14.
18. *Caritati vestrae.*
19. Apparently the foregoing sermon, and the two following sermons on the same psalm, were preached at some country church away from Hippo.

Exposition 2 of Psalm 32

Synopsis

The Psalm urges, *Dance for joy in the Lord*. The most fitting dance is praise for the Lord, for *praise befits the upright*. Rather than trying to bend God to their will, the "upright" refuse to do so; rather, they stand straight in God's uprightness. Christ came to teach God's will and to empower us to do it. He prayed, *not my will, but your will*, in order to show forth our human will and bend it toward God's (though his divine will always conformed to God). Will what God wills, and you are not separate from him (1–2). But bent people praise God in good times and then curse him in bad. If you are just, you praise God at all times. You ask whether you are just. I ask in reply whether you believe. The Apostle says, *the just live by faith* (3–4).

The Psalm calls us to praise God on the lyre and the ten-stringed psaltery. The first has its sounding board down low, while the other has it high up. We play the lyre by praising God equally for both the fortunes and the misfortunes of life "down below," as old Job did (5). The ten-stringed psaltery fits "higher" spiritual gifts like the Ten Commandments. These commandments are about love, not fear. The first three relate to charity toward God, and the last seven relate to charity toward our neighbor. "You fulfill through love what was beyond your powers through fear." The martyrs loved the beauty of justice, seen only with the heart (6). Who can describe it? To see it our hearts need cleansing. Don't be bashful about this. Think of the crazy things fickle people do for love! (7) Love makes persons new, and they *sing a new song* to the Lord about the New Covenant. Their song comes from jubilation, like workers at harvest singing a joyful song that defies speech. That's a model of praising God, who's beyond words (8).

Perform your works in faith so as to become just, for such faith "works through love." God's promise is utterly reliable, so we don't say to God, "Give what you owe," but rather, "Give what you promised" (9). God *loves judgment and mercy*, so practice these. Now seems the time for mercy, while judgment comes later; but in reality they're not separate. Mercy shown to the merciful is just, because it is discriminating. Let mercy and judgment be your business, not just God's. Let me end the sermon here out of respect for differing levels of physical stamina in our audience (10–12).

Augustine's Text of Psalm 32:1–5

(1) For David himself.

Dance for joy in the Lord; praise befits the upright.

(2) Confess to the Lord on the lyre,

And sing psalms to him with the ten-stringed psaltery.

(3) Sing to him a new song, sing skillfully in jubilation,

(4) Because the Lord's word is straight,

And all his works are done in faith.

(5) He loves judgment and mercy....

Exposition

First Sermon to the People, preached at Mappalia during the Vigil of the Feast of Saint Cyprian the Martyr[1]

Verse 1. Praising God means uniting our will to his

1. This psalm urges us to dance for joy in the Lord. But it is entitled, *For David himself.* All of us, then, who are numbered among the sacred progeny of David must listen to his words, and make those words our own, and dance for joy in the Lord. The psalm begins with the admonition, *Dance for joy in the Lord, you just.* Let the unjust dance for joy in this world, by all means; but when this world comes to an end, there will be an end to their dancing. Let the just dance for joy in the Lord, for the Lord abides for ever, and so will the exultation of the just. The most fitting way for us to dance for joy in the Lord is for us to praise him, in whom alone there is nothing whatever that can be displeasing to us, though in the eyes of unbelievers no one has so many aspects that are displeasing. There is a pithy saying: one is pleasing to God if one finds God pleasing to oneself. Do not dismiss this as frivolous, my friends. You can see for yourselves how many people argue in opposition to God, and how many are offended

---

1. According to the *Acta proconsularia sancti Cypriani*, after Cyprian's martyrdom his body was carried in triumph by the Christians to the *area Macrobii*, a graveyard "which is on the Mappalian Way, near the reservoirs," outside the walls of the city of Carthage. A basilica was later built there at the place of his burial, and in it the present sermon was preached, possibly on 13 September 403, though the date is disputed.

by what he does. When he has decided to act in a way human beings do not like, because he is the Lord and he knows what he is about, and is less concerned with our likes and dislikes than with what will be to our profit, people who want their own will carried out rather than God's seek to bend God to their will, instead of correcting theirs by aligning it with his. Such people are unbelievers, impious and wicked. I am ashamed to say this, but I will say it, for you know how true it is: an actor on stage[2] gives them more pleasure than God does.

2. With this in mind the psalmist first invites us, *Dance for joy in the Lord, you just*, because we could scarcely dance for joy in him without praising him, and we praise him by becoming more and more pleasing to him as we find him pleasing to us. Accordingly the psalmist then adds, *Praise befits the upright*. Who are the upright? Those who direct their hearts in accordance with the will of God. If human frailty unsettles them, divine tranquility consoles them; for although they may privately in their mortal hearts want something that serves their present purpose, or promotes their business, or meets their immediate need, once they have understood and recognized that God wants something different, they prefer the will of One better than themselves to their own, the will of the Almighty to that of a weakling, the will of God to that of a human being. As God is infinitely above his human creatures, so is God's will far above the will of men and women.

This is why Christ took the mantle of humanity, set us an example, taught us how to live and gave us the grace to live as he taught. To this end he let his human will be seen. In his human will he embodied ours in advance, since he is our Head and we all belong to him as his members, as you know well. *Father*, he said, *if it is possible, let this cup pass from me*. It was his human will speaking here, wanting something individual and private, as it were. But he wanted the rest of us to be right of heart, and whatever might be even slightly warped in us to be aligned with HIM WHO IS always straight, and therefore he added, *Yet not what I will, but what you will be done, Father* (Mt 26:39). But was Christ capable of wanting anything bad? Could he, in the end, will anything other than what the Father willed?

They are one in Godhead, so there can be no disparity of will. But in his manhood, he identified his members with himself,[3] just as he did when he said, *I was hungry, and you fed me* (Mt 25:35), and as he identified us with himself when he called from heaven to the rampaging Saul who was persecuting God's holy people, *Saul, Saul, why are you persecuting me?* (Acts 9:4), though no one was laying a finger on Christ himself. So too in

---

2. Literally a pantomime performer.
3. *Transfiguravit in se suos*, difficult to render in English, but a key phrase in Augustine's theology of Christ and the Church. Perhaps "he took us over into himself," or "he incorporated us into his own personality and will," may convey something of its richness.

displaying the will proper to a human being he displayed your nature, and straightened you out. "See yourself reflected in me," Christ says, "because you have the capacity to want something on your own account that is at variance with God's will. This is natural to human frailty, characteristic of human weakness, and difficult for you to avoid. But when it happens, think immediately about who is above you. Think of God above you, and yourself below him, of him as your Creator and yourself as his creature, of him as Lord and yourself as servant, of him as almighty and yourself as weak. Correct yourself, subject yourself to his will, and say, *Not what I will, but what you will be done, Father.* How can you then be separated from God, when you now will what God wills? You will be straight and upright, and praise will be your fitting occupation, for *praise befits the upright."*

Praise and thank God in adversity

3. On the other hand, if you are a bent person, you will praise God when good things come your way, and curse him when something bad happens to you; though in fact your lot cannot be bad if it is just, and it is just, because it is arranged for you by One who can do nothing unjust. But you will be like a spoiled child in its father's house, loving your father if he caresses you and hating him when he beats you, never thinking that he is all the while preparing an inheritance for you, whether caressing or beating.

Another psalm gives an example of how praise befits the upright. Listen to the voice of someone who knows how to praise in the right way: *I will bless the Lord at all times; his praise shall be in my mouth always.* In this saying *at all times* means the same as *always,* and *I will bless the Lord* is the same as saying, *His praise shall be in my mouth.* Praise him at all times and always, in good times and bad. If you praise God only in good fortune and not in adversity, how is that praising him always? We hear plenty of people making protestations like that when some happiness has come to them; they dance for joy, they are full of gladness; they sing to God and praise him. We should not disapprove of them; on the contrary, their behavior should delight us, for many people would not behave so even in the same good fortune. But people who have already begun to praise God in circumstances of prosperity must be taught to recognize their Father when he beats them too, and not to grumble under his correcting hand. Otherwise they may remain permanently warped, and deserve to be disinherited. Once straightened, however (and what does being straight mean? That nothing God does displeases them), they are enabled to praise God even when things go wrong, and to say, *The Lord gave, and the Lord has taken away. This has happened as the Lord willed: may the Lord's name be blessed* (Jb 1:21). Praise befits people of this stamp, not the kind who at first are ready to praise God, but later revile him.

4. Come on then, you just, you upright folk, dance for joy in the Lord, because praise befits you. No one should say, "Who is that? Am I just?

When am I just?"⁴ Do not rubbish yourselves or despair of yourselves. You are human beings made in the image of God, and he who made you human became human himself for your sake. The blood of God's only Son was poured out for you so that you, all of you, might be adopted as a great family of God's children with rights of inheritance. If you hold yourselves cheap in your earthly frailty, esteem yourselves precious by reason of the ransom paid for you. Give serious thought to what you eat, what you drink,⁵ what you endorse with your "Amen."⁶ Are we giving you this advice to prompt you to pride, or suggesting to you the audacity of attributing some perfection to yourselves? By no means; but neither must you think yourselves far removed from all righteousness. I do not mean to question you about your personal righteousness or justice; if I did, perhaps no one among you would dare to reply, "I am just." No, but I do question you about your faith. As no one among you dares to claim, "I am just," so equally no one will dare to say, "I am not a believer." I am not yet inquiring what your life is like; I am inquiring what your faith is. You will respond that you believe in Christ. Very well, then, have you not heard the apostle telling us that *the one who lives by faith is just?* (Rom 1:17) Your justice is your faith, because if you believe, you will undoubtedly be careful, and if you are careful you make efforts; and God knows your efforts, and sees deep into your will, and takes note of your struggle with the flesh, and encourages you to keep up the fight, and helps you to win, and has his heart in his mouth waiting for you⁷ when you are locked in conflict, and lifts you up when you are flagging, and crowns you when you are victorious. *Dance for joy in the Lord*, then, *you just*; I should have said, "Dance for joy in the Lord, you believers," for anyone who lives by faith is just. *Praise befits the upright.* Learn to give thanks to God both in prosperity and in trouble. Learn to have in your hearts what many people have on their tongues, "As God wills."⁸ That is a popular pious cliché, but even more it is the doctrine of salvation. Who is not ready to say every day, "As God wills, so may he act"? The one who says so will be upright,⁹ and find a place among those who dance for joy in the Lord, those for whom praise is the fitting occupation. To such as

---

4. *Quis ego iustus? Aut quando ego iustus?* The editors of the Latin text amend this to *Quis ergo iustus, aut quando ero iustus?* which yields the clearer sense, "Who is just, though, and when shall I be just?"
5. A eucharistic allusion.
6. Variant: "...drink, where your names are enrolled."
7. Variant: "watches you."
8. *Quod vult Deus.* So much was it a popular saying that it was sometimes given as a name; Augustine wrote at least two letters to a deacon called Quodvultdeus, who had asked him to compile a catalogue of heresies (Letters 222, 224).
9. Punctuating a little differently, some codices have "...to say every day, 'As God wills'? Let everyone do so, and he or she will be upright...."

these the psalm speaks in the following verses, inviting them to *confess to the Lord on the lyre, and sing psalms to him with the ten-stringed psaltery.* This is what we were singing just now, and as we gave expression to it with voices in unison, we were instructing your hearts.[10]

Verse 2. Praise God with both lyre and psaltery

5. Was not the purpose of the institution of these vigils in Christ's name,[11] to banish lyres from this place? Yet here we have even lyres being commanded to sound their melody: *Confess to the Lord on the lyre,* says our psalm, *and sing psalms to him with the ten-stringed psaltery.* But none of you must think that we are meant to turn to the musical instruments of the theatre. All of us have within ourselves the means of doing what we are bidden; in another place Scripture says, *The vows I must perform for you, and the praises I will render you, O God, are within me* (Ps 55(56):12). Those of you who were present on a previous occasion will remember how we discussed in our sermon, as best we could, the difference between a psaltery and a lyre, attempting throughout to make the distinction clear to everyone.[12] How far we succeeded is for those to judge who were listening then. But it is timely to repeat it now, so that we may find in the difference between these two musical instruments the difference between human activities. It is signified by the instruments but must be made real in our lives. The lyre[13] has a hollow, drum-like sounding-board with a vaulted back like a tortoise-shell. The strings are attached to the wood so that when they are plucked they yield resonant notes. I am not talking about the plectrum which is used, but about the concave sounding-chamber across which the strings are stretched, on which they lie, as it were, so that when they are set quivering they derive their resonance from the hollow cavity and yield a richer tone. Now the lyre has this wooden sounding-board below, while the psaltery has it at the top. That is the difference.

---

10. A variant in some codices makes better sense: "…just now, giving expression with voices in unison to what was in our hearts, and as we did so this is what we were teaching."
11. See the title of this sermon, and Augustine's *Sermon 311*, 5, where he reminds his hearers that the holy place where Cyprian's body rested had been invaded some years previously by dancers and singers who kept up wanton performances all night. The bishop of Carthage had made a clean sweep, and in their place the celebration of this vigil was instituted.
12. See his *Exposition of Psalm* 42, 5; *Exposition 2 of Psalm* 70, 11; *Exposition of Psalm* 80, 5.
13. *Cithara,* often translated "harp," but unlike the modern instrument of that name. The *cithara* was more like a zither or lyre. Its invention was attributed to Hermes, who stretched strings of sheep-gut across a tortoise-shell.

In the present passage we are commanded to confess on the lyre, and to sing psalms on the ten-stringed psaltery.[14] No mention is made of a ten-stringed lyre, either in this psalm or anywhere else, as far as I remember. The readers among my flock should look up that point, and consider it more carefully at leisure; but for my part I seem to recall that while we often find references to the psaltery with ten strings, there is nowhere any mention of a lyre with ten strings. Now, remember that the lyre has its sounding-board below, while the psaltery has it above. In our life below, our earthly life, we experience prosperity and adversity, and we have an opportunity to praise God in both, so that his praise may be in our mouths always, and we may bless the Lord at all times. There is earthly good fortune and earthly misfortune, and God is to be praised whichever we find ourselves in, so that we may play the lyre for him. What is earthly prosperity? It is enjoying bodily health and an abundance of all the things we need, being kept safe and having a profusion of crops; it is when God causes his sun to rise over good and bad alike, and sends his rain on both just and unjust.[15] All these things contribute to our earthly life, and anyone who does not praise God for them is ungrateful. Just because they are earthly, are they any the less God's gifts? Or are they to be deemed the gifts of someone else, because they are bestowed on wrongdoers too? No; God's mercy is manifold. He is patient and long-suffering. By letting us see how richly he endows even the wicked, he signifies more clearly what he is reserving for the righteous.

But adversities too are certainly our lot in this lower region. They come from the frailty of the human race, from pain and sickness, from harassment and disasters and temptations. The person who plays the lyre will praise God throughout all of it. We should not simply despise these things as lower realities, but remember that they can be controlled and governed only by that wisdom which reaches powerfully from end to end, disposing all things sweetly.[16] It is not the case that he rules the affairs of heaven and disregards those of earth; does not a psalmist ask him, *Whither shall I go from your spirit, and whither flee from your face? If I mount to heaven, you are there; if I sink down to hell, even there you are present?* (Ps 138(139):7–8) If there is no place from which he is absent, can he fail us anywhere? Confess to the Lord on the lyre, then. If you have plenty of some earthly commodity, give thanks to him who has given it to you; if you lack it, or if you have lost it through some mishap, still go on playing your lyre serenely. He who gave it to you has not been taken from you, even if what he gave has been withdrawn. Yes, even in these circumstances, I tell you, go on calmly playing your lyre. You are certain of your God, so pluck the strings in your heart, and say, like a lyre that gives its sweet sounds from

---

14. *Psalterium.*
15. See Mt 5:45.
16. See Wis 8:1.

below, *The Lord gave, and the Lord has taken away. This has happened as the Lord willed: may the Lord's name be blessed* (Jb 1:21).

Ten commandments and ten strings

6. But when you turn your thoughts to the higher gifts of God—to the commandments he has entrusted to you, the heavenly doctrine with which he has imbued you, the admonitions he has given you[17] from the fount of his truth in heaven—then take up the psaltery and sing psalms to God on this psaltery with its ten strings. There are ten commandments in the law, and in these ten commandments you find the psaltery. It corresponds perfectly. In the first three you have love for God, and in the other seven love of your neighbor;[18] and you certainly know, since the Lord has told us, that *on these two commandments depend all the law and the prophets* (Mt 22:40). From on high God instructs you that *the Lord your God is one God,*[19] and there you have one string. *You shall not misuse the name of the Lord your God:* there is string number two. *Observe the sabbath,* but not in carnal fashion, with the amusements the Jews indulge in, abusing their leisure to do mischief. They would be better off digging all day long than spending the day dancing. For your part you must ponder on the rest you are called to enjoy in the Lord your God, and do all you have to do with that rest in view. You must abstain from working like slaves. Anyone who commits sin is a slave of sin,[20] and it is better to be enslaved to another human being than to sin. These first three commandments are concerned with loving God. Think about his unity, his truth, and the enjoyment to be found in him;[21] for there is indeed pleasure for us in God, in whom we enjoy the true sabbath and true rest. This is why another psalm bids us, *Delight in the Lord, and he will grant you your heart's desire* (Ps 36(37):4). Can anyone else provide us with such delight as he can, who made everything that delights us?

In these first three commandments charity toward God is enjoined, and in the remaining seven charity to your neighbor, as you are taught to do nothing to another that you would not wish to suffer yourself. *You shall honor your father and mother,* because you hope to be honored by your own children. *Do not commit adultery,* because you would not want your wife committing adultery behind your back. *Do not kill,* because you do not want to be killed yourself. *Do not steal,* because you do not want your things stolen. *Do not bear false witness,* because you hate anyone who gives false evidence to damage you. *Do not lust after your neighbor's wife,*

---

17. Variant: "the gifts he has given to you more than to others."
18. See Ex 20:2–17; Dt 5:6–21.
19. Compare Dt 6:4.
20. See Jn 8:34.
21. Perhaps a trinitarian allusion, but also a reflection on the first three commandments.

because you do not want anyone lusting after yours either.[22] *Do not covet anything that belongs to your neighbor*, because if anyone covets your property, you are annoyed. Turn against yourself the denunciation you hurl against anyone who hurts or offends you.

Fear and love as motives for obedience

All these commandments are from God. They were granted to us as the gift of divine wisdom, and are trumpeted from heaven. Pluck your psaltery, then, and fulfill the law, for the Lord your God came not to supersede it but to bring it to perfect fulfillment.[23] You will fulfill through love what was beyond your powers through fear. A person who refrains from a bad action out of fear would really like to do it, if it were allowed; so even if the possibility of carrying it out is absent, the person's will is attached to the bad deed. "I'm not doing it," he or she will say. Why not? "Because I'm afraid to." Then you do not yet love righteousness, you are still a slave. Become a son or a daughter. Nonetheless a good slave may become a good son or daughter, so go on refraining from sin out of fear, and you will gradually learn to refrain also out of love, for there is beauty in righteousness. Let the fear of punishment deter you; but righteousness has its own fair character; it catches the eye and sets its lovers on fire. For love of it the martyrs trod this world underfoot and shed their blood. What were they in love with, when they renounced everything? They were truly lovers, I tell you. Am I trying to discourage you from loving? No, of course not. Anyone who does not love is a cold character, frozen stiff. Let us love beauty, but let it be the beauty that appeals to the eye of the heart. Let us love beauty, but let it be worthwhile, praiseworthy loveliness. Righteousness kindles our minds; people inflamed with righteousness are stimulated to speak, to shout aloud the beauty of it, to tell everyone within earshot, "It's lovely, it's splendid!" What have they seen? In what sense is an old, bent person beautiful?[24] Put a righteous old man on show: there is nothing lovable in his bodily appearance, yet everyone loves him. He is loved for that part of his being that we cannot see; or rather, he is loved for that part of him where he is seen only by our hearts. *For the Lord will grant sweetness and our earth shall yield its fruit*,[25] so that you are enabled to carry through by love what you found difficult when your motive was fear. Why do I say, "difficult"? Impossible

---

22. In the Deuteronomic text of the commandments (Dt 5:6–21), which Augustine is following in preference to the text in Exodus, a wife is mentioned first, and a man's other possessions after her; this makes possible the division of the commandment against covetousness into two, as noted earlier. Ex 20:17 regards a wife as one of the chattels.
23. See Mt 5:17.
24. The last three sentences translate a variant given in the best codices; the punctuation in the received text is slightly different.
25. See Ps 84:13(85:12).

rather, as long as our attitude is that we would prefer some command not to be laid upon us, impossible as long as we are not impelled to carry it out by love but constrained by fear. "Do not steal; fear hell"; and such a person would rather there were no hell to be thrown into. But when do they begin to love righteousness? Only when they would rather there were no robberies, even if hell did not exist to swallow up those who commit them. This is what it means to love righteousness.

7. But what is this righteousness like? Who is to describe it for us? What kind of beauty does God's wisdom have? Through it all those things that appeal to our eyes are beautiful, and to see it, to embrace it, our hearts need to be cleansed. We profess ourselves its lovers, so it sets us to rights,[26] so that we may not fail to please it. And when people berate us for anything we do to please the one we love, how lightly we take their complaints, how we despise them, how completely we discount them![27] Think of certain odious, fickle and amorous young men. When their hair and clothes are arranged by their girlfriends according to the girls' own liking they think this is fine provided that they are now pleasing to the girls they fancy, and they do not care if other people find them objectionable. Indeed they usually are unattractive to sensible people—or, rather, not usually but always—and are rebuked by persons of sounder judgment. "Your hairstyle is a disgrace," says a sober-minded man to a depraved youth. "It is unworthy of you to go about sporting those long curls." But the young man knows that his hairstyle pleases someone; he hates the man who rightly rebukes him and hangs onto the style that is attractive to perverted taste. He regards you as his enemy if you cut off that offending hair.[28] He keeps out of your way, and pays not the slightest attention to the reasonable standards that prompted the rebuke. So then, if such youths take no notice of those who administer well-judged admonitions, and prefer to remain pretty deceivers, should we pay any attention to unrighteous scoffers, people who have no eyes to see what we love, in matters where we are seeking to please the wisdom of God?

As you ponder all this, you upright of heart, *confess to the Lord on the lyre, and sing psalms to him with the ten-stringed psaltery.*

Verse 3. The song of the heart

8. *Sing him a new song.* Strip off your oldness, you know a new song. A new person, a New Covenant, a new song. People stuck in the old life have no business with this new song; only they can learn it who are new persons, renewed by grace and throwing off the old, sharers already in the New Covenant, which is the kingdom of heaven. All our love yearns toward that, and in its longing our love sings a new song. Let us sing this new song

---

26. *Componit.*
27. Variant: "...the one we love, how we are considered depraved by those who rebuke us, and worthy of their contempt, and entirely discounted by them!"
28. Or, more mildly with a variant, "censure" it.

not with our tongues but with our lives. *Sing him a new song, sing skillfully to him.* Each one of us is anxious to know how to sing to God. Sing to him, yes, but not out of tune. We don't want to grate on his ears. Sing skillfully, my friend. If you have to give a performance before some musical expert, and you are told, "Be sure to sing in a way that will please him," you are nervous about attempting it without any musical training, lest you displease the maestro,[29] because any shortcoming which someone ignorant of music might overlook will be criticized by the expert. Which of us, then, would volunteer to sing skillfully to God, who so shrewdly judges the singer, who so closely scrutinizes every detail, who listens with such discrimination? When will you ever be able to present him with so polished a performance that you at no point jar upon such a perfect ear?

Do not worry, for he provides you with a technique for singing. Do not go seeking lyrics, as though you could spell out in words anything that will give God pleasure. Sing to him *in jubilation*. This is what acceptable singing to God means: to sing jubilantly. But what is that? It is to grasp the fact that what is sung in the heart cannot be articulated in words. Think of people who sing at harvest time, or in the vineyard, or at any work that goes with a swing. They begin by caroling their joy in words, but after a while they seem to be so full of gladness that they find words no longer adequate to express it, so they abandon distinct syllables and words, and resort to a single cry of jubilant happiness. Jubilation is a shout of joy;[30] it indicates that the heart is bringing forth what defies speech. To whom, then, is this jubilation more fittingly offered than to God who surpasses all utterance? You cannot speak of him because he transcends our speech; and if you cannot speak of him, yet may not remain silent, what else can you do but cry out in jubilation, so that your heart may tell its joy without words, and the unbounded rush of gladness not be cramped by syllables? *Sing skillfully to him in jubilation.*

Verse 4. The fidelity of God

9. *Because the Lord's word is straight, and all his works are done in faith.* By its very straightness it is abhorrent to those who are not straight themselves. *And all his works are done in faith.* All your works should be performed in faith, because the one who lives by faith is just,[31] and faith works by choosing to love.[32]

Yes, whatever you do must be done in faith, because it is by believing in God that you become a faithful person. But how can God's works be

---

29. Variant: "...will please him, then, if you want to sing with some musical competence, you are nervous lest you displease the maestro."
30. *Iubilum* in classical Latin evokes rustic songs, mountain cries, whoops of joy, shepherds' shouts.
31. See Rom 1:17.
32. See Gal 5:6.

done in faith? Are we to suppose that God lives by faith? No, of course not, but we have experienced the faithfulness of God. This is not just my assertion; listen to what the apostle says: *God is so faithful that he does not allow you to be tempted more fiercely than you can bear, but along with the temptation ordains the outcome, so that you may withstand it* (1 Cor 10:13). So you have heard him call God faithful there, and now listen to what he says elsewhere: *If we hold out, we shall reign with him; if we deny him, he will deny us; if we do not believe, he still remains faithful, for he cannot deny himself* (2 Tm 2:12–13). It is clear from this that God is faithful, but obviously we must distinguish our faithful God from a faithful man or woman. A faithful human being is one who believes in God who promises; our faithful God is he who delivers what he promised to his human creature. Let us keep a tight hold on our supremely faithful debtor, because we hold onto him as the supremely merciful promisor. It is not as though we had lent him anything, so as to be able to hold him as a debtor; rather do we receive from him whatever we have to offer him, and whatever good there is in us is his gift. All the good things that gladden us are from him. Who has understood the mind of the Lord, or been his counselor? Who ever forestalled him in giving, and so deserved a recompense? From him and through him and in him are all things.[33]

We have given him nothing whatever, and yet we can hold him to his debt. How can he be a debtor? Because he is the promisor. We do not say to God, "Give back what we gave you," but "Give what you have promised." *Because the Lord's word is straight.* Straight in what sense? He does not deceive you, so you must not deceive him; indeed, you must not deceive yourself. But iniquity has lied to itself.[34] *The Lord's word is straight, and all his works are done in faith.*

Verse 5. Uniting mercy and judgment

10. *He loves judgment and mercy.* Practice these yourself, since God does. Look carefully at these two, mercy and judgment. This present time is the season for mercy, but the season for judgment will come later. Why do we say that this is the season for mercy? Because at this present time God calls those who have turned away from him, and forgives their sins when they return; he is patient with sinners until they are converted, and when they are converted at last he forgets everything in their past and promises them a future, encouraging the sluggish, comforting the troubled, guiding the eager and helping the embattled. He deserts no one who struggles and calls out to him; he bestows on us the wherewithal to offer him sacrifice; and he himself gives us the means of winning his favor. Let us not allow this time of mercy to pass away, my brothers and sisters, let it not pass us by. Judgment is coming. Then there will be repentance, certainly, but a

---

33. See Rom 11:34–36.
34. See Ps 26(27):12.

repentance that is sterile. *Groaning in anguish of spirit, the wicked will ruefully say within themselves*—these are the very words of Scripture, from the Book of Wisdom—*what good has our pride done us, or what benefit has come to us from our vaunted wealth? All these things have passed away like a shadow* (Wis 5:3.8.9). Let us admit even now that all things are passing away like a shadow. Let us say now, while we can say it with profit, "They are passing away," so that we may not be reduced to saying uselessly later, *They have passed away.* This present time is the season of mercy, but then will be the season for judgment.

11. Make no mistake, brothers and sisters: in God these two realities cannot be separated. We might think that they are mutually exclusive, so that a person who is merciful is not allowing judgment its rights, while someone who insists on judgment is forgetting mercy. But God is almighty, and he neither loses sight of judgment when exercising mercy, nor abandons mercy when passing judgment. He looks mercifully on his image, taking our frailty into account, and our mistakes and our blindness; he calls us, and when we turn back to him he forgives our sins. But he does not forgive those who refuse to turn back. Is he merciful to the unjust? He has lost sight of judgment, has he? Is he not right to judge between the converted and the unconverted? Or does it seem just to you that the converted and the unconverted should receive the same treatment, that one who confesses and one who lies, the humble and the proud, should all be welcomed without distinction? Even as he exercises mercy God has a place for judgment.

But within the judgment itself he will find room for mercy too, for he will deal gently with those at least to whom he can say, *I was hungry, and you fed me* (Mt 25:35). We know it, because in one of the apostolic letters we are told, *Merciless judgment will be passed on anyone who has not shown mercy* (Jas 2:13); and the Lord says, *Blessed are the merciful, for they shall obtain mercy* (Mt 5:7). Even in his judgment, then, there will be mercy as well, yet not at the expense of judgment. Mercy will be shown, if not to all and sundry, at least to anyone who has first shown mercy, and the mercy shown to such a person will itself be just, because discriminating. It is certainly a mercy that our sins are forgiven, and a mercy that we should be granted eternal life; but notice the judgment that enters into it: *Forgive, and you will be forgiven; give, and gifts will be given to you* (Lk 6:37–38). Unquestionably the promise that *gifts will be given to you* and *you will be forgiven* is a mark of mercy; but if there were no place in it for judgment, the Lord would not have said, *The same measure that you measure out will be measured in turn to you* (Mt 7:2).

Against favoritism, a cautionary tale

12. Well now, you have heard how God exercises both mercy and judgment; so exercise both mercy and judgment yourself. Do you imagine that while these qualities belong to God, they are no business of humans? Not at all. If they were no concern of ours, the Lord would not have said to the

Pharisees, *You have neglected the weightier matters of the law: mercy and judgment* (Mt 23:23). They are your business, then. Do not imagine either that, while you have a duty to exercise mercy, judgment is no affair of yours. Suppose it happens that you have to hear a case between two people, one rich and the other poor, and it turns out that the poor party has a weak case, while the case of the rich is sound. Now, if you are not well schooled in the kingdom of God, you may think you are acting virtuously if out of would-be kindness to the poor person you play down and conceal his wrongdoing, and try to vindicate him, and make his case appear better than it is. Then if you are criticized for giving an unfair judgment, you pretend that you were motivated by mercy, and reply, "Yes, I know, but he was poor, and deserved mercy." How did you hang onto mercy, if you let judgment slip? "But," you object, "how could I hold onto judgment without letting mercy go? Ought I to have decided the case against the poor defendant who had no means of making restitution, or, if he had, would have had nothing left to live on after restitution had been made?" Your God tells you, *You shall not show partiality to a poor person in giving judgment* (Lv 19:15). It is easy to say that we should not be prejudiced in a rich person's favor. Everyone can see the point of that; would that everyone acted on it! But where someone can go wrong who thinks to please God is in giving unfair preference to a poor litigant, and then saying to God, "Look, I showed favor to a poor man." You should have held tight to both, mercy and judgment. To begin with, what kind of mercy have you really shown to the poor person, by making yourself an accomplice in his dishonesty? You spared his purse but struck a blow to his heart. The poor man remained dishonest, and all the more so for seeing that you, a just man, seemed to approve of his dishonesty. He left your presence unjustly assisted, and remained in God's presence justly condemned. What kind of mercy have you dealt to him, by conniving at his injustice? You are to be judged more cruel than merciful. "What should I have done, then?" you reply. You should have given judgment on the merits of the case, and convicted the poor person, and then sought to mollify the rich man. There is a right place for judging, and a different place for making an appeal for clemency. If the rich litigant had watched you holding fast to justice, and giving no preference to a dishonest poor man, but justly finding him guilty as his crime deserved, would not that rich claimant have been inclined to mercy at your petition, as he had been rendered happy at your judgment?

Conclusion

Many verses of the psalm still remain, brothers and sisters, but we must take into account the mental and physical stamina of an audience comprising a wide variety of persons; for even though we are refreshed by the same wheat, we all taste it differently. And to drive away any weary aversion, let this be enough.[35]

---

35. Variant: "...we must take mental and physical stamina into account and provide refreshing variety for each hearer, for the same wheat yields many different flavors. So to drive away any aversion...."

Exposition of Psalm 72

Synopsis

The title reads, *The hymns of David, Son of Jesse, have failed*, because the first David represented the provisional earthly promises of the old covenant that were bound to pass away. But the New Covenant was hidden within the old, "like fruit in the root," just as Christ was in the loins of the patriarchs. Christ and the New Covenant now have burst forth into view (1–3). The old covenant's written record is full of prophetic narrative and characters that Christians read and unpack. The Psalmist's experience shows a person struggling under the incomplete outlook of the old covenant (4–6).

The Psalmist's feet had almost slipped into scorning God because he saw sinners enjoying undeserved peace (7–9). He was tempted to envy, and to consider God uncaring and unjust because the wicked prosper and the just suffer. Look at how evil people scoff at death, he says; they speak arrogantly and fairly ooze iniquity. They think themselves special, despise those beneath them, think and speak maliciously, and boast to the skies with their soaring tongues (10–15). So the Psalmist began to question things. Had he lived a godly, self-denying life and suffered for no reason? (16–20) But, just then, something checked his skepticism. Speaking this way contradicts the long line of my forebears, he thought. But the problem was too hard to solve alone. Not until he entered *God's holy place* did he see the final outcome of punishment being reserved for evildoers (20–23). Full of guile, they are beguiled; thrown down even as they lift themselves up, they fade like a dream (24–25).

Don't covet wealth, or, if you're wealthy, don't put your trust in it (26). The Psalmist realized he had become *like a beast* before God. But God grasped him before falling and gave him a new perspective (27–30). Now nothing but God satisfies his desires, and no other reward will do than to have God. This is "chaste love" for the one in whom we have all things. Get as many others as possible to desire God this way; there's room for all. Each possesses all of God, and all together possess God completely. Sorry—the stench in here tells me this was a long sermon. But you demanded it! (31–34)

Augustine's Text of Psalm 72

(1) The hymns of David, son of Jesse, have failed. A Psalm of Asaph.
   How good God is to Israel, to those of straightforward hearts!
(2) My feet had all but slipped;
   My steps had very nearly slid out of control.
(3) Because I envied sinners,
   Seeing the peace that sinners enjoy.
(4) There is for them no avoidance of death,
   And their scourging will be inevitable.
(5) But they have no part in the hardship of mortals,
   And will not be scourged as others are.
(6) Therefore pride has taken possession of them;
   They are entirely enveloped in their iniquity and impiety.
(7) Their iniquity will leak out as through folds of fat;
   They have crossed over into a certain attitude of heart.
(8) They thought and spoke maliciously,
   They shouted their iniquity.
(9) Their boastful talk is directed to the sky,
   And their tongues have soared above the earth.
(10) Therefore shall my people come back here;
   And full days will be found in them.
(11) And they said, How does God know?
   Is there any knowledge in the Most High?
(12) Look, they are sinners,
   Yet they have won abundant wealth in this world.
(13) So I said, To no purpose have I justified my heart,
   And I have washed my hands in innocence.
(14) All day long I have been chastised,
   And sharp reproof comes to me early in the morning.
(15) When I kept saying, That will be my story....
   Why, then, I condemned the long line of your children.
   (Var.:...then, with whom in the long line of your children will I have been in harmony?)

(16) I tried to solve the problem,
   But it is too hard for me.
(17) Until I come into God's holy place,
   And I understand what the final outcome must be.
(18) It is because of their guile that you conferred these things upon them;
   You threw them down even as they were lifting themselves up.
(19) How suddenly they have been desolated!
   They have faded away; they have perished because of their iniquity,
(20) Like the dream of one who awakens.
   In your city, O Lord, you will reduce their image to nothing.
(21) Because my heart was delighted, my kidneys were changed.
(22) I was brought to nothing, and I knew it not.
(23) I became like a beast in your presence.
   Yet I was always with you.
(24) You grasped the hand of my right hand.
   You led me by your will, and you have taken me up in glory.
(25) For what is there for me in heaven
   And what else but you have I desired on earth?
(26) My heart and my flesh have failed;
   But he is the God of my heart, and God is my portion for eternity.
(27) Lo, those who go far from you will perish;
   You have destroyed everyone who leaves you to go a-whoring.
(28) My good is to hold fast to God, to place in God all my hope,
   That I may proclaim all your praise in the courts of the daughter of Zion.

Exposition

A Sermon[1]

The title: how have David's hymns failed?

1. Listen, oh listen, you tenderly beloved members of Christ's body, you whose hope is the Lord your God, who have no eyes for empty things

---

1. Delivered in the Basilica Restituta at Carthage, possibly in the night of 13–14 September 411.

and lying foolishness.[2] If any of you still do have eyes for such things, you too must listen, that you may regard them no longer. Over this psalm is inscribed a title that reads, *The hymns of David, son of Jesse, have failed*.[3] The title then continues, *A psalm for Asaph himself.* We have many psalms that bear David's name in their titles, but the extra designation, *son of Jesse*, is never added anywhere else. We must believe that this was not done capriciously or without purpose, for God drops hints for us everywhere, and summons careful, earnest minds to deeper understanding. What, then, is the significance of this phrase, *the hymns of David have failed*?

Hymns are praises offered to God with singing; hymns are songs, with God's praise as their theme. If there is praise, but not praise of God, there is no hymn. If there is praise, and the praise is offered to God, but not sung, again there is no hymn. For there to be a hymn, three elements are required: there must be praise, it must be for God, and it must be sung. In what sense, then, have *the hymns failed*? What? Praises sung to God have failed? That looks like a gloomy piece of news, an announcement of mourning; for anyone who sings praise is not only praising, but praising cheerfully. The singer of praise is not only performing musically but showing love for the one who is sung about. To confess God by praise is a way of preaching him; to pour out passion in song is the way of a lover.

The hymns of David have failed, says the psalm; and it adds, *David, the son of Jesse*. David, who was king of Israel and Jesse's son, lived at a certain time in the Old Testament, and at that time the New Testament was hidden within the Old, as fruit is in the root. If you look for fruit in a root you will not find it; yet you will not find any fruit on the branches either, unless it has sprung from the root. At that early time the prophets spoke to the first people, the people who were Abraham's descendants in the carnal sense (for of course the second people, the people who belong to the New Covenant, are Abraham's posterity too, but spiritually). The few prophets who were sent to the first people understood what God desired and when he willed it to be publicly proclaimed, so they spoke to that still carnal people, foretelling future events and the coming of our Lord Jesus Christ. Christ himself, inasmuch as he was to be born according to the flesh, was hidden in the root, that is to say, in the bloodline of the patriarchs. At the appointed time he was to be revealed, like fruit forming from the flower, and so Scripture says, *A shoot has sprung from Jesse's stock, and a flower has opened* (Is 11:1). Similarly the entire New Covenant was hidden in Christ in those early days, and known only to the prophets and a few devout per-

---

2. See Ps 39:5(40:4).
3. These words occur as the last verse of the preceding psalm in the Septuagint and the Vulgate, but Augustine, like Ambrose, regarded them as part of the title to the present psalm. The word ἐξέλιπον in the Septuagint means "have come to an end," as the Latin *defecerunt* can also; but Augustine reads more into it, as the succeeding paragraphs show.

sons—not known, of course, as already manifest and present, but revealed as to come later. To take one simple example, brothers and sisters: what was the meaning of that gesture when Abraham, about to send his trusty servant to find a wife for his only son, required the servant to swear to him and, in administering the oath, ordered the servant, *Place your hand under my thigh, and so swear?* (Gn 24:2) What was present in Abraham's thigh, that the servant should have been ordered to place his hand there to take the oath? What else but that posterity promised to Abraham when God said, *In your seed shall all the nations of the earth be blessed?* (Gn 22:18) Now the thigh symbolizes the flesh; and from Abraham's flesh, through Isaac and Jacob and (to shorten the list) Mary, our Lord Jesus Christ was born.

Insertion of a Gentile graft into patriarchal stock

2. How are we to prove that the patriarchs constituted the root? Let us put our question to Paul. He rebuked the gentiles who had come to believe in Christ, and imagined that their faith gave them the right to despise the Jews who had crucified him. They were forgetting that from the Jewish people proceeded one wall, and from the uncircumcised gentiles the other wall, and that these two were destined to meet at the corner, that is, in Christ.[4] When these gentiles behaved arrogantly, then, Paul took them to task: *If you were cut out of the wild olive and engrafted into the Jewish stock*, he says, *do not boast at the expense of the branches. If you are tempted to boast, remember that it is not you who support the root, but the root you* (Rom 11:24.18). He reminds them that some branches were broken from the patriarchal root on account of their unbelief, and that the shoot of wild olive, which is the Church called from the gentiles, was grafted in to draw on the olive's richness. But who would ever graft a wild olive into the cultivated variety? We usually do it the other way round—the olive into the stock of a wild plant. We never see a wild olive grafted into a cultivated one. Anybody who does that will find no fruit except the wild berries. It is the graft that grows, and the fruit of the graft that we pick; we gather no fruit from the root, only from the scion.

Yet the apostle demonstrates that this was exactly what God had by his almighty power caused to happen: that a wild olive should be inserted into the stock of the true olive, and the graft bear not wild fruit but real olives. The apostle reminds us of God's omnipotence, saying, *If you were cut out of the wild olive and unnaturally grafted into the true olive, do not boast at the expense of the branches. But you maintain, "Those branches have been broken off so that I could be grafted in." Yes, but they were broken off because of their unbelief. You, for your part, stand in faith; be not high-minded, but stand in awe* (Rom 11:24.18–20). What does he mean by *Be not high-minded*? Do not be proud because you were grafted in; rather beware lest you be broken off for unbelief, as they were broken off.

---

4. See Eph 2:20.

They were broken off because of their unbelief. You, for your part, stand in faith; be not high-minded, but stand in awe, Paul warns them. *If God did not spare the natural branches, he may not spare you either* (Rom 11:21). Then follows a fine text, one eminently necessary and worthy of our attention: *Look at the kindness and the severity of God: severity indeed toward those who were broken off, but goodness toward you, who were grafted in. Be sure to abide in that goodness; for if you do not, you too will be cut out, whereas they, if they do not persist in their unbelief, will be grafted in again* (Rom 11:22-23).

3. During the period of the Old Covenant, brothers and sisters, the promises God made to that carnal people concerned earthly, temporal matters. They were promised an earthly kingdom; they were promised a land, and were led into it after their deliverance from Egypt; for Joshua, son of Nun,[5] led them into the land of promise, where the earthly Jerusalem was built and David reigned as king. They did indeed receive the land, for after being rescued from Egypt, and crossing the Red Sea, after tramping along all the winding ways[6] and wandering through the wilderness, they were given the land and the kingdom. But after they had been given their kingdom they sinned, because the good things bestowed on them were no more than earthly; and as punishment for their sins they began to suffer attacks, and defeats, and at last captivity. In the end their very city was overthrown.

Such were the provisional promises, promises that were not meant to last, but served as signs of other, future promises that would endure. This whole collapse of temporal promises was itself a sign, a prophecy of what was to come. The kingdom failed, the kingdom where David ruled—David son of Jesse. When we call him by that title we remember that he was only a man, even if a prophet and a holy man, since he beheld Christ who would come one day, and would indeed be born according to the flesh from David's own line. Still, David was no more than a man; he was not yet the Messiah, not yet our King, the Son of God, but only King David, son of Jesse. His kingdom was doomed to fail, that kingdom for which a carnal people was wont to praise God, since all they cared about was that they had been granted temporal deliverance from their taskmasters, and had escaped from their pursuers through the Red Sea, and had been led through the wilderness, and had found their own country and their kingdom. Only for benefits of this order were they accustomed to praise God, for they did not yet understand what God was foreshadowing and promising through these gifts.

We can see, then, that when these good things failed—the gifts for which a carnal people, David's subjects, were wont to praise God—*the hymns of David failed.* Not those of David, Son of God, but those of David,

---

5. In Augustine's version "Jesus, son of Nave."
6. Variant: "terrors."

son of Jesse. So now we have navigated through the title of this psalm, dangerous place though it was, in the way that the Lord willed us to; and you have been instructed as to why the title stated that *the hymns of David, son of Jesse, have failed.*

The title, continued: Asaph, the synagogue, represents believers under the Old Covenant

4. Whose voice is it that speaks in this psalm? Asaph's. But what is Asaph? Those who have translated the Hebrew into Greek and the Greek into Latin for us interpret *Asaph* as "the synagogue." So it is to the voice of the synagogue that we listen here. When you hear the name, "synagogue," do not immediately think of it as something detestable, the people that put the Lord to death. There was a synagogue that killed the Lord; no one doubts that. But remember also that it was from the synagogue that there came the rams, whose children we are. This is why another psalm says, *Bring the offspring of rams to the Lord* (Ps 28(29):1). Who are the rams that came from the synagogue?[7] Peter, John, James, Andrew, Bartholomew, and the rest of the apostles. From the synagogue too came the man who was at first Saul, then Paul; first a proud man, then a humble one. You remember that the earlier Saul, his namesake, had been a proud king, uncontrollable. It was not out of vanity that the apostle changed his name; on the contrary, his change from Saul to Paul was a transition from being proud to being cut down to size, for "Paul" means "small." Shall I remind you what he was like as Saul? Listen to Paul recalling what he had been through his own malice, and what he was now through God's grace; listen to how he had been Saul, and how he was now Paul. *I was originally a persecutor and a blasphemer, and harmed people* (1 Tm 1:13), he says. You have heard about Saul; now listen to Paul: *I am the least of the apostles.* What does he mean by saying that he is the least, if not, "I am just Paul"? He continues, *I am not worthy to be called an apostle.* Why not? "Because I was Saul." What does that mean—"I was Saul"? Let him tell us: *Because I persecuted God's Church*, he says. *But by God's grace I am what I am* (1 Cor 15:9–10). He has renounced all his towering stature. Now he is very small in himself, though great in Christ.

And what does Paul teach us? That *God has not cast off his people*, the people sprung from Jewish origins. *God has not cast off his own people, whom he foreknew. For I am myself sprung from the race of Israel, from the stock of Abraham, and the tribe of Benjamin* (Rom 11:2.1). So Paul came to us from the synagogue; Peter and the other apostles came from the synagogue. When you hear the name, "synagogue," think not of what it deserved, but of the children it brought to birth.

In this psalm, then, the synagogue is speaking. The hymns of David, son of Jesse, have failed, as the temporal goods for which a carnal people

---

7. On the apostles as rams, leaders of the flock, see *Exposition of Psalm* 64, 18.

used to praise God have failed. But why did they fail? So that other blessings might be looked for. What other blessings? Blessings in no way present as yet? No: blessings present but hidden under prophetic types; blessings not entirely absent, but concealed there in the root under mysterious signs. What are they? These things are symbols for us, says the apostle.[8]

The prophetic value of Israel's experiences

5. Now consider briefly how these things have symbolic import for us. The Israelite people dominated by Pharaoh and the Egyptians represents the Christian people which, before it came to faith, was indeed predestined for God, but still served demons and the devil, prince of demons. It was a people under the Egyptian yoke and enslaved to its sins, for the devil has no way of gaining control over us other than through our sins. The Israelites are freed from the Egyptians through Moses; the Christian people is freed from its former life of sin through our Lord Jesus Christ. The one people makes its passover through the Red Sea, the other through baptism. All the enemies of the former people die in the Red Sea; all our sins die in baptism. But notice this point, brothers and sisters: after crossing the Red Sea the Israelites are not given their homeland immediately, nor are they allowed carefree triumph, as though all their foes had disappeared. They still have to face the loneliness of the desert, and enemies still lurk along their way; so too after baptism Christian life must still confront temptations. In that wilderness the Israelites sighed after their promised homeland; and what else do Christians sigh for, once washed clean in baptism? Do they already reign with Christ? No; we have not reached our homeland yet, but it will not vanish; the hymns of David will not fail there.

Let all the faithful listen and mark this; let them realize where they are. They are in the desert, sighing for their homeland. Our foes died when we were baptized, but those were the enemies who pursued us from the rear. What do I mean by that—enemies who pursued from the rear? I mean that what we have in front of us is the future; the past is behind. All our past sins were blotted out in baptism. The things that tempt us now are not pursuing from behind, but lying in ambush along our path. This is why the apostle, still on this desert trek himself, declared, *Forgetting what lies behind and straining to what lies ahead, I bend my whole effort to follow after the prize of God's heavenly call* (Phil 3:13–14), which is another way of saying, "The country of God's heavenly promise." Though it all happened so long ago, brothers and sisters, whatever that people endured in the wilderness, whatever God lavished upon it, whatever the chastisements and whatever the gifts, all of them were prophetic types of what we receive for our consolation or suffer for our probation as we walk in Christ through the desert of this life, seeking our homeland. Small wonder, then, that the type which foreshadowed the future should itself pass away. The former

---

8. See 1 Cor 10:6.

people were led all the way to the promised land; but was it a country that would be theirs for ever? If it had been, it would not have been a symbol, but the real thing. No, it was a figure only, for what the people were brought into was something temporal; and if they were led only to a temporal goal, that goal had to fail sooner or later. When it failed, they would be forced to seek another, one that would never fail.

If temporal blessings were all God gave and promised, the happiness of the wicked was scandalous

6. The synagogue consisted, then, of the people in Israel who faithfully worshiped God, but did so for the sake of temporal goods and immediate advantages. They were not like impious people who seek such present goods from demons; clearly the Israelites were in this respect better than the gentiles, because they did at least seek the good things of the present life and temporal blessings from the one God, who is the creator of all things, both spiritual and corporeal. Devout persons among the Israelites were nonetheless preoccupied with carnal concerns, for the synagogue consisted of people who were good, but good only with regard to this temporal order of things, not of people who were good in a spiritual sense. There were a few of these latter, certainly: spiritual persons like the prophets, a few who understood about a heavenly kingdom that would last for all eternity. But for the most part the synagogue kept its thoughts fixed on what it had received from God, and what God had promised to his people: namely, an amplitude of earthly goods, a homeland, peace, and happiness in this world. Yet all these things were fraught with symbolic meaning, and the people did not understand what lay hidden under these signs. They thought these were the greatest things God had to give, and could not imagine that he reserved better gifts for those who love him and serve him. So Israelites concentrated on immediate rewards, and observed that there were sinners, impious people, blasphemers, demon-worshipers, children of the devil, who lived in wickedness and pride, yet had plenty of worldly and temporal goods. And it was precisely with an eye to such benefits that the synagogue itself paid cult to God. So a very pernicious thought arose in the heart of the synagogue, one which sent its feet slithering and all but slipping off God's path.

Now that thought, understandably, occurred to people under the Old Covenant. But how I wish it were not found even today in our carnally-minded brothers and sisters—today, when the happiness brought us by the New Covenant is openly proclaimed! What did the synagogue say, long ago? What did the earlier people say? "We serve God, yet we are rebuked and chastised. The things we loved, the things we prized so highly as God's gifts, are taken away from us. Yet those wicked, guilt-laden folk, proud, blasphemous, turbulent people, are awash with all the good things for which we serve God! There does not seem to be any point in serving him."

These are the sentiments expressed in our psalm, which is the protest of a people fainting and staggering. When it considers that the goods for which it was accustomed to serve God are available in abundance to others who do not serve him, it totters and almost falls. It fails, along with the hymns we spoke about, because hymns were bound to fail in hearts so troubled. Why should that be so? Because while they were entertaining such thoughts, they were not praising God. How could they praise God when they believed that he was acting perversely, in giving so much prosperity to the faithless while refusing it to those who served him? To their way of thinking God did not seem good, and those who did not consider God to be good would certainly not praise him. And when they stopped praising God, hymns fell silent as far as they were concerned.

Later on, however, they came to understand. When God withdrew temporal goods from his servants, yet bestowed them on his enemies, on blasphemous and unbelieving sinners, he meant to teach his servants to seek something different. They came to understand that besides all those things that he gives to the good and the wicked, and sometimes takes away from both good and wicked, there is something else that he reserves for the good alone. What does he reserve for good people? What does he keep for them? Himself.

Now, as I see it, we have launched into the psalm: in the name of the Lord we have already grasped what it is about. Listen to the plaint of one who had gone astray by thinking that God cannot be good, because he gives earthly goods to bad people, and takes them away from his own servants. Listen to this speaker remembering his error and repenting. He came to understand what God was keeping for his faithful ones all the while; and so he changed his mind, he castigated himself, and burst out....

Verse 1. Rectitude of heart and clarity of sight

7. *How good God is to Israel!* But to whom in Israel? *To those of straightforward hearts.* What is he to the perverse of heart? He seems perverse to them. A similar idea is expressed in another psalm: *With a holy person you will be holy, and with the innocent you will be innocent; but with the perverse you will deal perversely* (Ps 17:26–27(18:25–26)). What can it mean by saying, *You will deal perversely with the perverse*? It means that a crooked, perverse person will see God as perverse. Not that God can in any way be perverted: perish the thought! He is what he is. But it is like the effect of sunshine. The sun seems soothing to one whose eyes are clear, healthy, vigorous and strong, but on inflamed eyes sunlight strikes like sharp darts. Sunlight invigorates the one observer and tortures the other, yet the sun is unchanged; the change is in the beholder.[9] So when you begin to be crooked yourself, God will seem crooked to you; but it is you who have changed, not God. What brings joy to good people will be

---

9. Variant: "...but it changes the beholder."

painful to you. This is what the psalmist experienced, what prompted him to exclaim, *How good God is to Israel, to those of straightforward hearts!*

Verses 2–3. The psalmist totters

8. But how is it with you? *My feet had all but slipped.* And when did your feet begin to slip? "When my heart was not straightforward." In what sense was it not straightforward? "Listen, and I will tell you: *my steps had very nearly slid out of control.*" He has repeated the thought: *all but* becomes *very nearly*; and *my feet had all but slipped* is echoed by *my steps nearly slid out of control.* So his feet were slipping, his steps slithering wide; but why? His feet slipped, causing him to miss the path, and his steps went out of control, not to the point where he fell headlong, but very nearly. What exactly did happen? "I was beginning to go astray, but had not fully done so; I was on the point of falling, but had not quite fallen."

9. Why was that? *"Because I envied sinners, seeing the peace that sinners enjoy.* I studied their situation, and I saw that sinners had peace. What kind of peace? A peace that is temporal, fleeting, transient and earthly; yes, but that was just what I too longed to get from God. I saw that people who were not serving God enjoyed what I longed to have on condition that I served God, and so *my feet had all but slipped* and *my steps very nearly slid out of control."*

Verses 4–6. Temporal prosperity but eternal punishment for the wicked

10. He now tells us briefly why sinners enjoy peace at present: *There is for them no avoidance of death, and their scourging will be inexorable. But they have no part in the hardships of mortals, and will not be scourged as others are.* "Already I understand why they enjoy peace and flourish on earth," he says. For them death is unavoidable; that is to say, certain and eternal death awaits them. They will no more be able to dodge it than it will turn aside from them. *There is for them no avoidance of death, and their scourging will be inexorable.* Over the punishment reserved for them stands an immovable decree; their scourging is to be no temporal chastisement but one that will last for ever.

If such woes await them in the future, is there any compensation in the present? Yes, for *they have no part in the hardships of mortals, and will not be scourged as others are.* No indeed, for the devil himself is not chastised along with human beings, is he? Yet for him eternal punishment is being prepared.

11. How do they react, then, these people who are spared at present the afflictions and labors others undergo? *Therefore pride has taken possession of them,* says the psalm. Watch these proud, insubordinate folk, and see them as a bull marked out for sacrifice, allowed to wander freely and do as much damage as he likes until the day of slaughter. Yes, brothers and sisters, it is a good thing for us to hear in the prophet's words an evocation of the bull I have mentioned. Scripture uses the same image elsewhere,

likening sinners to victims destined for slaughter, and permitted an ominous freedom meanwhile.[10] *Therefore pride has taken possession of them*, says the psalm. What does it mean when it says that *pride has taken possession of them*? *They are entirely enveloped in their iniquity and impiety*. It does not say they are covered, but that they are *entirely enveloped*; every inch of them is contaminated by their impiety. Small wonder that these wretched folk can neither see nor be properly seen. So enveloped are they that the character of their inner life cannot be discerned. If anyone were able to inspect the inmost character of these bad people who seem to be so fortunate in the present life, such an observer would see the grim state of their consciences; anyone who could see into their souls would see how fiercely those souls are buffeted by the storms of desire and fear. The discerning observer would therefore recognize that such people are miserable, even though they are reputed to be happy. But because they *are entirely enveloped in their iniquity and impiety* they neither see nor are seen. The Spirit who inspired these words had the measure of such people; and we must regard them with the insight that is possible for us when the blindfold of impiety is lifted from our eyes. Let us look hard at them. When they are fortunate, let us steer clear of them; when they are fortunate, let us not imitate them. And let us not set our dearest hopes on getting from our God the kind of favors that people who do not serve him have deserved to receive. He is keeping something else in reserve, something that we must long for. Listen now to what this is.

Verse 7. Wealth, pride, and implicit denial of the human condition

12. First of all, let us have a description of them. *Their iniquity will leak out as though from folds of fat*. You can recognize the bull in that, can't you? Listen carefully, brothers and sisters; we certainly must not pass too hastily over these words, *their iniquity will leak out as though from folds of fat*. There are some people who are bad, but bad out of inadequacy. They are bad because they are deprived, because they are exiles, unimportant, laboring under some kind of need. Bad they are, yes, and reprehensible, for it is better to put up with any straitened circumstances than to commit iniquity. All the same, it is one thing to sin out of need, and quite another to sin amid abundance. A poor beggar steals: his iniquity proceeds from his penury. But what of a rich man, lapped in luxury: why does he seize other people's things? The iniquity of the former issues from his meager condition, that of the latter from his obesity. If you say to the destitute thief, "Why did you do it?" he replies, all humble and woebegone and abject, "I was forced into it by my need." But why did you not fear God? "Poverty drove me to it." You say to the rich person, "Why did you do that? Had you no fear of God?"—though in practice you may not be important enough to say anything of the kind. However, if the rich person does deign to listen,

---

10. Compare Prv 7:22.

see whether the iniquity that oozes out of his folds of fat does not wash over you as well. Such people declare war on all who instruct or rebuke them. They become enemies to all who speak the truth, because they are used to being cosseted by the words of flatterers; they are tender of ear, because unsound of heart. So who dare say to a wealthy person, "You did wrong in seizing the property of others"? But even supposing that someone does say it, someone of such stature that the accused cannot reject the question, what will the answer be? A rich person's reply will be entirely contemptuous of God. Why? Because such a person is proud. Proud about what? About being plump and fat. Why so? Because that is the sleek condition of one destined for sacrifice. *Their iniquity will leak out as though from folds of fat.*

13. *They have crossed over into a certain attitude of heart.* Within themselves they have crossed a boundary. What does *they have crossed over* suggest? They have gone off the path. *Crossed over*—in what sense? They have gone beyond the bounds assigned to the human race, they think they are not like other mortals. Yes, I tell you, they have violated the boundaries appointed to humans. You should say to a person of this type, "That poor beggar is your brother or sister. You both descend from the same ancestors, Adam and Eve. Forget your swollen status, forget your high and mighty pride. Although you are surrounded by a vast household, although your gold and silver are plentiful, although you live in a marble house and beneath a paneled roof, you[11] and the poor person are sheltered alike under the one roof of the sky. You are distinguished from the poor man by things that are not truly yours, but only added on from the outside; have regard to yourself, surrounded as you are by them, and not to them as though they were the reality of yourself. Turn your gaze on yourself, and on what you are in relation to that poor person—on yourself, not your possessions. How can you despise your brother? You and he were alike naked in the wombs of your mothers. And when both of you depart this life, when you have breathed forth your souls and your flesh has rotted, let anyone try then to tell the bones of rich and poor apart!"

What I am speaking of is the human condition common to all, the common lot of mortals into which all are born. Here on earth a person may be rich or poor, but it will not always be so. As the rich person did not come rich into the world, neither will he be rich when he leaves it. They both come into the world in the same way, and they will not be distinguished by their departure.

Don't forget that the two of you can change places. The gospel is preached everywhere today, so each of you wealthy folk can recall a certain poor, ulcer-ridden man who used to lie at a rich man's gate, longing to be filled with the crumbs that fell from the rich man's table.[12] Now remember

---

11. Plural, but some witnesses have the singular.
12. See Lk 16:19–31.

someone else, someone like yourself,[13] who was habitually clothed in purple and fine linen, and accustomed to feast sumptuously every day. Eventually the poor man died, and was carried by angels to Abraham's embrace. The rich man also died, and was buried (perhaps no one had bothered to arrange a funeral for the poor man). When the rich man was in torments below, did he not lift his eyes and behold a man now in unlimited joy, the very man whom he had formerly scorned outside his gate? Did he not beg for a drop of water from the finger of someone who had begged for the crumbs that fell from that opulent table?

Think about it, brothers and sisters. How much hardship had the poor man endured? How long had the rich man's luxury lasted? Not long; but the fates that had befallen them were fixed for ever. In the one case the rich man had no means of avoiding death, and now he was to be scourged inexorably, for he had had no part in the hardships of mortals, nor had he been scourged as others are. The other man had been scourged here, but found rest in the world beyond, for God whips every child whom he acknowledges as his.[14]

"To whom do you address this reminder?" you ask.[15] To anyone who feasts sumptuously and goes clad daily in purple and fine linen. "To whom are you speaking?" To one who has crossed over *into a certain attitude of heart*. Such a person may well say, *Send Lazarus; let him at least warn my brothers*,[16] but for himself it will be too late; the time accorded him for fruitful repentance has passed. Or, rather, it is not that space for repentance is denied him, but that there will be everlasting repentance and no salvation to follow it. These people *have crossed over into a certain attitude of heart*.[17]

Verses 8–9. Arrogant speech, lofty plans

14. *They thought and spoke maliciously.* Some people speak maliciously, though with cautious restraint; but how did these folk speak? *They shouted their iniquity.* They were not content with wicked talk; they proclaimed it at the top of their voices, proudly, in the hearing of all. "Look what I'm doing! I'll show you! You will find out whom you have to deal with. I won't leave you alive!" If only they would confine themselves to thinking like this, without blurting it out too! If only their baleful greed were penned

---

13. *Parem tuum.* Some codices have *patrem tuum*: "Remember your own father, who...."
14. See Heb 12:6.
15. This and the following question could be from members of the congregation who found Augustine's remarks disquieting.
16. See Lk 16:27–28.
17. As Augustine considered it earlier in this section, the "crossing over" was an interior event occurring in the present life; but now he seems to be thinking also of the "great gulf" separating Lazarus from the rich man in the world to come.

within the confines of thought, if only such a person could rein it in within his mind! But why should he? Is he a poor, skinny little man? No; *their iniquity will leak out as though from folds of fat. They shouted their iniquity.*

15. *Their boastful talk is directed to the sky, and their tongues have soared above the earth.* What does *soared above the earth* mean? The same thing as *talk directed to the sky*, for to *soar above the earth* is to put oneself above earthly realities. How would anyone do such a thing? It happens when people speak without remembering that they are human and may die suddenly; they utter threats as though expecting to live for ever. Their lofty plans outstrip their earthly frailty, and they take no account of the mortality that clothes them. Failing to understand what Scripture says elsewhere of people like themselves—*his spirit will go forth and return to its own country, and on that day all his plans will come to nothing* (Ps 145(146):4)—they do not remember their last day, and talk proudly. Their boastful words are flung up to the sky, and soar above the earth. If a robber held in prison were unmindful of his last day—the day, that is, which will see him judged—nothing would seem more monstrous than he. Yet he might still have the possibility of escape. Where will you flee to escape death? Your judgment day is absolutely certain. Why promise yourself a long life? Can anything that comes to an end truly be long? But in any case human life is not long, and even if reckoned long it is precarious. Why does a proud person not consider this? Because his boastful talk is directed to the sky, and his tongue has soared above the earth.

Verse 10. Glimmerings of truth: the passage to understanding begins

16. *Therefore shall my people come back here.* Already Asaph is coming back, after considering how wealthy are the wicked and the proud. He is coming back to God; he is beginning to inquire and argue. But when does this occur? When *full days will be found in them.* What are these *full days*? *When the fullness of time had come, God sent his Son* (Gal 4:4). The fullness of time it was when he came to teach us to make light of temporal things, not to rate over-highly what bad people crave, and to bear courageously what bad people fear. He became our Way. He recalled us to our deepest convictions, and advised us as to what we should seek from God. Look at the transition that this entails: a crossing over to preference for what is real, away from the attitude of mind that is constantly beating back on itself and calling back the flood of its own desires. *Therefore shall my people come back here, and full days will be found in them.*

Verses 11–14. Does God not know? Is innocence pointless?

17. *And they said, How does God know? Is there any knowledge in the Most High?* Now we get an example of the kind of thinking they pass through: "Look how well off the ungodly are! Obviously God does not care about human affairs. Is he really aware of what we do?" Consider what

is being said, brothers and sisters; and, we beg you, do not let Christians ever ask, *How does God know? Is there any knowledge in the Most High?*

18. Why does it seem to you that God does not know, and that there is no knowledge on the part of the Most High? The doubter replies, "*Look, they are sinners, yet they have won abundant wealth in this world.*[18] They are sinners, yet they have gained ample wealth in this world!" So the speaker has confessed that he refrained from sin only because he hoped for riches. A carnal soul had traded its righteousness for visible, earthly things. What kind of righteousness is that, if it is preserved only for the sake of money? He is almost rating gold above righteousness, or assuming that when someone swindles another, the person whose property is unlawfully withheld suffers more harm than the one who withholds it. Not so; for though the one loses a garment,[19] the other loses honesty and good faith. "*Look, they are sinners, yet they have won abundant wealth in this world.* So that proves that God knows nothing about it, and the Most High has no knowledge of the matter!"

19. "*So I said, To no purpose have I justified my heart.* If I serve God, and have to go without wealth, while those who do not serve him have plenty, it means that *to no purpose have I justified my heart, and washed my hands in innocence.*[20] What I did is pointless. Where is the reward for my good life? What wages do I get for my service? I live virtuously, and I am in need, while a godless person has plenty. *I have washed my hands in innocence.*"

20. "*All day long I have been chastised.* God's whips do not spare me, I give him good service, and I am whipped; that other fellow gives him no service at all, and is highly honored." This is a hard question that he has set himself. His soul is perplexed; but it is a soul destined to make the passage to a state where it will despise earthly things and long for those of eternity, and here we see something of that passover. The searching inquiry is itself the passage; the soul is tossed by storms but sure of reaching harbor. People who are seriously ill often seem calmer when their cure is very distant, but when they are nearly well their fever rises. Doctors call this the critical onset through which the patient progresses toward health;[21] the fever is more intense, but the direction is toward recovery; the patient's temperature is up, but cool refreshment is not far away. The psalmist too is in a fevered condition, for these are dangerous words, my brothers and

---

18. The Latin could equally well be translated, "Look how sinners, and those who abound in this world, have won their wealth"; both the Hebrew original and the Greek Septuagint have this sense. But Augustine seems to take *abundantes* as qualifying *divitias*, as his following sentence shows.
19. Perhaps Ex 22:26–27 is in mind.
20. Variant: "among the innocent."
21. Augustine comments on this phenomenon in his own progress toward spiritual healing; compare his *Confessions* VI,1,1.

sisters, almost blasphemous: *How does God know?* But the question has something tentative about it, like his earlier words, *all but*. He stops short of declaring, "God does not know," or "There is no knowledge in the Most High"; he is seeking the truth, hesitant and doubtful. It was the same earlier, when he said, *My feet had all but slipped*. Now he asks, *How does God know? Is there any knowledge in the Most High?* He does not give a negative answer, but his doubting is itself dangerous.

Yet through this peril he makes his passage to health. Listen now to the healing: *To no purpose have I justified my heart, and washed my hands among the innocent. All day long I have been chastised, and sharp reproof comes to me early in the morning.* Sharp reproof implies correction, for anyone subjected to it is put straight. What does *early in the morning* suggest? It is not long delayed.

For the godless, correction is delayed. Mine is not; but for them correction comes late, if at all, whereas for me it comes *early in the morning. All day long I have been chastised, and sharp reproof comes to me early in the morning.*

Verse 15. The doubter confronts tradition

21. *When I kept saying, That will be my story....* Or, in other words, "That is what I will teach... ." What are you going to teach? That there is no knowledge in the Most High? That God is unaware of what goes on? Will this be the position you adopt: that those who live righteously do so to no purpose, that the just have wasted their service, that God either favors the wicked or does not care about anyone? Will you say this, will this be your story?

No, he checks himself, because authority restrains him. What authority? Sometimes a person does feel inclined to burst out into such complaints, but is brought back to his senses by the Scriptures, which teach us that we must always live in accordance with right reason, that God does concern himself with human affairs, and that he does distinguish between the devout and the godless. This is why the speaker here, tempted to take that skeptical line, recalls himself to a better mind. What does he say? *"When I kept saying, That will be my story, why, then, I condemned the long line of your children.* I shall have turned my back on the whole race of your children if I talk in that fashion; I shall be condemning the long line of the just. Some codices have the reading, *Why, then, with whom in the long line of your children will I have been in harmony?*[22] With which of your children have I been in tune? With whom have I agreed," he means, "to which of them have I adjusted myself? I am out of tune with all of them, if I teach in that way. Only someone who keeps the tune is in harmony with others; anyone who loses the tune is out of harmony. Am I to contradict what Abraham said, what Isaac said, what Jacob said, what the prophets said? All of them

---

22. *Ecce generationis filiorum tuorum cui concinui*, but there are variants.

asserted that God does concern himself with human affairs; am I to say that he does not? Am I wiser than they were? Is my mind more penetrating than theirs? A very wholesome authority it is that has pulled my thoughts back from such impiety."

Verses 16–17. Understanding dawns

22. What comes next? *When I kept saying, That will be my story, why, then, I condemned the long line of your children.* What did he do, in order to avoid condemning them? *I tried to solve the problem.* He has begun to understand, and may God be with him, to enable him to understand more fully. Already, though, brothers and sisters, he is being plucked back from what would have been a grievous fall, because he no longer takes it for granted that he knows the answer; he has begun to realize that he does not know. Until this moment he wanted to seem knowledgeable, and to proclaim that God took no interest in the affairs of human beings. A very wicked and impious doctrine of this kind has been propounded, as you know, brothers and sisters. You must recognize that many people do argue like this, saying that God takes no interest in what happens to mortals, because everything is ruled by chance, or because our wills are controlled by the stars, since each of us is prompted to action not by any merit in ourselves but by astral influences.[23] This is an evil doctrine, thoroughly impious. The psalmist was sliding toward it, he who confessed, *My feet had all but slipped. My steps had very nearly slid out of control.* He was on the brink of that error, but he began to perceive that he was out of tune with the tradition perpetuated among God's children, so he repudiated the knowledge that put him out of harmony with the righteous who belong to God.

Let us listen to what he says, because he began to understand, and received help, and learned something, and explained it to us. *I tried to solve the problem*, he says, *but it is too hard for me*. It is a mighty task indeed, to understand how God takes care of human destinies, why things go well for bad people and why the good have such a hard time. A daunting question, certainly! This is why he says, "*It is too hard for me.* I might as well be up against a brick wall!" But you have the assurance of another psalm, *In my God I shall leap over the wall* (Ps 17:30 (18:29)). No, *it is too hard for me*.

23. You are right to say that it is too hard for you, but it is not too hard for God. Put yourself in the presence of God, for whom it is not too hard, and then it will not be too hard for you either. This is what he did, for he tells us how long the question continues to be too hard: *until I enter God's holy place, and understand what the final outcome must be.* This is all-important, sisters and brothers. "I have been struggling with the problem for a long time," he says. "In front of me I see what looks like an insoluble

---

23. Augustine discusses the denial of providence by astrologers and others in *Exposition 2 of Psalm* 31, 16.18.25. He alludes briefly to the Priscillianists as holding similar views in *Heresies* 70 and in Letter 166, 7.

difficulty: I am trying to understand how God can be just, and concerned about human conditions, and how he is not unjust even though sinners and criminals enjoy prosperity on this earth, while loyal believers and people who serve God are so often worn out with trials and hardships. I find it extremely difficult to solve the problem, but only *until I enter God's holy place*." What is given you in God's sanctuary, then, to help you solve it? "What I understand there," he replies, "is not the present state of affairs, but *what the final outcome must be*. From God's holy place I turn my gaze towards the end, passing over the present." All this crowd that we call the human race, all this mass of mortal creatures, will come to judgment; it will be brought to the scales where all human deeds will be weighed. A cloud envelops everything now, but the merits of every single person are known to God. "*I understand what the final outcome must be*," he says, "but not by my own efforts, for the problem is too hard for me. How can I understand *what the final outcome must be*? Let me go into God's sanctuary." In that place he understood the reason why malefactors are happy in the present life.

Verses 18–19. Fraudsters defrauded

24. *It is because of their guile that you conferred these things upon them.* Because they are full of guile—in other words, fraudulent—because they are full of guile, they are themselves beguiled. What do I mean when I say that because they are frauds, they are themselves defrauded? By all their wicked deeds they attempt to commit fraud against the human race, but they are defrauded themselves in that they choose earthly goods, leaving aside those which are eternal. So it can truly be said, brothers and sisters, that in their very trickery they are tricked. As I asked some time ago, my friends, what kind of heart must a person have who forfeits honesty[24] to gain a garment? Which party has been cheated—the person whose garment was taken, or the one who has lost integrity? If a garment is really more precious than good faith, the former has lost more heavily; but if good faith is worth incomparably more than the whole world, the case looks different. The one will be seen to have lost a cloak, but the other will be asked, *What advantage is it to anyone to gain even the whole world, and suffer the ruin of his own soul?* (Mt 16:26).

What happens to them? *It is because of their guile that you conferred these things upon them; you threw them down even as they were lifting themselves up.* The psalmist did not say, "You threw them down because they lifted themselves up," as though they had been lifted up first and thrown down afterward. It was in the very moment and by the very fact of

---

24. *Fidem*, but wider in meaning than "faith" here.

lifting themselves up that they were cast down. To be lifted up like that[25] is already to fall. *You threw them down even as they were lifting themselves up.*

25. *How suddenly they have been desolated!* He can marvel at their fate, because he understands what the outcome must be. *They have faded away*: smoke fades as it rises higher, and so too have they faded. How can he declare that *they have faded away*? Because he speaks as one who understands what the final outcome must be. *They have faded away, they have perished because of their iniquity.*

Verse 20. Worldly prosperity is only a dream

26. *Like the dream of one who awakens.* How did they fade away? As a dream fades when the dreamer wakes up. Take the case of a person who dreams that he has discovered some treasure. He is rich—but only until he wakes. So have the proud faded away, *like the dream of one who awakens.* The dreamer looks for his wealth, and it is not there: nothing in his hands, nothing in his bed. He had fallen asleep a poor man; in his dreams he became a rich man, and if he had not woken up he would still be rich. But he did wake up, and he found again the penury he had escaped from in his sleep. These arrogant folk too will find the misery they have earned for themselves. When they have awakened from this life everything they possessed here will be like dream-wealth; it will pass away *like the dream of one who awakens.*

The psalmist seems to think that someone may object, "What? Does their present status seem trifling to you, does their pomp seem a trivial thing? Do you think so dismissively of their titles, their images, the statues erected to them, the praise heaped on them, their queues of hangers-on?" He counters with the statement, *In your city, O Lord, you will reduce their image*[26] *to nothing.*

That being so, my brothers and sisters, let me speak plainly to you from this place of mine, or any other that gives me the right to speak so (for when we are mingling informally among you, to use such words would seem more like striking you than teaching you).[27] In the name of Christ, then,

---

25. *Sic efferri.* Probably as translated above; but the verb *effero* can also mean "to carry out," as a corpse is carried out for burial, so there could be an Augustinian pun here.
26. Variant: "images."
27. *Quia quando vobis miscemur, magis vos ferimus quam docemus.* It is not entirely clear what this parenthesis means, partly because *ferimus* could be either from *fero* (to carry, lift, support, bear, etc.) or from *ferio* (to strike, knock, smite). If the former, we might translate, "When we are mingling... we would rather support you than teach you." If the latter, the sense seems to be as in the translation above; he is saying, "I don't want to be getting at you when we are on friendly, informal terms; but I can properly say these things from my official position."

in the fear of Christ, I beg you: if you do not have these marks of distinction, do not covet them; but to any of you who do have them, I say, do not presume on them. Well, that is what I had to say to you. I am not saying, "You are heading for damnation because you have them." I am saying that you are heading for damnation if you presume on such advantages, if you are puffed up over them, if on account of such things you think yourself important, if because of them you disregard the poor, if you are so dazzled by your vain self-esteem that you forget the human condition common to all. In such a case God is bound to requite the proud at the end, and reduce their image to nothing in his city.

Anyone who is rich should be rich in the way the apostle commends: *Instruct the rich of this world not to be high-minded, nor to put their trust in unreliable wealth, but in the living God, who gives us everything to enjoy in abundance* (1 Tm 6:17). He has demolished the grounds for pride, but he goes on to give the rich good advice. We might suppose that they object, "We are rich. You forbid us to be proud, and order us not to make ostentatious use of our wealth. What are we to do with it, then?" Is it really so hard for them to find good use for it? The apostle has some suggestions: *Let them be rich in good works, give readily, and share what they have*, he says. And how will that profit them? *Let them use their wealth to lay a good foundation for the future, and so attain true life* (1 Tm 6:18–19). Where are they to make these profitable transactions? In the same place where the psalmist fixed his gaze, as he entered the sanctuary of God.[28] All our rich brothers and sisters must shudder with fear; all who have ample money, gold, silver, household slaves and marks of rank must shudder at the warning we have just heard: *In your city, O Lord, you will reduce their image to nothing*. Is not this a just sentence? Is it not right that God should reduce their image to nothing in his city, when in their own earthly city they have reduced the image of God to nothing? *In your city, O Lord, you will reduce their image to nothing*.

Verses 21–23. The change begins

27. *Because my heart was delighted, my kidneys were changed*. Perhaps he is admitting what tempted him when he says, *Because my heart was delighted, my kidneys were changed*: when those temporal things brought me delight, my emotions[29] were stirred.

But the verse could also be interpreted in this way: *because my heart was delighted* with God, *my kidneys too were changed*; that is, my lustful feelings were transformed and I became chaste all through. *My kidneys were changed*. Listen to how this happened.

---

28. In other words, in the Church.
29. In the biblical understanding of human nature, the kidneys were regarded as the seat of emotions and affections, the heart as the principle of thought.

28. "*I was brought to nothing, and I knew it not*. I, who now say these things about the wealthy, once coveted similar riches myself. That is why I can say that, at the time when *my steps had very nearly slid out of control, I was brought to nothing*. Moreover, since I too *was brought to nothing, and knew it not*, there is no need to despair of them either, the people against whom I have been speaking."

29. What does he mean by *I knew it not*? He says to God, *I became like a beast in your presence, yet I was always with you*. There is a great difference between him and some others. He became like a beast in his craving for earthly things, and when he was brought to nothing he did not yet know the things of eternity; but he did not abandon his God, for he would not seek those worldly things from demons or from the devil. I have reminded you already that the synagogue is speaking here, the people that refused to offer worship to idols. "I became a beast, surely, by desiring earthly goods from my God, yet from my God I never departed."

Verse 24. The grasp of God

30. "Reduced to beast-like state though I was, I did not abandon my God." And what was the consequence? *You grasped the hand of my right hand*. He does not say, "My right hand," but *the hand of my right hand*. If it is the hand of his right hand, it seems the hand must itself have a hand. *You grasped the hand of my right hand*, to lead me. Why did he speak of a hand? It signifies power. We say that someone has something in hand when we mean that it is within that person's power; so the devil said to God, concerning Job, *Stretch out your hand and touch all his belongings* (Jb 1:11). What did he mean by *stretch out your hand*? "Give me the power," he meant. He called God's power God's hand, as in another passage of Scripture it is said that *death and life are in the hands of the tongue* (Prv 18:21). Surely the tongue does not have hands? Why, then, does Scripture speak of *the hands of the tongue*? It means, "in the power of the tongue," for *out of your mouth you will be justified, and out of your mouth you will be condemned* (Mt 12:37).

Accordingly "*you grasped the hand of my right hand*, the power of my right hand. What was my right hand? My persistence in staying always with you. To my left hand must I attribute the fact that *I became like a beast in your presence* and that earthly concupiscence was in me; but my right hand was my continuance with you throughout. You grasped the hand of this right hand of mine, which is to say, you directed its power." What power would that be? *He gave them power to become children of God* (Jn 1:12). So the speaker had already begun to be numbered among the children of God, and already belonged to the New Covenant.

Now see how God's grasp of the hand of his right hand was maintained. *You led me by your will*. What is the meaning of *by your will*? Not by any merits of mine. *By your will*—what does it signify? Listen to the apostle answering: he was originally a beast in his desire for earthly goods, and lived in Old Covenant mode. What has he to say about that phase? *I was originally a persecutor and a blasphemer, and harmed people, but I received mercy* (1 Tm 1:13). And what about *by your will*? *By God's grace I am what I am* (1 Cor 15:10).

And you have taken me up in glory. Which of us can give any account of what that glory was? Who can say? But let us look forward to it, because at the resurrection it will be ours. At the final outcome we shall say, *You have taken me up in glory.*

Verse 25. Longing for God in heaven, purity of desire on earth

31. He began to think about the happiness of heaven, and to reproach himself because he had been a beast in his desire for earthly things, *for what is there for me in heaven, and what else but you have I desired on earth?* he asked. Ah, I know by your exclamations that you have understood! He compared his earthly objectives with the heavenly reward he was destined to receive; he saw what was being reserved for him there. As he pondered on it he caught fire from his contemplation of something beyond all description, something eye has not seen, nor ear heard, nor human heart conceived.[30] And so he did not say, "This happiness" or "that happiness" awaits me in heaven; but he put the question, *"What is there for me in heaven?* What is that Something which is mine in heaven? What is it? How great is it? What is it like? Moreover, since what there is for me in heaven does not pass away, *what else but you have I desired on earth?* You are keeping for me—forgive me; I will say it as best I can; accept my effort and my earnest striving, for I lack the skill to state it clearly—you are keeping for me in heaven imperishable riches, nothing other than yourself. Yet I aspired to get from you on earth what the godless also have, what the wicked have, what villains have: money, gold, silver, gems, servants; what many criminals have, and many disreputable women, and many ignoble men—these things I craved from my God on earth as though they were all that mattered, when all the time God is reserving himself for me in heaven! *What is there for me in heaven?"* He can only point to that ineffable Something. *And what else but you have I desired on earth?*

Verse 26. The chaste heart, at last

32. *"My heart and my flesh have failed; but he is the God of my heart.* This is what is kept for me in heaven: *he is the God of my heart, and God is my portion."* Take note of this, brothers and sisters. Let us assess our riches, and let the rest of humanity choose the portions it wants. Observe how people are torn apart by their conflicting desires: let some choose to serve in the army, others to practice at law. Let some choose various specialist studies, others trading, others farming; let them claim these avocations for themselves as their own portions out of all human possibilities, but let

---

30. See 1 Cor 2:9.

God's people cry out, *God is my portion*. Nor is he my portion for a time only, but *God is my portion for eternity*. I may possess gold, but even were I to possess it for ever, what would I have? But if I possess God, then even were I not to possess him for ever, how great a good would I have meanwhile! But that is not all: he promises himself to me, and promises that I will have that treasure for eternity. I have so much, and never will there be a time when I have it no longer. What a tremendous happiness this is! *God is my portion*. For how long? *For eternity*, for you can see now how he has loved him and how he has purified his heart.[31] *He is the God of my heart, and God is my portion for eternity*. His heart has become chaste, for now God is loved disinterestedly; the psalmist asks no other reward from God except God. Anyone who begs a different reward from God, and aspires to serve him in order to get it, is rating what he wants to get more highly than the God who, he hopes, will give it. Does this mean that God gives us nothing? Nothing, save himself. God's award is simply God himself. This is what the psalmist loves, this he chooses as his love. If he chooses anything else, his will not be a chaste love. If you distance yourself from the eternal fire you will grow cold, and decay. Do not move away, for that would mean corruption for you; and it would be fornication. The psalmist is on his way back now, already penitent; he is embracing repentance, and saying, *God is my portion*. How intense is his delight in the God he has chosen!

Verses 27–28. Union with God; praise in the new Jerusalem

33. *Lo, those who go far from you will perish*. The one who speaks here did go away from God, but not far away, for though he confesses, *I became like a beast in your presence*, he can still say, *Yet I was always with you*. But others have indeed gone to a far-off place, because not only have they coveted earthly things; they have even begged them from demons or the devil himself. *Those who go far away from you will perish*. What does it mean, to go far away from God? *You have destroyed everyone who leaves you to go a-whoring*. The opposite to such whoring is chaste love. What is chaste love? Already the soul loves its bridegroom, but what does it ask of him, of this bridegroom it loves? Can we suppose that it chooses him in the way women choose sons-in-law, or husbands, for themselves, setting their hearts perhaps on the man's wealth, loving his gold, his estates, his silver treasures, his money and horses and servants, and all the rest? No, far from it. The speaker in our psalm loves the bridegroom alone, and loves him for himself, disinterestedly; for in him we have all things, since all were made through him.[32] *You have destroyed everyone who leaves you to go a-whoring*.

---

31. The subject of "has loved" and "has purified" could be either the psalmist or God.
32. See Jn 1:3.

34. But what about you—what are you doing? *My good is to hold fast to God.* In this consists total goodness. Do you want more? I grieve for those who want more. What more can you want, brothers and sisters? When we see God face to face[33] there will be nothing whatever that can be better for us than to hold fast to him. But what of the present life? The psalmist answers, "I am speaking as one still on pilgrimage. *My good is to hold fast to God,* certainly; but it is good for me while on my journey *to place in God all my hope,* because the full reality[34] has not come yet for me." As long as you have not held fast to him inseparably, it is in him that you must put your hope. Tossed about, are you? Throw your anchor out ahead and hold fast. If you are not yet clinging to him in face-to-face presence, hold fast through hope.

To place in God all my hope. If you are putting your hope in God, how will you act here? What will your occupation be? Surely to praise him whom you love, and bring others to love him together with you. If you were enamored of a charioteer, would you not pester other people to become your fellow-fans? A charioteer's fan talks about his hero wherever he goes, trying to persuade others to share his passion. Dissolute human beings are loved gratis, yet people expect some reward from God as an incentive to love him! No, love God gratis. And do not begrudge God to anyone. Grab someone else, as many people as you can, everyone you can get hold of. There is room for all of them in God; you cannot set any limits to him. Each of you individually will possess the whole of him, and all of you together will possess him whole and entire.

Do this while you are here on earth, while you are placing your hope in God; for what does the psalmist say next? *That I may proclaim all your praise in the courts of the daughter of Zion.* So you are to proclaim God's praise without restriction, but where will you do that? *In the courts of the daughter of Zion,* because any proclamation of God outside the Church is worthless. It is not enough to extol God and trumpet all his praises; you must proclaim him *in the courts of the daughter of Zion.* Stretch out toward unity. Do not divide God's people, but seize them, pull them together, and make a single whole. I was forgetting that I had talked so long. The psalm is finished now, and from the stench in the building I surmise that I have given you rather a long sermon. But I can never keep up with your eager demands; you are extremely violent with me. I only wish you would be just as violent in seizing the kingdom of heaven.[35]

---

33. See 1 Cor 13:12.
34. *Res.*
35. See Mt 11:12.

Exposition of Psalm 140

Synopsis

We must search out Scripture's deep mysteries and allow them to exercise our minds. This Psalm's obscurities will accomplish that. Nothing is more profound than Scripture's commands to love God and neighbor. Anything you read there points only to charity. Paul defines it as *love from a pure heart*, namely, love that accords with God's will. This Psalm speaks of that love. The voice is Christ's. But Christ speaks for his members and vice versa. In the whole Christ, love cries out to Christ *from* us, and cries out from Christ *for* us (1–3). The Psalm's *evening sacrifice* was the Lord's passion, but his crucified body came from us; so the voice is ours too, in the charity of his body (4–6). He asks that his heart, the Church, not be turned to dishonesty by excusing our sin. If we candidly confess our sins, we shall *have no part with the elect among them*—that is, with self-styled elect who justify themselves before God and condemn others. For example, a Pharisee judged Jesus for accepting love from a sinful woman (7–8). But he contrasts her with the Pharisee and with all who defend their sin (9).

Beware the so-called elect among the odious Manicheans, who say it's not they who sin but some "race of darkness" produced by dueling powers before all time. If we deny our sin that way, we blame God for our faults. They think of God as buried inside matter and suffering within nature all over the world on a "cross of light." What mangled ideas and self-excusing teachings! (10–12) Faithful people welcome reproof for their sin and reject the oil of flattery. Accuse yourself, and you are just (13–14). But how can the same person be sinful and just at the same time? Look at Paul, who justly delighted in God's law and yet bore a sinful, death-ridden body. Grace has begun to heal us, and we groan for redemption; so master your body now, and prepare it to become whole in the resurrection (15–16).

On the surface we seem to do well enough in obeying the Ten Commandments. But look closely. No sins of the tongue? No unmanageable desires? No wandering thoughts in prayer? And these are the good people! (17–18) That's why we all must say the prayer, *Forgive us our trespasses*. Christ has undone human wisdom's greatest proponents by his humble cross. He has undone the fear of death. See how the blood of the martyrs has irrigated the earth; they have become fertilizer for the Church's rich crop. Now when the emperor visits Rome he goes to the tomb of a Christian martyr, Peter (19–23). But remember that Peter needed the Physician's healing to do what he did; after all, he denied the Lord. The word "passover" is important, for Christ "passed over" to the Father alone, though he produced an abundant harvest of believers. The prophets and John the Baptist, however, died for truth and justice rather than the name of Christ (24–26).

Augustine's Text of Psalm 140

(1) A Psalm for David himself.
    I have cried to you, O Lord; hear me.
    Listen to the voice of my entreaty whenever I cry to you.

(2) Let my prayer rise like incense before you,
    And the raising of my hands be an evening sacrifice.

(3) Set a guard over my mouth, O Lord, and a door to restrain my lips.

(4) Turn not my heart aside to dishonest words,
    To seek excuses in its sins with people who commit iniquity,
    And I will have no part with the elect among them.

(5) A just man will correct me with mercy, and will rebuke me.
    But let a sinner's oil never be nourishment for my head.
    Wait a little, and my prayer will be very popular among them.

(6) Their judges have foundered beside the rock.
    They will hear my words, for my words have prevailed.

(7) Like earthly dregs spread on the ground,
    So have our bones been scattered around the grave.

(8) To you, O Lord, my eyes are turned;
    In you have I hoped, do not take away my life.

(9) Guard me from the snare they have laid for me,
    And from the stumbling blocks set by those who sin.

(10) Sinners will fall into his nets.
    I am all alone, until my passover.

Exposition

A Sermon to the People[1]

Introduction: pray for the preacher

1. When a letter from the apostle was read just now, brothers and sisters, you heard in it an admonition and a request that could just as well have come from us. He said, *Be assiduous in prayer, and keep watch prayerfully. Pray also for us, that God may open to us a door for the word, whereby we may speak of his mystery and make it known, as it is my duty to speak* (Col 4:2–4). I ask you, please, to regard these words as my own. In the Holy Scriptures there are profound mysteries which are hidden so that no one may approach them disrespectfully. But we must search for them and allow them to exercise our minds, knowing that when they are opened they will nourish us. The psalm we have just sung is an example, for its meaning is somewhat obscure in many places. But, as with the Lord's help its message begins to be teased out and explained, you will see that what you are hearing is something you knew already. Nonetheless, this teaching was communicated in different ways so that the variety of expression might guard against any boredom with the truth itself.

Scripture teaches one thing: charity; the characteristics of true charity

2. Think of it this way, brothers and sisters. Are you ever likely to hear or understand anything vaster in scope, or more important for salvation, than the command, *You shall love the Lord your God with all your heart and all your soul and all your mind* (Mk 12:30), and again, *You shall love your neighbor as yourself?* (Mk 12:31) And in case you are tempted to underrate the importance of these two precepts, remember that *on these two commandments depend all the law and the prophets* (Mt 22:40). Whatever salutary idea anyone may conceive or formulate in words, whatever truth may be dug out from any page of the divine Scriptures, it tends toward one end only, and that is charity.

But this does not mean any kind of relationship that goes under the name of charity, for even persons of evil life are entangled with one another in a fellowship of ruined consciences. It is said that they love each other, are unwilling to leave the group, and are united in friendly discussion; they are said to miss those of their members who are away and to be glad when they return. But love like this is born from the infernal regions. It generates a sticky substance that plunges people into the depths instead of equipping them with wings to lift them to the sky. What is true charity, then, and what qualities mark it off from spurious forms that claim to be charity?

---

1. Probably preached during the vigil of a martyrs' feast at Hippo, between 397 and 405. See the note at section 13 below.

The true charity proper to Christians has been described by Paul and so clearly demarcated within its own boundaries that it is entirely distinct from all pseudo-charity—although, inasmuch as it is divine in origin, we should not speak of its having any bounds at all. *The end of the commandment is charity* (1 Tm 1:5), he says. He was able to leave it at that, just as in other passages, where he was speaking to well-instructed hearers, he could simply say, *The fullness of the law is charity* (Rom 13:10), without stating what kind of charity he meant. He had explained this elsewhere,[2] and it is neither possible nor desirable to repeat everything in every context. So too here: *The fullness of the law is charity.* Were you perhaps wondering what charity or what kind of charity? You find the answer in the other text I quoted: *The end of the commandment is charity from a pure heart* (1 Tm 1:5). Now consider whether robbers exercise charity from a pure heart when they hatch their plots together. To love with a pure heart means to love another person in accordance with God's will. This is how you are bound to love yourself, if the criterion that *you shall love your neighbor as yourself* (Mk 12:31) is to make sense. For if you love yourself in the wrong way you are doing yourself no good, and then, if you love your neighbor as yourself, you are not doing him much good either, are you?

But how is it possible to love yourself in the wrong way? Scripture, which flatters no one, gives us a hint. It proves that you do not truly love yourself—indeed, that you even hate yourself—by pointing out, *Whoever loves iniquity hates his own soul* (Ps 10:6(11:5)). So, if you love iniquity, can you pretend to love yourself? You are mistaken. And, if you love your neighbor in the same fashion, you will lead him or her into sin, and your friendship will entrap your friend. *Charity from a pure heart* is therefore charity exercised according to the will of God, from *a good conscience, and unfeigned faith* (1 Tm 1:5).

Charity thus defined by the apostle comprises two commandments: love of God and love of neighbor. You need look for nothing else in Scripture, and let no one lay upon you any other command. Wherever there is any obscure passage in Scripture, charity is concealed in it, and wherever the sense is plain, charity is proclaimed. If it were nowhere plain to see, it would not nourish you; if it were nowhere concealed, it would not exercise you. This same charity cries out from a pure heart in the words of the psalm and from hearts like his who prays here. And who this is, I can tell you in a word: it is Christ.

The whole Christ speaks in this psalm

3. But you will hear some words which cannot fittingly be attributed to our Lord Jesus Christ, and so anyone who lacks understanding will think I spoke rashly in identifying the "I" in the psalm as Christ. How can

---

2. For example, in 1 Cor 13.

the speaker be Christ? He is the spotless lamb[3] in whom alone no sin was found, who alone could say with perfect truth, *Now the prince of this world is coming, and he will find nothing in me* (Jn 14:30), for he was blameless and entirely free from guilt. He alone made restitution, though he had committed no robbery.[4] He, the only-begotten Son of God who took flesh, not diminishing himself by his Incarnation but ennobling us, he alone poured out innocent blood. How, then, could these words of the psalm be correctly understood as spoken by him: *Set a guard over my mouth, O Lord, and a door to restrain my lips, that my heart may not turn aside into dishonest words, to seek excuses in its sins?* (verses 3–4) The meaning is perfectly clear: Guard my mouth, O Lord, with a gate, and with the strong door of your commandment, so that my heart may not turn away to wicked words. What kind of wicked words? Those by which excuses are sought for sins. I pray, says the psalmist, that I may never choose to defend my sins instead of accusing myself of them. Such words obviously have no relevance at all to our Lord Jesus Christ himself, for what sins did he commit, that he had a duty to confess rather than defend?

No, these words are for us. "But Christ is speaking, isn't he?" Most certainly he is. "But if the words are ours, how can Christ be speaking?" If you ask that, I must ask you a question. Where is the charity of which I was speaking a moment ago? Do you not understand that it is charity that makes us one in Christ? Charity cries out to Christ from our hearts, and charity cries out from Christ on our behalf. How does charity cry out from our hearts to Christ? *It shall come to pass that whoever calls on the name of the Lord will be saved* (Jl 2:32; Acts 2:21; Rom 10:13). And how does charity cry out from Christ on our behalf? *Saul, Saul, why are you persecuting me?* (Acts 9:4) The apostle tells us, *You are Christ's body, and his members* (1 Cor 12:27). If then he is the head and we are the members, one single individual is speaking. Whether the head speaks or the members speak, the one Christ speaks. Moreover it is perfectly proper for the head to speak on behalf of the members; this is something we are accustomed to. Consider first how it is the head, and only the head, that is able to speak for the limbs. Think of how this happens in your own experience, how the head speaks up for the rest of you. If you are in a crowded place and someone treads on your toes, your head protests, "You're treading on me!" No one touched your head, but the organic unity of the body speaks. Your tongue, which resides in your head, has spoken in the name of all your members. It discharges the duty of speech on behalf of them all.

This is how we should hear Christ speaking. Yet each one of us should at the same time hear his or her own voice, since we are all organically parts of Christ's body. Sometimes he will speak words that none of us can recognize as our own, for they belong only to the head, but even then Christ

---

3. See 1 Pt 1:19.
4. See Ps 68:5(69:4).

does not divorce himself from our words and withdraw into his own, nor does he go so far away as not to return from his own words to ours. Of him and of the Church it was prophesied, *They will be two in one flesh* (Gn 2:24); and Christ himself, speaking about the same mystery in the gospel, reasserted, *So they are two no longer, but one flesh* (Mt 19:6).

These things are not new to you, for you are always hearing them from us. But it is necessary that they be recalled from time to time, partly because the Scriptures on which we preach are so closely connected among themselves that many truths recur in many different passages, and partly also because it is profitable for you to hear these things again. Preoccupation with worldly matters can cause thorns to spring up and choke the seed.[5] You need therefore to be reminded by the Lord fairly often of things which the world tries to make you forget.

Verses 1–3. Christ's evening sacrifice on the cross; he speaks in our name

4. *I have cried to you, O Lord; hear me.* We can all say this. Yet, if I say it, it is not I but the whole Christ. He says it primarily in the name of his body, just as when he was on earth he prayed in the name of his body to the Father. While he was praying drops of blood were forced from all over his body; this is what the gospel says: *Jesus prayed vehemently, and he sweated blood* (Lk 22:44). What was the meaning of this bleeding from his whole body if not that the whole Church would bleed in the suffering of the martyrs?

I have cried to you, O Lord; hear me. Listen to the voice of my entreaty whenever I cry to you. You thought, perhaps, that the business of crying out to him was finished when you had said, *I have cried to you*. Yes, you have cried to him, but do not be complacent. The need to cry to him is past only if the tribulation is past. But if tribulation remains the lot of the Church, Christ's body, until the end of the world, it must say not only, *I have cried to you; hear me*, but also, *Listen to the voice of my entreaty whenever I cry to you.*

5. *Let my prayer rise like incense before you, and the raising of my hands be an evening sacrifice.* Every Christian knows that this verse is customarily understood of Christ the head, for as the day drew on toward evening the Lord laid down his life on the cross in order to take it up again.[6] It was not snatched from him against his will. All the same, we too were prefigured there, for what was it that hung on the cross? The body Christ had taken from us. Moreover, how could it ever happen that God the Father should forsake and abandon his only Son, who most certainly is one God with him? Yet when he fastened our weak nature to the cross, *our old humanity was nailed to the cross with him* (Rom 6:6), as the apostle teaches, and he

---

5. See Mk 4:18–19 and parallels.
6. See Jn 10:17.

cried out in the voice of that old humanity of ours, *O God, my God, why have you forsaken me?* (Ps 21:2(22:1)) The evening sacrifice is the Lord's passion, the Lord's cross, the offering of the saving victim in a holocaust acceptable to God. Through his resurrection his evening sacrifice was transformed into a morning oblation. Because of him, every prayer purely directed from the heart of a believer rises like incense, as from a holy altar. Nothing is more delightful than this fragrance of the Lord. May all who believe send forth the same fragrance.

6. *Our old humanity was nailed to the cross with him*, the apostle teaches, and he goes on to say why: *so that our sinful self may be nullified, and we may be slaves of sin no longer* (Rom 6:6). Similarly in that earlier psalm, after crying, *O God, my God, why have you forsaken me?* the speaker immediately added, *The tale of my sins leaves me far from salvation* (Ps 21:2(22:1)).[7] If you think only of the head, what sins could these be? Yet the head himself testified on the cross that it is indeed his voice we hear in the psalm for he spoke these very words, he recited this verse.[8] No room is left for human guesswork, nor is denial of the attribution of the verse to Christ possible for anyone who claims to be Christian. What I read in the psalm I hear spoken by Christ. Furthermore, in the same psalm I recognize actions of which I read also in the gospel: *They dug holes in my hands and my feet, and numbered all my bones. These same people looked on and watched me, they shared out my garments among them, and cast lots for my tunic* (Ps 21:17–19(22:16–18)). All these things were prophesied, and they happened just as foretold. As we heard of them, so did we see them.[9]

We can say, then, that our Lord Jesus represented us, in the charity of his body, and that although he was personally without sin, he spoke in the name of his body of *the tale of my sins*. But if this is so, can anyone among his members pretend to have no sin? Only someone who is so bold as to flaunt himself and claim a spurious holiness and accuse Christ of falsehood. Confess, then, you who are a member of Christ, that your head spoke there for you.

In the next words he has shown us how we may make this confession and do it effectively and avoid the temptation of trying to justify ourselves in the sight of God, who alone is just and justifies the godless.[10] Still speaking with the voice of his body, he continues, *Set a guard over my mouth, O Lord, and a door to restrain my lips*. He does not say "a barrier to keep them closed" but *a door*. A door can be both opened and closed, so, if there is a door at our lips, let it be opened and closed: opened to confess our sins

---

7. Augustine accepted this sense in *Exposition 2 of Psalm 21*, though in *Exposition 1* he had preferred the sense resulting from an alternative punctuation: *Why have you forsaken me, and left me far from my salvation?*
8. See Mk 15:34.
9. See Ps 47:9 (48:8).
10. See Rom 4:5.

and closed to any excuses for them. Then the door will be a restraint for us, not our ruin.

Verse 4. Do not consort with the self-styled elect, and do not make excuses for your sins

7. How will the restraining door be useful to us? What is Christ praying for in the person of his body? *Turn not my heart aside to dishonest words*, he says. But what is *my heart*? The heart of my Church, which is the very heart of my body. Call to mind other texts of Scripture where this rule of identification is established for us: *Saul, Saul, why are you persecuting me?* (Acts 9:4) he asked, though no one had touched him. And again, *I was hungry, and you fed me; I was thirsty, and you gave me a drink*, and the rest. And the just will ask him, *When did we see you hungry or thirsty?* He will answer, *When you did that for even the least of those who are mine, you did it for me* (Mt 25:35.37.40). These truths should not be unfamiliar to Christians, especially not to those who have taken them to heart as a norm for understanding other passages as well. Such discerning Christians will either not be disconcerted by similar texts or at any rate will be quickly reassured.

Well then, as in the gospel passage we found the just asking, "Lord, why did you say, *I was hungry, and you fed me? When did we see you hungry?*" and we heard what his reply will be: *When you did that for even the least of those who are mine, you did it for me*, so must we question Christ within us, where he graciously dwells in our inmost selves through faith.[11] It is not as though he were absent from us, and we had no one to ask. On the contrary, he promised, *Lo, I am with you throughout all days, even to the end of the ages* (Mt 28:20). Now we have already ascertained that his voice is to be heard in the psalm, for no one can possibly deny that the words, *Let the raising of my hands be an evening sacrifice*, are his. Accordingly you must say to him, "What of these words, Lord? *Set a guard over my mouth, O Lord, and a door to restrain my lips, that my heart may not turn aside into dishonest words, to seek excuses in its sins*? Why do you pray in these terms, Lord? What sins have you, for which you would need to seek excuses?" He will answer, "When one of my members prays so, I pray so," just as he told us, *When you did that for even the least of those who are mine, you did it for me.*

8. But if your heart has not turned aside, you who are a member of Christ—if your heart has not turned aside *into dishonest words, to seek excuses in its sins with people who commit iniquity*—you *will have no part with the elect among them*. That is how the psalm continues: *And I will have no part with the elect among them*. Who are their so-called elect? People who seek to justify themselves. Who are their elect? Those who regard themselves as righteous and condemn others, like the Pharisee in

---

11. See Eph 3:17.

the temple who said, *O God, I thank you that I am not like other people* (Lk 18:11). Who are their elect? One such was he who thought, *If this man were a prophet, he would know who this woman is, who has approached his feet* (Lk 7:39). Do you not hear the voice of another Pharisee, the one who had invited the Lord to his table? When a sinful woman from the city came in and approached the Lord's feet, that was the host's reaction. She was unchaste, and she had been forward and brazen about fornication, but she was more brazen still in seeking salvation, and so she burst into a stranger's house. Yet the guest who was there at table was no stranger. She was no gatecrasher pursuing some ordinary guest but a servant following her Lord. She drew near to his feet because she was longing to follow in his footsteps; she bathed them in her tears and wiped them with her hair. Who are Christ's feet? The people through whose ministry he has traversed the whole world. *How beautiful are the feet of those who announce peace, who announce good news!* (Is 52:7; Rom 10:15) How many people there are who have given hospitality to the Lord's feet! By giving hospitality to a just person inasmuch as he or she was just, they received a just person's reward, and by giving hospitality to a prophet inasmuch as he was a prophet, they received a prophet's reward;[12] for the Lord promised, *Anyone who gives a cup of cold water to one of my little ones simply because he is a disciple, I tell you, he will not miss his reward* (Mt 10:42). But when someone has shown this kindness in welcoming the Lord's feet, what has he spent on hospitality? Only superfluities that he had in his house. I am sure this is implied by the woman's action in drying the Lord's feet with her hair, for hair is superfluous to the body. Your superfluous goods become vitally necessary to you if they are the means whereby you follow obediently in the footsteps of the Lord.

The woman in the gospel story sought to be healed, for she knew she was gravely wounded. Hers was a great wound, but he was no slight physician, was he? The Pharisees, however, shrank from being touched by unclean persons and shunned all physical contact with sinners. If any unavoidable contact occurred, they washed afterwards. They were for ever dipping and sprinkling not only themselves but also their vessels, beds, cups and dishes, as the Lord remarks in the gospel.[13] If the woman had approached the Pharisee's feet, he, knowing her, would have pushed her away, fearing that his holiness might be smirched. His supposed holiness resided only in his body, not in his heart, and, because he had no holiness in his heart, what he had in his body was meaningless. He would have repulsed the woman, and when the Lord did not do so the Pharisee thought it must be because he did not know who she was. He therefore said to himself, *If this man were a prophet, he would know who this woman is, who has approached his feet* (Lk 7:39). He did not say, "If he were a prophet, he would have pushed her

---

12. See Mt 10:41.
13. See Mt 23:25; Mk 7:3–4.

away"; he only said, *If he were a prophet he would know who she is*, as though the inevitable consequence of knowing would have been to repulse her; and so he took the fact that the Lord did not do so as clear proof that he was ignorant of her character.

But while the Lord's eyes were fixed on the woman his ears were alert to the Pharisee's heart and, as soon as he had heard the man's thoughts, he propounded a parable, one that you know well: *There was a certain creditor to whom two people were in debt. One owed him five hundred denarii, the other fifty. Since neither had the means to pay, he let them both off. I ask you, then, which of them will love him more? He replied, I suppose, sir, the one to whom he remitted the larger debt*—for he was cornered, you see, and forced to pronounce judgment against himself. *Then, turning to the woman, Jesus said to Simon, You see this woman? I entered your house, and you gave me no kiss, but she has not ceased to kiss my feet; you offered me no water for my feet, but she has washed my feet with her tears. You gave me no oil, but she has anointed my feet with ointment. Therefore, I tell you, many sins have been forgiven her, because she has loved so much* (Lk 7:41–47). How did she show her love? By confessing and weeping, by not letting her heart turn aside into dishonest words in order to seek excuses in her sins, and by not making common cause with their so-called elect by defending herself.

Do not blame God or the stars or fate for your sins

9. If this woman's heart had turned aside into dishonest words, she would not have needed to look far to find excuses. Do we not hear excuses every day from women who are her peers in disgraceful conduct but not her peers in confession: from prostitutes, adulterers, and all kinds of dissolute women? If they have sinned in secret, they deny it; if they have been caught and convicted or sinned in public, they defend their deeds. And how glibly, how quickly, they present their defense! Yet how dangerous their excuses are, how trite from daily repetition, and how sacrilegious! "If God hadn't made me do it, I wouldn't have done it, would I? God willed it, it was just my luck, it was my destiny."[14] Such a sinner never confesses, *I said, Lord, have mercy on me*, never comes to the physician's feet like the sinful woman in the gospel, pleading, *Heal my soul, for I have sinned against you* (Ps 40:5(41:4)).

I ask you, brothers and sisters, what sort of people have recourse to a defense like this? Not only the uneducated but the learned too. They sit down and base their calculations on the stars; they study, describe, and guess the distances, the courses, the rapid whirling, the fixed states, and

---

14. In section 8 above Augustine considered self-righteous Pharisees as typical of persons who make excuses for their sins. In the present section it is those who blame God or fortune or fate, and then the astrologers who held the stars responsible for the misdeeds of human beings.

the motions of the celestial bodies. So far, so good: they are regarded as scholars and eminent men. But all this learned, pretentious discourse is used to defend sins. "You will be an adulterer because Venus will influence you in this way," or, "You will be a murderer because of the position of Mars." So it is Mars that will be the murderer, not you, and Venus that will be the adulterer, not you. Take care, then, that you are not condemned for the sins of Mars and Venus! God will condemn you, for he knows that it is you who commit these sins, you who have the effrontery to say to the judge who knows everything, "It was not my sin."[15]

Now, what about the astrologer[16] who sells you these fables to entrap you? (And notice that he sells them, so you do not even get your death free. You disdain to get life free from Christ, but you buy death from an astrologer out of your own pocket.) Well now, if this astrologer catches his own wife in even slightly saucy behavior, or sees her looking impudently at other men, or notices that she is rather too often at the window, does he not seize her and beat her and enforce discipline in his own house? And suppose the woman protests, "Hit Venus, if you can, not me!" will he not retort, "You stupid woman! Can't you understand that I have to take one approach when I am dealing with my customers and quite another when I am ruling my household?"

Who, then, are *the elect among them*? They are the elect among bad people, the "chosen" among the godless, those with whom we must never throw in our lot, with whom we must not associate. But who are they? Can we identify them? Yes, they are people who consider themselves righteous and condemn others as sinners, like the Pharisee in the gospel. Or again, they are people whose sins are unmistakably shown up, or committed in public, who defend their actions and insist that no fault attaches to themselves. In order to escape blame they declare that it is all God's fault, either because he created human beings with such propensities or because he ordered the stars in a certain way or because he has simply neglected human affairs. These are the excuses proffered by the "elect" of this world.

A member of Christ, or the whole body of Christ, or Christ speaking in the name of his body, must make a different plea: *Turn not my heart aside into dishonest words, to seek excuses in its sins, with people who commit iniquity; I will have no part with the elect among them.*

The Manichean elect

10. There is another point here which we should not omit to notice, brothers and sisters. Among the Manichees there are certain people who are thought to be especially holy and to have reached the highest rung of

---

15. Similar thoughts on the folly of blaming the stars are expressed in *Exposition of Psalm* 40,6, where Augustine is considering the verse of Psalm 40(41) which he has just quoted here.
16. *Mathematicus.* See the note on this term at *Exposition 2 of Psalm* 33,25.

holiness, and these are called the elect.[17] Those of you who know about all this can recognize what I am referring to, and let those who do not know, listen.

All the saints are truly God's elect, as the Scriptures tell us. But the Manichees have usurped the title and applied it to themselves, as though they alone had the right to be called elect in the proper sense. Now who are these self-styled elect? The people who, when you say to them, "You have sinned," at once come out with an impious defense, an excuse which is worse and more sacrilegious than all the others. "It is not I who have sinned," they say, "but the race of darkness." But what is this race of darkness? The horde that fought against God. "So when you sin, it is really the dark power that sins?" "Yes, the dark power, because I am mixed with it," they reply. But if God caused this mingling, what was he afraid of? They say, you see, that the realm of darkness rebelled against God before the world was made, and that God was fearful lest his domain be partially laid waste by a hostile incursion. To guard against this he dispatched certain portions of himself, his own substance, his very being—gold, if gold is what we are thinking about, or light, if light is what we consider, and anything else that exists—these things he sent and mixed into the bowels of

---

17. In sections 8 and 9 Augustine has considered in turn various groups who excuse their sins: the Pharisees, the notorious sinners who blame God or fortune or destiny, and the *mathematici* who hold that the stars are responsible. In sections 10–12 he attacks another group, the elect among the Manichees, who have a more complicated theory to exculpate themselves. The radically dualistic Manichean system postulated two warring kingdoms: the kingdom of light and the kingdom of darkness. The latter had attacked the kingdom of light and, though unable to defeat it, had captured certain particles of light from among its defenders. These light-particles were thereafter imprisoned in the universe, in stars, trees, plants, and the earth, and in men and women. Thus each human being was inhabited by two souls: a dark, evil soul that animated the body and a light-soul that was a particle of divinity, and moral life consisted in the effort to liberate the light-soul. The sun and moon were apparently vehicles for conveying elements of light, purified and released from their imprisonment in the world, back to the kingdom of light. Human beings were bound to avoid any actions which might increase the mastery of the powers of darkness over any elements of light still held prisoner, including the plucking and eating of fruit from trees. Augustine ridicules these beliefs in his *Confessions*; see especially III,10,18. The practical difficulties raised by these forms of asceticism were overcome by the division of the sect into the elect (considered in the present Exposition) and the hearers who, content with a lower grade of sanctity, performed the proscribed actions and provided food for the elect. Augustine was himself a Manichee for about nine years (see *Confessions*, Books IV and V), but probably never advanced beyond the rank of hearer. Sections 10–12 are the only passage in his *Expositions of the Psalms* which he devotes to the Manichees.

the kingdom of darkness. And that, they say, was how God fashioned the world. As for ourselves, they continue, insofar as we are souls we belong to these members of God, but we are confined and oppressed by the bowels of the dark realm, and so, whenever we are accused of sinning, it is really the dark realm that sins.

They think that by this theory they exonerate themselves from sin, but they do not exonerate their God from the charge of cowardice, nor the very substance of God from liability to corruption. For, if God is incorruptible, immutable, and invulnerable, and beyond all possibility of being contaminated or defiled, what could that hostile race ever do to him? Whatever kind of attack it had chosen to mount against him, how could it have intimidated one who was impenetrable, inviolable, immune to contamination, unchangeable, and incorruptible? And if God had really done what you say he did, it would have been cruel of him, because he would have put you into that state unnecessarily, since he himself was immune to all harm. Why did he send you there? The dark powers could not hurt him, but he hurt you seriously. That means that God was even more your enemy than was the race of darkness, although that has hurt you too. Moreover, if you could be oppressed, imprisoned, defiled, and corrupted, so too could God, for a morsel or tiny part of his nature in some sense brings the whole into disrepute. If the portion he sent into the dark realm is guilty, so is that which remained with him. But this is the Manichees' doctrine. They confess that there are two primal substances, the one and the other. Their books record this belief. If they deny it, a study of their books is enough to refute them.

11. What are we to think of all this? I do not mean to speak more fully about this basic premise of theirs; I do not intend to speak of the more shameful, more disgraceful implications of it. But notice how even in this introductory thesis, where they postulate a primordial war, they are themselves overcome in warfare. By asserting that the realm of darkness fought against God, they are captured by their own belligerent words. There is no answer that they can make, no loophole of escape for them. You attempt to excuse your sin, you impious fellow, you false "elect," by saying that, when you have done something wrong, you should not be thought to have done it. You look for someone whom you can blame for your sin, and you shift the blame onto the race of darkness.[18] But think about God: Are you

---

18. Compare *Confessions* V,10,18, where Augustine describes his having joined some Manichees in Rome and being half-persuaded by their teaching: "It still seemed to me that it is not we who sin but some other nature within us that is responsible. My pride was gratified at being exculpated by this theory: when I had done something wrong it was pleasant to avoid having to confess that I had done it, a confession that would have given you [God] a chance to heal this soul of mine that had sinned against you. On the contrary, I liked to excuse myself and lay the blame on some other force that was with me but was not myself.... It was a detestable wrong, almighty God, to prefer the lie

not shifting the blame onto him? What if that realm of darkness you have invented were to challenge you like this: "Why accuse me? Did I have the power to harm your God, or didn't I? If I did, I am stronger than he. If I didn't, why was he afraid of me? And if he were not afraid, why did he send you here where you would suffer so much, if you were a member of him, made from his own substance? If he were not afraid, it must have been spite that motivated him; if he did not act out of fear, he acted from cruelty. How wicked he must be if, though nothing could hurt him, he caused his members to be so badly hurt here! If, on the other hand, he were in danger of being hurt, he couldn't be incorruptible."

You see, then, that if you try to defend yourself over your sin, you cannot praise God. You would not have experienced praising God as a captivity if you had not been so busy boasting in praise of yourself. Change course and censure yourself, and then you will praise God. Turn back to those words in a psalm that are so loathsome to you, and make them your own: *I said it myself, Lord, have mercy on me; heal my soul, for I have sinned against you* (Ps 40:5(41:4)). I have said it: it is I who have sinned, not bad luck or fate or the race of darkness. If you have sinned, look at the wide road that lies open before you, the road of praising God, that praise which you used to find cramping as long as you were trying to defend yourself. It is better for you to find your sins stifling and to find praising God an experience of broad freedom. Now that you have confessed your sin, see how God is to be praised, for he is both just when he punishes you in your obstinacy and merciful in freeing you when you confess. And so the psalm prays, *Turn not my heart aside into dishonest words, to seek excuses in its sins*, and to claim that the races of darkness did what I did myself.

12. *With people who commit iniquity.* Is any particular sort of iniquity meant here? Let us consider a detestable form of it prevalent among them. Listen to a vile Manichean iniquity, one they commit publicly and admit. They say that it is better for a person to be a moneylender than to be a farmer.[19] You ask why, and they state the reason, or what they call a reason: see whether madness would not be a more apt name. "Someone who lends money at interest," they say, "does not damage the cross of light." (Many people here will not understand this, but I will explain it.) "But," they con-

---

that you were suffering defeat in me for my destruction to the truth that I was being mastered by you for my salvation. You had not yet set a guard over my mouth or a chaste gate at my lips to keep my heart from straying into evil talk, and from making excuses for itself in its sins as it consorted with evildoers; and so I continued to associate with their elect." In this passage the same constellation of ideas and allusions is found as in the present *Exposition*: the references to Psalm 40:5(41:4) (see section 9 above); the reference to verses 3–4 of the present Psalm 140(141); the shifting of blame; the Manichean elect.

19. A startling assertion, in view of the low opinion of usury common in Augustine's day.

tinue, "a farmer seriously damages the cross of light." You ask what this cross of light is, and they tell you, "The members of God that were captured during the battle have been mingled into the whole of this world. They are trapped in trees, in plants, in fruits, and in other crops. Therefore anyone who breaks up the soil into furrows disturbs God's members. Anyone who plucks a plant from the earth disturbs God's members; anyone who picks fruit from a tree disturbs God's members."[20]

In order to avoid committing imaginary homicide in a field, the Manichee commits real homicide through usury! Moreover, he refuses to give bread to a beggar. Can there be any greater iniquity than this so-called righteousness? He refuses to give bread to a beggar, and, if you ask him why, he explains that the life in the bread is a member of God, a particle of the divine substance, and if the beggar eats it he will be binding it into flesh. So what about yourselves, you Manichees? Why do you eat? Are you not flesh too? "Ah," they say, "we have been purified by our faith in Mani. We, who are the elect, purge the life that is in the bread by our prayers and psalms and send it to the treasure-houses of heaven." So very elect are they that they do not need to be saved by God; rather they are saviors of God! And Christ himself, they hold, is crucified all over the world. I have accepted Christ, whom I find in the gospels, as my savior, but you, according to your books, are the saviors of Christ. It is quite plain, on the contrary, that you are blasphemers of Christ and therefore not on the way to being saved by him. You think that a beggar should not be given a mouthful in case a member of God that is present in the mouthful should be grieved, though the beggar is on the point of dying from hunger! The Manichee shows meaningless mercy to the mouthful while committing real homicide against a human being.

Who, in the end, are these elect among them? *Turn not my heart aside into dishonest words. I will have no part with the elect among them.*

Verse 5. Just correction is preferable to insincere flattery

13. *A just man will correct me with mercy, and will rebuke me.* Read this as coming from a sinner confessing his sin. He wants to be corrected and chastised mercifully rather than praised insincerely. If he is just and merciful, *a just man will correct me with mercy* when he sees me committing a sin. These are the authentic words of certain members of Christ, spoken about certain other members, and always within the one body. Our gracious Lord speaks in his own name as one who gives correction, but he does not disdain to speak also in the name of one who has received it, or needs it; for all the members of the body are in Christ, and speaking for them he can say, *A just man will correct me.* Who is the just one who will correct or chastise you? The head corrects all the members. *The just*

---

20. This passage is thought to be the only mention of the cross of light (*crux luminis*) in Augustine's extant works.

man will correct me with mercy, and will rebuke me. He will rebuke me, but mercifully; he will rebuke me, but he does not hate me. Indeed, he will be the more zealous in correcting me because he does not hate me. The sinner surely finds that a reason for thanksgiving. Why? Because, as Scripture reminds us, *Offer correction to a wise man, and he will love you for it* (Prv 9:8). Is it because he wants to hound you that a just man corrects you? By no means. If his correction were motivated by hatred, he would need correction himself. Why does he offer correction? Out of mercy. *He will correct me.* How? *With mercy.*

But let a sinner's oil never be nourishment for my head. What ever does that mean: *Let a sinner's oil never be nourishment for my head*? It means that my head will never be swollen by flattery. Flattery is hollow, insincere praise; and the duplicitous flattery offered by a sycophant is sinner's oil. When people have made a mockery of someone by disingenuous praise, they say, "I buttered him up!"[21] Be eager for the rebuke offered in mercy by a just person, but do not seek to be praised derisively by a sinner. Make sure you have the oil in your own keeping, and do not look for a sinner's oil. The wise maidens in the gospel carried oil with them;[22] because their consciences bore them witness, they were said to take their own oil with them. Oil is a symbol of bright glory, for it shines and glistens on any surface, but the true glory, the glory that is worth having, must be stored within, safe in its own containers. Scripture suggests what these containers might be: *Let each of us examine our own work, and then it is only within ourselves that we will have credit, not in the eyes of others* (Gal 6:4). But if you are still unsure what the containers are, listen to the apostle: *Our boast is this: the witness of our own conscience* (2 Cor 1:12).[23]

---

21. Literally, "I anointed his head!"
22. See Mt 25:4.
23. A.M. La Bonnardière notes that verse 5b of this psalm, *oleum peccatoris non impinguet caput meum*, was used by the Donatists as an excuse for keeping their distance from Catholics, whom they regarded as sinners. She finds it noteworthy, therefore, that Augustine does not mention the Donatists when dealing with the verse in the present Exposition but simply warns his hearers about the perils of flattery. This latter interpretation is in accord with Augustine's use of the parable in his early writings (e.g. *Confessions* X,37,62; Letter 27,6 to Paulinus of Nola and Letter 28,4(6) to Jerome, dated 394–395). La Bonnardière uses these facts as an argument for dating the *Exposition of Psalm* 140 to a period earlier than the major Donatist controversies. See A.M. La Bonnardière, "Les *Enarrationes in Psalmos* prêchées par saint Augustin à l'occasion de fêtes de martyrs" in *Recherches augustiniennes* 7 (1971) pp. 93–94.

Be your own just judge, and align yourself with God

14. One last point should be made on this matter of correction. You are within Christ's body, but you still carry the weight of your mortality. Be just toward yourself and just against yourself. You are a sinner, so punish yourself; go to the tribunal of your conscience, sentence yourself, and subject yourself to painful retribution. In so doing you are offering a sacrifice to God. *If you had wanted a sacrifice I would certainly have offered it*, declares a sinner, *but you take no pleasure in holocausts*. Does that mean that no sacrifice is acceptable to him? Far from it: *A sacrifice to God is a troubled spirit. A contrite and humbled heart God does not scorn* (Ps 50:18–19(51:16–17)). Humble your heart, bruise your heart, make your heart feel the pain, and then you will be correcting yourself with mercy, for when you deal severely with yourself you are not hating yourself. In assuming the role of corrector you are just, even though in the role of one who needs correction you are still a sinner. Certain things in yourself displease you and their presence in you renders you unjust, but the displeasure they cause you proves that you are just. Do you want me to demonstrate how just you are? Well now, if what you find displeasing in yourself is displeasing to God also, you have already aligned yourself with the will of God. What you hate in yourself is not what he created but something that he hates. When you hate those things in yourself that are of your own making—things which he did not make, things hateful to him—you begin to treat yourself severely, but he will be merciful and spare you because you have not spared yourself. So from the moment when you take his point of view, find delight in his law, censure whatever in yourself his law censures, and find offensive those things in you that are offensive in God's sight, see how just you are! But since you are a fallen creature and have acted in a way that displeases God, since you lapse into bad deeds through weak, fragile human nature, since you are still carrying about with you the infirmity of your flesh, and since you are woefully aware of a certain struggle, you are to that extent unrighteous and a sinner.

Yet the inner struggle continues in this life

15. "But," you object, "how is it possible to be a good person under one aspect and a sinner under another? What are you talking about?" This is difficult, and we would seem to be contradicting ourselves, were it not that the authority of the apostle comes to our aid. Listen to his teaching and then you will not accuse me of misrepresentation. *I take great delight in God's law as far as my inner self is concerned* (Rom 7:22), he says. That means he is a just man. Is not anyone who is delighted with God's law just? How then can he also be a sinner? *I am aware of a different law in my members that opposes the law of my mind, and imprisons me under the law of sin* (Rom 7:23). I am still waging war against myself, he implies. I have not yet been fully restored to the likeness of him who fashioned me. The process

of fashioning me anew has begun and, when I judge from the part of me where I have been reshaped, what is still misshapen is offensive to me. As long as I am in this condition, what can I hope for? *Who will deliver me from this death-ridden body, wretch that I am? Only the grace of God, through Jesus Christ our Lord* (Rom 7:24–25). The grace of God which has already begun to fashion you anew, the grace of God which infuses such sweetness that you are already delighted with God's law in your inner self—this is what has already healed you in part, and it will heal the rest. But for the present, go on groaning in your wounded condition, punish yourself, and find yourself less than pleasing.

16. *I do not deal blows like someone merely flailing at the air, but I chastise my body and bring it under control, lest while preaching to others I be disqualified myself* (1 Cor 9:26–27), says the apostle. If someone chastises his body, does that mean that he hates his body? Does a master who disciplines his slave hate his slave? Does someone who beats his child hate his child? But let us look at an even more intimate relationship: your flesh is like a wife to you. This is what the apostle tells us. *No one ever hated his own flesh; he nourishes it and takes good care of it, as Christ does of the Church* (Eph 5:29). This is the firm truth: your flesh is like your wife, and so no one hates his own flesh. Yet what does the apostle say elsewhere? *The flesh lusts against the spirit, and the spirit against the flesh* (Gal 5:17). Your flesh lusts against you like a wife opposing your wishes, so you must both love it and discipline it until undivided concord reigns, through the reformation of your whole self. But when will that be? You cry in distress, *Who will deliver me from this death-ridden body, wretch that I am?* (Rom 7:24) but you do not really think, do you, that you will get rid of your body and find peace that way? There is another Scriptural passage to set alongside that one. What about the words, *We groan inwardly as we await our adoption as God's children, the redemption of our bodies?* (Rom 8:23) Your body will be re-created and will make its passage from mortality to immortality, and then it will no longer give trouble, because the mortality that resists you now will no longer exist. This is why you must discipline your body. Gain the mastery now over what you hope to receive back later; give it a hard time now so that it may be happy then.[24] It cannot be fully re-created in this life as long as you carry your mortal burden. Do not let it pull you down or throw off your restraint, but carry it, educate it, subject it to discipline, and it will be re-created in the end. Because *no one ever hated his own flesh*, even our flesh will rise again.[25] What will this risen body be like? Will I have to struggle even then? No,

---

24. Variant: "For the present it is enough if your body does not faint from weakness."
25. The thought here seems to move on from the Christian's restraint of his individual body to Christ's love for his body/bride the Church, the love that will raise it up at the end.

for *this corruptible body must put on incorruptibility, and this mortal body be clothed in immortality* (1 Cor 15:53).

A further warning against being deceived by flattery

17. When the psalm says, *He will correct me, and will rebuke me*, it means that whether the correction comes from your brother, or your nearest and dearest, or your neighbor, or yourself, you must be rebuked and corrected with mercy. But remember, *Let a sinner's oil never be nourishment for my head*. That's all very well, you say, but what am I to do? I have to put up with flatterers all the time; they never cease their hubbub. Anything about me that I would prefer not to have, they praise. Anything about me that to me is unimportant, they make much of. But anything I hold dear, they belittle. They are sycophants, liars, deceivers. They say, for instance, "Gaius Seius is a great man, a fine man, learned and wise, but why on earth is he a Christian?[26] His teaching, his writings, and his wisdom are outstanding." You might reply that, if he is a man of great wisdom, give him credit for wisely becoming a Christian. And, if he is learned, can you not believe he made a well-informed choice? But the point is that what you censure is estimable to the person you praise.

How are we to react? Praise such as theirs does not seem sweet to you, for it is a sinner's oil. "But the flatterer never stops!" Perhaps not, but do not let his oil nourish and fatten your head. This means that you should not take pleasure in their flattery or agree with what they say; do not consent, do not bask in it. Then, even if someone has brought you the oil of adulation, your head has remained untouched. It has not become inflated or swollen. If it became inflated, if you suffered from a swelled head, it would become too heavy and throw you off balance. *Let a sinner's oil never be nourishment for my head*.

Everyone needs forgiveness for some kind of sin

18. *Wait a little, and my prayer will be very popular among them*. At present they do censure me, says Christ, but wait a little. In the earliest days of the faith Christians were denounced as blameworthy by all. But wait a little. Soon *my prayer will be very popular among them*. The time will come when there will be thousands of people beating their breasts and saying, *Forgive us our trespasses, as we forgive those who trespass against us* (Mt 6:12). Even today, how few are left who are too ashamed to beat their breasts! Let these few find fault with us; we can bear with them. Let them find fault, hate us, accuse us, and defame us: *Wait a little, and my prayer will be very popular among them*. The time will come when they will eagerly have recourse to my prayer. At first they will arrogantly pretend to be righteous by their own efforts, but they will be worsted in

---

26. This passage resembles a mention of Gaius Seius in Tertullian, *Apology* 3. Compare *Exposition of Psalm* 39,26 and *Exposition* 1 *of Psalm* 70,14.

the struggle, and then, because they reared up in their pride, they will be thrown down and dragged along by their sins. They will recognize their sinfulness, and the warnings of the prophets will be plainly verified. Sinners will begin to fear judgment. The keenest insight of their minds will be directed to their guilt, and they will seize with relief on the prayer, *Forgive us our trespasses, as we forgive those who trespass against us.*

So much for their long-winded defense of their iniquity! No one can deny that already crowds of people are saying this prayer, and the thunderous noise of nations beating their breasts never grows quiet. Those clouds have good cause to thunder, for they are God's habitation. What has become of that wordy bluster, that boastful claim, "I am righteous, I have done nothing wrong"? If you study the norm of righteousness set forth in the Holy Scriptures, you will find that you are a sinner, however advanced you may be. You have made progress, have you? You worship the one God? Splendid! You do not go a-whoring away from him after idols or astrologers or soothsayers or diviners or augurs or enchanters. All such pursuits are adultery against the Lord God, for you are now numbered among the members of Christ. All right, but take a look at the sins generally committed in the human family. You don't share them, do you? You do not kill anyone; you do not have adulterous relations with anyone else's wife or wrong your own wife by consorting with any other woman; you do not dishonor yourself by any kind of detestable corruption; you keep your hands from theft, your tongue from perjury, and your heart from coveting your neighbor's possessions. You are a righteous person, then. So far, so good.

But you haven't finished yet. Don't be proud too soon. Are you quite sure you commit no sins of the tongue—none at all? You never slip into any harsh word? "Oh, well," you say, "that is no great matter, is it?" No great matter? *If anyone says to his brother, You fool! he will be liable to hell fire* (Mt 5:22). All that pride of yours is beginning to quiver now, isn't it? Yes, it is true that a righteous person does not go to such extremes that God is obviously blasphemed by his impious conduct: he does not violently assail anyone so as to cause bodily harm, he does not treat anyone in a way he would not want to be treated himself. But what about the tongue? Does anyone succeed in controlling it?

You have now gained control of yours, you say? I wonder if anyone is able to do so perfectly, in every respect. Still, you think you have controlled your tongue. All right, but how do you manage with your thoughts? What do you do with the tumultuous rabble of rebellious desires? No, I am not saying you yield to them bodily; I am quite prepared to believe you do not, and in fact I can see you don't. But surely your thoughts sometimes throw you off course and bear you away, and often while you are kneeling in prayer? You prostrate yourself or bow your head, you confess your sins and you worship God. I can see your body lying there, but I wonder where the mind is flying. I see the limbs lying still, but is the attention standing still? Is it concentrated on him whom it is worshipping? Is it not more often torn away by thoughts like a stormy sea and tossed hither and thither by the blasts? If you were talking with me now and suddenly you turned away to talk to your slave instead, ignoring me, would I not think you had been rude to me? And this even though you were not a suppliant begging a favor from me but someone conversing with me as an equal. Yet this is how you behave to God every day!

What kind of person have I been describing, brothers and sisters? One who already worships the sole God, who confesses Christ, who knows the Father and the Son and the Holy Spirit to be one undivided God, who does not go a-whoring away from him or worship demons or seek help from the devil,[27] one who holds fast to the Catholic Church. Nobody complains of any dishonesty on his part; no weak neighbor groans under oppression from him. He makes no advances to any other man's wife but is content to enjoy his own—and even practices abstinence with her insofar as this is lawful, as the apostle's ruling allows, where both consent[28] or while they are not yet married. The person I have been describing has already attained this degree of righteous living, yet even he can be charged with the faults aforementioned.

19. The time has now come when the prophecy is verified, *Wait a little, and my prayer will be very popular among them*. This could be referred either to the prayer Christ taught us or to the prayer he himself offers as he intercedes for us.[29]

In all these daily sins that we commit, what hope have we? Only to say with humble hearts, not excusing our sins but confessing them, that petition of the Lord's prayer which is indeed popular and dearly loved among us, *Forgive us our trespasses, as we forgive those who trespass against us*, and to know that we have an advocate with the Father, Jesus Christ the just one, who is the propitiation for our sins.[30]

Verse 6. Christ's prayer, and Christ's words, have vanquished the wisdom of the ancients

Let the proud protest. They are refuted by our numbers and refuted by the mix of nations as the whole earth, from the sun's rising to its setting, praises the name of the Lord.[31] What power is left to the few who try to argue? They are like judges of the ungodly. What do they matter to you? Look at what the psalm says next: *Their judges have foundered beside the rock*. And remember, *The rock was Christ* (1 Cor 10:4). They *have foundered beside the rock*. The psalm uses the word *beside* to suggest a comparison with the rock, with Christ. Great men, powerful men, learned

---

27. Variant: "who seeks help only from the Lord."
28. See 1 Cor 7:5.
29. See Rom 8:34; Heb 7:25.
30. See 1 Jn 2:1–2.
31. See Ps 112(113):3.

men: these were all reputed *their judges* because they pronounced on moral matters, handing down judicious opinions. "Aristotle said this." But stand him close to the rock and clearly he has foundered. Who is Aristotle? Let him rather choose to listen. "Christ said this," and Aristotle trembles in the underworld. "Pythagoras said this...Plato said that...." Stand them beside the rock, compare their authority with the authority of the gospel, compare those inflated talkers with Christ crucified. Let us say to them, "You wrote your treatises in the hearts[32] of the proud, but Christ has planted his cross in the hearts of kings. Furthermore, he died and rose again. You have stayed dead, and I do not wish to inquire about your prospects at the resurrection."

We can confidently assert, then, that *their judges have foundered beside the rock*. They seem to be saying something valuable only until they are compared with the rock. If we find that one of them said something that Christ too said, we congratulate him, but we do not follow him. Someone protests, "But he was earlier than Christ." If somebody says something true, does that give him priority over truth itself? Think of Christ, you objector, not at the time when he came to you but when he created you. A sick man might as well say, "I took to my bed before the doctor had come to me." Of course he only came later, because you fell ill first.

20. Recall the psalm's prediction, *Wait a little, and my prayer will be very popular among them*. "But," someone might have said, "there will also be many to gainsay it." Indeed, but *their judges have foundered beside the rock*. Then what will happen? *They will hear my words, for my words have prevailed*. My words will prevail over theirs. They spoke learnedly, but I spoke the truth. It is one thing to commend an eloquent speaker but quite another to commend a truthful one. *They will hear my words, for my words have prevailed*. How can we say they have prevailed? Here is a proof: Is there any unbeliever who, on being caught out offering sacrifice in contravention of our laws, has not denied it? Has anyone among them been caught worshipping an idol and not cried out, "I didn't do it!" in terror of being convicted? The devil used to have[33] servants of that caliber. But in what sense have the words of the Lord prevailed? *See, I am sending you out like sheep among wolves. Do not be afraid of those who kill the body, but cannot kill the soul. Fear him rather who has the power to kill both soul and body in hell* (Mt 10:16.28). He enjoined fear, but he added hope and enkindled charity. "Do not fear death," he told them. "Are you afraid to die? I will die first. Are you anxious lest even a hair of your head perish? I will rise up first, with my flesh intact." You have indeed heard his words, for his words have prevailed. The martyrs spoke and were killed; they fell, yet they stood firm.

What has resulted from the slaughter of so many martyrs? Christ's words have prevailed and, as the earth was irrigated by the blood of his

---

32. Variant: "on the foreheads."
33. Variant: "The devil is welcome to have."

witnesses, the rich crop of the Church sprang up.[34] *They will hear my words, for my words have prevailed.* How did they prevail? We have indicated this already: because they were spoken by witnesses who were not afraid. What were they not afraid of? Not of exile, not of loss of their property, not of death, not even of crucifixion. It was not just death that they faced without fear but the cross as well, a death more horrible than any other that could be imagined. The Lord accepted it so that his disciples might not only be unafraid of death itself but would shrink from no manner of death. This is why we can say that, because Christ's words are spoken by those who are not afraid, they have prevailed.

Verse 7. The death of martyrs and the fertility of the Church

21. *Like earthy dregs*[35] *spread on the ground, so have our bones been scattered around the grave.* The bones of the martyrs—that is, the bones of Christ's witnesses—were scattered around the grave because the martyrs were put to death. Those who killed them had, to all appearances, prevailed. They prevailed by persecuting so that Christ's words might prevail through preaching. What resulted from the death of his saints? *Like earthy dregs spread on the ground, so have our bones been scattered around the grave.* What does this mean: *Like earthy dregs spread on the ground*? We understand *earthy dregs* to mean any waste products, things that are regarded as rubbish but help to fertilize the earth. Another psalm tells us that the bodies of the saints lay around because there was no one to bury them.[36] But all those deaths acted like dung on the earth. As the ground receives rich nourishment from things people despise and throw away, so did the earth receive material which the world despised, so that the rich crop of the Church might spring up. You know, brothers and sisters, what this despised material is: I do not want to name it for reasons of taste, but the earth receives it as nutritious and becomes fertile and productive. What people think of as disgusting and dirty, what they dispose of, enriches the soil.

But what did our psalmist do? Let us return to his words. God raised up *the needy from the earth, and* exalted *the pauper from the dungheap, to give him a place among princes, with the princes of his people* (Ps 112(113):7–8). The pauper lay prostrate on the ground, spread-eagled, like fertilizing material, like Lazarus who lay covered with sores yet was transported to Abraham's embrace.[37] *Precious in the sight of the Lord is the death of his saints* (Ps 115(116):15). Their death is ignominious in the world's eyes but precious to the farmer. He can see its potential value and the rich moisture

---

34. An echo of Tertullian's famous words, "The blood of Christians is a seed" (*Apology* 50).
35. *Crassitudo* ("thickness," "density," or any thickened substance). Augustine takes it as waste material.
36. See Ps 78(79):2–3.
37. See Lk 16:20–22.

it can generate; he knows what he should look for and select to make sure that a rich harvest will follow. The world has nothing but contempt for such deaths, but do you not remember that *it is the lowly and contemptible things of the world that God has chosen, even the nonentities, along with what matters, to bring to nothing things that are?* (1 Cor 1:28; Rom 4:17) Peter was lifted up from the dunghill, and so was Paul, and when they were slain the world scorned them. But now that the earth has been richly nourished by their deaths and the harvest of the Church is increasing, look at what is held noble and princely in the world. When the emperor comes to Rome, he hastens—where? To the imperial temple or to the memorial of the fisherman?[38] For *like earthy dregs spread on the ground, so have our bones been scattered around the grave.*

Verses 8–9. Christians under persecution prayed in fear

22. *To you, O Lord, my eyes are turned; in you have I hoped, do not take away my life.* Christians were subjected to great cruelty during the persecutions, and many apostatized. The psalmist has just said, in the name of those taken captive, *Like earthy dregs spread on the ground, so have our bones been scattered around the grave*; but now it occurs to him that many defected, and many were in danger of defecting. As though from the heart of these troubles under persecution a voice rises in prayer: *To you, O Lord, my eyes are turned.* I fix my gaze more firmly on your promises than on their threats. I know what you suffered for me and what you promised me, and so *to you, O Lord, my eyes are turned; in you have I hoped, do not take away my life.*

23. *Guard me from the snare they have laid for me.* What was their snare? It went like this: "If you consent, I will spare you." The bait they placed in the snare was this earthly life. If the bird is attracted by the bait, it falls into the snare; but if it is the kind of bird that can say, *I have never craved the human light of day, as you know* (Jer 17:16), its eyes will not stray from God, and he will pluck its feet clear of the snare.[39]

Guard me from the snare they have laid for me, and from the stumbling blocks set by those who sin. He has mentioned two perils, quite distinct from each other: the persecutors have laid a trap, and those who have yielded and apostatized have put stumbling-blocks in the way of others. The psalmist prays to be kept safe from both. On the one hand men rage and threaten, on the other, those who consent are falling. I am afraid lest the former make me afraid or the latter draw me to imitate them. "This is what I will do to you, if you do not consent," they say, so *guard me from the snare they have laid for me.* But look, your brother has already consented, so *guard me* also *from the stumbling blocks set by those who sin.*

---

38. Compare *Exposition of Psalm* 86,8.
39. See Ps 24(25):15.

Verse 10. Christ was alone in his passion,
abandoned and denied by his disciples

24. *Sinners will fall into his nets.* Now what is this about, brothers and sisters: *Sinners will fall into his nets*? It does not mean all sinners; it is saying that those who sin by being so much in love with this present life that they give it precedence over eternal life will fall into the persecutor's snare. But what are you saying, psalmist? You cannot mean that people of that type are the only ones who fall into his snare? What about your own disciples, O Christ? What about that time when persecution grew hot and they all left you alone, each to take his own way?[40] It is true that you had foreseen and foretold that they would, but you did not make them run away by announcing it in advance, nor did you deny yourself through the voice of a disciple. All those who had been continuously your close companions abandoned you in your time of trial and persecution, when your enemies were hunting for you to crucify you. One of them was that daring man who had promised to stand by you even to death, though he proved to be a sick man who needed to hear from the physician what was going on in him. Like a delirious patient he had declared himself healthy, but Christ listened to his heartbeat. The time came for temptations, for the searching test, for accusations, and the disciple was interrogated not by some important person in authority but by an insignificant slave—and a woman at that! Interrogated by a slave-girl, he collapsed. He denied Christ three times. He denied him once, and then, when someone took notice of him again, he denied a second time. After two denials attention was drawn to him once more, and he denied a third time. The Lord had foretold this, but he had not ordered it or coerced his disciple. If anyone tries to argue that Peter acted rightly because he fulfilled the Lord's prediction, we would have to conclude that Judas also did the right thing in betraying him, since the Lord had foretold this too. Far be it from us to say so, brothers and sisters; that sounds more like the voice of *the elect among them,* who defend their sins rather than confessing them.[41] We can interpret the episode better by concentrating on Peter himself. If what he did was no sin, why did he weep? Let us not ask questions of Peter but rather take Peter's tears as evidence; we shall find no more reliable witnesses concerning him than his tears. *He wept bitterly* (Lk 22:62), says the gospel. He was not yet ready for suffering. The Lord had promised him, *You will follow me later* (Jn 13:36). He would stand firm later, when the Lord's resurrection had confirmed him.

25. The time had not yet come for those bones to be scattered around the grave. Think how many people fell away. Even those who had been the first to hang on his words, even they failed. Why? *I am all alone, until my passover.* That is the next line in the psalm. He had prayed, *Guard me*

---

40. See Mk 14:50; Jn 16:32.
41. See sections 7–9 above.

from the snare they have laid for me, and from the stumbling blocks set by those who sin. Guard me against both, the snare and the scandals, those who terrify me and those who have lapsed.[42] But during the Lord's passion even his first followers, the men who were to be leaders of the Church and pillars of the earth, failed and fell. The prophecy spoken in another psalm had not yet been fulfilled: *I strengthened its pillars* (Ps 74:4(75:3)).

Why does he say, *I am all alone, until my passover*? He is speaking here in his own person as the head: *I am all alone, until my passover*. All alone, in what sense? In your passion, Lord, you will suffer alone; you alone will be killed by your enemies. *I am all alone, until my passover*. What does he mean by *until my passover*? An evangelist explains this: *When the hour had come, at which Jesus was to pass over from this world to the Father* (Jn 13:1). What else can *until my passover* signify if not his passage *from this world to the Father*? "Then it was that I strengthened the pillars, those pillars that were to support the earth," he says, "because at my resurrection they learned beyond a doubt that death was not to be feared. So although *I am all alone, until my passover*, once I have made my passover I shall be solitary no longer but multiplied, because many people will imitate me, many will suffer for my name. Until my passover I am one, one alone, but when I have accomplished it many will form one person in me." *I am all alone, until my passover.*

I want to point out to you that there is something mysterious about the word used. The word *pasch* sounds like "suffering" in Greek, since the Greek for "to suffer" is πασχειν. But in Hebrew the word *pasch* means "passing over," according to those who know the language. If you question Greeks carefully they will tell you that *pasch* is not a Greek word. It does sound rather like the Greek πασχειν, "to suffer," but the verb is not conjugated like that, and the noun "suffering" is παθος in Greek, not *pasch*. Those who know Hebrew and have translated for us what we should read have interpreted *pasch* as "passing over." Accordingly, as the Lord's passion drew near, the evangelist took care to use this apposite word: *When the hour had come, at which Jesus was to pass over from this world to the Father*; and this same *pasch* of the Lord is mentioned in the verse of our psalm: *I am all alone, until my passover*. After my *pasch* I shall no longer be all alone; once I have accomplished my passover I shall be solitary no more. Many others will imitate me, many will follow me. And if they do follow me later, what can I say? *I am all alone, until my passover.*

What then does the Lord mean in this psalm when he says, *I am all alone, until my passover*? What has our explanation clarified? If we have

---

42. *A lapsis.* The word probably awakened echoes for Augustine and his hearers. The problem of the *lapsi* who apostatized under persecution, and repented when it had ceased, had preoccupied Cyprian, bishop of Carthage, in the middle of the third century. The controversy had important consequences for the development of the Church's penitential discipline.

understood rightly, compare this with our Lord's own words in the gospel: *Truly, truly I tell you, unless the grain of wheat falls into the earth to die there, it will bear no fruit, but if it dies, it bears much fruit* (Jn 12:24–25). He said this on the same occasion when he promised, *When I am lifted up from the earth, I will draw all things to myself* (Jn 12:32). But *unless the grain of wheat falls into the earth to die there, it will bear no fruit, whereas if it dies, it bears much fruit.* This grain had the right to expect an abundant crop; but wait awhile, for it must be put to death first. Unless it falls into the soil and dies, it will remain alone.

Christ was alone until his passover because before him no one had died for confessing Christ

26. Clearly, then, Christ was alone until he was put to death. This had to be; and therefore not even Peter had the strength to stay with him. Peter would later be given the fortitude to follow Christ, but he could not go ahead of him.[43] Before Christ's death no one died for the sake of Christ: for the confession of his name, I mean, that name on account of which we are called Christians. You can't think of anyone, can you? It is true that many died as martyrs before Christ; many prophets suffered a similar fate. But they did not die because they had foretold Christ; they died because they had openly denounced people's sins and freely opposed the injustices prevalent in society. They are rightly regarded as martyrs, for, although they did not die for confessing Christ's name, they were slain in the cause of truth. But before the wheat-grain fell into the earth, before the death of him who said, *I am all alone, until my passover,* no one died for confessing the name of Christ. You can see how true this is by reflecting that not even John, killed so recently by a wicked king as a reward for a dancing girl,[44] was put to death for confessing Christ. He might well have been: there would have been no lack of people keen to kill him, for if he could be slain by one person for a different reason, how much more might he have been killed by those who were plotting to kill Christ? After all, John had been bearing witness to Christ. Some of those who heard Christ preaching wanted to kill him, yet they did not kill the man who was Christ's witness.

Why was that? Because, I think, if they had attacked John on account of Christ, John would not have denied him, for he was a man of extraordinary strength, which was why he was called the bridegroom's friend.[45] He was endowed with great grace and splendor of character, to which the Lord testified by saying, *There has never arisen a mother's son greater than John*

---

43. Augustine returns several times to the dialogue in Mt 16:22–23, and Jesus' command to Peter, *Get behind me, Satan.* Peter was ordered to follow Christ, not precede him. Compare *Exposition 1 of Psalm* 34,8 and *Expositions of Psalms* 62,17 and 126,4.
44. See Mk 6:22–28.
45. See Jn 3:29.

the Baptist (Mt 11:11). The attack was therefore mounted not against John the Baptist but against Peter, who did not possess such fortitude. He was to receive it later, but at the time of the Lord's passion he was still weak. So we see the man who lacked strength being interrogated about the name of Christ; but the one who has the strength does not suffer persecution for Christ's sake, because it would not be fitting that anyone suffer for the name of Christ before Christ himself. John freely bore witness to Christ, whom the Jews killed, yet John himself was not killed by the Jews but by Herod, whom he had warned, *It is not lawful for you to take your brother's wife* (Mk 6:18). (Herod's brother had not died without issue, you see.)[46] John died for the law of truth, for equity, and for justice, and therefore he was a saint and a martyr. But he did not die for that name after which we are called Christians. Why not? Because the prophecy was to be fulfilled, that *I am all alone, until my passover.*

---

46. See Dt 25:5; Mk 12:19.

PART IV

EXERCISING THE SPIRITUAL MIND

Steps to the Upper Floors

Exposition 3 of Psalm 30

Synopsis (Ps 30:8–16)

Let's recognize ourselves in the words of the prophet. Remember that Christ is speaking, the head and body in one voice. Some members are constrained by suffering while others are at ease; but charity feels both the distress and the comfort of others within the body. Churches may be full to bursting, but in truth many are impostors; still let's not give up hope or let love grow cold (1–2).

Impostors angered the Psalmist by their sins and hypocrisy. But be clear that anger is not hatred—not yet. Be wary of letting anger become hatred. Sorrow imperils a person angered by sin, especially someone unable to win over the enemy. The Church longs to "eat" its adversaries and make them part of Christ's body. Thus in Peter's rooftop vision the voice said, "Go on, Church, slaughter and eat." (Because the Lord had said that he would build his Church on Peter, Peter embodied the Church and so can be called "Church.") He was told to eat to signify the Church taking people in (3–5). But scorn for the Church caused by bad Christians is a worse calamity than scorn from outside enemies; it weighs down the Church heavily. Bad Christians repel those who might believe except for seeing the Church in disrepair. We're always at risk because even very good people in the Church fall into sin and cause others to doubt *all* the good people in it. But for our part, let's not multiply the doubts of others by thinking evil of our neighbors in the Church. Be the person you want your neighbors to be, so that you won't think that they're something you're not (6–7).

Now, some people caught in schisms outside the Church think evil of it their whole lives. Yet we're all Christians, or called such, signed with the mark of Christ. The prophets spoke more clearly about the Church than about Christ. For example, Abraham's sacrifice of Isaac obscurely foretells of Christ, but God's promise of numerous progeny to Abraham openly foretells the Church's growth in "all the nations of the earth" (8–9).

The Psalmist thinks he's been forgotten after being thought guilty by association. Curses upon bad Christians commonly fall upon all Christians and drive seekers away (10–11). Let's switch our hope back to the Lord alone and away from human beings like Donatus. Let human beings take their rightful lower place beneath the dignity of God, so that we say, "You alone are my God." His grace assigns to us our appropriate lots; lines of fortune are not in our hands but in God's. Grace is given freely; it can't be bought and sold as though it were in our power (12–14).

Augustine's Text of Psalm 30:8–16

(8) I will exult and be glad in your mercy, because you have looked kindly on my humble state;

You have saved my soul from its constraints.

(9) You have not shut me up in the clutches of my enemy,

But have guided my feet into open spaces.

(10) Have mercy on me, Lord, for I am in distress;

My eye is confused by anger, my soul too, and my belly.

(11) My life was imperiled by sorrow, and my years faded amid sighs;

My vigor is undermined by want and my bones are jarred.

(12) I have become the object of scorn, more so than all my enemies,

Beyond bearing in my neighbors' eyes, and a source of fear to my acquaintances.

Those who saw me fled outside away from me.

(13) I am consigned to oblivion, as though I had died out of their hearts.

I am no better than a pot thrown away.

(14) I heard hostile criticism from those who encircle me.

Colluding against me, they planned to seize my soul.

(15) I trusted in you, Lord; I said, "You are my God."

(16) The fate allotted to me is in your hands....

Exposition

The Second Sermon to the People

Verse 10. Varied experiences, common sympathy

1. We must turn our minds to the rest of the psalm now, and see if we can recognize ourselves in the words of the prophet. If we have examined ourselves when we are in trouble, we shall rejoice when the time comes for apportioning rewards. While explaining the earlier verses of the psalm

I reminded you, beloved,[1] that it is Christ who is speaking; and I stressed that we must understand this as the whole Christ, Head and body. I established this solidly, I think, with appropriate and crystal-clear texts from the Scriptures, so that there could be absolutely no doubt that Christ consists of Head and body, bridegroom and bride, the Son of God and the Church, the Son of God who became Son of Man for our sake, to make us who are children of men children of God. So by a great sacrament[2] these two were to be united in one flesh, the two who are hailed by the prophets as two in one voice. This voice exclaimed in grateful joy earlier, *Because you have looked kindly on my humble state you have saved my soul from its constraints, and have not shut me up in the clutches of my enemy, but have guided my feet into open spaces.* This is the grateful relief of someone freed from distress, the cry of Christ's members liberated from affliction and subtle attacks. Yet here is the speaker again, and now he is praying, *Have mercy on me, Lord, for I am in distress.* But being distressed is like being cramped in a narrow place, so how could he have said, *You have guided my feet into open spaces*? If he is still distressed, how can his feet be in open spaces?

The answer may be that there is, certainly, one single voice, because there is one body; but in some members there is a sense of spacious freedom, while others are squeezed and confined. Some live righteous lives and experience it as easy, but others toil away amid troubles. It must be like this, that different members suffer differently, because otherwise the apostle would hardly have told us, *If one member suffers, all the members suffer with it, and if one member is honored, all the rest rejoice too* (1 Cor 12:26). Some churches, for instance, enjoy peace; others are harassed. Those that are at peace have their feet in open spaces, while the harassed ones are confined and squeezed. But the distress of one group saddens the other, while the peace of some brings the distressed ones comfort. The body is one, so much so that it is not torn apart by this difference; the only thing that tears it apart is discord. Charity ensures the close connection of the parts; these organic links hold them together in unity; unity fosters charity; and charity brings us all to glory. From some members, then, it is right that the cry should go up: *Have mercy on me, Lord, for I am in distress; my eye is confused by anger, my soul too, and my belly.*

Why the distress or anger?

2. We may wonder all the same what this distress is, since not long ago the speaker seemed to be happy about the righteousness freely bestowed by God's gift, and the ample room it gave to his feet in the wide spaces

---

1. *Caritati vestrae.*
2. *In sacramento magno*: probably the mystery of the Incarnation, the "great sacrament" from which all sacraments derive, particularly as evoked by Eph 5:32, which he has already mentioned; but possibly an allusion also to the eucharist.

of charity. What can be the source of his distress now? Perhaps that state of affairs which the Lord mentioned: *With iniquity increasing mightily, the love of many will grow cold* (Mt 24:12). It is hinted first of all that the saints are few, but since the nets have been cast widely and the Church has grown, countless numbers have been caught, as another psalm foretold: *I announced the news and spoke the message, and they were multiplied, in numbers beyond reckoning* (Ps 39:6(40:5)). They have overloaded the boats and burst the nets, as that passage in the gospel tells us, when the Lord helped the fishermen's catch, before his passion.[3] These crowds have accumulated, and now they cram the churches full at Easter, until the walls can scarcely contain them. But the psalmist grieved over these crowds, and how could he not, when he also saw them filling up the playhouses and amphitheaters, the same people who so recently filled the churches? Or when he saw them committing sins, so soon after sharing in the praises of God? Or when he heard them blaspheming, after responding to God with their "Amen"?

But he must hold firm, stick it out and not weaken, even at the sight of this vast multitude of unworthy people; for the wheat does not give up hope when it views the quantity of straw, but waits for the day when after the harvest it will be stored in the barn, where it will have the company of the saints to enjoy, and no more harm to fear from whirling dust. The psalmist must stand fast, then, for the Lord has more to say. After his warning that *with iniquity increasing mightily, the love of many will grow cold*, the Lord immediately added something else, lest our feet should slip or waver at the increase of iniquity he had mentioned. He added something designed to uplift believers, to comfort and steady them. He said, *Whoever perseveres to the end will be saved* (Mt 24:13).

3. Let us turn our attention now to the speaker who, as I think, has found himself in such straits. If he was indeed in distress, surely he ought to have been sorrowful? Sorrow is the emotion appropriate to distress. But no, he is not sorrowful; he says he is angry: *Have mercy on me, Lord, for I am in distress; my eye is confused by anger.* If you are distressed, why are you angry?[4] He is angered by the sins of others. And who would not be angered by seeing people who confess God with their lips denying him by their conduct? Who could fail to be angry on seeing people renounce the world by their words, but not by their deeds? Who would not be angered

---

3. See Lk 5:6. Augustine thought of this episode, before the Lord's passion, as symbolizing the inclusion of both good and bad within the Church, to the danger of the nets. He contrasts it with the other fishing episode, after the resurrection (Jn 21:1–8), where the nets did not break; the catch there symbolizes the elect. See *Exposition of Psalm 49*, 9.
4. Throughout this sermon Augustine understands it to be the speaker who is angry; in his first exposition of the psalm he took it to be God's anger that caused the speaker's distress.

by seeing brothers and sisters plotting against each other, betraying the trust they express by exchanging the kiss during God's holy mysteries? And who could possibly count all the things that anger Christ's body, the body that inwardly lives by Christ's Spirit, but groans like wheat nearly choked by chaff? The people who are groaning are scarcely visible, just as the wheat is scarcely visible on the floor at threshing-time. Anyone who did not know how many ears had been thrown in would think there was nothing there but straw, yet from this massive bulk that looks like all straw, a great heap will be sifted out. These half-hidden groaners feel angry. In another passage they declare, *Zeal for your house has devoured me* (Ps 68:10(69:9)); and in similar vein they say elsewhere, *Disgust possessed me at the sinners who abandon your law*, and again, *With chagrin I watched the fools* (Ps 118(119):53.158).

Anger is not hatred

4. Now, about this anger: we must take care that our anger is not so vehement as to turn into hatred. Anger is not yet hatred. You may be angry with your son, but you do not hate your son. He is aware that you are angry with him, but all the while you are safeguarding an inheritance for him; indeed the reason why you are angry with him may be that you fear he may lose by his bad behavior what you are saving up for him. So anger is not yet hatred; we do not yet hate those with whom we are angry; but if the anger remains and is not quickly uprooted, it grows into hatred. This is why Scripture bids us, *Do not let the sun set on your wrath* (Eph 4:26); it is urging us to pluck out newly-aroused anger before it turns into hatred. Sometimes you come across one of the faithful who really does hate, and yet rebukes a brother or sister for being angry. The one is nurturing hatred, yet condemns anger in another; the one has a beam in his eye, but finds fault with the splinter in the eye of a brother or sister.[5] All the same, that splinter is a little shoot that may grow into a beam if it is not plucked out at once. This is why the psalmist does not say, "My eye has been blinded by anger"; he says it is *confused*. If it were being blinded, that would mean there was hatred there already, not anger. I can prove to you that hatred really does blind our eyes, for John says, *Whoever hates his brother is still in darkness* (1 Jn 2:11). Before we go off into darkness our eye is confused by anger, and we must be careful that anger does not develop into hatred, and blind us.[6] The psalmist therefore says, *My eye is confused by anger, my soul too, and my belly*, which means, "Everything inside me is in turmoil."

---

5. See Mt 7:3–5.
6. At this point a Louvain manuscript inserts the following: "Let everyone be careful about this, everyone who has been called in peace, that is, in Christ who bequeathed to us the peace of God, in Christ at whose birth supreme peace was proclaimed to the human race by angels. If such a person breaks out into hatred for any reason, light or grave, he or she will be unable to have

By his belly he means his inner life. It is sometimes legitimate to be angry with wicked and perverse people, and with those who transgress the law and lead bad lives, but we may not lose our temper with them. When we feel anger but are not allowed to lose our temper, all our inner being is confused. Sometimes perversity has gone so far that it is past correction.

Verse 11. The Church's hunger

5. *My life was imperiled by sorrow, and my years faded amid sighs.* He complains, *My life was imperiled by sorrow.* Remember how the apostle declared, *We are alive now, if you are standing firm in the Lord* (1 Thes 3:8). All those who have been made perfect through the gospel and the grace of God live on in this world only for the sake of others, for their life here is no longer necessary to themselves. Because what they have to give is necessary for others, that cry of the apostle comes true in them as well: *I long to die and to be with Christ, for that is much the best; but it is necessary for you that I remain in the flesh* (Phil 1:23–24). But when, on the contrary, someone sees that what he tries to give, through hard work and preaching, is of no profit to other people, his life is weakened and in want. And a miserable sort of want and hunger that is. When we win people over to the Lord, it is as though the Church eats them. How is that? Well, the Church draws them into its own body. Whatever we eat, we assimilate into our bodies. This is what the Church does, through the saints: it is hungry for those it longs to win over, and in a sense it eats those it has somehow won. Peter represented the Church when a dish was lowered to him from heaven full of all kinds of living creatures, all four-footed things, and crawlers, and flying creatures that by their diversity signified all the gentiles. The Lord was foreshadowing the Church, which was destined to swallow down all nations and convert them into its own body. So he said to Peter, *Slaughter and eat* (Acts 10:13). "Go on, Church," he said (he could call Peter, "Church," because he had said to him, "On you, the rock, I will build my Church"), "go on, Church, slaughter and eat. Slaughter them first, then eat them; kill what they are of themselves, then make them what you are."

When the gospel is preached, then, and the preacher sees that it is doing no good to people, he has reason to cry out, *My life is imperiled by sorrow, and my years have faded amid sighs. My vigor is undermined by want and my bones are jarred.* These years of ours that we spend here are passed amid groaning. Why? Because with the mighty increase of iniquity, the love of many grows cold. But it is groaning, rather than articulate complaints. When the Church watches many people going wrong, it swallows down its groans so silently that it can say to God, *My groaning is not hidden from you* (Ps 37:10(38:9)). That is said in another psalm, but it fits well here, and the meaning is: "My groaning is hidden from human beings, but never from

---

any fellowship with peace, which means with Christ, except through penance and worthy amendment."

you." *My vigor is undermined by want, and my bones are jarred.* We have spoken already about this want. The bones are the strong churches which, although undisturbed by any persecutions from outside, are shaken by the iniquities of their own members.

Verse 12. The deterrent effect of bad example

6. *I have become an object of scorn, more so than all my enemies, beyond bearing in my neighbors' eyes, and a source of fear to my acquaintances.* When he says, *I have become an object of scorn, more so than all my enemies,* whom does he mean? Who are the Church's enemies? Pagans? Jews? Bad Christians live worse than all those. Shall I show you how much worse bad Christians are than all the rest? The prophet Ezekiel compares them to useless branches.[7] Imagine that the pagans are woodland trees, outside the Church's garden. Something may still be made of them. From trees suitable for timber comes wood apt for the joiner's craft; it may still be knotty, or warped, or covered with bark, but he can work on these unsatisfactory features, and plane it, and in the end turn it into some object for human use. But a joiner can do nothing with the branches cut off from a tree; they are fit only for the fire. Think about it, brothers and sisters. As long as the branch remains attached to the vine, it is vastly superior to the forest tree, because the branch can bear fruit, and that tree bears none; but if the branch is lopped off the vine, and then compared with the forest tree, it is clear that the tree is better, because the joiner can make something out of it, whereas no one wants the branch, except someone who has to supply his hearth.

In the light of this the psalmist considers the hordes of people who lead bad lives in the Church, and exclaims, *I have become an object of scorn, more so than all my enemies.* "These people who frequent my sacraments live more disgracefully than others who have never approached them," he laments. Why should we not admit this openly, in plain English,[8] at least now, while we are expounding this psalm? We might shrink from saying it at other times, but the present need to comment gives us the freedom to correct. *I have become an object of scorn, more so than all my enemies.* The apostle Peter says of such people, *Their later doings are even worse than what they did earlier; for it would have been better for them not to have known the way of righteousness than having known it to be turned away from the holy commandment delivered to them* (2 Pt 2:20–21). In saying, *It would have been better for them not to have known the way of righteousness,* he has judged the enemies outside to be better than those inside who lead sinful lives, and weigh down the Church so heavily. *It would have been better for them not to have known the way of righteousness,* he says, *than having known it to be turned away from the holy commandment*

---

7. See Ezk 15:2–5.
8. He says, of course, "In plain Latin."

delivered to them. And as if this were not plain enough, look at the horrible comparison he offers: *the proverb is proved true by what happens to them: the dog has returned to its vomit* (2 Pt 2:22). Since the churches are full of such people, is it not a true lament that the few utter, or, rather, that the Church utters through those few, *I have become an object of scorn, more so than all my enemies, beyond bearing in my neighbors' eyes, and a source of fear to my acquaintances*? I have become the object of intense scorn to my neighbors, to those, that is, who had begun to approach me to find faith. These neighbors of mine have been thoroughly put off by the evil lives of bad and spurious Christians. How many people do you think would like to become Christians, my brothers and sisters, but are scandalized by the disgraceful way they see Christians behaving? These are the "neighbors" who had begun to approach the Church; but we have become an object of intense scorn in their eyes.

Scandals, and how not to react to them

7. *I have become a source of fear to my acquaintances.* What can be more frightening to one who sees others leading bad lives, than to find that even those for whom he had high hopes are also guilty of many bad deeds? Such a person is afraid that everyone who was considered good may after all be no better than the rest, and the result is that nearly all good people fall under suspicion. "What a fine fellow that man was! Then how comes it that he has fallen? How did it happen that he could be found out in that base dealing, that crime, that disgraceful business? Perhaps everyone is like that?" This is what *a source of fear to my acquaintances* implies, this is how we often come to be doubted even by those who know us well.

But it is only if you feel smug about your own virtue (supposing you have any) that you can suspect someone else of being bad like all the rest. Complacency of conscience, whatever form it takes, is so flattering to a good-living person that he may say to himself, "You were anxious just now lest everyone may be bad like that. So what about yourself? Are you like that?" Conscience replies, "Oh no, not me." "So if you aren't, you must be the only one who isn't?" When that happens you need to be on your guard lest pride of this kind be worse than the original wrongdoing. Beware of considering yourself the only one. Even Elijah, in his disgust at the vast number of the godless, once complained to God, *They have slain your prophets and undermined your altars. I am abandoned and alone, and they are seeking my life.* And what is God's reply to him? *I have seven thousand men left to me who have not bent their knees to Baal* (Rom 11:3–4).[9] So among all these scandals we have only one remedy, brothers and sisters: to believe no evil of our neighbor. Humbly try to be yourself what you want him or her to be, and then you will not think him or her to be what you are

---

9. See 1 K 19:10.18.

not. All the same, we must admit that such a person does necessarily arouse fear in his acquaintances, even those most familiar with him.

Scripture is clear on the Church

8. *Those who saw me fled outside away from me.* If those who had never truly seen me had fled outside away from me, that would have been excusable; but it is even those who did see me who fled outside. The flight of those who had not truly seen me would have been bad enough (though strictly speaking we should not say that they fled out of doors, because they had never truly been indoors. If they had been inside they would have known the body of Christ, the members of Christ, and our unity in Christ). But far more lamentable, indeed altogether beyond bearing, is that many who did see me fled away outside. Many who well knew what the Church was went outside and left it, and set up heresies and schisms in opposition to the Church. You may find someone today, for example, who was born within the Donatist party and does not know what the Church is. People like that hold fast to the sect in which they were born, and you will have a hard job to uproot from their minds a habit of thought which they imbibed with their mothers' milk.[10] But what about the person who is thoroughly versed in the Scriptures, who reads them constantly and preaches on them? Has he never come upon the text, *Ask of me, and I will give you the nations as your heritage, and the ends of the earth for your possession*? Will he not also light on the promise, *All the ends of the earth will be reminded and will turn to the Lord, and all the families of the nations will worship in his presence?* (Pss 2:8; 21:28(22:27)) If you see the unity of the entire world foretold in Scripture, what right have you to run out of doors away from it, so that you not only incur blindness yourself, but also inflict it on others?

Those who saw me—that is, those who knew what the Church is, and contemplated it in the Scriptures—*fled outside, away from me.* Do you really think, my brothers and sisters, that all those people who set up their little local heresies and sects were unaware that when the Church was prophesied in God's Scriptures, it was always as a Church spread throughout the world?[11] By no means! I tell you, beloved,[12] we are all Christians, we and they, or at any rate we are all called Christians, and all of us are signed with Christ's sign. Yet the prophets spoke more clearly about the Church than about Christ, because, I think, they saw in spirit that it was in opposition to the Church that people would found their conventicles. They would not

---

10. Their nurses' milk, literally. In this paragraph he is contrasting the invincible ignorance of some with the more culpable blindness of others who should be capable of finding the true Church prophesied in Scripture.
11. A favorite point in Augustine's polemic against the Donatists who, though powerful, were essentially an African phenomenon, in contrast to the catholicity of the Church.
12. *Caritati vestrae.*

engage in such intense argument about Christ himself; it would be about the Church that they would raise the fiercest quarrels. Accordingly the clearest predictions were made and the most open prophecies pronounced about this matter on which the most serious controversies would focus, so that the prophecies could convict those who had indeed seen, yet fled outside.

In Abraham's sacrifice Christ was prophesied obscurely, the Church plainly

9. I will mention one instance of this. Abraham is our father, not because we are descended from him in the flesh, but because we imitate his faith (see Rom 4). He was a just man, and pleasing to God. Through his faith he received Isaac, the son who had been promised to him and to his sterile wife, Sarah, in their old age.[13] Then he was ordered to immolate this very son to God. He did not hesitate, or argue, or question God's command, or think ill of what had been enjoined by one who had the best possible right to give the order. He led his son to the sacrifice; he laid the wood for the fire on the boy; he arrived at the place and raised his right hand to strike. At God's bidding he dropped it, as at God's bidding he had lifted it. As he had obeyed in preparing to slay the boy, so he now obeyed in sparing him. At every point he was obedient, at no point afraid. Yet in order that the sacrifice might be duly offered, and that he might not depart without some blood-shedding, a ram was found stuck by its horns in a thornbush. It was immolated, and so the sacrifice was carried through. Now what is this ram? It is a symbol of Christ, but one wrapped in mysteries. It is a symbol that needs discussion in order that the meaning may come clear; it has to be studied carefully so that it may be made plain to us, and what was wrapped in obscurity be unwrapped. Isaac as the only son, the dearly-loved son, prefigured the Son of God, and carried the wood for his sacrifice as Christ carried his cross. We can even say that the ram was a symbol of Christ, for to be held fast by the horns is like a crucifixion. So all this obscurely prefigures Christ. But it was necessary that the Church too be proclaimed, and proclaimed immediately; no sooner had the Head been foretold than the body must be too. The Spirit of God began—God himself began—to want to preach to Abraham about the Church, and to do so he discarded figurative language. He proclaimed Christ in a figurative way but foretold the Church quite openly, saying to Abraham, *Because you have hearkened to my voice, and for my sake have not withheld your beloved son, I will bless you exceedingly, and multiply your seed more and more, like the stars in the sky and the sand on the seashore; and in your seed shall all the nations of the earth be blessed* (Gn 22:16–18). The same is true nearly everywhere else: Christ was proclaimed by the prophets under a veil of mystery, but the Church clearly, so that even those who later would oppose the Church would see it, and in them would be realized that prophecy of

---

13. See Gn 21.

wickedness in the psalm: *those who saw me fled outside, away from me.* As the apostle John said of them, they went out from our midst, but they never truly belonged to us.[14]

Verse 13. Forgotten and useless

10. *I am consigned to oblivion, as though I had died out of their hearts.* I am forgotten, I have fallen into oblivion, those who once saw me have forgotten me. They have forgotten me so completely that it is as though in their hearts I have died. *I am consigned to oblivion, as though I had died out of their hearts; I am no better than a pot thrown away.* Why does he think he has become *no better than a pot thrown away*? He had been working hard, but doing no good to anyone; he saw himself as a tool or vessel fit to serve no one's purpose, so he calls himself a discarded pot.

Verse 14. Indiscriminate blame

11. *I have heard hostile criticism from those who encircle me.* Plenty of people live close around me, and every day they find fault with me. How many accusations are leveled against bad Christians, only to fall as curses upon all Christians! Do you find anyone who speaks ill of Christians, or rebukes them, saying, "Look what they are doing, those among the Christians who are unworthy"? No, not at all; they just say, "Look what the Christians are doing." They make no distinction, they tar us all with the same brush. The critics who talk like this live close by us, all around; that is, they walk round and round the church, but do not enter it. Why is that? Why do they walk round the church without entering? Because they are enamored of cyclic time; they are unwilling to enter and find the truth because they do not love eternity. They are given over to temporal concerns as though bound onto a wheel, and consequently another text says of them, *Whirl them round like dust,* and another again, *the wicked walk round in a circle* (Pss 82:14(83:13); 11:9(12:8)).

Colluding against me, they planned to seize my soul. What does that suggest, *they planned to seize my soul*?[15] It means that they planned to make me consent to their depraved acts. For those who curse the Church and do not enter it, merely refusing to enter is insufficient; they also want to drive others out of the Church by disparaging it. If they succeed in driving you out of the Church they have seized your soul; that is, they have secured your acquiescence. And then you will be wandering around the Church, not at home in it.

---

14. See 1 Jn 2:19.
15. *Ut acciperent animam meam consiliati sunt.* In his first exposition Augustine understands *animam* to mean "life" and *acciperent* to mean "spare," so extracting the idea that the persecutors cruelly prolonged the life of the just sufferer who longed for death. He takes the words differently here.

Verse 15. Put your trust in the Lord alone

12. What about me? Amid all these reproaches, all the scandals, all the calamities, amid all that would lead me astray, whether unjust treatment from without or crooked dealings within, amid all this I thought to find righteous people whom I might imitate. I looked for them, and there were none; so what did I do? *I trusted in you, Lord.* Nothing is more conducive to salvation, nothing safer. You wanted to imitate someone, and you found that person no good. Have done with imitation, then. You went on to look for someone else, but found in him or her something that displeased you. You sought out a third, and that one did not satisfy you either. Does that mean that you are destined to be lost, because this, that, or the other person has let you down? By no means. Switch your hope away from human beings, because all who fix their hopes on mortals are under a curse.[16] If you are still looking to some mortal, seeking to imitate him and to hang on his words, you are still thirsting for milk as your nourishment, and in danger of becoming a milksop,[17] as children are called who go on sucking too long, which is bad for them. What else is a persistent use of milk but a desire to get your food through the flesh of someone else? And that is to live off another human being. Grow up and eat at table; take your food from the same source where your hero took his (or perhaps failed to take it). It may have been lucky for you that you fell in with a bad fellow whom you believed to be good, so that you found only bitterness in what passed for a mother's breast, and were put off and disgusted by it, because then you were enticed to more sustaining fare. Nurses use this trick with milksops. They put something with a bitter taste on their nipples, so that the babies recoil from the breast in disgust, and struggle open-mouthed toward the table.

Let the psalm declare, then, *I trusted in you, Lord; I said, "You are my God."* You are my God. Begone, Donatus! Begone, Caecilian![18] Neither of them, nor my latest paragon, is my God. I am not walking under the banner of any ordinary name; I hold to the name of Christ. Listen to Paul's question: *was Paul crucified for you, or were you baptized in Paul's name?* (1 Cor 1:13). I would have been lost if I had thrown in my lot with Paul; shall I not be lost if I align myself with Donatus? Let human names, human claims and human devices fade away. *I trusted in you, Lord; I said, "You are my God."* Not any mere human, but you alone are my God. One human model fails, one perhaps makes some progress; but my God neither fails nor makes progress. He who is perfect has no scope for improvement, and the eternal cannot possibly fail. *I said to the Lord, "You are my God."*

---

16. See Jer 17:5.
17. *Mammothreptus.*
18. Donatus was the early-fourth-century schismatic bishop of Carthage from whom Donatism took its name. Caecilian was his orthodox counterpart.

Verse 16. God's will in the casting of lots

13. *The fate allotted to me is in your hands.* Not in other people's hands, but in yours. Now what is this talk about being allotted? Why lots? When lots are mentioned we must not think of soothsayers. The casting of lots is not a bad thing in itself; it is the means by which God's will is indicated when human beings are in doubt. Even the apostles drew lots after the death of Judas, who had betrayed the Lord and, as was written of him, had *gone to his own place* (Acts 1:25). The question arose as to who should be appointed in his stead. Two were chosen by human judgment, and from these two one was chosen by divine judgment. God was consulted as to which of them he wanted, *and the lot fell to Matthias* (Acts 1:26). So then, what does the psalm mean by *the fate allotted to me is in your hands*? He has called the grace by which we have been saved his "lot," or so I think. Why would he call God's grace a lottery? Because where lots are concerned, it is not our choice that operates, but God's will. Where it is a case of saying, "This person has this recommendation, but that one does not," we are weighing their merits, and where merits are taken into consideration there is choice, not lot. When God, though, found no merits on our part, he saved us by the "lot" of his will, saved us because he willed it, not because we were worthy. That is our lot. It was no accident that the Lord's tunic, woven throughout from the top to signify the heavenly charity that will last for ever, could not be divided by his persecutors.[19] So they drew lots for it. Those on whom the lot has fallen appear to be destined to share the lot of the saints.[20] *By grace you have been saved, through faith*, says Paul, the apostle. *By grace you have been saved, through faith, and this is not your own doing* (it is by lot, then), *and this is not your own doing, but the grace of God. It does not come from works* (as though you had behaved so well that you were worthy to attain it). *It does not come from works, lest anyone boast. We are his own handiwork, created in Christ Jesus for good works* (Eph 2:8–10). In a sense God's will is like a secret lottery held in the human race, a lottery decided by the hidden will of God, in whom there is no unfairness,[21] for he takes no account of human pretensions. Your lot comes from his hidden justice.

Grace is not for sale

14. Let me have your attention now, dearly beloved.[22] Notice how what we have been saying is confirmed by the apostle Peter. Simon the magician had been baptized by Philip, and he attached himself to Philip, believing

---

19. See Jn 19:23–24.
20. See Col 1:12.
21. See Rom 9:14.
22. *Caritas vestra.*

in the divine miracles he had himself witnessed. [23]The apostles came to Samaria, where the magician was and where he had been baptized. They laid their hands on the newly-baptized, who received the Holy Spirit and began to speak in tongues. Simon was amazed and dumbfounded at this divine miracle, that at the imposition of human hands the Holy Spirit should come and fill people; and he lusted after the power, not the grace. What he wanted was not something to set him free, but a gift to enhance his own reputation. But as he craved it his heart filled up with pride and devilish impiety and a haughtiness that needed to be taken down a peg. He asked the apostles, "How much money do you want from me for the power to lay my hands on people and cause them to receive the Holy Spirit?" This man lived close by, near the Church; he was after secular honors, and thought he could buy God's gift with money. And in thinking he could get the Holy Spirit with money he also judged the apostles to be avaricious, just as he was himself impious and proud. Peter immediately addressed him: *Take your money with you to perdition for thinking you could buy God's gift with it. You have no share or lot in this faith* (Acts 8:20–21). You, he implies, have no share in this grace which we have all received freely, because you think to purchase what is given gratis. Now grace is called a "lot" precisely because it is given gratis. *You have no share or lot in this faith.*

I have explained this to show that we have no need to be afraid when the psalm says, *The fate allotted to me is in your hands.* What is our allotted fate? The Church's inheritance. But how far does that stretch? Even to the furthermost coasts: *I will give you the nations as your heritage, and the ends of the earth for your possession* (Ps 2:8). I don't want some fellow promising me a little parcel of land: O my God, *the fate allotted to me is in your hands.*

Let that be enough for now, beloved ones.[24] We will finish it tomorrow, in the Lord's name and with his help.

---

23. See Acts 8:13–24.
24. *Caritati vestrae.*

Exposition 2 of Psalm 31

Synopsis

This is a Psalm about God's grace and being justified only by divine mercy. Don't think that we make ourselves just, or that grace licenses everything since we'll be forgiven anyway. Mercy and judgment stand together against these dangerous presumptions (1). Paul commended this Psalm by connecting it to Abraham's justice. In case anyone misunderstands, the apostle James assures us that faith goes with good works. "It is the intention that makes an action good, and the intention is directed by faith." In this sense faith is like a skilled but not overconfident sea captain who carefully steers his ship into port (2–4). Abraham's works followed faith, made fruitful by love. Add hope and love to your faith and you won't ask what works to perform. Faith and hope bring love to its proper "end." "Love as much as you like, but take care what you love." For Paul faith alone justifies, and yet he also says that faith without love *profits me nothing*. Are both true? Faith transforms the believer into a just person who loves by right actions (5–6). The forgiven are just by God's free gift, and "it is through being forgiven that you begin to live in faith." This "righteousness of faith" has good works as its consequence. No one can boast of good works before faith or should avoid good works after faith (7–8).

First, recognize you're a sinner; then, when faith moves you to good works, attribute them to grace and not to yourself. Jesus "saw" Nathanael under the fig tree; that was grace, and "all fruit grows from his grace." The truly strong person relies on God alone and watches out for pride (9–10). The Pharisee in the parable was proud, while the tax collector didn't lift his eyes to heaven because he was examining his conscience. The Pharisee showed the Doctor only healthy limbs and covered up his wounds, so he couldn't be healed (11–12).

People who refuse to confess and who shout about their merits—that is, who defend their sins—have things backward and have become decrepit. God lays a heavy hand on them so that they'll humble themselves in order to be exalted. Yes, it hurts to "perceive my sin." But looking straight at it is a turning point. "If he looks at it, God will overlook it." If we declare sin and not cover it, God has already covered it, even before we confess (13–15).

Some people, even very smart ones, think God allowed their sin, the stars forced them, Mars made them murder, and so on. True wisdom says, "God created me with free will; I myself have sinned" (16). Holy people pray *when the time is right*, forgiven by Christ's grace bestowed "in the fullness of time" in the New Covenant. Old covenant people were guilty *under* the law; New Covenant people are just *within* the law (17). Don't drown in the "many waters" of bad teachings about Fate, or Chance, the stars, or "the race of darkness," which threaten to swamp the soul. God's water, baptismal or doctrinal, teaches us to confess our sins and to humble our hearts. Some fine precepts may fill the pagan books of Epicureans, Stoics, Manicheans, or Platonists. But nowhere in them do you find the humility of Christ by which we draw near to God (18).

When we take refuge in God, we dance with joy even while groaning in prayer, "Save me" (19–20). God answers, *I will give you understanding*; that's what the Psalm is about—understanding to know yourself and to rejoice in hope, until hope gives way to heaven.

God rebukes proud, uncomprehending "horses and mules" who defend their sins. The unbroken among them get the bit and then the whip, though even that may not work (21–23). Meanwhile the just *rejoice in the Lord* because of being made *right of heart*. Crooked hearts complain that all woes are God's fault, or at least they grumble about life's unfair shake. They say either "God doesn't exist," or "God is unjust," or "God is impotent." Crooked hearts can't line up with God, who is straight and true. But the "right heart" says with Paul, "We rejoice in our sufferings." It knows that God allows scourges for the sake of either punishment or discipline. Christ himself showed sadness before his passion. Contrast that with Paul's joy! How is the commander sad while the soldier is happy? But Christ's sadness before his passion bent our will to God's, and that led Paul—and us—to rightness of heart (24–26).

Augustine's Text of Psalm 31

(1) For David himself, for understanding.

   Blessed are those whose iniquities are forgiven, and whose sins are covered.

(2) Blessed is the one to whom the Lord will impute no sin,

   And in whose mouth is no guile.

(3) My bones grew old because of my silence, in consequence of my shouting all day long.

(4) For day and night your hand lay heavy upon me.

I was reduced to bitterness, when the thorn stuck fast in me.
(5) I perceived my sin, and did not cloak my unrighteousness.
I will declare against myself my unrighteousness to the Lord;
And you have forgiven the impiety of my heart.
(6) Every holy person will pray to you about this matter, when the time is right.
Yet they will not draw near to him amid the flood of many waters.
(7) You are for me a refuge from the distress that besets me.
You who make me dance with happiness, save me.
(8) I will give you understanding, and set you on this road you must enter.
I will keep a firm eye on you.
(9) Do not be like a horse or a mule, devoid of understanding.
Rein in their jaws with bit and bridle, those who will not approach you.
(10) There is many a scourge for the sinner,
But everyone who hopes in the Lord is encompassed with mercy.
(11) Rejoice in the Lord and dance for joy, you just,
And make him your boast, all you who are right of heart.

Exposition

A Sermon to the People, preached on a Thursday in the Restored Basilica[1]

Treading a fine line between different kinds of presumption

1. This is a psalm about God's grace, and about our being justified by no merits whatever on our own part, but only by the mercy of the Lord our God, which forestalls anything we may do. It is a psalm to which the apostle's teaching has called our attention in a special way, as the reading that preceded the psalm has made clear to us all.[2] And this is the psalm which I, insignificant though I am, have undertaken to expound to you, dearest friends.[3] So I must begin by commending my weakness to your prayers. As the apostle says, *May the right word be given me when I open my mouth*

---

1. *Basilica Restituta*, the most famous of the Carthaginian basilicas, also called *Basilica Maior*. In it were held the African Councils of 390 and 401. This sermon has been tentatively assigned to the winter of 412–413.
2. An indication that the reading had been from Romans 4, by Augustine's choice, as appears from 2 below.
3. *Cum vestra Caritate.*

(Eph 6:19), so that I can speak in a way that will not be perilous for me, and will be salutary for you. The human mind dithers between opposite dangers, wavering between confession of its weakness and rash presumption, and for the most part it is tossed between these two and battered on either side, and whichever way it is driven there is a ruinous fall awaiting it. If it veers entirely to the side of its own weakness, it begins to think that God in his mercy forgives all sinners, provided only they believe that God sets them free, so that at the end his mercy is ready to ensure that no one among sinful believers shall perish. In other words, no one will be lost of those who promise themselves, "I can do anything, I can defile myself with any crimes or shameful deeds, I can sin as much as I like. God frees me in his mercy because I have believed in him." Now if a person takes the view that no one in these circumstances will perish, he will be inclined by this evil notion to think he can sin with impunity. And then our just God, whose mercy and judgment are sung about in another psalm[4]—and it is not mercy alone, mind you, but mercy and judgment—finds this person self-deceived by presumption and abusing the divine mercy to his own destruction, and then God must necessarily condemn.

An attitude like this brings a person crashing down. But then, suppose someone is terrified of that, and exalts himself in rash self-assurance, trusting in his own strength of character, and mentally resolving to fulfill all the righteous requirements of the law and to carry out all it enjoins without offending in any point whatever. If such persons think they can keep their lives under their own control and slip up nowhere, fall short nowhere, with never a wobble, never a blurring of vision, and if they claim the credit for themselves and their own strength of will, then even if they have carried out the whole program of righteous conduct as far as human eyes can discern, so that nothing in their lives can be faulted by other people, God nonetheless condemns their presumption and boastful pride.

What happens, then, if someone has thought to justify himself, and takes his stand on his own virtue? He falls. But if anyone considers himself and thinks about his weakness, and presumes on God's mercy, neglecting to purify his life from sin and sinking into a whirlpool of iniquity, he too falls. Presuming on one's righteousness is the danger on the right hand; thinking that one's sins will go unpunished is the danger on the left. We need to listen to God's voice warning us, *Turn not aside, to right hand or to left* (Prv 4:27). Do not presume on your virtue to get you into the kingdom; but do not presume on God's mercy and go on sinning. The divine command calls you back from both: from trying to climb the steep bank on the one hand, and from sliding down on the other. If you scramble up to the first you will fall headlong; if you slip down the second you will drown. *Turn not aside, to the right hand or to the left*, Scripture warns us. I will say it again so that you can all fix it in your minds in a brief formula:

---

4. See Ps 100(101):1.

don't presume on your virtue to win the kingdom, don't presume on God's mercy and think you can get away with sinning.

This psalm indicates the fine line

You will ask me, "What am I to do, then?" This psalm teaches us. Once we have read it through and discussed it, I think that with the help of the Lord's mercy we shall see the road clearly, the road on which we may be walking already, or which we must take. Each of us must listen according to our own capacity and, as our conscience dictates, either bemoan our need for correction or rejoice that we have something that deserves approval. Any who find that they have gone astray must return to the road and walk on it; and any who find that they are on the road must go on walking until they arrive. Do not be stubborn if you are off the road, or dilatory if you are on it.

Abraham and faith: Paul's teaching

2. The apostle Paul bore witness to the fact that this psalm deals with the grace that makes us Christians; that is why we arranged for this particular passage to be read to you. When the apostle was explaining about the righteousness that depends on faith, in opposition to those who boasted about a righteousness derived from works, he asked, *What are we to say that Abraham obtained, he who was our father according to the flesh? If Abraham was justified by works, he has ground for pride, but not before God* (Rom 4:1–2). May God keep that kind of pride far from us! Let us listen to a different injunction: *Let anyone who boasts, boast of the Lord* (1 Cor 1:31). Many people do boast about their works, and you will find plenty of pagans who are unwilling to become Christians because they think their upright lives are enough. "The important thing is to live a good life," such a pagan will tell you. "What further command would Christ lay upon me? That I should live a good life? But I am doing that already, so why do I need Christ? I commit no homicide, no theft, no robbery; I do not covet anyone else's property, or defile myself by adultery. Let anything that deserves rebuke be found in my way of life, and the one who rebukes me for it shall make me a Christian." A person like this has ground for pride, but not before God.

Not so our father Abraham. This passage of Scripture is meant to draw our attention to the difference. We confess that the holy patriarch was pleasing to God; this is what our faith affirms about him. So true is it that we can declare and be certain that he did have grounds for pride before God, and this is what the apostle tells us. It is quite certain, he says, and we know it for sure, that Abraham has grounds for pride before God. But if he had been justified by works, he would have had grounds for pride, but not before God. However, since we know he does have grounds for pride before God, it follows that he was not justified on the basis of works. So if Abraham was not justified by works, how was he justified?" The apostle goes on to tell us how: *What does Scripture say?* (that is, about how Abraham was justified). *Abraham believed God, and it was reckoned to him as righteousness* (Rom 4:3; Gn 15:6). Abraham, then, was justified by faith.

Paul and James do not contradict each other: good works follow justification

3. Now when you hear this statement, that justification comes not from works, but by faith, remember the abyss of which I spoke earlier. You see that Abraham was justified not by what he did, but by his faith: all right then, so I can do whatever I like, because even though I have no good works to show, but simply believe in God, that is reckoned to me as righteousness? Anyone who has said this and has decided on it as a policy has already fallen in and sunk; anyone who is still considering it and hesitating is in mortal danger. But God's Scripture, truly understood, not only safeguards an endangered person, but even hauls up a drowned one from the deep.

My advice is, on the face of it, a contradiction of what the apostle says; what I have to say about Abraham is what we find in the letter of another apostle, who set out to correct people who had misunderstood Paul. James in his letter opposed those who would not act rightly but relied on faith alone; and so he reminded them of the good works of this same Abraham whose faith was commended by Paul. The two apostles are not contradicting each other. James dwells on an action performed by Abraham that we all know about: he offered his son to God as a sacrifice. That is a great work, but it proceeded from faith. I have nothing but praise for the superstructure of action, but I see the foundation of faith; I admire the good work as a fruit, but I recognize that it springs from the root of faith. If Abraham had done it without right faith it would have profited him nothing, however noble the work was. On the other hand, if Abraham had been so complacent in his faith that, on hearing God's command to offer his son as a sacrificial victim, he had said to himself, "No, I won't. But I believe that God will set me free, even if I ignore his orders," his faith would have been a dead faith because it did not issue in right action, and it would have remained a barren, dried-up root that never produced fruit.

Apparent good works before faith are wide of the mark

4. What are we to make of this? That no good actions take precedence of faith, in the sense that no one can be said to have performed good works before believing? Yes, that's right, because although people may claim to perform good works before faith, works that seem praiseworthy to onlookers, such works are vacuous. They look to me like someone running with great power and at high speed, but off course. This is why no one should reckon actions performed before belief as good; where there was no faith, there was no good action either. It is the intention that makes an action good, and the intention is directed by faith. You should not pay too much attention to what a person does, but consider where he is aiming as he does it, and whether he is directing his efforts toward the right harbor, like a

skilled pilot. Imagine a very expert steersman who has lost his bearings. What is the use of keeping a firm hold on the jib, making fair speed, putting the vessel's prow to the waves, and taking good care that she is not caught sideways onto their force? Such a pilot may be so competent that he can turn the ship whatever way he will, and turn her away from anything he wants to avoid; but if you ask him, "Where are you making for?" he replies, " I don't know." Or rather, he does not say, "I don't know," but "I am making for such-and-such a port," when in fact he is speeding not into port but onto the rocks. The more handy and efficient he thinks he is in steering his ship, the more dangerous is his mastery of her, surely, since it just brings her more swiftly to shipwreck. A swift athlete who is off course is just like him. Would it not be better and safer if the pilot were somewhat less skilled, so that he steered the vessel laboriously and with difficulty, and yet held her to a straight and proper course, and if the athlete were running more lazily and feebly, but keeping to the track, rather than running so impressively off it? The best thing of all is to keep to the right road and maintain a good pace on it; but we may have good hopes for someone who straggles along in the rear, limping a little perhaps, but not so badly as to lose the way altogether or just sit down. Such walkers do make progress, even though slowly, and we may be confident that they will reach the goal sooner or later.

But faith cannot be sterile: it works through love

5. Well now, brothers and sisters, Abraham was justified by faith, but if no good works preceded his justification, they certainly followed it. Is your faith sterile? No, of course not. You are not sterile yourself, and neither is your faith. If you believe something bad, you scorch the root of your faith in the fire of that bad belief. So make sure to hold fast to your faith with a mind to work. You may object, "But that is not what the apostle Paul tells us." Oh, but it is. Paul speaks of *faith that works by choosing to love*[5] (Gal 5:6). In another place he says, *The fullness of the law is charity* (Rom 13:10); and elsewhere, *The whole law is summed up in one word, when scripture says, "You shall lovingly cherish*[6] *your neighbor as yourself"* (Gal 5:14). Can you really contend that Paul does not want good works from you, when he says, *You shall not commit adultery. You shall not murder. You shall not covet. And if there is any further commandment, it is covered by this one word, "You shall lovingly cherish your neighbor as yourself." Love of one's neighbor prompts no evil. The fullness of the law is charity?* (Rom 13:9–10) Does charity allow you to do anything harmful to a person whom

---

5. Augustine uses three different words for love in this section: *dilectio*, the love that is directed by choice, a cherishing love; *caritas*, charity; and *amor*, a general word for love which may have connotations of sensuality or lust, in some contexts.
6. *Diliges.*

you lovingly cherish? Perhaps, though, you refrain from doing harm, but do no good to your neighbor either. Does charity allow you to withhold from someone you lovingly cherish anything that it is in your power to give? Is it not charity that impels us to pray even for our enemies? Can charity leave a friend in the lurch, when it wishes well to an enemy?

If faith is devoid of the will to love,[7] it will equally be devoid of good actions. But don't spend too much time thinking about the works that proceed from faith: add hope and the will to love[8] to your faith, and you will have no need to ask yourself what kind of works you should perform. This deliberate love[9] cannot remain idle. After all, what is it in any one of us that prompts action, if not some kind of love?[10] Show me even the basest love[11] that does not prove itself in action. Shameful deeds, adulteries, villainies, murders, all kinds of lust—aren't they all the work of some sort of love?[12] Purify this love, then, divert onto your garden the water that is going down the drain, let the current that drove you into the arms of the world be redirected to the world's Maker. Do you want people to ask you, "Don't you love anything, then?" Of course not. If you loved nothing you would be sluggish, dead, loathsome and unhappy. Love[13] as much as you like, but take care what you love. Love of God and love of your neighbor are called charity; but love of the world, this passing world, is called greed or lust. Lust must be reined in, charity spurred on.

A good conscience and hope

Now when people perform good actions their charity endows them with the hope that proceeds from a good conscience; for it is a good conscience that gives rise to hope. As a bad conscience plunges a person into complete despair, so a good conscience fills us entirely with hope. Then there will be the three realities of which the apostle speaks: *faith, hope and charity* (1 Cor 13:13). In another place he mentions this triad again, but this time he substitutes a good conscience for hope. He refers to *the finishing of the commandment* (1 Tm 1:5). What does he mean by its being finished? He is thinking of the commandments being perfectly fulfilled, not done away with. We have two different ways of speaking about a thing being finished: we say, "The food is finished," and in a different sense, "This tunic which I was weaving is finished." Food is finished up and so exists no longer, but the tunic is finished by being brought to completion. Yet we use the word, "finished," in both cases. So when Paul spoke about the commandment

---

7. *Dilectione.*
8. *Dilectionem.*
9. *Dilectio.*
10. *Amor.*
11. *Amorem.*
12. *Amor.*
13. *Amate.*

being finished he did not mean that the commandments were being abolished, but that they were being brought to perfection, accomplished, not abrogated.[14] The commandment is "finished," then, because of these three realities: *the finishing of the commandment is single-hearted charity, and a good conscience, and unfeigned faith* (1 Tm 1:5). The apostle substituted "a good conscience" for hope, because anyone whose conscience is clear does have hope. Those who suffer from a bad conscience, on the contrary, have estranged themselves from hope, and can look for nothing but damnation. If we are to hope for the kingdom we must have good consciences, and in order to have good consciences we must both believe and do good. Believing is the province of faith, good work that of charity. So in one text the apostle began from faith, saying, *Faith, hope, and charity*; but in the other text he made charity itself his starting-point: *single-hearted charity, and a good conscience, and unfeigned faith*. But we began just now with the middle term, conscience and hope. Yes, and rightly, because anyone who wants to have good hope needs to have a good conscience, and to have a good conscience we must both believe and work. So from this middle term, hope, we can work backward to the beginning, that is, to faith; and forward to the end, which is charity.

Paul himself gives the complementary teaching on "works"

6. How can the apostle assert that a person is justified by faith, independently of works, when in another place he speaks of *faith that works by choosing to love?* (Gal 5:6) It is not just a case of pitting the apostle James against Paul; we can pit Paul against himself, and challenge him like this: "On the one hand you seem to give us permission to sin with impunity by saying, *Our argument is that a person is justified by faith, apart from any works* (Rom 3:28); and on the other hand you speak of *faith that works by choosing to love*. How can I be free from anxiety on the basis of the first, having done no good works, while according to the second I do not seem to have either sound hope or even sound faith itself, if I have performed no good works in love? I am listening to you, apostle. You obviously want to urge upon me faith without works, but faith's work is willed love,[15] and this willed love cannot remain idle; it must refrain from doing evil and do all the good it can. What does love do? *Turn away from evil, and do good* (Ps 36(37):27). You extol faith apart from works, yet in another place you declare, *If I have such perfect faith that I can move mountains, but have no love, it profits me nothing* (1 Cor 13:2). So if faith profits us nothing without charity, and charity must always be at work wherever it is found, then faith itself works by choosing to love. How then is it possible for anyone to be justified by faith apart from works?"

---

14. *Consummentur, non consumantur.*
15. *Dilectio.*

The apostle has an answer for us. "I told you this, stupid, to save you from the mistake of relying on your achievements and thinking that you earned the grace of faith by your works. Put no reliance on works accomplished before faith. You know well that when faith came to you it found you a sinner, and although it is true that once faith was given it made you righteous, it was an ungodly person that faith found to transform into a righteous one." *When someone believes in him who justifies the impious, that faith is reckoned as justice to the believer*—so says Paul (Rom 4:5). If the impious is justified, then the impious person is changed from being impious into being righteous, but in that case what good works can he or she have performed while still impious? An impious, ungodly person may boast about his good deeds, claiming, "I give alms to the poor, I rob no one, I do not covet anyone else's wife, I kill nobody, I commit no fraud, I return promptly anything entrusted to me even though there were no witnesses." All right, let the unbeliever say all this, but still I ask, is the speaker a godly person, or impious? "How can I be impious," he or she will reply, "if I conduct myself like that?" In just the same way, I reply, as those of whom Scripture says, *They served creatures rather than the Creator, who is blessed for ever* (Rom 3:25). In what sense are you impious? It may be that on the basis of all these good works of yours you either hope for what is worth hoping for, but not from God, from whom you should hope for it; or else you hope for something unworthy, even though you hope for it from God, from whom you should be hoping for eternal life. On the strength of your good actions you have hoped for worldly advantage, and so you are impious. The reward of faith is not like that. Faith is a precious thing, but you have cheapened it. You are impious, therefore, and those works of yours are null and void. Though you employ all your muscle in good works, and appear to pilot your ship with expertise, you are rushing toward the rocks.

But suppose what you hope for is the true object of hope, life eternal, but you do not hope for it from the Lord God through Jesus Christ, through whom alone eternal life is given, but think to arrive at eternal life through the host of heaven, through the sun and the moon, through the powers of air and sea and earth and stars? What then? You are still impious. Believe in him who justifies the impious, so that those good works of yours may be good too. I should not even have called them "good," as long as they do not spring from the root of faith. Think about it. Either you are hoping for temporal life from the eternal God, or you are hoping for eternal life from demons. Either way you are impious. Correct your faith, direct your faith, and set your course. If you have good strong feet, walk without fear, run, and stay on the road. The more strongly you run, the more easily you will arrive. Or perhaps you are slightly lame? At least do not leave the road; you may take longer, but you will get there. Only do not stand still, do not turn back, do not get sidetracked.

The grace of faith presupposes God's forgiveness

7. In the light of this, who are to be judged blessed? Certainly not people in whom God has found no sin, because he has found it in all of us. *All have sinned, and are in need of the glory of God* (Rom 3:23). Now, if sins are found in everyone, it follows that only those can be blessed whose sins have been forgiven. This is the point the apostle made by saying, *Abraham believed God, and it was reckoned to him as righteousness. But to anyone who does some work* (that is, anyone who takes his stand on works, pretending that the grace of faith was given to him on the strength of them) *wages are given not as a free grace, but as something owed* (Rom 4:3–4). And what does that mean, if not that the only recompense we have is called grace? And if it is grace, it is given gratis. Given gratis? How is that? It consists of a free gift. You have done nothing good, but forgiveness of your sins is granted to you. If your actions are scrutinized, they are all found to be bad. If God awarded you just retribution for those actions, he would certainly condemn you, for the wage due to sin is death.[16] What is owing to evil deeds, except damnation? And what to good deeds? The kingdom of heaven. You were found in your evil deeds, so if you are awarded what is due to you, you are to be punished. But what happens? God does not mete out to you the punishment you deserve; he bestows on you the grace you do not deserve. He owed you retribution, he awards you forgiveness. So it is through being forgiven that you begin to live in faith; that faith gathers to itself hope and the decision to love[17] and begins to express itself in good actions; but not even after that may you boast and preen yourself. Remember who planted you on the right road; remember how even with your strong, swift feet you were wandering off it; remember how even when you were sick and lying half-dead by the wayside you were lifted onto a mount and taken to the inn.[18] *To anyone who does some work,* Paul tells us, *wages are given not as a free grace, but as something owed* (Rom 4:4). If you want to be excluded from the domain of grace, vaunt your own merits. But God sees what is in you, and knows what he owes to each.

But what about the person who *does no work?* (Rom 4:5) Think here of some godless sinner, who has no good works to show. What of him or her? What if such a person comes to believe in God who justifies the impious? People like that are impious because they accomplish nothing good; they may seem to do good things, but their actions cannot truly be called good, because performed without faith. But *when someone believes in him who justifies the impious, that faith is reckoned as justice to the believer, as David too declares that person blessed whom God has accepted and endowed with righteousness, independently of any righteous actions* (Rom

---

16. See Rom 6:23.
17. *Dilectione.*
18. See Lk 10:30–37.

4:5–6). What righteousness is this? The righteousness of faith, preceded by no good works, but with good works as its consequence.

Good will is needed for right understanding

8. You must pay careful attention to what I am saying, my friends, because otherwise you will hurl yourselves into that abyss I mentioned, assuming that you can sin with impunity. It won't be my fault if you do, any more than it was the apostle's fault when many people misunderstood him. They misunderstood on purpose, so that they would not need to produce any good work after justification. Do not be like those folk, my brothers and sisters. One of the psalms speaks about them (about all such people, that is, but expressing it in the singular): *He refused to understand that he should act well* (Ps 35:4(36:3)). Notice that it does not say, "He was unable to understand." As for you, you must want to understand that you should act well. What you need to understand is perfectly clear, and well within your grasp. And what is this clear truth? That no one must boast of any good actions before faith, and no one must be lazy about performing good actions once faith has been given. So then, God grants forgiveness to all the ungodly, justifying them on the basis of faith.

Verses 1–2. Forgiveness and truth: the example of Nathanael

9. *Blessed are those whose iniquities are forgiven, and whose sins are covered. Blessed is the one to whom the Lord will impute no sin, and in whose mouth is no guile.* Now we get to the beginning of the psalm, and so to the beginning of understanding. This comprehension, this understanding, teaches you that you must neither vaunt your merits nor presume that you can get away with sinning. The title of the psalm is, *For David himself, for understanding*, so this is a psalm that promotes understanding. The first stage of understanding is to recognize that you are a sinner. The second stage of understanding is that when, having received the gift of faith, you begin to do good by choosing to love,[19] you attribute this not to your own powers but to the grace of God. Then there will be no guile in your heart, which means in your inward mouth, for you will not have one thing on your lips and something different in your thoughts. You will not be one of the Pharisees to whom the Lord said, *You are like whitewashed tombs; outwardly you appear righteous to other people, but inwardly you are full of guile and sin* (Mt 23:27). When people who are wicked pass themselves off as righteous, are they not full of guile? Nathanael was not like that; of him the Lord said, *Look, there is a true Israelite, in whom there is no guile* (Jn 1:47). But why was there no guile in Nathanael? *When you were under the fig tree, I saw you*, the Lord told him (Jn 1:48). He was under a fig tree, which symbolized being subject to the condition of our flesh. If he was subject to the fleshly condition, being held prisoner by the impiety

---

19. *Cum ex fide per dilectionem bene coeperis operari.*

we all inherit by human descent, then he was under that fig tree another psalm groans about: *Lo, I was conceived in iniquity* (Ps 50:7(51:5)). But he who saw Nathanael there was he who had come to bring grace. What does "saw him" mean? He had mercy on him. So when he commends a man free from guile, what he is commending is his own grace in that man. *When you were under the fig tree, I saw you.* What is special about saying, *I saw you*? Nothing, unless you understand it in a particular sense here, because otherwise what is remarkable about seeing anyone under a fig tree? If Christ had not espied the human race under that fig tree,[20] we should either have withered away completely, or else only leaves would have been found on us, but no fruit, as with the Pharisees in whom there was plenty of guile, for they justified themselves by their words, but were wicked in their deeds. It was just such a tree that Christ saw, and cursed; and it withered. "All I can see is leaves," he said; that is, words only, and no fruit. "Let it wither," he said, "so that it may not even produce leaves."[21] Why did he strip them even of words? It is a withered tree that cannot bring forth even leaves. The Jews were like that; the Pharisees were that tree; they produced a luxuriance of words but no deeds, so they deserved to be condemned by the Lord to wither.[22]

May Christ see us too under a fig tree; may he see us in our fleshly condition producing not leaves only but the fruit of good deeds, lest we wither away under his curse. But because all fruit grows from his grace, not from any merits of ours, the psalm declares, *Blessed are those whose iniquities are forgiven, and whose sins are covered*: not those in whom no sins have been found, but those whose sins are covered. Their sins are covered over, they are out of sight, they are done away with. If God has covered our sins, he does not want to see them or be aware of them; if he does not want to be aware of them, he does not want to punish them; if he does not want to punish them, he does not want to convict us, he wants not commination but commiseration.[23] *Blessed are those whose iniquities are forgiven, and whose sins are covered.* You must not interpret this statement that our sins are covered over to mean that they are still there, still

---

20. Perhaps we should translate here "under the guise of that fig tree"; see the next note.
21. See Mt 21:19.
22. When Augustine describes the climax of his struggle for conversion in *Confessions* VIII,12,28, he says he flung himself down under a fig tree. At least in retrospect he must have been aware of its ambivalent symbolism, alluded to here. Adam and Eve after their fall made themselves loincloths of fig leaves, a sign of their sinful condition (see Gn 3:7); the Lord curses a barren fig tree that represents unfaithful Israel (see Mt 21:19 = Mk 11:13–14); but Nathanael's call from beneath a fig tree suggests his vocation, like Augustine's own, to grace.
23. *Noluit agnoscere, maluit ignoscere.*

alive. Why, then, did the psalmist say that sins are covered? Because they are thrust out of sight. What would it mean for God to look at our sins? To punish our sins. I can prove to you that for God to look at our sins is the same thing as to punish them: another psalm prays to him, *Turn your face away from my sins* (Ps 50:11(51:9)). May God not look at your sins, so that he can see you. See you how? In the same way as he saw Nathanael: *When you were under the fig tree, I saw you.* The fig tree's shade was not so dense that the eyes of God's mercy could not see through it.

Forgiveness and truth: the example of the Pharisee and the tax collector

10. *In whose mouth there is no guile.* Very different is the case of those who refuse to confess their sins, and struggle vainly to excuse them. The more they exert themselves to defend their sins and brag about their merits, turning toward their sins a blind eye, the more do their strength and vigor wane. The only truly strong person is one who is strong not in himself but in God. So Paul admits that in his trouble *three times I begged the Lord to take it away from me, but he said to me, "My grace is sufficient for you."* Notice that God says, *My grace*, not "your own power." *My grace is sufficient for you, for my power finds complete scope in weakness* (2 Cor 12:8–9). Accordingly a little further on Paul himself confesses, *When I am weak, then I am strong* (2 Cor 12:10). Any who aspire to be strong, relying on themselves and displaying their own merits, whatever these may be, will be kin to that Pharisee[24] who managed to boast even about what he admitted was the gift of God, saying, *O God, I thank you.* Take note, my brothers and sisters, of the sort of pride God is warning us about here, the kind that can creep into a righteous person and sneak up even on someone of good promise. *O God, I thank you*, he kept saying. By repeating, *I thank you*, he was avowing that he had received what he had from God, for *what have you that you did not receive?* (1 Cor 4:7) Acknowledging that much, he said, *I thank you*, yes, *I thank you that I am not like other people: robbers, cheats, adulterers, or like that tax collector there.* Why was this a proud attitude? Not because he thanked God for the gifts he had, but because he was exalting himself above his neighbor on the strength of those gifts.

11. Close attention is required here, my brothers and sisters, because the evangelist tells us something at the outset to indicate what provoked our Lord's parable. Christ had asked, *When the Son of Man comes, do you think he will find faith on earth?* (Lk 18:8). But that might have given an opening to some heretics who would seize on it and think that it meant the whole world had fallen away (for all heretics are very elitist and out of touch) and might take occasion to brag that in themselves alone remained the faith that had vanished from the rest of the world. To guard against this the evangelist added to the Lord's question, *When the Son of Man comes,*

---

24. See Lk 18:10–14.

do you think he will find faith on earth? the further statement, *He spoke to certain people who considered themselves righteous and despised others the following parable. A Pharisee and a tax collector went up to the temple to pray* (Lk 18:9–10), and so on; you know the story.

So the Pharisee kept saying, *I thank you.* Was that pride? Yes. Why? Because he was despising others. How do I prove that? From his very words. The gospel tells us that the Pharisee despised another man who stood a long way off, but God came close to that man as he made his confession. *The tax collector stood a long way off,* we are told, but God was not standing a long way off from him. And why not? Because, as another verse of Scripture tells us, *The Lord is close to those who have bruised their hearts* (Ps 33:19(34:18)). Ask yourselves whether this tax collector had bruised his heart, and there you will see how close the Lord is to the brokenhearted. *The tax collector stood a long way off and would not even raise his eyes to heaven, but beat his breast*—beat his breast, you see, as a token of his bruised heart—*and said, O God, be merciful to me, a sinner.* And what was the Lord's verdict? *Truly I tell you, that tax collector went down to his house at rights with God, more than did the Pharisee* (Lk 18:13–14). Why? This is God's judgment. The one boasts, *I am not like other people: robbers, cheats, adulterers, or like that tax collector there; I fast twice a week, and give tithes from everything I own.* The other does not dare to lift his eyes to heaven; he examines his conscience and stands a long way off, and he is justified rather than the Pharisee. How can this be? I beg you, Lord, to explain to us this just sentence of yours; explain to us the equity of your law. And the Lord does explain. Would you like to hear him give his judgment? *Anyone who exalts himself will be humbled, but the one who humbles himself will be exalted.*

12. Now listen, beloved.[25] We have said that the tax collector did not dare to lift his eyes to heaven. Why was he not directing his gaze heavenward? Because he was directing it toward himself. He was scrutinizing himself so that he might initially find himself displeasing, and so become pleasing to God. But you, Pharisee, you bear yourself arrogantly, standing with head held high. And the Lord says to any such proud person, "So you are not willing to take a hard look at yourself? I am looking at you. Do you want me to stop looking at you? Then look hard at yourself." The tax collector did not dare to raise his eyes heavenward because he was looking into himself, and dealing severely with his own conscience. He took the role of judge over himself so that the Lord might be the intercessor; he was punishing himself so that another might set him free; he was accusing himself so that the other might defend him. The Lord did not merely plead the case in his defense; he went further and decided it in his favor: *the tax collector went down to his house at rights with God, more than did the Pharisee; because anyone who exalts himself will be humbled, but*

---

25. *Caritas vestra.*

the one who humbles himself will be exalted. "This man looked so hard at himself," says the Lord, "that I did not want to scrutinize him. I heard him entreating me, *Turn your face away from my sins.*" Who said that? The same who also said, *I know my iniquity* (Ps 50:11.5(51:9.3)).

Obviously, my brothers and sisters, the Pharisee was a sinner too. Not because he was able to say, *I am not like other people: robbers, cheats, adulterers*, nor because he fasted twice a week, nor because he gave tithes. None of these things made him a sinner. But even if he had been free of all other sins, pride such as this would have been gravely sinful in itself, and yet he did reel off this list. But in any case, who is free from sin? Who can boast of having a pure heart, or of being clean from sin in all respects?[26] The Pharisee was indeed guilty of sin; but he was looking the wrong way, and failed to realize where he was standing. He was like someone in need of healing who had come to a doctor's surgery, but presented only his sound limbs and covered up his wounds. Let God cover your wounds; don't cover them yourself. If you cover them up out of embarrassment, the doctor will not heal them. Allow the physician to cover and cure them, because he covers them with a dressing. Under the physician's dressing the wound heals; under the patient's covering it is merely hidden. Anyway, from whom are you trying to hide it? From him who knows everything?

Verse 3. Growing old in the wrong silence

13. Take heed now, brothers and sisters, to what this psalm says about the matter. *My bones grew old because of my silence, in consequence of my shouting all day long.* What does that mean? It sounds like a contradiction: *because of my silence, my bones grew old in consequence of my shouting.* If it was due to his shouting, how can he say he kept silence? The answer is that he kept silence about one thing but not about another. He refrained from saying something that would have helped him, but did not keep quiet about something that harmed him. He kept silence from confession, but shouted his presumption. When he says, *my silence*, he means, "I did not confess." That was how he ought to have spoken. He should have kept quiet about his merits and shouted his sins; but he got it all wrong: he was silent about his sins and shouted his merits. So what happened to him? His bones grew old. If he had shouted his sins aloud, and kept quiet about his merits, you see, his bones would have been rejuvenated—his virtues, that is.

He would have been invigorated in the Lord, because he knew he was weak in himself. But as things were he wanted to be strong and steady in himself, and so he became weak, and his bones grew old. He was stuck in decrepitude because he refused to embrace newness by confessing. You know who are renewed, brothers and sisters: *blessed are those whose iniquities are forgiven, and whose sins are covered.* This man did not want his sins forgiven, so he piled up more sins, and defended them, by boasting

---

26. See Prv 20:9.

about how good he was. And so, because he kept silence from confession, his bones grew old. *In consequence of my shouting all day long.* What can that mean, *shouting all day long*? Obstinately defending his sins.

Yet, after all, he does come to recognize himself. In a minute he will gain understanding, for he will turn his gaze on nothing else but himself; and in knowing himself he will find himself unlovely. You are going to hear about this, for your own healing.

Verse 4. The weight of God's hand

14. *Blessed is the one to whom the Lord will impute no sin, and in whose mouth is no guile. My bones grew old because of my silence, in consequence of my shouting all the day long. For day and night your hand lay heavy upon me.* What are we to understand by *your hand lay heavy upon me*? This is something momentous and real, my friends. Keep your eyes on that clear distinction drawn between the two of them, the Pharisee and the tax collector. What were we told about the Pharisee? That he is humiliated. And what of the tax collector? That he is exalted. Why is the former humiliated? Because he exalted himself. And why is the other exalted? Because he humbled himself. In order to humble a person who exalts himself, God puts a heavy hand on him. That person disdained to be humbled by confessing his iniquity, so he is brought low by the weight of God's hand. How could he ever endure the heavy hand that squashed him down? But how light the hand that lifts up! A mighty hand it was in both instances: powerfully pressing down the one, powerfully lifting up the other.

Verses 4–5. God forgives even before the confession is out

15. Accordingly, *day and night your hand lay heavy upon me. I was reduced to bitterness, when the thorn stuck fast in me.*[27] This heavy weight of your hand upon me, this very humiliation, has reduced me to bitterness;[28] I became wretched, the thorn stuck fast in me, and my conscience was stabbed. What happened when the thorn stuck into him? It hurt badly, and he realized his weakness. So what did he do, now that the thorn was lodged in him, this person who had kept silent from confession of sin, but shouted in defense of it, so that his strength waned and his bones wore out with age? *I perceived my sin.* Ah, so he does perceive it now. If he looks at it, God will overlook it.[29] Listen to how it goes on, and see if this is not his own admission. *I perceived my sin, and did not cloak my unrighteousness*: I explained this point just now. Do not cover it yourself, and God will cover it for you. *Blessed are those whose iniquities are forgiven, and whose sins are covered.* Those who draw a veil over their sins are stripped naked, but the speaker here stripped the cover off his so that he might be clothed. *I*

---

27. Variant: "in my bitter hardship I was converted, when the thorn...."
28. Variant: "caused me to writhe in my bitterness."
29. *Si ille cognoscit, ille ignoscit.*

did not cloak my unrighteousness. What does he mean by saying, *I did not cloak* it? Until very recently I kept my mouth shut, but now *I said....* Some reversal of his silence is taking place. *I said....* What did you say? *I will declare against myself my unrighteousness to the Lord; and you have forgiven the impiety of my heart*. He tells us, *I said....* Said what? He is not declaring anything yet, only promising that he will make a declaration; yet already God forgives.

Pay close attention, brothers and sisters, because this is very important. The psalmist says, *I will declare*. He does not say, "I declared"; yet you, Lord, have already forgiven him. This is what he says: *I will declare, and you have forgiven*. By the expression, *I will declare*, he made it obvious that he had not yet declared anything with his tongue, but he had made the declaration in his heart. The very resolve that *I will declare* is itself a declaration, and for that reason *you have forgiven the impiety of my heart*. My confession had not yet reached my lips; I had only got as far as saying, *I will declare against myself*, yet God heard the voice of my heart. My words were not yet in my mouth, but already God's ear was in my heart. *You have forgiven the impiety of my heart* because I said, *I will declare*.

Free will, not fate

16. It would not have been enough, though, for him to say, *I will declare my unrighteousness to the Lord*. He had good reason to say, *I will declare it against myself*. There is a difference. Plenty of people declare their unrighteous conduct, but against the Lord God himself. When they are found out in their sins they say, "God willed it so." People who say, "I didn't do it," or, "This action that you are finding fault with is no sin," are not making any declaration, either against themselves or against God. But if someone says, "Yes, I did it, to be sure, and it is a sin. But God willed it, so what fault is it of mine?" that is to make a declaration against God. You may object, "But no one would say that. How could anyone maintain that God willed it?" On the contrary, many people do say just that. And others there are who do not express it so bluntly, but what else does it amount to when they protest, "It was my fate. My stars were responsible"? They are simply getting at God by a roundabout route. They want to accuse God in this devious way, instead of taking a short cut to making their peace with him, so they say, "Fate did this to me." And what is fate? "Well, my stars did it." And what are the stars? "Those things we see in the sky, of course." And who made them? "God." Who set them in their courses? "God." Look what you are trying to say, then: "God made me sin." That means he is in the wrong and you are in the right, because if he had not made them, you would not have sinned! Have done with these excuses for your sins; remember the prayer in a psalm: *turn not my heart aside into dishonest words, to seek excuses in its sins with people who commit iniquity* (Ps 140(141):4).

Yet these people who defend their sins are persons of high repute, persons of good standing who count the planets, and calculate astral conjunctions and significant times; they predict who will sin, and when, and who will live honorably; when Mars will drive someone to murder or Venus someone to adultery. They are people of substance, learned men, who seem to be the privileged ones of this world. But what has the psalm to say? *Turn not my heart aside with people who commit iniquity; I will have no part with their privileged ones.* Let others call them wise, those privileged, learned ones who count the planets; let others call them wise, those pedants who fiddle human fate on their fingers[30] and map out human conduct from the stars. God created me with free will; if I have sinned, it is I myself who have sinned, so my business is not simply to declare my unrighteousness to the Lord, but to declare it against myself, not against him. *I myself said, Lord, have mercy on me*: this is a sick person crying out to the physician: *I myself said.* Why this emphasis, *I myself*? It would have been enough to write, *I said.*[31] But the emphasis is deliberate: I said it *myself.* I, I myself, not fate, not my horoscope, not the devil either, because he did not compel me, but I consented to his persuasion. *I myself said, Lord, have mercy on me; heal my soul, for I have sinned against you* (Ps 40:5(41:4)). Our psalmist made the same decision here too. He made up his mind: *I said, I will declare against myself my unrighteousness to the Lord, and you have forgiven the impiety of my heart.*

Verse 6. The time of grace

17. *Every holy person will pray to you about this matter, when the time is right.* What time would that be? The right time for *this matter.* What matter? Impiety. And what would one pray for about that? For sins to be forgiven, obviously. *Every holy person will pray to you about this matter, when the time is right*; and the only reason why all holy persons will pray to you is that you have forgiven their sins, for if you did not forgive sins there would not be a single holy person to pray to you. But *every holy person will pray to you about this matter, when the time is right,* when the New Covenant shall be revealed and the grace of Christ be made manifest. That will be the right time. *When the fullness of time had come, God sent his Son, made from a woman* (that means one of the female sex; the ancients applied the term to married women and virgins indiscriminately),[32] *made subject to the law, that he might redeem those who were subject to the law* (Gal 4:4–5). From what did he redeem them? From the devil, from perdition, from their sins, from him to whom they had sold themselves. *To redeem those who were subject to the law.* They were indeed subjects under the law, for it weighed heavily upon them. Its terms oppressed them by showing up their guilt without saving them. It certainly forbade wrongful deeds, but since

---

30. A pun: *qui digerunt in digitis.*
31. *Quare: Ego dixi? Sufficeret: dixi.*
32. Augustine is alluding to the virginal conception of Christ, not excluded by the general word, *mulier.*

they had in themselves no power of self-justification, they were forced to cry out to God in the same way as Paul did when he knew himself to be a prisoner under the law of sin: *Who will deliver me from this death-ridden body, wretch that I am?* (Rom 7:24). All men and women were under the law, not within it, as long as it oppressed them and declared them guilty. The law brought sin into the open; it drove the thorn home, evoked compunction of heart, and warned all that they must acknowledge their guilt and cry to God for pardon. *Every holy person will pray to you about this matter, when the time is right.* That is why, says the psalmist, I pointed to a right time: *when the fullness of time had come, God sent his Son.* The apostle says elsewhere, *At the acceptable and favorable time I have heard you, and on the day of salvation I have helped you.* And since the prophet envisaged all Christians[33] when he foretold this, the apostle added, *See, now is the acceptable time, lo, this is the day of salvation* (2 Cor 6:2).[34] *Every holy person will pray to you about this matter, when the time is right.*

The floods that keep us from God

18. *Yet they will not draw near to him amid the flood of many waters.* What is meant by *to him*? To God. This shift from second to third person is quite usual. We have another example of it in the verse, *salvation is from the Lord, and may your blessing be upon your people* (Ps 3:9(8)). It did not say there, "Salvation is from the Lord, and may his blessing be upon his people," did it? Nor did it say, "Salvation is from you, Lord, and may your blessing be upon your people"; but having begun in the third person, *salvation is from the Lord,* speaking about him, not to him, the psalmist then turned to him and continued, *and may your blessing be upon your people.* So too in the present psalm. When you hear it beginning, *to you,* and then shifting to *to him,* you must not think it is referring to someone different. *Every holy person will pray to you about this matter, when the time is right. Yet they will not draw near to him amid the flood of many waters.* What is meant by *the flood of many waters*? It means that people who swim in the flood of many waters do not draw near to God. Well, then, what are these many flood-waters? They stand for the multiplicity of variegated teachings. Try to concentrate, my brothers and sisters. The many waters are the variety of doctrines. God's doctrine is one. There are not many waters, but one single water, whether we think of the water of baptism or the water of salutary doctrine. Of this doctrine, with which we are irrigated by the Holy Spirit, Scripture says, *Drink water from your own cisterns and your own wellsprings* (Prv 5:15). The ungodly have no access to these springs, but those who believe in him who justifies the ungodly approach once they are justified. The many other waters are the many teachings that pollute human souls. I was speaking of some of them not long ago. One alien doctrine is: "Fate did this to me." Another is: "Chance

---

33. Variant: "Christian times."
34. Compare Is 49:8.

made this happen to me," or "My horoscope was responsible." If human beings are ruled by chance, nothing is effected by Providence; and this too is a doctrine. Another teacher said, "There is a hostile race of darkness which has rebelled against God, and it causes people to sin." Swimmers in this flood of many waters do not draw near to God.

What is the real water, the water that wells up from the most secret inner spring, from the pure channel of truth? Yes, what is that water, my brothers and sisters? It is the water that teaches us to confess to the Lord. What other water admonishes us that *it is good to confess to the Lord?* (Ps 91:2(92:1)) What water are we talking about, but the water that inspires the cry, *I said, I will declare against myself my unrighteousness to the Lord*, and *I myself said, Lord, have mercy on me; heal my soul, for I have sinned against you?* This is the water that urges us to confess our sins, the water that humbles our hearts, the water of a way of life that leads to salvation, of those who abase themselves, do not presume on themselves at all and refuse any proud attribution of their achievements to their own strength. You will not find this water in any of the books of the pagans, whether Epicurean, Stoic, Manichean or Platonist. You will find throughout those books excellent precepts of morality and self-improvement, but nowhere humility like this. The way of humility comes from no other source; it comes only from Christ. It is the way originated by him who, though most high, came in humility. What else did he teach us by humbling himself and becoming obedient even to death, even to the death of the cross?[35] What else did he teach us by paying a debt he did not owe, to release us from debt? What else did he teach us, he who was baptized though sinless, and crucified though innocent? What else did he teach us, but this same humility? He had every right to say, *I am the way, and the truth, and the life* (Jn 14:6). By this humility, then, we draw near to God, because the Lord is close to those who have bruised their hearts;[36] but amid the flood of many waters, amid the torrent of those who exalt themselves in opposition to God and peddle proud blasphemies, no one will draw near to him.

Verse 7. Joy amid groaning

19. But what about you, who are already justified: are you immersed in these flood-waters? They are all around us, my brothers and sisters; even when we confess our sins those torrential waters raise their din on every side. We are not in the flood, but it swirls all round us. Its waters splash us, yet do not swamp us; they drive against us but do not drown us. How are you going to manage, then, in the middle of the flood as you are, wading through this world? Is the psalmist deaf to those teachers, those proud professors? Does he not endure daily persecution in his heart from their pronouncements? What has this psalmist to say, already justified as he is

---

35. See Phil 2:8.
36. See Ps 33:19(34:18).

and relying wholly on God? What is he to say, surrounded by the flood? *You are for me a refuge from the distress that besets me.* Let those others take refuge with their gods, or with their demons, or in their own strength, or in defending their sins. As for me, I have no refuge in this flood except yourself, my refuge from the distress that besets me.

20. *You who make me dance with happiness, save me.* If you are already dancing with happiness, why ask to be saved? *You who make me dance with happiness, save me.* I can hear the voice of joy when he says, *You make me dance with happiness*; and I hear groaning when he prays, *Save me.* You are joyful, yet you groan. "Quite so," he replies, "I both groan and rejoice. I rejoice in hope, but still groan over present reality. *You who make me dance with happiness, save me.*" The apostle entreats us, *Rejoice in hope*, and so the psalmist is right to pray, *You who make me dance with happiness, save me.* Paul continues, *Be patient in anguish* (Rom 12:12), and the psalmist is in accord: *You who make me dance with happiness, save me.* The apostle too was already justified, and what had he to say? *Not creation only, but we ourselves, though we have the firstfruits of the Spirit, groan inwardly.* So why the psalmist's prayer, *save me*? Because we ourselves *groan inwardly as we await our adoption as God's children, the redemption of our bodies.* That is why the psalm begs, *Save me*: we are still groaning inwardly as we await the redemption of our bodies. But why then does he also say to God, *You make me dance with happiness*? The apostle's next words make it clear why: *in hope we have been saved. But if hope is seen, it is hope no longer, for when someone sees what he hopes for, why should he hope for it? But if we hope for what we do not see, we wait for it in patience* (Rom 8:23–25). If you hope, you rejoice; if you are waiting with patience, you still groan; for there is no need for patience when you have no evil to put up with. What we call endurance, what we call patience, what we call bearing up, what we call steadfastness, has no place except amid misfortunes. Where you are hard pressed, there you feel the pinch. If we are still waiting in patience, we still have reason to say, *Save me from those that hem me in*; but because we are saved in hope, we can say both these things simultaneously: *you make me dance with happiness*, and *save me.*

Verse 8. Keep your eyes on the Lord

21. Now comes God's answer: *I will give you understanding.* Remember, this is a psalm about understanding. *I will give you understanding, and set you on this road you must enter.*[37] What is meant by that: *I will set you on this road you must enter*? He does not mean to set you there so that you stay put, but so that you do not stray off it. I will give you understanding so that you may always truly know yourself, and always rejoice in hope toward God, until you arrive in your heavenly homeland, where there will

---

37. Variant, in this and the following sentence: "on this road where you must walk."

be no place for hope, but only the reality.³⁸ *I will keep a firm eye on you.* I will not take my eyes off you, because you will not take yours off me either. Now that you are justified, now that your sins are forgiven, lift your eyes to God. Your heart went moldy when it wallowed in the mud. There is good reason for the exhortation you know well: "Lift up your hearts,"³⁹ because they may go bad if you don't. You, for your part, must now lift your eyes to God all the time, so that he can keep a firm eye on you. Need you be afraid that when you keep your eyes on God you may trip over something, and fail to see what is before your feet, and even fall into a trap? No, you need not worry, for his eyes are alert, those eyes of God that he keeps fixed on you. *Do not be anxious* (Mt 6:31), says the Lord; and the apostle Peter tells us, *Cast all your anxiety on him, for he takes care of you* (1 Pt 5:7). In this same sense God promises here, *I will keep a firm eye on you.* Raise your eyes to him, and, as I said, you will have no cause to fear that you may stumble into a snare. Listen to what another psalm recommended: *My eyes are on the Lord continually*; and then, as though someone had objected, "But how can you take care of your feet, if you are not looking where you are going?" the psalmist continued, *He will pluck my feet from the snare* (Ps 24(25):15). *I will keep a firm eye on you.*

Verse 9. Mulish obstinacy

22. God has promised to this one who prays both understanding and protection; but now he turns to the proud folk who defend their sins, and gives us an idea of what kind of understanding is in view. *Do not be like a horse or a mule, devoid of understanding.* The horse and the mule toss their heads. Neither horse nor mule is like the ox that recognizes its owner, or the ass that knows its master's manger.⁴⁰ *Do not be like a horse or a mule, devoid of understanding*, for what kind of treatment are those creatures subjected to? *Rein in their jaws with bit and bridle, those who will not approach you.* Do you aspire to be a horse or a mule; Do you want to throw your rider? Your mouth and your jaws will be reined in with bit and bridle; yes, that mouth of yours with which you vaunt your merits but keep quiet about your sins will be reined in. *Rein in their jaws with bit and bridle, those who will not approach you* by humbling themselves.

Verse 10. Breaking in the horse

23. *There is many a scourge for the sinner.* We need not wonder if after the bit has been inserted the whip is also used. The sinner wanted to be like an unbroken animal, and so must be subdued with bit and whip; and let us hope that he or she can be broken in. The fear is that such persons may resist so obstinately that they deserve to be left in their unbroken state

---

38. *Ubi iam non spes, sed res erit.*
39. Familiar from the liturgy.
40. See Is 1:3.

and allowed to go their own sweet way, until of them it can be said, *Their iniquity will leak out as though from folds of fat* (Ps 72(73):7), as it is of those whose sins go unpunished for the present. May such people, when the whip catches them, be corrected and subdued, as the psalmist tells us he too was tamed. He admits that he was a horse or a mule, because he was obstinately silent; and how was he subdued? By the whip. *I was reduced to bitterness*, he says, *when the thorn stuck fast in me*. Whether we think of this as a whip or a spur, God tames the beast he rides, because it is to the beast's own advantage to be ridden. It is not because God is weary of walking on his own feet that he mounts. Isn't it a very mysterious episode, when a donkey is led to the Lord?[41] This donkey stands for the humble and docile people that provides a good mount for the Lord, and it is making for Jerusalem. *He will guide the meek in judgment*, as another psalm predicts; *he will teach his ways to the gentle* (Ps 24(25):9). Who are these gentle ones? Those who do not toss their heads in defiance of their trainer, who patiently accept the whip and the rein, so that later, when they have been broken in, they may walk without the whip, and hold to their course without the need for bit and bridle. If you refuse your rider, it is you who will fall, not he. *There is many a scourge for the sinner; but everyone who hopes in the Lord is encompassed with mercy*. How does the Lord prove himself a refuge from the distress that surrounds us? The person who was at first encompassed with distress is later encompassed with mercy, for he who gave the law will grant mercy too:[42] the law when he applied the whip, and mercy when he handles us gently. *Everyone who hopes in the Lord is encompassed with mercy*.

Verse 11. The true rejoicing

24. Now for the last verse. *Rejoice in the Lord and dance for joy, you just*. Woe betide you who rejoice in yourselves! You are impious and proud if you rejoice in yourselves; but once you come to believe in him who justifies the impious, your faith will be reckoned as righteousness. *Rejoice in the Lord and dance for joy, you just*. We must understand, "dance for joy in the Lord," of course. Why is that? Because they are now just. And how did that happen to them? Not by their own merits, but by his grace. In what sense are they just? Just because justified.

25. *And make him your boast, all you who are right of heart*. What is it to be *right of heart*? The right of heart are those who do not resist God. Let me have your attention, beloved ones,[43] and try to understand this rectitude of heart. I will explain it briefly, though it is a point of major importance; and I thank God that it comes at the end, so that it will stick in your minds.

---

41. See Mk 11:7.
42. See Ps 83:8(84:7).
43. *Caritas vestra*.

This is the difference between a right heart and a crooked one. When a person has to suffer many things willy-nilly, such as sickness, grief, toil and humiliations, and attributes them solely to the just will of God, not concluding that God is unwise or that he does not know what he is doing when he chastises this one and spares others, that man or woman is right of heart. People with perverse hearts, hearts crooked and misshapen, complain that all the woes they suffer are undeserved, and so they charge God, by whose will they undergo these things, with acting unjustly. Or perhaps they do not dare to accuse him directly of injustice, so they assume that he cannot be in control. "This must be the way of it," they say, "because he cannot do anything unjust, and yet it is unjust that I should suffer while someone else is exempt. I admit that I am a sinner, but there are others who are greater sinners still, and they make merry while I am in trouble. It is unfair that those who are even worse than I should be happy, and I, who am a righteous person, or at any rate less sinful than they are, should have to put up with all this. By my reckoning this is certainly unjust, and by my reckoning it is equally certain that God cannot act unjustly. So I conclude that God is not in control of human affairs, and does not care about us."

So the people with crooked, twisted hearts propose three opinions. Either God does not exist; so the fool says in his heart, "There is no God."[44] And as I have already said in connection with the flood,[45] there has been no lack of such teaching among the philosophers, no lack of teachers who denied the existence of a God who governs all things and created all things, but postulated a plethora of gods who were engrossed in their own affairs, distanced from the world and unconcerned with it. So then, either "There is no God," which is the opinion of the impious person who is angry about anything unpleasant that happens to him or her, but does not happen to someone else deemed to be less deserving; or, secondly, "God is unjust, since he enjoys this sort of thing, and acts like this"; or, thirdly, "God is not in control of human affairs, and does not concern himself with any of them." All three of these opinions entail grave impiety, whether it is denial of God's existence, or charging him with injustice, or doubting his governance of the world. Why does anyone hold such views? Because they are crooked of heart. God is straight and true, and therefore a crooked heart is not at peace with him. Another psalm exclaims, *How good is Israel's God to those who are right of heart!* But the psalmist had once held a perverse opinion himself: *How does God know? Can any knowledge be attributed to the Most High?* and remembering that, he added, *Even I almost lost my footing* (Ps 72(73):1.11.2). If you lay a warped beam on a hard, level surface, it does not fit or square up properly or lie flat; it will always shake and wobble, not because the surface where it was placed is uneven, but because the beam itself is lopsided. So too as long as a heart remains crooked and

---

44. See Ps 13(14):1.
45. See 18 above.

twisted, it cannot be aligned with the rectitude of God; it cannot be bedded close to him and cling to him.[46] In such a heart the saying cannot come true that *anyone who clings to the Lord is one spirit with him* (1 Cor 6:17).

Make the Lord your boast, then, *all you who are right of heart*. How do right-hearted people boast? Listen to their boasting: *What is more, we even glory in our sufferings*. It is no great thing to glory amid joy or boast when we are happy; right-hearted persons glory even in tribulations. And listen to how they do it, how no one who glories amid afflictions is doomed to disappointment or boasts in vain. Look at this rightness of heart, as evinced by Paul: *we even glory in our sufferings, knowing that suffering fosters endurance, and endurance constancy, and constancy hope; but hope does not disappoint us, because the love of God has been poured out into our hearts through the Holy Spirit who has been given to us* (Rom 5:3–5).

26. This is what a right heart is like, my brothers and sisters. If any misfortune befalls right-hearted people, let them say, "The Lord gave, and the Lord has taken away." This is rightness of heart: "as it has pleased the Lord, so it has turned out. May the name of the Lord be blessed."[47] They do not say, "The Lord gave, and the devil has taken away." Pay careful attention to this, my dearest ones,[48] so that you may never say, "The devil has done this to me." No, by no means; refer the scourge that falls on you to God, because the devil does nothing to you unless by permission from our powerful God, who may allow it either as punishment or as discipline: punishment for the ungodly or discipline for God's children. God scourges every son whom he acknowledges.[49] Do not hope that you will be spared the lash, unless you also plan to be disinherited. He scourges every son he acknowledges. Every single one? Yes. Where did you think to hide? Every one without exception, every single one, will be liable to scourging. What, is no one spared? No. Do you need to be convinced that this rule admits of no exceptions? Even the only-begotten Son, he who was sinless, even he was not exempt. The only-begotten Son himself, bearing your weakness and representing you in his own person, as the Head which included the body in itself, even he was deeply saddened in his human nature as he approached his passion, in order to give you joy. He was saddened that he might comfort you. Undoubtedly the Lord could have faced his passion free from sadness. If a soldier had the power to do so, surely the commander-in-chief had? But did a soldier have that power? Yes: listen to Paul shouting with joy as he approached his suffering: *Already I am being poured out like a sacrificial libation*, he says, *and the time for my dissolution is upon me. I have fought the good fight, I have run the whole*

---

46. Or, with the addition of one word by the editors of the Latin text, "…cling to him and be straightened."
47. See Jb 1:21.
48. *Caritas vestra.*
49. See Heb 12:6.

course, I have kept the faith; all that remains for me now is the crown of righteousness which the just judge will award me on that day, and not to me alone but to all those who love his coming (2 Tm 4:6–8). Look at that for triumphant cheerfulness in the face of suffering! So the man who is due to be crowned rejoices, while the One who is to crown him is deeply saddened. What does this suggest that he was carrying? The weakness of others, who are grieved when trouble or death looms.

But observe how he leads them toward rightness of heart. Think about it: you were wanting to live, and not wanting any calamity to fall upon you; but God willed otherwise. There are two wills, then; but your will must be straightened to fit the will of God, not God's will twisted out of shape to fit yours. Yours is crooked, his is the ruler. The ruler must stand steady so that the crooked thing may be conformed to it. Our Lord Jesus Christ teaches us this. Listen to him: *my soul is sorrowful to the point of death*; and *Father, if it is possible, let this cup pass from me.* His human will shows through here. But look at his rightness of heart: *not what I will, but what you will be done, Father* (Mt 26:38–39). Do likewise yourself, and rejoice in the troubles that befall you; and if your last day is upon you, rejoice. If any of the frailty of your human will tries to take over, surrender it swiftly to God, that you may be among those to whom the psalmist says, *Make him your boast, all you who are right of heart.*

Exposition of Psalm 54

Synopsis

The title speaks of Christ as the *end* in the sense of perfection rather than exhaustion. He is *the end of the law* because no one keeps the law without him. Praise to God in hymns comes forth from Christians whether he caresses or chastens them for their education. "David" stands for Christ, David's descendant who is also David's Lord. But Christ is head and body, one with his Church. When Christ's members understand this, it is Christ who understands in his members. He utters the Psalm in our name, so let's make its words our own (1–3).

The body is in distress from bad Christians who test the Church's mettle and cause it to labor for their conversion. They act like enemies, but even enemies are recipients of God's mercy. What are we doing to imitate God's generosity to enemies? Christ ordained "a ruling principle of love" for enemies: how can we get training in love if we never put up with any enemies? The Psalmist stretched himself to love his enemies, but he became weary. By grace Peter walked on water for a time by loving, but then he sank beneath the onslaught of "the enemy's shouting." But he did keep praying (4–5). Anger only tries to stop the wind, while prayer helps maintain love for the enemy—the flesh-and-blood one, not the devil. Love makes you superior to the devil. Anger hardens into hatred, so watch out. "If love is life, then hatred is death" (6–7).

Enemies distort vision, stab the heart, and kill the soul. Do you dream of growing wings that will fly you far from enemies to solitude or even death? But let these wings be given *as though to a dove*, whose moaning symbolizes love. Christians fill the deserts these days in order to withdraw from the world, but they don't really escape their enemies. "God knows that bearing with bad people is a necessity for us, and that thereby we make progress in goodness ourselves." Recall that our Lord chose a disciple who caused him suffering (8–9).

Might we retreat within? But charity disturbs there too. If an enemy's tempest rocks your boat, Christ is fast asleep there because you've forgotten him. Remember what he suffered for you, and he'll awaken to make calm within you. The Psalmist prays that God will confuse his enemies' languages, but not out of anger. God once confused tongues out of mercy, for people's good (10–11). The Church flees Babylon, the city of raging iniquity. One day it will fall, but until then usury and deceit will be rampant. But aren't you an unjust lender if you refuse to forgive a debtor? How then can you pray, *Forgive us our debts*? One skilled in heaven's laws composed that prayer; but he's also the judge, and he won't forgive unless you forgive others (12–14).

The Psalmist groans at the treachery of *a like-minded person* who was *wont to eat delicious foods with me*. He prays that figurative death might fall upon him like the rebels who were swallowed up under Moses. We endure enemies in the schismatic Donatists (15–16). They make Christ's body cry out in anguish, but the grain goes on preaching the gospel and endures the chaff—bad Christians among us, who are human like us but lack charity (17–19). We'll wait for God to humble them. But we know only one remedy will suffice: "Fear God and cut loose from Donatus." Clinging to a mere local church rejects prophecy and defiles God's covenant (21–22). God has come "near" in the trauma of this schism, because teachers have emerged who explain Scripture rightly. Some Scriptures were "hard" in their obscurity, but they become tender as they're explained, and they soak into the bones like oil. So suckle on Scripture's mysteries in order to gain strength to understand them. Then God's words will be like javelins striking the heart with peace. Until then, *cast your care upon the Lord* and not on some human leader (22–24). Schismatics are *blind leading the blind, and both will fall into the ditch*. Some are even killers, spiritually and physically, but they have no future (25–27).

Augustine's Text of Psalm 54

(1) Unto the end, in hymns, understanding for David himself.

(2) Hear my appeal, O God, and do not disdain my prayer.

(3) Pay heed to me and hear me;

 I am deeply saddened in my ordeal, and very distressed,

(4) By the shouting of the enemy and the trouble caused by a sinner.

 For they have brought down iniquity upon me,

 And cast a shadow over me with their anger.

(5) My heart is deeply disturbed within me; the fear of death fell upon me.

(6) Fear and trembling came upon me, and darkness covered me.

(7) And I said, Who will give me wings, as though to a dove?

 Then I will fly away and be at rest.

(8) Lo, I fled far away, and stayed in the desert.
(9) I was waiting for him who would save me from faintheartedness in the storm.
(10) Engulf them, Lord, and confuse their languages;
   For I have seen iniquity and denial in the city.
(11) Day and night iniquity will march round it upon its ramparts,
   And there will be labor within it,
(12) And injustice. Usury and deceit are never lacking in its streets.
(13) If an enemy had slandered me, I could have borne it.
   Or if someone who hated me had talked arrogantly against me,
   I could surely have hidden from him.
(14) But it was you, a like-minded person, my guide and my familiar companion,
(15) Who were wont to eat delicious foods with me;
   In the house of God we walked together in harmony.
(16) May death fall upon them, and may they go down alive into the underworld.
   For there is wickedness in their lodgings and in their midst.
(17) I cried out to the Lord, and the Lord hearkened to me.
(18) At evening, in the morning and at midday I will tell my tale,
   And proclaim it, and he will hear my voice.
(19) He will redeem my soul in peace from those who draw near to me.
   In many respects they were with me (*var.,* among the many they were with me).
(20) God will hear me and will humble them, God who exists before all ages,
   For with them there is no change, and they have not feared God.
(21) He stretches out his hand to requite them; they have defiled his covenant.
(22) They have been banished by the wrath of his countenance;
   His heart has come near.
   God's words are smoother than oil, but they are javelins.
(23) Cast your care upon the Lord, and he will nourish you.
   He will not allow the righteous one to waver for ever.
(24) You will assign them to the pit of corruption, O God.
   Men of blood and deceit, they will not see even half their days.
   But I will hope in you, O Lord.

Exposition

A Sermon to the People

The title: Christ our end and our perfection

1. The title of this psalm is *Unto the end, in hymns, understanding for David himself.* We need only remind you briefly what this "end" is, because you know already. *Christ is the end of the law, bringing justification to everyone who believes* (Rom 10:4). Our intention therefore must be directed to the end, directed to Christ. Why is he called "the end"? Because whatever we do is referred to him, and when we have reached him we shall have nothing further to seek. We speak of "an end" in the sense of something being exhausted, but also of "an end" meaning the completion of something. When we say, "The food we were eating has come to an end," we mean something quite different from "the weaving of that tunic is finished." In both cases we speak of something being ended or finished, but in the one instance it means that the food no longer exists, in the other that a garment has reached its perfection. So, in the case of ourselves, our "end" must mean our perfection, and our perfection is Christ. We are made perfect in him because he is our head and we are his members; and he is called the end of the law because without him no one perfectly keeps the law. Many of the psalms have this superscription, *Unto the end,* and when you hear it you must not think of something being consumed, but of something consummated.

2. *In hymns,* the title continues; that means with songs of praise. Whether we are troubled and hemmed in by difficulties, or glad and dancing for joy, God is to be praised, because he schools us through tribulations and comforts us with joy. God's praise should never depart from the heart and mouth of a Christian. We must not praise him when things go well with us and curse him when they go wrong; rather we must obey the injunction of another psalm: *I will bless the Lord at all times; his praise shall be in my mouth always* (Ps 33(34):1). When you feel happy, acknowledge the Father who is caressing you; when you are distressed, acknowledge the Father who is chastening you. Whether through caresses or through chastisement he is educating his child, for whom he is preparing an inheritance.

The title, concluded: Understanding for David,
who prefigures Christ, head and members

3. What does this imply: *understanding for David himself?* As we know, David was a holy prophet, a king of Israel, and the son of Jesse. But when our Lord Jesus Christ came for our salvation, he was from David's seed, according to the flesh,[1] and so he is often figuratively called by the name "David." And David himself figuratively stands for Christ, in virtue

---

1. See Rom 1:3.

of being Christ's carnal ancestor. In one respect Christ is the son of David, and in a different respect he is David's Lord: son of David according to the flesh, but Lord of David in his divinity. If all things were made through him,[2] then certainly David himself was made through him—David, whose descendant Christ was when he came to humankind. This is made clear when the Jews, questioned by our Lord as to whose son the Messiah would be, replied, *David's*. But he could see that they had remained at the level of the flesh and lost sight of the Messiah's divinity, so he corrected them by posing a further question: *Then how is it that David in the Spirit calls him "Lord," saying, The Lord said to my Lord, "Sit at my right hand, until I make your enemies into your footstool"? If David in the Spirit calls him "Lord," how can he be David's son?* (Mt 22:42–45). He is putting the question to them, not denying his sonship: "You have heard that the Messiah is David's Lord, so tell me how he is David's son; you have heard that he is David's son, so tell me how he is his Lord." The Catholic faith has the answer to this dilemma. How is he Lord? Because *in the beginning was the Word, and the Word was with God; he was God*. And how is he David's son? Because *the Word was made flesh, and dwelt among us* (Jn 1:1.14).

So David represents Christ. But as we have often reminded you, dearest friends,[3] Christ is both head and body, and we must not think ourselves alien to Christ, since we are his members. Nor must we think of ourselves as separate from him, because *they will be two in one flesh. This is a great mystery*, says the apostle, *but I am referring it to Christ and the Church* (Eph 5:31–32). Since, then, the whole Christ consists of head and body, we must understand that we too are included in David when in the psalm's title we hear of *understanding for David himself*. Christ's members must have this understanding, and Christ must understand in the persons of his members, and the members of Christ must understand in Christ, because head and members form one Christ. The head was in heaven when he insistently asked, *Why are you persecuting me?* (Acts 9:4). Through hope we are with him in heaven, and through charity he is with us on earth. This is why our psalm can speak about *understanding for David himself*. Let us take it to heart when we hear it, and let the Church understand, for it is our business to make the greatest possible effort to assess the evil situation we are in and from what evil we wish to be delivered, mindful of the Lord's prayer, which ends with our petition, *Deliver us from evil*.

Amid the manifold troubles of this world, our psalm about understanding utters its lament. Anyone who lacks understanding will not join in this lament. But we must remember, beloved,[4] that we have been made in the image of God, and that this image is to be found only in our understanding.

---

2. See Jn 1:3.
3. *Caritatem vestram.*
4. *Carissimi.*

We are outdone by[5] the beasts in many respects, but in that faculty where human beings know themselves to be made in God's image, there especially do they know that they have been granted something greater than anything given to the animals. When humans consider all their endowments, they find that they are most specifically distinguished from the animals by their possession of understanding. This is why certain people are rebuked by their Creator for belittling that faculty in themselves which is most properly human and is his most special gift to them: *Do not be like a horse or a mule, devoid of understanding*, he tells them (Ps 31(32):9). And in another passage he says, *Human beings failed to understand how they were honored; they were no better than the foolish beasts, and became like them* (Ps 48:13(49:12)).

Let us recognize our dignity, then, and try to understand. If we understand we shall see that where we live now is a place not for gladness but for groaning, not yet a place for exultation but still a place for lamentation. Even if a certain exultation is habitually present in our hearts, it is the joy of hope, not of fulfillment. We rejoice over God's promise, because we know that he who promises does not deceive us. But as far as the present time is concerned, listen to what a bad situation and what straits we are in. If you are keeping to the path, what you hear will find an echo in your own experience. Anyone who is not yet walking the way of dedication to God will be amazed that David's members have so much to groan over, for such a person has no experience of like troubles in himself. As long as he does not share the pain he is not there: he does not feel what the body feels because he is outside the body. Let him be incorporated, and he will feel the same. Let the body speak, then, and let us listen. Let us listen, and make these words our own.

Verses 2–3. The wicked put good people to the proof

4. *Hear my appeal, O God, and do not disdain my prayer; pay heed to me and hear me.* These are the words of someone who is anxious, apprehensive, beset by tribulation. He is suffering acutely as he prays, and longing to be delivered from his trouble. It is for us to find out what his plight is and, when he begins to tell us, to realize that we are in it too, so that as we share his tribulation we may unite our prayer with his. *I am deeply saddened in my ordeal, and very distressed.* Where is he deeply saddened? Where distressed? *In my ordeal*, he says. He is about to identify[6] the wicked people he is enduring, and he has called this endurance of them his ordeal. You must not think that bad people are in this world uselessly, or that God cannot employ them for good purposes. Every bad person is either allowed to live so that he or she may be corrected, or else allowed to live so that

---

5. *Superamur.* But the editors of the Latin text amend to *non separamur*, "we are not divided from."
6. Variant: "has identified."

through him or her a good person may be put to the proof. Would that those who are a trial to us now might be converted, and then tried along with us! However, as long as they remain the sort of people who put us through our paces we must not hate them, because we never know whether any one of them will persist in his evil way to the very end. It often happens that when you think you have been hating an enemy, you have unwittingly hated a brother or sister. It is the devil and his angels who are plainly indicated to us by Holy Scripture as destined for eternal fire. In their case alone may we despair of correction. Against them we wage hidden warfare, a struggle for which the apostle forearms us, saying, *It is not against flesh and blood that you have to struggle*—against human beings we can see, that is—*but against principalities and powers and the rulers of this world of darkness* (Eph 6:12). Possibly you might have thought that when he said *this world* he meant that they were rulers of heaven and earth; so to guard against this misconception he specified, *this world of darkness*. He thereby indicated the lovers of this world, the world of the godless and the unjust, that *world* of which the gospel says, *The world did not know him* (Jn 1:10). This world did not know the light; for although the light shone in the darkness, the darkness was never able to master it. This darkness which could not master the light even when present is called "the world." It follows, then, that this is the darkness of which the devil and his angels are rulers. Concerning these rulers we have Scripture's definite statement that there is absolutely no hope of conversion for any one of them; but the case is different for the darkness over which they rule, for we are uncertain whether those who once were darkness may not become light. After all, the apostle says to some who have become believers, *You were darkness once, but now you are light in the Lord* (Eph 5:8). Darkness when left to yourselves, but light in the Lord.

Well then, brothers and sisters, all bad people, while they are bad, put the good to the proof. I will make the point briefly: listen and grasp what I am saying. If you are good, you can have no enemy except a bad person. But observe the standard of goodness that is placarded up before you: you must imitate the goodness of your Father, who *causes his sun to rise over the good and the wicked, and sends rain upon just and unjust alike* (Mt 5:45). It is not as though you were the only one to have an enemy, and God had none. You have as your enemy someone who was created just like you; but God's enemy is someone he has himself created. We often find Scripture calling bad and unjust people enemies of God, yet he spares them—he against whom no enemy could have any grudge, he to whom every enemy is ungrateful, since it is from God that the enemy holds whatever good he has. Even in any trouble he has to undergo, this enemy is the recipient of God's mercy, because he is sent the trouble only to save him from getting proud. He is subjected to it so that he may be brought low and acknowledge the Most High. But what about you? What have you given to that enemy of yours whom you find insufferable? If that person is God's enemy, and yet

God has given him so much, causing *his sun to rise over the good and the wicked, and sending rain on just and unjust alike*, can you not keep just one thing for your enemy, you who have no power to make the sun rise or to send rain on the earth? Can you not allow the peace promised on earth to people of good will[7] to be yours?

Moreover, a ruling principle of love has been established for you, that you must imitate your Father by loving your enemy, for Christ commands, *Love your enemies* (Lk 6:27.35); and how are you going to get any training in observing it if you never have to put up with an enemy? So you see, he or she is doing you some good. And let the fact that God spares the wicked do you good as well; let it inspire you to show mercy, for though you are good now you may perhaps have been bad in earlier days, so if God did not spare bad people you would not have emerged to give him thanks today. May he who has spared even you be merciful to others as well. The road to a devout life must not be barred after you have traveled along it.

Verse 4. The storm all around

5. Now what about the speaker in this psalm, the one beset by bad people and feeling sorely tried by their hostility? What is his prayer, what does he say? *I am deeply saddened in my ordeal, and very distressed.* He stretched his love so far that he could love even his enemies, but now weariness has overtaken him. There are so many enemies, a great crowd is barking furiously all round him, and he has succumbed through human weakness. He saw that a wicked, diabolical suggestion was beginning to force an entry into his heart, persuading him to grant admission to[8] hatred for his enemies. He is struggling against the hatred, trying to make his love perfect, and as he wrestles and fights he is distressed. His voice is heard in another psalm too: *My eye was inflamed by anger.* And how does the psalm continue there? *I have grown old among all my enemies* (Ps 6:8(7)). He began to sink beneath the waves, like Peter, as the storm overwhelmed him; for the people who can tread underfoot the waves of this world are the ones who love their enemies. Christ walked on the sea without fear, because love for his enemies could not be torn out of his heart by any means whatever. Even when hanging on the cross he kept saying, *Father, forgive them, for they do not know what they are doing* (Lk 23:34). But Peter too wanted to walk on the water. Christ did so as head, Peter as body, for Christ had said, *Upon this rock I will build my Church* (Mt 16:18). He was commanded to walk, and walk he did, but by the grace of the one who gave the order, not by his own strength. When he felt the power of the wind, he was afraid, and began to sink, very worried when tested like this. What was this powerful wind? I was distressed, says the psalmist, *by the shouting of the enemy and the trouble caused by a sinner.* Just as Peter cried out from the waves,

---

7. See Lk 2:14.
8. *Inducat.* Some codices have *induat*, "to put on," like a garment or arms.

Lord, I'm sinking, save me! (Mt 14:30) so too had the psalmist cried out long before, *Hear my appeal, O God, and do not disdain my prayer; pay heed to me and hear me.* Why? What is the matter? What are you groaning about? *"I am deeply saddened in my ordeal, and very distressed.* You have put me among the wicked to test me, I know, but I have not the strength to withstand their onslaught. Give me tranquillity, for I am very upset; stretch out your hand to me, for I am sinking. *I am deeply saddened in my ordeal, and very distressed by the shouting of an enemy and the trouble caused by a sinner, for they have brought down iniquity upon me, and cast a shadow over me with their anger."*

You have heard about the waves and the winds. They buffeted him and he seemed to be brought low, but he kept on praying. The din of their insults raged all round him, but he continued to invoke in his heart someone they could not see.

Snatching victory from the jaws of defeat

6. When a Christian has to suffer anything like this, he or she must not be too ready to make an angry attack on the tormentor, or hope to subdue the wind. We should turn to prayer, so as not to lose our love. In any case, why be afraid of what a human enemy can do? What can he do? He can say nasty things, and hurl abuse at you, and make plenty of savage uproar; but how does that hurt you? Our Lord tells us, *Rejoice and dance for joy, because your reward is great in heaven* (Mt 5:12; Lk 6:23). As the enemy redoubles his ranting on earth, you are doubling your profits in heaven. But suppose he becomes yet more ferocious, and has power to inflict more harm that that? You are still completely safe, for you have been told, *Do not be afraid of those who kill the body, but cannot kill the soul* (Mt 10:28). What have you to fear, then, when you have to tolerate an enemy? Do not let the love that is in you be disturbed, the love you bear that enemy.

Now this enemy is a human being, a creature of flesh and blood, and what he attacks in you is something visible. The world of flesh and blood is attacking you, this dark world, but behind it stands another enemy, a hidden one, the ruler of this dark world. He attacks what is hidden in you; he is bent on destroying your interior treasures. Keep both these enemies in sight: the one overt, the other secret; the overt human foe, and the hidden foe, the devil. Your human adversary is the same as you are in respect of human nature; in respect of faith and love he or she is not yet what you are, but may still become so. Two enemies, then. Observe the one, and apprehend the other with your mind; love the one, and shun the other. The enemy you can see wants to humiliate in you whatever it is that gives you the advantage over him. If he is inferior to you in wealth, for instance, he wants to reduce you to poverty; if he is your inferior in rank, he wants to bring you down; if his strength is not equal to yours, he wants to weaken you. He is trying to spoil or steal whatever in you makes him feel inferior. The invisible enemy likewise wants to take away from you what sets you above him. As a human being you may be superior to other humans in your human good fortune, but you are superior to the devil by your love for your enemy. Just as that other human person strives to take from you, or curtail, or subvert your happiness because it surpasses his, so does the devil try to get the better of you, a human being, by stealing from you that very thing by which you get the better of him. Take great care, then, to preserve in your heart love for your enemy, because with that you overcome the devil. Let man or woman rage to their utmost, let them steal from you whatever they can; if the one who rages openly is loved, the one who rages in secret is vanquished.

Verse 5. Avoid hatred; it kills

7. But the psalmist went on praying, deeply distressed and saddened, as though his eye was inflamed by anger. If anger against a brother or sister becomes hardened, it is hatred. Anger inflames the eye, but hatred blinds it; anger is a splinter, hatred a beam. Perhaps at some time or other you felt hatred for someone you rebuked for being angry? There was hatred in you, anger in the person you corrected, and you deserved to hear the Lord's command, *Take the beam out of your own eye first, then you will see clearly to take the splinter out of your brother's* (Mt 7:5). Here is an illustration to help you understand the vast difference between anger and hatred: parents are angry with their children every day, but are there any parents who hate their children? I have yet to see them. This disturbed, saddened psalmist went on praying and struggling against all the insults of those who abused him, but not in order to get the better of them by trading insults. All he wanted was to avoid hating any of them. That is why he prays, that is why he pleads when confronted *by the shouting of the enemy and the trouble caused by a sinner, for they have brought down iniquity upon me, and cast a shadow over me with their anger. My heart is deeply disturbed within me.* This is the same lament that he made elsewhere: *my eye is inflamed by anger* (Ps 6:8(7)). And if his eye is inflamed, what is the consequence? *The fear of death fell upon me.* Love is our life, and if love is life, hatred is death. When a person begins to fear that he may hate the one he used to love, he is afraid of death; and the death he fears is one more dreadful and more interior, because it is a death that slays not the body but the soul. Think about it: you were faced with a fellow human who was furious with you; but what harm could he or she do you, in view of the security the Lord gave you against such enemies? He bade you, *Do not be afraid of those who kill the body* (Mt 10:28). In his rage the enemy may kill the body, but by hating him you have killed the soul; and whereas he has killed the body of another, you have killed your own soul. This is what is meant by *the fear of death fell upon me.*

Verses 6–7. The longing to flee from troublemakers

8. *Fear and trembling came upon me, and darkness covered me. And I said... .* Anyone who hates a brother or sister is in darkness still, for if love is light, hatred is darkness.⁹ Now what is he saying to himself, this man beset by weakness and distressed amid his trials? *Who will give me wings, as though to a dove?*¹⁰ *Then I will fly away and find rest.* He was either hoping for death or longing for solitude. "As long as it is indicated to me, or rather enjoined upon me, that I must love my enemies," he says, "their continually mounting insults are like a shadow falling across me; they trouble my eyes, distort my vision, thrust at my heart and kill my soul. I wish I could get away, and so avoid piling sins upon sins, but I am too weak for that.¹¹ At least I would like to withdraw for a little while from human society, so that my wound may not be constantly aggravated. Then when it had healed I could return to the fray."

This does happen, brothers and sisters. A desire for solitude does often arise in the mind of a servant of God from no other cause than a host of troubles and difficulties, so that he or she exclaims, *Who will give me wings, as though to a dove?* Is the speaker complaining of being wingless, or is it rather that his wings are tied? If he has none, let them be given him; if they are bound, let them be loosened; for anyone who frees a bird's wings from entanglements is giving the bird its wings, or at any rate giving them back. The bird did not really own them as long as it was unable to use them for flying. Tied wings are nothing but a burden. So the psalmist cries out, *Who will give me wings, as though to a dove? Then I will fly away and find rest.* Where will he find rest? As I have pointed out already, this can be taken in either of two senses: death or solitude. It may mean what the apostle meant when he longed *to die and to be with Christ, for that is much the best* (Phil 1:23). However strong he was, however great, however valiant of heart, however invincible as a soldier of Christ, Paul was distressed by his trials, as we read: *Let no one give me any further trouble* (Gal 6:17). He seemed to be echoing the complaint in another psalm: *Disgust possessed me at the sinners who abandon your law* (Ps 118(119):53). One may often strive to correct perverse, depraved people for whom one is responsible, yet on whom all human effort and vigilance seem wasted. If one cannot correct them, there is nothing for it but to endure them. But what if such an incorrigible person is one of your own, not merely because you are fellow-members of the human race, but even, as may often be the case,

---

9. See 1 Jn 2:9–11.
10. *Quis dabit mihi pennas sicut columbae?*, usually taken to mean "wings of a dove"; but *columbae* could be either genitive or dative, and Augustine apparently understands it as dative, since further on in this paragraph he says, "not as to a raven" (*corvo*, unambiguously dative).
11. So most manuscripts. A few have "sins upon sins, because I am weak, and so...," which makes better sense.

because you are bound together in the fellowship of the Church? He or she is within; so what are you going to do about it? Where will you go to get away? What place can you find to withdraw to, in order to suffer this no longer? No, stay here, talk to them, exhort them, be kind to them, threaten them, bring them to a better mind.

"But I have done all that. I have poured out all the strength I could command, wrung it all out of myself, but I can see that I have made no progress at all. All that effort has been spent, and nothing but grief is left to me. How can my heart find any rest from such people, unless I beg, *Who will give me wings*?"

But give them to him *as though to a dove*. Do not give him the wings you would give to a raven,[12] because though a dove certainly does seek to fly away from perplexities, it does not let go of love. A dove is considered to be the symbol of love, and its moaning is a loveable sound. No creature is as much given to moaning as a dove; it moans all day long and at night, evidently thinking the place where it lives to be one appropriate to moaning.

So then, this is the voice of a lover, and what has he to say? "I cannot bear all this abuse. People hiss at me, they are beside themselves with savagery, they are incandescent with rage, their anger is like a dark cloud over me. I can do nothing to help them, so I want to get some rest elsewhere, distant from them in body, but not in love,[13] simply so that the love that is in me may not be agitated any more. If I cannot do them any good through my instruction or in conversation with them, perhaps I shall be of more use by praying for them."

People say this, but often they are so tied down that flight is impossible. They may be held fast not by glue but by their office. If it is the responsibility of their position that binds them, and they cannot abandon it, they have to say, "*I longed to die and to be with Christ, for that is much the best; but it is necessary for you that I remain in the flesh*" (Phil 1:23–24). This dove was tied by affection, not greed for profit; it was rendered unable to fly not by any lack of merit but by its determination to discharge its duty. All the same, we must have this desire in our hearts. Only the person who has begun to walk in the narrow way[14] feels the pangs of this desire; and obviously we must feel them if we realize that the Church is never free from persecutions, even in this age when it seems to enjoy peace from the kind of persecution our martyrs endured. Persecutions are never lacking, because that saying of Scripture is true, *all who want to live devoted to God in Christ will suffer persecution* (2 Tm 3:12). If you do not experience

---

12. *Sicut columbae tamen, non sicut corvo.* See note 10 above.
13. *Amore*, the general word for love, often but not always carrying carnal overtones. Within the present sentence, as throughout this exposition, Augustine uses *dilectio*, a word conveying the love of deliberate choice, but it is not clear that any difference of meaning is implied in the present context.
14. See Mt 7:14.

persecution, you cannot be wanting to live a life devoted to God in Christ. And what does it mean, to live this devoted life in Christ? It means that you must in your heart of hearts experience the anguish the apostle felt: *Is anyone weak, and I am not weak too? Is anyone tripped up, without my being afire with indignation?* (2 Cor 11:29). The weaknesses of others, the stumbling-blocks set in other people's paths—these were the persecutions Paul suffered. And are they absent today? No, there are plenty of them for those who have to worry about these things. When one of us is viewed from a distance, an observer may say, "Everything seems to go well with him." Either the speaker tastes the bitterness of his own life but is incapable of tasting that of others, or else he has no bitterness to taste in his own, and so no sympathy for another who is not merely tasting it but obliged to swallow it in large doses. Let such an observer undertake to live devoted to God in Christ, and he will experience the truth of what is said here. Then he will begin to long for wings, long to travel far off and flee and stay in the desert.

Verse 8. You can never escape from troublesome companions

9. Why do you suppose the desert places have been filled with God's servants, my brothers and sisters?[15] If life among other people had suited them well, would they have withdrawn from others? Look what they are doing—they too! They flee as far away as they can, and live in the desert. But is each of them solitary there? By no means. Charity obliges them to stay with many companions, and among these multitudes are some who are a trial to them. In any large gathering of people there will inevitably be some bad ones. God knows that we need to be tested, so he mixes in among us some who will not persevere in the right way, and some spurious ones who have not even begun to walk in the path in which they ought to persevere. God knows that learning to bear with bad people is a necessity for us, and that we thereby make progress in goodness ourselves. Let us love our enemies, and correct them, punish them, excommunicate them, even cast them out from our society, provided we do so in love. Remember the apostle's advice: *If anyone disobeys our command conveyed in this letter, take note of such a one, and avoid his company.* He warns you, though, that anger must not creep in to inflame your eye in this situation: *But do not regard him as an enemy. Correct him as a brother, so that he may be ashamed* (2 Thes 3:14–15). The apostle prescribes separation from such a person, but does not cut off love from him. If that eye of yours is healthy, you are alive yourself. To lose love is the death of you. The psalmist was afraid of losing love when he lamented, *"The fear of death fell upon me,*

---

15. The monastic movement had become significant during the fourth century. The *Life of Antony*, attributed to Saint Athanasius and translated into Latin by Evagrius, had influenced many, including Augustine; see his *Confessions* VIII,6,15.

and so, to save me from losing this life that is love, *who will give me wings, as though to a dove? Then I will fly away and find rest.*"

But where will you go? Where will your flight take you? Where will you find rest? *Lo, I fled far away, and stayed in the desert.* But what desert? Wherever you are, others will gather there too; they will seek the desert along with you, and they will have an impact on your life. You cannot avoid the society of your brothers and sisters. And there will be some bad characters impinging on you as well, for some trials are still owing to you. *Lo, I fled away, and stayed in the desert.* What desert? Do you mean, perhaps, the inner place of your own soul,[16] where no other human being gains entry, where no one is with you, where there is only yourself and God? Well and good; but if "desert" means a geographical place, how are you going to stop people congregating there? You cannot separate yourself from the human race as long as you live the life of humankind. Console yourself, rather, by keeping your gaze fixed on our Lord and King, our Ruler and Creator, who became also a creature among us. Remember that he included among his twelve one who would be a cause of suffering to him.

Verse 9. Christ stills the storm

10. *Lo, I fled away, and stayed in the desert.* Perhaps the speaker sought refuge in his own soul, as I have already suggested, and there found some measure of solitude where he could rest. Yet charity itself disturbs him there. He is alone in his soul, but not alone as far as charity is concerned. In his innermost soul he was finding consolation, but tribulations continued to pester him without. Tranquil in himself, but on tenterhooks about others, and still distressed as a result, he says, *I was waiting for him who would save me from faintheartedness in the storm.* You are in the sea, and a storm is raging; there is no hope for you except to shout, *Lord, I'm sinking!* (Mt 14:30). May he who walks fearlessly upon the waves stretch out a hand to you, and lift you up in your terror, and grant you safety and stability in himself. May he speak to you interiorly and bid you, "Keep your eyes on me and on what I endured. Can it be that when you suffer a treacherous brother or sister, or the enemy's onslaughts from without, you are suffering anything I did not undergo? The Jews raged against me outwardly, and from within my own circle a disciple plotted to betray me."

So the tempest roars, but he saves us *from faintheartedness in the storm.* Perhaps your boat is rocking because he is asleep in you. When a rough sea was battering the boat in which the disciples were sailing, Christ was asleep; eventually they realized that the man who slept on board with them was the ruler and creator of the winds, so they approached him and woke him up. He gave orders to the gale, and there was a mighty calm.[17] Your heart is very likely to be turbulent if you have forgotten about him in whom

---

16. Literally "conscience."
17. See Mk 4:36–40; Mt 8:23–26; Lk 8:22–25.

your faith rests; you will find your troubles unendurable if you do not keep in mind what Christ suffered for you. If you do not keep Christ in mind, it is as though for you he is asleep. Awaken Christ and remember your faith. He sleeps in you when you forget his sufferings;[18] he is awake in you when you are mindful of his sufferings. When you contemplate with all your heart what he endured for you, will you too not bear your pain calmly, perhaps even gladly, since your experience of suffering likens you in some degree to your king? As with this in mind you begin to find comfort and joy, he arises, he gives orders to the gale, and tranquillity reigns. *I was waiting for him who would save me from faintheartedness in the storm.*

Verse 10. Pride issues in mutual unintelligibility; the Spirit restores unanimity

11. *Engulf them, Lord, and confuse their languages.* The psalmist is thinking of those who harass him and cast a shadow over him, and this is his wish. But notice this, brothers and sisters: it is not prompted by anger. If people have wickedly exalted themselves, it is good for them to sink; if they have conspired in wickedness, it is for their good that they lose their comprehension of each other's languages. Let them reach a common mind for good purposes, and then let their tongues chime in harmony. But if *with common purpose all my enemies kept whispering against me,* as another psalm complains (Ps 40:8(41:7)), they had better relinquish this common purpose and find their languages diversified, so that they cannot understand each other. *Engulf them, Lord, and confuse their languages.* Why does he pray, *Engulf them*? Because they have lifted themselves up. And why, *Confuse their languages*? Because they have conspired in wickedness. Remember the tower that certain proud people built after the flood. What was their intention? "Let us construct a high tower," they said. "We don't want to perish in another flood."[19] They thought their pride could protect them, so they built their high tower; but the Lord fragmented their speech. They began to find each other unintelligible, and that was the origin of all the different languages. Until that time there had been only one tongue; and one tongue was expedient for people who were of one mind, one single language was right for humble people. But when that unanimity degenerated into a conspiracy of pride God dealt mercifully with them by estranging their tongues, to make it impossible for them to form a dangerous unity by understanding each other. Through proud persons human languages were diversified, and through the humble apostles languages were harmonized; the spirit of pride fragmented language, and the Holy Spirit gathered dispersed languages into one. When the Holy Spirit came upon the disciples they spoke in the tongues of all who heard, and were understood by all.[20]

---

18. Some witnesses add here, "and if you deny that he is the true Son of God."
19. See Gn 11:4.
20. See Acts 2:4.

The fragmented languages were reunited. If there are still pagans on the rampage today, it is just as well that they speak different languages. If they aspire to one common language, let them come to the Church, for here, though we differ in our natural tongues,[21] there is but one language spoken by the faith of our hearts. *Engulf them, Lord, and confuse their languages.*

The glory of the cross

12. *For I have seen iniquity and denial in the city.* He had good reason to seek the desert, for all he saw in the city was iniquity and denial. There is a certain city full of unrest; it is the same as the city that built the tower, the one that was thrown into confusion and is called Babylon.[22] It was scattered among innumerable peoples,[23] and from there the Church has been called out into the desert of a good conscience, for it had met with denial in the city. "Christ has come," says the Church. "And who is Christ?" demands the objector. "The Son of God." "So God has a Son?" "Yes, he was born of a virgin, he suffered, and he rose again." But your contradictions continue: "How could that happen?" Have regard at least to the glory of his cross. That cross, once the butt of his enemies' ridicule, is now worn on the foreheads of kings. Its effect has demonstrated its power:[24] it has conquered the world, but by wood, not steel. The wood of the cross seemed to Christ's enemies an object of ridicule, and they stood before that tree wagging their heads, and saying, *If he is the Son of God, let him come down from the cross* (Mt 27:40). He kept on stretching out his hands to a people who refused to believe, a people that denied him.[25] If a person who lives by faith is just,[26] one who has no faith is iniquitous; so when the psalm here speaks of *iniquity* I take it to mean perfidious denial. Our Lord constantly saw iniquity and denial in the city, and he kept on stretching out his hands to a people that refused to believe and went on denying him. Yet he was waiting for them still, for he prayed, *Father, forgive them, for they do not know what they are doing* (Lk 23:34). The remnants of that city persist in their rage even today; still they deny him. But from the foreheads of us all he still stretches out his hands to the unbelieving, denying remnants. *For I have seen iniquity and denial in the city.*

---

21. *In diversitate linguarum carnis.*
22. As often in Augustine, the type of the earthly city set over against the city of God. See *Exposition 2 of Psalm* 26, 18; *Exposition of Psalm* 44, 25, and the note there.
23. See Gn 11:9.
24. Reading *effectus probavit virtutem*; but most codices have *effectis proba virtutem*: perhaps "verify its power by things accomplished."
25. See Is 65:2; Rom 10:21.
26. See Hb 2:4; Rom 1:17.

Verse 11. The city of pride

13. *Day and night iniquity will march round it upon its ramparts, and there will be labor.* On its ramparts, as though attached to its cornices, which represent its noble folk. "If that nobleman were a Christian, no one would remain pagan," people say. "No one would still be a pagan, if he were a Christian." Yes, they say that often: "If he became a Christian, would anyone remain a pagan?" So as long as such noble persons do not become Christians, they are like the ramparts of the city that does not believe, the city of denial. How long will those ramparts stand? Not for ever. As the ark was carried round the walls of Jericho, so too the time will come for this city of unbelief and denial when its walls will crumble at the seventh circuit of the ark.[27] But until this happens the psalmist is distressed in his ordeal. He finds the remnants of the argumentative, denying folk burdensome, and he yearns for wings to carry him in flight, yearns for the peace of the desert. Yet he must stand fast amid the objectors, bear the threats, drink in the insults, and wait for the one who will save him from faintheartedness and storm. He must keep his gaze fixed on the head, on whom his life[28] is modeled, and he must find tranquillity in hope, even if he is still harassed in reality. *Day and night iniquity will march round it upon its ramparts, and there will be labor within it, and injustice.* Because iniquity is there, labor will be there; because injustice is there, inevitably labor will be too. If only they would listen to him who stretches out his hands inviting them, *Come to me, all you who labor!* You shout, you deny, you jeer; how different is he who says to you, *"Come to me, all you who labor* in your pride, and you will rest in my humility. *Learn from me, for I am meek and humble of heart, and you shall find rest for your souls"* (Mt 11:28–29). Why are they laboring? Because they are not meek and humble of heart. God became humble; let men and women blush for being proud.

Verse 12. Debts, financial and spiritual

14. *Usury and deceit are never lacking in its streets.* Usury and deceit, evil though they are, are not even hidden; they are publicly rampant. When someone does a bad thing at home, at least he is ashamed of his evil deed, but here *usury and deceit* are flaunted even in the streets. Moneylending ranks as a profession, and is reckoned a technical skill. Its practitioners form a corporation, one allegedly necessary to the state, and as a profession moneylending is taxed. This is how something that should at least be hidden is instead paraded in the street.

There is an even worse kind of usury, however, and that is the refusal to forgive someone who is in your debt. Then your eye is inflamed indeed when you reach that line in the prayer, *Forgive us our debts.* What are

---

27. See Jos 6:3.
28. Variant: "his way."

you to do, when you want to pray, and you get to that line? You have been rudely spoken to, perhaps, and you want the offender to be committed for torture in return! At all events you should not demand more than you paid out, you unjust lender. Someone punched you, did he, and you want him killed? That is wicked usury. How are you going to find your way into prayer? Or, if you give up prayer, how do you propose to wend your way to the Lord? Consider your situation. You will say, *Our Father, who art in heaven, hallowed be thy name. Thy kingdom come. Thy will be done, on earth as it is in heaven.* So far, so good. You continue, *Give us this day our daily bread.* And then—here it comes—*Forgive us our debts, as we forgive those who are in debt to us* (Mt 6:9–12). Wicked, usurious attitudes may be commonplace in the city of pride, but they must not come within our walls; here we beat our breasts. So what are you going to do, when you and this verse meet here head-on? One skilled in heavenly law composed the prayer for you; the expert who knew what goes on in heaven tells you, "On no other condition will your request be granted. *Truly I tell you, if you forgive other people for their offenses, you will be forgiven; but if you do not forgive the offenses of others, neither will your Father forgive you*" (Mt 6:14–15). Who says this? One who understands the cause you stand there pleading. You must see this: he himself has undertaken to be your advocate. He who is your legal expert, he who is the Father's assessor, he who is your very judge—he has told you, "On no other condition will your plea be granted."[29] So what are you going to do? You will not get what you want if you do not say this prayer, nor will you get what you want if you say it insincerely. Either you must say it, and make your actions conform to your words, or you will not deserve to gain what you ask. Any who fail to meet the condition are compromised by their vile usury. Those who still worship idols, or have recourse to them, can continue in usury if they like, but not you, people of God, not you, Christ's people, not you, the body that belongs to that head. Remember the peace that binds you together, remember the promise that is your life. What good will it do you, if you insist on inflicting injuries in return for those you have received? Does revenge make you feel better? Or will you enjoy someone else's misfortune? A bad person has harmed you: very well, forgive him, or there will be two bad people. *Usury and deceit are never lacking in its streets.*

Verses 13–15. Treachery on the part of familiar friends

15. In view of this you longed for solitude and wished for wings. You grumble, you cannot bear it—all this argument and iniquity in the city. Take your rest, then, with those who live with you inside the Church, and do not seek solitude. However, you need to listen to what the psalm says

---

29. In his *Homilies on the Gospel of John* 7,11, Augustine elaborates this idea. If we wish to win our case in court, we must first approach a legal expert, to ensure that it is properly presented.

even of them: *If an enemy had slandered me...*, he says. Earlier he had been very distressed in his ordeal by the shouting of an enemy and the trouble caused by a sinner, but at that time he was perhaps still living in the proud city that erected the tower. The tower was sunk,[30] you remember, so as to fragment their languages. But now listen to how he groans within the Church on account of the dangers that threaten from treacherous brethren: *If an enemy had slandered me, I could have borne it; or if someone who hated me had talked arrogantly against me*—that is, if he had insulted me in his pride, and given himself airs while belittling me, and threatened me with any damage he could do to me—*I could surely have hidden from him*. Where would you have hidden, to escape from this enemy outside? Among those inside the Church, of course. But now consider. There may be no possibility open to you except to seek solitude, for the psalm continues, *But it was you, a like-minded person, my guide and my familiar companion*. Time was, when you gave me good advice, when you went ahead of me and gave me salutary counsel. We were at one in God's house. *You were to me a like-minded person, my guide and my familiar companion, who were wont to eat delicious food with me*. What delicious food is meant? Not all of you who are present know what it is.[31] But let those who do know not think it sour,[32] but say to those who do not know, *Taste and see how sweet the Lord is* (Ps 33:9(34:8)).

You were wont to eat delicious food with me. In the house of God we walked together in harmony. How, then, did the dissension arise? It looks as though someone who used to be inside became an outsider. That person walked with me in God's house in agreement, but then set up a rival house in opposition to the house of God.[33] Why did you leave this house, where we walked in concord? Why is it left deserted, this house where together we ate sweet food?

Verse 16. The revolt of Korah, Dathan, and Abiram prefigured the Donatist schism

16. *May death fall upon them, and may they go down alive into the underworld*. By this figure of speech he reflects upon the primal outbreak of schism, reminding us how among the ancient race of Israel a few proud persons separated themselves from the rest and wished to offer sacrifice apart. A novel kind of death overtook them, for the earth opened and

---

30. *Submersa*, alluding to verse 9. The editors of the CCL text unnecessarily amend to *subversa*, "overthrown."
31. A reference to the catechumens, to whom the mystery of the eucharist had not yet been proposed.
32. Reading *amaricent* with most witnesses. One has *amaricentur*, "become sour."
33. The Donatists, presumably, of whom he speaks in the next paragraph, or heretics and schismatics in general.

swallowed them up.[34] *May death fall upon them, and may they go down alive into the underworld.* What does the word *alive* suggest? It means that they know they are perishing, yet they perish all the same.

Listen now to an illustration of how ruin can overtake living persons, how they can be sucked down into a cleft of the earth by the earthly desires that devour them. Suppose you say to someone, "What's the matter, brother? We are brothers and sisters, we call upon the one God, we believe in the one Christ, we listen to the same gospel, we sing the same psalm, we respond with the one 'Amen,' we ring out the one 'Alleluia,' we celebrate the one Easter. So why are you outside, and I inside?" This often drives him into a corner and, seeing the truth of what you say, he replies, "It's the fault of our forebears—God will have to settle the account with them!" So even as he perishes, he is alive. You go further, and admonish him: "Isn't the disaster of separation bad enough? Must you compound it by repeating baptism? Acknowledge in me the reality you have yourself; and even if you hate me, be kind to the Christ in me." This pernicious practice is often the most grievous point of all to them, and they will admit, "Yes, it's true; this does happen. How we wish it did not! But what can we do about the statutes our ancestors handed down to us?" *May they go down alive into the underworld.* If you were already dead as you descended there, you would not know what you were doing. But as it is, you know that what you are doing is wrong, but still you do it; so you are alive as you go down there, aren't you?

Now why did the yawning earth swallow those leaders in particular, while fire from heaven consumed the other people who had taken their part?[35] The psalm which recalls their punishment began with the ordinary people and concluded with the leaders. *May death fall upon them*: this phrase refers to the people on whom fire fell from heaven; and then the psalm immediately adds, *May they go down alive into the underworld*, referring to the leaders who were swallowed up by the earth. This must be the right way to read it, because how could those of whom it had been said, *May death fall upon them*, be described as going down alive? If death had already overtaken them, they could hardly descend alive. No, we must take it that the psalm begins with the minor characters and ends with the important ones. *May death fall upon* those who consented and followed; but what of the leaders, the people of substance? *May they go down alive into the underworld*, because they are well versed in the Scriptures, and from their daily reading they know clearly that the Catholic Church is so widely diffused throughout the world that all gainsaying of it is absurd. They know perfectly well that no justification whatever can be alleged for their schism. And therefore they go down to the underworld alive, for they know that the wrong they do is wrong indeed.

---

34. See Nm 16:1–33.
35. See Nm 16:31–35.

As for the lesser folk, the fire of God's anger consumed them. Aflame with zeal for controversy, they were unwilling to abandon their wicked leaders; so fire fell upon them, the fire of destruction upon the fire of dissension.[36]

May death fall upon them, and may they go down alive into the underworld, for there is wickedness in their lodgings and in their midst. It says, *In their lodgings,* to indicate places where they stay temporarily before moving on; for they will not be here always, even though they fight so hard in their time-bound vehemence. Wickedness is *in their lodgings,* and wickedness is *in their midst,* for nothing is so central to them as their hearts.

Verse 17. The unity among the many

17. *I cried out to the Lord.* The body of Christ, the unity of Christ, is crying out in its anguish, its weariness, its affliction, in the distress of its ordeal. It is one single person, a unity grounded in an individual body, and in the distress of its soul it cries from the bounds of the earth: *from the ends of the earth I have called to you, as my soul grew faint* (Ps 60:3(61:2)). It is one, but the oneness is a unity made from many; it is one, but not because of confinement to any one place, for this is one person crying out from the ends of the earth. How could one individual cry out from the ends of the earth, unless that individual were one formed from many?

I cried out to the Lord. Yes, do just that: you cry out to the Lord, not to Donatus. Don't let him be your lord in place of our true Lord, he who refused to be your fellow-servant under our Lord. *I cried out to the Lord, and the Lord hearkened to me.*

Verse 18. Evening, morning, and high noon

18. *At evening, in the morning and at midday I will tell my tale, and proclaim it, and he will hear my voice.* Your job is to preach the good news. Do not be silent about what you have received. *At evening* tell of what is past, *in the morning* of what is still to come, and *at midday* of what is everlasting. So when the psalm says, *At evening,* it refers to a story that is to be told; when it says, *In the morning,* it thinks of an announcement; and when speaking of *midday* it looks to the effective hearing of its prayer. It puts *midday* as a finale, a high noon from which there is no sinking towards sunset. At noon the light is at its highest, like the splendor of wisdom and the ardor of love.

At evening, in the morning, and at midday. At evening the Lord was on the cross, in the morning he arose, at midday he ascended. At evening, then, my tale is of a dying man's patience, in the morning I proclaim the life of him who rises from the dead, and I will pray that at midday he

---

36. These remarks demonstrate Augustine's sympathy for the simple and innocent among the Donatists, whose schismatic status was merely inherited, as opposed to the deliberate stance of the well-informed.

who is seated at the Father's right hand may hear me. He who intercedes for us[37] will hear my voice. What security this is, what comfort, what an encouragement in the face of faintheartedness and storm! What strength against malicious people, against sadness both outside and within, and among those who were once inside but are now out!

Verse 19. Few are truly "with us"

19. When you see turbulent, proud self-seekers within this very congregation, my brothers and sisters, when you see within these four walls arrogant folk who instead of harboring a chaste, quiet zeal for God take too much on themselves, when you see them all ready to foment dissension but lacking only the opportunity, you know that they are the chaff in the Lord's threshing-floor. The wind of pride has blown a few of them away from us, but the main bulk of the chaff will not fly away until the Lord comes to winnow his crop at the end.[38]

What are we to do meanwhile? We must sing with the psalmist, pray with him, lament with him, and yet say in all confidence, *God will redeem my soul in peace*. Despite those who do not love peace, *he will redeem my soul in peace*, for with those who hate peace I dealt peaceably.[39]

He will redeem my soul in peace from those who draw near to me. Those who are far away from me present no difficulty: I am unlikely to be taken in by someone who says, "Come and worship the idol," for such a person is very far away from me. But when I inquire of someone, "Are you a Christian?" and the other says, "Yes, I am," then he or she is a very close adversary, one near at hand. *He will redeem my soul in peace from those who draw near to me, for in many respects they were with me*. Why did I say, *They draw near to me*? Precisely because *in many respects they were with me*. Two different explanations of this verse suggest themselves.

Here is the first. *In many respects they were with me*. We had a common baptism, so they were with me in that. We were both accustomed to read the gospel; they were with me in that. We both customarily celebrated the festivals of the martyrs; in that too they were with me. We always observed the solemnity of Easter, and they were with me in that also. But they are not with me in all respects: they are not with me in their schism, nor with me in their heresy. In many matters they are with me, but in a few they are not; and because of those few in which they are not with me, the many others in which they are with me do them no good. To make this point clear, brothers and sisters, look at the many items Paul listed, while insisting that there was only one that mattered, and that if this one was missing, all the rest were pointless: *if I speak with human tongue or angel's tongue... if I have the gift of prophecy, and have cognizance of all mysteries and*

---

37. See Rom 8:34.
38. See Mt 3:12.
39. See Ps 119:7(120:6–7).

all knowledge; if I have such perfect faith that I can move mountains... if I distribute all my resources to feed the poor, and deliver my body to be burnt (1 Cor 13:1–3)... what a lot of things he has enumerated! But one thing is lacking among these many things: one thing only, charity. The others are many in number, but charity exceeds them in weight. So too today: in all the sacraments they are with me, but in this one thing, charity, they are not. *In many respects they were with me.*

Here is the second possible interpretation of the verse. It could mean *among the many they were with me.*[40] The people who have cut themselves off from me were formerly with me, but they were not among the few—only among the many. Throughout the whole wide world there are only a few grains, but many husks. What is the psalm suggesting? As husks, as chaff, they were with me, certainly, but not with me as grain. The chaff is very near the grain; it emerges from the one seed, and strikes root in the one field, and is nourished by the same rain; it is subjected to the same reaper and undergoes the same threshing. It awaits the same sifting, but it does not find its way into the one barn. Only *among the many were they with me.*

Verses 20–22. Persevering refusal of the truth

20. *God will hear me and will humble them, God who exists before all ages.* Presumptuously they trust in some leader or other, an upstart of yesterday, but *God will humble them, God who exists before all ages.* This can be said of him because although Christ was born in time from the Virgin Mary, nonetheless before all ages, in the beginning, was the Word, and the Word was with God, and the Word was God.[41] *He will humble them, God who exists before all ages,* asserts the psalmist, *for with them there is no change,* "with them, I mean, who will not alter their course." He knew there would be some who would persist in their wickedness, and would die still persisting in it. We all know people like this: they will not change. Those who die in this state, in their perversity, in their schism, do not alter their course. But God will humble them, he will lay them low in condemnation because they reared up in dissension. There is no alteration in them, because they change not for the better but for the worse, and this holds not only for the present world, but even for the resurrection, because *though we shall all indeed rise again, we shall not all be changed.*[42] Why not? Because with such people *there is no change, and they have not feared*

---

40. *In multis erant mecum.* The Latin can mean "many things," "many people," "many respects," etc. The translation has been altered in the present paragraph to reflect Augustine's different interpretation.
41. See Jn 1:1.
42. 1 Cor 15:51. In the original Greek the sense of this verse is "We shall not all die, but we shall all be changed." Paul was thinking of the prospect for those who would be still alive at the Lord's second coming. But the Old Latin which Augustine was using, like the Vulgate, understood it differently.

God. There is but one remedy, brothers and sisters: let them fear God and cut loose from Donatus. To a Donatist you say, "You are heading for perdition in your heresy, in your schism. God must necessarily punish such sins. You will be damned; don't deceive yourself with words. Don't follow a blind guide, for if one blind person leads another, both fall into the ditch."[43] "What do I care?" he replies. "As I lived yesterday, so do I live today. What my parents were, I am too." "Then you do not fear God." Where there is fear of God, anyone must realize that all these things we read about are true, and that the faith of Christ cannot err. How can such a person remain in heresy[44] in the face of such overwhelming evidence in favor of the holy Catholic Church? God has spread it throughout the world; he promised it before diffusing it, announced it in advance, and then displayed it as he had promised. Let those who do not fear God be wary and watchful, then. *He stretches out his hand to requite them.*

21. *They have defiled his covenant*. Read the promise that announced this covenant they have defiled: *In your seed all nations shall be blessed* (Gn 12:3; 26:4). But *they have defiled his covenant*. What have you to say in contradiction to these words, spoken by the author of the covenant? "Africa alone has been worthy of this grace through Saint Donatus," you say. "The Church of Christ has survived only in him." The Church of Donatus you mean: go on, say it! Why bother to add the name of Christ—Christ to whom the promise referred, *in your seed all nations shall be blessed*? Do you want to follow Donatus? Bypass Christ, then, and off you go!

Look what follows. *They have defiled his covenant*. What covenant is this? The apostle answers: *To Abraham were the promises made, and to his seed. He argues, Brethren, even a human will and testament once proved cannot be nullified or overruled by anyone. To Abraham were the promises made, and to his seed. Scripture does not say, "To his descendants," as though indicating many, but as to one only: "And to your seed," which is Christ* (Gal 3:15–16). What then was the covenant promised in this seed, in Christ? *In your seed all nations shall be blessed*. It follows then, you Donatist, that because you have let slip the unity of all nations and clung to a part only, you have defiled his covenant. The fate that falls upon you—extermination and banishment from your inheritance—proceeds from God's anger. *They have defiled his covenant, and they have been banished by the wrath of his countenance*. What plainer language can you expect, brothers and sisters? Could heretics be more clearly indicated? *They have been banished by the wrath of his countenance*.

---

43. See Mt 15:4; Lk 6:39.
44. The editors of the CCL text reorganize these two sentences to make them part of the address to the heretic: "You must fear God. Realize that…err. How can you remain in heresy?"

Verse 22. But heretics have their usefulness

22. *His heart has come near.* Whose heart is meant? God's surely, by whose anger they were banished. In what sense has *his heart come near?* In enabling us to understand his will. Thanks to heretics, the Catholic faith has been clearly enunciated, and in reaction to people with wrong opinions, those with right opinions have been tested and approved. Many truths were contained in the Scriptures in an obscure way; and the heretics, after being cut off, rocked God's Church with their questions. But this served to lay open hidden truths, and so God's will came to be understood better. This is why in another psalm it is said that *a batch of bulls is among the cows of the peoples, so that those who have been proved sound by silver may be pressed out* (Ps 67:31(68:30)), in the sense, "may stand out clearly," or "may become visible."[45] In the silversmith's craft those who press out the form from the undifferentiated lump are called *exclusores*.[46] Among God's people there were many individuals capable of explaining the Scriptures with excellent discernment, but they were unknown. There was no occasion for them to put forward a solution to difficult questions as long as nobody arose to make false claims. Was any complete account of the Trinity offered, before the Arians began to bay at it?[47] Was there

---

45. *Excludantur.*
46. Augustine uses the word in this sense in his *Exposition of Psalm* 67, 39, and in *The Spirit and the Letter* 17. The root idea is that of separation ordered to the emergence of significant form or meaning.
47. The principal point of the Arian heresy was the effort to safeguard the unity of God by denying eternity and divinity in the full sense to the Second Person of the Trinity. The Son was held to have been created out of nothing by the Father as the first of his creatures, through whom the Father then created all else. Divinity was subsequently bestowed upon him in view of his righteousness. The heresy was influential in the 320s and spread widely. At the prompting of the Emperor Constantine a council was held at Nicea in A.D. 325 which condemned the Arian heresy, largely thanks to the leadership of Saint Athanasius, then still a deacon. This council coined the non-scriptural term *homoousios* ("of the same nature") to express the relationship of Son to Father, and the word became the touchstone of orthodoxy during the fierce controversies of the following decades. One of the bishops condemned at Nicea for Arian views was the influential Church historian Eusebius of Nicomedia. Others rallied to him and Arianism lived on, splitting eventually into three wings: (1) the extreme Anomoeans (proponents of "dissimilarity"); (2) the middle party of Homoeans (acknowledging "similarity" between Father and Son, but anxious to avoid the doctrinal precision of the homoousios); (3) the Semi-Arians, who were very close to the orthodox position, and eventually rallied to the orthodox ranks after the councils of Seleucia and Ariminum in 359 had seemed to mark the triumph of Arianism. Political influence, especially in the eastern half of the Empire, had contributed to this short-lived

any satisfactory treatment of penitential practice, before the Novatianists challenged it?[48] In the same way we had no complete teaching on baptism until the "rebaptizers" had put themselves outside the Church.[49] The things that needed to be said about the unity of Christ's body in this connection were not said with anything like the same clarity until the Donatist schism began to press hard on our weaker brothers and sisters. Others in our ranks, who were well able to discuss and find out the truth of the matter, were then prompted to bring obscure points of teaching into the open in their sermons and disputations, and thus save from ruin the weaker ones who were worried by the objections of the wicked. In this way our opponents were banished by the wrath of God's countenance, whereas his heart drew near to us so that we might understand.

In the light of these facts you must interpret the saying of the other psalm, *a batch of bulls* (of proud folk, pushing with their horns, that means) *is among the cows of the peoples.* Who are being called *cows*? Souls easily led astray.[50] But why does this occur? So that *those who have been proved sound by silver may be pressed out.* That is to say, so that those who were formerly hidden may appear openly. But why *by silver*? This means by God's word, for another psalm says, *The words of the Lord are pure words, silver tried by fire for the earth, purified seven times* (Ps 11:7(12:6)). This may seem an obscure interpretation, but look how the apostle presses it out[51] into the light: *Heresies there must be,* he says, *so that those who have been proved sound may be clearly identified among you* (1 Cor 11:19). What does *proved sound* mean? To be *proved sound by silver* means to be proved

---

triumph; but Athanasius had stood firm throughout in spite of being repeatedly exiled from his see at Alexandria, and the faith of Nicea was reasserted by a council at Alexandria in 362. After Athanasius' death in 373 the orthodox faith was defended and expounded by the three great Cappadocian fathers, Basil, Gregory of Nazianzus, and Gregory of Nyssa.

48. Novatian was an orthodox Roman theologian, who at first espoused Saint Cyprian's relatively lenient policy on the treatment of those Christians who had apostatized and denied the faith during the persecution of Decius (A.D. 249–250). Later, after the election of Saint Cornelius as pope (251), and the confirmation of this policy, Novatian joined the rigorist party which opposed the readmission of repentant apostates. Novatian led a schism and was consecrated as a rival bishop of Rome. A rigorist Novatianist church lingered on until Augustine's day. The importance of the schism was that it forced the Church to clarify its practice with regard to the forgiveness of sins in this crucial area.
49. The Donatist practice of repeating baptism in the case of any Catholic who transferred to their sect was a sore subject. Augustine frequently points out the illogicality of the Donatist position.
50. Augustine elaborates on this idea when commenting on that psalm; see *Exposition of Psalm* 67, 39.
51. *Excludat.*

by God's word. And what is meant by *may be clearly identified*? The same thing as *may be pressed out*. And how does that come about? Because of the heretics. Why do I say, "Because of the heretics"? Because of that *batch of bulls among the cows of the peoples*. This is how the schismatics have been banished by the wrath of his countenance, while to us *his heart has come near*.

God's word seems hard, but it is tender to believers

23. *God's words are smoother than oil, but they are javelins*. Some of the sayings in Scripture used to seem hard while they were still obscure; but once explained they are gentle and tender. The first heresy among Christ's disciples arose from the apparent hardness of something he had said. He had warned them, *No one can have life except by eating my flesh and drinking my blood*;[52] but they did not understand, and said to each other, *This is a hard saying; who could listen to it?* Complaining how hard it was, they withdrew from his company, and he was left with the twelve. When these pointed out to him that the ones who had left had been scandalized by his words, he asked them, *Do you want to go away too?* And Peter answered, *You have the word of eternal life. To whom should we go?* (Jn 6:61.68.69).

Take this to heart, we beg you. Be like little children and learn childlike piety. Did Peter understand then the mystery concealed in that saying of the Lord? No, he did not yet understand it, but in his childlike docility he believed. If some saying is hard, then, and not yet intelligible, let it be hard to the unbeliever, but tender to you because of your piety. When eventually it is made plain it will seem to you like oil, soaking right into your bones.

Verse 23. The power of the gentle words

24. Now it seems as though Peter has something further to say to us.[53] After those others had been, as he thought, scandalized by the hardness of the Lord's words, he asserted, *You have the word of eternal life. To whom should we go?* But now he adds, *Cast your care upon the Lord, and he will nourish you*. You are but a child, and you do not yet understand the mysteries concealed in these words. Bread is withheld from you, perhaps, and you still need milk as your food.[54] Do not disdain the breast, for it will bring you to the stage of being able to eat the food you cannot manage yet. Remember how many hard sayings have been softened, on the occasion of the heretics' departure. God's hard sayings have become softer than oil, yet they are javelins too. They have armed the preachers of the gospel: these very words are shot into the heart of any and every hearer by preachers who press home the message in season and out of season.[55]

---

52. See Jn 6:54.
53. In the following lines Augustine seems to be thinking of 1 Pt 5:7; 2:2.
54. See 1 Cor 3:2.
55. See 2 Tm 4:2.

By this preaching, by these arrow-sharp words, human hearts are struck and brought to love peace. The sayings were hard, and they have become tender; in so doing they have lost nothing of their strength, but have turned into javelins. *God's words are smoother than oil, but they*, yes, these very words which seem gentle, *they are javelins.*

But as for you, perhaps you are not yet grown up enough to be armed with these javelins, and the obscure, hard points in the saying have not yet become luminous to you? Then *cast your care upon the Lord, and he will nourish you.* Cast yourself upon the Lord. And, given that you want to cast yourself upon the Lord, make sure that no one else usurps the Lord's place. *Cast your care upon the Lord.* There was a certain mighty warrior for Christ who refused to let the cares of the little ones be cast upon himself; listen to what he says: *Was Paul crucified for you, or were you baptized in Paul's name?* (1 Cor 1:13). What else was he urging, if not *Cast your care upon the Lord, and he will nourish you*? But today it happens that some little one wants to cast his or her care upon the Lord, and some fellow comes along and says, "I'll take you on." He is like someone who meets a ship in distress and says, "I'll look after you." You must answer, "It's the harbor I'm making for, not the reef." *Cast your care upon the Lord, and he will nourish you.* You will see that the harbor does indeed welcome you, for God *will not allow the righteous one to waver for ever.* You seem to waver on the sea of this world, but the harbor is there for you. Just make sure that you do not break loose from the anchor[56] before you reach harbor. An anchored ship does toss about, but she is not driven far from the shore, nor will she be subject to turbulence for ever, even though she must suffer it for a time now. Some words we heard earlier refer to this present wavering: *I am deeply saddened in my ordeal, and very distressed. I was waiting for him who would save me from faintheartedness in the storm.* It is a storm-tossed person who speaks here, but one that will not waver for ever. He is lashed to the anchor, and the anchor is his hope. God *will not allow the righteous one to waver for ever.*

Verse 24. Donatists are bound for the pit as perpetrators of violence and deceit

25. Now what about the schismatics? *You will consign them to the pit of corruption, O God.* The pit of corruption is the same thing as the engulfing darkness. The psalm declares that *you will consign them to the pit of corruption* because when one blind person guides another, both fall into the ditch.[57] When God is said to lead them into the pit of corruption, it implies not that he is the author of their guilt, but that he is the judge of their iniquities. God has delivered them to the lusts of their own hearts[58]

---

56. See Heb 6:19.
57. See Mt 15:14; Lk 6:39.
58. See Rom 1:24.

because they loved darkness rather than light, and blindness, not vision. The Lord Jesus has shed his light on the entire world, and these people should be singing in unison with the whole world, because *no one can hide from his heat* (Ps 18:7(19:6)). Yet they have crossed over from the whole to a part, from the body to a wound, from live belonging to amputation; so what else can their fate be, but to go down to the pit of decay?

26. *Men of blood and deceit.* The psalm calls them *men of blood* because they kill; but if only it were corporal and not spiritual death that they meted out! When blood flows from a body we see it and shudder, but does anyone see the heart that bleeds when baptism is repeated? It takes a different kind of eyes to see those deaths. Not that the Circumcellions, armed and widespread as they are, hold their hand from visible killings;[59] and if we have visible killings in mind, they certainly are *men of blood.* If you are a peaceable person, and not bloodthirsty, look at that armed ruffian. If only he carried nothing worse than a cudgel! But no, he carries a sling,[60] he carries an axe, and stones, and a lance. Armed with these weapons the Circumcellions wander wherever they can, thirsting for the blood of the innocent, so even with regard to these visible murders they are *men of blood.* Yet we must still say, "If only these were all their killings, and they did not slaughter souls too!"

Just in case the *men of blood and deceit*[61] accuse us of misunderstanding this phrase, *men of blood,* by referring it to slayers of souls, let me remind them that they themselves so characterized their own Maximianists.[62] In the course of their condemnation of the Maximianists the Donatists included the following words in the decree of their own council: *Their feet are swift to shed the blood* of the messengers.[63] *Chagrin and unhappiness beset their ways, and they know not the path to peace.*[64] The Donatists made this accusation against the Maximianists, but I put this question to

---

59. The Circumcellions were a violent branch of the Donatists.
60. *Fundibalum,* literally a slinging or hurling machine, but this would hardly be portable. *Funda,* from which it is derived, usually means a sling, but can also mean the missile launched from it, the stone; hence *fundibalum* could mean the leather strap which holds and fires the stone.
61. The main Donatist party, as opposed to the Circumcellions.
62. The Maximianists broke away from the main body of the Donatists, constituting a schism within a schism. See Augustine's extensive treatment of the Acts of the Maximianist Council of Cebarsussa in his *Exposition 2 of Psalm 36,* 19–23.
63. *Annuntiatorum,* "of the announcers." This last word is not present in the decree of the Donatist Council of Bagai (A.D. 394) as quoted by Augustine in his *Answer to Cresconius* 4,4,5.
64. Ps 13(14):3. The Greek text of this psalm, from which the African Psalter used by Augustine and his opponents derived, contains extra words not found in the Hebrew. It is quoted by Paul with the extra words at Rom 3:10–18.

them: when did the Maximianists shed blood in a physical sense? (Not that they would have refrained from doing so had their numbers permitted. But they were too much afraid, being so few, so it was more a case of their suffering violence at the hands of others than of doing anything of the kind themselves.) So now I question any Donatist: in your council you applied to the Maximianists the words, *their feet are swift to shed blood.* Very well: show me one person on whom the Maximianists laid a finger? "No," you say, "that's not the point. Those who have cut themselves off from our united fellowship, and kill souls by leading them astray, shed blood not carnally but spiritually." Exactly! You have explained the matter very clearly. Now let your explanation show up to you what you have done yourself. *Men of blood and deceit*: your deceit lies in your trickery, your pretense, your misleading of others. What are we to say of people who *have been banished by the wrath of his countenance*? That these are the *men of blood and deceit*.

27. But what does Scripture say will happen to them? *They will not see even half their days.* What does that mean—*they will not see even half their days*? It means that they will not advance as far as they expect to; before the time they hope for is up, they will perish. They are like the partridge of which Scripture says, *Halfway through his days they will leave him, and he will be reckoned as a fool at the end.*[65] They do advance, but only for a time, for what does the apostle say? *People of ill-will and seducers go from bad to worse, in error themselves and leading others into error* (2 Tm 3:13). If one blind person leads another, both fall into the ditch.[66] They fall into *the pit of corruption* deservedly. But notice what the apostle says: *They go from bad to worse*, but not for very long; for just before this he says, *They will not last* (which means, *they will not see even half their days*), and he goes on to tell us why not: *for their lunacy will be obvious to everyone, as was that of the opponents of Moses* (2 Tm 3:9). *Men of blood and deceit will not see even half their days. But I will hope in you, O Lord.* With good reason they will not see even half their days, for they have put their trust in human resources. But I have passed beyond the days of time to the day of eternity. Why? Because I have hoped in you, O Lord.

---

65. See Jer 17:11. Part of the verse is omitted here, which leaves the comparison obscure. The image given by Jeremiah is that of a partridge hatching eggs not her own, like a person who amasses riches but will have to leave them at his premature death.
66. See Mt 15:14; Lk 6:39.

Exposition of Psalm 142

Synopsis

The Psalm title relates to David's conflict with his son, Absalom. But it's also a prophecy about the other David, our Lord Jesus, and the persecution he endured from his "son" (1–2).

The Book of Revelation speaks of a child born of a woman clothed with the sun, with the moon under her feet. This is the glorious city of God that tramples the mortality of the flesh underfoot. Christ was born to suffer in the flesh for us, but this same Christ is also the Word of God, equal to the Father. Christ deigned both to die for us and to speak in us: he's the head, we're the body, two in one flesh, two in one voice. Fix this great mystery in your minds! (3)

Judas, a "son of the bridegroom," persecuted the bridegroom. What about wicked "children" who seem to be one with us, and yet swear open hostility? We pray to God to hear us "in your justice," and prayer is heard because of God's grace and not our merit. Self-righteous people like to credit good to themselves and evil to God, but that's backward. The Psalmist is very different, a humble suppliant who is fearful of judgment and hopeful of mercy. He's right that no one living is just; even the apostles prayed, *Forgive us our debts* (4–6).

Christ prays in the Psalm, *The enemy has persecuted my soul*. Judas persecuted our head, but his body endures similar affliction, "for one Judas has been succeeded by another." All Judases think that Christ is *like the dead of this world*, though the Lord took clean flesh in order to cleanse us. He entered the dark tomb, but as one *free among the dead*, that is, he was free so that he might free others from sin (7–8). Remember his anguish before he died; he said, *My soul is sorrowful*. But notice the movement here between the head and the members. "We too were there. He took over into himself our lowly body and transformed it, configuring it to his own glorious body" (9). That body of Christ, justified by grace, clinging to God and meditating on his works, finds that all good comes from grace—even good works. True, you must "work out your own salvation in fear in trembling," but only because "God is at work in you" (10).

The Psalmist is *waterless earth* seeking rain, for "I cannot irrigate myself." If I'm already *poor in spirit*, he prays, then "remember that we are dust." Why does God delay? Is it to ward off pride? Once I boasted of plenty, he continues, and tried to establish my own justice; but no longer. *Do not turn your face away*, lest I sink without a trace in the lake of lost faith (11–13). In this nighttime let me hope for mercy in the morning at time's end. Until then, show me the way to walk.

Ancient prophecy shows that path, so let's "walk toward the prophecies, walk toward the words of God." The path leads to Christ. "Walk toward the form of a servant and you will be led to the divine nature of the Lord" (14–15). Humanity once fled from God in Eden but now flees to God in Christ. One escapes enemies only after battling an invisible foe—not Judas but the one who filled Judas. How many Judases has Satan filled! (16) But here's a magnificent confession and rule for life: *Teach me, that I may do your will*. This is a prayer to the one whose Word first created and then recreated us. Notice the emphasis on our need of grace: drink this in and take it to heart! God's good Spirit leads us by mercy that we've not deserved (17–18).

Augustine's Text of Psalm 142

(1) For David himself, when his own son was hunting him down.
   Hear my prayer, O Lord, let your ears be open to my petition.
   In your truth, hear me in your justice.
(2) Do not contend in judgment with your servant;
   No living person will be found righteous in your sight.
(3) The enemy has persecuted my soul, and grounded my life on the earth.
   They assigned me a place in the dark regions, like the dead of this world.
(4) My spirit was dismayed within me;
   Within me my heart was distressed.
(5) I called to mind the days of old, and meditated on all your works;
   I pondered on the works of your hands.
(6) To you I stretched out my hands;
   My soul is like waterless earth to you.
(7) Make haste to hear me, O Lord, for my spirit has fainted away.
   Do not turn your face away from me,
   Or I shall be like those who go down into the lake of the dead.
(8) Make your mercy known to me in the morning, for I have hoped in you.

Show me, Lord, the way in which I must walk, for to you I have lifted up my soul.

(9) Deliver me from my enemies, O Lord, for I have fled to you.

(10) Teach me, that I may do your will, for you are my God.

Your good Spirit will lead me straight forward into the right country.

(11) For the glory of your name, O Lord, you will give me life, in accordance with your justice.

You will lead my soul out of its distress,

(12) And in your mercy you will steer my enemies toward their destruction.

You will do away with all who trouble my soul, because I am your servant.

Exposition

A Sermon to the People[1]

Verse 1. David, persecuted by his son, foreshadows Christ

1. In the measure that the Lord grants me I am going to speak to you, beloved, about the psalm we have just sung. Yesterday we dealt with a short psalm,[2] but since we had plenty of time we were able to speak on it at some length, brief though it was. Today's psalm is somewhat longer, so we must not linger over individual verses, or the Lord may not make it possible for us to treat of the whole.

2. The psalm's title is *For David himself, when his own son was hunting him down.* We know about these events from the Books of the Kingdoms.[3] Absalom[4] arose as an enemy to his father, stirring up not only civil war against him but domestic strife as well. Yet David was not cast down in any spirit of impious resentment. Humbled and reverent, he accepted his misfortunes as a discipline imposed by the Lord, endured the healing pain, refused to meet iniquity with corresponding iniquity, and prepared his heart

---

1. Apparently preached at Carthage on 15 September, the day after the feast of Saint Cyprian. According to Perler, the most likely year is 416. But P.-M. Hombert prefers the year 412. In section 1 Augustine says that he preached on a short psalm the previous day; according to Hombert, this would have been Psalm 86. Thus the *Expositions of Psalms* 85, 86, and 142 would have been preached on 13, 14, and 15 September 412. See Pierre-Marie Hombert, *Nouvelles recherches de chronologie augustinienne* (Paris 2000).
2. Possibly Ps 86; see preceding note.
3. In our usage, 1 Samuel and 2 Samuel and 1 Kings and 2 Kings. The events to which Augustine is referring are narrated in 2 S 15–18.
4. This name, as usual in the *Expositions*, is given as Abessalon.

to follow the will of the Lord. David behaved in a praiseworthy manner, but we must recognize in him another David, another strong-handed man (that is what the name means), our Lord Jesus Christ. Those events of long ago prefigured what was to happen later, and there is no need for us to spend much time reminding you about them; you have heard the stories many times and remember them well. Let us rather look for our Lord and savior Jesus Christ in this psalm. The psalm is a prophecy, and in it he foretells himself. Through the medium of what happened long ago he proclaims what was to occur in our time. In the prophets he was proclaiming himself, for he is the Word of God, and everything they said was full of the Word of God. The prophets were full of Christ, and Christ it was whom they announced. They went ahead of him who was to come, but he did not desert his forerunners.

Let us try to understand how Christ too was persecuted by his own son. Yes, he did have children. He spoke of them when he declared, *The bridegroom's children cannot fast as long as the bridegroom is with them, but when the bridegroom has left them, then his children will fast* (Mt 9:15). From this we gather that the bridegroom's children were the apostles, and among them was a devil,[5] the persecutor, Judas. So Christ is going to preach to us in this psalm about his passion. Now let us listen to it.

Christ, the head of the body

3. We want you to focus your attention on a vital point, beloved. We are not teaching you something of which you are ignorant but reminding you of what you know already. Our Lord and savior Jesus Christ is the head of his body. He, the one mediator between God and humanity, the human Jesus,[6] was born of a virgin in a solitary place, as we learn from the Book of Revelation. I think this mention of solitude is a way of saying that he alone was born of a virgin. The woman bore him to rule his people with an iron rod.[7]

But this woman is the ancient city of God, of which a psalm sings, *Glorious things are spoken of you, city of God* (Ps 86(87):3). This city originates from Abel, as the wicked city derives from Cain.[8] This city of God is therefore very ancient. Tolerating the earth, its hope is fixed on heaven. It is called both Jerusalem and Zion. A psalm says of him who was born in Zion yet is also Zion's founder, *Zion, my mother, a man will say.* Who is this man? *He who was made man in her; the Most High himself established her* (Ps 86(87):5). He was indeed made man in Zion. As man he was made

---

5. See Jn 6:71.
6. See 1 Tm 2:5.
7. See Rv 12:5–6.
8. See Gn 4:17, and all the story in Gn 4. Compare *Exposition of Psalm* 86, which has affinities with the present exposition; see note 1 above.

lowly, yet all the while he was the Most High who established the city in which he was himself made man.

This is why the woman who bore him is said to have been clothed with the sun,[9] the very sun of righteousness[10] unknown to the godless, who will lament at the end, *No doubt of it, we strayed from the path of truth. On us the light of righteousness did not shine, nor did the sun rise for us* (Wis 5:6). Evidently there is a sun of righteousness that does not dawn upon the godless, though Scripture also tells us that God makes his sun rise over good and evil alike.[11] This woman who was clothed with the sun was pregnant with a male child and about to give birth. Her child was he who had founded Zion, and the woman was the city of God, protected by the radiant light of him whom she was bearing in the flesh. With good reason, too, was she depicted with the moon under her feet, because in her strength and holiness she trampled on the mortality of flesh which, moonlike, waxes and wanes.

Our Lord Jesus Christ is both head and body, and, having deigned to die for us, he has also willed to speak in us, for he has made us his members. Sometimes he speaks in the person of his members and at other times in his own person, as our head. He has some things to say without us, things which can come only from him, but without him we cannot say anything. The apostle desires *to fill up what is lacking to the sufferings of Christ in my own flesh* (Col 1:24). He speaks of *what is lacking* not to his own sufferings but *to the sufferings of Christ*, yet he prays that he may fill up this deficit not in the flesh of Christ but *in my own flesh*. He says that Christ is still suffering; but Christ cannot suffer in his own flesh, now glorified in heaven. Christ therefore suffers in my flesh, as it still struggles on earth. This is exactly what the apostle is telling us: Christ suffers in my flesh. *Now I live my own life no longer; it is Christ who lives in me* (Gal 2:20). If Christ himself were not truly suffering in his members, his faithful disciples, Saul could not possibly have been persecuting on earth the Christ who was enthroned in heaven. The former persecutor explains the matter clearly in another passage: *As your body is a unit and has many members, and yet all the members of the body, many though they be, are one body, so too is Christ* (1 Cor 12:12). Note that he does not say, "That is how it is with Christ and his body," but, *So too is Christ*. He says, *The body is a unit and has many members; so too is Christ*. All of it is simply Christ, and because the whole is Christ, the head shouted from heaven, *Saul, Saul, why are you persecuting me?* (Acts 9:4).

Hold onto this truth and imprint it indelibly on your minds like well-educated members of the Church, soundly instructed in the Catholic faith. Then you will understand that the Christ who is both head and body is the same Christ who is the only-begotten Word of God, equal to the Father.

---

9. See Rv 12:1.
10. See Ml 4:2.
11. See Mt 5:45.

And then too you will see how wondrous is the grace that has brought you so close to God that he who is one with his Father has willed to be one with us. How do we know he is one with the Father? Because he said, *I and the Father are one* (Jn 10:30). And how do we know he is one with us? Because *scripture does not say, To his descendants, as though indicating many, but as to one only, And to your seed, which is Christ* (Gal 3:16). Perhaps someone may raise an objection: "Well, yes, Christ is the descendant of Abraham. But that doesn't prove that we too are Abraham's offspring, does it?" Yes it does. Remember that Christ is Abraham's descendant, and, if we too are, that would mean that we are Christ. But we are Christ, for Paul has told us, *As the body is a unit and has many members; so too is Christ*, and he tells us elsewhere, *As many of you as have been baptized in Christ, have clothed yourselves in Christ* (Gal 3:27). Now we know for certain that Christ is from the stock of Abraham, for the apostle's plain words cannot be gainsaid: *And to your seed, which is Christ*. Look what he is telling us: *If you belong to Christ, you are the descendants of Abraham* (Gal 3:29).

That *they shall be two in one flesh* (Gn 2:24) is deeply mysterious, and so the apostle tells us, *This is a great mystery, but I am referring it to Christ and the Church* (Eph 5:32). Christ and the Church, two in one flesh. The fact that they are *two* points to the distance between us and the majesty of God. They are two, undeniably, for we are not the Word, we were not with God in the beginning, not through us were all things made.[12] But when we consider the flesh, there we find Christ, and in Christ we find both him and ourselves. Small wonder that we find this mystery in the psalms. There he says many things in his own name as head and many others in the name of his members, yet all of it is said as though one single individual were speaking. Wonder not that there are two with one voice, if there are two in one flesh.[13]

The enemies among our nearest and dearest

4. Now Judas was and is a "son of the bridegroom" who nonetheless persecutes the bridegroom.[14] It happened then, in Christ's time, but was that perhaps also a foreshadowing of future events? Surely it was, for the Church was destined to suffer many false brethren, so that even today the bridegroom's own son persecutes him and will do so until the end of time. *If an enemy had slandered me, I could have borne it; or if someone who hated me had talked arrogantly against me, I could surely have hidden from him* (Ps 54:13(55:12)). Who is the enemy? Who is the one who hates me? The person who sneers, "Who is this Christ? Christ was just a man

---

12. See Jn 1:1–3.
13. The foregoing paragraphs are a key to Augustine's understanding of the psalms.
14. The argument begun in section 2 is resumed here, after Augustine has established in section 3 the identification of Christ with the Church.

who wanted to stay alive and couldn't. He died in the end, however hard he tried not to. He was an outcast, crucified and killed." This is what our enemies say. Such people are my open enemies, Christ is saying. They swear open hostility to me, and it is easy to put up with them or avoid them altogether. But what am I to do about Absalom? What am I to do about Judas? What about false brethren? What about my wicked children, who are yet my children? What about people who do not contradict us by blaspheming Christ but worship Christ along with us, yet persecute Christ in us? The psalm just quoted goes on to point it out: it would have been easy enough to endure someone who plainly hated me, and anyway I could have hidden from him. You hide from a pagan when you come into a church. But what if you find the foe you fear even here? What is the use of looking for a place where you can hide from him? The apostle, groaning amid false brethren, complained of *fighting without, and fears within* (2 Cor 7:5). And the psalm speaks similarly: *If someone who hated me had talked arrogantly against me, I could surely have hidden from him. But it was you, a like-minded person* (Ps 54:13-14(55:12-13)). The psalmist called that covert enemy *a like-minded person* because he had seemed to be one with us in Christ. The Church has to contend with sufferings without and pain within, but it is forced to recognize that both those without and those within are enemies. The ones outside can be avoided more easily; those within are much harder to bear.

5. So then let our Lord say, let everyone say this who together with us constitutes the whole Christ, *Hear my prayer, O Lord, let your ears be open to my petition*. The idea contained in *hear* is echoed in *let your ears be open*; the repetition reinforces the plea. *In your truth hear me, in your justice*. Be very careful how you interpret that phrase, *in your justice*, brothers and sisters, for it includes the idea of grace, to prevent any of us imagining that our justice is our own achievement. Any justice or righteousness you have belongs to God; God gave it to you so that it might be yours. Remember what the apostle said about people who wanted to boast of their own righteousness: *I bear this witness against them: they have zeal for God*. He means the Jews. *They have zeal for God*, he says, *but it is not informed by knowledge* (Rom 10:2). What does he mean by *not informed by knowledge*? What kind of knowledge do you regard as valuable? Not, I hope, the knowledge which, on its own, merely puffs us up? That kind of knowledge does not build us up if it is not accompanied by charity.[15] No, not that, but the knowledge that is allied with charity, the teacher of humility. Let us see if that was what the Jews had. *They have zeal for God*, said Paul, *but it is not informed by knowledge*. Let him tell us what kind of knowledge it was that they lacked. *They failed to recognize the righteousness that comes from God and, by seeking to set up a righteousness of their own, they did not submit to God's righteousness* (Rom 10:3).

---

15. See 1 Cor 8:1.

What kind of people are anxious to set up a righteousness of their own? Those who, when they have done well, ascribe it to themselves but, when they have done badly, impute it to God. They are thoroughly twisted. They will get themselves straightened out only if they turn their conviction on its head. You are twisted because you attribute the wrong you have done to God and the good to yourself. You will be straight if you ascribe your wrongdoing to yourself and any good you have done to God. You, who were once godless, would not be living justly unless you had been made just by him who justifies the godless.[16]

And so the psalmist prays, *In your truth hear me, in your justice*. Not in any justice of mine; rather, *may I be found in him, not having any righteousness of my own, derived from the law, but that which comes through faith* (Phil 3:9). This is what the psalm means when it says, *In your justice, give me a hearing*, for, when I look at myself, I find nothing that is my own except sin.

Verse 2. In this life not one of us is just in God's sight

6. *Do not contend in judgment with your servant*. Who would ever want to go to law against God, except those who aspire to set up a justice of their own? *Why have we fasted and you did not notice, stinted our souls and you ignored it?* (Is 58:3) This is as good as saying, "We have done what you ordered. Why don't you give us the reward you promised?" God replies, "When you receive what I promised, it will be by my gift, just as I have already given you the means to deserve it."[17] It is undoubtedly to people as proud as these that a prophet addresses the Lord's question: *Why do you want to dispute your case at law with me? You have all abandoned me, says the Lord* (Jer 2:29). What are you doing, planning to take me to court and enumerating your own just actions? List everything that might justify you, if you like; I know your misdeeds. How can I approve any righteousness in you, where all I find is pride that I must condemn?

Very different is the plea of our psalmist, a humble supplicant in the body of Christ, who has learned from the head, from HIM WHO IS meek and humble of heart.[18] *Do not contend in judgment with your servant*, he prays. "Let us not go to law; I want no dispute with you, for, if I try to vindicate my justice, you convict me of iniquity. *Do not contend in judgment with your servant*." Why does he say this? Why is he fearful? Because *no living person will be found righteous in your sight*. By *no living person* he obviously means no one living here, living in the flesh, living a life that must end in death: no one who is born human and lives a life derived from other humans and initially from Adam, no living person who is Adam over again.

---

16. See Rom 4:5.
17. *Ut accipias quod promisi, ego dabo; ut faceres quare acciperes, ego dedi*. A terse, compact statement of Augustine's doctrine of grace.
18. See Mt 11:29.

A person living this life may possibly be justified in his own eyes but not in yours. How could he be justified in his own estimation? He might find himself pleasing, but he would be displeasing to you, for *no living person will be found righteous in your sight*. Do not contend in judgment with your servant, then, O Lord, my God. However straight I think I am, you have only to draw out a ruler from your storehouse and measure me against it, and I am shown up as crooked.

Do not contend in judgment with your servant. The psalm significantly says, *with your servant*. It is beneath your dignity to conduct a lawsuit against your servant and even more against your friend. We are indeed your friends, for you would not have said, *I tell you, my friends* (Lk 12:4), if you had not yourself raised us from servants to friends.[19] Yet though you call me friend, I confess that I am your servant. I need your mercy, I return to you like a runaway slave, I am not worthy to be called your son.[20] *Do not contend in judgment with your servant, for no living person will be found righteous in your sight*. Scripture warns us, *Praise no one before his death* (Sir 11:30), no living person at all. But what about those rams of the flock, the apostles, of whose young lambs another psalm cries, *Bring to the Lord the offspring of rams?* (Ps 28(29):1) Paul was one of these rams, yet even he acknowledges his imperfection: *Not that I have gained it already, or am already perfect* (Phil 3:12). Furthermore, brothers and sisters, there is a clinching argument by which you can grasp the point quickly: the apostles themselves learned to pray as we pray. The rule to be followed in presenting petitions was given them by the heavenly expert in law: *Pray like this* (Mt 6:9), he said. After indicating the earlier phrases of the prayer, he gave them a specific instruction—yes, even them, our foremost rams, the leaders of the sheep, the principal members of the chief shepherd and gatherer of the one flock.[21] They were taught to say, *Forgive us our debts, as we forgive those who are in debt to us* (Mt 6:12). Not even the apostles presumed to pray, "Thanks be to you, who have forgiven us our debts, as we too forgive those who are in debt to us." No, they simply prayed, *Forgive us as we forgive*. And when they used these words in their prayer they were certainly believers already; indeed, they were already apostles. The Lord's prayer is prescribed principally for believers. If the reference were to sins forgiven in baptism, it would be more fitting for catechumens only to pray, *Forgive us our debts*. But no; the apostles needed to say it. They too had to pray, *Forgive us our debts, as we forgive those who are in debt to us*. And if anyone had asked them, "Why do you make that petition? What debts have you?" they would have replied, *No living person will be found righteous* in God's sight.

---

19. Compare Jn 15:15.
20. See Lk 15:19.21.
21. Variant: "members of the chief shepherd, the gatherers of the one flock."

Verses 3–4. The downward pull, the upward call

7. *The enemy has persecuted my soul, and grounded my life on the earth.* Refer this to ourselves, certainly, but look also to the head who speaks on our behalf. *The enemy has persecuted my soul.* The devil quite obviously did persecute Christ's soul, as Judas too persecuted the soul of his master, and still today the devil is busy persecuting Christ's body, for one Judas has been succeeded by another. The prayer is still apposite today, for the Church can say, *The enemy has persecuted my soul, and grounded my life on the earth.* Notice that last phrase, *He has grounded my life on the earth.* In another passage the psalmist laments, *They bent my soul down* (Ps 56:7(57:6)), for, when anyone persecutes us, what else is he trying to do but persuade us to abandon our hope of heaven and savor only this earth, as we yield to our pursuer and love earthly things? That is undoubtedly their purpose, and they put their whole strength into achieving it. But, please God, it will not happen to us, for to us Scripture says, *If you have risen with Christ, have a taste for what is above, where Christ is seated at the right hand of God. Seek the things that are above, not the things on earth; for you are dead* (Col 3:1–3). No living person will be found righteous in God's sight. Our enemies strive by open savagery or by subterfuge to bend our life downward to the earth. Let us be on the watch against them, so that we may truly say, *Our way of life is in heaven* (Phil 3:20). But remember the psalm's warning: the enemy has tried to ground my life on the earth.

Christ, free among the dead

8. *They assigned me a place in dark regions, like the dead of this world.* You more readily hear the voice of the head in this verse and more readily understand its meaning in him. He indeed died for us, but he was not one of the *dead of this world.* Who are *the dead of this world,* and why can we say that he was not one of them? *The dead of this world* are those deservedly dead, who are receiving the due recompense for their iniquity. They have inherited death from the rootstock of sin, from the race that must confess, *Lo, I was conceived in iniquity, and in sins did my mother nourish me in the womb* (Ps 50:7(51:5)). But when Christ came he took flesh from a virgin, taking to himself not the iniquity inherent in our flesh but clean flesh with power to cleanse ours. People who believed him to be a sinner naturally reckoned him to be one of *the dead of this world.* But in another psalm he declared, *I was paying the price, though I had committed no robbery* (Ps 68:5(69:4)), and in the gospel he claimed, *Now the prince of this world is coming*—the sovereign over death, the prompter to evil, the exactor of punishment—*now he is coming, and he will find nothing in me* (Jn 14:30). What did he mean by *he will find nothing in me*? He will find no guilt in me, nothing for which I ought to die. Yet, he continued, *So that the world may know that I am doing my Father's will, rise, let us leave here* (Jn 14:31). In dying, I am doing my Father's will. I do not deserve to die;

I have done nothing to merit death. But I am going to meet death so that those who by their sins deserved to die may be freed through the death of one who is innocent.

They assigned me a place in dark regions, like the darkness of the underworld, the darkness of the tomb, the darkness of the passion itself. There they placed him *like the dead of this world*; there they left him who asserts, *I have become like a man bereft of help, free among the dead* (Ps 87:5-6(88:4-5)). Free? Why free? Because *whoever commits sin is the slave of sin* (Jn 8:34). Clearly he could not free others from their fetters if he were not free himself. Being free, he slew death, broke bonds, and captured captivity when they assigned him a place in dark regions, like *the dead of this world.*

We were there

9. *My spirit was dismayed within me.* Remember his cry, *My soul is sorrowful to the point of death* (Mk 14:34). Hearken to a single voice here. Is it not obvious that there[22] is movement between head and members, members and head? *My spirit was dismayed within me,* he says, and we cannot but be reminded of the words: *My soul is sorrowful to the point of death.* Yet we too were there. He took over into himself our lowly body and transformed it, configuring it to his own glorious body.[23] Our old self was nailed to the cross with him.[24]

Within me my heart was distressed. He says *within me*; the distress was not in others, for they all abandoned me. All who had been close to me ran away and changed their minds about what I was, because they saw me dying. The robber did better than they did: he believed[25] when they defected.

---

22. Some witnesses, by omitting the *non*, convey the sense, "to a single voice, though it is not obvious, is it, that there...."
23. See Phil 3:21. The expression, *transfiguravit in se* ("he took [us] over into himself and transformed us"), is a key phrase in Augustine's theology of the *totus Christus*. Compare *nos transfiguravit in se* (*Exposition of Psalm* 60,3); *transfiguravit in se suos* (*Exposition 2 of Psalm* 32,2); *praefigurans... et transformans in se nos ipsos* (*Exposition 1 of Psalm* 68,3). Christ "took us over into himself" or "incorporated us into his own person." The ideas of intercession and exemplary causality are certainly included, but Augustine goes further. His conviction is that "we were there" when Christ prayed, suffered, struggled, was tempted, and obeyed the Father's will. So, in the present section, *illic nos eramus*. There are other examples of the same assertion; compare *Exposition 2 of Psalm* 21,3 and *Exposition 2 of Psalm* 30,3.
24. See Rom 6:6.
25. See Lk 23:40-43.

Verse 5. All is grace

10. Now it is the turn of the members to speak. *I called to mind the days of old.* Could Christ, through whom every day has been created, be said to call to mind the days of old? No, this is the body speaking, this is everyone who, having been justified by his grace, clings to him in charity and dedicated humility: "*I called to mind the days of old, and meditated on all your works,* for you have made everything good, and nothing could have existed had you not created it. I surveyed your creation; I sought the artist in his work, the creator in all his creatures." Why did he do this? To what purpose? Surely in order to understand that whatever good there was in himself was created by God, lest, being ignorant of God's justice and trying to establish his own, he might fail to acknowledge himself as subject to the justice of God?[26] And having understood this, would he not have taken as his own the opening verse of our psalm, confessing that *in your truth and in your justice* all this was done? In all the works of God, and in his meditation on all these divine works, he instills into our minds the truth about God's grace. He reminds us about grace, and he glories in having found grace, that grace whereby we have been saved gratis. For indeed, *by grace* we *have been saved* (Eph 2:8). How can you boast about any justice of your own? How can you extol yourself and ignore the justice of God? Perhaps you did make some contribution to your own salvation, but did you have any hand in your coming to be human in the first place? Turn your eyes toward him who created your very life, the author of your being, your righteousness and your salvation. Meditate on the works of his hands, because then you will discover that even the justice that is in you is part of his handiwork. Listen to the apostle inculcating this lesson: *It does not come from works, lest anyone boast* (Eph 2:9). Have we nothing to show, then? To be sure we have, but notice how the apostle continues: *We are his own handiwork*, he says. *We are his own handiwork*—but was he perhaps referring only to our human nature and calling that God's handiwork? By no means. He was speaking about our works: *Not from works, lest anyone boast.* But let us not trust to guesswork, let the apostle make the point himself: *We are his own handiwork, created in Christ Jesus for good works* (Eph 2:10).

Do not claim any work as your own, then, except insofar as you are a bad worker. Turn away from your own work and look to the work of him who made you. He forms you; now let him reform what he formed and you marred. He acted to bring you into being; now he acts to make you good, if good you are. *Work out your own salvation in trembling and fear* (Phil 2:12), Scripture enjoins. But if we work out our own salvation, why in fear and why in trembling if the work is within our own power? Read on, and you will see why you must act in fear and trembling: *For it is God who is*

---

26. See Rom 10:3.

at work in you, inspiring both will and work, for his own good purpose (Phil 2:13). Keep yourself in fear and trembling, so that our artificer may enjoy working in a deep valley,[27] for he who executes judgment among the nations and rebuilds the ruins[28] works too in us when we are cast down. *I pondered on the works of your hands.* As I contemplated your works, what I saw was this: that there can be nothing good in us, unless it comes from you who made us.

Verses 6–7. Thirsting for God, the psalmist begs for grace and for God's benign regard

11. What did I do next, when I had seen that every good gift, every perfect endowment, comes from above, that it comes down from the Father of lights, with whom there is no variation, no play of changing shadow?[29] When I had seen this I turned away from the botched work for which I was responsible in myself, and *to you I stretched out my hands.* He says, *To you have I stretched out my hands; my soul is like waterless earth to you.* Rain on me, he prays, that I may yield good fruit, for *the Lord will give sweetness* (Ps 84:13(85:12)) so that our earth may produce its expected harvest. *To you have I stretched out my hands; my soul is like waterless earth to you*—not to me but *to you.* I can thirst for you, but I cannot irrigate myself. *My soul is like waterless earth to you,* for it thirsts for the living God.[30] *When shall I come?* (Ps 41:3(42:2)) Only when he comes first to me. My soul thirsts for the living God, for it is *like waterless earth to you.* The sea rises and floods the land; it is immense and its waters roar, but it is salt and bitter.[31] Then the waters were confined to their place and my dry soul was exposed.[32] Irrigate it, I beg, for it is *like waterless earth to you.*

12. *Make haste to hear me, O Lord.* Why this delay when I am so thirsty? Is it because you mean to inflame my thirst still more? Are you withholding your rain so that when it comes I may gulp it eagerly and not spit out anything you pour into me? If that is your reason for delaying, give it to me now, I beg, for *my soul is like waterless earth to you. Make haste to hear me, O Lord, for my spirit has fainted away.* Let your Spirit fill me, for my own spirit has fainted away; this is why you must hear me quickly: *My spirit has fainted away.* I have already been made poor in spirit; make me blessed in the kingdom of heaven.[33] If anyone's own spirit is alive in him, that person is likely to be proud, because he will use his own spirit to exalt himself against God. It will be very good for such persons if a prophecy

---

27. See *Exposition of Psalm* 126,6.
28. See Ps 109(110):6.
29. See Jas 1:17.
30. See Ps 41:3(42:2).
31. An image of the world without grace.
32. See Gn 1:9.
33. See Mt 5:3.

elsewhere in Scripture is verified in them: *When you withdraw their breath, they faint, and return to the dust whence they came* (Ps 103(104):29), for then they will confess, *Remember that we are dust* (Ps 102(103):14). Once they have made that confession, *that we are dust*, they will be disposed to pray, *My soul is like waterless earth to you*. What is more truly waterless earth than dust? But *make haste to hear me, O Lord*, rain upon me, give me strength, so that I may not be *dust which the wind sweeps away from the face of the earth* (Ps 1:4). *Make haste to hear me, O Lord, for my spirit has fainted away*. So urgent is my need that I cannot wait. You have taken my own spirit away to leave me faint, reduced to my native dust, and pleading that *my soul is like waterless earth to you*. Deal with me now as that other psalm goes on to prophesy: *You will breathe forth your Spirit and they will be created, and you will make the face of the earth new* (Ps 103(104):30). If a new creation is brought about in Christ, all that belongs to the old has passed away.[34] In your Spirit all old things have passed; in your Spirit all are made new.

13. *Do not turn your face away from me.* When I was proud, you did turn away. Time was when I was affluent, and in my affluence I was high and mighty. *I said in the midst of my plenty, I shall be unmoved for ever* (Ps 29:7(30:6)). That was my belief, and I boasted *in the midst of my plenty, I shall be unmoved for ever*, because I was unaware of your righteousness and was trying to establish my own.[35] *In your kindly will* you, Lord, *added strength to my beauty* (Ps 29:8(30:7)). *In the midst of my plenty I said, I shall be unmoved*, yet whatever wealth I had was your gift to me. And to prove that it had come to me from you, *you turned your face away from me, and I became distraught* (Ps 29:8(30:7)). After that distraught condition in which I found myself because you had turned away your face, after the dismay of my spirit and the distress of my heart within me, I became like waterless earth to you. *Do not turn your face away*. You turned away from me when I was proud; turn your gaze back now upon one who is humble. *Do not turn your face away from me, or I shall be like those who go down into the lake of the dead*. What does this mean, *like those who go down into the lake of the dead*? Scripture warns, *A person devoid of reverence goes deep into sin and is defiant* (Prv 18:3). The ones who go down into the lake of the dead are those who lose even the will to confess. Against such a fate the psalmist prays, *Do not let the pit close its mouth over me* (Ps 68:16(69:15)). A depth like this is often called a lake in Scripture. When a sinner has plumbed such depths, he is defiant. In what sense? He no longer believes in any divine providence; or, if he does believe in it, he does not think it extends to himself. He gives himself unrestrained license to sin; having lost hope of pardon, he gives free rein to iniquity. He does not say, "I will return to God, so that he may turn back to me." He does not hear the

---

34. See 2 Cor 5:17.
35. See Rom 10:3.

prophetic words, *Turn back to me, and I will turn back to you* (Ml 3:7), for he has plunged into the depths of evil and can show nothing but contempt. As Scripture warns us, *No confession can be made by a dead person: he is as though nonexistent* (Sir 17:26). Let this not be my fate. *Do not turn your face away from me, or I shall be like those who go down into the lake of the dead.*

Verse 8. Mercy in the morning; while night lasts, walk toward the lamp of the divine scriptures

14. *Make your mercy known to me in the morning, for I have hoped in you.* See, I am still in the night, but I have hoped in you, and I will go on hoping until the sin that belongs to night has passed away.[36] As Peter reminds us, *We have the trusty message of the prophets to rely on, and you will do well to attend to it, for it is like a lamp burning in a dark place until day breaks and the morning star rises in your hearts* (2 Pt 1:19). By *morning* the psalmist means the era after the end of the world, when we shall see what in this world we believe. *In the morning you will hear my voice. In the morning I will stand before you, and contemplate* (Ps 5:4–5(3)). *Make your mercy known to me in the morning, for I have hoped in you,* because *if we hope for what we do not see, we wait for it in patience* (Rom 8:25). The night demands patience, the day will give us joy. *Make your mercy known to me in the morning, for I have hoped in you.*

15. But what about our time here, before morning breaks? It is not enough to hope for morning;[37] we have work to do. Why need we do anything? Another psalm tells us, *On my day of trouble I searched for God; during my sojourn in the night I sought him. How did you search for him? With outstretched hands at night in his presence, and I was not disappointed* (Ps 76:3(77:2)). We must seek God in the night by using our hands, then. But how can we seek with our hands? By performing good works. Significantly, the psalm says, *In his presence,* for *when you give alms, be careful not to blow a trumpet before you, and then your Father, who sees in secret, will reward you* (Mt 6:2.4). If we must hope so firmly for the morning and endure the present night and persevere in it patiently until daybreak, what must we do while we are waiting? Beware! You do not imagine, do you, that you are going to do anything by your own powers that could earn you the right to be brought through until morning? *Show me, Lord, the way in which I must walk.* For this very reason did he light the lamp of prophecy; for this same reason did he send the Lord himself clothed in flesh as though in an earthenware covering,[38] a comparison he would use himself in his passion: *My strength was dried up like an earthenware pot* (Ps 21:16(22:15)). Walk toward the prophecies, walk toward the lamp of those predictions of

---

36. See Ps 56:2(57:1).
37. Many codices omit "for morning."
38. The earthenware lamp carried the light.

the future, walk toward the words of God. You do not yet behold the Word who was in the beginning, God with God,[39] but walk toward the form of a servant[40] and you will be led to the divine nature of the Lord. *Show me, Lord, the way in which I must walk, for to you have I lifted up my soul.* To you, not against you. *For with you is the fount of life* (Ps 35:10(36:9)), and *to you have I lifted up my soul.* I have brought it like an empty vessel to the fountain. Fill me, *for to you have I lifted up my soul.*

Verse 9. Fleeing to God from invisible enemies

16. *Deliver me from my enemies, O Lord, for I have fled to you.* Once I fled away from you, but now *I have fled to you.* Adam fled away from the face of God and hid among the trees of paradise[41] *like a slave fleeing from his master and grasping at a shadow* (Job 7:2, LXX). He fled from the face of his Lord and found shadow, for into that shadow among the trees of paradise his flight took him. Woe betide any of his descendants who have persisted in hugging the shadow, for later they may say, *All things have passed away like a shadow* (Wis 5:9).

Deliver me from my enemies. I am not thinking now of human foes, for *it is not against flesh and blood that we have to struggle.* Against whom, then? *Against principalities and powers and the rulers of this world.* This world? Do they rule this world? They certainly do not rule the heavens and the earth, for they cannot hold sway over what they did not make. Scripture says, *the rulers of this world,* but what does it mean? *This world of darkness* (Eph 6:12). But what darkness is it referring to? The world of godless people, undoubtedly, for we are reminded in the sacred writings, *You were darkness once, but now you are light in the Lord* (Eph 5:8). The rulers of *this world of darkness* are those who dominate wicked people, and against them we are bound to wrestle. A formidable battle is ahead of you, for you must defeat an invisible foe. You must contend *against the rulers of this world of darkness,* the devil and his angels. Your opponents do not rule the world of which the gospel says, *The world was made by him,* but the world of which it says, *The world did not know him* (Jn 1:10).[42]

Deliver me from my enemies, O Lord, for I have fled to you. In saying, *my enemies,* the psalmist envisages not Judas but the enemy who instigated Judas. I have to endure the visible enemy, but I must do battle with an enemy I cannot see. Judas received the morsel he was offered, and Satan entered him,[43] because our David was destined to suffer persecution stirred up by his own son.[44] How many other Judases there are whom Satan has filled!

---

39. See Jn 1:1.
40. See Phil 2:7.
41. See Gn 3:8.
42. Compare similar remarks in *Exposition of Psalm* 141:14–15.
43. See Jn 13:27.
44. See section 2 above.

They receive a certain morsel unworthily to their own condemnation, for whoever eats and drinks unworthily eats and drinks judgment on himself.[45] What he or she is given is not evil, but a good thing given to a bad person turns to that person's condemnation. A good gift cannot benefit anyone who receives it in a bad way.

Deliver me from my enemies, O Lord, for I have fled to you. Where else could I flee? *Whither shall I go from your spirit? If I mount to heaven, you are there; if I sink down to hell, even there you are present.* What is left to me? *If I take wings like a dove, and fly to the uttermost parts of the sea*—if I dwell in hope at the end of the present age, he means—*even there your hand will lead me, your right hand bring me through* (Ps 138(139):7–10). *Deliver me from my enemies, O Lord, for I have fled to you.*

Verse 10. God is all things to me

17. *Teach me, that I may do your will, for you are my God.* What a magnificent confession! What a comprehensive rule of life! *For you are my God,* he says. Let me run to someone else, if it was anyone other than you who made me. You are everything to me, because *you are my God.* Shall I look for a father, in hope of an inheritance? *You are my God* and not only the giver of an inheritance: you are yourself my inheritance, for *the Lord is my portion and my inheritance* (Ps 15(16):5). Shall I look for a master who can redeem me? *You are my God.* And most of all, am I, a creature, longing to be created anew? *You are my God,* you are my creator. You created me through your Word and recreated me through your Word. You created me through the Word abiding in yourself, and you recreated me through the Word who was made flesh for us.

Teach me, that I may do your will, for you are my God. If you do not teach me, I shall do my own will, and my God will abandon me. *Teach me, that I may do your will, for you are my God,* he prays. *Teach me,* for it is not that you are my God and that I shall be my own teacher. Notice how the psalmist emphasizes our need of grace. Hold onto this truth, drink it in, take it to heart, and let no one dislodge it from your hearts, for otherwise you might have zeal for God but not a zeal well informed. You might be ignorant of God's justice and, in striving to establish your own, fail to submit to the justice of God.[46] You know what the apostle had to say about that. Pray, then, *Teach me, that I may do your will, for you are my God.*

Verses 10–12. A hurried conclusion

18. *Your good Spirit*—not my own bad spirit—*your good Spirit will lead me straight forward into the right country.* My own bad spirit has led me[47] in a crooked way, into the wrong place. What have I deserved? Have I

---

45. See 1 Cor 11:29.
46. See Rom 10:2–3.
47. Variant: "will lead me."

any good works to my account, performed without your help, which I could adduce to plead that I am worthy to be led straight forward by your Spirit? What works can I claim, what merits? Yet *for the glory of your name, O Lord, you will give me life*. Listen hard, brothers and sisters, and observe the stress he puts on grace, the grace which saves us gratis. *For the glory of your name, O Lord, you will give me life*. Another psalm prays, *Not to us, Lord, not to us, but to your name give the glory* (Ps 113(115):1). *For the glory of your name, O Lord, you will give me life, in accordance with your justice*. Not in response to any justice of mine, not because I have deserved life, but because you show mercy. If I were to put forward any merits of my own, I would be proved to deserve nothing from you except punishment. But you have torn out my demerits and engrafted your gifts. *For the glory of your name, O Lord, you will give me life in accordance with your justice. You will lead my soul out of its distress, and in your mercy you will steer my enemies toward their destruction. You will do away with all who trouble my soul, because I am your servant.*

PART V

GAZING UPWARD IN LOVE

Steps to the Top Floor

Exposition of Psalm 38

Synopsis

The title features a mysterious figure named Idithun, "one who leaps across." Remember when we treated the Step-Songs that referred to inner ascent? Idithun's leaping is also an ascent. Scripture images of leaping feet and climbing steps and flying wings all signify "the loving impulses of a good will." The divine oracles yield unmatched sweetness to those laboring to find. The delightful law of the Most High has pleasures you'll find nowhere else (1–2).

Idithun leaped across less serious people, but so regretted a few things he said that he resolved not to speak at all. Yet that only made him deaf, and his exaggerated fears blocked the possibility of his saying even good things, which only further troubled his heart (3–4). So he spoke to God: *Make known to me my end, O Lord*. Paul, though not yet perfect, ran to reach this "end." Let's run as he did, with eyes on the finish line. Idithun wants to know his "end" in order to learn what he still lacks. Scripture's "droplets of divine dew" aroused thirst for God's waters. Let's pray that we all have and keep this desire! Only a few have it, but I speak to stir it up in those who don't (5–6).

Idithun looked for *the number of my days, the number that is*. What can that be? The past no longer "is," and the future "is" not yet. We're in constant flux, all things pass constantly into non-being, and even the word "is" no longer "is" as soon as I say it. Only the New Jerusalem "is," with no death, no yesterday, no tomorrow (7–8). We live in Adam's old world, with its sin, mortality, fleeting seasons, and stages of life that barrel toward old age. Let's savor the newness of Christ so that this oldness does not frighten us. Idithun leaped toward it, but he still sighed under the load of flesh, temptation, and scandal that comes with all life "under the sun." But he longs for things not found "under the sun": faith, hope, love, kindness, and chaste fear (9–10).

Despite wearing God's image, human beings stupidly focus on empty possessions. You miser, who's your wealth for? Children? That's an excuse for injustice. Look at the irony: you're passing away, you amass wealth that passes away for others who will also pass away. Lay up your treasure in heaven! God gave it to you anyway. The best treasure is God himself (11–12).

Idithun leapt across many things, but he still prayed for forgiveness. Thus the Apostle said, *As many of you who are perfect, be wise about this*. But didn't Paul just say that he was *not* perfect but straining toward perfection? Yes, but Paul was aware that "in this life you can be perfect in no other way than by knowing you cannot be perfect" (13–14). Being both imperfect and perfect, Idithun used his suffering to make spiritual progress; he saw punishment as grace. God thus gives form to pain, and molds it to his purpose like a potter (15–17). Idithun felt fragile, *brushed away like a spider*. But strength can lead to pride. God's first grace leads us to confess our weakness, and then to confess that all our strength comes from him (18).

Life is uncertain, except for our death—and we're uncertain when it will occur! Idithun groans over that (19–20). This earthly house is only a rental; when the owner says to move on, we must do it, just as our forebears did. Idithun prays to receive cool and refreshing forgiveness *before I go away to be no more*. He thinks of being and non-being; standing between them, he fears losing being, and even more, losing the one who is called I AM. Idithun "longed to be, there where being is being at its supreme perfection" (21–22). Sorry if I've burdened you, but this was work for me too! If you were bored I would have stopped (23).

Augustine's Text of Psalm 38

(1) *To the end, Idithun's song for David himself.*

(2) I said, I will keep guard over my conduct, so that I do not offend with my tongue.

> I have set a guard over my mouth, when the sinner took his stand against me.

(3) I have become deaf, and have been humbled, and have fallen silent even from good words.

> And my pain has come back.

(4) (My heart glowed within me;)

> Fire will blaze up during my meditation.

(5) I spoke with my tongue, "Make known to me my end, O Lord,

> And make known to me the number of my days, the number that is,
>
> That I may know what I lack."

(6) How old you have made my days!

> And my substance is as nothing in your sight.
>
> Nonetheless all things are empty, for everyone who lives.

(7) Although each human being walks as an image, nonetheless his perturbation is vain.

He heaps up treasure, but does not know for whom he will be gathering it.

(8) And now, what am I waiting for? Surely for the Lord.

And all I have is continually before you.

(9) Pluck me free from all my iniquities;

You have made me an object of reproach to the unwise.

(10) I grew deaf and did not open my mouth.

Because it is you who made me,

(11) Take your scourges away from me.

(12) I fainted under your strong hand as you accused me.

You have chastised human beings for their sin, and brushed my soul away like a spider.

Yet all human anxiety in this life is pointless.

(13) Hear my prayer and my entreaty; let your ears listen for my weeping.

Do not be silent toward me, because I am no more than a lodger in your house,

And a pilgrim, like all my forebears.

(14) Forgive me, so that I may find some cool refreshment,

Before I go away to be no more.

Exposition

A Sermon preached at Carthage, at the shrine of Saint Cyprian,[1] on a Wednesday[2]

Verse 1. Learning to leap

1. The psalm which we have just sung, and are now undertaking to expound, is entitled, *To the end, Idithun's song for David himself.* We are to expect the words of someone called Idithun, then, and we must listen to what he has to tell us. If anyone among us is able to be an Idithun, that person will find and hear himself or herself in what is sung. Who the original Idithun was in that far-off generation they only can determine who lived at that time,[3] but we shall be in a better position to understand the truth he tells

---

1. *Ad mensam sancti Cypriani.*
2. Possibly in September 416.
3. Thus the CCL editors of the Latin text, amending an original "is for you to determine."

us if we look first at the interpretation of his name. As far as we have been able to discover by studying these names, which have been translated for us from Hebrew into Latin by students of sacred Scripture, Idithun means "one who leaps across." So who is this leaping speaker, and across whom did he leap? Notice that the name means not simply "one who leaps," but "one who leaps across." Does he sing while leaping across, or leap across by singing? Whichever it is, we sang a few minutes ago the song of someone leaping across; and God, to whom we sang it, must judge whether we too are people who leap across. If anyone here did leap across while singing it, let such a one rejoice to be what he has sung about; but if anyone who sang it is still stuck fast in the earth, that person must aspire to be a leaper in accord with the psalm. This psalmist whose name is Leaping Across has jumped over people who cling to the soil, people bowed down to the earth with their minds attached to what is lowest and their trust in things that pass away. Whom could he have leapt across, otherwise? He could only leap over those who stand still.

2. You know that certain psalms are called "Songs of Ascents."[4] In Greek this is quite plain, for they are called $\dot{\alpha}\nu\alpha\beta\alpha\theta\mu\tilde{\omega}\nu$. This means songs about steps, but steps up, not down. The distinction cannot be made in Latin; we just have to say "steps" without being specific, and leave it vague whether people on them are going up or down. But since no speech, no utterance, goes unheard[5] the earlier language clarifies the one that came later, and what is ambiguous in one is made clear by another. So just as in one type of psalm the singer was going up, in this one the singer is leaping across. But the leaping across is also an ascent, though not on foot or by using scaling-ladders or wings. Yet if you refer it to our inner life, feet and scaling-ladders and wings are available. If we had no feet in this inward sense, why does a person of spiritual discernment pray, *Let not the foot of pride come near me?* (Ps 35:12(36:11)) If there were no spiritual ladders, what was it that Jacob saw, with angels going up and down on it?[6] And if we could not use spiritual wings, what does a psalmist mean by the question, *Who will give me wings like a dove's? Then I will fly away and find rest?* (Ps 54:7(55:6)) When we are dealing with material matters, feet are one thing, scaling-ladders another, and wings something else again; but within ourselves feet and ladders and wings are all the loving impulses of a good will. By means of these we walk and climb and fly. When any of you hear about this man who is leaping across, and you aspire to imitate him, you must not think to leap across ditches in a bodily sense by leaping lightly into the air, or to fly over some highish obstacle by jumping. But I am talking now in bodily

---

4. The group of psalms 119–133 (120–134) was traditionally referred to as "Gradual Psalms" or "Songs of Ascents," probably because they were used by pilgrims "going up" to Jerusalem for festivals.
5. See Ps 18:4(19:3–4).
6. See Gn 28:12.

terms because there is a sense in which a spiritual person does leap even across ditches. Another psalm declares, *Burnt up by fire and dug out, they will perish at your frowning rebuke* (Ps 79:17(80:16)). But what are these things that are *burnt up by fire and dug out*, these things that will perish at the Lord's *frowning rebuke*? Sins, obviously. Anything that has been set alight by disordered greed is burnt up by fire, and whatever is dictated by supine fear is like a ditch dug out. All sins spring from one or other of these two, greed or fear. Spiritual persons must therefore leap across all the things that could trap them on earth. Let all of us erect our ladders and spread our wings, and see whether we recognize ourselves here.

But we should more truly say that by the grace of the Lord many people do recognize themselves in these words: people who, detached from this world and all the delights it offers, choose to live rightly, even as they live here amid spiritual joys. Where will they find such joys, while still walking the earth? Surely from the divine oracles, from the word of God, from some parable in Holy Scripture which they have studied and pondered, from the sweetness of finding after the labor of the search. There are indeed good and holy pleasures in these books, pleasures that are not to be found in gold and silver, feasting and luxury, hunting and fishing, games and jesting, frivolous theatrical entertainments, or the high offices which people try to seize, though they crumble to nothing. It is not the case that true enjoyment is to be derived from all these, and none from the sacred books; quite the contrary. A soul that has leapt over these baser things and found itself delighted by the Holy Scriptures is compelled to say, *The unrighteous have told me titillating tales, but they cannot compare with your law, O Lord,*[7] and it says this confidently, knowing it to be true. Let our Idithun come forward and leap across people who still look to the base things for their pleasure; let him or her take delight in the higher things and find joy in the word of the Lord, in the delightful law of the Most High.

But is there more to say? Must we make yet another leap, from here to somewhere else again? If we desire to leap across, is there still a further place to which we must leap? We need to listen to what our psalmist has to say, for it seems to me that he is still leaping across the place where he was accustomed to dwell in the divine oracles, where he learned the lessons we are about to hear.

Verse 2. No one avoids all faults in speaking; the hearers must take it in good part

3. *I said, I will keep guard over my conduct, so that I do not offend with my tongue.* One can well believe that in the course of reading, discussion, preaching, administering reproof, encouraging people, or while engaged

---

7. Ps 118(119):85. Augustine had heard this verse from the symbolic figure of Continence, who encouraged him as he stood on the brink of decision; see his *Confessions* VIII,11,27.

in work, or beset by human problems, living as a man among fellow men and women, the psalmist had said some things he regretted and admitted that some expressions had fallen from his lips that he wished to recall, but could not. This is likely to have been the case even though he was already leaping across people who did not delight in the same things as he did, for it is difficult for anyone not to slip up and sin with the tongue. As Scripture says, *If anyone has not sinned with his tongue, he is a perfect man.*[8] The moist saliva that surrounds the tongue makes it slippery. The psalmist was aware how difficult it is for a person who is obliged to speak to say nothing in his discourse that he will afterwards regret having said, so he felt disgusted about these sins and sought to avoid them. This very Leaper-Across felt how hard it was, so no one who is not yet leaping across ought to pass judgment on me. Let any such critic make the leap across and experience for himself or herself what I mean; then such a person will be both a witness to the truth and a child of truth.

In the light of this experience Idithun had made up his mind not to talk, in order to avoid saying anything he might wish unsaid. His opening words indicate his resolution: *I said, I will keep guard over my conduct, so that I do not offend with my tongue.* Well said, Idithun: keep guard over your conduct, and do not offend with your tongue; weigh what you are going to say, scrutinize it, refer it to the truth within you, and then bring it forth to the hearer outside. No doubt you often try to do this[9] amid the turmoil of business and when minds are preoccupied, but the soul itself is weakened and weighed down by the corruptible body,[10] and although it wishes both to hear and to speak—to hear within and to speak outside—it is sometimes troubled by the effort that speaking demands and fails through insufficient attention and inadvertence, and says something that should not be said. A surer remedy against these failures is silence; for a sinner will stand up, someone notorious for some particular sin, someone proud and malicious, and will hear the Leaper speaking. He will take careful note of the words, and set traps. It is hardly possible that anyone with this intention will be unable to find anything that has not been fittingly said, and as he listens he does not make allowances, but cavils out of ill-will. Confronted with people like this Idithun had chosen to say nothing as he leapt over them, so he sang of his intention: *I said, "I will keep guard over my conduct, so that I do not offend with my tongue.* As long as I am liable to be ensnared by those who misrepresent me, or as long as they snatch at me, even though I am not ensnared, *I will keep guard over my conduct, so that I do not offend with my tongue.* Although I have leapt beyond earthly pleasures, although fleeting desires for temporal gain do not hold me fast,

---

8. Jas 3:2. The last word in Augustine's Latin version is *vir*, denoting a male person. So too the Greek behind it, ἀνήρ.
9. Variants: "Who tries to...?"; "The person who observes this rule...."
10. See Wis 9:15.

although I now despise those lower things and climb to what is better, I find it enough to enjoy in God's presence the understanding I have from these better things. Why need I speak and lay myself open to their traps, why give the accusers their opportunity? So I resolved, *I will keep guard over my conduct, so that I do not offend with my tongue. I have set a guard over my mouth.*" What is the purpose of that? To defend yourself against the devout, the zealous, the faithful, the holy? Of course not. They listen with a mind to approve and commend, and if among the many things they find to commend there may be some they cannot approve, they are more inclined to forgive than to prepare malicious accusations. Against whom, then, do you seek to protect yourself in keeping guard over your conduct and in setting a guard over your mouth, so that you do not offend with your tongue? He explains: "It was *when the sinner took his stand against me.* He did not take his stand at my side, but *against me.* What shall I ever find to say that will satisfy him? I am speaking to a carnally-minded person about the things of the spirit, to one who sees and hears only on the outside, but is deaf and blind within. A materialist has no perception for what concerns the Spirit of God. If he were not a materialist, would he misrepresent me so? Happy the person who speaks a word into the ear of a listener,[11] not into the ear of a sinner who has taken his stand against him."

Many people of this kind stood round grinding their teeth when Christ was led like a sheep to the slaughter, when like a lamb voiceless before its shearer he did not open his mouth.[12] What can you say to the inflated, the turbulent, the vexatious, the litigious, the chatterboxes? What can you say that is holy and edifying, what can you say to them concerning religious truth that leaps beyond them,[13] when the Lord himself said even to willing hearers, people who longed to learn, who hungered for the food of truth and received it avidly, *I have many things to tell you, but at present you are not able to bear them?* (Jn 16:12) The apostle likewise said, *Not as spiritual persons could I speak to you, but only as carnal,* yet they were not to be despaired of, for all that, but nourished; for he went on to say, *As if to little children in Christ I gave you milk to drink, rather than solid food. You were not capable of it then.* Tell it to us now. *Nor are you capable even now* (1 Cor 3:1–2). Do not be in a hurry, then, to hear what you cannot yet take in, but grow up so that you may become capable of it. This is how we address a little child, who needs to be nourished with holy milk at the breast of Mother Church, and so eventually made capable of sharing the Lord's table. But what am I to say even in childish mode to a sinner who has taken his stand against me, thinking or pretending that he is suited to

---

11. See Sir 25:12.
12. See Is 53:7.
13. Variants: "What is a holy and pious person, one who from his religious faith leaps beyond them…?" and "What can you say to the holy and the pious, to anyone who from his religious faith leaps beyond them…?"

what is beyond him, who, when I say things to him that he cannot take in, will attribute it not to incapacity on his own part but to failure on mine? It is with this sinner in view, the one who has taken his stand against me, that *I have set a guard over my mouth*, declares Idithun.

Verse 3. Woe betide a preacher who falls silent

4. And what followed that decision? *I have become deaf, and have been humbled, and have fallen silent even from good words.* This leaping speaker has encountered a difficulty in the place to which he has now leapt, and he is looking for some way to leap out of it, to escape this difficulty. "I was so afraid of committing sin that I imposed silence on myself. I had resolved, *I will keep guard over my conduct, so that I do not sin with my tongue*; but in my fear of speaking *I have become deaf, and have been humbled, and have fallen silent even from good words.* Through my excessive fear of saying something bad, I have been left with nothing good to say. *I have become deaf, and have been humbled, and have fallen silent even from good words.* How did I say anything worthwhile before, except because I had heard it? *You will give me delight and gladness to hear*" (Ps 50:10(51:8)). And the bridegroom's friend stands and hears him, and is transported with joy at that voice not his own, but the bridegroom's.[14] In order to say anything true, he must first hear what he has to say. Anyone who lies, on the contrary, speaks from his own store.[15] The psalmist has suffered a sad and irksome fate, and by confessing it here he is warning us to avoid it, not imitate it. As I have said, in his exaggerated fear of saying something that might not be good, he decided to say nothing, not even good things; and because he resolved to keep quiet, he began to lose his hearing. If you are a leaper, you stand and wait to hear from God what you are to say to your fellow men and women. You leap between our rich God and the needy people who look to you, so that you may hear in one quarter and speak in the other. But if you choose not to speak on the one side, you will not deserve to hear on the other: you are scorning the poor, so you will be scorned yourself by God, who is rich. Have you forgotten that you are a servant, whom the Master has appointed over his household to give your fellow-servants their rations?[16] Why do you seek to receive anything, if you are unwilling to dole it out? Give what you have, that you may deserve what you have not.[17] "Accordingly," says Idithun, "when I had placed a kind of guard over my mouth, and imposed silence on myself because I saw how dangerous speech was, something happened to me that I had not bargained for: *I became deaf, and*

---

14. See Jn 3:29.
15. See Jn 8:44.
16. See Mt 24:45.
17. These remarks clearly come from Augustine's own heart and experience. The double duty of hearing and speaking was an essential ingredient in his idea of a bishop's office.

was humbled. I did not humble myself; rather *I was humbled. I became deaf, and was humbled, and fell silent even from good words.* I have stopped saying even good things, so afraid am I that I may say something amiss, and my teaching be censured. *I have fallen silent even from good words, and my pain has come back.* In silence I had found a respite from one kind of pain, that which my slanderers and critics had inflicted on me; the pain I endured from them had ceased. But when I began to keep silence from good words, my pain was renewed. My policy of keeping quiet about what I ought to have said began to cause me more intense pain than having said the wrong things would have done. *My pain has come back."*

Verses 4–5. Longing for the goal

5. *Fire will blaze up during my meditation.*[18] My heart began to be troubled. Often I saw people behaving foolishly; it sickened me, but I did not rebuke them, and zeal for your house devoured me as I remained silent.[19] I thought of my Lord saying, *You wicked, lazy servant, you should have handed my money over to the bankers, so that I could have recovered it with interest on my return.* And may God shield his stewards from the fate mentioned in the next verse: *Let him be cast into outer darkness* (Mt 25:26–27.30) bound hand and foot. Remember that he was not one to squander and bring financial ruin, but a servant indolent in paying out what was due. What are people to expect who have used up the Lord's property in self-indulgence, if those who have simply held it back through laziness are condemned so severely? *Fire will blaze up during my meditation.* The psalmist finds himself caught in this vacillation between speaking and keeping silence, between those who are poised to censure him and those who long to receive instruction, between those who have plenty and those in need. To the affluent he has become an object of abuse, to the proud the butt of their scorn,[20] yet he is conscious of the blessed ones who are hungering and thirsting after righteousness.[21] Whichever way he turns he is hard pressed, in trouble either way, in danger of casting his pearls before swine[22] and equally endangered if he does not dispense their rations to his fellow-servants. In such a ferment he sought a better place, somewhere better than this stewardship where one works so hard and is in such peril. He sighed for some kind of end, where he would not have to suffer all this, and the end he longed for was that final reckoning when the Lord will say to his good steward, *Enter into the joy of your Lord* (Mt 25:21). *I spoke with my tongue,* says the psalmist. "Amid the ferment, the dangers, the difficulties (for though the law of the Lord is a delight to us, it still permits

---

18. Some codices supply the first half of this verse, which Augustine omits.
19. See Ps 68:10(69:9).
20. See Ps 122(123):4.
21. See Mt 5:6.
22. See Mt 7:6.

the charity of many to grow cold[23] as scandals abound), amid this ferment, I say, *I spoke with my tongue.*" To whom? "Not to any hearer whom I want to instruct, but to that unfailing hearer by whom I want to be instructed. *I spoke with my tongue* to him, to whom I must listen within if I am to hear anything good, anything true." And what did you say? *"Make known to me my end, O Lord.* I have leapt across certain things, and arrived at certain others, and the things I have reached are better than those from which I leapt away, but there is still something over which I must leap; for we shall not always remain here to endure temptations, obstacles, and accusing listeners. *Make known to me my end,* show me the goal still far away, not the race immediately in front of me."

6. The "end" he mentions is that goal the apostle kept in view as he sped along his way, though he confessed his own imperfection and knew the distance between his present life and that other place to which he was running. *Not that I have gained it already, or am already perfect, brethren; I do not judge myself to have taken hold of it yet,* he says. On hearing that you might say, "If the apostle has not taken hold of it, can I?" But look at what he is doing, and pay attention to what he says. So what are you saying,[24] apostle? Do you really mean that you have not laid hold on it yet, that you are not yet perfect? What are you saying? To what kind of activity are you exhorting me? What model do you propose to me, for me to imitate and follow? *One thing only I do,* he says. *Forgetting what lies behind and straining to what lies ahead, I bend my whole effort to follow after the prize of God's heavenly call in Christ Jesus* (Phil 3:12–14). *I bend my whole effort,* not claiming to have arrived, not claiming to have laid hold of the prize. Let us not slip back again into the place from which we have already leapt across, but neither let us remain in the place we have reached. Let us run ahead, keeping our eyes on the finishing-post, for we are still on the way. Do not be complacent about the things you have left behind; rather be concerned for those you have not yet gained. *Forgetting what lies behind and straining to what lies ahead,* says Paul, *I bend my whole effort to follow after the prize of God's heavenly call in Christ Jesus.* For Christ is the end. The "one thing" Paul mentions is the one thing the apostles longed for: *Lord, show us the Father, and that is enough for us* (Jn 14:8). It is the "one thing," the one request made in another psalm: *One thing have I begged of the Lord, and that will I seek after. Forgetting what lies behind and straining to what lies ahead, one thing have I begged of the Lord, and that will I seek after, to live in the Lord's house all the days of my life.* For what purpose? *That I may contemplate the Lord's delight* (Ps 26(27):4). There I shall rejoice in my ally, no longer fearing him or her

---

23. See Mt 24:12.
24. This is the variant suggested by the CCL editors, here and in the following line. The codices have "What are you doing?"

as an adversary; there he will be a friend who joins me in contemplation, not an enemy to accuse me.

This was Idithun's desire. He wanted that end to be revealed to him while he was still here, that he might know what was still lacking to him; he wanted not so much to rejoice in the things he had attained as to long for those he had not reached yet. Though he had leapt beyond some things, he prayed not to halt on the way, but to be carried on by desire to the things of heaven, until after leaping over some things he might at last leap over all. Droplets of divine dew were falling on him from the Scriptures, arousing his thirst to run like a hart to the fountain of life, and in that light to see light, and to be sheltered in the recess of God's face, far from human disturbance.[25] There he would be able to say, "At last! I want nothing else. Here I love everyone and fear no one."

This is a good desire, a holy desire. If any of you have it already, rejoice with us, and pray that we may persevere in our desire, and never slacken in it by reason of the scandals around us. For our part we make the same prayer for you; for it is not as though we were fit to pray for you, and you unworthy to pray for us, The apostle habitually commended himself to his hearers, to whom he was preaching the word of God. So you too, brothers and sisters, pray for us, that we may clearly see what should be seen, and aptly say what is to be said. However, I know that this desire exists in only a few people, and only those who have tasted the realities of which I speak understand me perfectly. Nonetheless we speak to all of you, to those who have such a longing and to those who do not have it yet: to those who have it, that they may sigh together with us for the things we speak of, and to those who do not yet long for them, that they may shake off their sluggishness, leap beyond base things, and come to experience the sweetness of the divine law, rather than linger amid the pleasures of the wicked. For many people tell many titillating tales, and there are plenty of people singing the praises of plenty of attractions, and wicked people offering wicked suggestions. And it is true that those wicked things do afford pleasure, but none to compare with your law, O Lord.[26] Let those who are convinced that we too are testifying about these realities come and testify along with us, for though this is a process that goes on inside ourselves, and cannot be expressed in words, anyone who engages in it must believe that it goes on in others too. None of us must think ourselves to be the sole recipients of this gift from God. Let Idithun say on their behalf, *Make known to me my end, O Lord.*

---

25. See Pss 41:2(42:1); 35:10(36:9); 30:21(31:20).
26. See Ps 118(119):85.

Time, the dimension of contingent being

7. *And make known to me the number of my days, the number that is.*[27] Now I am looking for a number of days "that is." I can speak about, and understand, a number that is not really a number, just as I can speak of years where there are not really any years, for ordinarily where there are "years," a number is implied, yet a psalm says to God, *You are the Selfsame, and your years will not fail* (Ps 101:28(102:27)).

But here the prayer is not simply, "Make me know the number of my days," but "Make me know the number of them that *is*." What does that mean? That numbered day in which you are now—does it not exist? Well, I have to say that if I look hard, it does not exist. If I am sticking fast on the road, I have the illusion that it does exist, but when I leap across, it does not exist. If I shake myself free of earthly things to contemplate the things of heaven, if I compare transient things with those that abide, I see what has true being, and what has more the appearance of being than true existence. Am I to say that these present days of mine have true being? I repeat, am I to say that these days really exist? Shall I be so rash as to use the great word "being" of this flux of things that slide toward extinction? For myself, in my weakness I am so nearly nonexistent that God has eluded my memory, God who said, *I AM WHO AM* (Ex 3:14).

Is there some "number of days" that truly exists, then? Indeed there is, it exists without end. But in these present days I can only say that something "is" if I am able to hold onto something of the day on which you ask me whether it exists, or if you can hold onto something of that day in order to ask me. But do you hold onto it? If you have held onto yesterday, you hold onto today as well. "But," you will reply, "I am not holding onto yesterday, because it no longer exists; I hold onto this day where I am now, the day that is present to me." Really? Has not the part of it which has passed since first light already escaped from you? Did not "today" begin from its first hour? Give me its first hour; give me its second hour too, for by now that may have flown away as well. "At least I will give you its third hour," you say, "if that is where we are now. Certainly these days do exist, and there is a third day,[28] and if you accept that, you must grant me that the third hour also exists." But no, I will not concede to you even that, if you have in any degree leapt across these things with me. Give me just this third hour where you are now. If some portion of it has already slipped by, and some other portion still remains, you cannot give me either what has passed (because it no longer exists) or what remains (because it does not exist yet). What are you going to give me, then, of this present hour? How much of it will you

---

27. *Et numerum dierum meorum qui est.* The phrase is awkward. The translation here offered assumes that this is the correct reading, though two codices ease it by amending *qui* (relative) to *quid* (interrogative): "the number of my days, what it is."
28. Allusion to the resurrection?

give me—enough for me to speak the word, "is"? When you say the word "is" you utter one syllable, and that only takes a moment. But this syllable has three letters,[29] and even in that tiny moment you will not reach the second letter of the word until the first has ended, nor will the third make itself heard until the second has died away. What can you give me, then, of this one syllable? And do you think you can hold onto a day, if you cannot hold onto a syllable? As the moments fly past all things are snatched away. The torrent of things flows on, but from this torrent he drank for us on his way, he who has now lifted up his head.[30] These days of ours do not have being; they depart almost before they arrive, and when they do arrive they cannot stand still. They join onto each other,[31] they follow one another and cannot hold themselves together. Nothing of the past can be called back, and the future that we await will pass away; as long as it has not come, we do not possess it, and when it has come we cannot keep hold of it.

I want to know *the number of my days, the number that is,* not this number that is not, or rather this number that both is and is not. It is this last aspect that disturbs me more and is to me more difficult and dangerous, for we cannot say something "is" if it does not stand still, but neither can we say it has no being at all, if it comes and goes. What I am seeking is the simple "is." I seek the true "is"; I am looking for the genuine "is," the "is" that we shall find in that Jerusalem which is the bride of my Lord, where there will be no death, no deficiency, where the day passes not, but abides, the day that is preceded by no yesterday and hustled on by no tomorrow. *Make known to me the number of my days,* this number, *the number that is.*

What I have and what I lack

8. *That I may know what I lack,* for this is what is wanting to me as I struggle along here, and as long as I lack it I do not claim to be perfect. As long as I have not received it, I confess, *Not that I have already gained it, or am already perfect; but I bend my whole effort to follow after the prize of God's heavenly call* (Phil 3:12.14). I shall receive it as my prize at the end of my race. The end of our running will be a stillness, and in this stillness a homeland where there will be no journeying, no unrest, no temptation. So then, *make known to me the number of my days, the number that is, that I may know what I lack.* I am not there yet, so let me not become proud about the place I have attained, but let me be found in Christ, not having

---

29. Two in English of course, three in Latin: *est.*
30. See Ps 109(110):7. The quotation points the contrast between the elusive quality of our time, characteristic of creaturely existence which is close to non-being, and the eternity of God, whose Word has neither beginning nor ending. Yet the incarnate Word "drank from the torrent" of our transient human existence.
31. Variant: "press upon each other."

any righteousness of my own.[32] With my eyes on HIM WHO IS, and comparing with him these present things which have no being in that sense, I shall see that what I lack is greater than what I have, and so I shall be more humbled about what is missing than elated about what is at hand. People who while living here think they possess anything deserve by their pride not to receive what they lack, for they think what they have is something great; but any who think themselves something, whereas they are nothing, deceive themselves.[33] The illusion does not make them great, for while inflation and swelling look like greatness, they are no bearers of health.

Verse 6. The passage from the old to the new

9. Our leaping psalmist is carrying on a secret business in his heart which only someone who is engaged in the same will know. He has obtained what he asked: his end has been made known to him, and so has the number of his days—not the number of days that passes, but that which "is." He has a true estimate of the things he has leapt over and has compared it with a higher knowledge. Now you might ask him, "Why did you want to know the number of your days, the number that is? What have you to say about these present days?" With regard to this other number,[34] the days of this present life, he replies, *"How old you have made my days!* They are growing old, and I want new ones, days that never grow old, so that I may say, *The old things have passed away, and lo, everything is made new!"* (2 Cor 5:17), even now in hope, and hereafter in reality. Though already made new by faith and hope, how much old business we still have to deal with! We have not so put on Christ as to wear nothing any longer of Adam. Look at Adam growing old, and Christ being made new in us: *Though our outer self is decaying,* says Scripture, *our inner self is being renewed daily* (2 Cor 4:16). As we regard our sin, our mortality, our fleeting seasons, our groaning and toil and sweat, the stages of our life that succeed one another and will not stand still, but slip by imperceptibly from infancy to old age as we regard all these, let us see in them the old self, the old day, the old song, the Old Covenant. But when we turn to our inner being, to all that is destined to be renewed in us and replace the things subject to change, let us find there the new self, the new day, the new song, the New Covenant, and let us love this newness so dearly that the oldness we meet there does not frighten us. As we run our race we are passing from the old things to the new. This transition is effected as the old things decay and the inner are made new, until our outer decaying self pays its debt to nature and meets its death, though it too will be renewed at the resurrection. Then all things which for the present are new only in hope will be made new

---

32. See Phil 3:9.
33. See Gal 6:3.
34. Variant: "having regard to that high knowledge."

in very truth. You further the process now as you strip yourself of the old and run toward the new.

Our psalmist was running toward these new things and straining toward what lay ahead when he said, *Make known to me my end, O Lord, and the number of my days, the number that is, that I may know what I lack.* He is still dragging Adam along, but look how he is hastening toward Christ. *How old you have made my days!* he says. These old days derive from Adam, and you have rendered them old; every day they grow older, so much so that eventually they will be consumed altogether. *And my substance is as nothing in your sight.* In your sight, Lord, it is as nothing, nothing in the presence of you who see this. When I see it too, it is in your sight that I see it. I do not see the truth in the presence of fellow-mortals, for what can I say, what words can I use to demonstrate that what I am is nothing when compared with HIM WHO IS? But within myself it can be said,[35] within myself it can be experienced in some measure. *In your sight*, Lord, where your eyes see me, not where human eyes see.... What do I see there, where your eyes are? That *my substance is as nothing.*

Emptiness all round

10. *Nonetheless all things are empty, for everyone who lives.* Why does he say, *Nonetheless*? Well, what has he been saying? "By now I have leapt across mortal things, I have learned to despise what is lowest, I have trampled earthly things underfoot and have soared to the enjoyment of the law of the Lord. I have been afloat in the number of days the Lord gives,[36] and I have longed for that end which knows no ending. I have desired to know the number of my days, the number that truly is, for the present numbered days have no true being. This is what I am like; I have leapt beyond so much and now I pant with longing for the realities that are still and lasting. *Nonetheless*, in my present state, as long as I am here, as long as I am in this world, as long as I carry mortal flesh, as long as human life on earth is all temptation,[37] as long as I gasp, beset by scandals, as long as I who stand must be wary lest I fall,[38] as long as both my bad points and

---

35. Variant: "learned."
36. *Fluctuavi in dispensatione numerorum dierum dominicorum.* If this is the correct reading, the reference is presumably to the contemplation of eternal realities that he has mentioned, and this would suit the immediate context here. But the phrase is difficult and has given rise to a number of variants. Some codices omit *dierum*, others substitute *nummorum* ("coins," "money"). This last may be right; he would then be harking back to the dilemma he faced in 5, where the words *fluctuo* and *dispensatio* also occur, together with the idea of investing money. We could then translate "I have wavered in my stewardship of the Lord's money, but...."
37. See Jb 7:1.
38. See 1 Cor 10:12.

my good deeds are opaque to me, *all things are empty, for everyone who lives.* Everyone, I say, both the person who sticks fast and the one who leaps along. Even Idithun still belongs in this universal state of emptiness; for all things are empty, and vanity of vanities, and what wealth does anyone get from all the work he toils at under the sun?[39] Is Idithun still under the sun? He has some stake in this world under the sun, and some stake in the world beyond it. Here under the sun he has the business of waking and sleeping, eating and drinking, feeling thirst and hunger, thriving and being tired, growing from a child into a youth, and then into an old man, being unsure what to hope and what to fear. All these even Idithun experiences under the sun, even though he is one who leaps beyond. Where does he get the impetus for his leaping? From his desire: *Make known to me my end, O Lord.* The desire is something beyond this sunny world; it does not arise from the world under the sun. All the things we can see are under the sun, but whatever is invisible is not under the sun. Faith is not visible, hope is not visible, charity is not visible, kindliness is not visible, neither is that chaste fear that abides for ever.[40] In all these Idithun finds sweetness and consolation; he lives beyond this sun, because he is a citizen of heaven.[41] The things that still preoccupy him under the sun wring groans from him; he scorns them and suffers pain, longing ardently for the things he truly desires. Of these latter he has already spoken, and now he must speak of things here below. You have heard what he yearns for; listen now to what he spurns. *Nonetheless all things are empty, for everyone who lives.*

Verse 7. For whom are you amassing your wealth?

11. *Although each human being walks as an image.* What image is meant? Surely the image of him who said, *Let us make humans in our own image and likeness?* (Gn 1:26) *Although each human being walks as an image*: he puts in the word *although* because this image is something great, yet after the "although" comes a "nonetheless," to show that what you heard after "although" refers to what is beyond the sun, and what follows "nonetheless" refers to what is under the sun. The one belongs to truth, the other to emptiness. So *although each human being walks as an image, nonetheless his perturbation is vain.* Listen to what makes him fret, and see if it is not empty; listen so that you may leap over it and dwell in heaven, where there is no such emptiness. What is the emptiness here? *He heaps up treasure, but does not know for whom he will be gathering it.* A crazy vanity this is! *Blessed is the one whose hope is the Lord, who has had no regard for empty things and lying foolishness* (Ps 39:5(40:4)). No doubt, you miser, I seem to you to be mad when I say things like this; such statements are old wives' tales as far as you are concerned. Clearly you are

---

39. See Eccl 1:2–3.
40. See Ps 18:10(19:9).
41. See Phil 3:20.

a person of considerable shrewdness and acumen; every day you think up ways of making money from business, or from agriculture, perhaps even by oratory or by practicing at law, or from warfare; you might even dabble in moneylending. Like the intelligent man you are you let slip no opportunity to pile money upon money, and to stow it away secretly[42] with ever greater care. You plunder the next man and take precautions against anyone who may rob you; you fear the possibility of yourself suffering what you do to others, and you do not learn better ways from what you do suffer. But I am wrong: of course you do not suffer, do you? You are a prudent man, well able not only to acquire wealth but also to hang onto it. You have safe places to put it, and safe hands to entrust it to, so that nothing you have amassed may be lost. Well now, I want to put a question to your heart, and subject your shrewdness to scrutiny. You have gathered these riches, and preserved them so ably that you can lose nothing of what you have preserved; tell me, then: for whom are you keeping your wealth? I am not tackling you about any other evil aspect of your vain greed, I will not make a point of this or magnify its importance. I am putting this one question; this is all I want to discuss, since our reading of this psalm gives me a good opportunity. Quite clearly you are picking up all the wealth you can; I am not telling you to watch out while you are picking it up in case you are picked up yourself; I am not saying, Take care that when you plan to be a predator you do not become the prey. No, I will emphasize it even more plainly, in case you are blinded by your greed and have not heard or understood—I am not, I tell you, saying, Take care that when you plan to prey on smaller fry you do not become the prey of someone more powerful. After all, you do not consider yourself to be in the sea, do you, where you might watch small fish being swallowed by larger ones? No, that is not what I am saying. I am not even concerned with the difficulties and dangers inherent in acquiring money, or the hardships endured by those who collect it and are exposed to perils on every side as they do so, almost coming face to face with death. All these aspects I am passing over. Granted, then, that you make money and no one challenges you, and you save it and no one robs you, now shake out the creases from your heart, and from that great prudence of yours which leads you to deride me and think me a simpleton for saying these things, tell me this: you are laying up treasure, but for whom? I see what you intend to say (did you think it would not have occurred to me?). You will say, "I am keeping it for my children." This sounds like family loyalty, but it is an excuse for injustice. "I am keeping it for my children," you say. Really? You are keeping it for your children, are you? Did not Idithun know about this? Certainly he did, but he reckoned that such a practice belonged to the old days, and so he despised it, because he was hurrying toward the new days.

---

42. *Castigetur* usually means "punish, chastise" but occasionally "confine" (as a punishment). It evidently surprised copyists, who offered variants: *congregetur* or *collocetur* ("gather together") or even *cartigetur* ("record in a charter").

There is a safer place to store it

12. All right then, now I will include your children in this question I am discussing with you. You who will pass away are storing up wealth for children who will pass away; or rather you who are already fading away are storing it up for those who are already fading away. I should not have said, "You will pass away," as though you were stable at present. You are not; for even today, from the point when we began speaking until the present moment, you know we have grown older. You cannot see your hair growing, yet even now as you stand here, or while you are busy with some work, or talking, your hair is growing. It does not grow suddenly, so as to send you scurrying for a barber. Our lifetime is flying past, for those who understand, and for those who take no notice, and for those intent on evil designs. You are passing away, and keeping your wealth for a son who is also passing away. I ask you, first, do you know that this son for whom you are saving will in fact ever possess it? Or, if he is not born yet, do you know that he will be born? You are keeping it for your children, yet you know neither that they will exist nor that they will possess it. Moreover you are not storing your treasure where it ought to be stored, for your Lord did not advise his servant to squander the allowance he made to him. You are the servant of a great householder, and as such you are entrusted with money. What you love, what you have, he has given you, and it is not his wish that you waste what he gave you, he who intends even to give you himself. But even what he gave you temporarily he does not want you to waste, believe me. Perhaps there is a lot of it; it is overflowing and your needs cannot keep up with it; it must certainly be deemed superfluous. "But I do not want you to waste even that," your Lord says. "What am I to do?" Move it. The place where you have stored it is unsafe. You want to act in the best interests of your avarice; very well, see whether what I advise does not consort well even with your avarice. You want to keep what you have, not lose it, so I will show you where to store it. Do not pile up treasure on earth, without knowing for whom you are collecting it, or how the person who will possess it later, the future holder, may run through it. Perhaps the person who possesses it then will be possessed by someone else, and will be unable to hold onto what he inherits from you. Or perhaps even while you are saving it for him you may lose it, before he even comes into the money. Let me give you a piece of advice in your anxiety: *Lay up for yourselves treasure in heaven* (Mt 6:20). If you wanted to keep your valuables safe here on earth you would look for a storage-place; perhaps you would not entrust them to your own home because of your servants, so you would commit them to the banking quarter,[43] for accidents are unlikely to happen there and a thief cannot easily break in, so everything is kept safe. Why do you plan to do this? Because you have no better place to keep them? What if I show you a

---

43. Variant: "to a neighboring banker."

better place? I will tell you of one: do not entrust your wealth to someone unsuitable. There is someone eminently suitable, leave it with him. He has vast storerooms from which no riches can be lost, and he himself is very great, and richer than all the wealthy in the world. So perhaps you will reply, "How could I dare to entrust my goods to such a personage?" But suppose he himself asks you to? Recognize him: he is not simply a householder, he is also your Lord. "I do not want you to waste the money I allowed you, my servant," he says. "Be careful where you put it. Why are you putting it where you may lose it, and where you cannot yourself remain permanently in any case? There is another place, to which I am going to transfer you. Let your wealth travel there ahead of you. Do not fear to lose it, for I was the giver, and I will be its guardian." This is what your Lord says to you; question your faith, and see if you are willing to trust him. You will object, "What I can't see is as good as lost. I want to see it here." But if you are determined to see it here, you will neither see it here nor have anything at all there. You have some treasures hidden in the earth perhaps—I don't know what they are. When you go out, you do not carry them with you. You have come here to listen to this sermon, to acquire interior riches. Think about your exterior riches: have you brought them with you? No? Well then, you cannot actually see them now, can you? You believe that you have them at home, because you remember where you put them; but are you sure you have not lost them? How many people have returned to their homes and failed to find what they left there! Ah, some covetous people felt a clutch at their hearts when I said that![44] Because I said that it has often happened that people have gone home and not found what they left there, some of you may perhaps say in your hearts, "Stop it, bishop! Say something of good omen, and pray for us. Don't bring it on, please don't let it happen! I trust in God to let me find what I left there safe and sound." So you trust in God, but do not believe him? "I trust in Christ, that what I left at home will be safe, and no one will break in or steal it." So you want to play safe by trusting in Christ in order to lose nothing from your house. You will be much safer if you believe Christ, and put your money where he advised you to put it. Do you trust your servant, yet feel suspicious of your Lord? Are you secure about your house, and uneasy about heaven? "But how can I put money into heaven?" you will ask. I have given you good advice; put your money where I tell you. I do not want you to know how it gets to heaven. Put it into the hands of the poor, give it to the needy. What does it matter to you how it gets there? Will I not deliver what I receive? Have you forgotten the promise, *When you did it for even the least of those who are mine, you did it for me?* (Mt 25:40) Suppose some friend of yours had certain tanks or cisterns or other containers made to store liquid—wine or oil, perhaps—and you were looking for somewhere to store your produce, and your friend said to you, "I will store it for you." But suppose he had

---

44. Evidently a frisson in the congregation evoked the next few remarks.

connected to his cisterns pipes and conduits that were out of sight, so that what was poured in as you watched drained away unseen; and he said to you, "Pour what you have in here," but you saw that the place where you had meant to store your produce was not what you thought, and you were afraid to pour it in. He would know the secret workings of his own plant, so he would say to you, "Don't worry, just pour it in. It flows from here to that other place over there. You can't see how it gets there, but trust me, I built it." Now he who made all things has built mansions for us all, and he wants our possessions to go there ahead of us, lest we lose them on earth. But if you have hoarded them on earth, tell me for whom you will be gathering them. You have children? Very well, then, increase their number by one, and give Christ something. *He heaps up treasure, but does not know for whom he will be gathering it. His perturbation is vain.*

Verse 8. Still waiting

13. *And now*, says Idithun, as he looks down at vanity and looks up at truth, standing midway between the two, with something below him and something else above him (for below him is what he has leapt away from, and above is what he is straining toward). *"And now,"* he says, "that I have leapt beyond some things, and trampled many things underfoot, now that I am no longer held captive by temporal things, I am still not perfect, for I have not yet received what I want." *In hope we have been saved. But if hope is seen, it is hope no longer, for when someone sees what he hopes for, why should he hope for it? But if we hope for what we do not see, we wait for it in patience* (Rom 8:24–25). So he asks, *"And now, what am I waiting for? Surely for the Lord.* For him I am waiting, for him who gave all these things by which I now set little store. He will give me himself, he who is above all things, he through whom all things were made and by whom I was made among all these things. He, the Lord, is my hope." You see our Idithun, brothers and sisters, you see how he waits for God. Let none of us claim to be perfect here: we should be deceiving ourselves, making a mistake, misleading ourselves, for none of us can reach perfection here. And what advantage would we gain by losing humility? *And now, what am I waiting for? Surely for the Lord.* When he has come we shall not have to wait for him any more, and then the perfection we seek will be ours. But for the present, Idithun is still waiting, however much he has already leapt over. *And all I have is continually before you.* I am making some progress, and already tending toward him; already I am beginning to attain true being, in some measure; but *all I have is continually before you.* What you have on earth is before the eyes of men and women. You have gold, silver, slaves, estates, trees, cattle, servants; all these can be seen by other men and women. Yet all you truly have is in God's sight all the time. *All I have is continually before you.*

Verse 9. Perfection through knowing one's imperfection

14. *Pluck me free from all my iniquities.* I have leapt across many things, yes, many indeed, yet *if we say that we have no sin, we deceive ourselves, and the truth is not in us* (1 Jn 1:8). I have leapt beyond many things, but still I beat my breast and say, *Forgive us our debts, as we forgive those who are in debt to us.* For you I wait, you who are my end, for *Christ is the end of the law, bringing justification to everyone who believes* (Rom 10:4). Free me from all my sins: not only from those of the past, lest I roll back again into the ones I have leapt across, but from absolutely all of them, for which I now beat my breast and say, *Forgive us our debts. Pluck me free from all my iniquities,* as I make my own the wisdom of the apostle's words. *Let those of us who are perfect be wise about this,* he says (Phil 3:15). He had just confessed that he was not yet perfect, yet he immediately added, *Let those of us who are perfect be wise about this.* How can he speak of *those of us who are perfect*? What do you mean, Paul? You said a moment ago, *Not that I have gained it already, or am already perfect.* "Read the whole verse in order," he replies. *One thing only I do: forgetting what lies behind and straining to what lies ahead, I bend my whole effort to follow after the prize of God's heavenly call in Christ Jesus* (Phil 3:12–14). He is not yet perfect, because he is following after the prize of God's heavenly call, and he has not yet caught up with it; he has not yet arrived. But if he is not perfect, and has not reached his goal, which of us is perfect? Yet he goes on to say, *Let those of us who are perfect be wise about this.* If you are not perfect yourself, apostle, do you suppose we are? Remember, he has just said that he is! He did not say, "As many of you as are perfect, be wise about this"; what he said was, *Let those of us who are perfect be wise about this,* and he gave this exhortation just after saying, *Not that I have gained it already, or am already perfect.*

We learn, then, that in this life you can be perfect in no other way than by knowing you cannot be perfect. Your perfection will consist in having leapt over certain things in order to hasten on toward certain others, but in having leapt over them in such a way that there still remains something further, to which after all your efforts you must still leap. Faith like this is safe, for those who think they have already reached the goal are exalting themselves and are heading for a fall.

On show before mortals and angels

15. Since I am wise on this score, since I acknowledge that I am both imperfect and perfect (imperfect because I have not yet attained what I want, but perfect because I know this thing that I lack), since then I am wise enough to spurn human pleasures and refuse to find my joy in things that perish, since I am ridiculed by the miser who prides himself on his shrewdness and mocks me for being a simpleton—since this is how I live, he says, *you have made me an object of reproach to the unwise.* Your will

is that I live among those who are set on vanity, and that I preach the truth to them. Inevitably we shall be taunted by them, for *we have become a spectacle to this world, to both angels and mortals.*[45]

The angels praise us and mortals insult us; or rather angels both praise and revile, while mortals too both praise and revile. *We have weapons in both right hand and left with which to fight, through glory and ignominy, through bad repute and good, as seducers and trustworthy people.*[46] These varied fortunes are ours among angels as among mortals, for among the angelic hosts there are angels who are pleased when we live our lives well, and traitor-angels whom we offend by our good lives, just as among mortals there are holy people who applaud our life, and wicked people who deride our goodness. All these reactions are our weapons, some for the right hand, others for the left; both kinds are useful, and I employ both: right-handed and left-handed, the commendations and the insults, those which do us honor and those which defame us. With both sorts I do battle with the devil and with both I strike home at him, in favorable times if I do not let success go to my head, and in adversity if I do not flinch.

Verses 10–11. Struck dumb

16. *You have made me an object of reproach to the unwise. I grew deaf and did not open my mouth.* But it was only to the unwise that *I did not open my mouth*, for to whom could I speak about what goes on within me? Rather will I *listen to what the Lord God speaks within me, for he will speak peace to his people*, whereas *there is no peace for wicked people*, says the Lord (Ps 84:9(85:8); Is 48:22). *I grew deaf and did not open my mouth, because it is you who made me.* Do you mean that was why you did not open your mouth—because it was God who made you? That is a strange thing to say. Did not God make a mouth for you so that you could speak? *Does he who planted ears in us not hear? Does he who fashioned the eye not see?*[47] God gave you a mouth to speak with, yet you say, *I grew deaf and did not open my mouth, because it is you who made me*?

But perhaps the phrase, *Because it is you who made me*, should be taken with the following verse, so that we read, *Because it is you who made me, take your scourges away from me.* Because you are my Maker, do not kill me; beat me only enough to help me succeed, not succumb;[48] buffet me only to bring me up, not to break me down.[49] *Because it is you who made me, take your scourges away from me.*

---

45. See 1 Cor 4:9.
46. See 2 Cor 6:7–8.
47. See Ps 93(94):9.
48. *Ut proficiam, non ut deficiam.*
49. This phrase could also mean "Hammer me only to stretch me out further, not to pound me to pieces."

Verse 12. Salutary correction

17. *I fainted under your strong hand as you accused me*; that is, when you rebuked me, I tottered. What does it mean to be accused by you, Lord? The psalm goes on to explain: *You have chastised human beings for their sin, and brushed my soul away like a spider.* This Idithun understands a great deal; are any of us prepared to understand, and leap across with him? He confesses that he has fainted under God's censure, and asks that the divine rod be removed from him, since it is God who made him. It is for the Maker to remake his work, for the Creator to recreate. But are we to suppose, brothers and sisters, that Idithun's fainting, the tottering that made him long to be recreated and formed anew, was pointless? *You have chastised human beings for their sin*, he says. All my fainting, all my weakness, all my need to cry from the depths—all of this is because of my iniquity, and in this situation you did not condemn me, but chastised me. *You have chastised human beings for their sin.* This truth is stated even more clearly in another psalm: *It is good for me that you have humbled me, so that I may learn your righteous judgments* (Ps 118(119):71). I was humbled, yet I recognize that it did me good: it is both punishment and grace. What must he be holding in reserve for us when the punishment is over, if his very punishment is grace? God it is of whom a psalm says, *I was humbled, and he saved me* (Ps 114(116):6), and *it is good for me that you have humbled me, so that I may learn your righteous judgments.* For *you have chastised human beings for their sin.* There is another text which could be spoken to God only by one who leaps over, because only by such a leaper could its truth be seen: *You who shape our pain as your precept* (Ps 93(94):20). Yes, he says to God, *you shape our pain as your precept,* you fashion pain into a precept laid on me. You give form to my pain; you do not leave it shapeless but mold it to your purpose, and this carefully formed pain inflicted on me will be for me a commandment from you, so that you may set me free. You form pain, Scripture says, you shape our pain, you mold our pain, you do not send any unreal pain to us. As an earthenware pot is so called because it is a potter's work, so do you like a potter mold our pain into shape. This is why it can be said, *You have chastised human beings for their sin.* I see myself full of bad things, I see myself undergoing punishment, and in you I see no injustice at all. So if I am undergoing punishment, and in you there is no injustice, what other explanation is there but that you chastise men and women in their sin?

Experienced weakness leads to humility

18. How have you chastised them? Tell us about the chastisement itself, Idithun. How were you disciplined? *You brushed my soul away like a spider.* This was the chastisement. What is more fragile than a spider—the creature itself, I mean, though I could also ask, what is more fragile than a spider's web? But look how frail the spider itself is: if you lay a finger on

it even lightly, it disintegrates; nothing else at all is so easily crushed. You have treated my soul like that by chastising me for my iniquity, says the psalmist. When such weakness is the effect of God's correction, there is a kind of strength that is really a vice. (I can see that some of you are flying ahead and have grasped the point already, but you swift ones must not leave the slower ones behind; they need to follow the course of the sermon with the rest.) As I was saying, try to understand why this is. If it is the correction administered by a just God that has reduced a person to such weakness, there is a certain kind of strength that is simply vicious. Human beings displeased God by a show of that kind of strength, and therefore needed to be corrected by weakness; they displeased him by their pride, and therefore needed to be disciplined by humility. All proud people claim to be strong. This is why the many who are coming from the east and the west have been victorious, the many who are to sit down with Abraham and Isaac and Jacob in the kingdom of heaven. Why have they been victorious? Because they refused to be strong. What do I mean by that: they refused to be strong? They were afraid to rely on their own strength, and they did not set up any righteousness of their own, but chose to be subject to God's righteousness.[50] When you hear the Lord's words, *Many will come from east and west and will sit down with Abraham and Isaac and Jacob in the kingdom of heaven; but the children of the kingdom* (the Jews who knew nothing of God's righteousness and wanted to establish their own) *will be thrown into the outer darkness* (Mt 8:11–12)—when you hear him say that, remember the faith of the centurion, a gentile, who was so weak in himself, so lacking in any strength, that he confessed, *I am not worthy to have you coming under my roof* (Mt 8:8). He was unworthy to receive Christ in his house, but he had already welcomed him into his heart. Indeed, the Son of Man who teaches us humility had already found in the centurion's breast a place to lay his head.[51]

When the centurion spoke like this, the Lord looked round at those who were following him and said, *Truly I tell you, I have not found faith to match this in Israel* (Mt 8:10). He found[52] this man weak, and the Israelites strong, so he drew the contrast between the two: *It is not the healthy who need the physician, but the sick* (Mt 9:12). For this reason, then, because they were humble, the Lord declared that *many will come from east and west and will sit down with Abraham and Isaac and Jacob in the kingdom of heaven; but the children of the kingdom will be thrown into the outer darkness*. Face the fact that you are mortal, that you carry about decaying flesh. You shall fall as any lordly ruler falls, you shall die as mortals die, and fall as the devil fell.[53] What good does the medicine of mortality do

---

50. See Rom 10:3.
51. See Mt 8:20.
52. Variant: "I found."
53. See Ps 81(82):7.

you? The devil is proud of being an angel without mortal flesh; but you[54] have been given mortal flesh, and it has done you no good because you are not humbled by this glaring weakness; therefore you shall fall as any lordly ruler falls. The first grace that God in his kindness confers on us is to bring us to confess our weakness, to confess that whatever good we can do, whatever strength we have, is ours only in him, so that anyone minded to boast may boast in the Lord.[55] *When I am weak, then I am strong*, says Paul (2 Cor 12:10). *You have chastised human beings for their sin, and brushed my soul away like a spider.*

Only death is certain

19. *Yet all human anxiety in this life is pointless.* The psalmist returns now to the truth of which he reminded us earlier. However much progress a person has made here, *all human anxiety in this life is pointless*, for we live in uncertainty. Which of us can be secure even about the good in ourselves? We fret in vain. Each of us must cast our anxiety upon the Lord, cast on him whatever worries us, believing that he will sustain and protect us.[56] What is certain on this earth? Only death. Consider all the vicissitudes of this life, both good and bad, all that befalls us in our righteousness or in our iniquity. What among all these is certain? Only death. You have made some progress, have you? You know what you are today, but you do not know what you will be tomorrow. A sinner, are you? You know what you are today, but not what you will be tomorrow. You hope to get money, but whether it will come your way is uncertain. You hope to find a wife, but it is uncertain whether you will find one, or what she will be like if you do. You hope to have children, but you cannot be certain that any will be born. If they are born, it is not certain that they will survive. If they do live, you cannot know whether they will grow up well or prove to be weaklings. Whichever way you turn, everything is uncertain, except for one sole certainty: death. If you are poor, there is no certainty that you will ever be rich; if you are uneducated, you cannot be certain of being taught; if you are in poor health, it is uncertain whether you can recover your strength. You have been born, and so you can at least be certain that you will die, but even in this certainty of death uncertainty lurks, because you do not know the day of your death. We live beset with uncertainties, holding one thing only as certain, that we shall die, but without even the certainty of when that will be. The only thing we ultimately fear is the one thing that we cannot possibly avoid. *All human anxiety in this life is pointless.*

---

54. Here the "you" which has been plural, initially addressing the Jews, becomes singular.
55. See 1 Cor 1:31.
56. See Ps 54:23(55:22).

Verse 13. Weeping for the distant prospect

20. Although he is already leaping over these things, already to some extent living in things above and spurning those below, the psalmist still finds himself amid these earthly realities, and so he prays, *"Hear my prayer.* What have I to rejoice over, and what to groan about? I rejoice over the stages passed, but groan over what still remains. *Hear my prayer and my entreaty; let your ears listen for my weeping.* Just because I have leapt over so many things, and mounted above so many, am I not to weep? Have I not reason to weep all the more bitterly? In piling up knowledge we only pile up grief.⁵⁷ The more I long for what is still distant, the more I groan until it comes, and the more I weep. Am I not right to weep? Should I not weep the more as scandals become more widespread, as iniquity increases, as the charity of many grows colder?⁵⁸ *Who will give water to my head, and to my eyes a fount of tears?* (Jer 9:1). *Hear my prayer and my entreaty; let your ears listen for my weeping. Do not be silent toward me.* Do not let me become permanently deaf. *Do not be silent toward me,* but allow me to hear you." God speaks in secret, and he speaks to many in their hearts. Very loud is his voice in a very quiet heart, where with mighty power he cries, *I am your salvation.* That is how another psalm prays: *Say to my soul, I am your salvation* (Ps 34(35):3). Now he prays, "Let that voice never fall silent for me," that voice with which God says to the soul, *I am your salvation.* "I beg you," says he, *"Do not be silent toward me."*

No security of tenure

21. *Because I am no more than a lodger in your house.* Whose lodger? I was the devil's lodger once, and a bad landlord I had then. But now I am with you, and am I a lodger still? What does "lodger" mean?⁵⁹ A lodger I am with respect to this place from which I shall be moving on, but not in that other place where I shall live for ever. The place where I shall abide for eternity should be called my home; but this place which I shall leave is the place of my sojourning. Yet even while I am a sojourner here, I am my God's lodger, as I shall be at home with him when I have gained my final dwelling. What is this home to which we shall move when the time comes for us to leave this present lodging? The apostle mentions it. You can recognize it when he says, *We have a building from God, a home not made by hands, an everlasting home in heaven* (2 Cor 5:1). If this home will be eternal in heaven, we shall not be lodgers or tenants any longer when we reach it. How could you be a lodger in your eternal home? But as for your earthly lodging, when the Master of the house says to you, "Move on,"

---

57. See Eccl 1:18.
58. See Mt 24:12.
59. *Inquilinus*, one who lodges in the house of another. Sometimes it means a serf, or sometimes a non-Roman in Roman territory.

you must be prepared to go; and you do not know when he will say it. But your longing for your eternal home will itself prepare you. You must not be indignant with him for choosing any moment he likes to say, "Move on." It is not as though he had given you any guarantee, or had bound himself by any agreement, and not as though you had paid advance rent to cover any definite period. When the owner of the house decides, you will be out. For the time being you stay only by his favor. *Because I am no more than a lodger in your house, and a pilgrim.* There beyond is my homeland, there is my house; but here I am no more than a tenant in your property, a traveler lodging with you. Many travelers are the guests of the devil; but those who have believed and stayed faithful, though travelers still because they have not yet reached their own land and their home, are travelers who lodge with God. *As long as we are in the body we are on pilgrimage and away from the Lord; but we make it our business to please him, whether we stay here or are on our way* (2 Cor 5:6.9). I am only a traveler and a lodger, *like all my forebears.* If I am like all my forebears, have I any right to say that I shall not be departing, when they have all moved on? Are the conditions of my sojourning likely to be different from theirs?

Verse 14. The goal of true being

22. What petition remains for me to make, then, since I shall undoubtedly move on from here? *Forgive me, so that I may find some cool refreshment before I go away.* But, Idithun, look carefully at those knots you need to have untied if you are to find cool refreshment before you go. What are they? You presumably suffer from some fever that makes you long for coolness, so that you cry out, "Let me find cool refreshment," and "Forgive me." What has God to forgive, unless it is some minute fault[60] that prompts you to pray, *Forgive us our debts*? Yet he begs, *Forgive me, before I go away to be no more.* Set me free entirely from my sins before I go, for I do not want to go with my sins on me. Forgive me, that I may have peace in my conscience, that my conscience may shed its burden of feverish anxiety, for I must take serious thought for my sin.[61] *Forgive me, so that I may find some cool refreshment*, and above all forgive me *before I go away to be no more*; for if you do not forgive me and allow me this cool refreshment, I shall go and not be. *Before I go away* to a place where I shall not be, *forgive me that I may find some cool refreshment.*

This raises the question: in what sense will he not be? Was he not going to his rest? God forbid that Idithun should have failed to find that rest! Obviously Idithun was going away, but going away to his rest. But think instead of some malefactor, not Idithun: someone who does not leap over earthly things, someone who lays up treasure here and watches over

---

60. *Scrupulum* (or *scripulum*), the 24th part of an ounce, applied metaphorically to a source of worry or unease.
61. See Ps 37:19(38:18).

it jealously, someone unjust, proud, boastful, haughty, disdainful of the pauper lying at the gate. Will such a person "not be"? Of course he or she will still exist. Then what does the psalm mean by saying, *Before I go away to be no more*? If that rich man in the gospel did not exist anymore, who was burning? Who was longing for a drop of water to be trickled onto his tongue from Lazarus' finger? Who was it who kept saying, *Father Abraham, send Lazarus*? (Lk 16:24) If he could speak he undoubtedly existed; this man who was on fire existed, the man who will rise again at the end, to be condemned to eternal flames along with the devil. What does *to be no more* mean, then? I think Idithun had in mind the difference between being and non-being. He was looking forward with all the longing of his heart, with all the power of his mind, to that end which he had desired should be shown him when he prayed, *Make known to me my end, O Lord*. He was looking to the number of his days, the number that truly *is*; he considered that all the things that exist here below have no being at all when compared with that eternal being; and he habitually declared that he himself did not truly exist either. The things of heaven abide, but the things of earth are changeable, subject to death and fragile. As for that eternal pain, it is full of decay, and the only reason it does not end is that it is doomed to be coming to an end unendingly.[62]

Idithun gazed toward that blessed country, his blessed land, his blessed home, where the saints share eternal life and unchangeable truth; and he feared to go away from it and be exiled to a place where there is no true being. He longed to be, there where being is being at its supreme perfection. Comparing the two, and finding himself standing between them, he was still fearful, so he said, *"Forgive me, so that I may find some cool refreshment before I go away to be no more*, for if you have not forgiven my sins, I will go away from you for ever. And from whom would I then be going away for ever? From him who said, *I AM WHO AM*, from him who said, *Thus shall you say to the children of Israel, HE WHO IS has sent me to you"* (Ex 3:14). Anyone who takes the road away from him who truly *is* necessarily goes toward non-being.

23. Well, brothers and sisters, if I have burdened and wearied you, put up with it, for this sermon has been hard work for me too. But in fact you have only yourselves to blame if you feel overworked, because if I felt you were getting bored with what was being said, I would stop immediately.

---

62. *Ad hoc non finitur, ut sine fine finiatur.*

Exposition of Psalm 41

Synopsis

The Psalm portrays holy desire in the deer that longs for springs of water. Whose words are these? They're ours, if we but claim them. Remember that this is the Church's voice. Many believe it's her catechumens longing for baptism, but I think this Psalm's intense longing goes beyond that. This is another Psalm *for understanding for the children of Korah*, so we know it refers to those who grasp the cross of Christ. What are we to "understand"? God's invisible realities, known through created things. So share my longing, run thirsty with me to the font of understanding (1–2). Consider the behavior of deer. They kill snakes and get thirsty; spiritual deer also thirst after they kill off their vices and sins. Deer also walk in a line, the head of each one resting on the hindquarters of the one before it; spiritual deer likewise carry each other's burdens. Deer endure other animals but keep thirsting to reach the waters (3–5). Day and night the Psalmist consumes tears like bread, that is, like nourishment. He can't point to God in a way that will satisfy his critics who "lack the right kind of eyes."

But is there a way to discern God? Let's see. All creation points beyond itself; even our inner self points away from itself in order to perceive reality, both visible (e.g., objects) and invisible (e.g., justice). God is beyond the physical world and beyond even the soul. But when the Psalmist *poured out my soul above myself* an answer began to emerge: above the soul he found *the home of God* (6–8). But how did he get there? The road to God's house lies right through his tent on earth, his tabernacle, the Church. Another Psalmist found this out when he confronted the thorny question of why sinners flourish and the just suffer. Only in God's house did he understand that judgment of the unjust is being held in reserve, while affliction trains the skills and attitudes of the just. He arrived at God's house, he says, by following the sound of people praising God with beautiful spiritual music of praise (9). In that tent the spiritual "tip of his mind" became enrapt by strains of music from a heavenly source. Hope quieted the Psalmist's troubled soul. He confessed that salvation comes from God, not from himself, and it helped him to persevere (10–12).

Let's get through this Psalm. *Deep calls to deep*: this may be God's holy preachers calling to the deep abyss of other human hearts. Alternatively it refers to God's judgments (13–15). Like the wise ant let's collect food from God's word during our tranquil day, so that we'll be nourished during the troubling night. All that we need to pray is within: the victim, the sacrifice, the incense, the spices, and the words. God doesn't withdraw from his promise, but delays fulfillment for training purposes (16–17). But the Psalmist, having tasted sublime understanding, pants for more and so feels cast off. When strong people in the Church yield to temptation, the whole body of Christ cries out. It adds an insulting tone to the scoffer's old mocking question, *Where is your God?* Martyrs had to endure those insults too, though they could not show the crown they were receiving (18–19).

Augustine's Text of Psalm 41

(1) Unto the end, understanding for the children of Korah.

(2) As a deer longs for springs of water, so does my soul long for you, O God.

(3) My soul has been athirst for the living God.

    When shall I reach him and appear before the face of God?

(4) My tears have been bread to me day and night,

    As every day I hear the taunt, Where is your God?

(5) I reflected on these things, and poured out my soul above myself.

    Because I will walk into the place of the wonderful tent, even to the home of God,

    By the voice of exultation and praise, the sounds of one celebrating a festival.

(6) O my soul, why are you sorrowful, and why do you disquiet me?

    Hope in God, because I will confess to him, the salvation of my countenance,

(7) My God. My soul was troubled as it turned to me, therefore I remembered you, O Lord,

    From the territory of the Jordan and the little hill of Hermon.

(8) Deep calls to deep at the sound of your cataracts;

    All your breakers and waves have coursed over me.

(9) The Lord has assured us of his mercy in the daylight, but he will demonstrate it at night.

    My prayer to the God of my life is within me.

(10) I will say to God, You are my protector; why have you forgotten me?

Why have you thrust me back?

Why must I walk in deep sadness, while my enemy harasses me,

(11) And breaks my bones?

Those who trouble me have insulted me, as every day they taunt me: Where is your God?

(12) O my soul, why are you sorrowful, and why do you disquiet me?

Hope in God, because I will confess to him, the salvation of my countenance, my God.

Exposition

A Sermon to the People

Introduction: longing on both sides

1. Our soul has been longing for some time past to rejoice with you in God's word, and to salute you in SCRIPTURE our help and our salvation.[1] So listen now to what God gives you through us, and together with us be glad about his words, and about his truth and charity; for we have undertaken to talk to you about this psalm in response to your own longing.[2] The psalm begins in fact with holy longing, for the singer says, *As a deer longs for springs of water, so does my soul long for you, O God.* Who is it saying that? If we will, it is we ourselves. Why bother to inquire any further who it is, when it is within your power to be yourself the answer to the question? Remember, though, that the speaker is not a lone individual, but a single body: the Church, which is the body of Christ. A longing like this is not found in everyone who comes into church, yet those who have tasted the sweetness of the Lord,[3] and recognize that savor in this song, should not think they are alone in this experience. They must believe that similar seeds have been sown widely in the Lord's field all over the world, and that it is a single, united Christian voice which sings, *As a deer longs for springs of water, so does my soul long for you, O God.* We could well hear the voice of our catechumens here too, for they are hurrying toward the holy, grace-giving bath.[4]

This is why we customarily sing the psalm to arouse in them a longing for the fountain of forgiveness for their sins, like the longing of a deer

---

1. A pun in the Latin links verb with noun: *in illo vos salutare, qui est nostrum adiutorium et salutare*: "to wish you good health in HIM WHO IS our help and our health."
2. Variant: "our desire."
3. See Ps 33:9(34:8).
4. *Lavacrum.*

for the springs of water.⁵ Fair enough, and may this interpretation keep its place in the Church; it is both true and sanctioned by usage. All the same, brothers and sisters, I cannot believe that a longing of such intensity is satisfied in believers even at baptism. If the candidates know where their pilgrimage is tending, and what that land is to which they must cross over, their longing will be kindled to even greater intensity.

Verse 1. Understanding offered to the "children of Korah"

2. The psalm is entitled, *Unto the end, understanding for the children of Korah*. We have come upon these children of Korah in the titles of other psalms;⁶ and we remember having discussed the name and its meaning before. Nonetheless we ought to mention the title now. The fact of having expounded it earlier should not deter us, for you were not all present in the various places where we discussed it previously. Now Korah may have been an historical person, as indeed he was, and may well have had children who were called "the sons of Korah." But we must peer into the holy secret implicit here, and persuade this name, pregnant with mystery, to bring forth what it holds. It is a great and holy mystery that Christians should be designated "children of Korah." Why can they be called that? Because they are children of the bridegroom, children of Christ; that is what Christians are called: the bridegroom's children.⁷ But why does Korah stand for Christ? Because the name Korah means Calvary; but that is a more obscure point. I was inquiring why Korah stood for Christ, but I am far more interested in inquiring why Christ is seen to be connected with Calvary. You already know, don't you? Of course you do. Christ was crucified at a place called Calvary. So "the children of the bridegroom," the children of his passion, the children redeemed by his blood, the children of his cross who wear upon their brows the sign of that gibbet his enemies set up on Calvary—these are called "children of Korah." For them this psalm is sung, to bring them understanding.

---

5. The catechumens were instructed during Lent and baptized at Easter. The psalm was sung as they processed to the baptistery, where they received the sacrament by immersion. Ambrose has left an account of baptismal practice in two works: *On the Sacraments* and *On the Mysteries*.
6. The collection "of the sons of Korah" was one of the groups incorporated into the final form of the Psalter. It includes Pss 43–48, 83, 84, 86, 87 (44–49, 84, 85, 87, 88). In his *Exposition of Psalm* 83, 2 and *Exposition of Psalm* 84, 2, Augustine discusses the meaning of the name Korah, interpreted as "bald," and associates this with Calvary, "the place of a skull." In the present context he seems to assume that this link is known to his hearers: he did not comment on the psalms in numerical order. See also the *Expositions of Psalms* 43, 1; 44, 1; 46, 2.
7. See Mt 9:15; Lk 5:34.

Let us bestir ourselves to understand, then. If it is sung for us, we should try to understand it. What are we going to understand? Into what kind of comprehension will the singing of this psalm lead us? I will tell you, boldly I will tell you: since the world was first created men and women have seen the invisible realities of God, understood through things that are made.[8] Well then, brothers and sisters, catch my eagerness, share my longing. Let us love, all of us together; let us burn together with this thirst; let us run together to the fountain of understanding. Let us long for it as a hart yearns for a spring. I do not mean that spring which the baptismal candidates long for, that their sins may be forgiven; let us who are baptized long rather for the well-spring of which Scripture says, *With you is the fountain of life*; for God is both a spring and light, as that other psalm goes on to say: *In your light we will see light* (Ps 35:10(36:9)). If he is both fountain and light he obviously is understanding, for while he fully satisfies the soul athirst to know, everyone who understands is illumined by a light that is not corporeal or carnal or external, but is an inward radiance. There is an interior light, brothers and sisters, which people without understanding do not know. The apostle has some exhortation to offer to believers who long for the fountain of life and already experience it in some degree: *Walk no more now as the pagans walk*, he says. *Their minds are empty; they are darkened in their understanding and estranged from the life of God by the ignorance that is in them, owing to the blindness of their hearts* (Eph 4:17–18). If they are darkened in their understanding—darkened, that is, precisely because they do not understand—it follows that they who do understand are illuminated. Run to the springs, long for the fountains of water. With God is the fountain of life, a fountain that can never dry up; and in his light is a radiance never dimmed. Long for this light; long for the well-spring, and for a light such as your eyes have never known. Your inner eye is being prepared to see that light, and your inner thirst is burning ever more fiercely for that fountain. Run to the fountain, long for the fountain; but do not run to it in any random fashion, do not run like any animal you may chance to think of: run only like a deer. Why like a deer? Because there must be no tardiness about your running. Run energetically, long untiringly for the fountain. I say this because the deer stands for fleetness of foot.

Verse 2. Deer kill snakes, and then feel thirstier

3. Perhaps this is not the only characteristic of deer that Scripture wished us to consider. There may be something else. Listen now to another peculiarity of theirs. A hart kills snakes, and after font them he burns with a more intense thirst than before; so after dealing with the snakes he runs to the well-springs even more urgently. These snakes represent your vices; put the snakes of your iniquity to death, and you will long all the more keenly for the font of truth. Perhaps a miserly spirit is hissing dark suggestions in

---

8. See Rom 1:20.

you, hissing something opposed to God's word and forbidden by his commandments? You know what you are told: "Give that thing up, and stay clear of sin." But if you would rather commit the sin than turn your back on some temporal gain, you are choosing to be bitten by the snake instead of killing it. If you prefer your vice, your lust, your greed, your snake, when am I going to find in you the kind of longing that will send you running to the well-spring? How are you going to yearn for the font of wisdom, if you are still floundering in the venom of ill-will? Kill off whatever in you is opposed to the truth; but when you judge yourself to be free of crooked desires, do not sit down as though that were all, and you had nothing else to long for. There is something for which you must arouse yourself and go, if you have already done your best to rid yourself of anything in you that could hold you back. I know that if you are a good deer you are going to say to me, "God knows that I'm not a money-grubber now, that I no longer covet other people's property, that I'm not on fire with adulterous lust, not tormented by hatred or envy of anyone," and so forth. You are going to tell me, "I no longer have these sins"; and so you look for something you can enjoy, don't you? Long for what will truly give you delight, long for the fountains of water. God has everything that will refresh you. He is able to fill anyone who comes to him, anyone who comes parched from slaughtering snakes, like a fleet-footed deer.

Kindly arrangements among deer

4. There is another point to notice about deer. People have seen them doing what I am about to describe; it would not have been recorded about them in writing unless previously observed. It is said, then, that when deer are walking in single file, or want to swim to a different place to find fresh grazing, they rest their heavy heads on each other. One goes in front, another rests its head on him, and others on them, and so on until the whole line is supported. When the hart who has been bearing the weight in the foremost position is exhausted, he moves to the rear, and another takes his place to carry what the first one was carrying, while this previous leader rests himself by supporting his head on another, as all the others have been doing. They go on like this, carrying the heavy weight for each other; so they make good progress, and do not let each other down. Was it not deer like these that the apostle had in mind? *Bear one another's burdens*, he says, *and so you will fulfill the law of Christ* (Gal 6:2).

Verse 3. The longing is intensified by waiting

5. Once a deer of this kind is established in faith, but does not yet see the object of that faith and yearns to understand what he or she loves, this deer has to endure other people who are not deer at all, people whose understanding is darkened, who are sunk in their inner murk and blinded by vicious desires. Nor is this all, for they jeer at the believer who cannot yet point to the reality in which he or she believes: *Where is your God?* Let

us listen to how our hart handled these attacks, so that we may meet them in the same way if we can. To begin with he expressed his thirst: *as a deer longs for springs of water, so does my soul long for you, O God.* Did I hear someone ask, "Perhaps the deer is longing for springs of water because he needs a wash?" We can't tell whether it was for drinking or for washing, but listen to the next line; and don't ask questions: *my soul has been athirst for the living God.* The line, *as a deer longs for springs of water, so does my soul long for you, O God*, means the same as *my soul has been athirst for the living God.* What was this soul thirsting for? *When shall I reach him and appear before the face of God?* "This is what I am thirsting for, to reach him and to appear before him. I am thirsty on my pilgrimage, parched in my running, but I will be totally satisfied when I arrive. But *when shall I reach him?*" What is soon to God seems late to our longing. *When shall I reach him and appear before the face of God?* A like longing evoked the cry in another psalm: *One thing have I begged of the Lord, and that will I seek after: to live in the Lord's house all the days of my life.* To what purpose? *That I may contemplate the Lord with delight* (Ps 26(27):4). *When shall I reach him and appear before the face of the Lord?*[9]

Verse 4. A diet of tears

6. Meanwhile I mull over these things as I run my course, as I am still on the way, not yet arriving, not yet appearing there. And all the while *my tears have been bread to me day and night, as every day I hear the taunt, Where is your God?* Notice that he says, *My tears have been bread*, bread, not bitterness. "My very tears were delicious to me. I was thirsting for that spring, and because I could not yet drink from it, I ate my tears the more hungrily." He did not say, "My tears have been my drink." If he had, we might have thought he had thirsted for his tears as he thirsted for the wellsprings; but no: "My thirst, my burning thirst, remains unquenched, and it drags me toward the springs of water; but as I wait, my tears have become bread to me." And in eating his tears he would certainly find his thirst for the springs all the keener. "My tears became bread for me, by day and by night." It is in the daytime that people eat food, which is represented by the term "bread"; at night they sleep. Yet the psalmist eats his bread of tears by day and by night. You could take this to mean "all the time"; or you could understand "day" as prosperity in this world, and "night" as worldly misfortune. "In both prosperity and adversity, as this world sees them, I pour out my tears," he says. "Never do I take the keen edge off my desire. Even if things are going well by worldly standards they are bad for me,

---

9. Perhaps because of contamination from the quotation immediately preceding, the last word here is *Domini*, not *Dei* as in his citation of the same verse above. One of the characteristic features in the psalms of the Korah collection is the use of "God" rather than the divine name usually rendered in English by "the Lord." But a few codices amend to *Dei* here.

until I appear before the face of God. Why try to force me into enjoying the daylight, if some worldly prosperity smiles on me? Is prosperity not a deceiver? Is it not labile, unsteady, mortal? Is it not ephemeral, fleeting, transient? Does it not harbor more of deceitfulness than delight? Why then should my tears not be bread for me, even in prosperity?" It is true, indeed, that even if the happiness of this world bathes us in its light, as long as we are in the body we are still on our journey and absent from the Lord,[10] and *every day I hear the taunt, Where is your God?* If a pagan says this to me, I cannot retort, "What about you? Where is *your* God?" because the pagan can point to his god. He indicates some stone with his finger and says, "Look, there's my god! *Where is yours?*" If I laugh at the stone, and the pagan who pointed it out is embarrassed, he looks away from the stone toward the sky; then perhaps he points to the sun and says again, "Look, there's my god! *Where is yours?*" He has found something he can demonstrate to my bodily eyes. For me it is different, not because I have nothing to demonstrate, but because he lacks the kind of eyes to which I could demonstrate it. He was able to point the sun out to my bodily eyes as his god, but how can I point out to any eyes he has the sun's Creator?

Where is your God? The search through creatures and in oneself

But as I listened daily to the taunt, *Where is your God?* and was nourished by my daily diet of tears, as I pondered day and night on this question hurled at me, *Where is your God?* even I came to wonder if was possible for me not merely to believe in my God, but even to see something of him. I see the things my God has made, but my God himself, who made them, I do not see. Yet like a deer I long for the springs of water, and the fountain of life is with him; and since this psalm was written to bring understanding to the children of Korah, and the invisible realities of God are seen and understood through things that are made,[11] what shall I do to find my God? I will consider the earth, for the earth was made. Great is the beauty of earth's many faces, but it was an artist who made it. Great wonders there are in seeds and in the generation of living things, but all of them come from their Creator. I point to the immensity of the sea all around us; I am astonished and filled with wonder, and I look for the artificer. I look up to the sky and the loveliness of the stars; I marvel at the sun's radiance with its power to awaken the day, and the moon that relieves the darkness of night. These things are marvelous, we must praise them, even be astounded at them, for they are not earthly things; they belong to the heavens. But not yet is my thirst slaked, for though I admire them and sing their praises, it is for him who made them that I thirst. So I return to myself, and examine who I am, I who can ask such questions. I find that I have a body and a soul: the one I must rule and by the other be ruled: the body serves and the soul

---

10. See 2 Cor 5:6.
11. See Rom 1:20.

commands. I observe that my soul is a better thing than my body, and that the investigator of these mysteries is not my body but my soul; and yet I recognize that when I surveyed all these things, I surveyed them through my body. I was praising the earth, but I knew it only through my eyes; I praised the sea, but my eyes had revealed it to me; I praised the sky, the stars, the sun and the moon, but only through my eyes had I come to know them. The eyes are bodily organs, the windows of the mind; it is the inner self that looks out through them, and if the mind is preoccupied with some other thought, the eyes are open to no purpose. My God, who made these things I see with my eyes, is not to be sought with my eyes.

My mind even has the power to see objects through itself alone. It may be aware of something like colors and light not actually present to my eyes, music or other sounds not available to my ears, sweet scents not perceived by my nose, a savor not in contact with my palate or tongue, a feeling of hardness or softness, of cold or heat, of roughness or smoothness, which my body might have perceived, but does not. Or again it may be aware of something that I see within myself. See within? How is that? Something, I mean, that is neither a color, nor a sound, nor a scent, nor a taste, nor heat, nor cold, nor hardness nor softness. When we think about justice, and appreciate the beauty of it within ourselves, in our thought, what sound do our ears catch? Does any steamy scent rise to our nostrils? What enters the mouth? What pleasant surface meets the exploring hand? Yet justice is within us; it is beautiful, it moves us to praise, we see it; and even if our bodily eyes are in darkness, the mind enjoys its light. What was it that Tobit saw, when in his blindness he was giving advice to a son who could see?[12]

The mind which governs the body, guides it and dwells in it, is aware of something that reaches it not through the body's eyes, or ears, or nose, or palate, or sense of touch, but through itself; and unquestionably what the mind knows through itself is better than what it comes to know through its servant. But still there is more: the mind sees itself through itself; it sees itself so as to know itself. In no way does it seek the help of the bodily eyes to see itself; on the contrary, it withdraws from all its bodily faculties, finding them a hindrance and a noisy one, and betakes itself to itself that it may see itself in itself and know itself in its own presence.

But is the mind's God something similar, something like the mind itself? To be sure, God can be seen only with the mind, but he cannot be seen as the mind itself can be seen. This mind is seeking a reality that is God, a reality of which the mockers cannot say, *Where is your God?* It is seeking the unchangeable truth, the substance that cannot fail. But the mind itself is not like that: it fails and makes progress, it knows and then knows not, it remembers and forgets, it wants something at one moment and then wants it no more. No such mutability is found in God. If I say,

---

12. See Tb 4:1–23.

"God is subject to change," they will have the right to jeer at me, those who say, *Where is your God?*

Verse 5. The soul is poured out above itself

8. I sought my God in visible, material creatures, and I did not find him. I sought the substance of him in myself, as though he were something like what I am, and did not find him there either; so I have become aware that my God is some reality above the soul. *I reflected on these things, and poured out my soul above myself* that I might touch him,[13] for how could my soul ever attain what it seeks, the reality above the soul, unless it poured itself out above itself? If it remained within itself it would see nothing other than itself; and in seeing only itself it would certainly not be seeing its God. Let the onlookers who deride me go on saying, *Where is your God?* Yes, let them say it, and as long as I do not see him, as long as I am made to wait, I will eat my tears day and night. Let them go on saying, *Where is your God?* I look for my God in every bodily creature, whether on earth or in the sky, but I do not find him. I look for his substance in my own soul, but do not find him there. Yet still I have pondered on this search for my God and, longing to gaze on the invisible realities of God by understanding them through created things, *I poured out my soul above myself*; and now there is nothing left for me to touch, except my God. For there, above my soul, is the home of my God; there he dwells, from there he looks down upon me, from there he created me, from there he governs me and takes thought for me, from there he arouses me, calls me, guides me and leads me on, and from there he will lead me to journey's end.

In the admirable tabernacle he catches the sound of another festival

9. For he who has his most lofty home in a secret place has also a tent on earth. His tent[14] is the Church, the Church which is still a pilgrim; yet he is to be sought there, because in this tent we find the way that leads to his home. When I resolved to pour out my soul above myself to reach my God, why did I do it? *Because I will walk into the place of the tent.* If I seek my God away from that camp-site I will go astray. *I will walk into the place of the wonderful tent, even to the home of God.* I will walk into the place where this tent is pitched, this wonderful tabernacle, and so reach God's home. And already I find many wonderful things in the tent, great things that move me to admiration and amazement. The faithful are God's tent on earth; and in them I admire the obedience of their bodily parts, for sin does not reign in them to exact obedience to its desires, nor do they put their members at sin's disposal as implements of iniquity, but rather subject

---

13. One manuscript specifies, "touch him with my mind's understanding."
14. *Tabernaculum.* See Augustine's observations on homes and tents in his *Exposition 2 of Psalm* 26,6.

them to the living God in good works.[15] So I marvel at bodily members enlisted for action under the soul that serves God. Moreover I watch the soul obeying God, organizing its activities, restraining its wayward desires, banishing ignorance, stretching out to endure all that is harsh and testing, and exercising justice and kindness toward other people.

These virtues I do indeed admire in the soul, yet still I am walking in the wonderful tent. Then I go further still and pass beyond it; and though the tent is admirable, I am dumbfounded when I arrive at God's house. In another psalm the speaker tells us that he had put a hard, puzzling question to himself: why on this earth good fortune usually comes the way of the wicked, while misfortune dogs the good. Then he speaks of the house of God: *I tried to solve the problem, but it is too hard for me until I enter God's holy place, and understand what the end must be* (Ps 72(73):16–17); for there, in God's holy place, in God's house, is the spring of understanding. There that psalmist understood what the end must be, and solved his problem about the happiness of villains and the travail of the just. What was his solution? He saw that while the life of the wicked is prolonged here, they are being reserved for punishment without end, but while the good struggle along they are being trained until they are ready at last to gain their inheritance. This is what the psalmist understood in God's holy place: he understood the final outcome. He climbed up to the tent, then arrived at God's house. Yet it was while he marveled at the members of that company in the tent that he was led to God's house. He was drawn toward a kind of sweetness, an inward, secret pleasure that cannot be described, as though some musical instrument were sounding delightfully from God's house. As he still walked about in the tent he could hear this inner music; he was drawn to its sweet tones, following its melodies and distancing himself from the din of flesh and blood, until he found his way even to the house of God. He tells us about the road he took and the manner in which he was led, as though we had asked him, "You admire the tent on earth, but how did you reach the secret precincts of God's house?" *By the voice of exultation and praise*, he says, *the sounds of one celebrating a festival.*[16]

When people celebrate in this world with their various forms of indulgence, they usually set up musical instruments outside their houses, or assemble singers there, or provide some kind of music which enhances the pleasure of the guests and entices them to immoderate behavior. If we are passing by and happen to hear it, we say, "What's going on?" And they tell us that it's some kind of party. "It's a birthday party," they say, or "There's a wedding reception." They tell us this so that the songs may not seem out of place, and the lavish expenditure[17] may seem to be justified by the festive occasion. In God's home there is an everlasting party. What is celebrated

---

15. See Rom 6:12–13.
16. Variant: "of a banquet."
17. Variant: "the joy."

there is not some occasion that passes; the choirs of angels keep eternal festival, for the eternally present face of God is joy never diminished. This is a feast day that does not open at dawn, or close at sundown. From that eternal, unfading festival melodious and delightful sound reaches the ears of the heart, but only if the world's din does not drown it. The sweet strains of that celebration are wafted into the ears of one who walks in the tent and ponders the wonderful works of God in the redemption of believers, and they drag the deer toward the springs of water.

Verse 6. Subsequent sadness

10. Nonetheless, brothers and sisters, as long as we are in the body we are still on pilgrimage and away from the Lord.[18] Our corruptible body weighs down the soul, and this earthly dwelling oppresses a mind that considers many things.[19] At times we may in some measure scatter the clouds as our yearning draws us on, and even come within earshot of that melody, so that by pressing forward we may conceive something of the house of God. Yet under the weight of our weakness we fall back into familiar things, and slide down again into our ordinary way of life. As we have found there a cause for joy, so here there is no shortage of things to groan about. The deer made tears his food by day and by night; he was possessed by yearning for the well-springs, those springs of God's spiritual delight, and he poured out his soul above himself in his longing to touch what was above his soul. He walked into the admirable tent, and even to the house of God; he was drawn onward by the charm of a spiritual, intelligible music until he despised all external things and was rapt by love for what is within. But for all that, he is still a human being, still groaning, still carrying frail flesh, still imperiled amid the stumbling-blocks of this world. So he looked again at himself as he returned from that place, and as he found himself amid his woes he compared them with the glories he had gone in to see, the wonder he had seen and left behind as he came out. *O my soul, why are you sorrowful, and why do you disquiet me?* he asked. "Remember how we were gladdened by an inner sweetness, remember how we found it possible to perceive with the sharp point of our mind something that does not change, even though we could but brush against it for a swift moment. Why, then, do you still disquiet me? Why are you still sorrowful? You do not doubt your God. It is not as though you had no retort to make to those who ask, *Where is your God?* Already in my deepest being I have known something beyond change, so how can you still disquiet me? *Hope in God.*"

His soul seems to reply silently to him, "Why do I disquiet you? Why else, than because I am not there, in that place of delight to which I was carried away, but so briefly? Am I yet drinking from that fountain, free from fear? Am I yet beyond all danger of falling? Am I secure, as though

---

18. See 2 Cor 5:6.
19. See Wis 9:15.

all sinful desires were subdued and overcome? Is my adversary, the devil, not still on the watch? Does he not set cunning traps for me every day? Can you seriously ask me not to disquiet you, while my place is still in this world, while I am a pilgrim still, and far from God's house?"

But he has an answer for the soul that disquiets him, and gives him such plausible reasons for its unease by pointing to the evils that abound in this world. "*Hope in God*," he says. "Dwell in hope for this in-between time." If hope is seen, it is hope no longer; but if we hope for what we do not see, we wait for it in patience.[20]

Verse 7. Hope and salvation

11. *Hope in God*. Why? *Because I will confess to him*. And what will you confess to him? "That he is *the salvation of my countenance, my God*. There can be no salvation for me derived from myself, so this is what I will say, this I will confess: he is *the salvation of my countenance, my God*." The speaker knows that caution is necessary in spite of the things he has in some measure understood, so he is on his guard lest the enemy approach by stealth, and he does not yet make bold to say, "I am saved in every respect." We do indeed possess the first fruits of the Spirit, yet we groan within ourselves, waiting for our full adoption in the redemption of our bodies.[21] When that salvation has been brought to perfection in us we shall live in God's house for ever, praising without end the God to whom another psalm cries out, *Blessed are they who dwell in your house; they will praise you for ever and ever* (Ps 83:5(84:4)). This is not our situation yet, for the salvation promised us is not yet fully accomplished, but I confess to my God in hope, and say to him, "You are *the salvation of my countenance, my God*." We are saved in hope; but if hope is seen, it is hope no longer.[22] Persevere until you get there, persevere until salvation comes to you. Listen to God himself speaking to you inwardly: *Hold out for the Lord, act manfully; let your heart be strengthened, and hold out for the Lord* (Ps 26(27):14), for *whoever perseveres to the end will be saved* (Mt 10:22; 24:13). In view of all this, *O my soul, why are you sorrowful, and why do you disquiet me? Hope in God, because I will confess to him*. This is my confession: You are *the salvation of my countenance, my God*.

Turn away from yourself

12. *My soul was troubled as it turned to me*. It would not be, would it, if it turned to God? It is troubled when it turns to myself. When turned toward the unchangeable it received new strength, but when turned to what is prone to change it was disturbed. I know that my God's righteousness abides, but whether my own will abide, I know not, for the apostle's warning

---

20. See Rom 8:24–25.
21. See Rom 8:23.
22. See Rom 8:24.

terrifies me: *Anyone who thinks he stands must take care not to fall* (1 Cor 10:12). Since there is in me no stability, neither is there any hope for me in myself. *My soul was troubled as it turned to me.* Would you like to free your soul from its anxiety? Then do not let it linger in yourself. Say rather, *To you, Lord, have I lifted up my soul* (Ps 24(25):1). Listen, I will make the point clearer. Put no trust in yourself, but only in your God. If you trust in yourself, your soul will be turned toward yourself and gravely troubled, because it cannot yet find any grounds for security in you. So then, if my soul turned toward myself and found itself disturbed, what is left to me but humility, the humble refusal of the soul to place any reliance on itself? What course is open to it, except to make itself very small indeed, and to humble itself so that it may be raised up? Let it attribute nothing to itself, and then what is profitable may be granted to it by God.

My soul was troubled when it focused on itself, and what aroused that turbulence was pride. *Therefore I remembered you,*[23] *O Lord, from the territory of the Jordan and the little hill of Hermon.* From where did I remember you? From an insignificant mountain and from the Jordan region. Perhaps that means from baptism, where our sins were forgiven. I think this may be right, because no one runs toward the forgiveness of sins except those who are displeased with themselves; no one runs toward the forgiveness of sins except those who acknowledge that they are sinners; and none can confess their sinfulness without humbling themselves before God. This is why *I remembered you from the territory of the Jordan, and from a little hill*, not from a high mountain. From this paltry hill I want you to bring about great things, because *anyone who exalts himself will be humbled, but the one who humbles himself will be exalted* (Lk 14:11; 18:14). An additional point is that if you investigate the interpretation of the names, you find that Jordan means "their descent." Descend then, so that you may be lifted up; do not lift yourself up, or you may be suppressed. *And from the little hill of Hermon*. The name Hermon is said to mean "putting under a ban." Put yourself under a ban in your displeasure with yourself; for if you are self-satisfied you will be displeasing to God. God grants us all good things because he is good, not because we are worthy, because he is merciful and not because we have deserved them in any way. Therefore *I remembered God from the territory of the Jordan and from Hermon*. Because he remembers God in humility, he will be found worthy to be exalted and to enjoy God to the full, for those who make the Lord their boast are not exalted on their own account.

Verse 8. The human heart is a great deep

13. *Deep calls to deep at the sound of your cataracts*. I may be able to get through this whole psalm if you help me by your concentration, for I can see how eager you are. I am not too worried about any fatigue you

---

23. Variant: "I will remember you."

may feel as you listen, for you can see how I am sweating in the effort that speaking costs me. And as you watch me laboring, you will certainly help me, for you know I am laboring not for my own benefit, but yours. Go on listening, then; I can see you want to.

Deep calls to deep at the sound of your cataracts. The one who remembered God from the Jordan region and from Hermon now says this to God. He says it wonderingly: *Deep calls to deep at the sound of your cataracts.* What is this deep that is invoking another deep, and what is the depth invoked? The latter must be the depth of understanding,[24] for a depth is an unsearchable place, a profundity beyond comprehension. The word "depth" is usually applied to some vast ocean, because there we find such depth, such profundity, that we can never fathom it.

Now in another place it was said, *Your judgments are an unfathomable abyss* (Ps 35:7(36:6)), and by this metaphor Scripture meant to teach us that God's judgments are deeper than our minds can comprehend. What then is the deep that is calling out here, and what the deep that is invoked? If "deep" signifies profundity, surely the human heart is a deep abyss? Could anything be more profound? Human beings can speak, they can be observed as they use their limbs, and heard in their speech; but can we ever get to the bottom of a person's thoughts, or see into anyone's heart? Who can grasp what another person is intent upon there within the heart, what are the possibilities, the activity, the purposes of the heart, its will and its refusals? The profundity of a human being is surely referred to in a saying we find elsewhere: *A mortal will draw near to the heart's depths, and God will be exalted* (Ps 63:7–8(64:6)).

But if a human being is a deep abyss, how does a deep call upon a deep? Can it mean one human invoking another? Can a human being do that, in the way we invoke God? No, certainly not. But we do use the word "invoke" to mean "invite" or "call something to oneself." For instance, it might be said of someone that he invites death;[25] this means that he lives in such a way as to call death down upon himself, for no one will actually pray for it, or explicitly invite it; but by living in a wicked fashion people implicitly call it down upon themselves. So in this sense deep does call to deep when one human being calls to another. This is how wisdom is imparted, and faith is learned, when one deep invokes another. Holy preachers of God's word call to a deep abyss. But are they not a deep abyss themselves? They certainly are, as you know. The apostle says, *It matters very little to me that I am judged by you or by any human day of reckoning.* What a deep abyss he is! But he goes further: *Neither do I judge myself* (1 Cor 4:3). Do you find it difficult to believe that there could be such profundity in any human being that it is hidden from the person himself? Think, then, what a depth of human weakness lay hidden in Peter. He did not know what was

---

24. Mentioned in the title of the psalm.
25. See Wis 1:16.

going on within him when he kept promising so rashly that he would die with the Lord or for the Lord.[26] What a deep abyss he was! Yet even that depth lay open and naked to God's eyes, for Christ told him in advance what Peter himself did not know.

Any human being, even a holy, good-living person, even one who has made great progress, is a deep place, and such a person calls upon another depth when he preaches to another some part of the faith, some part of the truth, with a view to eternal life. But the deep that preaches is profitable to the deep he calls to if he calls in the sound of God's cataracts. *Deep calls to deep*, one person wins over another, but not with his own voice only: he calls in *the sound of your cataracts*.

The depth of God's judgments

14. Now consider an alternative interpretation. *Deep calls to deep at the sound of your cataracts.* I already began to tremble when my soul turned to myself and was troubled, but I am thoroughly terrified by your judgments, for *your judgments are an unfathomable abyss* (Ps 35:7(36:6)), and *deep calls to deep*. As we struggle in this mortal flesh, this travailing, sinful flesh, full of troubles and handicaps and liable to immoderate desires, we are already subject to the penalty imposed by your judgment, for of old you said to a sinner, *You shall certainly die* and *In the sweat of your face you shall eat your bread* (Gn 2:17; 3:19). But this is only the first abyss of your judgment. If people live sinfully here, *deep calls to deep*, because they pass from punishment to punishment, from darkness to darkness, from depth to depth, from torment to torment, from burning lust to the flames of hell. Perhaps it was of this that the psalmist was afraid when he said, *My soul was troubled as it turned to me; therefore I remembered you, Lord, from the territory of the Jordan and from Hermon*. I must be humble, for I am exceedingly frightened by the prospect of your judgments. I was in sheer terror at the thought, and as it turned to me *my soul was troubled*. What judgments of yours struck fear in me? Were they some trivial judgments on your part? No, your present judgments are already great, and severe, and grievous; but if only they were all! *Deep calls to deep at the sound of your cataracts.* You threaten us, you tell us that after our present travail a further condemnation awaits us: *at the sound of your cataracts deep calls to deep*. Where shall I go, then, from your face, whither flee from your spirit,[27] if even after our present pains more severe pains are to be feared?

Waves and breakers

15. *All your breakers and waves have coursed over me*. The waves wash over me in the sufferings I undergo now, but your threats are judgments

---

26. See Jn 13:37.
27. See Ps 138(139):7.

poised above me.[28] All my present hardships are your waves, but all your menaces hang over me, ready to break on my head. In the waves this abyss that I am calls out, but behind your impending threats is that other abyss to which this one calls. Already I flounder amid your waves, but your threats are far more serious and they hang over me, for a threat is something not yet pressing down, but poised overhead. Yet you set me free, and therefore I have said to my soul, *Hope in God, because I will confess to him, the salvation of my countenance, my God.* The more my woes are multiplied, the gentler will be your mercy.

Verse 9. Gather the word while you can

16. With this in mind the psalmist continues, *The Lord has assured* [29] *us of his mercy in daylight, but he will demonstrate*[30] *it at night.* When tribulation strikes, no one has time to listen. Take note while things are going well for you, listen while you are prospering, learn while you are tranquil. Collect the teachings of wisdom and the word of God like food, for when we are in trouble we need to feel the benefit of what we heard in our carefree days. So it is that in your times of prosperity God assures you of his mercy, telling you that if you serve him faithfully he delivers you from trouble; but only at night does he demonstrate to you that mercy of which he assured you in the daytime. When the trouble is visited upon you, he does not leave you bereft; he proves to you that his daytime assurance was true. This is why Scripture says, *Very lovely is the Lord's mercy in time of trouble, like a rainy cloud in drought* (Sir 35:26). *The Lord has assured us of his mercy in daylight, but he will demonstrate it at night.* He can only prove to you that he comes to your help when tribulation overwhelms you, because then he who made his promise to you in daylight has the chance to deliver you.

We are urged to imitate the ant, for the same reason.[31] Worldly prosperity is symbolized by daylight, and worldly adversity by the darkness of night; but another image is provided by the changing seasons. Summer represents prosperity, and winter adversity. What does the ant do? Throughout the summer she collects what will be useful in winter. So you must do likewise: in summertime, when your enterprises are going well and you are tranquil, listen to the word of the Lord. How is it possible that in this stormy world you could make your entire crossing of the sea without running into trouble? How is that possible? Does anyone? If anyone did, that person's tranquil course would be all the more suspect. *The Lord has assured us of his mercy in daylight, but he will demonstrate it at night.*

---

28. *Suspensiones.*
29. Variant: "will assure."
30. Variant: "has demonstrated."
31. See Prv 6:6.

Verses 9–10. The inner prayer: "Why have you forgotten me?"

17. What must you do, then, while you are on your pilgrimage? How must you conduct yourself? *My prayer to the God of my life is within me.* This is what I do, I, a thirsty deer, longing for the springs of water, remembering the sweetness of the sound that has led me through the tent, even to God's house. As long as my corruptible body weighs heavily on my soul[32] *my prayer to the God of my life is within me.* To offer supplication to God I have no need to seek exotic gifts from overseas; for God to hear me I have no need to sail afar and bring back incense and aromatic spices, or to bring calf or ram from the flock, for *my prayer to the God of my life is within me.* Here within me I have the victim I must offer, here within the incense I must burn, here within me is the sacrifice with which I may propitiate my God: *a sacrifice to God is a troubled spirit* (Ps 50:19(51:17)). Listen to what this inner sacrifice is like, this offering from a troubled spirit: *"I will say to God, You are my protector; why have you forgotten me?* I am struggling here as though you were no longer mindful of me. But you are training me, and I know that you are only delaying what you promised, not disavowing it.[33]

All the same, *why have you forgotten me?* Just as our head cried out in our voice, *My God, my God, why have you forsaken me?* (Ps 21:2(22:1); Mt 27:46), so too *I will say to God, You are my protector; why have you forgotten me?"*

Verses 10–11. Even my bones are broken

18. *Why have you thrust me back?* Why have you thrust me away from that sublime source of understanding and unchangeable truth? I am already panting for it, so why have I been thrown down to my old life by the burdensome weight of my sinfulness? This same plea is made in another psalm: *Beside myself with fear* or after some kind of ecstasy, where he had seen some glorious vision, *Beside myself with fear, I said, I have been flung far out of your sight* (Ps 30:23(31:22)). That suppliant compared his present lot with the wonders he had attained in his uplifted state, and he saw himself now flung far away from God's gaze, as the psalmist does here: *Why have you thrust me back? Why must I walk in deep sadness, while my enemy harasses me and breaks my bones,* my enemy the devil, the tempter? As scandals increase all around, the charity of many grows cold.[34] When we see even the powerful people in the Church so often giving way under pressure, does not Christ's body cry out, "The enemy is breaking my bones"? Bones are our strong framework, yet even these strong supports sometimes yield to temptation. When any member of Christ's body thinks of this, does he

---

32. See Wis 9:15.
33. *Differs mihi, non mihi aufers, quod promisisti.*
34. See Mt 24:12.

or she not cry out with the voice of Christ's body, *"Why have you thrust me back? Why must I walk in deep sadness, while my enemy harasses me and breaks my bones?* It is not just my flesh that is under attack, but my bones too." You watch them crumble under temptation, even those bones in which you thought there would be some strength, and so the weak members lose heart when they see the strong succumb. How dangerous this is, my brothers and sisters!

Verses 11–12. Where is your God?

19. *Those who trouble me have insulted me.* And here it comes again, the same mocking question: *They insulted me, as every day they taunt me: Where is your God?* Most of all do they say this when the Church is beset by temptations: *Where is your God?* What a lot of insults the martyrs heard, as they suffered valiantly for Christ's name: "Where is your God? Let him deliver you, if he can." People saw them enduring torments outwardly, but did not see them inwardly crowned. *Those who trouble me have insulted me, as every day they taunt me: Where is your God?* When I have this to contend with, and as my troubled soul turns to me, what else am I to say to it, except, *O my soul, why are you sorrowful, and why do you disquiet me?* But my soul seems to reply, "And how could I not disquiet you, trapped as I am amid such great evils? I am longing for the good, I am thirsting, laboring; and you think I could refrain from disquieting you?" But *hope in God, because I will still confess to him.* My soul makes the same confession; it reiterates its hope yet more strongly: "You are *the salvation of my countenance, my God.*"

Exposition of Psalm 42

Synopsis

The Psalmist's soul is sad here, perhaps because of spiritual hunger. The body of Christ is hungry everywhere. Listen to the voice: it's familiar because it's our own voice—if we're in Christ's body. Christians making progress are like good seed that groans among the weeds of bad Christians until harvest. Just and unjust share the rain that God sends, yet believers ask to be distinguished from unbelievers (1–2).

Endurance takes patience and battle requires fortitude; God grants both. Yet, as the Psalmist asks, why then does sorrow remain? He and we deal with consequences left over from sin. So let's imitate the Psalmist's prayer, *Send forth your light and your truth*. These two are linked; indeed, Christ himself is both the light and truth that leads us to his "mountain," the Church. The mention of "tents" reminds us that a war is on, so beware the enemy (3–4). Through the tent we come to the invisible high altar; only the just may approach it, but doing so renews fresh and youthful joy. The lyre differs from the psaltery, though the spiritual music of each pleases God. Spiritual harmony with God's commandments emits music, as it were, from high up, where the psaltery's sound is made. But praising God in earthly difficulties is playing the lyre, whose sound comes from down low (5).

The Psalmist speaks down low to his soul. So who exactly speaks here? It can't be flesh speaking to soul, or soul to flesh. Rather it's God's image within us, our rational-spiritual powers of reason; the spiritual mind or understanding here addresses the earthbound soul. Paul had the same conversation within himself when he was confounded by delighting in God's law with his mind but at the same time obeyed a law of sin in his members. The Lord portrayed the same conflict in Gethsemane. We too will feel it at the point of death; but just then the inner voice of God will draw us onward indescribably with healing encouragement. So humbly confess your hope in the Lord, not in yourself. Acknowledge your sickness candidly to the Physician (6–7). Be vigilant to do good works willingly and not grudgingly. Let your fasting, almsgiving, and prayer be for another's benefit (8).

Augustine's Text of Psalm 42

(1) *A Psalm for David himself.*

    Judge me, O God, and distinguish my cause from that of an unholy people;

    Deliver me from the wicked and deceitful.

(2) Since you are my fortitude, O my God, why have you thrust me back?

    Why must I walk in deep sadness, while my enemy harasses me?

(3) Send forth your light and your truth.

    They have led me, bringing me all the way to your holy mountain and into your tents.

(4) I will go in to God's altar, to God who makes my youth joyful.

    I will confess to you on the lyre, O God, my God.

(5) Why are you sorrowful, O my soul; why do you disquiet me?

    Hope in the Lord, because I will confess to him,

    The salvation of my countenance, my God.

Exposition

A Sermon to the People

The song of Christ's body

1. This psalm is a short one, so as you listen it will satisfy your minds without putting too much strain on your fasting stomachs. Let us hope that our soul may find nourishment in it, that soul which the psalmist speaks of as sad. I think it is probably sad because of some fasting on the part of the psalmist, or I should say because of his hunger, because fasting is a voluntary state, whereas hunger is something we cannot help. The Church is hungry, Christ's body is hungry. This person who is spread worldwide, whose head is on high and whose limbs are here below—this whole person is hungry. We should hear his voice, her voice, in all the psalms, jubilating or groaning, rejoicing in hope or sighing with love in fulfillment; we should hear it as something already well known to us, a voice most familiar because it is our own. There is no need to make heavy weather over indicating to you who the speaker is. Only let each of us be within Christ's body, and we shall be the speaker here.

A common lot for all, but different desires

2. Now you know that all those Christians who are making progress are like good seed. These are the people who groan with longing for the

heavenly city, who know they are on pilgrimage, who hold steadily to their road, and who by their desire for that abiding country have cast their hope ahead like an anchor.[1]

Christians of this stamp are the good seed, Christ's wheat which moans amid the weeds until the time arrives for harvest at the end of the world. Truth himself has explained this to us, Truth who is never deceived.[2] The good seed mourns amid weeds, amid bad people I mean, cheats and seducers, violent and angry folk and those poisoned by intrigue; it looks round and sees itself growing with them in the same field all over the world, watered by the same rain, blown on by the same wind, finding the same nutriment with them and going through the same hardships. It knows that it shares with them all this bounty of God in one common provision, and that all of it is granted to wicked and to good people without distinction by him who makes his sun rise over good and bad alike, and sends his rain on just and unjust.[3] The good seed, the holy seed, the seed of Abraham, is aware of how much it has in common with those from whom it will one day be separated; it is aware of being born in the same way as they are, of inheriting the same human condition, of carrying a mortal body exactly as they do, of enjoying the one daylight, the springs and fruits and abundance of this world, and of enduring its adversities in hunger or plenty, in peace or war, in health and disease. The holy people knows how much it has in common with the wicked, yet knows too that it does not make common cause with them; and so it bursts out, *Judge me, O God, and distinguish my cause from that of an unholy people.* It says, "Judge me, O God; I am not afraid of your judgment, because I have experience of your mercy. In this in-between time while I am on pilgrimage you do not yet assign me any distinguished place, because I have to live with the weeds until the season for harvest. You do not yet distinguish the rain that falls on me, you do not yet distinguish my daylight; but please distinguish my cause." Let a distinction be drawn between one who believes in you, and one who does not. In weakness they are equal, but in conscience far apart; there is parity of travail, disparity of desire. The desire of the ungodly will be extinguished; but what of the desire of the just? We should certainly be apprehensive about that, if the one who makes the promise were not totally reliable. The goal of our desire is the one who has promised; he will give us himself because he has already given us himself. He will give his immortal self when we are immortal, as he has already given himself to us as mortal in our mortality. *Judge me, O God, and distinguish my cause from that of an unholy people; deliver me from the wicked and deceitful.* The wicked and deceitful are the same as the *unholy people.* The psalm mentions them to

---

1. See Heb 6:19.
2. See Mt 13:24–30.
3. See Mt 5:45.

indicate that it means people of a certain type, for there will be two people working together, and one will be taken, the other left.[4]

Verse 2. The cause of your sorrow

3. It takes patience to endure until the harvest a kind of undistinguished distinction, if we can put it that way. I mean that since the two sorts of growth are still together, they are still undistinguished; but since the weeds are weeds and the grain is grain, in that sense they are distinguished already. We need fortitude as we wait, and we must beg it from him who ordered us to show fortitude, for if he does not make us into brave people we shall not be so. Let us entreat him to grant us fortitude, then, since he has said, *Whoever perseveres to the end will be saved* (Mt 10:22; 24:13). The psalmist saw the danger that if his soul arrogated fortitude to itself, it might be enfeebled thereby, so he immediately added, *Since you are my fortitude, O my God, why have you thrust me back? Why must I walk in deep sadness, while my enemy harasses me?* He is looking for the cause of his sorrow. *Why must I walk in deep sadness, while my enemy harasses me?* he asks. I am walking in sorrow, and the enemy attacks me with daily temptations, throwing into my path either attractive things which I should not love, or bogeys that it would be wrong to fear. The soul battles against both, and though not captured it is endangered and huddled up in sadness, so it says to God, *Why?* Let it ask him, and let it hear the reason why, for here in this psalm we have someone looking for the cause of the same sadness we know, and demanding of God, *Why have you thrust me back, and why must I walk in deep sadness?*

He may find the answer in Isaiah; possibly the reading we have just heard may help him in his quest: *From me, who gave life to all, a breath of life will go forth. For a little while I afflicted him on account of his sin, and struck him, and turned my face away from him; and so he went away disconsolate and walked in his own ways* (Is 57:16–17). So did you need to ask, *Why have you thrust me back, and why must I walk in deep sadness?* You have heard the reason why: *on account of sin.* The cause of your sadness is sin; try to let righteousness be the cause of your joy. You had the will to sin but did not want the unpleasant consequences. So not content with being unrighteous yourself, you wanted God, from whose punishment you shrank, to be unrighteous too. A better counsel is offered you in another psalm: *It is good for me that you have humbled me, so that I may learn your righteous judgments* (Ps 118(119):71). I learned my iniquities in my arrogance; now let me learn your righteous judgments in my humiliation. *Why must I walk in deep sadness, while my enemy harasses me?* Complaining about your enemy, are you? Yes, he certainly does harass you,

---

4. See Mt 24:40.

but it was you who gave him a foothold.[5] You have a recourse now, though. Accept sound advice, open the door to your King and shut out the tyrant.

Verse 3. Light and truth; the mountain and the tent

4. Now notice what the psalmist says, what prayer he makes to God, so that this may indeed happen. And offer the very prayer that you hear, make the same prayer yourself even as you hear it, because this must be the petition of us all: *Send forth your light and your truth. They have led me, bringing me all the way to your holy mountain and into your tents.* "Your light" and "your truth": we have two names here, but one single reality, for what else is God's light, if not God's truth? And what is God's truth, if not God's light? But both of these are the one Christ, who says, *I am the light of the world. Whoever believes in me will not walk in darkness. I am the Way, the Truth and the Life* (Jn 8:12; 14:6). He is light and he is truth. May he come, then, and deliver us, distinguishing our cause from that of an unholy people even now; may he deliver us from the wicked and deceitful. May he separate wheat from weeds, for he will send in his angels at harvest-time to collect from his kingdom all the things that make people stumble, and throw them into a blazing fire, but his wheat they will gather into the barn.[6] He will send forth his light and his truth, for these have already led us, already brought us to his holy mountain and into his tents. We have the advance payment, and we hope for the final award. His holy mountain is his holy Church. This is the mountain that grew out of a tiny stone to smash earthly kingdoms, as Daniel saw in his vision; so great did it grow that it filled the whole surface of the earth.[7] It is on this mountain that a psalmist knew his prayer had been heard when he told us, *With my voice I cried to the Lord, and he heard me from his holy mountain* (Ps 3:5(4)). Those who pray elsewhere than on this mountain should not hope to be heard in such a way as to be brought to eternal life. It is true that many people are heard when they pray with other objects in view, but they have no cause to congratulate themselves on that, for the demons too were heard when they begged to be sent into the pigs.[8] Let us long to be heard so that the issue is eternal life, in accord with the longing expressed here: *Send forth your light and your truth.* This Light seeks the eye of our hearts, for he says, *Blessed are the pure of heart, for they shall see God* (Mt 5:8). We are on his mountain at present—in his Church, that is—and in his tent. A tent is something nomads lodge in, but a house is where people live together at home. A tent is for travelers and for soldiers. So when you hear mention of a tent, understand that there is a war on, and watch out for the enemy.

---

5. See Eph 4:27.
6. See Mt 13:41–42.
7. See Dn 2:31–45.
8. See Mk 5:11–13.

But what will our home be like? *Blessed are they who dwell in your house; they will praise you for ever and ever* (Ps 83:5(84:4)).

Verse 4. God is praised with both lyre and psaltery

5. We have already been brought to the tent and assigned our place on his holy mountain, so what further hope do we cherish? *I will go in to God's altar.* There is an invisible altar on high, to which no unrighteous person has access. The only person who approaches that altar is one who has no qualms about approaching this altar here below; there will he find his life, Christ, who at this altar distinguishes his cause.[9] *I will go in to God's altar.* From his holy mountain, from his tent, from his holy Church, I will make my entrance to God's altar on high. What kind of sacrifice is offered there? The one who enters is taken up into the holocaust. *I will go in to God's altar.* What does he mean by this approach to God's altar? He goes on to develop the idea: *to God who makes my youth joyful.* "Youth" symbolizes newness. It is as though he said, "To God who gives joy to my new condition." He who saddened my old state now gladdens my newness. At present I step sorrowfully in my old state, but then I shall stand joyfully in my newness.

I will confess to you on the lyre, O God, my God. What is the difference between confessing to him on the lyre,[10] and confessing to him on the psaltery?[11] We cannot praise him all the time on the lyre, nor always on the psaltery. These two musical instruments work quite differently, and the distinction between them is worth considering and committing to memory.[12] Each of them is carried in the hands and plucked manually, which suggests that they represent our bodily activities. Each of them is good, provided that the player is skilled at the psaltery and equally skilled on the lyre. But here is the difference: the psaltery has its vaulted part[13] at the top: that wooden, concave, sounding-chamber, its drum-like piece, I mean, on which the strings are stretched and which gives them their resonance. The lyre has its hollow sounding-chamber at the bottom. Accordingly our activities can be distinguished into those which are played on the psaltery

---

9. *Illic inveniet vitam suam, qui in isto discernit causam suam.* Since God was the subject of *discernit* in earlier paragraphs, and Christ has been referred to as the Life, this seems the best interpretation; but it would be grammatically possible to take the believer as the subject of both verbs, and translate, "The person who at this altar distinguishes his cause will find his life at that other altar." In either case the background is probably 1 Cor 11:28–29, but the allusion would be clearer if this latter interpretation is the right one.
10. *In cithara.*
11. *In psalterio.*
12. He draws it out in several places in his expositions: see *Exposition 2 of Psalm 32*, 5; *Exposition 2 of Psalm 70*, 11; *Exposition of Psalm 80*, 5.
13. *Testitudinem.*

and those played on the lyre; but both are pleasing to God and melodious in his ears. When we do something in harmony with God's commandments, obeying his orders and careful to comply with his precepts, and when we feel no pain in the doing,[14] that is the music of the psaltery. The angels do this all the time, and they never feel pain. But sometimes we do suffer from the troubles and temptations and obstacles on earth. Our pain is then only in our lower part, because it is due to our mortal condition and the debt of tribulation we contract from our primitive origins. Moreover the things that give us pain are not above us. In these cases we are playing the lyre. The sweet sounds proceed from the lower part; we suffer as we sing our psalms; or rather, we sing and play the lyre. The apostle used to say that he preached the gospel, and preached it the world over, in response to God's command, because he had received this gospel not from human sources nor through human agency but through Jesus Christ;[15] and when he spoke in those terms, the strings were resonating from above. At other times he would say, *We even glory in our sufferings, knowing that suffering fosters endurance, and endurance constancy, and constancy hope* (Rom 5:3–4); and then it was the lyre sounding from below, but still very melodiously, for all patient endurance is melody to God's ears. But if you give way under tribulations like that, you have broken your lyre.

Why, then, does the psalmist now say, *I will confess to you on the lyre*? Perhaps because he had asked earlier, *Why must I walk in deep sadness, while my enemy harasses me?* He was experiencing some pain from lowly troubles, yet even in these circumstances he wanted to please God. He was strong amid his afflictions and very keen to give God thanks; and since he could not be free from trouble he paid to God his debt of patient endurance. *I will confess to you on the lyre, O God, my God.*

Verse 5. The higher part of the mind converses with its soul

6. The psalmist turns again to his sad soul, hoping to coax some notes from that sounding-chamber underneath. *Why are you sorrowful, O my soul; why do you disquiet me?* he asks. "I find myself amid troubles, sickness and grief. O my soul, why do you disquiet me?" Who is speaking here, and to whom? He is speaking to his soul; we all know that. It is obvious that the words are addressed to his soul. *Why are you sorrowful, O my soul; why do you disquiet me?* But what I am asking is this: exactly who is the speaker? It can't be the flesh talking to the soul, can it? Apart from the soul, the flesh has no power to speak. It would be more fitting for the soul to address the flesh than for the flesh to address the soul. Yet he did

---

14. *Ubi facimus et non patimur.* This could also be understood as "when we are active and not passive," and the following remark about the angels translated in the same sense. But the emphasis on suffering in the next few lines suggests otherwise.
15. See Gal 1:12.

not say, "Why are you sorrowful, O my flesh?" What he said was, *Why are you sorrowful, O my soul?*

We might suppose that if he had indeed been addressing his flesh, he might have said not, *Why are you sorrowful?* but rather, "Why are you in pain?" The pain of the soul is called sorrow; the body's distress may be called pain, but not sorrow. It is true, of course, that the soul is often saddened by bodily pain, but even then there is a difference between what is in pain and what is sorrowful, for the flesh is feeling pain, but the soul is sad; and our psalm says quite plainly, *Why are you sorrowful O my soul?* So it cannot be the soul addressing the flesh, because the psalm did not say, "Why are you sorrowful, my flesh?" Nor can it be the flesh addressing the soul, because it is absurd to suppose that the lower part could speak to the higher.

We are therefore given to understand that we have something within us where the image of God is to be found: our mind or reason. It is this mind that was just now calling upon God's light and God's truth. It is with our mind that we apprehend what is just and what unjust, and with it we distinguish the true from the false. This mind is called our understanding, and it is a faculty not granted to the beasts. Anyone who neglects his understanding, or subordinates it to other things, or throws it away as though he had none, is admonished in another psalm: *Do not be like a horse or a mule, devoid of understanding* (Ps 31(32):9). So it is our understanding that is addressing our soul here. The soul is drooping in its troubles, wearied amid anxieties, cringing under temptations and sick with its toil. But the mind, which apprehends truth from on high, cheers its soul, saying, *Why are you sorrowful, O my soul; why do you disquiet me?*

You cannot be wholly free from sin

7. A conversation of this kind was surely taking place in the conflict where the apostle typified others, and perhaps even ourselves. *I take great delight in God's law as far as my inner self is concerned*, he says, *but I am aware of a different law in my members* (Rom 7:22-23), that is, certain carnal impulses. In his wrestling, nearly desperate, he invokes the grace of God: *Who will deliver me from this death-ridden body, wretch that I am? Only the grace of God, through Jesus Christ our Lord* (Rom 7:24-25). Even the Lord himself deigned to prefigure all who engage in a fight like this, for he said, *My soul is sorrowful to the point of death* (Mt 26:38; Mk 14:34). He knew what was coming. But could he have been afraid of suffering, he who had said, *I have the power to lay down my life, and I have the power to take it up again. No one takes it away from me, but I lay it down of my own accord and take it up again?* (Jn 10:18) No, but he who said, *My soul is sorrowful to the point of death,* was representing his members in advance. Often enough our minds firmly believe, and hold it as certain in faith, that we shall make our way to Abraham's embrace; yet though we believe it, the soul is troubled by the imminence of death owing to its familiarity with the

present world. But then it bends its ear to the inner voice of God, and hears within itself the song of reason. In our silence something sounds softly to us from above, reaching not our ears but our minds. Any who hear that music are so disenchanted with material noise that the whole of human life seems to them a confused uproar, which stops them hearing another sound that is delightful, a sound like no other and beyond description. Indeed, whenever someone in a very stressful situation feels battered, he or she addresses the soul: *Why are you sorrowful, O my soul, and why do you disquiet me?*

This is all the more so because our life can never pass muster as truly pure, since he who judges us will deliver a perfectly clear, unclouded judgment. A person's life may win general approval in human society, so that other people can find in it no just grounds for reproach. But God's eyes judge the matter, and from him proceeds a standard of measurement supremely fair and incapable of error. In any human being God finds things he must indeed reproach, reprehensible things unseen by anyone else, things which even the person who stands under judgment was unaware of. Perhaps this was what the soul feared when it felt so troubled; but the mind spoke to it, as though to offer encouragement:

"Why be afraid about your sins, when you know you have not the strength to avoid them all? *Hope in the Lord, for I will confess to him.*" This encouragement effects some healing at once, and the rest of its sins are purged by faithful confession. You have good cause to fear if you claim to be just, and do not make your own the plea in another psalm, *Do not sit in judgment on your servant* (Ps 142(143):2). Why this prayer, *Do not sit in judgment on your servant*? Because I need your mercy. If you hand down judgment without mercy, what will become of me? *If you make an inventory of our law-breaking, O Lord, Lord, who will stand?* (Ps 129(130):3). *Do not sit in judgment on your servant, for no living person will be found righteous in your sight.* So then, if no living person is found righteous in his sight, woe betide anyone who lives here, however righteously he or she may live, if God undertakes to judge. In the words of another prophet God frequently reprimands the arrogant and proud: *Why do you want to dispute your case at law with me? You have all abandoned me, says the Lord* (Jer 2:29). Do not dispute with him at law; concentrate on being righteous. But then, however righteous you have managed to be, confess that you are a sinner, and always hope for mercy. Freed from anxiety by this humble confession,[16] speak to the soul that troubles you and raises its hubbub against you: *"Why are you sorrowful, O my soul, and why do you disquiet me?* You wanted to trust in yourself, did you? *Hope in the Lord*, not in yourself. What are you in yourself? What are you by your own efforts? Let him be your healing, who was willingly wounded for you." *Hope in the Lord, because I will confess to him.* And what will you confess? That he is *the salvation of my countenance, my God.* You are my face-saving God,

---

16. Variant: "persist in this humble confession."

and you will heal me. I speak as a sick person to you; I acknowledge you to be my physician; I do not boast of my health. What do I mean by saying that I acknowledge the physician, and do not boast of my health? I mean exactly what another psalm means: *I said it myself: Lord, have mercy on me; heal my soul, for I have sinned against you* (Ps 40:5(41:4)).

Fasting, almsgiving and prayer

8. This is a safe saying,[17] brothers and sisters; but be vigilant also about good works. Pluck your psaltery by obeying the commandments, and pluck your lyre by accepting suffering. You heard Isaiah's advice: *Break your bread for the hungry* (Is 58:7), so do not delude yourself that fasting is all that is required. Fasting punishes you, but brings no refreshment to anyone else. Your restriction will be fruitful if it brings amplitude to another. So you have deprived yourself, have you? But to whom do you mean to give what you denied to yourself? How do you intend to dispose of what you went without? How many poor people might grow fat on that luncheon we missed! Fast in such a fashion that while another person is fed you may feel the contentment of having lunched on your prayers, which are now more likely to win a hearing, for in the same prophecy the Lord says, *While you are yet speaking, lo, I am here, if you willingly break your bread for the poor* (Is 65:24; 58:9,10,7). This kind of gift is often made grudgingly and in a sulky spirit by those who want to be rid of beggars rather than to refresh hungry bellies, but *God loves a cheerful giver* (2 Cor 9:7). If you give your bread grudgingly, you have lost both the food and the merit. Do it with a good will, so that he who sees within you may say, *Lo, I am here*, even before you have finished speaking. How swiftly are the prayers of those who do good works accepted! This is what human righteousness consists of in this life: fasting, almsgiving and prayer.[18] Do you want your prayer to fly to God? Then make two wings for it, fasting and almsdeeds.

May the Light of God and the Truth of God find us so employed, and therefore free from anxiety, when he comes to deliver us from death, he who has already come to undergo death for us. Amen.

---

17. Variant: "This is your voice."
18. The three classic "good works" already in Jewish piety. See, for example, Tobit 12:8.

EPILOGUE

View From the Roof

Exposition of Psalm 122

Synopsis

Love either ascends by holy desires or descends by bad desires, though the Lord descended to us in love. He ascended back to heaven, but not alone: he was "clothed in the Church." Or we might say that he ascended alone with us—for we're one person together with him forever. So let's hear Christ praying this Step-Song, knowing that it's the Church that prays in weariness (1–2). This climber prays with eyes lifted to heaven, but he is fearful that he will fall if he looks at himself. God dwells in heaven, that is, in all holy souls, just as Christ dwells in our hearts by faith. But God doesn't need any assistance from us in order to have a place to dwell. After all, God doesn't even need heaven, but rather heaven needs God in order to be heaven (3–4).

The Psalm says that our eyes are glued to the Lord like a maid's to her mistress. Though it's odd to compare God to a mistress, Scripture elsewhere speaks of God's "power" and "wisdom," both feminine nouns. The Church has great dignity as the bride of Christ, but she must still comport herself like an obedient servant. Note that Paul called himself a servant, and we can't compare ourselves to Paul. But our mistress has ordered a flogging: such is the fragile, mortal life we must endure. We're chastised for sin, just as Adam was; and like him feel "brushed away like a spider" (5–7).

Moreover, we're stabbed by contempt from those who remain in love with this world. Many possessions make them think they're permanently rich—even though they'll take nothing along when they die. Others mock our faith because the just suffer and the unjust are at ease. Those people act like haughty rich people too (8–10). But let us recognize our poverty, and recognize that we live off God's richness alone. Though sickly, both physically and spiritually, we're made healthy moment by moment only by God's medicines. And let's be encouraged: the poor and destitute are the very ones who have been promised God's abundance (11–12).

Augustine's Text of Psalm 122

(1) *A Song of Steps*
   To you have I lifted up my eyes, you who dwell in heaven.
(2) Even as the eyes of servants are on the hands of their masters,
   And as the eyes of a maid are on the hands of her mistress,
   So are our eyes on the Lord our God, until he take pity on us.
(3) Have mercy on us, O Lord, have mercy,
   For we are overwhelmed with contempt.
(4) Our soul is saturated with it,
   A disgrace to the affluent and contemptible to the proud.

Exposition

A Sermon to the People

Introduction: Christ ascends, with his body; the two-way link of charity

1. I have undertaken to study the *Songs of Ascent* with you, holy brethren.[1] They are the songs of one who ascends and loves, one who, being a lover, cannot but ascend. All love either descends or ascends, for by good desire we are raised to God, but by bad desire we are plummeted into the depths. Sinful desire has brought us down already; we have fallen, but there is another chance left to us. We must acknowledge who it is who has descended to us—not fallen, but descended—and then we can ascend by clinging to him, for we cannot rise by our own strength. The Lord Jesus Christ himself testified, *No one has gone up to heaven except the one who descended from heaven, the Son of Man who is in heaven* (Jn 3:13). But that could be taken to mean that he ascended alone. Are we to think that the rest of us have been left behind, if only he who came down has ascended? What are the rest to do? We must be united to his body so that there may be only the one Christ who both descended and ascended. The head came down, but he went up with his body; he went up clothed in the Church, whom he made ready for himself, free from spot or wrinkle.[2] Did he ascend alone? Yes, in a way, but not without us, as long as we are so closely united with him that we are members of his body. He is alone, yet he is with us, forming one person, and one for ever. Unity binds us to the

---

1. *Cum sanctitate vestra.*
2. See Eph 5:27.

one Lord. The only people who do not ascend with him are those who have refused to be one with him.

We must not therefore feel our situation to be hopeless, even though that flesh in which he was for a time mortal has now been raised to immortality, and in this immortal state he has taken his place in heaven. There in heaven he suffers no persecution, no malice or insult, such as he graciously willed to endure for our sake while on earth. Yet though his passion is over he still has compassion for his hard-pressed body on earth. *Saul, Saul, why are you persecuting me?* (Acts 9:4) he cried. No one was touching him, yet he cried out from heaven that he was being persecuted! We have no reason to despair, then; rather must we with great confidence take it for granted that, if he is with us on earth through charity, we are, through the same charity, with him in heaven. We have explained to you how he is so truly present with us on earth that he could shout from heaven, *Saul, Saul, why are you persecuting me?* although Saul was not touching him in any way and could not even see him. But what about the other side of it? How can it be proved that we are with him in heaven? The same apostle, Paul, demonstrates it, for he says, *If you have risen with Christ, seek what is above, where Christ is seated at the right hand of God. Have a taste for the things that are above, not the things on earth; for you are dead, and your life is hidden with Christ in God* (Col 3:1–3). Both things are quite evident, therefore: he is still down here, and we are already up there. He is down here by compassionate charity, and we are on high by hopeful charity, *for in hope we have been saved* (Rom 8:24). But because our hope, even though it bears upon the future, is absolutely certain, Paul's statement is made about us as though it were realized already.

Verse 1. The one Christ prays from the ends of the earth

2. Let the singing psalmist make the ascent; but let him sing from the heart of each one of you like a single person. Indeed, let each of you be this one person. Each one prays the psalm individually, but because you are all one in Christ, it is the voice of a single person that is heard in the psalm. This is why you do not say, "To you, Lord, have we lifted up our eyes," but *To you, Lord, have I lifted up my eyes*. Certainly you must think of this as a prayer offered by each of you on his or her own account, but even more should you think of it as the prayer of the one person present throughout the whole world. This same one person is praying who says elsewhere, *From the ends of the earth I have called to you, as my heart was wrung with pain* (Ps 60:3(61:2)). Who is this, crying out from the ends of the earth? How can any one person be present even to earth's bounds? Each individual can cry out from his or her own country, but how is it possible to cry from every extremity of the world? Ah, but Christ's inheritance can. To him a promise is made in another psalm, *I will give you the nations as your heritage, and the ends of the earth for your possession* (Ps 2:8), and it is the voice of this heritage that we hear in the verse, *From the ends of the earth I have called*

to you, as my heart was wrung with pain. Let our heart too be wrung with pain, and let us cry out with him. What should cause our heart anguish? Not any of the woes that afflict the wicked equally—for instance, suffering some loss—for if our heart is tormented over something like that, it is dust and ashes. Or suppose you have by God's decree lost someone dear to you. Is that so exceptional that your heart should be in anguish over it? The hearts of unbelievers anguish over it too. Those who have not yet come to believe in Christ suffer just as much over these things.

What strikes anguish into the heart of a Christian? The fact of not yet living with Christ. Over what is a Christian heart wrung with pain? Over being a pilgrim still, and longing for our homeland. If that is what wrings your heart with anguish, you groan even if you are well off as the world sees it. Even if everything is turning out prosperously for you and the world is smiling upon you in your every enterprise, you groan nonetheless, because you see yourself still in your pilgrim state, and you are aware that though in the eyes of the foolish you enjoy good fortune, you still lack the happiness Christ has promised. Groaning, you seek it; seeking it, you long for it; and as you long, you ascend, singing this *Song of Steps.* You sing, *To you have I lifted up my eyes, you who dwell in heaven.*

The humble climber; keep your eyes off yourself

3. In which direction was this praying climber to lift his eyes? Where else but to the place he was making for, the place to which he longed to ascend? He is ascending from earth to heaven. But look, the earth is below us, our feet tread on it, and the sky is above, the sky we can see. Yet we mean to ascend, and we sing, *To you have I lifted up my eyes, you who dwell in heaven.* Where are the ladders? We observe the enormous distance between heaven and earth, the vast space between, the huge separation; we want to ascend to heaven, but there are no ladders to be seen. Are we not indulging in wishful thinking when we sing a *Song of Steps,* a song of ascending?

No. We ascend to heaven if we think of God, who arranges ascents in our hearts.[3] But what does it mean, to ascend in the heart? To draw closer to God. Anyone who slackens and gives up does not descend but falls; just so does everyone who is making progress ascend, but only as long as his progress does not make him proud, only if he ascends in such a way as to beware of a fall. If people take pride in their progress, their very ascent will bring them tumbling down again. How are they to conduct themselves in order to avoid pride? Let them lift their eyes to him who dwells in heaven and not focus on themselves. Every proud person is self-absorbed and self-satisfied and thinks himself important. But anyone who is satisfied with himself is feeling pleased with a fool, because when he finds himself pleasing he is foolish. The only man or woman who can be pleasing without risk is the one who is pleasing to God. And who is pleasing to God? A

---

3. See Ps 83:6(84:5).

person who finds God pleasing. God cannot be dissatisfied with himself; let him be satisfying to you as well, so that you may be satisfactory to him. But you cannot find God pleasing unless you are displeased with yourself. But then, if you find yourself unpleasant, take your eyes off yourself! Why focus on yourself? If you look at yourself as you truly are, you find unpleasant things, and then you say to God, *My sin confronts me all the time* (Ps 50:5(51:3)). Make sure your sin is before your eyes so that it will not be before the eyes of God; but do not keep yourself before your eyes, if you want to be before the eyes of God. Just as we do *not* want God to turn his face away from us, so we *do* want him to turn it away from our sins. The psalms pray for both. One psalm prays, *Do not turn your face away from me* (Ps 26(27):9), and certainly we recognize our own voice in that plea. But after saying, *Do not turn your face away from me*, the psalmist begs in another place, *Turn your face away from my sins* (Ps 50:11(51:9)). If you want God to turn his face away from your sins, turn your own face away from yourself; but do not turn your face away from your sins, for if you do not avert your eyes from them, you will be angry with your sins. And if you do not turn your face from your sins, then, even as you look at them, God overlooks them.[4]

The spiritual heaven

4. Lift your eyes away from yourself, then, and regard him. Say to him, *To you have I lifted up my eyes, you who dwell in heaven*. Now what is heaven, brothers and sisters? If we take it in a material sense, take it to be the sky we can see with our bodily eyes, we shall certainly go wrong and think that we cannot ascend there except by setting up ladders or some kind of scaffolding. But if our ascent is spiritual, we must also understand heaven in a spiritual sense. If our ascent is made by our loving will, heaven consists in righteousness. What, then, is God's heaven? All holy souls, all just souls. The apostles were heaven even while they were still on earth as to their bodies, because the Lord was enthroned in them and through them traversed the whole earth.

God dwells in heaven, then. But how? In the manner indicated by another psalm: *You dwell in your holy place, you who are the praise of Israel* (Ps 21:4(22:3)). God, who dwells in heaven, dwells in his holy place, and what else is his holy place but his temple? But *God's temple is holy, and that temple is yourselves* (1 Cor 3:17). All those who, though still weak, are walking in faith[5] are God's temple now in virtue of their faith; but one day they will be his temple in direct vision. How long do they remain his temple by their faith? As long as through their faith Christ continues to be present in them, according to the apostle's prayer, *May Christ dwell in your hearts through faith* (Eph 3:17). But those in whom God already

---

4. *Tu agnoscis, et ille ignoscit.*
5. See 2 Cor 5:7.

dwells through direct vision are already heaven. These are the holy angels who see him face to face, all the holy powers, sovereignties, thrones, and dominations;[6] they constitute the heavenly Jerusalem for which we sigh on our pilgrimage, and for which we pray in our longing. This is where God dwells. Thither has the psalmist lifted up his faith, thither is he ascending by love and desire. This very desire makes the soul rid itself of[7] the filth of sin and cleanse itself of every stain, so that it too may become a heaven, for it has raised its eyes to him who dwells in heaven.

If we suppose that God's habitation is the material sky we see with our eyes, we shall be forced to say that God's dwelling is impermanent, because the Lord tells us in the gospel that *heaven and earth will pass away* (Mt 24:35). And then we shall be faced with the question, "Where was God living before he made heaven and earth?"[8] Perhaps someone may pose a variant of this question: "Where was God living before he made his holy ones?" God was dwelling in himself; he dwells with himself; with himself he is God. Moreover, when he graciously wills to dwell in the saints, they do not become a kind of supportive house for God in such a way that, if the house disappeared, God would fall. We dwell in a house in our human fashion, but God dwells in the saints in a way entirely different. You live in your house and, if it is swept away, you fall. But God dwells in the saints in such a way that, if he departs, they fall. If anyone is a bearer of God, God's temple, let him not imagine that God relies on him and that he would frighten God by withdrawing his support. Rather, woe betide this God-bearer if God withdraws from him, because then he will be the one who falls. God abides eternally in himself. The places we dwell in contain us, but those in whom God dwells are contained by him.

Now you can see what a wide difference there is between our manner of dwelling and God's. Let the soul say, *To you have I lifted up my eyes, you who dwell in heaven*, and say it in the knowledge that God does not need heaven to live in, but heaven needs God: it needs him to dwell in it in order to be heaven.

Verse 2. Expectant servants, chastised but watching for mercy

5. The psalmist has said, *To you have I lifted up my eyes, you who dwell in heaven*. How does he continue? How did you lift up your eyes, psalmist? *Even as the eyes of servants are on the hands of their masters, and as the eyes of a maid are on the hands of her mistress, so are our eyes on the Lord our God, until he take pity on us*. We are servants, and we are a maid; God is both our master and our mistress. What do these words mean? What is

---

6. See Eph 1:21; Col 1:16.
7. Literally "sweat out."
8. Comparable to the question, "What was God doing before he made heaven and earth?" which Augustine shows to be a non-question in his *Confessions* IX,12,14 and the following sections. Time itself is a creature of God.

the force of these comparisons? You must concentrate for a little while, beloved.⁹ There is nothing strange in our being servants, with God as our master; what is strange is that we should be a maid and God our mistress. Yet there is nothing really incongruous about our being a maid, because we are the Church. And indeed, there is not even anything strange about Christ being our mistress, because he is the power and the wisdom of God.¹⁰ Listen to what the apostle has to say: *We preach Christ crucified, to Jews a stumbling-block and to Gentiles folly; but to those who are called, both Jews and Greeks, a Christ who is the power of God and the wisdom of God* (1 Cor 1:23–24). Thus the people are a servant and the Church is a maid. When you hear the name of Christ, lift your eyes to the hands of your master; but when you hear him called the power and the wisdom of God, lift your eyes to the hands of your mistress, because you are both a servant, being his people, and also a maid, being the Church.

This maid has been endowed with great dignity before God, because she has become a wife. But for the present, until she attains the spiritual embrace where she may without fear enjoy him whom she has loved, and for whom she has sighed on her tedious pilgrimage, she is still a bride. Yet she has received a great pledge,¹¹ the blood of her bridegroom, for whom she sighs with no sense of constraint. There is no need to warn her, "Wait, the time for love has not come yet," as a virgin betrothed but not yet married is sometimes cautioned. People may have good reason to say to a betrothed girl, "Do not love him yet; when you have become his wife you can love him." That is sound advice, because if she loves a man before she is certain of marrying him, her desire for him is premature, precipitous and unchaste. Another suitor may claim her and make her his wife. But there is no one who can take precedence over Christ, and the bride therefore loves him without anxiety. Let her love him before their union and sigh for him while still far off. He alone will wed her at the end of her long journey, because he alone has laid down such an enormous pledge.¹² Who else marries a bride by dying for her? If he wants to die for her, he will not be there to marry her. But Christ unhesitatingly died for his bride, because he was to marry her when he rose from the dead.

---

9. *Caritas vestra.*
10. *Virtus et sapientia*, both feminine nouns.
11. *Arrha*, in the Septuagint (see Gn 38:17.18), is a loan-word from Hebrew. The *arrha* was a first installment of the purchase-price, a pledge or deposit or down-payment which made a contract valid and obligated the contracting party to make further payments. God has *deposited the first installment of the Spirit* (or *the Spirit as the first installment*) *in our hearts* (2 Cor 1:22); and the Spirit is *the pledge/first installment of our inheritance* (Eph 1:14). Here the *arrha* is Christ's blood.
12. *Arrham.*

All the same, brothers and sisters, we must conduct ourselves in the meantime like servants or like a maid. It is true that the Lord said, *I call you servants no longer; I call you friends* (Jn 15:15), but perhaps he meant this only for the disciples. No; listen to Paul, who says, *You are a servant no longer, but a son; and if a son, an heir too, through God's act* (Gal 4:7); and Paul was speaking to the whole people, to all the faithful. Already we have been redeemed and claimed as the Lord's possession by his blood, we have been washed in the laver of his baptism, we are sons and daughters—or rather we are the one single son, because though many we are one in him. How, then, can we still comport ourselves as servants?

From our servile state we have been raised to be true sons and daughters, to be sure. But do we stand as high in merit in the Church as did the apostle Paul? Hardly. But what does he say in his letter? *From Paul, a servant of Jesus Christ* (Rom 1:1). If the man through whom the gospel was preached to us still calls himself a servant, how much more must we acknowledge our condition, that Christ's grace may increase in us? Initially he claimed those whom he redeemed as his servants, for his blood was a purchase-price for slaves, as well as a pledge[13] for his bride. We must acknowledge our condition: though sons and daughters through grace, we are still servants because we are creatures, and all creation serves God. Let us say, therefore, *Even as the eyes of servants are on the hands of their masters, and as the eyes of a maid are on the hands of her mistress, so are our eyes on the Lord our God, until he take pity on us.*

6. The psalm has explained why *our eyes are on the Lord our God*, after the manner of servants who watch the hands of their masters, or maids who watch the hands of their mistress. Now you may ask, "But to what purpose?" The psalmist accordingly adds, *Until he take pity on us.* What kind of servants[14] watching their masters' hands did he want us to think of, brothers and sisters, what kind of maids eyeing the hands of their mistress, until she take pity on them? Who are these servants and maids, watching so intently? They must be ones who have been condemned to a beating. *Our eyes are on the Lord our God, until he take pity on us.* And how do we keep our eyes focused on him? *Even as the eyes of servants are on the hands of their masters, and as the eyes of a maid are on the hands of her mistress.* It is implied that these servants and maids are also looking for mercy from their master or mistress. Imagine a master who has ordered that his servant be beaten. The servant is whipped and feels the pain of the

---

13. *Pignus.* In his Sermons 23,8.9; 156,16; 378, Augustine explains that a *pignus* is a pledge given as a guarantee, which is returned when that which is guaranteed is fulfilled (e.g. if you lend a book you ask a *pignus* from the borrower, which you return to him when he restores the book). Thus *pignus* differs from *arrha.* In the present exposition the distinction is less clear.
14. Or "slaves"; so throughout this section.

welts, so he fixes his gaze on his master's hands, longing for the master to signal, "That's enough." The hand symbolizes authority.

What about ourselves, brothers and sisters? Our Lord has ordered us to be beaten; our mistress, the wisdom of God, has ordered us to be beaten; and the whole of this mortal life is a flogging for us. Listen to what another psalm has to say: *You have chastised human beings for their sin, and brushed my soul away like a spider* (Ps 38:12(39:11)).[15] Think how fragile a spider is, brothers and sisters: a light touch is enough to squash it and kill it. And the psalm did not intend us to think only of our flesh in its fragile, mortal weakness, for it did not say, "You have brushed me away"—a statement that could be referred to the flesh—but *you have brushed my soul away like a spider*. Nothing is weaker than the human soul tossed among the temptations of the world, amid groans and anguish and afflictions; nothing is weaker, until our soul is indissolubly bound to the solid strength of heaven and finds its way into God's temple, never to fall away from there again. Our soul was reduced to this infirmity and subjection to decay, which left it as weak as a spider when it was cast out of paradise. That was when God's servant was ordered to undergo a beating.

Consider when our whipping began, brothers and sisters. Adam has endured a whipping in all those who have been born since the dawn of the human race; Adam is whipped in all who are alive today; and his whipping will continue in all who come after us. Adam is the human race under the whip, and many have so hardened themselves that they do not even feel their lacerations. But those members of the human race who have been made God's children have been given sensitivity to the pain. They feel their lashes, they know who ordered their chastisement, and they keep their eyes fixed on him who dwells in heaven. Their eyes are therefore on the hands of their Lord, longing for him to take pity on them, as servants' eyes are on the hands of their masters, or a maid's eyes on the hands of her mistress. You may see some prosperous people in this world laughing and behaving pretentiously; they are not aware of being under the lash. But in truth they are being whipped much more severely, for their flogging is all the worse in that they have lost all sensitivity to it. Let them wake up and take their whipping; let them feel it and know that they are being thrashed and let them suffer under it; for *the more one knows, the keener the pain* (Qoh 1:18), as Scripture teaches. This is why the Lord declared in the gospel, *Blessed are those who mourn, for they shall be comforted* (Mt 5:5).

7. As we listen to the cries of the sufferer under the lash, let these cries be our own, echoed by each one of us, even when things are going well. Is there anyone who is unaware of being whipped when he is ill, or in prison, or perhaps in chains, or being attacked by robbers? It is quite unmistakable

---

15. *Aranea* commonly means the spider's web rather than the spider; but in his *Exposition of Psalm* 38,18 Augustine explicitly says that he is thinking primarily of the animal.

then. Or when troubles are inflicted on someone by dishonest aggressors, he knows he is under the lash. But it takes great insight to know one is being whipped when one's affairs are prospering. In the Book of Job Scripture does not say, "There are plenty of trials in human life." It does say, *Is not human life on earth all temptation?* (Jb 7:1) It calls our entire life one long trial. All your life on earth is your beating. Mourn, then, as long as you live here on earth, whether you are enjoying good fortune or are beset by troubles; cry to God, *To you have I lifted up my eyes, you who dwell in heaven.* Cry out to the hands of your Lord, who has ordered your beating, to whom you lament in another psalm, *You have chastised human beings for their sin, and brushed my soul away like a spider* (Ps 38:12(39:11)). Cry out to the hand that beats you, *Have mercy on us, O Lord, have mercy!* Is not this the plea of someone being whipped: *Have mercy on us, O Lord, have mercy?*

Verses 3–4. Those who are affluent in any sense will despise us

8. *Have mercy on us, O Lord, have mercy, for we are overwhelmed with contempt. Our soul is saturated with it, a disgrace to the affluent and contemptible to the proud.* To be viewed with contempt is to be despised. All those who try to live a godly life according to Christ's teaching[16] will inevitably suffer disgrace; they will of necessity be despised by those who want to live in ungodly fashion and look to find their whole happiness in earthly things. People of a different persuasion, who regard something invisible as their happiness, are taunted: "You fool, what do you believe? Can you see this thing you believe in? Has anyone come back from the underworld to tell you what goes on there? What I love are things I can see and enjoy." You are treated with contempt because you hope for what you do not see, treated with contempt by someone who seems to have a firm grasp of what he can see. But consider how secure his grip is. Do not worry; just watch whether he does truly hold it. Do not take his insults to heart, lest while judging him to be happy in this present life you lose your true happiness in the life to come. Do not worry; just reflect on whether his hold is secure. Does his property slip through his fingers, or does he slip away from his property? Either he will leave his possessions behind or they will leave him; one or the other is bound to happen. Who is abandoned by his possessions? A person who is ruined in his lifetime. And who leaves his possessions behind? The one who dies rich; because when he dies he does not take his wealth with him to the underworld. "I own my house," he boasted. You ask him, "What house would that be?" "The house my father left me." "And where did he get it from?" "Our grandfather bequeathed it to him." Go back to his great-grandfather, and then to his great-great-grandfather, and now he cannot even tell you their names. Do you not find it more frightening than a matter for pride when you reflect that so many

---

16. See 2 Tm 3:12.

have passed through that house and not one of them has taken it with him to be a home for eternity? Your father left it behind here; he went his way, as you too will go your way. If all you have in this house of yours is a temporary occupancy, it is a lodging for passers-by, not an abode for permanent residents. And yet we, for our part, *are overwhelmed with contempt* by those who seek or possess happiness in this world, because we hope for what is still future, because we sigh for a happiness yet to come, and because, although we are God's children already, *what we shall be has not yet appeared* (1 Jn 3:2), for our life *is hidden with Christ in God* (Col 3:3).

9. *Our soul is saturated with it, a disgrace to the affluent, and contemptible to the proud.* We were perhaps wondering who *the affluent* are, and the psalm made it clear to you by calling them *the proud*. Similarly *disgrace* is parallel to *contemptible*, as *the affluent* are parallel to *the proud*. The thought is repeated: *a disgrace to the affluent, and contemptible to the proud*. Why are the proud affluent? Because they want to be happy here. But they are wretched too, surely, so how can they be affluent? Well, perhaps when they are reduced to wretchedness, they will not taunt us any more. But this is not so certain, so pay attention now, beloved. Perhaps they jeer at us when they are enjoying good fortune themselves, when they flaunt their ostentatious wealth, when they make their windy boasts over trumpery privileges. Then they mock us, as though saying, "Look how well off I am! I'm enjoying good things here and now. Away with people who promise what they cannot show me! I hold onto what I see and make the most of what I see. I'm out to have a good time in life." But what about you? You must be more secure than he is. Christ is risen, and he has taught you what he means to give in another life; be certain that he does indeed give it. The proud mocker insults you because he has his good fortune now. Put up with him and his insults, for you will laugh at him later when he is groaning. The time will come when people like him will say, *These are the people we once held in derision* (Wis 5:3). That text comes from the Book of Wisdom; Scripture has made known to us what they will be saying one day, these people who laugh at us now, who despise us and dismiss us as disgraceful and contemptible. We are told what they will be saying then, when they are shamed by the truth. They will see, shining gloriously at Christ's right hand, those whom they despised when living among them, for in those formerly contemptible folk the apostle's prophecy will have been verified: *When Christ appears, Christ who is your life, then you too will appear with him in glory* (Col 3:4). They will say, *These are the people we once held in derision, as a byword and a butt for our mockery! Fools that we were, we thought their life madness and their end a disgrace. How has it happened that now they are reckoned among the children of God, and their lot is among the saints?* (Wis 5:3–5) The text continues to relate their chagrin: *No doubt of it, we strayed from the path of truth. On us the light of righteousness did not shine, nor did the sun rise for us. What good has our pride done us,* and what benefit has come to us from our vaunted

wealth? (Wis 5:6–8) There will be no need for you to reproach them then, for they will be reproaching themselves.

Until this comes to pass, brothers and sisters, let us lift our eyes to him who dwells in heaven and never turn our gaze away from him until he take pity on us and set us free from all temptation and reproach and contempt.

10. There is more to be said, though: sometimes even people who are under the lash of temporal misfortune insult us too. You may come across someone who for his sins is thrown into prison and shackled, either as a result of God's secret judgment or because his guilt is manifest. Perhaps someone says to him, "Why did you not live a good life? Look where your wrongdoing has led you." He retorts, "And why do some who do live good lives suffer the same fate?" We may reply that these latter suffer to be proved sound; the trials that come their way serve to put them through their paces; repeated scourging turns out to their advantage, for God *whips every child whom he accepts* (Heb 12:6). If he caused his sinless only-begotten Son to be scourged and delivered him to death for us all,[17] are we not rightly scourged, we whose deeds have merited a beating? But when we make these points, an answer comes from people who, far from being humbled by their affliction, are proud even of their misfortune: "That is the way those stupid Christians talk. They believe in what they do not see."

If even people in that situation insult us, brothers and sisters, can we suppose that they are not included in the groups envisaged in the psalm, when it says that we are *a disgrace to the affluent, and contemptible to the proud*? We know that insults are hurled at Christians by those also who are not affluent yet never stop railing at us even in their poverty and distress. Is the psalm right, then, to say that we are *a disgrace to the affluent*? Would we find no one in a calamitous situation ever insulting others if we did not know about the robber who insulted Christ, crucified alongside him?[18] If those who are not affluent insult others as much as those who are, why does the psalm say that we are *a disgrace to the affluent*?

If we examine the matter carefully, we find that persons who mock even when in distress are affluent—yes, even they are. Why can they be regarded as affluent? Because if they were not affluent, they would not be proud. One person is affluent in money and is proud about that; another is well off with regard to prestigious offices, and that makes him proud; another thinks himself wealthy in righteousness and is proud on that score, which is worse. Some who do not appear to be wealthy as far as money is concerned think themselves affluent in righteousness in despite of God. When overtaken by disasters they justify themselves and accuse God. "Of what am I guilty? What have I done?" such a person asks. You answer, "Take a good look, recall your sins and ask yourself whether you have really done nothing wrong." His conscience is stirred a little. He returns

---

17. See Rom 8:32.
18. See Lk 23:39.

to himself and reflects on his misdeeds. But even after having thought it over he is unwilling to confess that his punishment is deserved. Instead he says, "Well, yes, I have obviously done many bad things, but I know many others have done worse yet suffer no harm for it." So he sets himself up as just, in opposition to God. He too is therefore affluent, for he has a heart full of self-righteousness, since in his eyes God is doing wrong, while he himself is suffering unjustly. If you were to entrust him with the navigation of a ship, he would wreck it along with himself; yet he wants to wrest the control of this world from God and steer creation himself, distributing to all their pains and joys, their punishments and rewards. Unhappy soul! But is it surprising? He is one of the affluent, but his affluence is in wickedness and malice. And the more affluent he thinks himself to be in righteousness, the more affluent he is in sin.

The true poverty of a Christian

11. A Christian has no business to be affluent but has a duty to recognize that he is poor. Even if he has worldly wealth he must realize that it is not true wealth, and so he must long for wealth of a different kind. Anyone who longs for false riches does not seek true riches; but a person who is in search of true riches knows himself or herself to be still a pauper and rightly admits, *I am poor and sorrowful* (Ps 68:30(69:29)). But what of a person who is materially poor yet full of wickedness? Why can such a one be regarded as affluent? Because he hates his poverty but believes himself richly supplied with justice in his heart, in opposition to the justice of God. What kind of riches does our righteousness amount to? However abundant righteousness may be in us, it is no more than dew in comparison with the fountain of God's justice, no more than a few drops compared with that great feast, drops that only dampen our life and soften the hard surface of our iniquity. Let us in this life long to be fully fed from that plenteous fount of justice; let us yearn to be satisfied with that abundance of which another psalm predicts, *They will be inebriated by the rich abundance of your house, and you will give them the torrent of your delights to drink* (Ps 35:9(36:8)).

But, as long as we live here, let us understand that we are penurious and needy not only in the matter of true riches but even with respect to our health. Even when we are well, let us realize that we are infirm. As long as this body hungers and thirsts, as long as it is tired by keeping vigil, tired by standing, tired by walking, tired by sitting; as long as it gets tired of eating, and finds some new form of fatigue wherever it turns to relieve its tiredness, we do not have perfect health, not even bodily health. This state is not riches but beggary, because the more there is of it, the more our need and avarice increase. It is not bodily health, but infirmity. Every day our condition is alleviated[19] by God's remedies as we eat and drink, for these are medicines prescribed for us. If you want to diagnose the disease that has hold of us, brothers and sisters, think how a person who fasts for a week is consumed by hunger. The hunger is there all the time, but you do not feel it because you cure it every day. Even our bodily health is not perfect.

Riches, health, and righteousness elude us in this life,
but we hope for them in the new Jerusalem

12. I want you to be quite clear, beloved, as to how we should understand that we are poor, so that we may lift our eyes to him who dwells in heaven and rejoice unto him. Worldly riches are not true riches, for they only increase cupidity in those who possess them. Nor is what is reckoned bodily health true health, because we carry within us infirmity which lets us down on every side; whichever way we turn, there is deficiency. Even in applying the remedy you will not find stable strength. A person is weary of standing and wants to sit down. But can he bear to remain sitting indefinitely? He adopted a sitting position to relieve his fatigue, but even sitting down is no answer. He was wearied from keeping vigil, and so he is going to sleep awhile. Now he has slept, but does that mean the end of his weakness? By no means. He is fatigued by fasting and goes to take refreshment. If he goes on eating, that too is bad for him. This weak condition of ours cannot bear any activity for long.

What about righteousness? What does our righteousness amount to amid such fierce temptations? We can refrain from murder, from adultery, from theft, from perjury, from fraud. But can we restrain ourselves from evil thoughts? Or from the wicked desires that suggest themselves? What is our righteousness, then?

We must therefore long for wholeness, for true riches and true health and true righteousness. What are true riches? Our heavenly abode in Jerusalem. Who is reckoned rich on earth? When a rich person is the subject of gossip, what do people say? "He is very wealthy, he lacks nothing." That may be genuine praise in the intention of the one who says so; but to assert of someone, "He lacks nothing," is a hollow sort of praise. Look into the statement carefully and find out whether he is really in want of nothing. If he lacks nothing, he craves nothing; but if he is still craving for more than he has, his accumulation of riches has only increased his need. In that city, though, there will be true riches for us, because we shall need nothing whatever, and our health will be true health. What is true health? That state wherein death has been swallowed up in victory and this corruptible nature has clothed itself with incorruptibility and our mortality is clothed

---

19. *Paregorizamur*, derived from the Greek παρηγορίζω. This unusual verb has given rise to a crop of variants: *quare curamus*; *pare gloridiamur*; *parum ergo rigamur*; *par ego rideamur*, etc.

in immortality.[20] Then there will be true health for us; and then also there will be true and perfect righteousness, for not only shall we be incapable of doing wrong: we shall not even be able to think of it.

But now, needy, poor, destitute, and in pain, we sigh and groan and pray and lift our eyes to God; for those who enjoy this world's goods—the affluent, that is—despise us; but so too do the unfortunate. Even those who do not prosper in this world despise us, because they too are affluent in their way, with an abundance of righteousness in their hearts, but a righteousness that is counterfeit. They do not attain true righteousness because they are full of the kind that is false. But you, for your part, be needy, be a beggar for true righteousness, that you may reach it. Listen to the gospel: *Blessed are those who hunger and thirst for righteousness, for they shall be satisfied* (Mt 5:6).

---

20. See 1 Cor 15:54.53.

Select Bibliography

Arnold, W. H. A. and Pamela Bright, eds. *De doctrina christiana: A Classic of Western Culture*. Notre Dame: University of Notre Dame Press, 1995.
Asmis, Elizabeth. "'Psychagogia' in Plato's *Phaedrus*." *Illinois Classical Studies* 11 (1986) 153–172.
Auerbach, Erich. *"Sermo Humilis,"* in *Literary Language and Its Public in Late Latin Antiquity and the Middle Ages*, trans. Ralph Manheim. Princeton: Princeton University Press, 1965: 27–57.
Ayres, Lewis. "Patristic and Medieval Theologies of Scripture," in *Christian Theologies of Scripture: A Comparative Introduction*, ed. Justin S. Holcomb. New York: New York University Press, 2006: 11–20.
Babcock, William S. "The Christ of the Exchange: A Study in the Christology of Augustine's *Enarrationes in psalmos*." Ph.D. diss., Yale University, 1971.
van Bavel, Tarsicius J. "L'humanité du Christ comme *lac parvulorum* et comme *via* dans la spiritualité de saint Augustin." *Augustiniana* 7 (1957) 247–281.
Bochet, Isabelle. *"Le Firmament de l'Écriture": L'herméneutique augustinienne*. Paris: Institut d'Études Augustiniennes, 2004.
Brown, Peter. *Power and Persuasion in Late Antiquity: Towards a Christian Empire*. Madison: University of Wisconsin Press, 1992.
_____. *Augustine of Hippo: A Biography,* new ed. Berkeley: University of California Press, 2000.
_____. "Foreword," in Henry Chadwick, *Augustine of Hippo, A Life*. New York: Oxford University Press, 2009.
Bright, Pamela. "Augustine: The Hermeneutics of Conversion," in Charles Kannengiesser, *Handbook of Patristic Exegesis*. Leiden: Brill, 2006: 1219–1233.
_____. "St. Augustine," in *Christian Theologies of Scripture: A Comparative Introduction,* ed. Justin S. Holcomb. New York: New York University Press, 2006: 39–59.
Bright, Pamela, trans. and ed. *Augustine and the Bible*. Notre Dame: University of Notre Dame Press, 1999.
Byassee, Jason. *Praise Seeking Understanding: Reading the Psalms with Augustine*. Grand Rapids: Eerdmans, 2007.
Cameron, Averil. *Christianity and the Rhetoric of Empire: The Development of Christian Discourse*. Berkeley: University of California Press, 1991.

Cameron, Michael. "*Enarrationes in psalmos*," in *Augustine through the Ages: An Encyclopedia,* ed. Allan Fitzgerald. Grand Rapids: Eerdmans, 1999: 290–296.

_____. "*Totus Christus* and the Psychagogy of Augustine's Sermons." *Augustinian Studies* 36 (2005) 59–70.

_____. "Augustine and Scripture," in *The Blackwell Companion to Augustine.* Oxford: Wiley-Blackwell, 2012: 200–214.

_____. *Christ Meets Me Everywhere: Augustine's Early Figurative Exegesis.* New York: Oxford University Press, 2012.

Carruthers, Mary. *The Craft of Thought: Meditation, Rhetoric and the Making of Images, 400–1200.* Cambridge: Cambridge University Press, 1998.

Cavadini, John C. "The Sweetness of the Word: Salvation and Rhetoric in Augustine's *De doctrina Christiana,*" in *De doctrina christiana: A Classic of Western Culture,* eds. Duane W. H. Arnold and Pamela Bright. Notre Dame: University of Notre Dame Press, 1995: 164–181.

_____. "Eucharistic Exegesis in Augustine's *Confessions.*" *Augustinian Studies* 41 (2010) 87–108.

Chadwick, Henry. *Augustine of Hippo: A Life.* New York: Oxford University Press, 2009.

Daley, Brian. "A Humble Mediator: The Distinctive Elements in St. Augustine's Christology." *Word and Spirit* 9 (1987) 100–117.

_____."Is Patristic Exegesis Still Usable? Some Reflections on Early Christian Interpretation of the Psalms," in *The Art of Reading Scripture,* eds. Ellen F. Davis and Richard B. Hays. Grand Rapids: Eerdmans, 2003: 69–88

Daley, Brian E. and Paul Kolbet, eds. *The Harp of Prophecy: Early Christian Interpretation of the Psalms.* Notre Dame: University of Notre Dame Press, 2015.

Dodaro, Robert. "Literary Decorum in Scriptural Exegesis: Augustine of Hippo, *Epistula* 138," in *L'esegesi dei Padri Latini, Dalle origini a Gregorio Magno.* Rome, Institutum Patristicum Augustinianum, 2000, 1:159–174.

_____. "*Quid deceat videre* (Cicero, *Orator* 70): Literary Propriety and Doctrinal Orthodoxy in Augustine of Hippo," in *Orthodoxie, christianisme, histoire,* eds. Susanna Elm et al. Rome: École Française de Rome, 2000: 57–81.

_____. "The Theologian as Grammarian: Literary Decorum in Augustine's Defense of Orthodox Discourse." *Studia Patristica* 38 (2001) 70–83.

_____. "Language Matters: Augustine's Use of Literary Decorum in Theological Argument." *Augustinian Studies* 45 (2014) 1–28.

Drobner, Hubertus R. "Grammatical Exegesis and Christology in St. Augustine," *Studia Patristica* 18 (1990) 49–63.

_____. "Psalm 21 in Augustine's *Sermones ad populum*: Catecheses on *Christus Totus* and Rules of Interpretation." *Augustinian Studies* 37 (2006) 145–169.

Dupont, Anthony. *Gratia in Augustine's* Sermones ad populum *during the Pelagian Controversy.* Leiden: Brill, 2013.

Eden, Kathy. *Hermeneutics and the Rhetorical Tradition: Chapters in the Ancient Legacy and Its Humanist Reception.* New Haven: Yale University Press, 1997.
Enos, Richard Leo and Roger Thompson et al., eds. *The Rhetoric of St. Augustine of Hippo:* De doctrina christiana *and the Search for a Distinctly Christian Rhetoric.* Waco: Baylor University Press, 2008.
Fiedrowicz, Michael. *Psalmus Vox Totius Christi: Studien in Augustins 'Enarrationes in psalmos.'* Freiburg: Herder, 1997.
_____. "General Introduction." *Expositions of Psalms 1–32,* trans. Maria Boulding. Works of Saint Augustine III/15. Hyde Park, N. Y.: New City Press, 2000: 13–66.
Fiedrowicz, Michael and Hildegund Müller. "*Enarrationes in psalmos,*" in *Augustinus-Lexikon* 2, ed. C. P. Mayer. Basel: Schwabe, 1996–2002: 804–857.
Fredriksen, Paula. *Augustine and the Jews: A Christian Defense of Jews and Judaism,* with a new postscript. New Haven: Yale University Press, 2010.
Gallagher, Michael Paul. *Faith Maps: Ten Religious Explorers from Newman to Joseph Ratzinger.* New York: Paulist Press, 2010.
Gowans, Coleen Hoffman. *The Identity of the True Believer in the Sermons of Augustine of Hippo: A Dimension of his Christian Anthropology.* Lewiston, N. Y.: Edwin Mellen Press, 1998.
Harmless, William, S.J. *Augustine: In His Own Words,* Washington: The Catholic University of America Press, 2010. See esp. "Augustine the Preacher," 122–155; "Augustine the Exegete," 156–200.
_____. "Augustine's Jazz of Theology." *Augustinian Studies* 43 (2012) 149–177.
_____. *Augustine and the Catechumenate,* rev. ed. Collegeville: Liturgical Press, 2014.
Harrison, Carol. *The Art of Listening in the Early Church.* Oxford: Oxford University Press, 2013.
Hombert, P-M. "La christologie des trente-deux premières *Enarrantiones in psalmos* de saint Augustin," in *Augustin philosophe et prédicateur. Hommage à Goulven Madec,* ed. Isabelle Bochet. Turnhout: Brepols, 2012: 431–63.
Kolbet, Paul R. "Formal Continuities between Augustine's Early Philosophical Teaching and Late Homiletical Practice." *Studia Patristica* 43 (2006) 149–154.
_____. *Augustine and the Cure of Souls.* Notre Dame: University of Notre Dame Press, 2010.
Kotzé, Annemaré. "Reading Psalm 4 to the Manicheans." *Vigiliae Christianae* 55 (2001) 119–136.
Lawless, George. "Augustine of Hippo as Preacher," in *Saint Augustine as Bishop: A Book of Essays,* eds. Fannie LeMoine and Christopher Kleinhenz. New York: Garland, 1994: 13–37.
_____. "Preaching," in *Augustine through the Ages: An Encyclopedia,* ed. Allan Fitzgerald. Grand Rapids: Eerdmans, 1999: 675–677

Leff, Michael C. "Decorum and Rhetorical Interpretation: The Latin Humanistic Tradition and Contemporary Critical Theory." *Vichiana* 3 (1990) 107–126.

Leff, Michael C., and Andrew Sachs. "Words the Most Like Things: Iconicity and the Rhetorical Text." *Western Journal of Speech Communication* 54 (1990) 252–273.

Lonergan, Bernard. *Method in Theology.* New York: Herder and Herder, 1972.

Louth, Andrew. "'Heart in Pilgrimage': St Augustine as Interpreter of the Psalms," in *Orthodox Readings of Augustine*, eds. G. E. Demacopoulos and A. Papanikolaou. Crestwood, N.Y.: St Vladimir's Seminary Press, 2008.

MacMullen, Ramsay. "The Preacher and His Audience (AD 350–400)." *Journal of Theological Studies* 40 (1989) 503–511.

Martin, Thomas F. "Reading the Psalms of David through Paul: Augustine's Commentary on Psalm 31." *L'Esegesi dei Padri Latini*, in *Studia Ephemeridis Augustinianum* 68. Rome: Institutum Patristicum Augustinianum, 2000: 245–252.

McCarthy, Michael C. "The Revelatory Psalm: A Fundamental Theology of Augustine's *Enarrationes In Psalmos*." Ph.D. Diss., University of Notre Dame, 2003.

_____. "An Ecclesiology of Groaning: Augustine, the Psalms, and the Making of Church." *Theological Studies* 66 (2005) 23–48.

_____. "Creation through the Psalms in Augustine's *Enarrationes in Psalmos*," *Augustinian Studies* 37 (2006) 191–218.

_____. "The Psalms of Ascent as Word of God in Augustine's *Enarrationes in psalmos*." *Augustinian Studies* 41 (2010) 109–120.

McGinn, Bernard. *The Foundations of Mysticism: Origins to the Fifth Century.* New York: Crossroad, 1991.

McLarney, Gerard. *St. Augustine's Interpretation of the Psalms of Ascent.* Washington, D.C.: The Catholic University of America Press, 2014.

Morrison, Karl F. *"I Am You": The Hermeneutics of Empathy in Western Literature, Theology, and Art.* Princeton: Princeton University Press, 1988.

Müller, Hildegund. "Theory and Practice of Preaching: Augustine, *Enarrationes in psalmos* and *de doctrina christiana*." *Studia Patristica* 38 (2001) 233–237.

_____. "Preacher: Augustine and His Congregation," in *The Blackwell Companion to Augustine,* ed. Mark Vessey. Oxford: Wiley-Blackwell, 2012: 297–309.

Pellegrino, Michele. "General Introduction." *Sermons,* trans. Edmund Hill. The Works of Saint Augustine III/1. Hyde Park, N. Y.: New City Press, 1990: 13–163.

Pollmann, Karla. "Hermeneutical Presuppositions," in *Augustine Through the Ages: An Encyclopedia,* ed. Allan Fitzgerald. Grand Rapids: Eerdmans, 1999: 426–429.

Rebillard Éric. "*Sermones*," ibid. 773–792.

_____. "Religious Sociology: Being Christian in the Time of Augustine," in *The Blackwell Companion to Augustine*, ed. Mark Vessey. Oxford: Wiley-Blackwell, 2012: 40–53.

Rondeau, M.-J. *Les commentaires patristiques du Psautier*, vol. 2: *Exégèse prosopologique et théologie*. Orientalia Christiana Analecta 220. Rome: Pontificium Institutum Studiorum Orientalium, 1985.

Rosenberg, Stanley R. "Orality, Textuality, and the Memory of the Congregation in Augustine's Sermons." *Studia Patristica* 49 (2010) 169–174.

Sanlon, Peter T. *Augustine's Theology of Preaching*. Minneapolis: Fortress Press, 2014.

Stroumsa, Gedaliahu G. "Milk and Meat: Augustine and the End of Esotericism," in *Hidden Wisdom: Esoteric Traditions and the Roots of Christian Mysticism*, eds. Aleida and Jan Assmann. Leiden: Brill, 1996: 132–146.

Sundén, Hjalmar. "Saint Augustine and the Psalter in the Light of Role-Psychology." *Journal for the Scientific Study of Religion* 26 (1987) 375–382.

Teske, Roland J. "Spirituals and Spiritual Interpretation in Augustine." *Augustinian Studies* 15 (1984) 65–82.

_____. "Criteria for Figurative Interpretation in St Augustine," in *De doctrina christiana: A Classic of Western Culture*, eds. Duane W. H. Arnold and Pamela Bright. Notre Dame: University of Notre Dame Press, 1995: 109–122.

_____. "Augustine, the Manichees and the Bible," in *Augustine and the Bible*, trans. and ed. Pamela Bright. Notre Dame: University of Notre Dame Press, 1999: 208–221.

Toom, Tarmo. "Augustine on Scripture," in *The T & T Clark Companion to Augustine and Modern Theology*. London: Bloomsbury T & T Clark, 2013: 75–90.

Tracy, David. "Charity, Obscurity, Clarity: Augustine's Search for Rhetoric and Hermeneutics," in *Rhetoric and Hermeneutics in Our Time*, eds. Walter Jost and Michael J. Hyde. New Haven: Yale University Press, 1997: 254–274.

_____. "Augustine's Christomorphic Theocentrism," in *Orthodox Readings of Augustine*, eds. Aristotle Papanikolaou and George E. Demacopoulos. Crestwood, N. Y.: St. Vladimir's Seminary Press, 2008: 263–289.

Uhalde, Kevin. *Expectations of Justice in the Age of Augustine*. Philadelphia: University of Pennsylvania Press, 2007.

Van der Meer, F. *Augustine the Bishop*, trans. Brian Battershaw and G. R. Lamb. New York: Harper Torchbooks, 1961.

Van Fleteren, Frederick. "Ascent of the Soul," in *Augustine through the Ages: An Encyclopedia*, ed. Allan Fitzgerald. Grand Rapids: Eerdmans, 1999: 63–67.

Williams, Rowan. "Augustine and the Psalms." *Interpretation: A Journal of Bible and Theology* 58 (2004) 17–27.

Young, Frances M. *Biblical Exegesis and the Formation of Christian Culture*. Cambridge: Cambridge University Press, 1997.

Abbreviations of Biblical Books

Gn	Genesis	Hb	Habakkuk
Ex	Exodus	Ml	Malachi
Lv	Leviticus	Mt	Matthew
Nm	Numbers	Mk	Mark
Dt	Deuteronomy	Lk	Luke
Jos	Joshua	Jn	John
1 S	1 Samuel	Acts	Acts of the Apostles
2 S	2 Samuel	Rom	Romans
1 K	1 Kings	1 Cor	1 Corinthians
2 K	2 Kings	2 Cor	2 Corinthians
Jb	Job	Gal	Galatians
Ps	Psalms	Eph	Ephesians
Prv	Proverbs	Phil	Philippians
Eccl	Ecclesiastes	Col	Colossians
Sg	Song of Songs	1 Thes	1 Thessalonians
Sir	Sirach	2 Thes	2 Thessalonians
Wis	Wisdom	1 Tm	1 Timothy
Is	Isaiah	2 Tm	2 Timothy
Jer	Jeremiah	Heb	Hebrews
Lam	Lamentations	1 Pt	1 Peter
Ezk	Ezekiel	2 Pt	2 Peter
Dn	Daniel	1 Jn	1 John
Hos	Hosea	Rv	Revelation
Jl	Joel		

Names and Places Index

Ancient

Ambrose 18–22; 54n48; 55n59; 244n3; 420n5

Arians, Arianism 86; 363

Aristotle 288

Athanasius 22; 351n15; 363–64n47

Basil of Caesarea 22; 364n47

Caecilian 308n18

Carthage 18; 149; 210n1; 226n1; 243n1; 371n1

Cassiciacum 21

Cicero 18; 34; 36; 38

Circumcellions 219n13; 367

Clement of Alexandria 22

Constantine 24; 363n47

Crispina 73; 74n1; 75n5; 88–90

Cyprian 22; 24; 226; 230n11; 292n42; 364n48; 371n1; 391

Donatists 24; 52n17; 71; 86n34; 138n17; 157; 201n49; 282n23; 298; 305; 308; 340; 357–59; 362–68

Donatus 298; 308; 340; 359; 362

Eugippius 137n15; 138n18

Gregory of Nazianzus 22; 364n47
Gregory of Nyssa 22; 364n47
Gregory the Great 54n48

Hilary of Poitiers 22

Irenaeus 22

Jerome 22; 50n3; 69n17; 117n11; 282n23

Justin Martyr 22

Manicheans 18; 24; 42; 267; 277–81; 312; 331

Maximianists 367–68

Monica 18; 38; 137n16

Novatian, Novatianists 364

Origen 22

Paulinus of Nola 282n23

Plato, Platonists 288; 312; 331

Possidius 52n16; 94n1

Pythagoras 288

Stoics 312

Tertullian 22; 285n26; 289n34
Thomas Aquinas 53n38
Tyconius 52n17

Valerius 22–23

Modern

Bardy, G. 52n19
Brown, P. 15
Brown, R.E. 53n35

Cameron, M. 55n59
Canning, R. 54n40
Chadwick, H. 50n4; 52n25

Deferrari, R. 50n6
Dodaro, R. 54n44

Eden, K. 54n43

Fiedrowicz, M. 51n9; 52nn19–20
Fredriksen, P. 24; 52n22

Gilson, E. 53n38

Harmless, W. 50n5.6; 51n8; 52nn14.27.28; 53nn30.36; 55n54

Harrison, C. 51n8; 53nn32.34; 54nn47.52
Hays, R. 52n18
Hombert, P. 371n1

Johnson, L. T. 26; 52n23

Kotzé, A. 52n15

La Bonnardiére, A.-M. 282n23
Lonergan, B. 26–27; 52n24

McCarthy, M. C. 51n9
McLarney, G. 52n13

Stroumsa, G. G. 55n53

Toom, T. 50n7

Watts, W. 52n25

Index to Works of Augustine Cited*

Answer to Cresconius
  (Contra Cresconium)
  4,4,5   367

Answer to Faustus
  (Contra Faustum Manichaeum)
  VI,4   19
  XII,48   55n53
  XV,8   21
  XXXII,18   54n41

The Catholic Way of Life and the
  Manichean Way of Life
  (De moribus ecclesiae catholicae et
  de moribus Manichaeorum)
  I,17,31   42

The City of God (De civitate Dei)
                    13, 14, 24, 150

Confessions (Confessiones)
                    13
  I,1,1   34
  II,3,8   150
  III,5,9   54n48
  III,10,18   278
  IV-V   278
  V,10,18   279
  VI,1,1   256
  VI,4,6   21
  VI,5,8   54n48
  VII,7,11   23
  VII,17,23   52n25; 99
  VII,18,24   20
  VIII,6,15   351
  VIII,11,27   393
  VIII,12,28   323
  IX,4,8   21
  IX,4,11   99
  IX,9,20   137
  IX,10,23–26   54n51
  IX,10,24   99
  IX,12,14   454
  X,37,62   282
  XII,7,7   99
  XII,14,17   38
  XIII,9,10   98

Expositions of the Psalms
  (Enarrationes in psalmos)
                    14, 278
  8,6   42
  8,10–11   168
  (2)21   273
  (2)21,3   379
  (2)26,6   426
  (2)26,18   354
  (2)30,3   379
  (3)30,2   202
  (2)31,16–25   258
  (3)32,1   53n31
  (2)32,2   379
  (2)32,5   173
  (2)33,25   277
  (2)36,19–23   367
  (1)34,8   293
  35,1   42
  35,12–14   168
  38,18   457
  (2)48,5   196
  42,5   173, 230
  43,1   420
  44,1   420
  44,25   354
  46,2   420
  49,9   202, 300
  54,8–9   192
  54,23   42
  60,3   379
  62,17   293
  67,39   363, 364
  (1)68,3   379
  (2)70,11   173, 230
  79,1   20, 37
  80,5   173, 230
  83,2   420
  84,2   420
  85   371
  86   371
  105,36   51n11
  166,7   258
  119–133   60
  126,4   293
  140,1   13
  142   371

---

*   Reference in work cited is on left, and page found in this text is on right. If no reference is made in left, then the work itself is cited.

Faith and the Creed (De fide et symbolo)
   1,1   42

The Happy Life (De beata vita)
   10   54n51

Heresies
   70   258

Homilies on the Gospel of John
  (In Iohannis evangelium tractatus CXXIV)
   7,11   356
   80,3   28
   98,6   41

Instructing Beginners in Faith
  (De catechizandis rudibus)
   2,3   34
   3,6   34
   4,8   20, 51n11
   8,12–9,13   54n50
   10,15   35, 36
   12,17   34, 35
   15,23   54n49

Letters (Epistulae)
   21,4   15
   27,6   282
   28,4(6)   282
   41,2   52n17
   120,1,4   55n60
   137,3   17
   222   229
   224   229

Miscellany of Questions in Response to Simplician (Ad Simplicianum)
   I,1,1   54n42

Questions on the Heptateuch (Quaestiones in Heptateuchum)
   II,73   51n11

Sermons (Sermones)
   23,8,9   456
   156,16   456
   311,5   230
   378   456

The Spirit and the Letter (De spiritu et littera)
   17   363

The Teacher (De magistro)
   11,37   42

Teaching Christianity (De doctrina christiana)
                      15
   I,35,39   19–20; 29
   I,39,43   55n57
   II,6,7   53n37
   IV,17,34   53n39

True Religion (De vera religion)
   24,45   42
   50,98   29

Index of Scripture References

Old Testament

Genesis (Gn)
1:3	139
1:9	381
1:26	404
1:26–27	191
2:17	432
2:21	167
2:24	181, 272, 374
3:7	323
3:8	384
3:19	53n31, 105, 180; 217, 432
4	372
4:17	372
11:4	353
11:9	354
12:3	100, 362
14:18	118
15:6	316
16:15	69
18:10–15	69
21	306
21:2	69
21:10	70
22:16–18	306
22:18	100, 245
24:2	245
24:2–3	139
25:13	70
25:27	145
26:4	100, 362
28:11–12	144
28:12	62, 392
32:24–31	145
38:17–18	455
49:10	139

Exodus (Ex)
3:13	99
3:14	99, 400, 416
3:15	100
20:2–17	232
20:12	83
22:26–27	256
20:17	233
32:11–13	203
32:26–28	203
33:13	185
33:20.22–23	79, 185

Leviticus (Lv)
19:15	238
19:18	19
22:4	72

Numbers (Nm)
16:1–33	358
16:31–35	358

Deuteronomy (Dt)
5:6–21	232, 233
6:4	232
6:5	19
25:5	148, 294
25:6	148

Joshua (Jos)
6:3	355

1 Samuel (1 S)
17:41–54	115
18:7	115
21:10–15	115
21:11	116
21:12–13	114
21:12–15	116
24	161

2 Samuel (2 S)
15–18	371
15:14	115

1 Kings (1 K)
	371
19:10, 18	304

2 Kings (2 K)
	371
2:23–24	128

Job (Jb)
1:11	85, 262, 336
1:21	82, 193, 228, 232
7:1	403, 458

Psalms (Ps) (LXX/Hebrew)

1:4	382
2:8	68, 310, 451
2:9	142
3:1	115
3:5 (3:4)	155, 441
3:6 (3:5)	80, 168, 181
3:9 (3:8)	330
5:4–5 (5:3)	383
6:6 (6:5)	189
6:8 (6:7)	346, 348
10:6 (11:5)	270
11:7 (12:6)	364
13:1 (14:1)	335
13:3 (14:3)	367
15:5 (16:5)	385
17:26–27 (18:25–26)	142, 250
17:29 (18:28)	191
17:30 (18:29)	258
17:45 (18:43–44)	150
18:2 (19:1)	105
18:3 (19:2)	87
18:4 (19:3–4)	392
18:5 (19:4)	105
18:6 (19:5)	130
18:7 (19:6)	367
18:10 (19:9)	404
21 (22)	22
21:2 (22:1)	19, 273, 434
21:4 (22:3)	453
21:16 (22:15)	383
21:17–19 (22:16–18)	220, 273
21:23 (22:22)	148
24:1 (25:1)	430
24:9 (25:9)	334
24:15 (25:15)	290, 333
26:4 (27:4)	398, 423
26:9 (27:9)	143, 453
26:12 (27:12)	236
26:14 (27:14)	429
28:1 (29:1)	247, 377
29:7 (30:6)	382
29:8 (30:7)	382
30 (31)	22
30:23 (31:22)	434
31:1 (32:1)	134
31:4 (32:4)	186
31:9 (32:9)	344, 444
33:1 (34:1)	342
33:2 (34:1)	193
33:9 (34:8)	357, 419
33:19 (34:18)	164, 325, 331
34:3 (35:3)	414
35:4 (36:3)	322
35:7 (36:6)	431, 432
35:8 (36:7)	77
35:9 (36:8)	77, 82, 461
35:10 (36:9)	77, 78, 384, 421
35: 10.12–13 (36:9.11–12)	96
35:12 (36:11)	78, 392
35:13 (36:12)	78
36:4 (37:4)	232
36:27 (37:27)	319
37:10 (38:9)	302
37:19 (38:18)	415
38:12 (39:11)	457, 458
39:5 (40:4)	244, 404
39:6 (40:5)	300
40:5 (41:4)	276, 280, 329, 446
40:8 (41:7)	353
41:3 (42:2)	381
41:4 (42:3)	182
44:14 (45:13)	204
47:9 (48:8)	53n36, 273
48:13 (49:12)	344
50:5 (51:3)	143, 453
50:7 (51:5)	323, 378
50:10 (51:8)	396
50:11 (51:9)	143, 324, 453
50:11.5 (51:9.3)	326
50:18–19 (51:16–17)	283
50:19 (51:17)	434
54:7 (55:6)	95, 392
54:13 (55:12)	374
54:13–14 (55:12–13)	375
54:23 (55:22)	413
55:12 (56:12)	230
56:2 (57:1)	383
56:7 (55:6)	378
60:3 (61:2)	68, 359, 451
61:6 (62:5)	196
61:12 (62:11)	132
63:7–8 (64:6)	431
63:8 (64:7)	169
67:31 (68:30)	363
68 (69)	22
68:5 (69:4)	271, 378
68:10 (69:9)	203, 301, 397
68: 16 (69:15)	382

68:30 (69:29)	75, 461	118:53 (119:53)	203, 349
72 (73)	27	118:53.158 (119:53.158)	
72:1 (73:1)	142		301
72:1.11.2 (73:1.11.2)		118:71 (119:71)	411, 440
	335	118:85 (119:85)	393, 399
72:7 (73:7)	334	119:2–5 (120:2–5)	135
72:16 (73:16)	188	119:7 (120:6–7)	204, 360
72:16–17 (73:16–17)		122:4 (123:4)	397
	427	125:6 (126:6)	75
74:4 (75:3)	292	126:2 (127:2)	182
76:3 (77:2)	383	129:3 (130:3)	445
77:24–25 (78:24–25)		138:7 (139:7)	432
	119	138:7–8 (139:7–8)	217, 231
78:2–3 (79:2–3)	289	138:7–10 (139:7–10)	
79:17 (80:16)	393		385
81:7 (82:7)	412	140 (141)	13
83:5 (84:4)	97, 429, 442	140:4 (141:4)	328
83:6 (84:5)	70, 452	141:6 (142:5)	83
83:6–7 (84:5–6)	39, 60, 64	142:2 (143:2)	445
83:8 (84:7)	334	143:11 (144:11)	82
84:9 (85:8)	410	143:11–14 (144:11–14)	
84:12 (85:11)	139		82
84:13 (85:12)	233, 381	143:15 (144:15)	83
86 (87)	371	145:4 (146:4)	255
86:3 (87:3)	155, 372	147:15	133
86:5 (87:5)	372	*Proverbs (Prv)*	
87:5–6 (88:4–5)	379	1:7	64
90:16 (91:16)	83	3:16, LXX	83
91:2 (92:1)	331	4:27	314
93:9 (94:9)	410	5:15	330
93:20 (94:20)	411	6:6	433
94:2 (95:2)	137	7:22	252
100:1 (101:1)	314	9:8	282
101:27–28 (102:26–27)		9:10	64
	100, 101, 185	12:23, LXX	105
101:28 (102:27)	400	18:3	189, 382
102:14 (103:14)	382	18:21	85, 262
103:29 (104:29)	382	20:9	326
103:30 (104:30)	382	*Ecclesiastes (Eccl)*	
109:4 (110:4)	118	1:2–3	404
109:6 (110:6)	381	1:18	414
109:7 (110:7)	401	*Song of Songs (Sg)*	
110:10 (111:10)	64	1:3	147
112:3 (113:3)	287	2:2	204
112:7–8 (113:7–8)	289	2:5	140
113:1 (115:1)	386	2:6	83
114:6 (116:6)	411	4:8, LXX	122
115:12–13 (116:12–13)		4:12	24
	135	5:8	140
115:15 (116:15)	289	6:6	151
117:13 (118:13)	219		
117:22 (118:22)	145		

6:9	24	5:6	174
6:10	151	10:22	120
8:6	108	11:1	244
Sirach (Sir)		11:2–3	39, 41, 64
1:16	64	40:5	163
10:15	46	40:6–8	221
11:30	377	48:22	410
17:26	201, 383	49:8	330
18:6	18	52:7	275
23:25	189	52:11	72
25:12	395	53:2	130
27:6	89	53:7	140, 395
35:26	433	57:16–17	440
		58:3	376
Wisdom (Wis)		58:7	446
1:5	201		
1:7	188	*Jeremiah (Jer)*	
1:16	431	17:16	290
2:18	162	*Lamentations (Lam)*	
2:20	162	3:30	61
2:21	162	*Ezekiel (Ezk)*	
4:20	215	15:2–5	303
5:3	237, 459	*Daniel (Dn)*	
5:3–5	459	2:31–45	441
5:6	87, 373	2:35	155
5:6–8	460	*Hosea (Hos)*	
5:8–9	87, 237	6:6	152
5:9	384	*Joel (Jl)*	
7:27	185	2:32	271
8:1	231	*Habakkuk (Hb)*	
9:15	61, 394, 428, 434	2:4	354
Isaiah (Is)		*Malachi (Ml)*	
1:3	333	3:7	383
1:18	151	4:2	76, 373
2:2	61		
3:14	105		

New Testament

Matthew (Mt)		5:12	347
1:11	98	5:14	155
3:12	201, 202, 360	5:16	153
4:3.9.6	219	5:17	233
4:11	166	5:22	286
5:3	381	5:44	203, 222
5:3–8	41	5:45	87, 231, 345, 373, 439
5:5	457		
5:6	397, 463	6:1	153
5:7	237	6:2.4	383
5:8	150, 441	6:3	81, 84

6:9	377	15:22	151
6:9–12	356	15:28	151
6:12	285, 377	16:16–17	199
6:14–15	356	16:18	346
6:19–21	152	16:22–23	293
6:20	406	16:22	199
6:31	333	16:23	199
7:2	237	16:26	259
7:3–5	301	18:3	128
7:5	348	19:5–6	214
7:6	397	19:6	130, 181, 272
7:7	80, 114	19:17	132
7:7–8	114	19:21	65
7:14	76, 223, 350	19:28	105, 148
7:23	202	20:22	62
8:8	412	21:19	194, 323
8:10	412	21:38.40–42.39	220
8:11–12	412	22:37–40	20
8:20	412	22:40	86, 95, 189, 232, 269
8:23–26	352		
8:24–26	81	22:42–45	343
9:12	412	22:42–46	119
9:13	152	23:12	62
9:15	129, 372, 420	23:23	237
9:20	147	23:27	322
10:16.28	288	23:35	275
10:22	429, 440	23:37	97
10:28	89, 347, 348	24:12–13	164
10:30	200	24:12	190, 300, 398, 414, 434
10:34	137		
10:41	275	24:13	190, 300, 429, 440
10:42	107, 275	24:35	454
11:11	77, 293	24:37–39	76
11:12	265	24:40	440
11:25–27	54n53	24:43	75
11:28–29	355	24:45	106, 396
11:29	376	25:4	282
12:7	152	25:21	397
12:37	85, 262	25:26–27.30	397
12:48	138	25:34	85, 149
13:23	204	25:34–35.37.40	106
13:24–30	439	25:34–38	152
13:26	67	25:35	227, 237
13:29	202	25:35.37.40	274
13:30	201	25:40	407
13:41–42	441	25:41	149, 184
13:47	202	25:41–42	215
13:47–48	205	26:26	122
14:25	199	26:34	198
14:30	346, 352	26:38	212, 444
15:3	362	28:38–39	337
15:14	366, 368	26:39	20, 227

27:24	168	8:22–25	352
27:34	22	8:23–24	81
27:40	354	8:44	147
27:40.42	162	10:30	102
27:42	128	10:30–34	100
27:46	19, 22, 434	10:30–35	218
27:51	180	10:30–37	321
27:57	77	11:8	114
28:10	148	11:41	152
28:20	160, 274	12:4	377
		12:52–53	137
Mark (Mk)		14:11	62, 430
1:13	166	15:8–9	191
3:33	138	15:11–32	183
4:18–19	272	15:12	188
4:36–40	352	15:18	183
4:37–39	81	15:19.21	377
4:39	199	15:20	183
5:11–13	441	15:24.32	136
5:28	147	16:9	106, 108
6:18	294	16:19–31	253
6:22–28	293	16:20–22	289
7:3–4	275	16:24	416
10:18	132	16:27–28	254
11:7	334	17:26–27	76
11:13	195	18:8	324
11:13–14	323	18:9–10	325
12:19	294	18:10–14	324
12:30	269	18:11	275
12:31	269, 270	18:13–14	325
13:21	86	18:14	62, 430
14:34	379, 444	19:8	107
14:50	291	22:33	197, 200
15:34	22, 273	22:43	166
16:19	180	22:44	53n35, 272
		22:62	198, 291
Luke (Lk)		23:34	140, 346, 354
1:32	119	23:39	460
2:14	346	23:40–43	379
3:6	163	23:46	22, 220
4:13	219	24:39	163
5	202	24:44	22
5:6	202, 300		
5:7	220	John (Jn)	
5:34	129, 420	1:1	25, 61, 79, 118,
6:23	347		130, 146, 343, 361,
6:27.35	346		384
6:37–38	237	1:1–3	63, 374
6:39	362, 366, 368	1:3	161, 185, 264, 343
7:39	275	1:3–4	133
7:41–47	276	1:9	77
7:47	66	1:10	345, 384
8:15	204		

1:12	85, 262	16:12	42, 395
1:14	25, 61, 79, 100, 119, 130, 146, 163, 343	16:32	200, 291
		17:2	163
		18:31	168
1:16	77	19:6	169
1:17	19, 134	19:21	161
1:29	61, 133	19:23–24	309
1:46–51	78	19:30	220
1:47	104, 145, 322	19:34	163, 167, 181
1:47–51	146	20:17	148
1:48	322	20:27–28	163
2:19.21	165	20:28	166
3:2	122	21:1–8	202, 300
3:13	450	21:18–19	213
3:29	293, 396		
6	113	*Acts of the Apostles (Acts)*	
6:51	180	1:25	309
6:53	121	1:26	309
6:54	365	2:4	187, 353
6:54.56	120	2:25–28	22
6:61.68.69	365	2:21	271
6:71	372	2:37	187
8:6	217	2:38	187
8:12	441	4:25–26	22
8:34	232, 379	4:34–35	152
8:44	96, 138, 396	7:49	104, 105
8:48–49	218	8:13–24	310
10:15	122	8:20–21	310
10:17	272	9:4	146, 181, 212, 213, 227, 271, 274, 343, 373, 451
10:18	198, 444		
10:18.17	167		
10:30	182, 200, 374	9:6	141
11:25	171	10:13	302
11:39–44	199	13:33–37	22
11:47	199	15:9	150
12:24–25	293	22:25	84
12:32	293		
12:35	198	*Romans (Rom)*	
13:1	79, 186, 292	1:1	456
13:36	291	1:3	161, 342
13:27	384	1:17	229, 235, 354
13:37	432	1:20	48, 421, 424
14:6	166, 204, 331, 441	1:24	366
14:8	398	1:31	121
14:9	25, 129	2:6	140
14:10	200	3:10–18	367
14:28	182, 199	3:23	130, 216, 321
14:30	271, 378	3:25	320
14:31	378	3:28	319
15:5.1	214	4	306
15:12	159	4:1–2	315
15:15	377, 456	4:3	316
		4:3–4	321

4:4	321	11:34–36	236
4:5	215, 273, 320, 321, 376	12:12	332
		13:9–10	317
4:5–6	321	13:10	20, 270, 317
4:17	290	15:8–11	22
4:25	79, 164		
5:3	197	*1 Corinthians (1 Cor)*	
5:3–4	443	1:13	72, 148, 149, 308, 366
5:3–5	172, 197, 336	1:23–24	455
5:6	130	1:23.25	131
5:14	181	1:24	186
6:6	272, 273, 379	1:25	139
6:9	80	1:28	290
6:12–13	427	1:31	315, 413
6:21	215	2:2	63
6:23	321	2:6	87, 146
7:13–25	46	2:8	129, 162, 186
7:22	283	2:9	39, 61, 263
7:22–23	444	2:13	87
7:22–25	134, 216	3:1	63
7:23	283	3:2	63, 365
7:24	284, 330	3:1–2	39, 41, 42, 395
7:24–25	222, 284, 444	3:2	146
8:6	47	3:10	41
8:23	284, 429	3:11	98
8:23–25	332	3:17	97, 453
8:24	429, 451	4:3	431
8:24–25	408, 429	4:5	155
8:25	383	4:7	324
8:32	460	4:9	410
8:34	287, 360	4:15	148
9:14	309	6:17	336
9:27	120	7:3	107
9:32	215	7:5	287
10:2	215, 375	7:7	107
10:2–3	385	7:27	107
10:3	215, 222, 375, 380, 382, 412,	7:30	193
		7:31	76
10:4	160, 211, 342, 409	8:1	21, 375
10:9	79	9:11	106
10:13	271	9:26–27	284
10:15	275	10:1–2	116
10:21	354	10:3	116
11:2.1	247	10:4	61, 116, 133, 287
11:3–4	304	10:6	248
11:21	245	10:11	116
11:22–23	246	10:12	403, 430
11:24.18	245	10:13	86, 90, 236
11:24.18–20	245	10:33	109
11:25–26	187	11:1	36
11:32	187	11:3	145
11:33–36	187		

11:19	364	3:29	374
11:28–29	442	4:4	255
11:29	385	4:4–5	329
12:12	214, 373	4:7	456
12:26	299	4:21–22.24	69
12:27	180, 271	4:22–31	69
13	20, 270	4:24	117
13.1.3	107	4:26	97
13:1–3	361	4:29	70
13:2	319	5:6	235, 317, 319
13:12	55n60, 122, 174, 265	5:14	317,
		5:17	284
13:13	318	6:2	422
14:20	128	6:3	402
15:9	147	6:4	282
15:9–10	247	6:14	108, 130
15:10	263	6:17	349

Ephesians (Eph)

15:51	361	1:14	455
15:53	285	1:21	454
15:54.53	463	2:2	128

2 Corinthians (2 Cor)

		2:8	380
1:12	282	2:8–10	309
1:22	455	2:9	380
2:15	147	2:10	380
3:6	21, 120	2:14	72
3:15	180	2:20	155, 245
4:16	402	3:17	81, 274, 453
5:1	97, 414	4:17–18	421
5:1–4	222	4:18	201
5:6	424, 428	4:26	301
5:6.9	415	4:27	441
5:7	79, 453	5:8	76, 345, 384
5:13	39, 62, 63, 146	5:23	212
5:13–14	211	5:27	147, 450
5:17	382, 402	5:29	284
11:29	88, 351	5:31	130
12:2	212	5:31–32	181, 197, 212, 214, 343
12:2.4	212		
12:4	63	5:32	138, 299, 374
12:8–9	324	6:12	345, 384
12:10	324, 413	6:19	314
13:4	80		

Galatians (Gal)

Philippians (Phil)

1:10	109	1:21	109
1:12	443	1:23	109, 349
1:15–16	194	1:23–24	109, 154, 302, 350
2:20	373	2:4.21	108
3:15–16	362	2:6	100, 182, 186
3:16	374	2:6–7	138, 199, 211
3:24	166	2:6–8	119
3:27	374	2:7	182, 384

2:8	331	*2 Timothy (2 Tm)*	
2:8–9	165	2:19	90
2:12	380	2:12–13	236
2:13	381	3:2	136
3:9	376, 401	3:9	368
3:12	377	3:12	350, 458
3:12–14	398, 409	3:13	368
3:12.14	401	4:2	365
3:13–14	248	4:6–8	337
3:15	409	*Hebrews (Heb)*	
3:20	378, 404	1:5–13	22
3:21	379	1:9	144
4:15	106	4:13	218
Colossians (Col)		6:19	366, 439
1:12	309	7:25	287
1:16	132, 174, 454	12:6	254, 336, 460
1:24	373	*1 Peter (1 Pt)*	
2:13–14	180	1:19	271
3:1–3	378, 451	2:2	365
3:3	103, 459	2:4	145
3:4	459	2:5	97, 154
4:2–4	13, 269	5:7	333, 365
1 Thessalonians (1 Thes)		*2 Peter (2 Pt)*	
2:7	36	1:19	383
3:8	302	2:20–21	303
5:2	75, 76	2:22	304
5:4–5	76	*1 John (1 Jn)*	
5:5	76	1:8	409
2 Thessalonians (2 Thes)		2:1–2	205, 287
2:14–15	351	2:9–11	349
1 Timothy (1 Tm)		2:11	301
1:5	21, 29, 270, 318, 319	2:19	307
1:7	72	3:2	122, 459
1:13	247, 263	3:15	202
2:5	372	*Revelation (Rv)*	
6:17	261	1:16	169
6:17–19	152	5:5	61, 133
6:18–19	261	5:6	61
		12:1	373
		12:5–6	372
		19:16	148

Subject Index

abandonment 32; 87; 129; 151; 154; 174; 193; 188; 203; 218; 235; 237; 262; 272; 291; 301; 304; 349–50; 376–79; 385; 445; 458

Abel 372

Abessalon (= Absalom) 115; 371
See also Absalom

Abimelech 113–23

Abraham 59; 69. 100; 119; 257
descendants, offspring, seed, stock 100; 125; 139; 244–47; 362; 374; 439
faith and righteousness 129; 306; 311; 315–17
embrace (in heaven) 254; 289; 416; 444
justice (righteousness) of 311; 316–17
and Melchizedek 113; 118
promises to 100; 139; 297 362
prophecy and 297; 306
sacrifice of Isaac 297; 306
two sons of (see also Isaac and Ishmael) 59; 69; 116
patriarch, with Isaac and Jacob 412

Absalom 369; 371; 375
See also Abessalon

Absolute Being 99; 101
See also Being-Itself; I AM WHO AM; *idipsum*; Selfsame

abundance 69; 77; 82; 94; 107–08; 127; 146; 152; 192–93; 231; 242; 250; 252; 256; 261; 268; 293; 439; 449; 461–63

accommodation, rhetorical
as characterizing rhetoric 34–40; 44; 54n49
as service to others 211
incarnation as model of 18; 211
of Scripture 18

accusation 157; 171; 201; 253; 267; 271; 273; 279–80; 283; 285; 291; 307; 325; 328; 335; 367; 391; 395; 398–99; 411; 460

Achis 113–23

actor 227

Adam
See also Adam and Eve
fall 59; 62; 384
symbol of old life 376; 389; 402–03; 449; 457
sleep of 167; 181
and time 137; 217
as type of Christ 167; 181

Adam and Eve 53n31; 101; 181; 253; 323n22

adoption 284; 332; 429

adultery 129; 217; 232; 276–77; 286; 315–29; 422; 462

adversity 177; 192; 228; 231; 410; 423; 433

affections 23; 70–71; 107; 121–22; 148; 193–94; 261n29; 350

affliction 164; 172; 251; 299; 336; 359; 369; 417; 443; 457; 460

Africa 53n31; 88; 149; 305; 313; 362
See also North Africa

allegory 59; 69; 117

Alleluia 358

almsgiving 152–53; 320; 383; 437; 446

altar 28–29; 139; 273; 304; 437–38; 442

Amen 229; 300; 358

angels
ascending and descending 125; 145–46; 392
devil as angel 77; 101; 413
devil's angels 128; 184; 215; 345; 384; 410
as divine heralds and emissaries 166; 219; 254; 301; 441
food of 63; 113; 118–19; 209; 218
human fellowship with 68; 95; 102; 174
as looking upon God 122; 174; 428; 443; 454
among powers of heaven 132; 174
as spirit beings 222; 410

487

anger (divine) 188–89; 210; 223; 359; 362–63

anger (human) 46; 297–302; 339–40; 346–53

anguish 237; 332; 340; 351; 359; 369; 452; 457

animals 61; 117; 128; 152; 333; 344; 417; 421; 457n15

anointing 125–26; 144–46; 276; 282n21

anxiety 33; 89; 152; 319; 333; 391; 406; 413–15; 430; 445–46; 455
See also fear; fear of death

apostles 22; 76; 93; 96; 104–06; 126; 132; 147–55; 159; 161; 174; 187; 196; 200; 213; 247; 309–10; 316; 353; 369; 372; 377; 398; 453

ark of Noah 76

ark of the covenant 355

arrangement (rhetorical) 30; 159

arrogance 55n53; 149; 165; 241; 245; 254; 260; 285; 325; 341; 357; 360; 374–75; 440; 445
See also pride

arrow 59–60; 65–70; 126; 135; 140–41; 158; 169–70; 366

ascension of Christ 148; 181; 187; 212; 358; 449–51

ascent, spiritual 54n51; 17; 26–27; 37–41; 59–73; 93; 102–04; 146; 392; 452
See also authority; descent; reason; sacrament; Scripture; *spiritales*
charity and 70; 389; 449–54
Christ and 35; 39; 59; 61–62; 65; 146; 450–51
Church and 35; 102; 109; 146; 449–51
conversion and 42; 44–48; 60; 65; 73; 392
descent and 43; 62; 125; 145–46; 392
heart and 60; 62; 64; 70; 74–75; 452
humility as beginning 39; 69; 73; 74–75; 90; 96
not physical 39; 60; 70 95; 392; 449–54
pride and 62; 74; 78; 90; 392; 452

Ascents, Songs of 60; 69; 74–78; 90; 392
See also Step-Songs

astrologers 258n23; 276n14; 277; 286
See also stars

athlete 216; 317

attachment 95; 233; 303; 39

authority 39; 42; 47; 65; 117; 257–58; 283; 288; 291; 457

avarice 85; 191; 406; 461

awe 38; 245–46

babies 36–37; 41; 63; 118; 123; 128; 131; 218; 308

Babylon 98 150; 177; 194–95; 340; 354

"bad Christians" 23; 297; 303; 307; 339–40; 437

Bagai, Council of 367n63

banquet 90; 118; 130n9; 427n16

baptism 28; 40; 45; 72; 116; 138; 149; 151; 187; 248; 308–12; 330–31; 358; 360; 364–67; 374; 377; 417; 420–21; 430; 456

baptized 53n37; 54n53; 55n54; 310; 420–21

barn 67 ; 72; 300; 361; 441

basilica 55n54; 98; 127; 226n1; 243n1; 313

battle 236; 281; 384; 410; 437; 440

beard 113–16; 121–23

beast 128; 171; 241; 243; 262–64; 334; 344; 444

beauty 52n25
Christ and 25; 47; 125–31; 136; 139; 147
Church and 125–30; 148–53; 203; 275; 382; 417
justice and 225; 233–34; 425

bed 173; 217; 260; 275; 288

behavior 36; 113–23; 128; 222; 228; 277; 301; 417; 427

being 15; 42; 93; 99; 101; 103; 133; 195; 233; 278; 380; 390; 400–03; 408; 415–16; 428
See also Absolute Being; Being-Itself; *idipsum*; non-being

Being-Itself 42; 93–94; 99–103; 108–09
  See also Absolute Being; I AM WHO AM; Selfsame

believer 25; 41–42; 48; 55n60; 85; 120; 126; 129; 138; 177; 191–92; 194; 215; 229; 259; 268; 311–21; 330; 334; 342; 345; 354; 358; 377; 407–09; 415; 420; 422; 437; 442n9

believing 20; 42; 85–86; 97; 122; 129; 145–53; 159; 163–65; 169–71; 180–81; 211; 236; 273; 297; 365; 379; 383; 444; 458–60
  See also Abraham, faith of; faith
  in Christ 73; 79–80; 93; 221; 411
  for justification 215; 225; 229; 235; 311–16; 409
  without seeing 150; 170; 422–24; 458

belly 210; 223; 298–302

bird 190; 290; 349

birthday 88; 90; 427

bishop 14; 22–23; 49; 52n19; 55n58; 104; 126; 154; 230n11; 308n18; 363n47; 364n48

bitterness 177; 192; 308; 313; 327; 334; 351; 423

blessing 118; 145; 248–49; 330

blind 45; 131; 162; 166; 171; 173; 177; 184–187; 201; 216; 237; 252; 301; 305; 324; 340; 348; 362; 366–68; 395; 405; 421—22; 425

blood 244
  of Jesus 32; 53n35; 117–23; 147; 152; 168; 180; 186; 190; 229; 271–72; 420; 427; 455–56
  See also body and blood of Jesus
  of martyrs 32; 233; 268; 288–89
  sacrificial 152; 306

blood violence 179; 201–02; 341; 367–68

boasting 130; 216; 241–45; 255 ; 280–82; 286; 309; 311–15; 320–26; 334–37; 370; 375; 380; 382; 413; 416; 430; 446; 458–59

body (flesh) and blood of Jesus (Eucharist) 28; 117–23; 365

body (human) 19; 61; 70; 88–89; 101; 107; 134; 146; 186; 212; 214; 221–22; 226n1; 230n11; 267; 275; 278n17; 284–88; 330; 347–48; 350; 361; 394; 415; 424–28; 434; 439; 444; 461
  See also flesh and blood

body of Christ (Church) 15; 20; 27–30; 32; 35; 59; 126; 140; 146; 150; 157; 159–160; 164; 177–84; 197–204; 209; 212–14; 218–20; 243; 267; 271–74; 277; 281–84; 297–302; 305–06; 336; 339–46; 356; 359; 364; 367; 369; 372–80; 418–19; 434; 437–438; 450–51
  See also whole Christ

body of Christ (Incarnation) 19; 32; 89; 120; 122; 162–63; 165; 172–73; 198; 267; 272

bone 167; 178–79; 195–200; 220; 253; 268; 273; 289–91; 298; 302–03; 312; 326–27; 340; 365; 419; 434–35

bow 143; 170
  See also arrow

bread 53n31; 118–19; 160; 177; 182–83; 219; 281; 356; 365; 417–18; 423–24; 432; 446

bread of angels 113; 119; 209

brethren 94; 109; 357; 362; 374–75; 398

bride 25; 46; 83; 125–30; 140; 147–55; 167; 180; 212n4; 214; 284n25; 299; 401; 449; 455–56

bridegroom 25; 83; 89; 127–40; 147–54; 177; 180; 212n4; 214; 264; 293; 299; 369–72; 396; 420; 455

brother 138; 148–49; 171; 254; 285; 286; 294; 351

building 41; 45; 67; 98–99; 131–32; 217; 222; 265; 414

Cain 372

captivity 190; 194; 246; 280; 379

carnal 63; 69; 119; 142; 203; 232; 244; 246–49; 343
  external or visible 106; 119; 232; 244; 421
  fleshly (vs. spiritual) 47; 63; 66; 69–70; 80; 85; 106; 142; 249; 256; 343;

350n12; 162;368; 395; 444
Israel in the Old Testament 203; 244; 246–47; 249
mind 47; 66; 70; 80; 85; 395; 444
sense 244; 350n13; 368; 421

catechumens 28; 42; 55n54; 357n31; 377; 417; 419; 420n5

Catholic Church 71–72; 137–38; 154; 170; 287; 358; 362
See also Church

Calvary 25; 125; 128; 420

censure 121; 234n28; 280; 283; 285; 397; 411

chaff 71; 103–04; 301; 340; 360–61

Chance 258; 312; 330–31

change 11; 16; 18; 20; 25; 34; 37;100–03; 113–20; 125–29; 141; 145; 177; 180; 185; 215; 243; 247; 250; 261; 280; 320; 341; 361; 379; 402; 426–29

chastisement 148; 183; 191–92; 242; 248–51; 256–57; 281; 284; 335; 342; 391; 405n42; 411–13; 449; 454–58

chastity 25; 129; 241; 261–64; 275; 280n18; 360; 389; 404; 455

childishness 29; 128; 395; 404

childlikeness 55; 123; 128; 365

children 30; 36; 69; 88n41; 131; 228; 232; 284; 348; 369; 373; 389; 405–08; 413
of the devil (evil, world, darkness) 76; 138; 151; 169–70; 249; 369; 375
of God (Christ, light, truth, Church, etc.) 76; 81; 85–88; 122; 125; 129; 136; 148–50; 153; 229; 254; 258; 262; 284; 299; 332; 336; 342; 372; 394; 420; 457–60
of Israel (synagogue) 99; 242; 247; 257–58; 412; 416
of Korah 25–26; 125–28; 417–20; 424
"of men" 77; 146; 194; 299
spiritual infancy 42; 54n48; 218; 308; 395

charity 29–30; 35; 69; 77; 107–09; 126; 154; 159; 188–90; 211; 213; 288; 309; 339–40; 343; 361; 375; 380; 398; 414; 419; 434

See also love
as exercise of patience 71; 351–52
as goal ("end") of Scripture 21; 269–70; 319
as law toward God and neighbor 70; 189;197; 225; 232; 267; 270; 317
as linked with faith and hope 20; 47; 55n57; 73; 75; 150; 318–19; 343; 404
as uniting Christians 155; 271–73; 297–300
as uniting Church and Christ 160; 213; 267;451

choice (divine) 63; 121; 134; 145; 168; 185–86; 290; 339; 394; 415

choice (human) 43; 85; 88; 142; 154; 161; 211; 222; 235; 259; 263–64; 271; 285; 288; 309; 317–22; 350n13; 393; 396; 422
See also free choice

chosen *See also* elect, Manichean

Christ 39; 46; 61; 64–65; 67; 73; 78–79; 84–87; 97; 105; 113; 129; 133; 140; 146; 148; 153; 165–70; 198–201; 211–12; 287–88; 323–24; 354; 378; 419–22
See also end; Jesus; whole Christ
"anointed" 125; 144–46
charity's source 19–21; 29; 34; 38; 159; 190; 211; 270; 346
Church and 18; 25–29; 35; 44; 46; 52n12; 68; 72; 83; 87; 125–26; 129; 138; 140; 153; 155; 180–81; 198; 204–05; 209; 214; 219; 274; 284; 305; 343; 374
See also Church; whole Christ
divine and human 18; 23; 157–58
divinity 20; 41 62; 73; 119; 140; 182; 185–86; 361
faith, indwells heart by 81; 83; 192; 352–53; 449; 453
flesh nurturing faith, "little ones" 39; 41; 46; 87; 93; 99–100; 190–91; 395
and grace 134–35; 215–16; 284; 312; 456
humanity 18; 22–23; 41; 45–46; 73; 93; 125; 134; 163; 173; 177; 181; 227
humility of 39; 45–46; 59; 62–63; 87; 117; 122; 312; 331; 412

and Jews; stock of Israel, David, patriarchs 119–21; 138; 145; 161; 165–168; 177; 243–46; 342–43; 374
  kingdom, reign 68; 140–42; 148; 170
  passion and death 20; 25; 39; 130; 167; 181; 190; 197–98; 291–94; 306; 373
  resurrection 76; 79–80; 157; 165; 173
  sacramental presence of 29; 120–22; 180; 442
  Scripture's center and prophetic fulfillment 19; 23; 35; 116; 144; 161; 165–67; 181; 306; 372–74
  as teacher and example 37; 39; 42; 160; 225; 228; 337; 346; 458
  voice in Scripture 19; 22; 29; 32; 177; 181; 197; 213–14; 267; 271–72; 299
  See also body and blood of Jesus; head; humility; *totus Christus*; whole Christ

Church 14; 18; 20; 23–30; 32; 34; 36–37; 44; 46; 52n12; 68; 59; 68; 70–71; 73; 83; 86–89; 100; 102; 104; 109; 119; 125–26; 129–30; 138; 146–47; 152–55; 159–60; 167; 170; 177–83; 200–05; 213–14; 219; 227; 245; 247; 265; 267–68; 272–74; 284; 289–92; 297–310; 339–40; 343; 346; 349–50; 354–58; 362–64; 373; 375; 378; 395; 417–20; 426; 434–35; 437–38; 441–42; 449–50; 455–56
  See also Catholic Church; whole Christ

church (physical space) 28; 52n26

churches (local) 104; 126; 129; 148; 159; 210n1; 219; 223; 297; 299–300; 303–04; 307; 375; 419

city 69; 93–102; 108–09; 113–22; 126; 149–50; 155; 165; 177; 194–95; 204; 243; 246; 260–61; 340–41; 354–57; 369; 372–73; 439; 462
  See also Babylon; city of God; Jerusalem

city of God 155; 354n22; 369; 372–73

climbers 39–43; 59; 62–65; 78; 449; 452

clothing 25; 127; 147; 152; 63; 168; 173; 212; 215; 222; 234; 254–55; 285; 323; 337; 369; 373–74; 383; 449–50; 462

cloud 29; 116; 158; 173–74; 185; 259; 286; 350; 428; 433; 445

commandments 19; 86; 95; 174; 183; 189–90; 225; 232–33; 269–70; 318–19; 422; 437; 443; 446
  See also Ten Commandments

communion 28; 170; 201–04

community 18; 22; 27–28; 35; 39; 42; 45; 55n54

compassion 47; 107; 121; 451

complacency 143; 198; 272; 304; 316; 398

compunction 330

concupiscence 90; 262; 462

condemnation 19–20; 78; 85; 162; 216; 238; 242; 257–58; 262; 267; 274; 277; 301; 314; 321; 323; 361; 363n47; 367; 376; 385; 397; 411; 416; 432; 456

confession 46; 77; 104; 155; 177; 184; 199; 201; 273; 276; 279n18; 293; 314; 325–28; 370; 382–85; 429; 435; 445

confusion 165; 191; 210; 223; 298–302; 340–41; 353–54; 445

conscience 126; 153; 168; 171; 217; 252; 269–70; 282–83; 304; 311; 304; 318–19; 325–27; 352n16; 354; 415; 439; 460

consolation 76; 105; 227; 248; 352; 404

constancy 172; 197; 336; 443

contemplation 14; 35; 40; 47; 55n60; 62; 80; 93; 100; 118; 132; 133; 136; 174; 188; 211; 263; 305; 353; 381; 383; 398–400; 403n36; 423

contempt 215; 234n27; 253; 290; 383; 449–50; 458–460

conversion 14–18; 21–25; 29–48; 54n48; 55n53; 67; 125–26; 149; 236–37; 302; 323n22; 327n27; 339; 345

correction 43; 257; 281–85; 302; 315; 345; 411–12

corruption 264; 279; 286; 341; 366–68

courage 198; 255

court (of law) 356; 376

courts of Jerusalem 93–101; 243; 265

coveting 84; 233; 249; 261–64; 286; 315–20; 407; 422
See also envy

covenant 19; 59; 69; 117; 203; 225; 234; 241; 244–49; 262–63; 312; 329; 340–41; 362; 402

creation 63; 85; 105; 132–33; 143; 149; 152; 166; 181; 185–86; 203; 332; 335; 345; 380; 382; 417; 421; 426; 456; 461

creation (new) 126; 151; 181–82; 284; 309; 370; 380; 382; 385; 411

creator (divine) 73; 136; 138; 159; 179; 181; 191; 196–98; 228; 249; 277; 283; 288; 312; 320; 329; 344; 352; 363n47; 370; 380; 385; 411; 424; 426

creature 15; 103; 133; 151; 181; 185; 190; 227–28; 236; 259; 283; 302; 320; 333; 347; 350; 352; 363n47; 380; 385; 401n30; 411; 424–26; 454; 456

crop 71n26; 231; 268; 281; 289; 293; 360

cross 19–20; 25; 28; 32; 45; 75; 119; 121; 131; 140; 147; 157; 161–63; 167; 169; 180–81; 187; 209; 220; 267; 272–73; 288–89; 306; 331; 346; 354; 359; 417; 420
See also crucifixion

cross of light (Manichean) 267; 280–81

crucifixion 21–22; 39; 41; 46; 53n35; 61; 87; 102; 122; 125; 128–30; 145; 150; 157; 161–62; 165; 169; 173; 186–87; 245; 267; 281; 288–89; 291; 306; 331; 375; 420; 460
See also cross

cry 30; 71; 97; 115; 136; 151; 158; 163–64; 172; 187; 213; 220; 222; 235; 264; 268; 271–73; 284; 299; 302; 329–31; 340; 359; 379; 411; 415; 423; 434–35; 451–52; 458

cup 20; 62; 93; 107; 135; 212; 227; 275; 337

curse 85n31; 194; 215; 225; 228; 297; 307–08; 323; 342

damnation 215; 222; 261; 319; 321; 362

dance 115; 169; 225–30; 312–13; 332–34; 347

danger 15; 27; 46; 66; 77; 86; 202n52; 216; 247; 256–57; 276; 280; 290; 300; 308; 311–17; 353; 357; 396–97; 401; 405; 428; 435; 440

Daniel 155; 441

darkness 39; 69–71; 76; 78; 120; 155; 177; 191–95; 267; 278–80; 301; 345; 349; 366–67; 379; 384; 424–25; 432–33

darkness race of (Manichean) 312; 331

David 14; 82; 94; 97; 98; 113–23; 157–62; 167; 178; 210–11; 226; 241–48; 268; 312; 321–22; 339–44; 369–72; 384; 390–91; 438

day 24; 74–76; 87–88; 100–01; 173; 177–79; 192–200; 221; 242; 251–57; 290; 300; 330; 337; 380; 383; 389–90; 400- 06; 418; 423–24; 431
See also night

dead 148–49; 173; 199; 201; 378–83

death, dying 62; 85; 108–09; 138; 164; 171; 209; 221–22; 241–42; 251–55; 262; 268; 277; 281; 288–93; 307n15; 309; 337; 339–41; 348–51; 357–59; 364; 368n65; 376–79; 389–90; 401–02; 405; 413; 416; 431; 444
See also death; fear of death

deceit, deception 86–90; 135; 145; 166; 188; 234–36; 285; 314; 340–44; 355–56; 362; 366–68; 402; 408–09; 424; 438–41

decorum (rhetorical "fittingness") 36–37; 44; 54n44

deer 26–27; 417–24; 428; 434

defeat 145; 169; 246; 278n17; 280n18; 347; 384

delight 27; 34; 43; 77; 96; 108; 128; 134; 136; 142–43; 179; 190–95; 205;

Subject Index

232; 243; 261–64; 283–84; 389–98; 422–28; 444–45; 461

demons 83; 128; 184; 218; 248–49; 264; 287; 320; 332; 441

depth 17–18; 23; 25; 38; 94; 170; 186; 189–90; 269; 382–83; 411; 431–32; 450

desert 248; 339–41; 351–55

desire 17–18; 23; 37; 39; 42–48; 73–75; 94; 101; 151; 177; 185–92; 232; 241–44; 252; 255; 262–63; 267; 286; 349–50; 358; 389; 394; 399; 403–04; 417–32; 438–39; 449–50; 454–55; 462

despair 69; 100; 189–90; 318; 451

devil 67; 77; 82; 85; 101–02; 117; 122; 125; 128; 138; 146; 151; 180; 184; 209; 215; 219; 222; 248–51; 262; 264; 287–88; 310; 329; 336; 339; 345–48; 372; 378; 384; 410; 412–16; 429; 434
See also Satan

dignity (divine) 62; 125–26; 139; 213; 298

dignity (human) 344; 449; 455

disciple 42; 62; 109; 120; 141; 159; 166; 178; 187; 197–201; 275; 289–91; 352–53; 365; 373; 456

discipline 150; 192; 277; 284; 292n42; 312; 336; 371; 411–12

discouragement 65; 233

disease 101; 439; 462

disgrace 165; 192; 234; 276; 279; 303–04; 450; 456–60

dishonesty 67; 238; 256–59; 267–81; 287; 328; 458
See also lies

dispensation, temporal (plan of salvation) 87; 403n36

distress 85; 196; 210; 223; 284; 297–300; 313; 332–34; 339–59; 370–71; 379–86; 444; 460

doctor 198; 256; 288; 311; 326
See also physician

doctrine (Christian) 47; 150; 229; 232; 330; 376n17

doctrine (false) 184; 258; 279; 330–31
See also heresy; schism

Donatists 507

donkey 334

door 13; 44; 80; 113–22; 219; 268–74; 305; 441

doubt 99; 159; 256–57; 297; 304; 309; 335; 428

dove 24; 95; 192; 339–40; 349–52; 385; 392

dream 125; 241–43; 260; 339

drink 62–63; 76–77; 91; 101; 110; 120–23; 146; 152; 215; 229; 274; 330; 355; 365; 370; 385; 395; 404; 423; 428; 461–62

drunkard 67
See also inebriated

dust 300; 307; 370; 382; 452

duty 13; 42; 93; 106–07; 136; 238; 269; 271; 350; 396n17; 461

ears 27–28; 63; 71; 185; 210; 233; 410; 425; 428; 445

ears, God's 71; 235; 276; 370; 375; 391; 414; 443

earthenware 383; 411

ecstasy 209–14; 217; 434

Eden 53n31; 370

education 16; 43; 47; 133; 177; 191; 201; 276; 304; 339; 342; 373; 413

Elijah 304

elect (good and bad) 103; 147; 202; 267–68; 274–78; 281; 290; 300n3

elect, Manichean 267; 277–81

emotion (feeling, passion, affection) 23; 26; 31; 261; 300

emperor 191; 219; 268; 290; 363n46

emptiness 66–67; 82–83; 108; 121; 201; 209; 221; 243; 384; 389–90; 403–04;

421

emptying self- 35; 119; 138; 182; 211

encouragement 42–43; 47; 73; 93–95; 170; 199; 229; 360; 437; 445; 449

end 18; 39; 68; 83–84; 102; 133; 189–192; 217; 219; 231; 244n3; 255; 305; 310; 359; 389–91; 397–404; 420; 426–27; 451; 459
   Christ as (Rom 10:4), 160–61; 209–12; 339–42; 398; 409
   as Scripture's goal 20–21; 269–70; 311; 319
   of time 87; 89; 159–60; 164; 178; 189–90; 202–04; 219; 222; 226; 259; 261; 272; 274; 284; 300; 314; 360; 368; 370; 373–74; 383; 385; 416; 429; 439–40; 455

endurance 172; 196–97; 332; 336; 344; 437; 443

enemies 68–69; 79; 85; 89; 98; 116; 118–19; 126; 137; 140–41; 165–67; 171–72; 178–79; 193; 202–04; 209–10; 219–23; 234; 248–53; 279; 291–92; 297–99; 303–04; 318; 339–57; 369–75; 378; 384–86; 399; 419–20; 429; 434–35; 437–43

enigma 186

enjoyment 96; 123; 192; 232; 393; 403

enlightenment 26; 47; 78; 191–95

envy 101; 241; 422
   See also coveting

equity (legal) 294; 325
   See also letter and spirit

error 73; 87; 120; 165; 201–02; 209; 219; 250; 258; 368; 445

escape 68; 115–16; 188–190; 217–21; 246; 255; 260; 278; 339; 351; 357; 370; 396; 400

eternal (vs. temporal, changing) 40; 46; 73–75; 83–84; 94; 99; 256; 262; 264; 307; 403n36
   See also unchanging
   being (God, Word) 48; 119–21; 132–34; 140–41; 308; 320; 363n47; 401n30; 416; 428; 454
   goods, food 118; 192; 259
   life 73; 82–84; 88n42; 108; 122; 138; 155; 182; 204; 237; 291; 320; 365; 416; 432; 441
   punishment (shame; fire; judgment; death) 121; 149; 184; 214–15; 251; 345; 416
   state (eternal city; joy; blessedness; Jerusalem) 27; 39; 73–75; 95; 204; 414–15; 428
   "way" (Christ) 178–79; 204–05

eternity 83–84; 90; 106–08; 125; 155; 204; 214–15; 243; 249; 264; 368; 414; 459

Eucharist 28–29; 41; 113; 120–22; 229n5; 299n2; 357n31

evangelist 163; 165; 186; 219; 292; 324

evening sacrifice 32; 180; 267–74

evil 67–72; 74; 88–98; 128; 135; 141; 157;162; 169; 189–90; 201; 258; 278n17; 280n18; 297; 314–21; 332; 343–45; 355; 369; 378; 383; 385; 405–06; 429; 435; 462

evildoers 27; 104 ; 157;171; 203; 241; 269; 280n18; 304; 373
   See also sin; sinners; wicked

example 13; 39; 59; 62–67; 75; 88; 157–60; 170; 193; 199; 209; 219; 227–28; 303; 322–24

exchange 19; 30; 35; 209; 21
   impersonation 11; 20; 31; 36; 54n42
   See also redemption

exercises, spiritual 13; 17; 21; 23; 27–30; 33; 37; 40–41; 43; 46–48; 267; 269–70; 427

experience 27; 31; 47; 54n48; 55n55; 62–64; 69; 129; 139; 164; 171; 191–92; 196; 211; 231; 236; 241; 248; 251; 271; 280; 298–99; 344; 350–53; 394–404; 411; 419–21; 439

Eve 53n31; 181; 253; 323n22
   See also Adam and Eve

exegesis 13–41; 50n3; 53n31; 55n58; 114

existence 100–01; 133; 185; 211; 335; 400–01

Exodus, Israel's 29

eye 11; 21; 24–29; 39; 43; 61; 73–77; 97–99; 117–19; 125–31; 143; 157–

Subject Index

58; 171; 174; 179; 186; 188; 210; 217; 221–23; 233–34; 243–44; 250; 252; 263; 268; 290; 298–304; 314; 325–27; 332–33; 346–55; 367; 380; 389; 398; 402–03; 408–10; 414; 417; 421; 424; 425; 441; 449–63

eyes, God's 27; 66; 179; 183; 198–200; 217–18; 276; 313; 324; 333; 403; 432; 445; 453

eyelids, God's 21

face 153; 166; 177; 188; 215; 382; 432; 453

face to face 43; 55n60; 122; 158; 174; 178; 265; 405; 454

face, God's 68; 79; 137; 143; 178; 185–89; 217; 231; 324–26; 370; 382–85; 399; 418; 423–28; 432; 453

fainthearted 341; 352–55; 360; 366

faith 14; 15; 17; 18; 20; 23; 24; 31; 33; 41–43; 45–47; 54n48; 55n57; 55n60; 69; 73; 75; 76n13; 79–86; 90; 122; 139; 150–51; 165; 171; 190; 192; 195; 225–26; 229; 235–36; 245–48; 256; 259; 270; 274; 304; 309; 311; 315–24; 334; 347; 353–54; 361–62; 370; 376; 379; 395n13; 402; 404; 407; 409; 412; 422; 431–32; 444; 449; 453–54

See also Abraham, faith of; authority; believing; believer

faith, Catholic 132; 149; 165; 285; 310; 315; 337; 343; 363; 364nn47–48; 373

faith, Manichean 281

faithfulness (divine) 86; 90; 125–26; 139–40; 236

faithfulness, fidelity 83; 125–26; 139; 235–36

false, falsehood 47; 64; 89; 103; 144; 174; 201; 232; 273; 279; 363; 374–75; 444; 461–63

fame 46; 83–84

Fate 276–80; 312; 328–30

fate (outcome) 254; 260; 293; 298; 309; 362; 367; 382; 383; 396–97; 460

fear 23; 187–88; 191; 198–99; 209–15; 219; 225; 233–34; 252; 255; 261; 280; 286; 290; 298; 303–05; 340; 347; 369; 37576; 380–81; 389–407; 416; 428; 432–34; 440; 445; 449; 455

See also anxiety; fear of death; fear of the Lord; terror

fear of death 20; 198; 221; 268; 288; 292; 340; 348–51; 413

fear of the Lord 39; 50; 64; 89; 125; 195; 217; 252; 261; 288; 340–41; 361–62; 432

fidelity 83; 235

fig tree 146; 311; 322–24

figurative reading 19; 32

figure of speech 30–31

fire 29; 67; 88–89; 108; 303; 317; 351; 364; 390; 393; 397; 422
    eternal fire 149; 184; 214–15; 286; 345; 358–59; 416; 441
    of love 53n37; 96–97; 140; 233; 263–64
    of sacrifice 306

firmness 55; 77; 154; 178–79; 185; 196–200; 284; 288–91; 300–02; 313; 333; 364n47; 383; 444; 458

fish 201n49; 202–05; 219; 405

fishermen 219; 290; 300

flattery 46; 253; 267; 270; 281–85; 305

flesh and blood (i.e., humanity) 27; 199; 339; 345; 347; 384

flight 95; 115; 161; 181; 190; 305; 350–52; 355; 384

flood 76; 255; 313; 330–32; 335; 353

food 41; 45; 59; 63–64; 106; 116–20; 131; 146; 215; 218; 278; 308; 318; 340–42; 357; 365; 395; 418; 423; 428; 433; 446

fool, foolishness 24; 82; 130–31; 244; 286; 301; 335; 344; 368; 397; 404; 452; 458–59

foot, feet 16; 20; 27; 39; 60; 73–78; 81;

90; 94–101; 107; 146; 152; 158; 170–71; 210; 213; 219–20; 223; 241–42; 249; 251; 257–58; 273; 275–76; 290; 298–300; 320–21; 333–35; 367–68; 369; 373; 389; 392; 397; 421–22; 441; 452

footing 73; 77; 335

footsteps 117; 275

footstool 104; 119; 343

forecourts *See* courts of Jerusalem

foreshadowing 152; 163–65; 181; 246–48; 302; 371; 374

foretelling 32; 126; 162; 186; 200; 213; 244; 273; 291–93; 297; 300; 306; 330; 372

forgetfulness 73–74; 101; 126–27; 150–51; 236–37; 245; 248; 253; 261; 265; 272; 353; 398; 409; 425

forgiveness 66; 134; 140; 155; 182; 187; 217; 236–37; 267; 276; 285–87; 311–14; 321–29; 333; 346; 354; 340; 355–56; 364n48; 369; 377; 390–91; 395; 409; 415–16; 419–21; 430

fornication 264; 275

fortitude 198; 293–94; 437–40

fortune 191; 276n14; 278n17; 298; 410
See also astrologers; fate; chance

fortune (good) 27; 82–83; 177; 191–92; 225–31; 348; 427; 452; 458–59
See also misfortune

foundation 41; 46; 52n19; 82; 97–98; 152; 154; 165; 261; 316

free (from encumbrance) 89; 94–95; 104; 121; 126; 145; 147; 155; 162–63; 190; 193; 209–23; 248; 251–52; 271; 280; 293–94; 298–99; 303; 310; 314; 316; 319; 323–26; 336; 349–50; 369; 378–79; 391; 400; 409; 411; 415; 422; 428; 430; 433; 443–46; 450; 460

free (without cost) 277; 311; 321

free (social status) 69; 118; 369

free will, choice 85; 88; 106n31; 190; 312; 328–29; 350n13

friend 52n16; 65; 68; 106; 130; 141; 143; 147; 152; 159; 179; 185; 200; 221; 270; 293; 313; 356; 377; 396; 399; 407; 456

fruit 25; 67; 110; 128; 135; 194–95; 204; 233; 241–45; 278n17; 281; 293; 303; 311; 316; 323; 332; 381; 429; 439

fulfillment 19–20; 22–23; 42; 84; 87; 96; 139; 157; 164; 166; 195; 220; 225; 233; 291; 292; 294; 314; 318; 344; 418; 422; 438; 456n13

future 73; 96; 100; 133; 135; 152–54; 236; 261; 340; 389; 401; 406; 451; 459

future (predictions, promises, prophecies of) 120; 165; 186; 213; 244–48; 374; 384

future life 44; 48; 212

future realities 128; 251

game 29; 216; 393

gates 116; 253–54; 271; 275; 280n18; 416

gentleness 125–26; 139; 140; 160; 334; 365–66; 433

gentiles 113; 119–20; 123; 130; 138–39; 141; 150–51; 158; 173–74; 183; 187; 245; 249; 302; 455
See also nations

gift 41–48; 64; 76; 83–86; 104; 127; 136–40; 151–52; 195; 213–15; 225; 231–37; 246–48; 299; 310; 311; 321–24; 344; 360; 376; 381–86; 399; 434; 446

gladness 96; 107; 127; 136; 153; 210; 221–22; 228; 235–36; 269; 298; 342; 344; 353; 396; 419; 428; 442

glory 39; 73; 93; 105; 115; 127–29; 149; 153; 157–58; 162; 169–75; 185–87; 197–201; 215–16; 243; 263; 282; 299; 321; 336; 354; 371; 386; 410; 443; 459

Godhead 131; 141; 162; 181; 199; 227

godless, ungodly 76; 151; 164; 171; 184; 204; 216; 255–57; 263; 273; 277; 287; 304; 320–22; 330; 336; 345; 373; 376; 384; 439; 458
See also sin; sinner; wicked

godliness 216; 241; 320; 458

gods 88n41; 332; 335

gold 108; 127; 149–53; 253–64; 278; 393; 408
  See also silver

good fortune 27; 82; 177; 192; 228; 231; 348; 427; 452; 458–59

good will 322; 346; 389; 392; 446

goodness 72; 132; 140; 246; 265; 339; 345; 351; 410

goods 82; 107; 152; 193–95; 247–50; 259–62; 275; 407; 463

gospel (preached) 19; 32; 65–66; 76; 125; 140; 147–50; 161; 165; 174; 253; 288; 302; 340; 365; 443; 456

grace 14–20; 27; 41–45; 90n47; 125–26; 134–41; 147; 157–58; 174; 177; 183–88; 195–201; 209–16; 222; 227; 234; 247; 263; 267; 284; 293; 298; 302; 309–10; 311–34; 339; 346; 362; 369–70; 374–86; 390–93; 411–13; 419; 444
  See also Christ, grace and

gratitude 211; 299
  See also thanksgiving

grave 226n1; 268; 289–91

greed 75; 219; 254; 318; 350; 393; 405; 422

grief 171; 335; 350; 414; 443

groaning 68–71; 95; 109; 155; 164; 191; 201; 204; 222; 237; 267; 284; 287; 301–02; 312; 323; 331–32; 340; 344; 347; 357; 375; 390; 402–04; 414; 428–29; 437–38; 452–63

guard, guardian 73–90; 218; 268–80; 290–91; 301; 304; 316; 390–96; 407; 429

guidance 141; 147; 160–61; 189; 209–10; 223; 236; 298–99; 334; 341; 357–66; 425–26

guile 60–66; 104; 135; 145; 178; 184; 241–43; 259; 312; 322–27

guilt 143; 168; 180; 215; 238; 249; 271; 279; 286; 297; 304; 312; 326–30; 366; 378; 460

habit 55n57; 203; 209; 222; 254; 305; 344; 399; 416

hand 73–74; 78–90; 96–97; 113–22; 127; 135; 139–40; 149; 159; 168; 177–79; 184–88; 190; 209–10; 215; 219–222; 242–45; 256–57; 262; 268; 272–74; 298; 309–10; 311–14; 327; 341; 347–52; 362; 370; 372; 380–85; 391; 410; 411; 414; 442; 450; 455–58

hand, God's right 159; 180; 190; 201; 343; 347; 352; 360; 378; 451; 459

happy, happiness 36; 61; 67; 77; 82–83; 95; 130; 155; 184; 192–95; 228; 235–38; 249; 252; 259; 263–64; 284; 299; 312–13; 332–36; 342; 348; 395; 424–27; 452; 458–59

harmony 23; 71; 159; 175; 242; 257–58; 341; 353; 357; 437; 443

harvest 25; 69; 106; 128; 202–04; 225; 235; 268; 290; 300; 381; 437–41

haste 42; 97; 137; 209–10; 217; 290; 370; 381–82; 403; 409

hate, hatred 59–60; 71–72; 115–16; 125–26; 142–46; 178–79; 202–04; 210; 221; 232; 234; 270; 282–85; 297; 301; 339; 341; 345–49; 357–58; 360; 374–75; 422; 461
  See also contempt

head (of Christ's body) 20; 27–30; 32; 35; 43–46; 83–90; 130; 140; 145–46; 153; 157–60; 164; 177–83; 197; 202; 212–14; 220; 227; 268–73; 281; 292; 297–99; 306; 336; 339–46; 355; 369–79; 434; 438; 450

healing 46–47; 186; 256n21; 257; 268; 326–27; 371; 437; 445

health 66; 69n22; 192; 231; 250; 256–57; 291; 311; 351; 402; 412–13; 419n1; 439; 446–49; 461–63

hearing 13; 20; 30; 35; 40; 187; 254; 269–72; 359; 376; 396; 445

heart 16–17; 20–21; 27–43; 59–72; 73–82; 96–100; 114; 118–22; 125–55; 158; 164; 169; 172–74; 179–80; 186–87; 193; 197; 204; 209; 213; 217; 221; 225–35; 242–43; 250–64; 267–91; 298; 307; 310; 312–13;

322–37; 339–67; 370–71; 376; 379–85; 389–90; 397; 402–16; 418; 421; 428–31; 441; 449–63

heaven (divine home) 20; 35; 62; 93; 104; 119; 125; 131; 139; 141–46; 153; 158–75; 178–81; 187–88; 199; 212–18; 231–33; 243; 263; 302; 311–12; 325; 340–47; 356–58; 372–73; 390; 406–07; 414–16; 424; 449–62

heaven (human goal) 27; 39; 93–98; 152; 104; 222; 263; 281; 312; 332; 378; 404; 407

heaven (image of the just) 104–08; 453

"heavenly" (city, doctrine, reward, etc.) 68; 93–98; 137; 155; 178; 194; 204; 209; 211–12; 218; 222; 232; 248; 263; 309; 377; 398–401; 409; 417; 439; 462
  See also kingdom of heaven

heavens (sky, stars, etc.) 74; 76n11; 93; 101; 131; 195; 320; 345; 384–85; 454

Hebrew names and words 25; 48–49; 50n3; 69; 79; 113; 117; 128; 149; 186; 192n22; 247; 256n18; 292; 367n64; 392; 455n11

height 39; 45; 47; 61–63; 102; 174

hell 89; 94; 178; 188–89; 217; 231; 234; 286–88; 385; 432
  See also underworld

heresy, heretics 86; 109; 137; 154; 170; 201–04; 324; 357–65
  See also doctrine (false)

hidden (i.e., mysterious) 13–26; 80; 107; 126; 155; 162; 171; 179–88; 195–201; 210–211; 219–20; 241–49; 269; 301–02; 309; 326; 341–47; 355–64; 374–75; 407; 431; 451; 459
  See also obscurity

history 14–16; 19; 33; 116; 128; 420

holiness 23; 142; 201; 273–78; 373

holocaust 32; 273; 283; 442

holy (city, Church, desire, life, mountain, etc.) 94–97; 135–38; 155; 164–66; 180; 185; 191; 201–05; 230n11; 241–43; 258–59; 269–73; 286; 301–03; 315; 342–45; 362; 393–99; 417–20; 427; 432; 438–42; 449–454

holy persons 19; 62; 68; 75; 98; 107; 128; 164; 183; 202; 227; 246; 250; 312–13; 329–30; 395; 410; 432; 439; 449; 453
  See also saints

Holy Spirit 61; 64; 70; 86–87; 97; 118n13; 119–20; 161; 169; 172; 187–88; 205; 212; 252; 287; 306; 310; 330; 332; 336; 343; 353; 395; 429; 455n11

hope 20; 47; 69; 77; 83–84; 96–101; 114; 134; 155; 158; 164; 172; 182; 189–90; 195–99; 213; 243; 252; 256; 265; 268; 284–90; 297–300; 308; 311–21; 332–36; 341–55; 366–68; 369–72; 378–85; 389; 402–13; 417–19; 428–35; 437–45; 451; 458–62
  See also charity

horse 264; 312–13; 333–34; 344

house 27; 44–45; 61; 77; 82; 94–100; 107–09; 116–20; 127; 148–51; 203; 217; 228; 253; 275–77; 301; 341; 357; 390–91; 397–98; 407; 412–15; 417; 423–34; 441–42; 454–61

humility (of Christ) 19–20; 23; 35; 38–39; 43; 45–46; 59; 62; 75; 87; 117–19; 121–22; 125; 167; 267; 312; 331; 355; 376; 412
  See also Christ; "little ones"; *spiritales*

humility (of the Father) 133–34

humility (human) 38–40; 42; 44–45; 55n53; 61–62; 64; 72; 74–75; 77; 90; 96; 101; 104; 114; 117; 122; 131; 150; 182; 185; 195; 210; 221–22; 237; 247; 252; 283; 287; 298–99; 304; 311–12; 325–27; 331; 333–34; 353; 369; 371; 375–76; 380; 382; 390; 396–97; 402; 408; 411–13; 430; 432; 437; 440; 445; 460

hunger 15; 21; 106; 152; 172–73; 183; 188; 215; 227; 237; 274; 281; 302; 395–97; 404; 423; 437–39; 446; 461–63

hymn 136; 149; 194; 241–50; 339–42

Subject Index 499

I AM WHO AM (HE WHO IS) 48; 93; 99–100; 103 390; 400; 403; 416
  See also Absolute Being; Being-Itself; *idipsum*; Selfsame

Idithun 389–99; 404–11; 415–16

idipsum 42; 99
  See also Being-Itself; Selfsame

idol, idolatry 83; 129; 183–86; 262; 286–88; 356; 360

ignorance 47; 73–75; 120–21; 128; 209; 215; 221; 235; 276; 305n10; 372; 380; 385; 421; 427

image, imagery 17–18; 23–48; 52n25; 53n31; 55n54; 76; 165–67; 181; 243; 251; 260–61; 368n65; 381n31; 389–91; 404; 433

image of God 15; 24; 47; 177; 191; 229; 237; 343–44; 389; 404; 437; 444
  See also likeness

imitation 78; 308

immortality 126; 140; 146; 220; 284–85; 439; 451; 463

immutability 55n60; 99; 185; 279

imperfection 46; 178–79; 197–200; 377; 390; 398; 408–09

impersonation. 20; 31; 36; 54n42

impiety 242; 252; 258; 310; 313; 322; 328–29; 335

Incarnation 35; 41; 44; 79n18; 271; 299n2

incorruption 279–80; 285; 462

inebriated 77; 82; 91; 461
  See also drunkard

infinite 99; 227

infirm, infirmity 21; 101; 121; 283; 457–62

inherit, inheritance 27; 68–69; 136–37; 220; 228–29; 301; 310; 323; 336; 342; 359n36; 362; 378; 385; 406; 427; 439; 451; 455n11

iniquity 78; 96; 125–26; 142–46; 164; 190; 203; 236; 241–43; 252–60; 268; 270; 274–81; 286; 300–02; 314; 323; 326–29; 334; 340–41; 347–48; 354–56; 371; 376; 378; 382; 411–14; 421; 426; 461
  See also sin; sinner

injustice 24; 131; 140; 238; 293; 335; 341; 355; 389; 405; 411

inner life 22; 252; 302; 392

innocence 128; 142; 168; 180; 201; 204; 242; 250–57; 271; 331; 359n36; 367; 379

instruction 37; 60; 350; 377; 397

intention 14; 19; 23; 73; 75; 114; 153; 160; 311; 316; 342; 353; 394; 462

intercession (of Christ) 20; 287; 325; 360; 379n23

interpretation 14–16; 19; 22; 33; 37; 40; 44; 50n3; 52n18; 60n2; 69; 78; 83; 87; 90; 103; 113; 117; 128; 132; 136; 148–49; 172n29; 181; 201; 203; 247; 261; 282n23; 291–92; 323; 361; 364; 375; 392; 420; 430; 432; 442n9

Isaac 69–70; 100; 119; 245; 257; 297; 306; 412

Isaiah 39; 64; 119

Israel, Israelite 14; 19; 73–80; 90; 93–94; 99–105; 116; 119; 125; 142–48; 160; 184–87; 242–51; 322; 323n22; 335; 342; 357; 412; 416; 453

Jacob 62; 100–02; 119; 125; 144–46; 245; 257; 392; 412

James (epistle writer) 311–19

Jerusalem 59; 68–69; 93–109; 118; 165; 178; 194; 204; 246; 264; 334; 372; 389; 392n4; 401; 454; 462

Jesus 19–20; 22; 27; 32; 53n35; 54n53; 61; 79; 119; 157; 162; 164; 168; 172; 186; 199–200; 267; 272–73; 276; 292; 293n43; 311; 367; 369; 372
  See also Christ

Jews, Judaism 24; 38 50n3; 60n1; 79; 113; 117–19; 121; 130; 135–50; 157; 160–70; 174–77; 186–87; 194; 215–22; 232; 245–47; 294; 303; 323; 343; 352; 375; 412–13; 446n18; 455
  See also gentiles; synagogue

Job 73; 82–85; 177; 193; 225; 262

John the Baptist 77; 268; 293–94

journey, sojourn 13; 16; 33; 39; 44; 59; 68–70; 95; 160; 190; 265; 383; 401; 414–15; 424–26; 455
See also pilgrim

joy 23; 39; 75; 91; 96–97; 115; 118; 126–27; 136; 146–48; 153; 169–71; 191–96; 212; 225–29; 235; 250; 254; 299; 312–13; 331–36; 342–47; 353; 383; 393–97; 409; 427n17; 428; 437–42; 461
See also jubilation

jubilation 225–26; 235; 438
See also joy

Judas 291; 309; 369–78; 384

judge (divine) 71–72; 105; 134; 137; 140; 143; 152; 169; 201; 235–37; 277; 309; 325; 334; 337; 340; 356; 366; 370; 376–77; 381; 411; 418; 431–32; 438–39; 445; 460

judge (human) 93; 143; 161; 168; 171; 192; 267–68; 287–88; 309–10; 394; 398; 422; 431; 458

judgment (discernment) 18; 36; 42–43; 46; 55n58; 83; 155; 178; 196; 234; 283–85; 303; 311; 314; 321; 392

judgment (reckoning) 73; 93–94; 104–08; 137; 148; 225–26; 236–38; 255; 259; 276; 286; 325; 369; 385; 417

justice (divine) 19; 125–26; 131; 139–46; 183; 209–10; 215–19; 309; 369–71; 375–76; 380; 385–86; 417; 425; 461

justice (human) 14; 27; 40; 47; 170; 209–10; 215–16; 225; 229; 238; 268; 294; 311; 320–21; 370; 375–76; 380; 385–86; 427; 461

justification (general) 85; 242; 256–57; 262; 358; 427

justification (by God) 79; 105; 151; 164; 166; 177; 183–84; 209; 211; 215–16; 273; 311–34; 342; 369; 376; 380; 409

justification (of self) 267; 273–74; 314; 323; 330; 377; 460

Kedar 69–71

kill, killing 21; 72; 89; 97; 115–16; 161–71; 201–03; 220; 232; 247; 286–94; 302; 320; 339; 340; 347–49; 356; 367–68; 375; 410; 417; 421–22; 457

kindness 161; 238; 246; 275; 350; 358; 389; 413; 427

king 14; 108; 115–21; 125–27; 132–36; 141–55; 157–61; 165; 204; 244–47; 288; 293; 342; 352–54; 441

kingdom, earthly 69; 113–20; 126; 136; 141; 144; 155; 165; 170; 219; 246; 249; 278–79; 441

kingdom of God, heaven 55; 69; 85; 105–06; 119; 125; 128; 136–39; 149–52; 222; 234; 238; 265; 314–21; 356; 381; 412

knock 80; 113–20; 260n27

knowledge 18; 21; 26; 33; 35; 39–40; 46; 53nn37–38; 64; 87; 119; 177–78; 185–88; 195; 215; 242; 255–58; 335; 361; 375; 402; 414; 454

Korah 25; 128; 420; 423n9; 424

ladder 62–64; 144–46; 152; 392–93; 452–53

lament 22; 52n18; 68; 87; 303–05; 343–51; 360; 373; 378; 458

lamp 191; 383

law, divine 19–20; 69; 134; 136; 141; 146; 148; 183; 203; 211; 215–16; 222; 232–33; 238; 267; 270; 283–84; 294; 301–02; 312; 314; 317; 325; 329–30; 334; 339–40; 342; 349; 356; 376–77; 389; 393; 398–99; 403; 409; 422; 437; 444
See also grace

law, human 137; 168; 263; 288; 376–77; 405; 445

"law and prophets" 20; 22; 86; 189; 232; 269

"law of sin" 134; 216; 222; 283; 330; 437; 444–45

Lazarus (and Rich Man) 254; 289; 416

Subject Index

left hand 73; 80–89; 215; 262; 410
  See also right hand

letter (of Scripture); 20–21; 29; 68; 120; 134

lies, lying 160–61; 166; 171; 203; 209; 221; 232–37; 244; 280n18; 285; 396; 404
  See also dishonesty

"Lift up your hearts" 28; 333

light 23; 39; 46; 69–70; 76; 82; 87; 96; 171–73; 179; 190–98; 250; 267; 278–81; 290; 345–49; 359; 364; 367; 373; 381–84; 399; 418; 421; 424–25; 433; 437–46; 459

likeness 98; 283
  image and (of God) 404
  as principle of Christology 119; 182
  sacramental 53n37

lion 61; 133; 158; 166–67

lips 19; 60–71; 125–26; 134–41; 193; 268–74; 280; 300; 322; 328; 394

"little ones" (*parvuli,* i.e., simple believers) 39; 41–43; 46; 54nn48.53; 59; 63–64; 72; 87; 113; 118; 146; 275; 366

longing 23; 26; 42; 46; 95; 97; 109; 153–54; 183; 185; 222; 234; 251–53; 263; 275; 297; 302; 344; 349–51; 385; 389–90; 395–99; 403–04; 411; 414–16; 417–28; 434–35; 438; 441; 452–54; 457; 461–62
  See also desire

Lord's Prayer 287; 343; 356; 377

lots, lottery 220; 273; 298; 309

love 14–21; 25–27; 29–30; 34–35; 38; 40; 43–44; 46–48; 52n25; 53nn37.38; 54n41; 59; 66; 70–72; 73; 83; 86; 93–97; 98n10; 104; 106–09; 125–26; 129–30; 136–37; 140–47; 152–53; 157–59; 164; 169; 172; 174; 177–78; 189–90; 195; 202–205; 220; 223; 225–26; 232–36; 241; 244; 249; 264–65; 267–70; 276; 282; 284; 287; 291; 297; 300; 302; 307; 311; 317–19; 321–22; 336–37; 339; 345–52; 359–60; 366–67; 378; 389; 399; 402; 406; 421–22; 428; 438; 440; 446; 449–50; 454–55; 458
  See also charity

LXX *See* Septuagint

lyre 158; 172–73; 225–34; 437–46

malice 115; 140; 162; 247; 451; 461

marriage 76; 125–29; 181; 214; 287; 329; 455

martyrs 32; 73–75; 88; 91; 95; 140; 164; 171; 225–26; 233; 268–72; 288–94; 350; 360; 418; 435
  See also blood of martyrs

Mary, Virgin 130–31; 161; 180–81; 214; 245; 329n32; 354; 361; 372; 378

material (vs. spiritual) 91; 96–99; 107; 146; 185; 392; 395; 426; 445; 453–54

medicine 43; 46; 177; 191; 412; 449; 462

meditation 29; 369–70; 380; 390; 397

meek 140n25; 334; 355; 376

Melchizedek 113; 117–19

memory 51n11; 68; 74; 101; 115; 123; 128; 246; 250; 255; 353; 356; 400; 407; 425; 428–434

mercy 62; 76; 91; 121; 130; 143–44; 152; 157–58; 163; 166; 173–74; 184; 187–88; 209–23; 225–26; 231; 236–38; 263; 268; 276; 280–85; 298–300; 311; 325; 329–34; 339–40; 345–46; 353; 369–71; 383–377; 386; 418; 430; 433; 439; 445–46; 450; 454–58
  See also compassion; forgiveness

mercy, works of 105–06

merit 107; 209; 216; 238; 258–62; 309; 311–13; 321–26; 333–34; 350; 369; 379; 386; 446; 456; 460

messiah, messianic 22; 41; 52n18; 246; 343

metaphor 43; 46–47; 133; 415n60

milk 41; 46; 59–64; 87; 113; 118; 146; 209; 218; 305; 308; 365; 395

mind 11; 13; 23; 29; 47–48; 61–62; 70; 80; 84; 97–101; 117; 128; 134; 146;

155; 183–87; 209–16; 222; 233–36; 244; 249; 255–58; 267–69; 283; 286; 314; 347; 353; 392–95; 416–17; 421; 425–31; 437; 443–44

miracle 105; 131; 162; 173–74; 199; 310

mirror 23; 122; 166

miser 389; 404; 409; 421

misery 67–69; 174; 191; 196; 252; 260

misfortune 27; 191–96; 225; 231; 332; 336; 356;371; 423; 427; 460
See also fortune

mixed body (Church) 23; 59; 71–72; 93–95; 103; 178; 200–04; 339; 344–46

mockery 24; 127–28; 173; 187; 282; 409; 418; 425; 435; 449; 459–60

model 14; 22; 27; 29; 35–39; 43; 117; 138; 177; 225; 308; 355; 398

moon 24; 46; 73–74; 86–88; 95; 132; 278n17; 320; 369–73; 424–25
See also sun; stars

moneylending 280; 355; 405
See also usury

mortality 146; 181–84; 204; 221–22; 251–55; 259; 283–85; 369; 373; 389; 402–03; 412–13; 424; 432; 439; 443; 449; 457; 462

Moses 19; 73; 79; 99–100; 116; 134; 177; 185–86; 203; 248; 340

mother 18; 24; 36; 38; 41; 63; 77; 83; 88n41; 97; 118; 125; 131; 137–39; 153; 179; 185; 194–95; 204; 209; 218; 232; 253; 293; 305; 308; 372; 378; 395

mountain 39; 59–61; 73–78; 97; 155; 174; 217; 235; 319; 361; 430; 437–42

mourn, mourning 193; 216; 244; 439; 457–58

mousetrap 170n24; 219n12

mouth 19; 71; 82–85; 140; 169; 193; 196; 228–31; 262; 268–74; 280n18; 281; 308; 312–13; 322–28; 333; 342; 382; 390–96; 410; 425

mule 312–13; 333–34; 344

multiple, multiply 292; 300; 3–6; 330

music 16; 26–27; 30; 172–73; 230; 235; 244; 417; 425–28; 437; 442–45

mystery 13; 18; 20–21; 29; 31; 33; 45–46; 80; 113–16; 120; 138; 145; 149; 178; 181; 186; 211; 214; 267–72; 299n2; 301; 306; 340; 343; 360; 365; 369; 374; 420; 425

mysteries (sacraments) 76n13; 144; 299n2; 357n3

mysterious 27; 35; 37; 54n48; 73; 99; 115; 116–17; 177; 184; 248; 292; 334; 374; 389

Nathanael 104; 145–46; 311; 322–324

natural 116; 195; 197; 228; 245–46; 354–378

nature 20; 23; 24; 1000; 143; 165; 179–82; 197–99; 228; 261n29; 267; 272; 279; 283; 336; 347; 363n47; 370; 380; 384; 402; 462

nations 68; 100; 108; 139–40; 153; 165; 173; 187; 245; 286–87; 297–310; 362; 381; 451
See also gentiles

New Covenant 69; 203; 225; 234; 241; 244; 249; 262; 312; 329; 402

New Testament 22; 50n3; 51n11; 52n18; 244

night 46; 74–76; 87–88; 177–82; 190–95; 205; 312; 327; 341; 350; 355; 370; 383; 417–33
See also day

Noah 76

non-being 389–9; 401–03; 416
See also being; Absolute Being; Being-Itself; nonexistent

nonexistent 99; 201; 383; 400

North Africa 13; 16; 24; 26; 50n3; 54n53; 149
See also Africa

number 102; 200; 220; 273; 287; 300; 304; 361; 368; 389–90; 400–03; 408; 416

nurse 36; 41; 305n10; 308

obedience 26; 119–21; 165; 233; 275; 306; 33; 426; 449

obscurity (textual) 13; 19–21; 30; 33; 37; 80; 114; 178; 185; 205; 267–70; 297; 306; 340; 363–68; 420
See also hidden

oil 126; 144–46; 267–68; 276; 282–85; 340–41; 365–66; 407

old age 17; 84; 233; 306; 389; 402–04

Old Covenant 69; 203; 241; 246; 249; 263; 312; 402

Old Latin Bible (*Vetus Latina*) 30; 42; 49; 50n3; 361n42

Old Testament 18–19; 21–23; 42; 48; 136; 161; 167; 183; 244

Old and New Testaments (unity) 18–19; 33; 244

one and many 19; 68; 104; 214; 292; 359; 373–74; 456

oppression 61; 171; 279; 287; 329–30; 428

order 14; 39; 44; 54n47; 55n55; 64; 133; 195; 246–49; 393; 409; 420n6

pagan 24–25; 55n54; 65; 79; 125; 129; 171; 303; 312; 315; 331; 354–55; 375; 421; 424

pain 68; 135; 167; 173; 191; 210; 223; 231; 251; 283; 344; 353; 371; 375; 390; 397; 404; 411; 416; 432; 443–44; 451–63

parables 67; 177; 183; 276; 282n23; 311; 324–25; 393

paradise 77; 384; 457

parents 84; 131; 138; 348; 362

Passover 46; 73; 79; 177; 186–87; 248; 256; 268; 291–94

patience 158; 172; 178; 192; 196; 202; 204; 332; 359; 383; 408; 429; 437; 440

patriarchs 117; 145; 241; 244–45

Paul 13; 20–22; 29; 36; 39–40; 42; 48; 59; 72; 84; 97–98; 108–09; 113; 122; 125; 141; 146–150; 154; 172; 194–97; 209; 211; 214–16; 245–47; 267; 270; 290; 308–09; 311–12; 315–21; 324; 330; 332; 336; 349; 351; 360; 366–67; 374–75; 377; 389–90; 398; 409; 413; 437; 449; 451; 456

peace 24; 33; 35; 59–60; 71–72; 93–94; 106–09; 137; 204; 220; 241–42; 249–51; 275; 284; 299; 301–2n6; 328; 335; 340–41; 346; 350; 355–56; 360; 366–67; 410; 415; 439

perdition 147; 310; 329; 362

perfect 87; 126; 146; 155; 178; 181; 198; 203; 211; 233; 302; 308; 346; 394; 409; 461–63

perfection 25; 81n26; 97; 128; 160; 229; 286; 319; 339; 342; 390; 408–09; 416; 429

persecution 70; 89; 116; 161–62; 170; 178; 196–97; 203; 219; 290–94; 303; 331; 350–51; 369; 384; 451

perseverance 117; 150; 164; 190; 204–05; 300; 351; 361; 383; 399; 417; 429; 440

perversity 142; 250; 302; 335; 349; 361

Peter 149; 150n44; 154; 178; 187; 197–99; 213; 247; 268; 290–93; 297; 302–03; 309–10; 333; 339; 346; 365; 383; 431

Pharisee 238; 267; 274–78; 311; 322–27

philosophy 14; 15; 23; 38; 40; 46; 53n38; 54n51; 55n59; 335

physician 197; 268; 275–76; 291; 326; 329; 412; 437; 446
See also doctor

piety 39; 64; 365; 446n18

Pilate, Pontius 157–61; 168; 180

pilgrim, pilgrimage 27; 33; 38; 60; 67–71; 93; 95; 109; 178–83; 204; 265; 391–92; 415; 420–34; 439; 452–55
See also journey

pity 146; 199; 218; 450–60

planets 277; 312; 328–29
See also stars

pleasure 27; 46; 47; 75; 101; 177; 192–93; 272; 232; 235; 285; 389; 393–94; 399; 409; 424

possessions 68; 82–85; 233n22; 253; 286; 305; 310; 389; 408; 449–58

poverty 107–08; 183; 252; 347; 449; 460–61

power 15; 20; 30; 33; 35–47; 80; 85–89; 93–95; 106–08; 118; 126; 131–41; 148; 161; 163; 167–74; 188–90; 195–98; 210; 221–222; 225; 231–33; 245; 262; 280; 287–88; 305n11; 310; 316; 324; 327; 336; 345–47; 354; 365; 378; 383–84; 405; 414; 416; 424–25; 434; 437; 444; 449; 454–55

praise 27; 65–67; 96–97; 11; 136; 153–55; 158; 173–74; 193–94; 225–31; 243–50; 260; 264–65; 280–87; 300; 339; 342; 377; 399; 410; 417–18; 424–29; 443; 453; 462

prayer 13; 20–32; 44–45; 52n18; 65; 70–71; 78; 81; 90; 106–08; 114; 117; 130; 135; 140; 155; 157; 163–65; 178; 203–04; 209; 215–22; 225; 267–74; 280–91; 299; 312–13; 318; 324–33; 339; 340–60; 369–86; 389–92; 399–400; 407; 414–18; 431–34; 437; 441–46; 449–54; 463

predestination 48; 248

presumption 46; 104; 189; 198; 311–14; 326; 361

pride 20; 45–46; 62; 72; 75–78; 87; 90; 96; 101–04; 108; 115; 117; 121–22; 140; 149; 153; 165; 185–89; 195; 201–02; 229; 237; 242–55; 260–61; 279n18; 286–88; 304; 310; 311–15; 324–26; 331–34; 345; 353–60; 364; 370; 376; 381–82; 390–402; 412–16; 430; 445–452; 458–59
See also arrogance; humility

priesthood 14; 20; 113–18; 142–44; 218

progress 17–18; 23; 30; 37–47; 59–70; 77–81; 198; 256; 286; 308; 317; 339; 350–51; 390; 408; 413; 422; 425; 432; 437–38; 452

property 82; 165; 188; 193; 233; 253; 256; 289; 315; 397; 415; 422; 458

prophecy 14; 19–20; 22–23; 25; 39; 59; 68; 86; 97–98; 113; 117–18; 120; 125; 129; 139; 144; 151; 162; 164–66; 173; 177; 200; 213; 220; 241; 246; 248; 272–73; 287; 292; 294; 305–06; 340; 360; 369–70; 372; 381–83; 446; 459
See also history

prophet 22; 96; 126; 128; 130–32; 135–37; 139; 150–51; 155; 157; 169; 174–75; 177; 180–81; 189; 212–14; 244; 246; 248; 251; 257; 268; 275–76; 286; 293; 297–99; 303–06; 330; 342; 372; 376; 383; 445
See also "law and prophets"; patriarchs

prosperity 64; 70; 192–93; 228–31; 250–51; 259–60; 423–24; 433

prostitute 136; 183; 276

protection 30; 65; 73; 77; 83; 88; 108; 146; 157; 333

providence 157; 258n23; 331; 382

psaltery 158; 172–73; 225–34; 437; 442–43; 446

punishment 27; 134; 141; 168; 180; 184; 187; 191–92; 202–05; 217; 233' 241; 246; 251; 312; 321; 336; 358; 378; 386; 390; 405n42; 411; 427; 432; 440; 461

purification 103; 264; 278; 281; 314; 318; 364

purity 21–34; 67; 71n26; 94; 126; 150–51; 178; 201n49; 263; 267–73; 326; 331; 364; 441; 445

race of darkness (Manichean) 267; 278–80; 312; 331

rain 91; 105; 135; 141; 174; 231; 345–46; 361; 370; 381–82; 433; 437–39

ram 152; 200; 247; 306; 377; 434

reason (spiritual) 33; 47; 55n60; 257; 437; 444–45

redemption 19–20; 22; 27; 36; 209; 267; 284; 332; 428–29

Subject Index

repent, repentance 24; 182; 187; 236–37; 250; 254; 264; 292n42; 364n48

rest 16; 19; 33; 47; 53n37; 72; 80; 83; 95; 98n10; 167–68; 181; 189; 232; 254; 340; 349–56; 415; 417; 422

resurrection, final 32; 174; 212; 263; 267; 288; 361; 402

revelation 22; 33; 51n11; 145; 199

reward 48; 55n55; 84; 107; 121; 136; 153; 160; 185; 195; 216; 41; 249; 256; 263–65; 275; 293; 298; 320; 347; 376; 383; 461

rhetoric 17; 30–37; 44; 54nn44.47

riches 82–84; 89; 93–94; 107–08; 141n28; 193–94; 256; 262–63; 368n65; 405–07; 461–62
See also wealth

right hand 73–74; 80–90; 108; 119; 127; 140; 149; 159; 179–80; 190; 201; 243; 262; 306; 314; 343; 360; 378; 385; 410; 451; 459
See also left hand

righteous (persons) 68; 89; 104–05; 164; 213; 308; 324; 335; 337; 341; 366
See also saints

righteousness (divine) 35; 76; 87; 104; 125–26; 141–47; 184; 189; 205; 215; 222; 314; 373; 375; 382; 412; 429; 440; 459

righteousness (human) 103–04; 164; 195; 213; 216; 221–22; 229–34; 256–58; 286–87; 299; 303; 311; 363; 397; 413; 440; 445–46; 453; 461–63
See also self-righteousness

righteousness of faith 35; 104; 215; 222; 315–16; 320–22; 334; 375–76; 380
See also justice; justification; self-righteousness

rock 61; 116; 133; 162; 185; 199; 215; 268; 287–88; 302; 317; 320; 346

Roman 84; 88n41; 102n21; 414n59

ruler 101; 141–42; 177; 180; 337; 345–52; 377; 384; 412–13

sabbath 19; 232

sacrament 24; 28–29; 40; 44; 46; 53n37; 76; 116n10; 121; 144; 167; 181; 202–03; 299; 303; 361; 420n5

sacrifice 20; 32; 113; 117–19; 145; 152; 180; 236; 251–53; 267–74; 283; 288; 297; 306; 317; 336; 357; 418; 434; 442

sadness 193–97; 312; 336; 360; 419; 428; 434–43

saints 27; 65- 68; 93; 105–09; 126; 132; 140; 147–48; 211–13; 278; 289; 300–02; 309; 416; 454
See also holy persons

salvation 15–23; 35–38; 45; 52n12; 64–65; 69; 109; 118; 122; 134–35; 147; 163; 187; 212; 229; 254; 269; 273; 275; 280n18; 308; 330–31; 342; 369; 380; 414; 417–19; 429–35; 438; 445

Samaritan, Good (Christ as) 209; 218

sanctuary 188; 259–61

Sarah 69; 306

Satan 199; 293n43; 370; 384
See also devil

Saul (king) 114–16; 158–63; 172

Saul (Paul); 140–41; 146; 181; 213; 227; 247; 271; 274; 373; 451

scandal 67–68; 73; 86–88; 120; 130; 190; 215; 249; 292; 304; 308; 365; 389; 398–403; 414; 434

schism 44; 59; 71n26; 72; 126; 137n16; 204–05; 297; 305; 308n18; 340; 357–67
See also Donatists; heresy

scorn 64; 241; 254; 283; 290; 297–98; 303–04; 396–97; 404

scourge 131; 169–73; 219; 242; 251–52; 312–13; 333–36; 391; 410; 460

Scripture 11; 13–21; 23; 25–29; 31; 33–34; 37–48; 50nn3.7; 54n48; 55nn53.57; 73; 76–77; 83–84; 86; 115; 128; 135; 144; 157; 160–61; 163–66; 251; 257; 267; 269–70; 272; 274; 299; 305; 315–16; 340; 345;

358; 363; 365; 382–85; 389; 392–93;
399; 421; 431; 449
humble form of 38
See also interpretation

secret 21; 27; 51n11; 77; 80; 153; 179–80;
193–200; 209–11; 217; 276; 309;
331; 348–49; 383; 402–08; 414; 420;
426–27; 460

self-righteousness 71; 103–04; 187–89;
215; 221–22; 274–81; 285–86; 314;
322; 325; 369; 375–76; 382; 402;
412; 429–30; 460–63
See also justification; righteousness
of faith

Selfsame 42; 93–94; 99–104
See also Absolute Being; Being-Itself;
I AM WHO AM; *idipsum*

Septuagint (LXX) 42; 48–49; 50n3;
80n19; 83; 105; 122; 144n34;
192n22; 244n3; 256n18; 455n11. 384

sermon 13–18; 22; 26; 28; 30; 33; 36; 38;
40–41; 43–45; 48–49; 50n6; 51n8;
53n38; 54nn45.46; 55n54.59; 60n1;
90; 123; 209; 223n19; 226; 230; 241;
265; 313n1; 364; 407; 412; 416

servant 24; 69; 99; 109; 139; 159; 166;
182; 185–88; 199; 203; 211–14; 218;
228; 245; 250; 263–64; 275; 288;
349–51; 359; 370–77; 384–86; 396–
97; 406–08; 425; 445; 449–57
See also slave

shade 146; 164; 186; 324

sheep 122; 140; 215; 230n13; 288; 377;
395

shepherd 235n30; 377

shouting 71; 93; 96; 128; 143; 151;
168–70; 191; 233–35; 242; 254–55;
311–12; 326–27; 336; 339–40; 346–
57; 373; 451

sickness 46; 99; 101; 115; 152; 173; 192;
197–98; 215; 231; 288; 291; 321;
329; 335; 397; 412; 437; 443–46;
449

signification, significance 69–70; 80; 83;
89; 113; 116–17;120–23; 135; 133;
136; 139; 145; 152; 161; 186; 189;

230–31; 244; 262; 292; 297; 302;
309; 363n46; 389; 431

signs; 31; 44; 117; 144; 157; 177; 180;
187; 205; 246; 248–49; 305; 323n22;
420; 457

silence 133;-96 312; 326–28; 394–97; 445

silver 253; 261–64; 363–64; 393; 408
See also gold

sin, original 24; 184

sin, sinners 19–35; 43–47; 53n31; 66–67;
78; 96; 104–05; 121; 125–35; 141–
43; 151; 155; 170; 177–205; 214–
17; 232–37; 241–59; 267–93; 297–03;
311–35; 340; 346–49; 357; 362;
364n48; 369; 376–83; 389–96; 402;
409–16; 417–22; 426–34; 437–46;
449–61
See also evil; evildoers; godless;
wicked

sing, song 25; 62; 69; 71; 75; 77–78; 90;
103; 126–31; 136; 149–50; 155;
158–60; 172–73; 182; 225–35; 244;
342; 358; 360; 367; 372; 390–92;
399; 402; 419; 421; 424; 427; 438;
443; 445; 450–52
See also hymn; lyre; music; praise;
psaltery

sinless 134; 331; 336; 460

sky 87; 132; 174; 242; 253–55; 269; 306;
328; 424–26; 452–54

slander 202; 341; 357; 374; 397

slave 69–70; 119; 138; 165; 182; 188;
211–12; 232–33; 248; 261; 273; 284;
287; 291; 377–79; 384; 408; 456
See also servant

sleep 74–81; 88–90; 144–45; 157–58;
167–68; 173; 181; 260; 339; 352–53;
404; 423; 462

snare 158; 170–72; 268; 290–92; 333; 394

soldiers 168; 312; 336; 349; 441

sorrow 23; 75; 182; 196; 212; 297–302;
337; 369; 379; 418–19; 428–29; 435;
437–45; 461

soul 17–29; 35; 41–48; 53n37; 60–71; 74;
88–89; 93–105; 135; 148; 157–70;

179; 192–96; 209–12; 221–23; 252–64; 269–70; 276–80; 288; 298–99; 301; 307; 312; 329–31; 337; 339–41; 347–68; 369–86; 391–94; 411–14; 417–35; 437–46; 449–61

sound 19; 27–30; 69; 85; 105; 133–34; 173; 183–85; 225; 230–31; 350; 417–18; 425–34; 437; 442–45

sovereign, sovereignty 132; 142; 174; 378; 454

speech 18; 31; 36–37; 60; 65; 71; 131; 185; 225; 235; 254; 271; 353; 392; 396; 431

"spiritual ones" (i.e., advanced believers) 39; 41; 43; 48; 59
See also "little ones"

springs 26–27; 330–31; 417–28; 434; 439

stars 95; 132; 258; 276–78; 306; 312; 320; 328–29; 424–25
See also astrologers; moon; planets; sun

stealing 152; 232–34; 252; 347–48; 407
See also thief

Step-Songs 39; 51n9; 59; 389
See also Ascents, Songs of

stone 61; 93–98; 125; 144–46; 154–55; 215; 219–20; 367; 424; 441

storm 31; 46; 81; 252; 256; 287; 341; 346; 352–55; 360; 366; 433

straw 67; 71; 95; 105; 202; 301

suffering 27; 64; 70; 79; 158; 164; 172; 192; 196–97; 201; 213; 241; 267; 280; 291–92; 297–99; 312; 335–38; 344; 347; 352–53; 366; 373; 375; 390; 404–05; 417; 432; 443; 446; 449; 457; 460
See also Christ; exchange; martyrs; redemption

sun 31; 73–76; 86–88; 95; 101; 129; 132; 164; 192; 195; 231; 250; 278n17; 287; 301; 320; 345–46; 359; 369; 373; 389; 404; 424–28; 439; 459
See also moon; stars

sword 108; 125–26; 137–39; 158; 168–71

synagogue 125; 138; 194; 247–49; 262
See also children of Israel; Jews

tabernacle 26; 148; 417; 426

table 42; 91; 218; 253–54; 275; 308

table of the Lord 395

taste 199; 234; 239; 308; 351; 357; 378; 399; 418–19; 425; 451

tax collector 311; 324–27

teaching 15; 125; 138; 149; 153; 160n1; 230n10; 260; 267–69; 283–85; 313–15; 319; 364; 372; 397; 433; 458

teaching, false 267; 279n18 312 330; 335

tears 71; 75; 182; 198; 275–76; 291; 299; 414; 417–28

teeth 85; 157–58; 169; 395

temple 38; 77; 82; 97; 113; 127; 129; 149–55; 165; 180; 186; 275; 290; 325; 453–57

temporal "things" (concerns, goods, etc.) 62–64; 73; 82–83; 89; 91nn49–50; 192–94; 246–51; 255; 261; 307; 320; 394; 408; 422; 460

temptation 73; 82–90; 146; 164; 190; 193; 209; 219–21; 231; 236; 241; 245'; 248; 253; 257; 269; 273; 261; 291; 379n23; 389; 398; 401; 403; 418; 434–35; 440; 443–44; 458–62
See also test

Ten Commandments 225; 232–34; 267
See also commandments

tent 26–27; 60; 67–71; 106–08; 130; 417–18; 426–28; 434; 437–38; 441–42

terror 209; 219; 288; 352; 432

test 66; 71; 73; 107; 177–84; 204; 291; 339; 346–47; 351; 363; 427
See also temptation

testify 77; 161; 167; 194; 211; 216; 273; 293; 399; 450

testimony 19; 94; 103–04; 122; 142; 171

thanksgiving 135–36; 175; 190; 229; 231; 282; 346; 377; 443
See also gratitude

thief, theft 25; 75–76; 129; 152; 252; 286; 315; 406; 462
See also stealing

thirst 77; 93; 152; 172–73; 215; 274; 308; 367; 381; 389; 397–99; 404; 417–24; 434–35; 461–63

thorn 61; 135; 169; 174; 204; 272; 306; 313; 327–34; 417

threshing 23; 70–72; 104; 301; 360–61

threshold 45; 113–22

throne 93; 104–05; 119; 125–26; 132; 141; 146–52; 159–60; 170; 174; 213; 373; 453–54

time
  See also today
  as conceptual reality 15; 19; 24; 137; 159; 164; 178; 181; 209; 267; 307; 359; 361; 368; 370; 374; 400–01; 406; 454n8
  as moment, season 19; 70–71; 74–75; 89–90; 107; 125; 136; 141; 149; 161; 173; 180–81; 186–89; 193; 201n49; 202–05; 225–37; 244; 254–55; 264; 285–91; 298; 301; 312–13; 329–30; 336; 342; 344; 355; 366–68; 372; 383; 414; 423; 429; 433; 439–41; 455; 459
  as duration 11; 13; 28; 60; 70–72; 145; 216–21; 258; 442–43; 451–53; 462

today 19; 70; 72; 100; 119–20; 132; 154; 159; 217; 221–22; 249; 253; 285; 305; 346; 351; 354; 361–62; 366; 374; 378; 400; 406; 413; 457

tolerance 71n26; 72; 204; 347; 372

torment 147; 216; 254; 347; 422; 42; 435; 452

torture 250; 356

totus Christus 20; 30; 379n23; 157; 212n4
  See also "whole Christ"

touch 72; 85; 145; 147; 152; 166; 173; 262; 275; 425–26; 428

tranquility 84; 227; 347–55; 418; 433
  See also peace

transfiguration (incorporation into Christ) 35; 36 212–13; 220; 227n3; 379n23
  See also exchange

transgression 79; 180; 302

trap 72; 85; 90; 153; 170–72; 209–10; 219–23; 270; 277; 281; 290; 333; 393–95; 429; 435

treasure 14; 152; 260; 264; 282; 347; 390–91; 404–08; 415

tribulation 89; 272; 336; 342–44; 352; 433; 443

Trinity 44; 363

trouble 60–68; 89; 146; 192; 195; 229; 236; 250; 283–84; 290; 298–99; 324; 335; 337; 340–57; 371; 383–86; 389; 397; 417–19; 429–35; 443–45; 458

trust 77; 152; 158; 163; 190; 210–22; 232; 241; 261; 298; 301; 308; 314; 361; 368; 380; 392; 407–08; 430; 445
  See also faith; believing

trustworthy 68; 201; 245; 383; 410

truth 19; 23; 29; 37; 42; 47; 54n41; 59; 71; 81; 86–87; 96–97; 130; 134; 138–40; 146–48; 154; 160–61; 166; 169; 173–74; 217; 220; 232; 253–57; 268–69; 280n18; 288; 293–94; 307; 322; 324; 331; 361; 370; 373; 375–76; 380; 394–95; 403–04; 408–16; 419–25; 432–34; 459

truth, Christ as 25; 43; 144; 157–58; 174; 178; 204; 331; 437–46

turmoil 213; 301; 394

unbeliever 76; 129; 138; 226–29; 236; 236; 288; 320; 365; 437; 452

unchanging 40; 82; 87; 99; 142; 250; 279; 416; 425; 429; 434

understanding (spiritual-rational) 25–26; 30; 33–48; 54n48; 55n60; 64; 75;87; 120–21; 125–34; 201; 244; 255; 258; 270; 312–13; 322; 332–33; 340–44; 395; 417–34; 437; 444

underworld 288; 341; 357–59; 379; 458
  See also hell

unhappiness 69; 171; 191; 222; 318; 367; 461

union 130–31; 181; 226; 264

Subject Index

unity 20; 137; 146; 149; 299; 305; 353–54

unity (of Christ and Church; of Church) 20; 30; 43–44; 52n26; 68–72; 96; 109; 142–43; 149–50; 154; 170; 178; 201–02; 214; 265; 271; 299; 305; 359; 362–74; 419; 450

unity (of Christ; of God) 23; 130; 132; 157; 232; 363n47

unrighteousness 71; 370; 376–78; 393; 440–45

usury 280n19; 281; 340–41; 355–56
See also moneylending

valley 39; 45; 59–64; 73–75; 78; 90; 381

vanity 247; 404–10

vice 203; 412; 417–22

vigilance 74–76; 349; 437; 446

vigil, keeping 226; 230; 269n1; 461–62

vine 214; 303

vineyard 24; 174; 220; 235

violence 52n25; 265; 286; 366–68; 439

virgins 126–31; 153–54; 329; 455

virtue 304; 314–15; 326; 427

"visible words" 28–29

voice 27; 31; 35–36; 71; 78; 86; 102; 150; 155; 157; 186–87; 201–02; 228–30; 247; 275; 290–91; 314; 328; 332; 341; 346; 350; 359–60; 383; 396; 414; 427; 432; 437; 445

voice of Christ (for humanity, Church) 14; 19–20; 27; 30; 68; 146; 157; 163–64; 177–82; 197–98; 209; 214; 267–74; 297–99; 369; 374; 378–79; 434–35; 437–38; 451–53

voice of Christ (in Scripture) 19–22; 28; 30; 33; 173; 182

voice of the Church 71–72; 102; 417–19; 441

vow 230; 324

Vulgate 50n3; 244n3; 361n42

walk, walking 27; 33; 42; 77; 85; 96; 116; 165; 173; 184; 198–99; 204; 218; 248; 307–08; 315–20; 332n37; 334; 339–57; 370–71; 383–84; 391–93; 404; 417–28; 434–35; 438–43; 453; 461

wash, washing 53n37; 147; 151; 168; 243; 248; 256–57; 275–76; 322; 423; 456

water 26–27; 93; 97; 108; 116; 199; 254; 275–76; 312–13; 318; 330–31; 339; 346; 370; 381–82; 389; 414–16; 417–28; 434; 439

weakness 19–20; 43; 46; 66; 80; 85–89; 100; 107–08; 123; 131; 139; 159; 162; 178; 196–99; 211–13; 221; 227–28; 272; 283–94; 300–02; 313–14; 324–27; 336–37; 346–51; 364; 390; 394; 400; 411–13; 428; 431; 435; 439; 453–57; 462

wealth 82–89; 107; 152; 184; 193; 237; 241–42; 252–64; 347; 382; 389; 404–407; 458–62
See also riches

wedding 25–27; 125–30; 149; 154; 427

weeping 39; 45; 60–64; 73–78; 90; 193; 276; 391; 414

weight 98; 107; 159; 166; 212; 238; 283; 327; 361; 422; 428; 434

wheat 67; 71; 95; 102; 104; 201–02; 239; 293; 300–01; 439–41

"whole Christ" (*totus Christus*) 20; 23; 27–28; 30; 32; 35; 37; 43; 157; 159–60; 163–64; 177; 180; 212; 267; 272; 299; 343; 373; 375

wicked, wickedness 60; 65–72; 76; 82; 87; 102; 135; 151; 174; 202–04; 215; 219; 227; 231; 237; 241; 249–51; 254–59; 263; 270–71; 280; 293; 302; 307; 322–23; 341–47; 356–64; 369–75; 384; 397–99; 410; 427–31; 438–41; 452; 461–62
See also evildoers; godless; sin

will, human 84; 184; 225–27; 229; 258; 312; 337

will of God, of Christ 15; 29; 38; 47; 125; 141–42; 158; 162; 172; 177–80;

225–28; 243; 262–63; 267–72; 283; 309; 335–37; 356; 363; 370–71; 379n23; 385; 409

wind 339; 346–47; 352; 360; 382; 439; 459

wine 118; 407

wing 36; 70; 77; 95; 158; 164; 177; 179; 188–92; 269; 339–40; 349–56; 385; 389–93; 446

winnowing 67; 70–71; 104; 202; 360

wisdom 18; 21; 24; 33; 38–40; 46–47; 59; 64; 87; 105; 131; 150; 186; 194; 233; 267; 285; 312; 359; 409; 422; 431; 433

Wisdom (divine) 45; 83–84; 118; 185–86; 191; 218; 231; 234; 449; 455; 457

witness 157; 289–93; 320; 394

woman, women 45; 63–69; 80; 88–89; 101; 115–16; 126; 147; 151–53; 177–81; 191–92; 217; 227; 236; 263–67; 275–77; 278n17; 286; 291; 329–30; 335; 348; 355; 369; 372–73; 394–96; 408–11; 421

womb 130–31; 179; 185; 194–95; 253; 378

word(s) of God 66; 119; 185; 194; 370; 384; 393; 399; 433
   See also Scripture

Word of God (Logos) 18; 125; 132–34; 185; 369; 372–73
   See also Christ; Christ the Mediator; Wisdom

work (labor) 53n31; 98; 183; 235; 302; 394; 404; 411; 416; 440

works (divine) 125–26; 132–36; 179; 195; 214–15; 235–36; 369–70; 380–81; 411; 428

works, good 75; 84; 106; 152–53; 173; 180; 214; 225–26; 235; 261; 282; 309; 311; 315–22; 369; 380–86; 427; 437; 446

world
   as alienated from God 27; 46; 52n26; 66; 115; 177; 192; 249; 260–62; 272; 320; 423–24; 433; 461–62
   as created earth 86–87; 94; 100; 105; 117; 126–27; 139; 149; 152–54; 159; 170; 186; 189; 259; 267; 275; 278–79; 305; 318; 358; 361–62; 367; 419–21; 438–39; 443; 451
   as present human home 62–66; 75–85; 94; 108; 129; 152; 155; 186–87; 189–96; 202; 211–12; 217; 226; 233; 242; 249; 252; 256; 261; 271–72; 277; 281; 289–92; 300–02; 318; 324; 329; 331; 339; 341–47; 354; 361; 366; 369–70; 378–84; 389; 393; 403–10; 417; 423–33; 439–41; 445; 449–52; 457–63

worship 69; 88n41; 129; 145; 155; 183; 193; 219; 249; 262; 286–88; 305; 356; 360; 375

wound 84; 99; 140–41; 163–70; 218; 222; 275; 284; 311; 326; 349; 367; 445

wrongdoing 143; 238; 304; 376; 460

year 83; 93; 100–01; 210; 221–23; 298; 302; 400

yearning 140; 234; 355; 404; 421–22; 428; 461

youth 234; 404; 437–38; 442

Zacchaeus 107

zeal 203; 215; 282; 301; 359–60; 375; 385; 395; 397

Zion 243; 265; 372–73

Works of St. Augustine: A Translation for the 21st Century

New City Press, in conjunction with the Augustinian Heritage Institute, will provide the complete works of Saint Augustine for the first time in the English language. New translations, introductions and notes are written by renowned Augustinian scholars. Foreseen are 48 volumes. See the list below for books already published. Future publication plans available upon request. Standing Order customers receive a 10% discount on each volume in the Works of Saint Augustine series.

(All books are 6 x 9 in. unless otherwise noted)

(updated March 2015)

Part I — Books

Autobiographical Works

Confessions (I/1)
   cloth, 978-1-56548-468-9, 432 pp.; $59.00
   paper, 978-1-56548-445-0, 425 pp.; $24.95
   pocket 4½ x 7, 978-1-56548-154-1,
                              320 pp.; $9.95

Revisions (I/2)
   cloth, 978-1-56548-360-6, 227 pp.; $44.00

Dialogues I (I/3) forthcoming

Dialogues II (I/4) forthcoming.

Philosophical-Dogmatic Works

The Trinity (I/5)
   cloth, 978-0-911782-89-9, 471 pp.; $64.00
   paper, 978-1-56548-446-7, 471 pp.; $36.95

The City of God 1-10 (I/6)
   cloth, 978-1-56548-454-2, 348 pp.; $49.00
   paper, 978-1-56548-455-9, 348 pp.; $29.95

The City of God 11-22 (I/7)
   cloth, 978-1-56548-479-5, 615 pp.; $59.00
   paper, 978-1-56548-481-8, 615 pp.; $39.95

On Christian Belief (I/8)
   cloth, 978-1-56548-233-3, 376 pp.; $49.00
   paper, 978-1-56548-234-0, 372 pp.; $31.95

Pastoral Works

Marriage and Virginity (I/9)
   cloth, 978-1-56548-104-6, 251 pp.; $44.00
   paper, 978-1-56548-222-7, 256 pp.; $26.95

Morality and Christian Asceticism (I/10) forthcoming

Exegetical Works

Teaching Christianity (I/11)
   cloth, 978-1-56548-048-3, 272 pp.; $44.00
   paper, 978-1-56548-049-0, 259 pp.; $26.95

Responses to Miscellaneous Questions (I/12)
   cloth, 978-1-56548-277-7, 301 pp.; $49.00

On Genesis (I/13)
   cloth, 978-1-56548-175-6, 540 pp.; $54.00
   paper, 978-1-56548-201-2, 539 pp.; $36.95

The Old Testament (I/14) forthcoming.

New Testament I and II (I/15 and I/16)
   cloth, 978-1-56548-529-7, 452 pp.; $49.00
   paper, 978-1-56548-531-0, 452 pp.; $29.95

The New Testament III (I/17) forthcoming

Polemical Works

Arianism and Other Heresies (I/18)
  cloth, 978-1-56548-038-4, 480 pp.; $54.00

Manichean Debate (I/19)
  cloth, 978-1-56548-247-0, 346 pp.; $49.00

Answer to Faustus, a Manichean (I/20)
  cloth, 978-1-56548-264-7, 468 pp.; $54.00

Donatist Controversy I (I/21) forthcoming

Donatist Controversy II (I/22) forthcoming

Answer to the Pelagians I (I/23)
  cloth, 978-1-56548-092-6, 605 pp.; $59.00

Answer to the Pelagians II (I/24)
  cloth, 978-1-56548-107-7, 596 pp.; $54.00

Answer To The Pelagians III (I/25)
  cloth, 978-1-56548-129-9, 774 pp.; $89.00

Answer to the Pelagians IV (I/26)
  cloth, 978-1-56548-136-7, 264 pp.; $49.00

Part II — Letters

Letters 1-99 (II/1)
  cloth, 978-1-56548-163-3, 440 pp.; $49.00

Letters 100-155 (II/2)
  cloth, 978-1-56548-186-2, 438 pp.; $49.00

Letters 156-210 (II/3)
  cloth, 978-1-56548-200-5, 424 pp.; $49.00

Letters 211-270 (II/4)
  cloth, 978-1-56548-209-8, 352 pp.; $49.00

Part III — Homilies

Sermons 1-19 (III/1)
  cloth, 978-0-911782-75-2, 399 pp.; $49.00

Sermons 20-50 (III/2)
  cloth, 978-0-911782-78-3, 400 pp.; $49.00

Sermons 51-94 (III/3)
  cloth, 978-0-911782-85-1, 520 pp.; $54.00

Sermons 94A-150 (III/4)
  cloth, 978-1-56548-000-1, 480 pp.; $54.00

Sermons 151-183 (III/5)
  cloth, 978-1-56548-007-0, 374 pp.; $59.00

Sermons 184-229 (III/6)
  cloth, 978-1-56548-050-6, 357 pp.; $59.00

Sermons 230-272 (III/7)
  cloth, 978-1-56548-059-9, 336 pp.; $59.00

Sermons 273-305A (III/8)
  cloth, 978-1-56548-060-5, 368 pp.; $59.00

Sermons 306-340A (III/9)
  cloth, 978-1-56548-068-1, 340 pp.; $49.00

Sermons 341-400 (III/10)
  cloth, 978-1-56548-028-5, 527 pp.; $59.00

Sermons Newly Discovered Since 1990 (III/11)
  cloth, 978-1-56548-103-9, 452 pp.; $64.00

Homilies on the Gospel of John 1-40 (III/12)
  cloth, 978-1-56548-319-4, 604 pp.; $59.00
  paper, 978-1-56548-318-7, 604 pp.; $39.95

Homilies on the Gospel of John (41-124) (III/13)
  forthcoming

Homilies on the First Letter of John (III/14)
  cloth, 978-1-56548-288-3, 176 pp.; $39.00
  paper, 978-1-56548-289-0, 173 pp.; $21.95

Expositions of the Psalms 1-32 (III/15)
  cloth, 978-1-56548-126-8, 466 pp.;$54.00
  paper, 978-1-56548-140-4, 462 pp.; $36.95

Expositions of the Psalms 33-50 (III/16)
  cloth, 978-1-56548-147-3, 462 pp.; $59.00
  paper, 978-1-56548-146-6, 462 pp.; $39.95

Expositions of the Psalms 51-72 (III/17)
  cloth, 978-1-56548-156-5, 518 pp.; $54.00
  paper, 978-1-56548-155-8, 518 pp.; $36.95

Expositions of the Psalms 73-98 (III/18)
  cloth, 978-1-56548-167-1, 510 pp.; $54.00
  paper, 978-1-56548-166-4, 510 pp.; $36.95

Expositions of the Psalms 99-120 (III/19)
  cloth, 978-1-56548-197-8, 558 pp.; $54.00
  paper, 978-1-56548-196-1, 552 pp.; $36.95

Expositions of the Psalms 121-150 (III/20)
  cloth, 978-1-56548-211-1, 536 pp.; $59.00
  paper, 978-1-56548-210-4, 536 pp.; $41.95

Essential Texts Created for Classroom Use

Augustine Catechism: Enchiridion on Faith Hope and Love
  paper, 978-1-56548-298-2, 143 pp.; $14.95

Essential Sermons
  paper, 978-1-56548-276-0, 440 pp.; $31.95

Instructing Beginners in Faith
  paper, 978-1-56548-239-5, 173 pp.; $13.95

Monastic Rules
  paper, 978-1-56548-130-5, 149 pp.; $13.95

Prayers from The Confessions
  paper, 978-1-56548-188-6, 144 pp.; $13.95

Selected Writings on Grace and Pelagianism
  paper, 978-1-56548-372-9, 523 pp.; $39.95

Soliloquies: Augustine's Inner Dialogue
  paper, 978-1-56548-142-8, 108 pp.; $11.95

Trilogy on Faith and Happiness
  paper, 978-1-56548-359-0, 141 pp.; $13.95

Ebooks Available

City of God, Books I-X, Essential Sermons, Homilies on the First Letter of John, Revisions, The Confessions, Trilogy on Faith and Happiness, The Trinity, The Augustine Catechism: The Enchiridion on Faith, Hope and Love.

Custom Syllabus

Universities that wish to create a resource that matches their specific needs using selections from any of the above titles should contact New City Press.

NEW CITY PRESS
of the Focolare
Hyde Park, New York

About New City Press of the Focolare

New City Press is one of more than 20 publishing houses sponsored by the Focolare, a movement founded by Chiara Lubich to help bring about the realization of Jesus' prayer: "That all may be one" (Jn 17:21). In view of that goal, New City Press publishes books and resources that enrich the lives of people and help all to strive toward the unity of the entire human family. We are a member of the Association of Catholic Publishers.

Further Reading

15 Days of Prayer with St. Augustine, Jaime Garcia, 978-1-56548-489-4, $12.95
Roots of Christian Mysticism, Olivier Clement, 978-1-56548-485-6, $29.95
From Big Bang to Big Mystery, Brendan Purcell, 978-1-56548-433-7, $34.95
A Critical Study of the Rule of Benedict, Adalbert de Vogüé, 978-1-56548-494-8, $39.95

Periodicals
Living City Magazine,
www.livingcitymagazine.com

Scan to join our mailing list for discounts and promotions or go to www.newcitypress.com and click on "join our email list."